More Than Just a Textbook

Internet Resources

Step 1 Connect to  SC Math Online **macmillanmh.com**

Step 2 Connect to online resources by using *QuickPass* codes. You can connect directly to the chapter you want.

 **SC7120c1** — Enter this code with the appropriate chapter number.

For Students

Connect to the student edition *eBook* that contains all of the following online assets. You don't need to take your textbook home every night.

- Personal Tutor
- Extra Examples
- Self-Check Quizzes
- Multilingual eGlossary
- Concepts in Motion
- Chapter Test Practice
- Test Practice
- Study to Go
- Math Adventures with Dot and Ray
- Math Tool Chest
- Math Songs

For Teachers

Connect to professional development content at **macmillanmh.com** and the *eBook Advance Tracker* at **AdvanceTracker.com**

For Parents

Connect to **macmillanmh.com** for access to the *eBook* and all the resources for students and teachers that are listed above.

Macmillan McGraw-Hill

south Carolina Math Connects

4

Authors
Altieri • Balka • Day • Gonsalves • Grace • Krulik
Malloy • Molix-Bailey • Moseley • Mowry • Myren
Price • Reynosa • Santa Cruz • Silbey • Vielhaber

 Macmillan/McGraw-Hill

About the Cover

Fractions and decimals and the relationship between fractions and decimals are featured topics in Fourth grade. On the cover, the pitcher is wearing a fraction. It is equivalent to 0.5. Have students find the other fraction on the cover that is equivalent to 0.5.

The McGraw·Hill Companies

 Macmillan/McGraw-Hill

Send all inquiries to:
Macmillan/McGraw-Hill
8787 Orion Place
Columbus, OH 43240-4027

ISBN: 978-0-02-107712-0
MHID: 0-02-107712-6

South Carolina Math Connects, Grade 4

Printed in the United States of America.

2 3 4 5 6 7 8 9 10   071/055   17 16 15 14 13 12 11 10 09

Contents in Brief

Focal Points and Connections
See page iv for key.

The Curriculum Focal Points identify key mathematical ideas for this grade. They are not discrete topics or a checklist to be mastered; rather, they provide a framework for the majority of instruction at a particular grade level and the foundation for future mathematics study. The complete document may be viewed at www.nctm.org/focalpoints.

KEY

G4-FP1
Grade 4 Focal Point 1

G4-FP2
Grade 4 Focal Point 2

G4-FP3
Grade 4 Focal Point 3

G4-FP4C
Grade 4 Focal Point 4
Connection

G4-FP5C
Grade 4 Focal Point 5
Connection

G4-FP6C
Grade 4 Focal Point 6
Connection

G4-FP7C
Grade 4 Focal Point 7
Connection

G4-FP8C
Grade 4 Focal Point 8
Connection

G4-FP1   *Number and Operations* and *Algebra:* **Developing quick recall of multiplication facts and related division facts and fluency with whole number multiplication**

Students use understandings of multiplication to develop quick recall of the basic multiplication facts and related division facts. They apply their understanding of models for multiplication (i.e., equal sized groups, arrays, area models, equal intervals on the number line), place value, and properties of operations (in particular, the distributive property) as they develop, discuss, and use efficient, accurate, and generalizable methods to multiply multidigit whole numbers. They select appropriate methods and apply them accurately to estimate products or calculate them mentally, depending on the context and numbers involved. They develop fluency with efficient procedures, including the standard algorithm, for multiplying whole numbers, understand why the procedures work (on the basis of place value and properties of operations), and use them to solve problems.

G4-FP2   *Number and Operations:* **Developing an understanding of decimals, including the connections between fractions and decimals**

Students understand decimal notation as an extension of the base-ten system of writing whole numbers that is useful for representing more numbers, including numbers between 0 and 1, between 1 and 2, and so on. Students relate their understanding of fractions to reading and writing decimals that are greater than or less than 1, identifying equivalent decimals, comparing and ordering decimals, and estimating decimal or fractional amounts in problem solving. They connect equivalent fractions and decimals by comparing models to symbols and locating equivalent symbols on the number line.

G4-FP3   *Measurement:* **Developing an understanding of area and determining the areas of two-dimensional shapes**

Students recognize area as an attribute of two-dimensional regions. They learn that they can quantify area by finding the total number of same-sized units of area that cover the shape without gaps or overlaps. They understand that a square that is 1 unit on a side is the standard unit for measuring area. They select appropriate units, strategies (e.g., decomposing shapes), and tools for solving problems that involve estimating or measuring area. Students connect area measure to the area model that they have used to represent multiplication, and they use this connection to justify the formula for the area of a rectangle.

G4-FP4C *Algebra:* Students continue identifying, describing, and extending numeric patterns involving all operations and nonnumeric growing or repeating patterns. Through these experiences, they develop an understanding of the use of a rule to describe a sequence of numbers or objects.

G4-FP5C *Geometry:* Students extend their understanding of properties of two-dimensional shapes as they find the areas of polygons. They build on their earlier work with symmetry and congruence in grade 3 to encompass transformations, including those that produce line and rotational symmetry. By using transformations to design and analyze simple tilings and tessellations, students deepen their understanding of two-dimensional space.

G4-FP6C *Measurement:* As part of understanding two-dimensional shapes, students measure and classify angles.

G4-FP7C *Data Analysis:* Students continue to use tools from grade 3, solving problems by making frequency tables, bar graphs, picture graphs, and line plots. They apply their understanding of place value to develop and use stem-and-leaf plots.

G4-FP8C *Number and Operations:* Building on their work in grade 3, students extend their understanding of place value and ways of representing numbers to 100,000 in various contexts. They use estimation in determining the relative sizes of amounts or distances. Students develop understandings of strategies for multidigit division by using models that represent division as the inverse of multiplication, as partitioning, or as successive subtraction. By working with decimals, students extend their ability to recognize equivalent fractions. Students' earlier work in grade 3 with models of fractions and multiplication and division facts supports their understanding of techniques for generating equivalent fractions and simplifying fractions.

Authors

Mary Behr Altieri
Putnam/Northern
    Westchester BOCES
Yorktown Heights,
    New York

Don S. Balka
Professor Emeritus
Saint Mary's College
Notre Dame, Indiana

Roger Day, Ph.D.
Mathematics Department Chair
Pontiac Township High School
Pontiac, Illinois

Philip D. Gonsalves
Mathematics Coordinator
Alameda County Office
    of Education and
    California State
    University East Bay
Hayward, California

Ellen C. Grace
Consultant
Albuquerque,
    New Mexico

Stephen Krulik
Professor Emeritus
Mathematics Education
Temple University
Cherry Hill, New Jersey

Carol E. Malloy, Ph.D.
Associate Professor of
    Mathematics Education
University of North
    Carolina at Chapel Hill
Chapel Hill, North
    Carolina

Rhonda J. Molix-Bailey
Mathematics Consultant
Mathematics by Design
Desoto, Texas

Lois Gordon Moseley
Staff Developer
NUMBERS: Mathematics
    Professional
    Development
Houston, Texas

Brian Mowry
Independent Math Educational
    Consultant/Part-Time Pre-K
    Instructional Specialist
Austin Independent School District
Austin, Texas

Christina L. Myren
Consultant Teacher
Conejo Valley Unified
    School District
Thousand Oaks,
    California

Jack Price, Ed. D.
Professor Emeritus
California State
    Polytechnic University
Pomona, California

Mary Esther Reynosa
Instructional Specialist for
    Elementary Mathematics
Northside Independent
    School District
San Antonio, Texas

Rafaela M. Santa Cruz
SDSU/CGU Doctoral
    Program in Education
San Diego State
    University
San Diego, California

Robyn Silbey
Math Content Coach
Montgomery County
    Public Schools
Gaithersburg, Maryland

Kathleen Vielhaber
Mathematics Consultant
St. Louis, Missouri

Contributing Authors

Donna J. Long
Mathematics
    Consultant
Indianapolis, Indiana

FOLDABLES **Dinah Zike**
Educational Consultant
Dinah-Might Activities, Inc.
San Antonio, Texas

Master the South Carolina Academic Standards in 3 Easy Steps

1 ## Practice the Standards Daily

- Each lesson addresses the South Carolina Academic Standards covered in that lesson.

- Questions aligned to the standards in a format like those on the Palmetto Assessment of State Standards provide you with ongoing opportunities to sharpen your test-taking skills.

SC Academic Standards

4-6.2 Interpret data in tables, line graphs, **bar graphs,** and double bar graphs **whose scale increments are greater than or**

PASS PRACTICE

② Practice the Standards throughout the Chapter

- Every chapter contains two full pages of PASS Practice.

 **PASS Practice**

③ Practice the Standards Before the Test

- If you've followed steps 1 and 2, you should be more than ready for the test. But just in case you want to make sure, use pages SC2–SC21 to practice questions that are organized by standard. Lesson references are included for you should you need a little refresher.

Countdown *PLUS* **to the PASS**

South Carolina Reviewers

Each South Carolina Reviewer gave feedback and suggestions for improving the effectiveness of the Pre K–8 *Math Connects* program.

 Laurel W. Blackburn
Teacher/Mathematics
  Department Chair
Hillcrest Middle School
Simpsonville,
  South Carolina

 Hailey Caldwell
7th Grade Mathematics
  Teacher
Greenville Middle Academy
  of Traditional Studies
Greenville, South Carolina

 Joyce Wolfe Dodd
6th Grade Mathematics
  Teacher
Bryson Middle School
Simpsonville,
  South Carolina

 Carol A. Fincannon
6th Grade Mathematics
  Teacher
Southwood Middle School
Anderson, South Carolina

 Lorraine Moore
Grade 3 Math Teacher
Cowpens Elementary
  School
Cowpens, South Carolina

 Shannon L. Moorhead
4th Grade Teacher
Centerville Elementary
Anderson, South Carolina

 E. Elaine Rafferty
Mathematics Consultant
Summerville,
  South Carolina

 Natalie Rohaley
6th Grade Mathematics
Riverside Middle School
Greer, South Carolina

 Kelly Eady Shaw
7th Grade Mathematics
  Teacher
Rawlinson Road Middle
  School
Rock Hill, South Carolina

Macmillan/McGraw-Hill wishes to thank the following professionals for their feedback. They were instrumental in providing valuable input toward the development of this program in these specific areas.

Mathematical Content

Viken Hovsepian
Professor of Mathematics
Rio Hondo College
Whittier, California

Grant A. Fraser, Ph.D.
Professor of Mathematics
California State University, Los Angeles
Los Angeles, California

Arthur K. Wayman, Ph.D.
Professor of Mathematics Emeritus
California State University, Long Beach
Long Beach, California

Assessment

Jane D. Gawronski, Ph.D.
Director of Assessment and Outreach
San Diego State University
San Diego, California

Cognitive Guided Instruction

Susan B. Empson, Ph.D.
Associate Professor of Mathematics
   and Science Education
University of Texas at Austin
Austin, Texas

English Learners

Cheryl Avalos
Mathematics Consultant
Los Angeles County Office of Education, Retired
Hacienda Heights, California

Kathryn Heinze
Graduate School of Education
Hamline University
St. Paul, Minnesota

Family Involvement

Paul Giganti, Jr.
Mathematics Education Consultant
Albany, California

Literature

David M. Schwartz
Children's Author, Speaker, Storyteller
Oakland, California

Vertical Alignment

Berchie Holliday
National Educational Consultant
Silver Spring, Maryland

Deborah A. Hutchens, Ed.D.
Principal
Norfolk Highlands Elementary
Chesapeake, Virginia

Consultants and Reviewers

Each Reviewer reviewed at least two chapters of the Student Edition, giving feedback and suggestions for improving the effectiveness of the mathematics instruction.

Ernestine D. Austin
Facilitating Teacher/Basic Skills
   Teacher
LORE School
Ewing, NJ

Susie Bellah
Kindergarten Teacher
Lakeland Elementary
Humble, Texas

Megan Bennett
Elementary Math Coordinator
Hartford Public Schools
Hartford, CT

Susan T. Blankenship
5th Grade Teacher – Math
Stanford Elementary School
Stanford, KY

Wendy Buchanan
3rd Grade Teacher
The Classical Center at Vial
Garland, TX

Sandra Signorelli Coelho
Associate Director for
   Mathematics
PIMMS at Wesleyan University
Middletown, CT

Joanne DeMizio
Asst. Supt., Math and Science
   Curriculum
Archdiocese of New York
New York, NY

Anthony Dentino
Supervisor of Mathematics
Brick Township Schools
Brick, NJ

Lorrie L. Drennon
Math Teacher
Collins Middle School
Corsicana, TX

Ethel A. Edwards
Director of Curriculum and
   Instruction
Topeka Public Schools
Topeka, KS

Carolyn Elender
District Elementary Math
   Instructional Specialist
Pasadena ISD
Pasadena, TX

Monica Engel
Educator Second Grade
Pioneer Elementary School
Bolingbrook, IL

Anna Dahinden Flynn
Math Teacher
Coulson Tough K–6
   Elementary
The Woodlands, TX

Brenda M. Foxx
Principal
University Park Elementary
University Park, MD

Katherine A. Frontier
Elementary Teacher
Laidlaw
Western Springs, IL

Susan J. Furphy
5th Grade Teacher
Nisley Elementary
Grand Junction, CO

Peter Gatz
Student Services Coordinator
Brooks Elementary
Aurora, IL

Amber Gregersen
Teacher – 2nd Grade
Nisley Elementary
Grand Junction, CO

Roberta Grindle
Math and Language Arts
   Academic Intervention
   Service Provider
Cumberland Head Elementary
   School
Plattsburgh, NY

Sr. Helen Lucille Habig, RSM
Assistant Superintendent/
   Mathematics
Archdiocese of Cincinnati
Cincinnati, OH

Holly L. Hepp
Math Facilitator
Barringer Academic Center
Charlotte, NC

Martha J. Hickman
2nd Grade Teacher
Dr. James Craik Elementary
   School
Pomfret, MD

Margie Hill
District Coordinating Teacher
   for Mathematics, K–12
Blue Valley USD 229
Overland Park, KS

Carol H. Joyce
5th Grade Teacher
Nathanael Greene Elementary
Liberty, NC

Stella K. Kostante
Curriculum Coach
Roosevelt Elementary
Pittsburgh, PA

Pamela Fleming Lowe
Fourth Grade eMINTS Teacher
O'Neal Elementary
Poplar Bluff, MO

Lauren May, NBCT
4th Grade Teacher
May Watts Elementary School
Naperville, IL

Lorraine Moore
Grade 3 Math Teacher
Cowpens Elementary School
Cowpens, SC

Shannon L. Moorhead
4th Grade Teacher
Centerville Elementary
Anderson, SC

Gina M. Musselman, M.Ed
Kindergarten Teacher
Padeo Verde Elementary
Peoria, AZ

Jen Neufeld
3rd Grade Teacher
Kendall
Naperville, IL

Cathie Osiecki
K–5 Mathematics Coordinator
Middletown Public Schools
Middletown, CT

Phyllis L. Pacilli
Elementary Education Teacher
Fullerton Elementary
Addison, IL

Cindy Pearson
4th/5th Grade Teacher
John D. Spicer Elementary
Haltom City, TX

Herminio M. Planas
Mathematics Curriculum
   Specialist
Administrative Offices-
   Bridgeport Public Schools
Bridgeport, CT

Jo J. Puree
Educator
Lackamas Elementary
Yelm, WA

Teresa M. Reynolds
Third Grade Teacher
Forrest View Elementary
Everett, WA

Dr. John A. Rhodes
Director of Mathematics
Indian Prairie SD #204
Aurora, IL

Amy Romm
First Grade Teacher
Starline Elementary
Lake Havasu, AZ

Delores M. Rushing
Numeracy Coach
Dept. of Academic Services-
   Mathematics Department
Washington, DC

Daniel L. Scudder
Mathematics/Technology
   Specialist
Boone Elementary
Houston, TX

Laura Seymour
Resource Teacher Leader –
   Elementary Math &
   Science, Retired
Dearborn Public Schools
Dearborn, MI

Petra Siprian
Teacher
Army Trail Elementary School
Addison, IL

Sandra Stein
K–5 Mathematics Consultant
St. Clair County Regional
   Educational Service
   Agency
Marysville, MI

Barb Stoflet
Curriculum Specialist
Roseville Area Schools
Roseville, MN

Kim Summers
Principal
Dynard Elementary
Chaptico, MD

Ann C. Teater
4th Grade Teacher
Lancaster Elementary
Lancaster, KY

Anne E. Tunney
Teacher
City of Erie School District
Erie, PA

Joylien Weathers
1st Grade Teacher
Mesa View Elementary
Grand Junction, CO

Christine F. Weiss
Third Grade Teacher
Robert C. Hill Elementary
   School
Romeoville, IL

Lessons in which the standard is the primary focus are indicated in **bold.**

Standards and Indicators		Lesson(s)	Page Number(s)
Mathematical Processes			
Standard 4-1: The student will understand and utilize the mathematical processes of problem solving, reasoning and proof, communication, connections, and representation.			
4-1.1	Analyze information to solve increasingly more sophisticated problems.	*Used throughout the text.* For example: **1-3, 1-7, 2-3, 2-6, 7-3, 7-6, 8-3, 8-6, 10-6, 11-3, 12-5, 13-7, 14-6, 15-3, 15-5**	**26-27, 40-41, 62-63, 76-77, 280-281, 294-295, 320-321, 330-331, 416-417, 446-447, 502-503, 564-565, 594-595, 626-627, 634-635**
4-1.2	Construct arguments that lead to conclusions about general mathematical properties and relationships.	*Used throughout the text.* For example: 2-1, 4-2, **Extend 11-6, CSB10**	55-57, 150-153, **464-465, R65**
4-1.3	Explain and justify answers to problems on the basis of mathematical properties, structures, and relationships.	*Used throughout the text.* For example: **2-1, 4-2, Explore 7-4, CSB1**	**55-57, 150-153, 282-283, R56**
4-1.4	Generate descriptions and mathematical statements about relationships between and among classes of objects.	*Used throughout the text.* For example: 9-6, **13-3**	376-378, **544-545**
4-1.5	Use correct, complete, and clearly written and oral mathematical language to pose questions, communicate ideas, and extend problem situations.	*Used throughout the text.* For example: **P1, P2, P3, P4**	**P2-P9**
4-1.6	Generalize connections between new mathematical ideas and related concepts and subjects that have been previously considered.	*Used throughout the text.* For example: **Ch. 1 CC, Extend 2-4**	**42-43, 68**
4-1.7	Use flexibility in mathematical representations.	*Used throughout the text.* For example: **9-7, 14-3**	**380-381, 586-587**
4-1.8	Recognize the limitations of various forms of mathematical representations.	*Used throughout the text.* For example: **9-7, 14-3**	**380-381, 586-587**
Number and Operations			
Standard 4-2: The student will demonstrate through the mathematical processes an understanding of decimal notation as an extension of the place-value system; the relationship between fractions and decimals; the multiplication of whole numbers; and accurate, efficient, and generalizable methods of dividing whole numbers, adding decimals, and subtracting decimals.			
4-2.1	Recognize the period in the place-value structure of whole numbers: units, thousands, millions, and billions.	**1-1, 1-2,** Ch. 1 CC, 10-1	**17-19, 22-25,** 42-43, 395-397
4-2.2	Apply divisibility rules for 2, 5, and 10.	**CSB2**	**R57**
4-2.3	Apply an algorithm to multiply whole numbers fluently.	**Explore 4-1, 4-1, 4-3, 4-4, 4-5, Ch. 4 CC, 4-6, 4-7, 4-8, 6-1, 6-2, 6-3, 6-4, 6-5, 6-6, Ch. 6 CC, 6-7, 7-1, 7-2, Explore 7-4, 7-4, 7-5, Ch. 7 CC, 7-7**	**145-149, 154-162, 164-174, 237-244, 246-248, 250-261, 273-279, 282-286, 288-293, 296-298**

Standards and Indicators		Lesson(s)	Page Number(s)
4-2.4	Explain the effect on the product when one of the factors is changed.	**6-1**	**237-239**
4-2.5	Generate strategies to divide whole numbers by single-digit divisors.	**Explore 4-1, 4-1, 4-3, 4-5, Ch. 4 CC, 4-6, 4-7, Explore 8-1, 8-1, 8-2, 8-4, 8-5, 8-7, Extend 8-7, 8-8, Ch. 8 CC, 8-9**	**145-149, 154-157, 160-162, 164-171, 311-319, 322-324, 326-329, 332-338, 340-345**
4-2.6	Analyze the magnitude of digits through hundredths on the basis of their place value.	1-1, **Explore 1-2**, 1-2, **1-5, Explore 14-1, 14-1, CSB6**	17-19, **20-21**, 22-25, **32-34, 577-581, R61**
4-2.7	Compare decimals through hundredths by using the terms *is less than, is greater than,* and *is equal to* and the symbols <, >, and =.	**1-4, Ch. 1 CC, 14-5, 14-8**	**28-30, 42-43, 590-592, 602-604**
4-2.8	Apply strategies and procedures to find equivalent forms of fractions.	**Explore 13-4, 13-4, Ch. 13 CC**	**546-551, 558-559**
4-2.9	Compare the relative size of fractions to the benchmarks $0, \frac{1}{2},$ and 1.	**13-5,** 14-8	**554-557,** 602-604
4-2.10	Identify common the fraction/decimal equivalents $\frac{1}{2} = .5, \frac{1}{4} = .25, \frac{3}{4} = .75, \frac{1}{3} \approx .33, \frac{2}{3} \approx .67,$ multiples of $\frac{1}{10},$ and multiples of $\frac{1}{100}.$	**Explore 14-1, 14-1, 14-2, 14-4, 14-7, Ch. 14 CC, CSB4**	**577-585, 588-589, 596-601, R59**
4-2.11	Represent improper fractions, mixed numbers, and decimals.	**13-6,** Explore 14-1, 14-1, 14-2, 14-4, **15-1**	**560-563,** 577-585, 588-589, **617-620**
4-2.12	Generate strategies to add and subtract decimals through hundredths.	**15-2, Explore 15-4, 15-4, Explore 15-6, 15-6, Ch. 15 CC**	**622-625, 628-632, 636-643**

Algebra

Standard 4-3: The student will demonstrate through the mathematical processes an understanding of numeric and nonnumeric patterns, the representation of simple mathematical relationships, and the application of procedures to find the value of an unknown.

4-3.1	Analyze numeric, nonnumeric, and repeating patterns involving all operations and decimal patterns through hundredths.	**5-4, 9-3, FOSC4**	**204-206, 366-367, 663-664**
4-3.2	Generalize a rule for numeric, nonnumeric, and repeating patterns involving all operations.	**5-4**	**204-206**
4-3.3	Use a rule to complete a sequence or a table.	**5-5, 5-8, 12-9**	**208-211, 220-223, 518-519**
4-3.4	Translate among letters, symbols, and words to represent quantities in simple mathematical expressions or equations.	**5-1, 5-5, Ch. 5 CC, 5-6, 5-8**	**193-195, 208-216, 220-223**
4-3.5	Apply procedures to find the value of an unknown letter or symbol in a whole-number equation.	**Explore 5-2, 5-2, 5-3,** 5-5, 5-8	**196-203,** 208-211, 220-223
4-3.6	Illustrate situations that show change over time as either increasing, decreasing, or varying.	**CSB15**	**R70-R71**

FOSC = Focus on South Carolina, CSB = Concepts and Skills Bank, P = Projects, CC = Cross-Curricular

Standards and Indicators		Lesson(s)	Page Number(s)
Geometry			
Standard 4-4: The student will demonstrate through the mathematical processes an understanding of the relationship between two- and three-dimensional shapes, the use of transformations to determine congruency, and the representation of location and movement within the first quadrant of a coordinate system.			
4-4.1	Analyze the quadrilaterals squares, rectangles, trapezoids, rhombuses, and parallelograms according to their properties.	**9-6**	**376-378**
4-4.2	Analyze the relationship between three-dimensional geometric shapes in the form of cubes, rectangular prisms, and cylinders and their two-dimensional nets.	**9-1**	**359-361**
4-4.3	Predict the results of multiple transformations of the same type—translation, reflection, or rotation—on a two-dimensional geometric shape.	**Explore 10-5, 10-5, 10-7**	**410-415, 418-420**
4-4.4	Represent the two-dimensional shapes trapezoids, rhombuses, and parallelograms and the three-dimensional shapes cubes, rectangular prisms, and cylinders.	**9-1,** 9-2, **9-6, Ch. 9 CC**	**359-361,** 362-365, **376-378, 382-383**
4-4.5	Use transformation(s) to prove congruency.	**10-7, Extend 10-7**	**418-421**
4-4.6	Represent points, lines, line segments, rays, angles, and polygons.	**9-2,** 9-4, **9-5, 10-1, 10-2**	**362-365,** 368-370, **372-375, 395-397, 400-403**
4-4.7	Represent with ordered pairs of whole numbers the location of points in the first quadrant of a coordinate grid.	**10-4, CSB7**	**406-408, R62**
4-4.8	Illustrate possible paths from one point to another along vertical and horizontal grid lines in the first quadrant of the coordinate plane.	**10-4**	**406-408**
Measurement			
Standard 4-5: The student will demonstrate through the mathematical processes an understanding of elapsed time; conversions within the U.S. Customary System; and accurate, efficient, and generalizable methods of determining area.			
4-5.1	Use appropriate tools to measure objects to the nearest unit: measuring length in quarter inches, centimeters, and millimeters; measuring liquid volume in cups, quarts, and liters; and measuring weight and mass in pounds, milligrams, and kilograms.	**Explore 11-1, 11-1, Explore 11-4, 11-4, Explore 12-1, 12-1, 12-3, Explore 12-4, 12-4, 12-7**	**439-443, 448-452, 485-489, 492-500, 508-510**
4-5.2	Compare angle measures with referent angles of 45 degrees, 90 degrees, and 180 degrees to estimate angle measures.	**9-4**	**368-370**
4-5.3	Use equivalencies to convert units of measure within the U.S. Customary System: converting length in inches, feet, yards, and miles; converting weight in ounces, pounds, and tons; converting liquid volume in cups, pints, quarts, and gallons; and converting time in years, months, weeks, days, hours, minutes, and seconds.	**11-2, Ch. 11 CC, 12-2, 12-6, Ch. 12 CC, CSB8**	**444-445, 454-455, 490-491, 504-507, 516-517, R63**
4-5.4	Analyze the perimeter of a polygon.	**11-5, CSB11**	**456-459, R66**

Standards and Indicators		Lesson(s)	Page Number(s)
4-5.5	Generate strategies to determine the area of rectangles and triangles.	**11-6, 11-7, FOSC5, CSB12, CSB13, CSB14**	**460-462, 466-467, 665-666, R67-R69**
4-5.6	Apply strategies and procedures to determine the amount of elapsed time in hours and minutes within a 12-hour period, either a.m. or p.m.	**12-10**	**520-523**
4-5.7	Use Celsius and Fahrenheit thermometers to determine temperature changes during time intervals.	**11-8**	**468-471**
4-5.8	Recall equivalencies associated with liquid volume, time, weight, and length: 8 liquid ounces = 1 cup, 2 cups = 1 pint, 2 pints = 1 quart, 4 quarts = 1 gallon; 365 days = 1 year, 52 weeks = 1 year; 16 ounces = 1 pound, 2,000 pounds = 1 ton; and 5,280 feet = 1 mile.	11-2, **12-2, 12-6,** CSB8	444-445, **490-491, 504-507,** R63
4-5.9	Exemplify situations in which highly accurate measurements are required.	**11-7**	**466-467**
Data Analysis and Probability			
Standard 4-6: The student will demonstrate through the mathematical processes an understanding of the impact of data-collection methods, the appropriate graph for categorical or numerical data, and the analysis of possible outcomes for a simple event.			
4-6.1	Compare how data-collection methods impact survey results.	3-1	95-97
4-6.2	Interpret data in tables, line graphs, bar graphs, and double bar graphs whose scale increments are greater than or equal to 1.	**3-2, 3-5, 3-6, 3-7, Ch. 3 CC, FOSC1, FOSC2, FOSC2 Extend, CSB15**	**98-101, 108-110, 112-114, 118-121, 654-656, 657-658, 659-660, R70-R71**
4-6.3	Organize data in tables, line graphs, and bar graphs whose scale increments are greater than or equal to 1.	**3-1, 3-3, Extend 3-6, 5-7**	**95-97, 102-103, 116-117, 218-219**
4-6.4	Distinguish between categorical and numerical data.	**FOSC3, CSB16**	**661-662, R72-R73**
4-6.5	Match categorical and numerical data to appropriate graphs.	**FOSC3, CSB16**	**661-662, R72-R73**
4-6.6	Predict on the basis of data whether events are *likely, unlikely, certain, impossible,* or *equally likely* to occur.	**3-9**	**128-130**
4-6.7	Analyze possible outcomes for a simple event.	**Explore 3-8, 3-8, Extend 3-9, 10-3**	**122-127, 131, 404-405**

FOSC = Focus on South Carolina, CSB = Concepts and Skills Bank, P = Projects, CC = Cross-Curricular

Contents

Start Smart

H.O.T. Problems

WRITING IN ▸MATH 3, 5, 7, 9, 11, 13

CHAPTER 1

Use Place Value to Represent Whole Numbers

SCAS

Focal Points and Connections
See page iv for key.

G4-FP8C Number and Operations

 PASS PRACTICE 25, 31, 39, 49, 50, 51

H.O.T. Problems
Higher Order Thinking 19, 25, 30, 34, 39

WRITING IN ▸MATH 19, 21, 25, 27, 30, 31, 34, 39, 41, 49

Contents

CHAPTER 2

Solve Addition and Subtraction Problems

SCAS

Focal Points and Connections
See page iv for key.

G4-FP4C Algebra
G4-FP8C Number and Operations

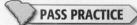 **PASS PRACTICE** 61, 67, 69, 83, 89, 90, 91

H.O.T. Problems
Higher Order Thinking 57, 61, 67, 74, 82

WRITING IN MATH 57, 61, 63, 67, 68, 69, 71, 74, 77, 82, 89

CHAPTER 3

Organize, Display, and Interpret Data

SCAS

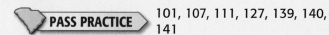

Focal Points and Connections
See page iv for key.

G4-FP7C Data Analysis

Contents

CHAPTER 4

Apply Multiplication and Division Facts

Focal Points and Connections
See page iv for key.

G4-FP1 Number and Operations and Algebra

PASS PRACTICE 153, 157, 163, 169, 179, 187, 188, 189

H.O.T. Problems
Higher Order Thinking 149, 153, 157, 162, 169, 174, 179

WRITING IN MATH 146, 149, 153, 157, 159, 162, 163, 169, 171, 174, 179, 187

CHAPTER 5

Describe Algebraic Patterns

SCAS

Focal Points and Connections
See page iv for key.

G4-FP4C Algebra
G4-FP1 Number and Operations and Algebra

 PASS PRACTICE   201, 207, 211, 223, 231, 232, 233

H.O.T. Problems
Higher Order Thinking 195, 200, 206, 210, 222

WRITING IN ►MATH 195, 197, 200, 203, 206, 207, 210, 216, 219, 222, 231

Contents

CHAPTER 6
Multiply by One-Digit Numbers

 SCAS

Focal Points and Connections
See page iv for key.

G4-FP1 Number and Operations and Algebra

PASS PRACTICE 249, 255, 261, 267, 268, 269

H.O.T. Problems
Higher Order Thinking 239, 244, 248, 255, 261

WRITING IN ►MATH 239, 241, 244, 248, 249, 251, 255, 261, 267

CHAPTER 7
Multiply by Two-Digit Numbers

SCAS

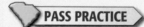

Focal Points and Connections
See page iv for key.

G4-FP1 Number and Operations and Algebra

PASS PRACTICE   279, 287, 291, 305, 306, 307

H.O.T. Problems
Higher Order Thinking 275, 279, 286, 290, 298

WRITING IN ►MATH 275, 279, 281, 283, 286, 287, 290, 295, 298, 305

Contents

CHAPTER 8 — Divide by One-Digit Numbers

 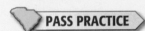
Focal Points and Connections
See page iv for key.

G4-FP8C Number and Operations

PASS PRACTICE 319, 325, 329, 345, 353, 354, 355

H.O.T. Problems
Higher Order Thinking 315, 319, 324, 329, 334, 338, 345

WRITING IN MATH 312, 315, 319, 321, 324, 325, 329, 331, 334, 338, 345, 353

CHAPTER 9
Identify and Describe Geometric Figures

SCAS

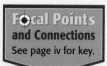
Focal Points and Connections
See page iv for key.

G4-FP6C Measurement
G4-FP5C Geometry

H.O.T. Problems

Contents

CHAPTER 10
Understand and Develop Spatial Reasoning

SCAS

Focal Points and Connections
See page iv for key.

G4-FP5C Geometry

H.O.T. Problems
Higher Order Thinking 397, 403, 408, 415, 420, 424

WRITING IN MATH 397, 399, 403, 405, 408, 409, 411, 415, 417, 420, 424, 433

CHAPTER 11

Measure Length, Area, and Temperature

SCAS

Focal Points and Connections
See page iv for key.

G4-FP3 Measurement
G4-FP5C Geometry

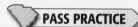

PASS PRACTICE 453, 459, 479, 480, 481

H.O.T. Problems
Higher Order Thinking 443, 445, 452, 458, 462, 471

WRITING IN ▸MATH 440, 443, 445, 447, 449, 452, 453, 458, 462, 465, 467, 471, 479

Contents

Measure Capacity, Weight, and Volume

SCAS

Focal Points and Connections
See page iv for key.

G4-FP3 Measurement
G4-FP5C Geometry

PASS PRACTICE 489, 495, 501, 507, 515, 523, 531, 532

H.O.T. Problems
Higher Order Thinking 489, 491, 494, 500, 506, 510, 515, 523

WRITING IN ▸MATH 485, 491, 497, 503, 506, 519, 531

Describe and Compare Fractions

SCAS

Focal Points and Connections
See page iv for key.

G4-FP2 Number and Operations
G4-FP8C Number and Operations

PASS PRACTICE 543, 553, 557, 571, 572, 573

H.O.T. Problems
Higher Order Thinking 539, 543, 551, 557, 563

WRITING IN ►MATH 539, 543, 545, 547, 551, 553, 557, 563, 565, 571

Contents

CHAPTER 14 Use Place Value to Represent Decimals

Focal Points and Connections
See page iv for key.

G4-FP2 Number and Operations
G4-FP8C Number and Operations

PASS PRACTICE 585, 593, 599, 604, 611, 612, 613

H.O.T. Problems
Higher Order Thinking 581, 585, 589, 592, 599, 604

WRITING IN MATH 578, 581, 585, 587, 589, 592, 593, 595, 599, 611

CHAPTER 15

Add and Subtract Decimals

SCAS

Focal Points and Connections
See page iv for key.

G4-FP2 Number and Operations
G4-FP8C Number and Operations

PASS PRACTICE 620, 625, 633, 641, 649, 650, 651

H.O.T. Problems
Higher Order Thinking 620, 625, 632, 641

WRITING IN ▶MATH 620, 625, 627, 629, 632, 633, 635, 637, 649

Contents

FOCUS ON

South Carolina
Beyond the Focal Points

SCAS

Problem-Solving Projects

H.O.T. Problems
Higher Order Thinking 656

WRITING IN ▶MATH 656, 660, 664

Student Handbook

Built-In Workbook

Reference

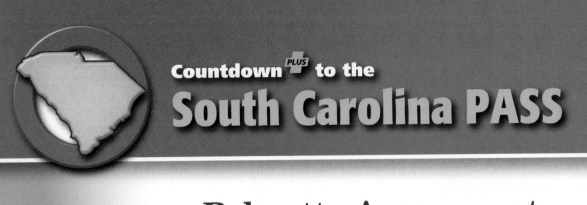

Palmetto Assessment of State Standards

In May, you will take the Grade 4 Palmetto Assessment of State Standards (PASS) for Mathematics. The PASS covers the South Carolina Academic Standards. It has multiple-choice and constructed-response questions. You will apply the concepts and skills that you have learned throughout the year.

Multiple-Choice Items

For multiple-choice questions, you will select the correct response from four answer choices. Your teacher will provide you with an answer sheet to fill in your answer choices.

Constructed-Response Items

For constructed-response questions, you will write an answer to open-ended questions. You are required to show your work to receive full credit. In some cases, you will be required to explain, in words, how you arrived at your response.

Should I Study for the PASS?

The good news is that you've been studying all along for the PASS – a little bit every day. Here are some of the ways your textbook has been preparing you for the test.

- **Every Day** Each lesson had practice questions that are similar to the questions on the PASS.

- **Every Week** The Mid-Chapter Quiz and Practice Test had several practice questions. Also, the following pages include a section called Countdown Plus to the PASS. These pages give you practice questions similar to those found on the test and specifically address the South Carolina Academic Standards for Grade 4 Mathematics.

- **Every Chapter** Each chapter had two full pages of practice questions that are similar to the questions on the PASS.

How Should I Use Countdown PLUS ?

Countdown Plus has 20 practice pages. You can use these pages in the weeks before the test to determine if you are ready.

Begin 20 weeks before the PASS. You should plan to complete one practice page each week to help you review the Grade 4 South Carolina Palmetto Assessment of State Standards.

One-a-Day

Plan to spend a few minutes each day working on the practice problem for that day unless your teacher asks you to do otherwise.

Reviewing Skills

If you are struggling with any of the items, lesson references are provided so that you can go back and review from the pages in your textbook.

Week 20

Monday

1. Which number is less than the number represented by point *A*? (Lesson 1-4)
(4-2.1, 4-1.2)

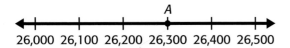

	A	
26,000 26,100 26,200 26,300 26,400 26,500		

- Ⓐ 26,350
- Ⓒ 26,400
- Ⓑ 27,125
- Ⓓ 26,200

Tuesday

2. What is the value of 3 in 593,659?

(Lesson 1-1) (4-2.6, 4-1.1)

- Ⓐ 300
- Ⓑ 3000
- Ⓒ 30,000
- Ⓓ 300,000

Wednesday

3. Which set of numbers is in order from greatest to least? (Lesson 1-5) (4-2.6, 4-1.2)

- Ⓐ 27,503; 27,305; 27,530; 27,035
- Ⓑ 38,934; 38,439; 37,934; 38,349
- Ⓒ 76,487; 76,478; 67,847; 76,874
- Ⓓ 93,840; 93,804, 93,408; 93,084

Thursday

4. Which sentence below is true?

(Lesson 1-4) (4-2.1, 4-1.2)

- Ⓐ 15,384 < 15,934
- Ⓑ 38,394 = 38,943
- Ⓒ 84,239 > 85,239
- Ⓓ 93,320 < 93,230

Friday

5. **a.** What is the value of 6 in the number shown at the right? (Lesson 1-1) (4-2.6, 4-1.1)

Thousands			Ones		
hundreds	tens	ones	hundreds	tens	ones
2	6	8	0	9	5

b. Is 269,047 >, <, or = the number shown at the right? Explain. (Lesson 1-4) (4-2.1, 4-1.2)

Week 19

1. Which number sentence shows the Associative Property of Addition? (Lesson 2-1) (4-3.5, 4-1.3)

   Ⓐ $(57 + \blacksquare) + 36 = 57 + (25 + 36)$

   Ⓑ $8 + 0 = 8$

   Ⓒ $4 + 1 = 5, 1 + 4 = 5$

   Ⓓ $5 + 7 + 3 = 15$

2. What is 45,715,503 rounded to the thousands place? (Lesson 1-6) (4-2.1, 4-1.1)

   Ⓐ 45,715,000

   Ⓑ 45,715,900

   Ⓒ 45,716,000

   Ⓓ 45,720,000

3. What is 4396 rounded to the thousands place? (Lesson 1-6) (4-2.1, 4-1.1)

   Ⓐ 4400

   Ⓑ 4000

   Ⓒ 4390

   Ⓓ 4300

4. What property explains why the number sentences $23 + 2 = 25$ and $2 + 23 = 25$ have the same sum? (Lesson 2-1) (4-3.2, 4-1.3)

   Ⓐ Associative Property

   Ⓑ Identity Property of Addition

   Ⓒ Multiplication Property of Zero

   Ⓓ Commutative Property

5. **a.** What is the value of 7 in 1,527,064? (Lesson 1-1) (4-2.1, 4-1.1)

   b. How would you complete the place value chart below to support your answer? Explain. (Lesson 1-2) (4-2.1, 4-1.2)

Millions			Thousands			Ones		
hundreds	tens	ones	hundreds	tens	ones	hundreds	tens	ones

Monday

1. What outcome is certain to take place when Margarita spins the spinner? (Lesson 3-9) (4-6.6, 4-1.6)

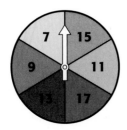

- Ⓐ 9, 13, or 15
- Ⓑ even number
- Ⓒ number less than 11
- Ⓓ odd number

Tuesday

2. What scale is needed to create a bar graph from the line plot? (Lesson 3-5) (4-6.2, 4-1.7)

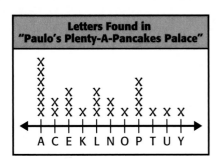

- Ⓐ 0–6
- Ⓑ 0–11
- Ⓒ 0–24
- Ⓓ 5–15

Wednesday

3. Which set of data is best represented in a double bar graph? (Lesson 3-6) (4-6.2, 4-1.3)

- Ⓐ Times tornadoes occurred in seven states in one year
- Ⓑ Number of days Carson was absent each quarter in one school year
- Ⓒ Number of books read each month by 5th and 6th grade students
- Ⓓ Number of inches that water in Lake Wylie dropped and number of boating licenses bought in York County from June to November

Thursday

4. Based on the results shown in the table, what is the probability that the spinner will land on red? (Lesson 3-9) (4-6.6, 4-1.6)

Dylan's Spinner	
Color	**Results**
Blue	卌 卌 ||||
Green	卌 卌 卌 |||
Red	|||

- Ⓐ likely
- Ⓑ equally likely
- Ⓒ unlikely
- Ⓓ impossible

Friday

5. a. The side dishes on a menu are grits, sliced tomatoes, hash browns, and biscuits. How many combinations are possible if a customer chooses two side dishes? (Lesson 3-8) (4-6.7, 4-1.7)

b. How many combinations are left if you take away side dish combinations that are the same? (Lesson 3-8) (4-6.7, 4-1.7)

Week 17

1. What is the value of the underlined digit in 31,7<u>5</u>2,001? (Lesson 1-2) (4-2.1, 4-1.5)

   Ⓐ 500
   Ⓑ 5000
   Ⓒ 50,000
   Ⓓ 5,000,000

2. What number will make the expression $(5 + 9) + 6 = 5 + (9 + \blacksquare)$ true? (Lesson 2-1) (4-3.5, 4-1.3)

   Ⓐ 9
   Ⓑ 6
   Ⓒ 5
   Ⓓ 0

3. Which number contains the digit 6 in the place value that has the least value? (Lesson 1-2) (4-2.1, 4-1.7)

   Ⓐ six million, three hundred twenty-seven thousand, eight hundred two
   Ⓑ one hundred five thousand, six hundred sixty
   Ⓒ twenty-six thousand, nine hundred twenty-three
   Ⓓ four thousand, three hundred forty-two

4. What symbol makes the number sentence below true? (Lesson 1-4) (4-3.5, 4-1.3)

   $$300 + 60 + 2 \ \bullet\ 600 + 20 + 3$$

   Ⓐ >   Ⓒ =
   Ⓑ <   Ⓓ ×

5. **a.** What number is the outlier in the data table? (Lesson 3-2) (4-6.2, 4-1.5)

Flower Deliveries Made in December				
Week	1	2	3	4
Deliveries	37	123	167	139

   b. Explain why this number is the outlier. (Lesson 3-2) (4-6.2, 4-1.5)

Week 16

Monday

1. Which number sentence is NOT represented by the array? (Lesson 4-6) (4-2.3, 4-1.7)

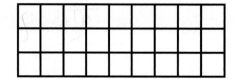

Ⓐ 5 × 11 = 55 ⓒ 11 × 5 = 55
Ⓑ 55 ÷ 5 = 10 Ⓓ 5 = 55 ÷ 11

Tuesday

2. Roxanne has 63 jelly beans. If she shares them equally with 7 of her friends, how many jelly beans will each person get? (Lesson 4-5) (4-2.5, 4-1.5)

Ⓐ 9
Ⓑ 8
ⓒ 7
Ⓓ 6

Wednesday

3. Which set of factors will result in the products 15, 10, and 25 when multiplied by 5? (Lesson 4-3) (4-2.4, 4-1.7)

Ⓐ 1, 2, and 3
Ⓑ 2, 3, and 4
ⓒ 3, 4, and 5
Ⓓ 6, 7, and 8

Thursday

4. Shawna has 50 CDs. If she places an equal amount of CDs on each of 5 shelves, how many CDs will be on each shelf? (Lesson 4-5) (4-2.2, 4-1.5)

Ⓐ 10
Ⓑ 30
ⓒ 50
Ⓓ 55

Friday

5. **a.** What multiplication equation is represented by the array? (Lesson 4-5) (4-2.4, 4-1.5)

b. Suppose one row in the array is deleted. What multiplication expression would represent the new array? Explain. (Lesson 4-5) (4-2.4, 4-1.1)

Week 15

Monday

1. Sonia made the function table below. What pattern is taking place between the output numbers? (Lesson 5-4) (4-3.3, 4-1.1)

Input	Output
2	2000
3	3000
4	4000
5	5000

Ⓐ add 1000
Ⓒ multiply by 1000
Ⓑ subtract 1000
Ⓓ divide by 1000

Tuesday

2. A pet store has nine aquarium tanks of 36 fish each. Which expression can be used to find the total number of fish in the pet store? (Lesson 5-6) (4-3.4, 4-1.5)

Ⓐ 36 + 9
Ⓒ 36 × 9
Ⓑ 36 − 9
Ⓓ 36 ÷ 9

Wednesday

3. Randy is drawing the figures below. Which sentence explains the rule for the pattern? (Lesson 5-4) (4-3.3, 4-1.4)

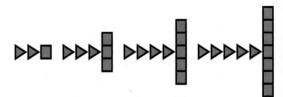

Ⓐ add one ▷ and two ▢
Ⓑ add two ▷ and one ▢
Ⓒ add three ▷ and two ▢
Ⓓ add four and (2 ▷ × 1 ▢)

Thursday

4. Which expression shows fifty-six divided by a number? (Lesson 5-6) (4-3.4, 4-1.7)

Ⓐ $n \div 56$
Ⓑ $n + 56$
Ⓒ $56 \times n$
Ⓓ $56 \div n$

Friday

5. **a.** How much does Taylor save of her allowance each week? (Lesson 5-4) (4-3.4, 4-1.1)

Taylor's Allowance Savings								
Week	1	2	3	4	5	6	7	8
Total Saved	$12	$24	$36	$48	$60	$72	$84	$96

b. Write an expression that represents the total amount of money Taylor has saved by n weeks. How much will Taylor have saved by week ten? (Lesson 5-4) (4-3.4, 4-1.1)

Week 14

1. Which pair of numbers best completes the equation below? (Lesson 6-1)
(4-2.3, 4-1.4)

$$\square \times 70 = \bigcirc$$

Ⓐ 60 and 420

Ⓑ 60 and 4200

Ⓒ 60 and 42,000

Ⓓ 600 and 4200

2. What two partial products can be used to find 24 × 3? (Lesson 6-4) (4-2.3, 4-1.2)

Ⓐ 50 and 7

Ⓑ 23 and 24

Ⓒ 60 and 12

Ⓓ 50 and 12

3. What number completes the number sentence below? (Lesson 6-4) (4-2.3, 4-1.2)

$$4 \times 52 = (4 \times \blacksquare) + (4 \times 2)$$

Ⓐ 5

Ⓑ 10

Ⓒ 20

Ⓓ 50

4. There are 200 booths at a state fair. Each booth is given 5000 tickets to sell to customers. How many tickets is this in all? (Lesson 6-1) (4-2.3, 4-1.5)

Ⓐ 10,000

Ⓑ 100,000

Ⓒ 1,000,000

5. **a.** Use the chart below to answer the question. What equation can be written to show the relationship between June 2006 and June 2009 sales? (Lesson 6-4) (4-2.3, 4-1.3)

Danny's Boiled Peanuts Summer Sales, 2006–2009				
Year	June	July	August	Over-all Sales Total
2006	3	4	30	37
2007	12	9	48	69
2008	16	10	32	48
2009	36	7	31	74

b. How do total sales in 2006 compare to total sales in 2009? Explain. (Lesson 6-4) (4-2.3, 4-1.1)

Week 13

Monday

1. Which number has the greatest value? (Lesson 1-4) (4-2.1, 4-1.4)

```
←——+————+————+————+——→
  3,200   3,300   3,400   3,500
```

Ⓐ 3400

Ⓑ 3250

Ⓒ 3500

Ⓓ 3350

Tuesday

2. What is the value of 3256 subtracted from the number shown below?

(Lesson 2-5) (4-2.1, 4-1.6)

Thousands			Ones		
hundreds	tens	ones	hundreds	tens	ones
		9	3	4	9

Ⓐ 7093

Ⓑ 6113

Ⓒ 6093

Ⓓ 693

Wednesday

3. Which number makes the number sentence true? (Lesson 4-2) (4-3.5, 4-1.2)

$$(4 \times 20) + (4 \times 8) = 4 \times \blacksquare$$

Ⓐ 28

Ⓑ 20

Ⓒ 8

Ⓓ 4

Thursday

4. Bradley made the function table below. What pattern is taking place between the output numbers? (Lesson 5-4)

(4-3.2, 4-1.1)

Input	1	2	3	4	5
Output	95	91	87	83	79

Ⓐ add 4 then subtract 1

Ⓑ subtract 5 then add 1

Ⓒ add 2 then subtract 4

Ⓓ subtract 1 then add 5

Friday

5. **a.** A boss purchased a 12-month pass to an amusement park for each employee. There are 8 employees. One 12-month pass costs $98. Write an expression that can be used to find the total cost of the passes. (Lesson 6-4) (4-2.3, 4-1.1)

b. Explain how the total cost could be shown with base-ten blocks. What is the total cost? (Lesson 6-4) (4-2.3, 4-1.1)

Week 12

Monday

1. A coach bought 15 helmets that cost $120 each. About how much is the total cost of the helmets? (Lesson 7-5) **(4-2.2, 4-1.2)**

Ⓐ $100 × 20 = $2000

Ⓑ $200 × 50 = $10,000

Ⓒ $120 × 15 = $1810

Ⓓ $200 × 5 = $1000

Tuesday

2. Shelly is buying 13 bushels of peaches. How many peaches will Shelly have altogether? (Lesson 7-4) **(4-2.3, 4-1.5)**

Container	Peaches
Sack	6
Basket	12
Bushel	36

Ⓐ 13 + 6 = 19 peaches

Ⓑ 36 ÷ 12 = 3 peaches

Ⓒ 12 × 13 = 156 peaches

Ⓓ 13 × 36 = 458 peaches

Wednesday

3. What is the product of 362 × 17? (Lesson 7-5) **(4-2.3, 4-1-7)**

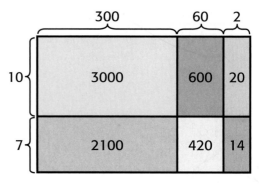

Ⓐ 6045

Ⓑ 6140

Ⓒ 6154

Ⓓ 6254

Thursday

4. What is the estimate of 55 × 49 when each factor is rounded to the nearest ten? (Lesson 7-2) **(4-2.3, 4-1.5)**

Ⓐ 60 × 50 = 3000

Ⓑ 50 × 50 = 2500

Ⓒ 50 × 40 = 2000

Ⓓ 60 × 40 = 2400

Friday

5. **a.** The map shows the distance between Columbia and Mount Pleasant. Estimate how many miles a truck driver will travel during 32 round trips. (Lesson 7-2) **(4-2.3, 4-1.5)**

b. What is the exact number of miles traveled? Is the estimate greater than or less than the exact miles traveled? Explain. (Lesson 7-5) **(4-2.3, 4-1.8)**

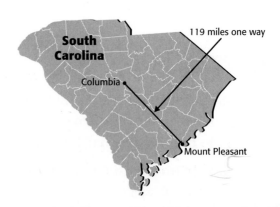

Week 11

1. Jamison read a book that was 450 pages long. He read 50 pages a day. How many days did it take him to read the book? (Lesson 8-2) (4-2.2, 4-1.5)

   Ⓐ 6

   Ⓑ 7

   Ⓒ 8

   Ⓓ 9

2. Round the dividend to the nearest hundred, then solve $4489 \div 5 = \blacksquare$.
   (Lesson 8-4) (4-2.2, 4-1.5)

   Ⓐ 700

   Ⓑ 800

   Ⓒ 900

   Ⓓ 1000

3. What is the division expression represented by the model below?
   (Lesson 8-1) (4-2.5, 4-1.4)

   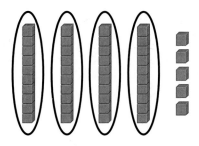

   Ⓐ $\$45 \div 10$ Ⓒ $\$45 \div 4$

   Ⓑ $\$40 \div 5$ Ⓓ $\$40 \div 10$

4. Tina wants to estimate the quotient for $352 \div 7$. What compatible number can be used for the dividend?
   (Lesson 8-4) (4-2.5, 4-1.7)

   Ⓐ 300

   Ⓑ 350

   Ⓒ 375

   Ⓓ 400

5. **a.** There are 320 students going to a school picnic. Each student will be served one hamburger. If there are 8 hamburger buns in one package, how many packages will be needed? (Lesson 8-5) (4-2.5, 4-1.1)

   b. There are 16 hamburger patties in each box. Explain a way to find the number of boxes of hamburger patties needed for 320 students. (Lesson 8-2) (4-2.5, 4-1.3)

Monday

1. How many more vertices does a cube have than a square? (Lesson 9-1) (4-4.2, 4-1.4)

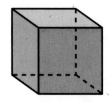

Ⓐ A cube has 2 times more vertices than a square.

Ⓑ A cube and a square have an equal number of vertices.

Ⓒ A cube has 8 more vertices than a square.

Ⓓ A cube has no vertices and a square has 4.

Tuesday

2. Which net will form a cube when folded? (Lesson 9-1) (4-4.2, 4-1.7)

Ⓐ 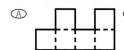   Ⓒ

Ⓑ 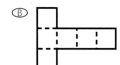   Ⓓ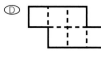

Wednesday

3. Which word does NOT describe the figure below? (Lesson 9-6) (4-4.1, 4-1.2)

Ⓐ parallelogram

Ⓑ rectangle

Ⓒ square

Ⓓ trapezoid

Thursday

4. A right angle is formed by the hands of which clock? (Lesson 9-4) (4-4.6, 4-1.6)

Ⓐ    Ⓒ

Ⓑ    Ⓓ

Friday

5. **a.** Identify the figures shown at the right. (Lesson 9-6) (4-4.1, 4-1.2)

   b. Explain how the figures are the same and how they are different. (Lesson 9-6) (4-4.1, 4-1.4)

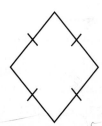

Week 9

1. Which number below is another way to represent 76,943? (Lesson 1-1) (4-2.1, 4-1.7)

ⓐ 7600 + 9423

ⓑ seventy-six thousand, six hundred ninety and forty-three

ⓒ 7000 + 600 + 90 + 4 + 2 + 3

ⓓ seventy-six thousand, nine hundred forty-three

2. How many band members received a score of 63 at a band competition? (Lesson 3-4) (4-6.2, 4-1.1)

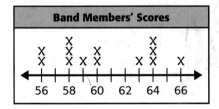

Band Members' Scores

ⓐ 1   ⓒ 3

ⓑ 2   ⓓ 4

3. What expression is represented by the model below? (Lesson 4-6) (4-2.3, 4-1.3)

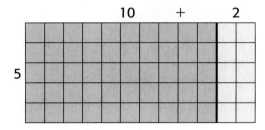

ⓐ 11 × 5   ⓒ 5 × 12

ⓑ 5 × 10   ⓓ 10 × 5

4. How many DVDs will 3 store clerks place on the shelves of a video store if 5734 DVDs are divided up equally? (Lesson 8-4) (4-2.5, 4-1.4)

ⓐ 6000 ÷ 3 = 2000 DVDs

ⓑ 5700 ÷ 3 = 1900 R11 DVDs

ⓒ 5734 ÷ 3 = 1911 R1 DVDs

ⓓ 5734 ÷ 3 = 19,001

5. **a.** What two types of figures are used in the pattern below? (Lesson 9-6) (4-4.1, 4-1.5)

b. Classify the two types of angles in the parallelogram. Then explain the rule for parallelograms in the pattern. (Lesson 9-4) (4-3.1, 4-1.1)

Week 8

1. What type of transformation is shown below? (Lesson 10-5) (4-4.3, 4-1.5)

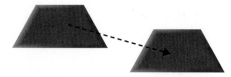

Ⓐ mutation   Ⓒ rotation
Ⓑ reflection   Ⓓ translation

2. Which pair of pattern blocks shows a reflection? (Lesson 10-5) (4-4.3, 4-1.4)

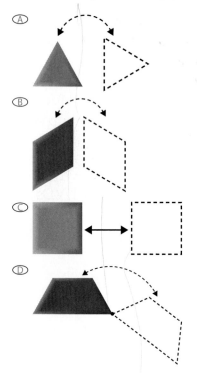

Ⓐ

Ⓑ

Ⓒ

Ⓓ

3. Which point is located at (6, 3)? (Lesson 10-4) (4-4.7, 4-1.7)

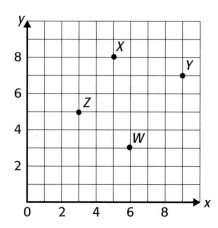

Ⓐ W   Ⓒ Y
Ⓑ X   Ⓓ Z

4. Which line is parallel to line *A*? (Lesson 10-2) (4-4.6, 4-1.1)

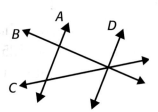

Ⓐ line *A*   Ⓒ line *C*
Ⓑ line *B*   Ⓓ line *D*

5 **a.** What transformation is represented by the triangles at the right? (Lesson 10-5) (4-4.3, 4-1.4)

b. Explain why the two triangles are congruent. (Lesson 10-7) (4-4.5, 4-1.2)

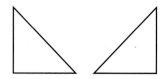

Week 7

Monday

1. Before school, the outside temperature was 43°F. The thermometer below shows the outside temperature during lunchtime.

Which of the following statements is true? (Lesson 11-8) (4-5.7, 4-1.4)

Ⓐ The temperature increased by 105°F.
Ⓑ The temperature increased by 19°F.
Ⓒ The temperature decreased by 19°F.
Ⓓ The temperature decreased by 62°F.

Tuesday

2. A rectangular photograph has a length of 7 inches and an area of 35 square inches. What is its perimeter?

(Lesson 11-5) (4-5.4, 4-1.1)

Ⓐ 5 inches   Ⓒ 17 inches
Ⓑ 12 inches   Ⓓ 24 inches

Wednesday

3. A rectangle has a width of 36 feet and a length of 84 feet. Which expression can be used to find the area of the rectangle? (Lesson 11-6) (4-5.5, 4-1.2)

Ⓐ 84 + 36
Ⓑ 84 − 36
Ⓒ 84 × 36
Ⓓ 84 ÷ 36

Thursday

4. Jana needs 57 inches of ribbon for a project. Each roll of ribbon is 1 yard long. How many rolls will Jana need to buy? (Lesson 11-2) (4-5.3, 4-1.1)

Ⓐ 1 roll
Ⓑ 2 rolls
Ⓒ 3 rolls
Ⓓ 4 rolls

Friday

5. **a.** A sheet of poster board is 3 feet long and 2 feet wide. What is the perimeter of the poster board in inches? (Lesson 11-5) (4-5.4, 4-1.6)

   b. Explain how you found the perimeter in inches. (Lesson 11-5) (4-5.4, 4-1.3)

Week 6

Monday

1. What time will it be 2 hours and 35 minutes from the time shown on the clock? (Lesson 12-10) (4-5.6, 4-1.1)

   Ⓐ 5:15   Ⓒ 6:00

   Ⓑ 5:50   Ⓓ 6:15

Tuesday

2. What is the most reasonable estimate for the mass of a wren? (Lesson 12-7)
(4-5.1, 4-1.2)

   Ⓐ 10 grams

   Ⓑ 10 kilograms

   Ⓒ 100 grams

   Ⓓ 100 kilograms

Wednesday

3. The cuckoo clock shown below sounds every 30 minutes. How many times will this clock sound when it is 5:30?
(Lesson 12-10) (4-5.6, 4-1.1)

   Ⓐ 4 times   Ⓒ 6 times

   Ⓑ 5 times   Ⓓ 7 times

Thursday

4. A cook needs to order 364 ounces of grits. One box contains 16 ounces of grits. How many boxes should the cook order? (Lesson 12-6) (4-5.8, 4-1.6)

   Ⓐ 8 boxes

   Ⓑ 6 boxes

   Ⓒ 4 boxes

   Ⓓ 2 boxes

Friday

5. **a.** Would liters or milliliters be the more appropriate unit of measure for a carton of juice that is 2 inches wide, 3 inches long, and 3 inches tall? (Lesson 12-3) (4-5.1, 4-1.3)

   b. Explain why the unit of measure chosen is more appropriate for the carton of juice.
(Lesson12-3) (4-5.1, 4-1.3)

Week 5

1. What is the elapsed time between clock A and clock B? (Lesson 12-10) (4-5.6, 4-1.2)

Clock A   Clock B

- Ⓐ 2 hours
- Ⓑ 2 hours 30 minutes
- Ⓒ 3 hours
- Ⓓ 3 hours 30 minutes

2. Which pair of lines shows perpendicular lines? (Lesson 10-2) (4-4.6, 4-1.3)

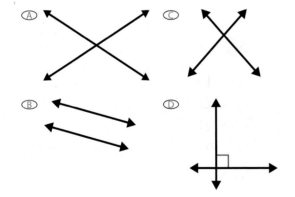

3. Ellis made a clay sculpture of a three-dimensional figure in art class. The sculpture has 6 faces, 12 edges, and 8 vertices. What three-dimensional figure did Ellis make? (Lesson 9-1) (4-4.2, 4-1.1)

- Ⓐ triangular prism
- Ⓑ triangular pyramid
- Ⓒ rectangular prism
- Ⓓ cylinder

4. How many squares will make up the next figure in the pattern? (Lesson 5-4) (4-3.1, 4-1.2)

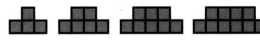

- Ⓐ 12
- Ⓑ 14
- Ⓒ 16
- Ⓓ 18

5. **a.** What is the perimeter of the screen on Mike's game player if the screen is 6 centimeters wide and 4 centimeters long? (Lesson 11-4) (4-5.4, 4-1.2)

b. How does the area of an index card that is 6 centimeters wide and 8 centimeters long compare to the area of the game player screen? Explain. (Lesson 11-6) (4-5.5, 4-1.4)

Week 4

Monday

1. Which fraction is NOT equivalent to the fraction shown by the model?
(Lesson 13-4) (4-2.8, 4-1.2)

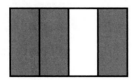

Ⓐ $\frac{6}{8}$ Ⓒ $\frac{12}{16}$

Ⓑ $\frac{9}{12}$ Ⓓ $\frac{16}{20}$

Tuesday

2. Which of the following does the model show? (Lesson 13-5) (4-2.9, 4-1.2)

Ⓐ $\frac{3}{5} < \frac{5}{10}$ Ⓒ $\frac{3}{5} = \frac{5}{10}$

Ⓑ $\frac{5}{10} > \frac{3}{5}$ Ⓓ $\frac{3}{5} > \frac{5}{10}$

Wednesday

3. What is the improper fraction and mixed number represented by the model? (Lesson 13-6) (4-2.11, 4-1.2)

Ⓐ $\frac{8}{7}$ and $2\frac{1}{7}$ Ⓒ $\frac{8}{7}$ and $1\frac{1}{7}$

Ⓑ $\frac{8}{7}$ and $8\frac{1}{7}$ Ⓓ $\frac{8}{7}$ and $1\frac{8}{7}$

Thursday

4. What is the order of the fractions $\frac{5}{12}$, $\frac{3}{6}$, and $\frac{1}{3}$ from least to greatest? (Lesson 13-5) (4-2.9, 4-1.2)

Ⓐ $\frac{3}{6}$, $\frac{1}{3}$, $\frac{5}{12}$ Ⓒ $\frac{1}{3}$, $\frac{3}{6}$, $\frac{5}{12}$

Ⓑ $\frac{3}{6}$, $\frac{5}{12}$, $\frac{1}{3}$ Ⓓ $\frac{1}{3}$, $\frac{5}{12}$, $\frac{3}{6}$

Friday

5. **a.** What symbol compares $\frac{2}{6}$ and $\frac{2}{4}$? Use >, <, or =. (Lesson 13-5) (4-2.9, 4-1.2)

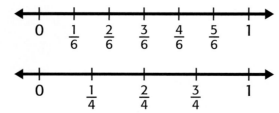

b. Explain why $\frac{3}{4}$ is greater than $\frac{3}{6}$. (Lesson 13-5) (4-2.9, 4-1.5)

Week 3

Monday

1. A fourth grade class ate $5\frac{7}{10}$ pizzas. Which decimal represents $5\frac{7}{10}$?

(Lesson 14-2) (4-2.10, 4-1.4)

Ⓐ 75.10

Ⓑ 57.10

Ⓒ 5.7

Ⓓ 5.07

Tuesday

2. A sunflower in Sabrina's garden is 6.7 feet tall. Which decimal is greater than 6.7? (Lesson 14-5) (4-2.7, 4-1.5)

Ⓐ 6.08

Ⓑ 6.10

Ⓒ 6.18

Ⓓ 6.81

Wednesday

3. Which set of numbers is equivalent?

(Lesson 14-7) (4-2.10, 4-1.7)

Ⓐ 0.25, $\frac{5}{2}$

Ⓑ 0.4, $\frac{2}{5}$

Ⓒ 0.75, $\frac{3}{10}$

Ⓓ 0.8, $\frac{5}{8}$

Thursday

4. The model below shows $\frac{4}{10}$. Which decimal also describes the model?

(Lesson 14-1) (4-2.11, 4-1.7)

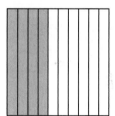

Ⓐ 4.00

Ⓑ 0.44

Ⓒ 0.40

Ⓓ 0.04

Friday

5. **a.** Compare 0.3 and 0.03. Use >, <, or =. (Lesson 14-5) (4-2.7, 4-1.4)

b. Explain how you know which decimal is greater. (Lesson 14-5) (4-2.6, 4-1.3)

Week 2

Monday

1. What numbers are missing in the pattern below? (Lesson 15-4) (4-2.6, 4-1.2)

$$0.7, \blacksquare , 2.3, \blacksquare , 3.7, 4.4$$

Ⓐ 1.6 and 3.0   Ⓒ 1.6 and 2.7

Ⓑ 1.3 and 3.0   Ⓓ 1.3 and 2.0

Tuesday

2. What equation does the model represent? (Lesson 15-6) (4-2.12, 4-1.1)

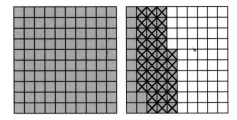

Ⓐ 14.6 − 0.34   Ⓒ 1.40 − 3.04

Ⓑ 1.46 − 3.4   Ⓓ 1.46 − 0.34

Wednesday

3. Which statement is NOT true? (Lesson 15-1) (4-2.7, 4-1.2)

Ⓐ 1.78 > 2.01

Ⓑ 2.01 > 1.78

Ⓒ 17.8 < 20.1

Ⓓ .178 < .201

Thursday

4. What symbol makes the number sentence 14.23 + 7.02 ⬤ 5.75 + 16.92 true? (Lesson 15-4) (4-2.12, 4-1.2)

Ⓐ >

Ⓑ <

Ⓒ =

Ⓓ ×

Friday

5. **a.** Which three decimals have a sum of 29.17? (Lesson 15-4) (4-2.12, 4-1.5)

| 12.72 | 6.13 | 7.42 | 9.03 |

b. Round each of the three decimals to the nearest whole number. How does the actual sum compare to the estimated sum? Explain. (Lesson 15-4) (4-2.10, 4-1.2)

Week 1

1. What fraction is represented by the shaded part of the figure below? (Lesson 13-1) (4-2.11, 4-1.3)

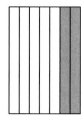

Ⓐ $\frac{1}{7}$ Ⓒ $\frac{1}{4}$

Ⓑ $\frac{2}{7}$ Ⓓ $\frac{3}{8}$

2. Which decimal has the greatest value? (Lesson 14-5) (4-2.6, 4-1.2)

Ⓐ 3.64

Ⓑ 4.36

Ⓒ 3.46

Ⓓ 4.63

3. Which number will make this statement true? (Lesson 4-1) (4-2.2, 4-1.2)

If $4 \times 5 = 20$, then $20 \div 4 = \blacksquare$.

Ⓐ 4

Ⓑ 5

Ⓒ 6

Ⓓ 7

4. Carla solved the problem below:

$$654 \div 5 = 130 \text{ R4}$$

Which expression could be used to check her answer? (Lesson 8-7) (4-2.3, 4-1.2)

Ⓐ $(5 \times 130) \times 4$

Ⓑ $(5 + 30) + 4$

Ⓒ $(5 \times 130) + 4$

Ⓓ $(5 + 130) \times 4$

5. **a.** On Friday, Zack played video games for 14.05 minutes. On Saturday, he played for 30.95 minutes and on Sunday he played for 22.17 minutes. About how many minutes did he play during those three days? (Lesson 15-4) (4-2.12, 4-1.1)

b. There are 60 minutes in one hour. Explain how to convert 66 minutes to hours and minutes. (Lesson 8-5) (4-2.5, 4-1.5)

To the Student

As you gear up to study mathematics, you are probably wondering, "What will I learn this year?"

- **Number and Operations:** Estimate and find products of whole numbers, including multidigit whole numbers.

- **Number and Operations:** Understand decimals and relate fractions and decimals.

- **Measurement:** Understand and find areas of two-dimensional figures.

Along the way, you'll learn more about problem solving, how to use the tools and language of mathematics, and how to THINK mathematically.

How to Use Your Math Book

Have you ever been in class and not understood all of what was being presented? Or, you understood everything in class, but got stuck on how to solve some of the homework problems? Don't worry. You can find answers in your math book!

- **Read** the MAIN IDEA at the beginning of the lesson.

- **Find** the New Vocabulary words, **highlighted in yellow**, and read their definitions.

- **Review** the EXAMPLE problems, solved step-by-step, to remind you of the day's material.

- **Refer** to the EXTRA PRACTICE boxes that show you where you can find extra exercises to practice a concept.

- **Go** to SC Math Online where you can find extra examples to coach you through difficult problems.

- **Review** the notes you've taken on your FOLDABLES.

- **Refer** to the Remember boxes for information that may help you with your examples and homework practice.

Let's Get Started

Use the Treasure Hunt below to learn where things are located in each chapter.

1. What is the title of Chapter 1?

2. What is the Main Idea of Lesson 1-1?

3. How do you know which words are vocabulary words?

4. What are the vocabulary words for Lesson 1-1?

5. What is the key concept shown in Lesson 1-6?

6. How many Examples are presented in Lesson 1-4?

7. What is the Web address where you could find extra examples?

8. On page 29, there is a Remember tip box. How does the Remember tip help you?

9. How many exercises are there in Lesson 1-5?

10. Suppose you need more practice on a concept. Where can you go for Extra Practice?

11. Suppose you're doing your homework on page 38 and you get stuck on Exercise 16. Where could you find help?

12. What is the web address that would allow you to take a self-check quiz to be sure you understand the lesson?

13. On what pages will you find the Chapter 1 Study Guide and Review?

14. Suppose you can't figure out how to do Exercise 36 in the Study Guide and Review on page 48. Where could you find help?

MATH? SYMBOLS.

South Carolina

Start Smart

Let's Review!

Loggerhead Turtle

Problem Solving

Climbing to the TOP!

Hiking is a popular sport in the mountains of South Carolina. The table shows the heights of the four tallest mountain peaks in the state.

What is the difference in height between Sassafras Mountain and Pinnacle Mountain?

South Carolina Mountain Peaks	
Mountain	Height (ft)
Sassafras Mountain	3,560
Hickorynut Mountain	3,483
Pinnacle Mountain	3,425
Table Rock Mountain	3,124

Source: U.S. Geological Survey

You can use the four-step problem-solving plan to solve math problems. The four steps are Understand, Plan, Solve, and Check.

Understand

- **Read the problem carefully.**
- **What facts do you know?**
- **What facts do you need to find?**

The table lists the heights of the mountain peaks. You need to find the difference in height between Sassafras Mountain and Pinnacle Mountain.

Plan

- **How do the facts relate to each other?**
- **Plan a strategy to solve the problem.**

To find the difference, subtract the height of Pinnacle Mountain from the height of Sassafras Mountain.

Solve

- **Use your plan to solve the problem.**

$$\begin{array}{r} \overset{5\,10}{3,5\cancel{6}\cancel{0}} \text{ feet} \\ -\ 3,425 \text{ feet} \\ \hline 135 \text{ feet} \end{array}$$ Sassafras Mountain
Pinnacle Mountain

So, Sassafras Mountain is 135 feet taller than Pinnacle Mountain.

Check

- **Look back.**
- **Does your answer make sense?**
- **If not, solve the problem another way.**

Sassafras Mountain is about 3,600 feet tall. Pinnacle Mountain is about 3,400 feet tall. So, an answer close to 200 feet makes sense.

CHECK What You Know

1. List the four steps of the four-step plan.

2. **WRITING IN ►MATH** The table shows the elevations of cities in South Carolina. Write a real-world problem using the table.

City Elevations	
City	Elevation (ft)
Columbia	1,931
Rock Hill	433
Anderson	787
Charleston	1,944

Source: U.S. Geological Survey

Lesson 2

Number and Operations

South Carolina Critters

The Carolina mantis is South Carolina's state insect. There are over 1,500 types of mantises.

CHECK What You Know **Addition and Subtraction** · · · · · · · · · · · ·

For Exercises 1–3, use the table. It shows how many eggs two South Carolina insects will lay at a time.

Insect Eggs	
Insect Type	Number of Eggs Laid at a Time
Carolina mantis	60
Twostriped walking stick	10

Source: Florida Department of Agriculture and Consumer Services

1. How many eggs could 3 Carolina mantises lay?

2. What is the total amount of eggs that two Carolina mantises and two walking sticks could lay?

3. How many more eggs can a Carolina mantis lay than a twostriped walking stick?

Another animal found in the state of South Carolina is the big brown bat. It survives on a diet of flying beetles, mosquitoes, bees, flies, and other insects.

4. The typical wingspan of a big brown bat is 12 inches. What is the total length of 5 big brown bats if lined up wingtip-to-wingtip?

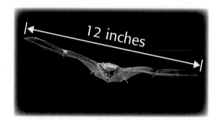

12 inches

5. An adult big brown bat weighs 12 grams. How much would 3 adult bats weigh?

6. A group of adult big brown bats weighs 60 grams. How many big brown bats are in the group?

7. Female big brown bats usually give birth to two pups each year. How many pups could a female give birth to in 8 years?

8. The weight of a young big brown bat increases by 1 gram every 2 days. How much weight will it gain in 18 days?

9. If an adult big brown bat can fly 40 miles in 1 hour, how many miles can it fly in 15 minutes?

10. **WRITING IN ►MATH** Use the table to write a real-world problem about the weights of big brown bat predators.

Big Brown Bat Predators	
Predator	Weight (g)
Common grackle	108
Great horned owl	1,250
Barn owl	550

Source: University of Michigan

South Carolina Start Smart

Algebra

Music, Sun, and Patterns!

The Spoleto Festival is held in Charleston, South Carolina. This seventeen-day festival begins in late May and runs through early June. More than 100 musicians perform at various locations in Charleston.

CHECK What You Know Patterns

A pattern is a set of numbers or figures that follows a rule. Finding a pattern is a useful problem-solving strategy.

For Exercises 1 and 2, use the table. It shows the cost of souvenir T-shirts.

Cost of T-Shirts	
Number of T-Shirts	Cost ($)
1	$12
2	$24
3	$36
4	$48

1. How much would 6 souvenir T-shirts cost?

2. Find the total cost of 9 T-shirts.

3. Two chicken sandwiches cost $12. Three chicken sandwiches cost $18. Four chicken sandwiches cost $24. If the pattern continues, how much will 5 chicken sandwiches cost?

4. Refer to Exercise 3. Find the cost of seven chicken sandwiches.

The Spoleto Festival highlights music and dance. Suppose 20 ballerinas each leap 4 times through the air. How many leaps did the ballerinas make in all?

Number of ballerinas		Number of leaps per ballerina		Total number of leaps by all ballerinas
20	×	4	=	▢

Did you Know?

The Spoleto Festival, inspired by the Italian city of Spoleto, began in the United States in 1977.

You know that $20 \times 4 = 80$. So, the ballerinas made a total of 80 leaps in all.

Choose the number sentence that can be used to solve each problem. Then solve each problem.

5. There is a booth selling music CDs. If 9 people visit the booth each hour for 5 hours, how many people will have visited the booth in all?

6. Julio is handing out 14 flyers for a play. He gave some of them away. If he has 9 flyers left, how many did he give away?

7. Before lunch, Emory heard 9 jazz songs. After lunch, she heard a total of 14 jazz songs. How many jazz songs did Emory hear after lunch?

8. Ms. Siegel spent $45 on festival posters. If she bought a total of 5 posters at the same price, how much did each poster cost?

9. **WRITING IN ►MATH** Write a real-world multiplication problem that can be represented by using a number sentence.

A $14 - ▢ = 9$

B $9 \times 5 = ▢$

C $9 + ▢ = 14$

D $45 \div 5 = ▢$

Lesson 4

Measurement

One of the main crops grown in South Carolina is tomatoes. The varieties of tomatoes grown in South Carolina include beefsteak, plum, and cherry.

 **Mass**

Mass is the amount of matter an object has.
Metric units of mass are gram (g) and kilogram (kg).
1,000 grams (g) = 1 kilogram (kg)

1. What is the total mass of the tomatoes shown?

2. What is the best estimate for the mass of 10 tomatoes: 1,200 grams or 2 kilograms? Explain your answer.

Compare. Use >, <, or =.

3. 800 g ● 1 kg   4. 2,010 g ● 2 kg   5. 4,000 g ● 4 kg

CHECK What You Know **Capacity** ·

Capacity is the amount of fluid a container can hold. Common measures of customary capacity are fluid ounces (fl oz), cups (c), and pints (p).

8 fluid ounces (fl oz) = 1 cup (c)
2 cups (c) = 1 pint (pt)

Did you Know

The world's most popular fruit is the tomato. About 60 million tons of tomatoes are grown each year.

For Exercises 6–8, write the unit you would use to measure the capacity of each object.

6. a glass of tomato juice

7. a melted ice cube

8. water in a kitchen sink

9. Choose the best estimate for the amount of of water in a bucket.

A 10 fluid ounces

B 30 pints

C 2 cups

D 4 pints

10. **WRITING IN** ►**MATH** Find two objects in the classroom that have a mass of more than one gram. Find two objects that have a mass of less than one gram. Explain each choice.

Geometry

Lesson 5

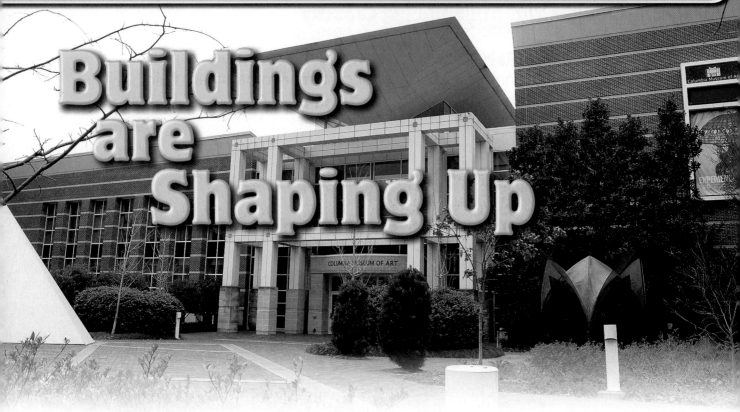

Buildings are Shaping Up

The Columbia Museum of Art, located in Columbia, South Carolina, houses European and American paintings, prints, sculptures, and much more.

CHECK What You Know **Lines and Line Segments** · · · · · · · · · · · ·

Line segments can be found in architecture. A **line segment** is a part of a line between two endpoints. A **line** is a straight set of points that extend in opposite directions without ending.

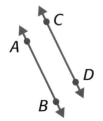

Parallel lines are always the same distance apart.

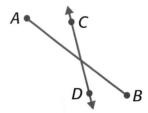

Intersecting lines meet or cross each other.

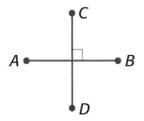

Perpendicular lines meet or cross each other to form right angles.

10 Start Smart

1. Draw two lines that intersect.

2. Draw a line and a line segment that are parallel.

3. Do perpendicular lines always intersect? Explain.

Two-Dimensional Figures · · · · · · · · · ·

A two-dimensional figure has length and width. Two-dimensional figures are all around us. Just take a look at the traffic signs below.

stop sign

railroad sign

speed limit

yield sign

4. Which sign is an example of a circle?

5. How many sides does a speed limit sign have? What shape is it?

6. Explain the difference between a square and a triangle. Which of these shapes is a yield sign?

7. Look for two-dimensional figures in your classroom. Draw and label each figure.

8. **WRITING IN ►MATH** Describe a real-world two-dimensional figure. Then exchange papers with a classmate to see if he or she can guess the figure.

Did you Know?

The Columbia Museum of Art is home to more than 7,000 pieces of artwork.

Data Analysis

Hockey is a popular sport. There are three minor league hockey teams in South Carolina.

CHECK What You Know **Pictographs**

A pictograph shows data by using pictures. The pictograph at the right shows the number of hockey games a hockey team played each month during a recent regular season.

Source: South Carolina Stingrays

1. What does each 🏒 represent?

2. What is the range for this set of data?

3. What is the maximum for this set of data?

A bar graph compares data by using bars of different heights. The graph below shows the number of South Carolina's sports teams.

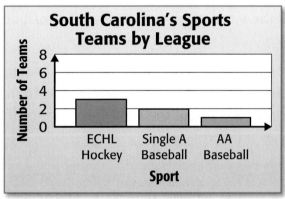

South Carolina's Sports Teams by League

Source: South Carolina Information Highway

4. Which sports have less than 3 teams each? Explain.

5. What is the total number of teams?

6. What is the minimum for this set of data?

7. What is the range for this set of data?

8. Follow these steps to take survey. Then make a bar graph to show the results.

- Ask each student to name his or her favorite sport.
- Make a tally chart to show how many students like each sport.
- Make a bar graph from the tally chart.

9. WRITING IN ►MATH Write a sentence that describes what your graph shows.

Did you **Know**

A hockey puck is 1 inch thick. Some of the best hockey players can shoot pucks at speeds over 100 miles per hour.

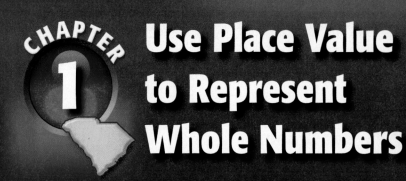

CHAPTER 1

Use Place Value to Represent Whole Numbers

BIG Idea What is place value?

Place value is the value given to a digit by its position in a number.

Example The honeybee is the state insect for 16 states. Among these are North Carolina, Oklahoma, and Utah. The table shows some facts about the honeybee. Notice that each number has a different value.

Honeybee Facts
• Travels 15 miles per hour
• Makes 154 trips to make one tablespoon of honey
• Wing stroke of 11,400 times per minute

Source: National Honey Board

What will I learn in this chapter?

- Read and write whole numbers to millions.
- Compare and order whole numbers.
- Round whole numbers.
- Use the four-step plan to solve problems.

Key Vocabulary

place value

standard form

expanded form

is greater than (>)

is less than (<)

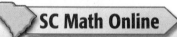 **SC Math Online**

Student Study Tools
at macmillanmh.com

FOLDABLES®
Study Organizer

Make this Foldable to help organize information about place value. Begin with one sheet of notebook paper.

1 **Fold** a sheet of paper lengthwise. Leave a two-inch tab at the top.

2 **Fold** the right side and the left side to make three equal sections.

3 **Unfold** the sides. Then cut along the creases as shown.

4 **Label** as shown. Take notes as you move through the chapter.

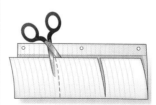

Use Place Value to Represent Whole Numbers

| Place Value through Hundred Thousands | Place Value through Millions | Compare, Order, and Round Whole Numbers |

You have two ways to check prerequisite skills for this chapter.

Option 2

SC Math Online Take the Chapter Readiness Quiz at macmillanmh.com.

Option 1

Complete the Quick Check below.

QUICK Check

Write each number in word form and expanded form.

(Prior Grade)

1.

Ones		
hundreds	tens	ones
	6	4

2.

Ones		
hundreds	tens	ones
9	9	5

3. 79　　　　**4.** 30　　　　**5.** 90　　　　**6.** 165

7. 347　　　　**8.** 692　　　　**9.** 1,840　　　　**10.** 4,505

11. Write $300 + 20 + 1$ in standard form and word form.

Compare. Use >, <, or =. (Prior Grade)

12. 40 ● 4　　　　**13.** 59 ● 59　　　　**14.** 888 ● 898　　　　**15.** 682 ● 700

16. Nora earned $425. She wants to buy a video game system that costs $375. Does she have enough money? Explain.

Round to the nearest ten. (Prior Grade)

17. 26　　　　**18.** 4　　　　**19.** 18　　　　**20.** 75

21. 152　　　　**22.** 175　　　　**23.** 347　　　　**24.** 508

25. Measurement Ann Arbor, Michigan, is 65 miles from Lansing, Michigan. Would it be reasonable to say that Ann Arbor is about 70 miles from Lansing? Explain.

Place Value Through Hundred Thousands

GET READY to Learn

The average lead pencil can draw a line that is almost 184,800 feet (about 35 miles) long. Do you know the value of each digit in 184,800?

MAIN IDEA

I will read and write whole numbers to hundred thousands.

SC Academic Standards

4-2.1 Recognize the period in the place-value structure of whole numbers: units, thousands, millions, and billions. *Also addresses 4-2.6.*

New Vocabulary

digit
place value
period
standard form
word form
expanded form

SC Math Online

macmillanmh.com
• Extra Examples
• Personal Tutor
• Self-Check Quiz

A **digit** is any of the symbols used to write numbers 0, 1, 2, 3, 4, 5, 6, 7, 8, 9. A **place-value** chart shows the value of the digits in a number. Each group of three digits is called a **period**. Each period is separated by a comma.

Period			Period		
Thousands			**Ones**		
hundreds	tens	ones	hundreds	tens	ones
1	8	4	8	0	0

EXAMPLE   Identify Value of Digits

1 Write the value of the underlined digit in 18<u>4</u>,800.

Step 1 Write the number in a place-value chart.

Thousands			**Ones**		
hundreds	tens	ones	hundreds	tens	ones
1	8	④	8	0	0

Step 2 Identify the column where the 4 is located. Circle it.

Step 3 Replace all the digits that are to the right of the 4 with zeros.

The underlined digit has a value of 4,000. This is because the 4 is in the thousands place.

Standard form is the usual way to write a number using digits. **Word form** is the way you read or say a number. **Expanded form** shows the value of each digit.

EXAMPLES Read and Write Numbers

2 **Write 628,371 in word form and expanded form.**

Thousands			Ones		
hundreds	tens	ones	hundreds	tens	ones
6	2	8	3	7	1

Word form: six hundred twenty-eight thousand, three hundred seventy-one

Expanded form: 600,000 + 20,000 + 8,000 + 300 + 70 + 1

3 **Write *one hundred five thousand, twenty-six* in standard form and expanded form.**

Standard form: 105,026

Expanded form: 100,000 + 5,000 + 20 + 6

CHECK What You Know

Write the value of the underlined digit. See Example 1 (p. 17)

1. 32,0<u>8</u>6   **2.** 78,<u>3</u>87   **3.** 1<u>0</u>9,378   **4.** <u>5</u>90,320

Write each number in word form and expanded form. See Examples 2 and 3 (p. 18)

5. 5,789   **6.** 18,046   **7.** 49,909   **8.** 270,006

9. Write *one hundred thousand, two hundred fifty-six* in standard form and expanded form. See Examples 2 and 3 (p. 18)

10. China has 555,200 fast food restaurants. Write 555,200 in word form.

11. **Talk About It** Do 800,600 and 860,000 represent the same values? Explain.

Write the value of the underlined digit. See Example 1 (p. 17)

12. 59,<u>8</u>33   **13.** <u>7</u>2,134   **14.** 93,7<u>4</u>3   **15.** 1<u>7</u>4,305

16. 593,8<u>0</u>2   **17.** <u>8</u>26,193   **18.** 830,25<u>9</u>   **19.** <u>9</u>26,794

Write each number in word form and expanded form. See Examples 2 and 3 (p. 18)

20. 5,050   **21.** 3,791   **22.** 57,402   **23.** 89,074

24. 243,895   **25.** 485,830   **26.** 649,320   **27.** 784,132

Write each number in standard form and expanded form. See Examples 2 and 3 (p. 18)

28. twenty-five thousand, four hundred eight

29. forty thousand, eight hundred eleven

30. seven hundred sixty-one thousand, three hundred fifty-six

Write each number in word form and standard form.

31. 7,000 + 600 + 30 + 5   **32.** 20,000 + 900 + 70 + 6   **33.** 60,000 + 80 + 4

Real-World PROBLEM SOLVING

Science The photo shows an African elephant.

34. African elephants can weigh up to <u>1</u>4,432 pounds. What is the value of the underlined digit?

35. Write 14,432 in expanded form.

36. A zookeeper weighed a newborn African elephant. He was 232 pounds. After one year, the elephant had gained 1,000 pounds. Write the elephant's new weight in standard form and word form.

H.O.T. Problems

37. OPEN ENDED Write a six-digit number that has a 9 in the hundreds place and a 6 in the hundred thousands place.

38. **WRITING IN ►MATH** Explain how the value of the 4 in 694,213 will change if you move it to the tens place.

Math Activity for 1-2
How Big is One Million?

You can use models to help understand the value of 1,000,000.

ACTIVITY Model 1,000,000.

Step 1 **Model 1,000.**

Cut out a thousand cube model. Fold the edges where the sides meet and form a cube. This shows 1,000.

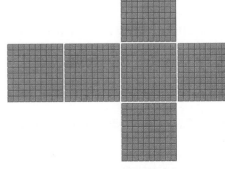

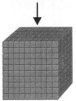

Step 2 **Model 10,000.**

Work with your classmates. Use 10 of the cubes to show 10,000.

Step 3 **Model 100,000.**

Make more cubes to build a model of 100,000.

Step 4 **Create 1,000,000.**

Suppose you were to build a model of 1,000,000. How many more 100,000 models would you need? (*Hint:* There are ten 100,000s in 1,000,000.)

Think About It

1. How did you build a model of 10,000?

2. Describe what your model of 1,000,000 looks like.

3. How are the models you built and drew like the models for ones, tens, and hundreds?

4. What number patterns did you see as you built and drew these models?

CHECK What You Know

Write the number shown by each model.

5.
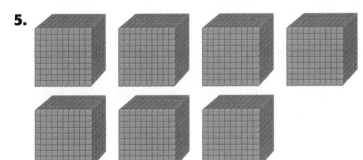

6.
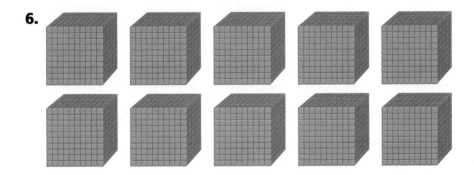

7. The model at the right shows 1,000. How many tens are in 1,000?

8. How many thousands are in 1,000,000?

9. Explain how to determine how long it would take to count to one million.

10. **WRITING IN ►MATH** How many hundreds are there in 1,000,000? Explain your answer.

GET READY to Learn

Baseball is one of America's favorite sports. The graph shows how many fans attended games for three teams during recent years. The attendance numbers are in the millions.

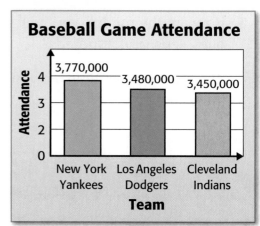

Baseball Game Attendance

Source: *Scholastic Book of World Records*

MAIN IDEA

I will read and write whole numbers through the billions.

SC Academic Standards

4-2.1 Recognize the period in the place-value structure of whole numbers: units, thousands, millions, and billions. *Also addresses 4-2.6.*

SC Math Online

macmillanmh.com

• Extra Examples
• Personal Tutor
• Self-Check Quiz

A place-value chart can be used to read and write numbers in the millions. The place-value chart below shows the value of each digit in 3,770,000, the attendance at the New York Yankees baseball games.

Period			Period			Period		
Millions			**Thousands**			**Ones**		
		ones	hundreds	tens	ones	hundreds	tens	ones
		3	7	7	0	0	0	0

Real-World EXAMPLE   Read and Write Numbers

1 **SCIENCE** The human eye blinks an average of 5,500,000 times a year. Write 5,500,000 in three ways.

Standard form: 5,500,000

Word form: five million, five hundred thousand

Expanded form: 5,000,000 + 500,000

② ANIMALS Chickens are the most popular farm animal in the world. There are *sixteen billion, one hundred ninety-four million, nine hundred twenty-five thousand* chickens living on farms around the world.

Sixteen billion, one hundred ninety-four million, nine hundred twenty-five thousand is written in the place-value chart below.

Billions			Millions			Thousands			Ones		
hundreds	tens	ones	hundreds	tens	ones	hundreds	tens	ones	hundreds	tens	ones
	1	6	1	9	4	9	2	5	0	0	0

Standard form: 16,194,925,000

Expanded form: 10,000,000,000 + 6,000,000,000 + 100,000,000 + 90,000,000 + 4,000,000 + 900,000 + 20,000 + 5,000

 CHECK What You Know

Write the value of the underlined digit. See Examples 1 and 2 (pp. 22–23)

1. 469,9<u>9</u>9
2. <u>1</u>,040,710
3. 35,0<u>9</u>8,098
4. <u>4</u>1,653,000,241

Write each number in word form and expanded form. See Example 1 (p. 22)

5. 2,007
6. 43,980
7. 302,806
8. 38,000,875

Write each number in standard form and expanded form. See Example 2 (p. 23)

9. nine hundred thousand, five hundred fifty-two

10. two hundred forty-six million, nine hundred thousand, eighteen

11. On Sunday, 2,617,000 newspapers were sold. Write the number of newspapers sold in word form and expanded form.

12. **Talk About It** Explain how to find the value of the underlined digit in the number 26,0<u>5</u>7,928.

Write the value of the underlined digit. See Examples 1 and 2 (pp. 22–23)

13. 132,<u>6</u>85

14. <u>3</u>09,573

15. 309,8<u>4</u>1

16. 7,824,0<u>1</u>5

17. 40,<u>2</u>45,854

18. <u>6</u>8,210,397

19. 73,581,<u>2</u>09

20. 814,<u>2</u>10,307,000

Write each number in word form and expanded form. See Example 1 (p. 22)

21. 29,205

22. 82,009

23. 901,452

24. 200,013

25. 30,842,085

26. 63,930,053

27. 319,999,990

28. 107,000,523,094

Write each number in standard form and expanded form. See Example 2 (p. 23)

29. two hundred thirty-eight thousand, three hundred seventy

30. four million, ninety-four thousand, two hundred fifteen

31. eighty three million, twenty-three thousand, seven

32. fifty billion, one hundred million, ninety-five

Write each number in word form and standard form.

33. 200,000 + 60,000 + 3,000 + 200 + 70 + 3

34. 1,000,000 + 900,000 + 50,000 + 6,000 + 200 + 20 + 5

35. As of 2005, the population of Philadelphia was 1,463,281. Write Philadelphia's population in word form.

36. **Measurement** The land area for Florida is 100,000 + 30,000 + 9,000 + 800 + 50 + 2 square kilometers. Write the area in word form.

Real-World PROBLEM SOLVING

Planets The Sun and Earth are shown.

37. The distance from Earth to the Sun is 92,955,793 miles. Write this number in word form and expanded form.

38. The amount of time that American astronauts have spent in space is about 13,507,804 minutes. Is this number read as *thirteen million, fifty-seven thousand, eight hundred four*? Explain.

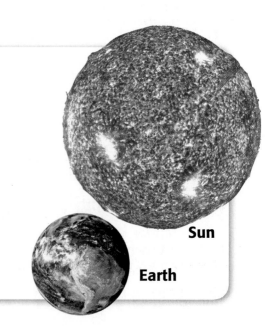

Sun

Earth

H.O.T. Problems

39. OPEN ENDED Write an eight-digit number that has a 7 in the ten millions place and a number in the thousands place with a value of 2,000.

40. CHALLENGE Write the number with the smallest value using the digits 1 through 9. Use each digit only once.

41. NUMBER SENSE Is the following statement *true* or *false*? Explain your answer.

$$1,000 \text{ thousands} = 1,000,000$$

42. **WRITING IN ►MATH** Explain how you know what number is missing in $3,947 = 3,000 + \blacksquare + 40 + 7$.

PASS Practice ⟩ 4-2.1

43. Which number below is the word form of 57,302? (Lesson 1-1)

　A five thousand, three hundred two

　B fifty-seven thousand, three hundred twenty

　C fifty-seven thousand, three hundred two

　D five hundred thousand, three hundred two

44. Yosemite National Park hosts three million, three hundred seventy thousand visitors each year. What is this number in standard form?

(Lesson 1-2)

　F 3,307,000

　G 3,370,000

　H 30,307,000

　J 30,370,000

Spiral Review

Write each number in standard form and expanded form. (Lesson 1-2)

45. three thousand five

46. four million, six hundred thirty-seven thousand, five hundred four

47. seventeen million, twenty thousand, four hundred fifty-eight

Write the value of the underlined digit. (Lesson 1-1)

48. 10,<u>4</u>98

49. 12,00<u>4</u>

50. <u>3</u>0,182

Problem-Solving Skill

MAIN IDEA I will solve problems using a four-step plan.

 SCAS 4-1.1 **Analyze information to solve increasingly more sophisticated problems.**

There are six girls in Dina's scout troop. They are planning a trip to the local amusement park. Admission for children is $12. What is the total cost of admission for everyone to go?

Understand	**What facts do you know?** • There are six scouts who want to go. • The price of admission is $12 for each girl. **What do you need to find?** • The total cost of admission for all the girls.
Plan	To find the total cost, you can use addition. There are 6 girls, and it will cost $12 each. So, add 12 six times.
Solve	$12 + $12 + $12 + $12 + $12 + $12 = $72 or 6 × $12 = $72 So, the troop needs $72 to go to the amusement park.
Check	Look back. One way to check the answer is to use a drawing. 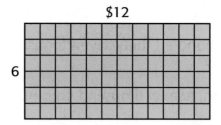 There are 6 × 12 or 72 squares, so the answer is correct.

Refer to the problem on the previous page.

1. Explain why addition was used to solve the problem.

2. In the problem, the price for an adult admission was not included. Suppose the price of an adult ticket is $8 more than a child's ticket. Find the total cost of three adult tickets. Explain.

3. Refer to Exercise 2. Draw a model to check. Explain how the model shows that your answer is correct.

4. If three adults were to go on the trip with the scouts, how much would admission cost for everyone to go? Explain how you found your answer.

PRACTICE the Skill

SCAS • PASS

Extra Practice, p. R2

Solve. Use the four-step plan.

5. A class is playing a game. Each correct answer is worth 5 points. Team 1 has 55 total points. Team 2 has answered 12 questions correctly. Who has answered more questions correctly?

6. **Measurement** Rosa is downloading music. It takes about 3 minutes to download one song. About how long will it take her to download an album with 10 songs?

7. Casey's mom is the baseball coach for his team. She spent $50 on 10 baseballs. How much would 1 baseball cost?

8. William can make 4 bracelets in an hour. With Daisy's help, they can make twice as many in an hour. If they work for 2 hours, how many bracelets can they make?

9. The opening phrase of the Gettysburg Address is shown. A score is 20 years. How many years would be in four score and seven years?

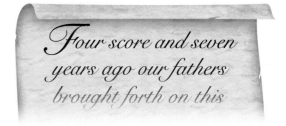

Four score and seven years ago our fathers brought forth on this

10. **Measurement** Scott spends 1 hour a day in math class. How many hours does he spend in math class in four weeks in which there are no days off except weekends?

11. Karl Freidrich Benz invented the first gasoline-powered automobile in 1885. Estimate how many years ago this automobile was invented.

12. **WRITING IN ▶MATH** Select one problem from Exercises 5–11. Explain how you solved the problem.

1-4

Compare Whole Numbers

GET READY to Learn

On average, a first-year police officer earns $41,793 in one year. A first-year firefighter earns $41,294 in one year. Which occupation pays more for the first year?

MAIN IDEA

I will compare whole numbers.

SC Academic Standards

Reinforcement of 3-2.1 Compare whole number quantities through 999,999 by using the terms *is less than, is greater than,* and *is equal to* and the symbols <, >, and =.

New Vocabulary

number line
is greater than (>)
is less than (<)
is equal to (=)

SC Math Online

macmillanmh.com
• Extra Examples
• Personal Tutor
• Self-Check Quiz

You can use a number line to compare numbers. A **number line** is a line with numbers on it in order at regular intervals. The symbols below are used to show relationships of numbers.

is greater than	**is less than**	**is equal to**
>	<	=

Real-World EXAMPLE   Use a Number Line

① JOBS Which occupation pays more for the first year: police officer or firefighter?

On a number line, numbers to the right are greater than numbers to the left.

41,793 is to the right of 41,294.

So, 41,793 is greater than 41,294.

Therefore, 41,793 > 41,294.

So, police officers earn more money than firefighters.

To compare numbers, you can also use place value.

Real-World EXAMPLE   Use Place Value

2 **DATA** The table shows the two most popular names in the United States. Which name is more popular?

Last Name	Number of People
Miller	1,253,913
Jones	1,836,509

Source: *Top 10 of Everything*

Remember

Before comparing numbers, always line up the ones place.

Step 1 Line up the numbers so that the digits in the ones place align.
1,253,913
1,836,509

Step 2 Begin at the greatest place. Compare the digits.
1,253,913
1,836,509
Since 1 = 1, go to the next place.

Step 3 Compare the digits in the next place on the right.
1,**2**53,913
1,**8**36,509
8 > 2

So, 1,836,509 is greater. Therefore, the more popular last name is Jones.

CHECK What You Know

Compare. Use >, <, or =. See Examples 1 and 2 (pp. 28–29)

1. 1,798 ● 1,789

2. 7,440 ● 7,436

3. 25,409 ● 26,409

4. 50,402 ● 50,406

5. 655,543 ● 556,543

6. 10,027,301 ● 10,207,301

7. Jun collects stamps and baseball cards. He has 1,834 stamps and 1,286 baseball cards. Does he have more stamps or more baseball cards?

8. **Talk About It** Explain why any five-digit number is less than any six-digit number.

Compare. Use >, <, or =. See Examples 1 and 2 (pp. 28–29)

9. 3,030 ● 3,030

10. 5,980 ● 5,090

11. 6,789 ● 6,798

12. 9,623 ● 9,623

13. 23,001 ● 23,010

14. 18,041 ● 18,040

15. 76,101 ● 77,000

16. 12,683 ● 12,638

17. 304,999 ● 305,049

18. 701,010 ● 701,010

19. 2,999,214 ● 2,999,214

Copy and complete to make the number sentence true.

20. 658,431 < ■00,000

21. 1,342,646 > 1,■89,035

22. Delaney received 1,127 E-mails in a year. Patricia received 1,132 E-mails. Who received more E-mails?

23. Hassan read 2,365 pages during the school year. Anjelita read 2,382 pages during the school year. Who read more pages during the school year?

Real-World PROBLEM SOLVING

Technology The table shows the top four online languages.

24. Which language is used most on the Internet?

25. Which language is used less on the Internet, Japanese or Spanish?

Top Online Languages

Language	Internet Users
Chinese	105,736,236
English	286,642,757
Japanese	66,763,838
Spanish	55,887,063

Source: *Top 10 of Everything*

H.O.T. Problems

26. OPEN ENDED Write a seven-digit number that is greater than 8,458,942.

27. WHICH ONE DOESN'T BELONG? Which number does not belong? Explain.

| 10,000 | 10 hundreds | ten thousand | 100 hundreds |

28. WRITING IN ►MATH Explain how to compare numbers using place value.

Write each number in word form and expanded form. (Lesson 1-1)

1. 2,384   **2.** 917,022

Write each number in standard form and expanded form. (Lesson 1-1)

3. nineteen thousand, two hundred six

4. two hundred seventy-two

5. There are 3 schools. Each school has 297 students. How many students are in all three schools? Write in standard form and word form. (Lesson 1-1)

6. MULTIPLE CHOICE Which number below is the standard form of twelve thousand, five hundred seven?
(Lesson 1-1)

A 1,257

B 12,057

C 12,507

D 12,570

Write the value of the underlined digit. (Lesson 1-2)

7. 31,<u>6</u>87   **8.** 8,3<u>2</u>0,579

9. Erika is writing the greatest number possible using the digits shown.

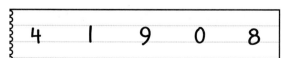

Write the number in expanded form.
(Lesson 1-2)

10. What is 20,000,000 + 8,000,000 + 300,000 + 6,000 + 30 + 7 in standard form and word form? (Lesson 1-2)

11. MULTIPLE CHOICE Which word form represents 7,402,644? (Lesson 1-2)

F seven million, forty-two thousand, six hundred four

G seven thousand, four hundred two

H seven million, four hundred two thousand, six hundred forty-four

J seven million, two hundred four thousand, six hundred four

Compare. Use >, <, or =. (Lesson 1-4)

12. 2,481 ● 2,814

13. 200 + 70 + 8 ● 700 + 80 + 2

Algebra Find the value of x. (Lesson 1-4)

14. 5,000 + x + 9 = 5,709

15. 40,000 + 6,000 + x = 46,009

16. Coty traveled 2,643 miles by air. Ramiro traveled 2,643 miles by car. Who traveled farther? Explain. (Lesson 1-4)

17. On Monday Dylan used a pedometer to record 15,725 steps. On Tuesday he took 15,806 steps. On which day did he take more steps? (Lesson 1-4)

18. WRITING IN ►MATH Explain how to find the number missing in the following expanded form sentence.
8,000,000 + 5,000 + 90 + 3 = 8,■05,093
(Lesson 1-2)

Order Whole Numbers

GET READY to Learn

Having a dog is very popular. The table shows the number of Yorkshire Terriers, Beagles, and German Shepherds in the United States. Which dog breed is most popular? least popular?

Dog Breeds in the U.S.	
Dog Breed	**Number**
Yorkshire Terrier	47,238
Beagle	42,592
German Shepherd	45,868

Source: American Kennel Club

MAIN IDEA

I will order whole numbers through the millions.

SC Academic Standards

4-2.6 Analyze the magnitude of digits through hundredths **on the basis of their place value.**

SC Math Online

macmillanmh.com

• Extra Examples
• Personal Tutor
• Self-Check Quiz

To order numbers, you can use a number line or place value.

Real-World EXAMPLE   Use a Number Line

1 **DOGS Order the dog breeds in the table above from most popular to least popular.**

Graph each number on a number line.

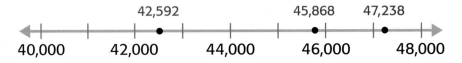

47,238 is the farthest to the right.

45,868 is between 42,592 and 47,238.

42,592 is the farthest to the left.

The order is Yorkshire Terrier, German Shepherd, Beagle.

2 **OIL** The table shows the number of barrels of oil used each day in different countries. Use place value to order the data from greatest to least.

Oil Usage	
Country	**Barrels per Day**
Brazil	2,199,000
Canada	2,200,000
India	2,130,000
United States	19,650,000

Source: *CIA World Fact Book*

Remember

When ordering numbers, you can use number lines or place value.

Step 1
Line up the ones place. Compare the digits in the greatest place.

Step 2
Compare the digits in the next place.

Step 3
Compare the digits in the next place.

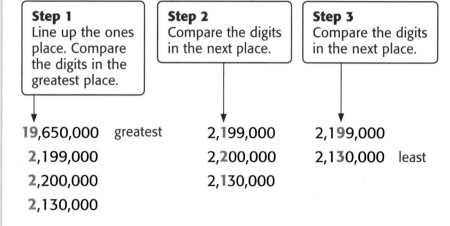

19,650,000 greatest

2,199,000

2,200,000

2,130,000

2,199,000

2,200,000

2,130,000

2,199,000

2,130,000 least

The numbers ordered from greatest to least are 19,650,000; 2,200,000; 2,199,000; and 2,130,000.

So, the order is the United States, Canada, Brazil, and India.

CHECK What You Know

Order the numbers from greatest to least. See Examples 1 and 2 (pp. 32–33)

1. 3,456; 4,356; 3,465; 6,543

2. 52,482; 50,023; 56,028; 63,340

3. 87,035; 80,562; 78,035; 79,003

4. 145,099; 154,032; 145,004; 159,023

5. Measurement Order the lakes shown in the table from greatest to least surface area.

6. **Talk About It** When ordering whole numbers, explain what you do when the digits in the same place have the same value.

Florida Lakes	
Lake	**Surface Area (acres)**
Lake Apopka	30,875
Lake Harris	13,788
Lake Tohopekaliga	18,810
Lake Okeechobee	467,200
Lake Seminole	37,500

Source: World Atlas Travel

Order the numbers from greatest to least. See Examples 1 and 2 (pp. 32–33)

7. 2,004; 1,906; 2,006; 1,507

8. 3,521; 3,512; 1,243; 3,306

9. 79,920; 82,234; 97,902; 90,125

10. 12,378; 12,783; 12,873

11. 138,023; 138,032; 139,006; 183,487

12. 258,103; 248,034; 285,091; 248,934

13. 6,052,264; 6,025,264; 6,052,462

14. 12,345,678; 1,234,567; 123,456,789

15. Rank the following cities in the United States from least to greatest population.

16. Order the cars from most expensive to least expensive.

City Population	
City	Population
Baltimore	635,815
Boston	559,034
Indianapolis	784,118
Seattle	573,911

Source: U.S. Census Bureau

Most Expensive Cars	
Car	Price
Bugatti Veyron 16.4	$1,192,057
Leblanc Mirabeau	$645,084
Pagani Zonda Roadster	$667,321
Saleen S7	$555,000

Source: Forbes

South Carolina Data File

The Myrtle Beach Pelicans are part of the Carolina League of Minor League Baseball. The table shows the Pelican's and other teams' stadium capacities and attendances.

17. Order the stadium capacities from greatest to least.

18. Order the average game attendances from least to greatest.

Carolina League Statistics		
Team	Stadium Capacity	Average Game Attendance
Myrtle Beach Pelicans	5,200	3,098
Winston-Salem Warthogs	6,000	2,442
Kinston Indians	4,100	1,745
Wilmington Blue Rocks	6,532	4,558

Source: Minor League Baseball

H.O.T. Problems

19. **OPEN ENDED** Write three numbers that are greater than 750,000 but less than 760,000.

20. **NUMBER SENSE** Use the digits 2, 3, 4, and 9 to create four numbers. Order them from least to greatest.

21. **WRITING IN ►MATH** Write a real-word problem in which you would order three numbers from least to greatest.

Greater Number Game

Compare Whole Numbers

Get Ready!

Players: 2 players

Get Set!

Each player gets 20 index cards. Separate the cards into 2 piles of 10. On each card in the first pile, write a number in standard form that has no more than 4 digits.

Next, write the expanded form of each number on one of the cards in the second pile.

You will need: 40 index cards

Go!

- Combine both sets of cards.
- Shuffle and deal the cards.
- Place your cards facedown. Turn over the top card at the same time as your partner.
- The person who turns over the greatest number takes both cards. If the cards are equal, keep turning over cards until a player can take the cards.
- Play until one person has all the cards.

Round Whole Numbers

MAIN IDEA

I will round whole numbers through the millions.

SC Academic Standards

Reinforcement of 3-2.4 Apply procedures to round any whole number to the nearest 10, 100, or 1,000.

New Vocabulary

estimate

rounding (or round)

SC Math Online

macmillanmh.com
• Extra Examples
• Personal Tutor
• Self-Check Quiz

GET READY to Learn

A certain tractor weighs 17,554 pounds. About how much does it weigh?

When you do not need an exact answer, you can **estimate** by **rounding**. You can use a number line to round.

Real-World EXAMPLES Round Whole Numbers

1️⃣ **MEASUREMENT** To the nearest thousand, how much does the tractor weigh?

17,554

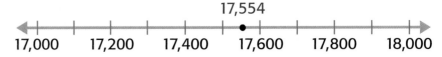

17,000   17,200   17,400   17,600   17,800   18,000

On the number line, 17,554 is closer to 18,000 than 17,000. So, round 17,554 to 18,000.

2️⃣ **WORLD RECORDS** The most dominoes that were set up and toppled by one person is 303,621. How many dominoes is this to the nearest ten thousand?

303,621

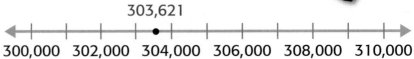

300,000   302,000   304,000   306,000   308,000   310,000

On the number line, 303,621 is closer to 300,000 than 310,000. So, round 303,621 to 300,000.

Place value can also be used to round numbers.

Vocabulary Link
Round
Everyday Use shaped like a circle

Math Use to find the nearest value of a number based on a given place value

Rounding Whole Numbers
Key Concept

Step 1	Underline the digit to be rounded.
Step 2	Look at the digit to the right of the place being rounded.
Step 3	If the digit is 4 or less, do not change the underlined digit. If the digit is 5 or greater, add 1 to the underlined digit.
Step 4	Replace all digits after the underlined digit with zeros.

Real-World EXAMPLE   Round Whole Numbers

3 **MEASUREMENT Saturn is 120,536 kilometers wide. Round this number to the nearest thousand.**

You need to round 120,536 to the nearest thousand.

Step 1 Underline the digit in the place to be rounded. In this case, the 0 in the thousands place is to be rounded.   12**0**,536

Step 2 Look at the digit to the right of the underlined digit, which is 5.   120,**5**36

Step 3 Since the digit is 5 or greater, add 1 to the underlined digit.   12**1**,536

Step 4 Replace all digits after the underlined digit with zeros.   121,000

To the nearest thousand, 120,536 is rounded to 121,000.

Remember

Check your answer to make sure it is reasonable.

Check
The number line shows that the answer is correct.

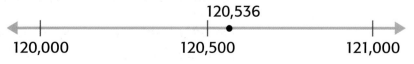

120,536

120,000   120,500   121,000

Round each number to the given place-value position. See Examples 1–3 (pp. 36–37)

1. 927; ten

2. 934; hundred

3. 4,282; thousand

4. 43,032; ten thousand

5. 593,205; hundred thousand

6. 1,709,385; million

7. The largest house made out of playing cards used 91,800 cards. To the nearest thousand, how many cards were used?

8. **Talk About It** Write the smallest number that you can round to the thousands place to get 8,000. Explain.

Practice and Problem Solving

SCAS • PASS

Extra Practice, p. R3

Round each number to the given place-value position. See Examples 1–3 (pp. 36–37)

9. 568; ten

10. 396; ten

11. 297; hundred

12. 148,245; hundred

13. 4,752; thousand

14. 493,580; thousand

15. 519,158; hundred thousand

16. 791,275; hundred thousand

17. 77,690; hundred

18. 95,230; thousand

19. 3,190,236; million

20. 4,303,985; million

21. **Measurement** Earth's highest peak is Mount Everest. It is 29,028 feet high. Is this about 30,000 feet high? Explain.

22. **Measurement** The highest point in New Jersey is High Point. It is 1,803 feet high. Is this about 1,000 feet high? Explain.

Real-World PROBLEM SOLVING

Literature The graphic shows the number of characters that are in the longest novel in the world.

23. Round this number to the nearest hundred thousand.

24. To which place would this number be rounded if the rounded number was 14,156,100?

Longest Novel

14,156,074 characters

Source: *Guinness Book of World Records*

H.O.T. Problems

25. OPEN ENDED Write five numbers that would round to one million.

26. FIND THE ERROR Amanda and Martin round 83,275,925 to the hundred thousands place. Who is correct? Explain.

Amanda
80,000,000

Martin
83,300,000

27. **WRITING IN ▸MATH** Create a real-world problem that involves rounding a number and results in an answer of 670,000.

PASS Practice   4-2.6, 3-2.4

28. Which shows the correct order from least to greatest? (Lesson 1-5)

A 1,245; 2,451; 5,412; 4,152

B 2,124; 4,215; 4,512; 5,214

C 5,214; 4,512; 4,215; 2,124

D 2,512; 2,215; 4,124; 4,421

29. Yuma, Arizona, is the sunniest place in the world. Round Yuma's average hours of sunlight each year to the nearest thousand. (Lesson 1-6)

Top Two Sunniest Places	
Location	**Hours of Sunlight Each Year**
Yuma, Arizona	4,127
Phoenix, Arizona	4,041

Source: *The Top 10 of Everything*

F 4,000   **H** 4,200

G 4,100   **J** 5,000

Spiral Review

Order the numbers from greatest to least. (Lesson 1-5)

30. 685; 700; 660   **31.** 1,363; 1,468; 1,333   **32.** 12,009; 12,090; 12,900

Compare. Use >, <, or =. (Lesson 1-4)

33. 163 ● 165   **34.** 16,094 ● 16,090   **35.** 1,866 ● 1,866

36. The tallest mountain in the United States is 20,320 feet tall. Round this number to the nearest thousand. (Lesson 1-3)

1-7 Problem-Solving Investigation

MAIN IDEA I will choose the best strategy to solve a problem.

SCAS 4-1.1 Analyze information to solve increasingly more sophisticated problems.

P.S.I. TEAM +

TORY: My family is going on vacation to Mexico. Before we go, we have to trade our dollars for Mexican pesos. For every dollar we will get about 11 pesos.

YOUR MISSION: Find about how many pesos Tory's family will get for $8.

Understand	You know that one dollar is about 11 pesos. You need to find about how many pesos they will get for $8.
Plan	For every 1 dollar, they get 11 pesos. Make a table to solve the problem.
Solve	

Dollars	$1	$2	$3	$4	$5	$6	$7	$8
Pesos	11	22	33	44	55	66	77	88

+11 +11 +11 +11 +11 +11 +11

The pattern is to add 11. You can also solve this using multiplication. $8 \times 11 = 88$.
The family can expect to get about 88 pesos for $8.

Check	There is a second pattern in the table. When the digit in the dollar row is changed to pesos, the dollar digit is repeated twice. For example, $5 is 55 pesos. The answer, $8 is 88 pesos, follows this pattern. So, the answer is correct.

Use the four-step plan to solve.

1. **Measurement** A black bear weighs 25 pounds more than a gorilla. Use the information in the table to find how much a black bear weighs.

Large Animal Weights	
Animal	Weight (pounds)
Gorilla	400
Black bear	▦
Lion	440

2. A watch costs $34. A pair of sunglasses costs $6. How much change would you receive if you bought one watch and one pair of sunglasses and paid with a $50 bill?

3. Jade has 3 sticker sheets with 6 stickers on each sheet. How many stickers does she have in all?

4. **Measurement** A robin can fly 20 miles in one hour. An eagle can fly 40 miles in one hour. How many hours will it take a robin to fly as far as an eagle in 3 hours?

5. A video game store buys used video games for $10 each. Vivian wants a new video game for $77. How many used games must she sell to buy the new game?

6. Lee wants a motorized scooter. He earns $8 a week, and already has $11. How many weeks will he have to save all of his money to buy the scooter?

$75

7. Turi burns about 350 calories for every hour he skis. The last time he skied, he burned 1,200 calories. Did he ski over 3 hours? Explain.

8. **Algebra** Leticia earns $20 each time she babysits. How many times will she need to babysit to earn $120?

9. Jack's basketball games are 4 quarters that are each 8 minutes long. Is it possible for Jack to play 35 minutes in a game? Explain.

10. Xavier saved three $10-bills, six $5-bills, and twelve $1-bills. Does he have enough money to buy this MP3 player?

$82

11. **WRITING IN ►MATH** Refer to Exercise 10. Suppose Xavier has 5 bills and the total is $37. Explain the steps you would take to find which bills he has.

CREATURES Under the SEA

Earth's oceans are filled with many different sea creatures. Of these creatures in the ocean, marine mammals such as whales, dolphins, seals, and sea lions are the most skilled divers. Both sperm whales and elephant seals can stay underwater for almost two hours. That is a long time to hold your breath!

Population of Pacific Coast Marine Mammals

Species	Estimated Population
California sea lion	111,016
Gray whale	20,869
Hawaiian monk seal	1,300
Northern fur seal	988,000
Pacific harbor seal	131,826
Spinner dolphin	631,000
Spotted dolphin	731,000

Source: National Biological Service

Real-World Math

Use the information on pages 42 and 43 to solve each problem.

1. Which marine mammal species has the greatest population? Write in expanded and word forms.

2. There are about 20,000 blue whales. Your friend tells you that there are more blue whales than gray whales. Is your friend right? Explain.

3. A humpback whale can eat up to 9,000 pounds of food a day. Is this more or less than a blue whale eats? How much more or less?

4. A sea lion can dive 400 feet. Some seals can dive 5,314 feet. Dolphins can dive up to 1,000 feet. List these dives from greatest to least.

5. You are told that there are about 132,000 Pacific harbor seals. Is this true when you round to the nearest thousand? Explain.

6. Which animal populations, when rounded to the nearest thousand, have a one in the thousands place?

Did You Know?

A blue whale eats about 7,500 pounds of food each day.

Study Guide and Review

FOLDABLES Study Organizer
GET READY to Study

Be sure the following Key Vocabulary words and Key Concepts are written in your Foldable.

Place Value and Number Sense

| Place Value through Hundred Thousands | Place Value through Millions | Compare, Order, and Round Whole Numbers |

Key Concepts

Place Value (pp. 17–19 and 22–25)

• A **place-value** chart shows the value of the digits in a number.

Thousands			Ones		
hundreds	tens	ones	hundreds	tens	ones
	2	1	8	3	3

Read and Write Numbers (pp. 17–19 and 22–25)

• **Standard form:** 21,833
• **Word form:** twenty-one thousand, eight hundred thirty-three
• **Expanded form:** 20,000 + 1,000 + 800 + 30 + 3

Compare Numbers (pp. 28–30)

• To compare numbers, use **is greater than (>)**, **is less than (<)**, or **is equal to (=)**.

123 > 122   478 < 874   925 = 925

Key Vocabulary

estimate (p. 36)
is greater than (>) (p. 28)
is less than (<) (p. 28)
place value (p. 17)
rounding (p. 36)

Vocabulary Check

Choose the vocabulary word that completes each sentence.

1. When you do not need an exact answer, you can _____.

2. To help you read and write numbers, you can use _____.

3. When you do not need an exact answer, you can estimate by _____.

4. The _____ of the 7 in 7,495 is the thousands.

5. The symbol > is used to show that a number is _____ another number.

6. The symbol < is used to show that a number is _____ another number.

Lesson-by-Lesson Review

1-1 **Place Value Through Hundred Thousands** (pp. 17–19)

4-2.1,
4-2.6

Example 1
Write 5,789 in three different ways.

Thousands			Ones		
hundreds	tens	ones	hundreds	tens	ones
		5	7	8	9

Standard form: 5,789

Word form: five thousand, seven hundred eighty-nine

Expanded form: 5,000 + 700 + 80 + 9

Write each number in word form and expanded form.

7. 18,045   **8.** 94,804

9. Write *four hundred thirty thousand, two hundred fifty-six* in standard form and expanded form.

Write the value of the underlined digit.

10. 1<u>9</u>0,843   **11.** 84,2<u>9</u>9

12. The Petrified Forest National Park in northeast Arizona is 93,533 acres. Write this number in word form and expanded form.

1-2 **Place Value Through Millions** (pp. 22–25)

4-2.1,
4-2.6

Example 2
Write *nine million, three hundred seventy-two thousand, five hundred* in standard form and expanded form.

Word form: nine million, three hundred seventy-two thousand, five hundred

Standard form: 9,372,500

Expanded form: 9,000,000 + 300,000 + 70,000 + 2,000 + 500

Write each number in standard form and expanded form.

13. two thousand, six hundred ninety-seven

14. nine million, four hundred six thousand, two hundred seventy-one

15. León has a baseball card collection of 4,826 cards. He sells 215 cards to another collector. How many cards does he have left? Write in word form and expanded form.

Problem-Solving Skill: The Four-Step Plan (pp. 26–27)

4-1.1

Example 3

Dorota saves $2 each week. How much will she save after 2 months?

Understand

Dorota saves $2 each week. You need to find how much money will she save after 2 months.

Plan

There are 4 weeks in 1 month. Use repeated addition to find how much money she has saved after 2 months.

Solve

First, find how much she saved in one month.

$2	1 week
$2	1 week
$2	1 week
+ $2	1 week
$8	

Now, find the amount saved in two months.

$8	1 month
+ $8	1 month
$16	

So, Dorota will save $16 after 2 months.

Check

Count by two's 8 times.
2, 4, 6, 8, 10, 12, 14, 16

So, the answer is correct.

Solve. Use the four-step plan.

16. Cynthia earns 5 points at the library for each book she reads. She wants to earn 75 points in order to win the grand prize. How many books does she need to read?

17. Darius has $72. He wants to buy the bike shown. How much more money does he need?

$100

18. Kristina earned $22 dollars babysitting. She owes her mom $17. How much will Kristina have left after she pays her mom?

19. Trent has to read a book by Friday. It is Tuesday and he has 60 pages left to read. If he reads 20 pages a night for the next 3 nights, will he finish the book? Explain.

20. Measurement Presta's family is going to the mountains 280 miles away. The family's car can go 25 miles on a gallon of gas, and the gas tank holds 10 gallons. Can they travel to the mountains without stopping to fill up the gas tank? Explain.

1-4 **Compare Whole Numbers** (pp. 28–30)

3-2.1

Example 4
Compare 1,278 ● 1,500.
Use >, <, or =.

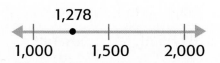

1,278

1,000   1,500   2,000

1,500 is to the right of 1,278.
So, 1,500 is greater than 1,278.
1,278 is less than 1,500.
Therefore, 1,278 < 1,500.

Compare. Use >, <, or =.

21. 25,689 ● 25,679

22. 54,820 ● 58,240

23. 109,050 ● 109,050

24. 234,461 ● 234,641

25. Jaya ate 2,142 calories on Monday. On the same day her brother ate 2,111 calories. Who had more calories on Monday?

1-5 **Order Whole Numbers** (pp. 32–34)

4-2.6

Example 5
Order 54,282; 65,820; and 52,466 from greatest to least.

First, line up the ones place. Compare the digits in the greatest place.

54,282
65,820 ← greatest
52,466

Then, compare the digits in the next place.

54,282
52,466

4 > 2. So, 54,282 is the next greatest number.

The numbers ordered from greatest to least are 65,820; 54,282; and 52,466.

Order the numbers from greatest to least.

26. 12,378; 12,784; 12,837

27. 138,023; 138,032; 139,006

28. 456,980; 612,701; 611,036

29. The table shows the population of three states. Order these states from greatest to least population.

State	Population
Illinois	12,831,970
Kentucky	4,206,074
South Carolina	4,321,249

Source: U.S. Census Bureau

Study Guide and Review

1-6 Round Whole Numbers (pp. 36–39)

3-2.4

Example 6
Round 587 to the nearest ten.

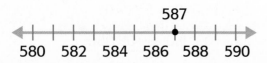

587

580 582 584 586 588 590

On the number line, 587 is closer to 590 than 580. Therefore, round 587 to 590.

Round each number to the given place-value position.

30. 874; hundred

31. 12,025; ten thousands

32. 617,589; ten thousands

33. 547,203; thousands

34. In 1790, the population of the United States was 3,929,214. To the nearest million, what was the population in 1790?

1-7 Problem-Solving Investigation: Choose a Strategy (pp. 40–41)

4-1.1

Example 7
Each time Esteban goes to the grocery store for his grandmother, she gives him $4. He has $12. How many times has Esteban gone to the grocery store?

Esteban has $12, and he gets $4 each time he goes to the store. You need to find how many times he has gone to the store. Use addition.

$$\begin{array}{ll} \$4 & 1 \text{ trip} \\ \$4 & 1 \text{ trip} \\ \underline{+\ \$4} & 1 \text{ trip} \\ \$12 & \end{array}$$

So, Esteban has gone to the store 3 times.

Use the four-step plan to solve.

35. Lindsay earns $5 for every A she gets on her report card and $3 for every B. On her last report card, she received a total of $19 for 5 subjects. How many As and Bs did she get?

36. Precious spends 35 hours in school every five-day week. How many five-day weeks will she have been in school if she has been in school for 175 hours?

37. In 1916, Jeannette Rankin of Montana became the first woman elected to Congress. Use rounding to estimate how many years ago the first woman was elected to Congress.

For Exercises 1 and 2, tell whether each statement is *true* or *false*.

1. The four steps of the four-step problem-solving plan in order are Plan, Understand, Solve, Check.

2. The standard form of nine hundred seventy is 970.

Write the value of the underlined digit.

3. 1<u>8</u>,765

4. <u>3</u>01,936

5. Students voted on their favorite frozen yogurt flavors. The results are shown. Order the results from most favorite to least favorite.

Flavor	Number of Students
Vanilla	410
Chocolate	240
Strawberry	99
Chocolate chip	401

6. **MULTIPLE CHOICE** Which of these is 7,201,446?

   A seven thousand, two hundred one, four hundred forty-six

   B seven million, two hundred one thousand, four hundred forty-six

   C seven hundred two thousand, one hundred forty-six

   D seven million, two hundred ten thousand, four hundred forty-six

Order the numbers from greatest to least.

7. 1,002; 1,037; 1,200; 1,102

8. 7,613; 7,702; 8,045; 7,499

9. A computer costs $1,295. Round this price to the nearest hundred.

Compare. Use >, <, or =.

10. 6,782 ● 6,702

11. 2,487 ● 2,784

12. **MULTIPLE CHOICE** What is 7,620,113 rounded to the nearest hundred thousand?

   F 7,600,000

   G 7,620,000

   H 7,700,000

   J 8,000,000

13. Sora earned a score of 98 on a test. Ryan earned a score of 89. Who earned a higher score?

Write each number in word form.

14. 3,476

15. 97,602

16. **WRITING IN ►MATH** Andrew rounded 647,963 to the nearest hundred thousand. Is his answer correct? Explain.

    700,000

PASS PRACTICE

What is four hundred sixty-one thousand, eight hundred five in standard form?

A 416,805   **C** 461,805

B 461,580   **D** 461,850

Read the Test Question

You need to find the number in standard form.

Solve the Test Question

Make a place-value chart to help you find the standard form of the number.

Thousands			Ones		
hundreds	tens	ones	hundreds	tens	ones
4	6	1	8	0	5

As you read the numbers, listen to the place value.

The answer is C.

PART 1   Multiple Choice

Read each question. Then fill in the correct answer on the answer sheet provided by your teacher or on a sheet of paper.

1. What is 54,678,491 rounded to the nearest hundred thousand?

A 54,000,000   **C** 54,680,000

B 54,600,000   **D** 54,700,000

2. What is the standard form for sixteen million, three hundred twenty-seven thousand, four hundred three?

F 16,723,043   **H** 16,327,403

G 16,372,430   **J** 16,237,340

3. The table shows the number of coupons mailed out by four large grocery store chains.

Grocery Store Coupons	
Store	Number of Coupons
Fast Mart	35,411
Saver Center	35,408
Gardens	35,416
Big Value	35,420

Which store mailed out the most coupons?

A Big Value   **C** Gardens

B Fast Mart   **D** Saver Center

4. Which symbol makes the following true?

12,935,374 ● 12,953,748

F >   **H** =

G <   **J** +

5. Which is the value of the digit 7 in 273,158?

A 70   **C** 7,000

B 700   **D** 70,000

PART 2   **Short Response**

Record your answers on the answer sheet provided by your teacher or on a sheet of paper.

6. What is $4,775,000 rounded to the nearest million?

7. What is the word form for 724,385?

8. Which point on the number line represents 22?

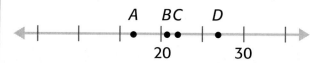

PART 3   **Extended Response**

Record your answers on the answer sheet provided by your teacher or on a sheet of paper.

9. What is the value of the digit 9 in 349,865? Create a place-value chart to support your answer.

10. Explain how to round $3,876,342 to the nearest million.

NEED EXTRA HELP?										
If You Missed Question...	1	2	3	4	5	6	7	8	9	10
Go to Lesson...	1-6	1-2	1-5	1-4	1-1	1-6	1-1	1-4	1-1	1-6
SC Academic Standards	3-2.4	4-2.6	4-2.6	3-2.1	4-2.6	3-2.4	4-2.6	3-2.1	4-2.6	3-2.4

CHAPTER 2 Solve Addition and Subtraction Problems

What is addition? What is subtraction?

Addition is an operation on two or more numbers that tells how many in all. Subtraction is an operation on two numbers that tells how many are left when some are taken away.

Example Celeste and her parents are painting a fence. The fence has three sides. To find the total length of the fence, use addition.

$$\begin{array}{r} \scriptstyle 1 \\ 25 \\ 30 \\ + 25 \\ \hline 80 \end{array}$$

25 ft   25 ft

30 ft

The total length of the fence is 80 feet.

What will I learn in this chapter?

- Use addition properties and subtraction rules.
- Estimate sums and differences.
- Determine when to estimate or find an exact answer.
- Add and subtract whole numbers, including multi-digit numbers.

Key Vocabulary

Commutative Property of Addition

Associative Property of Addition

estimate

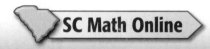
SC Math Online

Student Study Tools
at macmillanmh.com

FOLDABLES
Study Organizer

Make this Foldable to help you organize information about addition and subtraction. Begin with one sheet of 11″ × 17″ paper.

① **Fold** lengthwise about 3″ from the bottom.

② **Fold** the paper in thirds.

③ **Open** and staple to form 3 pockets.

④ **Label** as shown. Place 2 index cards in each pocket.

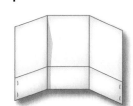

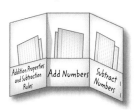

Addition Properties and Subtraction Rules

Add Numbers

Subtract Numbers

You have two ways to check prerequisite skills for this chapter.

Option 2

SC Math Online ▷ Take the Chapter Readiness Quiz at **macmillanmh.com**.

Option 1

Complete the Quick Check below.

QUICK Check

Estimate. Round to the tens place. (Lesson 1-6)

1. 65
     + 23

2. 58
     + 31

3. $64
     − $21

4. 98 − 22

5. $60 + $29

6. 88 − 26

7. Kavel wants to buy a pair of swimming goggles and a snorkel. Kavel has $22. About how much more money does he need to buy the items?

$28 $19

Add. (Prior Grade)

8. 24
     + 47

9. 36
     + 57

10. 67
      + 24

11. $56 + $25

12. 46 + 78

13. $89 + $53

14. Zita read an 82-page book. Then she read a 69-page book. How many pages did she read in all?

Subtract. (Prior Grade)

15. 26
      − 9

16. $31
      − $ 7

17. 47
      − 19

18. 42 − 19

19. 64 − 27

20. $73 − $45

21. Algebra Omar took 34 pictures on Monday and some more on Tuesday. He took 71 pictures in all. How many did Omar take on Tuesday?

Algebra: Addition Properties and Subtraction Rules

MAIN IDEA

I will use addition properties and subtraction rules to add and subtract.

SC Academic Standards

4-1.3 Explain and justify answers to problems on the basis of mathematical properties, structures, and relationships. *Also addresses 4-1.2.*

New Vocabulary

Commutative Property of Addition

Associative Property of Addition

Identity Property of Addition

SC Math Online

macmillanmh.com
• Extra Examples
• Personal Tutor
• Self-Check Quiz

GET READY to Learn

Carlos is buying the items shown. Does the order in which the cashier scans the items change the total cost?

$15 $10 $20

Addition Properties   Key Concepts

Words	**Commutative Property of Addition** The order in which numbers are added does not change the sum.
Examples	$4 + 1 = 5$ $1 + 4 = 5$
Words	**Associative Property of Addition** The way in which numbers are grouped when added does not change the sum.
Examples	$(5 + 2) + 3$ $5 + (2 + 3)$

$$7 + 3 \qquad 5 + 5$$

$$10 \qquad\qquad 10$$

> Parentheses ( ) show which numbers are added first.

Words	**Identity Property of Addition** The sum of any number and 0 is the number.
Examples	$8 + 0 = 8$ $0 + 8 = 8$

Real-World EXAMPLE   Use Addition Properties

1 **MONEY Does the order in which the camping supplies are scanned change the total cost?**

The Associative Property tells us that the way in which numbers are grouped when added does not change the sum.

$$(\$20 + \$15) + \$10 = \$20 + (\$15 + \$10)$$
$$(\$35 + \$10) = \$20 + \$25$$
$$\$45 = \$45$$

EXAMPLE **Use Addition Properties**

Remember

Use parentheses ( ) to show the two numbers you are adding first.

2 **Complete** $0 + \blacksquare = 6$**. Identify the property used.**

Zero is added to a number, and the sum is 6. So, the missing number is 6. $0 + 6 = 6$

This is the Identity Property of Addition.

The following rules apply to subtraction.

Subtraction Rules   Key Concepts

Words	When you subtract 0 from any number, the result is the number.
Examples	$6 - 0 = 6$ $4 - 0 = 4$
Words	When you subtract any number from itself, the result is 0.
Examples	$6 - 6 = 0$ $5 - 5 = 0$

EXAMPLE **Use Subtraction Rules**

3 **Find the missing number in** $10 - \blacksquare = 10$**.**

When you subtract 0 from 10, the result is 10.

$10 - 0 = 10$ So, the missing number is 0.

CHECK What You Know

Copy and complete each number sentence. Identify the property or rule used. See Examples 1–3 (pp. 55–56)

1. $19 - \blacksquare = 19$ **2.** $(5 + \blacksquare) + 2 = 5 + (9 + 2)$ **3.** $74 + 68 = \blacksquare + 74$

Add mentally. See Example 1 (p. 55)

4. $12 + 13 + 28$ **5.** $21 + 16 + 19$ **6.** $24 + 17 + 36$

7. *Talk About It* What subtraction rule is like the opposite of the Identity Property of Addition? Explain your reasoning.

Copy and complete each number sentence. Identify the property or rule used. See Examples 1–3 (pp. 55–56)

8. $(\blacksquare + 8) + 7 = 9 + (8 + 7)$ **9.** $4 + 3 + 1 = 3 + 1 + \blacksquare$ **10.** $\blacksquare + 0 = 9$

11. $5 - \blacksquare = 0$ **12.** $7 + (1 + 8) = (7 + \blacksquare) + 8$ **13.** $15 - \blacksquare = 15$

Add mentally. See Example 1 (p. 55)

14. $17 + 24 + 13$ **15.** $35 + 22 + 15$ **16.** $13 + 11 + 27$

17. $22 + 16 + 28$ **18.** $14 + 33 + 26$ **19.** $31 + 22 + 29$

20. Measurement There are 24 minutes left in Alicia's class. Then she has 2 more classes before lunch that are each 35 minutes. How many minutes does Alicia have before lunch?

21. Measurement Paco has 75 minutes before practice. He cleans his room for 40 minutes and reads for 30 minutes. Can he do both of these activities before his baseball practice? Explain.

Write a number sentence. Then identify the property or rule used.

22. Susan ate 1 hot dog and 2 apples. Amelia ate 2 hot dogs and 1 apple. Who ate more food items?

23. Carla has 4 triangles, 3 squares, and 5 circles. Ethan has 3 circles, 4 squares, and 5 triangles. Who has more shapes?

H.O.T. Problems

24. OPEN ENDED Copy and complete the number sentence $(23 + \blacksquare) + 19 = 23 + (\blacksquare + 19)$. Can any number complete the number sentence? Explain.

25. FIND THE ERROR Trey and Mika are showing an example of the Identity Property of Addition. Who is correct? Explain.

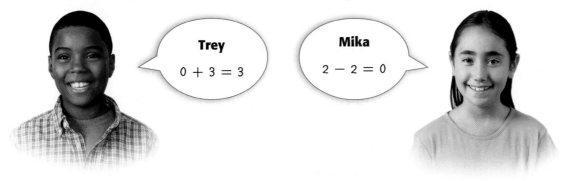

Trey
$0 + 3 = 3$

Mika
$2 - 2 = 0$

26. **WRITING IN ►MATH** Explain how you could group $775 + 639 + 225$ to find the sum mentally.

2-2

Estimate Sums and Differences

GET READY to Learn

Natalie has been saving her money so that she can buy snowboarding equipment. She wants to buy the items shown. About how much money does she need?

$119

$67

MAIN IDEA

I will estimate sums and differences of numbers.

SC Academic Standards

Reinforcement of 3-2.3 Apply an algorithm to add and subtract whole numbers fluently.

New Vocabulary

estimate

SC Math Online

macmillanmh.com

• Extra Examples
• Personal Tutor
• Self-Check Quiz

Sometimes you do not need an exact answer. When the word *about* is used in a problem, you can find an estimate. An **estimate** is an answer close to the exact answer.

Real-World EXAMPLE   Estimate Sums

① **MONEY About how much money does Natalie need to buy a snowboard and boots? Round to the tens place.**

Round each amount to the nearest tens. Then add.

$$
\begin{array}{r}
\$119 \\
+\$\ 67
\end{array}
\quad
\boxed{\begin{array}{l} \text{rounds to} \\ \text{rounds to} \end{array}}
\longrightarrow
\begin{array}{r}
\$120 \\
+\$\ 70 \\ \hline
\$190
\end{array}
$$

So, Natalie needs to save about $190.

When estimating, you can also round to the nearest hundred or thousand.

EXAMPLE   Estimate Sums

② **Estimate 2,342 + 637. Round to the hundreds place.**

Round each number to the nearest hundreds. Then add.

$$
\begin{array}{r}
2,342 \\
+\ 637
\end{array}
\quad
\boxed{\begin{array}{l} \text{rounds to} \\ \text{rounds to} \end{array}}
\longrightarrow
\begin{array}{r}
2,300 \\
+\ 600 \\ \hline
2,900
\end{array}
$$

So, 2,342 + 637 is about 2,900.

58 Chapter 2 Solve Addition and Subtraction Problems

EXAMPLE Estimate Differences

③ **Estimate $7,542 − $3,225. Round to the tens place.**

Round each amount to the nearest ten dollars. Then subtract.

$$\begin{array}{r} \$7,542 \\ -\ \$3,225 \end{array} \quad \boxed{\begin{array}{l} \text{rounds to} \\ \text{rounds to} \end{array}} \longrightarrow \begin{array}{r} \$7,540 \\ -\ \$3,230 \\ \hline \$4,310 \end{array}$$

So, $7,542 − $3,225 is about $4,310.

Remember

Use place value to help you round whole numbers.

Real-World EXAMPLE Estimate Differences

④ **MEASUREMENT The table shows populations for two cities in Kentucky. About how many more people live in Covington than in Ashland?**

City Populations	
City	**Population**
Ashland	21,510
Covington	42,811

Source: U.S. Census Bureau

Round each population to the nearest thousand. Then subtract.

$$\begin{array}{r} 42,811 \\ -\ 21,510 \end{array} \quad \boxed{\begin{array}{l} \text{rounds to} \\ \text{rounds to} \end{array}} \longrightarrow \begin{array}{r} 43,000 \\ -\ 22,000 \\ \hline 21,000 \end{array}$$

So, Covington has about 21,000 more people.

✓ CHECK What You Know

Estimate. Round to the indicated place value. See Examples 1–4 (pp. 58–59)

1. $21 + $73; tens

2. 312 + 27; tens

3. 383 + 122; hundreds

4. 1,561 − 305; hundreds

5. $2,746 − $1,529; tens

6. 37,215 − 6,972; thousands

7. The Davis family will buy the camping equipment shown. About how much will the equipment cost?

8. **Talk About It** Estimate 829 + 1,560 to the nearest hundred and the nearest thousand. Compare both estimates to the actual sum. What do you notice?

Camping Equipment	
Item	**Cost**
Family-size tent	$399
Camping stove	$179

Estimate. Round to the indicated place value. See Examples 1–4 (pp. 58–59)

9. $34 + $23; tens

10. $35 + $42; tens

11. $636 + $27; tens

12. $687 + $331; hundreds

13. $455 + $229; tens

14. 1,624 + 534; hundreds

15. $772 − $593; hundreds

16. 985 − 639; tens

17. 2,647 − 256; hundreds

18. 27,629 − 5,364; thousands

19. $48,986 − $7,664; thousands

20. $47,236 − $20,425; thousands

Solve. Round to the nearest thousand.

21. The largest NBA arena can seat 22,076 people. Suppose two games are sold out. About how many people will attend the two games?

22. Luz is going to buy a car that costs $18,460 new and $15,788 used. About how much money would Luz save if she bought the car used?

23. **Measurement** A mountain climber is climbing Mt. Everest. It is 29,035 feet tall. About how many feet will the climber have traveled after going up and down the mountain?

24. Jupiter and Saturn are the two largest planets in our solar system. Jupiter is 88,846 miles across and Saturn is 74,898 miles across. What is the approximate difference in the distance across these two planets?

Real-World PROBLEM SOLVING

Buildings This table shows the tallest buildings in the world. Round to the nearest hundred.

25. About how much taller is the Sears Tower than the Jin Mao Building?

26. Estimate the difference between the height of the Taipai 101 Building and the Empire State Building.

27. About how much taller is Petronas Towers than the Empire State Building?

Tallest Buildings in the World		
Building	**Location**	**Height (ft)**
Taipai 101	Taiwan	1,669
Petronas Towers	Malaysia	1,482
Sears Tower	United States	1,450
Jin Mao Building	China	1,381
CITIC Plaza	China	1,282
Shun Hing Square	China	1,259
Empire State Building	United States	1,250

Source: *The Ultimate Book of Lists*

H.O.T. Problems

28. OPEN ENDED Write two numbers that when rounded to the thousands place have an estimated sum of 10,000.

29. NUMBER SENSE If both addends are rounded down, will the sum of the numbers be greater or less than the actual sum? Explain.

30. **WRITING IN** ►**MATH** When rounding to estimate the sum or difference of numbers, explain a situation where less exact answers would be better than more exact answers.

PASS Practice 4-1.3, 3-2.3

31. What number completes the number sentence below? (Lesson 2-1)

$$(24 + \blacksquare) + 18 = 24 + (36 + 18)$$

A 18   **C** 36

B 24   **D** 38

32. The Casey family traveled last week. They drove 182 miles on Friday, 138 miles on Saturday, and 119 miles on Sunday. Approximately how many miles did they travel? (Lesson 2-2)

F 200 miles   **H** 320 miles

G 300 miles   **J** 400 miles

Spiral Review

Algebra Copy and complete each number sentence. Identify the property or rule used. (Lesson 2-1)

33. $35 - \blacksquare = 35$

34. $(57 + \blacksquare) + 36 = 57 + (25 + 36)$

Round each number to the given place-value position. (Lesson 1-6)

35. 354; ten   **36.** 4,396; thousand   **37.** 257,468; hundred

Compare. Use >, <, or =. (Lesson 1-4)

38. 8,650 ● 8,623   **39.** 44,068 ● 44,086   **40.** 248,632 ● 284,632

41. Jameson's basketball team scored a total of 58 points. Jameson scored 18 points, and his sister scored 12 points. How many points did the rest of the team score? (Lesson 1-3)

42. Teresa's cell phone bill is $32 each month. About how much money does she spend on cell phone service every two months? (Lesson 1-3)

Problem-Solving Skill

MAIN IDEA I will determine when to estimate or find an exact answer.

 SCAS **4-1.1 Analyze information to solve increasingly more sophisticated problems.**

Keith and his brother are going to build a tree house. They will need $12 for nails, $95 for tools, and $46 for wood. About how much money do they need to build the tree house?

Understand	**What facts do you know?**
	• Nails cost $12.
	• Tools cost $95.
	• Wood costs $46.
	What do you need to find?
	• Find about how much money they need to build the tree house.
Plan	Since the question says *about* how much money is needed, you can estimate the sum.
Solve	Round each amount to each greatest place value. Then add.
	$12 $\longrightarrow$ $ 10 $95 $\longrightarrow$ $100 $\longleftarrow$ Round each number to its greatest place value. + $46 $\longrightarrow$ + $ 50 $160 So, about $160 is needed to build the tree house.
Check	Look back. Suppose the question asked for an exact answer. Add $12, $95, and $46. $\overset{1}{\$12}$ $95 + $46 $153 Since $153 is close to $160, an estimate of $160 is correct.

Refer to the problem on the previous page.

1. Why does it make sense to round in this situation?

2. Suppose it costs $16 for nails, $109 for tools, and $62 for wood. What would a good estimate be? Explain.

3. Why did the boys round each dollar amount up?

4. Why is it a good idea to round up when dealing with money even if the number would be rounded down?

PRACTICE the Skill

SCAS • PASS
Extra Practice, p. R5

Tell whether an estimate or exact answer is needed. Then solve.

5. Determine if Tammy, Anessa, and Jaleesa have more than 110 CDs.

Name	CDs Owned
Tammy	21
Anessa	42
Jaleesa	33

6. Samuel bought a sweater for $36 and paid with a $50 bill. About how much change should he get back?

7. A theater can hold 200 people. Two groups rented out the theater. The first group has 92 people and the other has 107 people. Are there enough seats for everyone? Explain.

8. Carissa pays $2 each day for lunch. Her money is in an account that is deducted each time she buys a lunch. There are 6 days until the end of the school year and her account has $13 in it. How much money will she get back at the end of the year?

9. Jacob is taking a test at school. The question is shown below. What is the answer?

$$23 + 34 + 17$$

10. Tracy is allowed to watch 2 hours of television each night. About how much television does she watch in a year?

11. **Measurement** Rodney needs to measure the distance around his garden. How much fencing should Rodney buy?

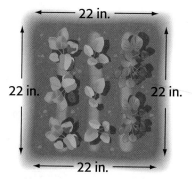

22 in.

22 in.   22 in.

22 in.

12. **WRITING IN ►MATH** A newspaper stated that the population of California was 33,871,600. Explain why this is probably an estimate.

2-4 Add Whole Numbers

Hands-On Mini Activity

The model shows 135 + 127.

1. Estimate 135 + 127.

2. To find 135 + 127, is it necessary to regroup the ones? How do you know?

3. Is it necessary to regroup the tens? How do you know?

Hundreds	Tens	Ones
1	3	5
+ 1	2	7

MAIN IDEA

I will add numbers, including multi-digit numbers.

SC Academic Standards

Reinforcement of 3-2.3 Apply an algorithm to add and subtract whole numbers fluently.

SC Math Online

macmillanmh.com

- Extra Examples
- Personal Tutor
- Self-Check Quiz

When you add whole numbers, it may be necessary to regroup.

EXAMPLE Add Whole Numbers

① **Find 6,824 + 349.**

Estimate
$$
\begin{array}{r}
6{,}824 \longrightarrow 6{,}800 \\
+\ 349 \longrightarrow +\ 300 \\
\hline
7{,}100
\end{array}
$$

Step 1 Add ones.

$$
\begin{array}{r}
\overset{1}{6}{,}824 \\
+\ 349 \\
\hline
3
\end{array}
$$

4 + 9 = 13
Regroup 13 ones as 1 ten and 3 ones.

Step 2 Add tens.

$$
\begin{array}{r}
\overset{1}{6}{,}824 \\
+\ 349 \\
\hline
73
\end{array}
$$

1 + 2 + 4 = 7

Step 3 Add hundreds.

$$
\begin{array}{r}
\overset{1}{6}\overset{1}{,}824 \\
+\ 349 \\
\hline
173
\end{array}
$$

8 + 3 = 11
Regroup 11 hundreds as 1 thousand and 1 hundred.

Step 4 Add thousands.

$$
\begin{array}{r}
\overset{1}{6}\overset{1}{,}824 \\
+\ 349 \\
\hline
7{,}173
\end{array}
$$

6 + 1 = 7

Check for Reasonableness

The estimate is 7,100. Since 7,173 is close to the estimate, the answer is reasonable. ✔

2 **TICKETS** Weekend ticket sales for a play are shown in the table. What was the total?

Ticket Sales	
Day	**Amount**
Saturday	$5,713
Sunday	$4,827

Estimate

$$\begin{array}{r} \$5,713 \longrightarrow \$6,000 \\ + \underline{\$4,827} \longrightarrow + \underline{\$5,000} \\ \$11,000 \end{array}$$

Vocabulary Link

prefixes The prefix *re-* means *again*. Examples: *regroup* means *to group again*; *review* means *to view again*

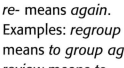

Step 1 Add ones.

$$\begin{array}{r} 1 \\ \$5,713 \\ + \underline{\$4,827} \\ 0 \end{array}$$

$3 + 7 = 10$
Regroup 10 ones as 1 ten and 0 ones.

Step 2 Add tens.

$$\begin{array}{r} 1 \\ \$5,713 \\ + \underline{\$4,827} \\ 40 \end{array}$$

$1 + 1 + 2 = 4$

Step 3 Add hundreds.

$$\begin{array}{r} 1 \quad 1 \\ \$5,713 \\ + \underline{\$4,827} \\ 540 \end{array}$$

$7 + 8 = 15$
Regroup 15 hundreds as 1 thousand and 5 hundreds.

Step 4 Add thousands. Place $ sign.

$$\begin{array}{r} 1 \quad 1 \\ \$5,713 \\ + \underline{\$4,827} \\ \$10,540 \end{array}$$

$1 + 5 + 4 = 10$
Place $ in front.

So, the total ticket sales were $10,540.

Check for Reasonableness

The estimate is $11,000. Since $10,540 is close to the estimate, the answer is reasonable. ✓

Find each sum. Check your work by estimating. See Examples 1 and 2 (pp. 64–65)

1. 397
+ 84

2. 1,592
+ 429

3. $2,971
+ $ 864

4. $29,380
+ $ 8,253

5. Mr. Russo's class is collecting bottles to recycle. The class collected 178 bottles in March and 236 bottles in April. How many bottles were collected?

6. **Talk About It** Explain why it is important to line up digits in numbers when you add.

Practice and Problem Solving

SCAS • PASS
Extra Practice, p. R5

Find each sum. Check your work by estimating. See Examples 1 and 2 (pp. 64–65)

7. 364
+ 58

8. 290
+ 693

9. 6,742
+ 975

10. 8,346
+ 7,208

11. $23,824
+ $ 7,346

12. 82,828
+ 4,789

13. $37,178
+ $82,370

14. $693,782
+ $ 47,816

15. There are 4,585 students who rode the bus to school today. There were 3,369 students who came to school another way. How many students were there in all at school?

16. Becky wants to buy a new bike that costs $150 and a pair of roller blades that costs $30. She made $200 baby-sitting. If she buys a book that is $15, will she have enough money for the bike and roller blades?

 South Carolina Data File

The table shows the populations of various cities in South Carolina.

17. What is the total population of Rock Hill and Sumter?

18. What is the total population of Florence, Summerville, and Goose Creek?

19. Which has a greater population, Rock Hill and Sumter or North Charleston and Anderson? Explain.

City	Population
Anderson	25,563
Florence	30,267
Goose Creek	30,574
North Charleston	81,577
Rock Hill	56,114
Summerville	31,734
Sumter	39,790

Source: U.S. Census Bureau

H.O.T. Problems

20. OPEN ENDED Write two 5-digit addends whose sum would give an estimate of 60,000.

21. **WRITING IN** ►**MATH** Explain why an addition problem that has 4-digit addends could have a 5-digit sum.

PASS Practice 4-1.1, 3-2.3

22. Jackson is buying a new board game. It costs $26. If he has 2 ten-dollar bills and 5 one-dollar bills, which of the following statements is true? (Lesson 2-3)

  A He will have less than $5 left over.

  B He does not have enough money.

  C He has the exact amount of money.

  D He will have more than $5 left over.

23. There are 17 extra chairs in the library and 45 extra chairs in the cafeteria. Which of the following shows how to find the total number of extra chairs? (Lesson 2-4)

  F $17 + 45$

  G $17 - 45$

  H 17×45

  J $17 \div 45$

Spiral Review

Tell whether an estimate or exact answer is needed. Then solve.

24. A school collected 189 cans of corn, 500 cans of soup, 168 cans of beans, and 269 jars of spaghetti sauce in a food drive. How many items did the school collect? (Lesson 2-3)

Estimate. Round to the indicated place value. (Lesson 2-2)

25. $137 + 192$; tens

26. $489 + 1,963$; hundreds

Add mentally. (Lesson 2-1)

27. $10 + 25 + 18$

28. $26 + 14 + 3$

29. $15 + 12 + 30$

Round each number to the given place-value position. (Lesson 1-6)

30. 987; ten

31. 2,159; hundred

32. 78,368; thousand

You can use *Math Tool Chest* to compose and decompose numbers.

MAIN IDEA

I will use technology to explore addition.

SC Academic Standards

4-1.6 Generalize connections between new mathematical ideas and related concepts and subjects that have been previously considered.

EXAMPLE

1 **There are 275 books. Each book is either non-fiction or fiction. How many of each type might there be?**

Click on place-value tool box from the *Math Tool Chest.*

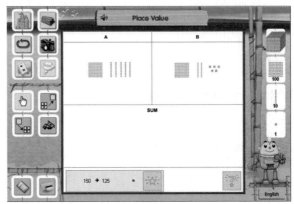

- Click on the addition mat.
- In section A, use hundreds and tens to stamp out 150.
- In section B, use hundreds, tens, and ones to stamp out 125.
- Click on sum. The models show that $150 + 125 = 275$.
- Click on the star at the bottom to check the sum.
- Explore different ways to make 275.

CHECK What You Know

Use the *Math Tool Chest* to explore different ways to compose and decompose each amount. Name two different ways.

1. There are 895 students in the 4th grade at South Elementary. How might this population be divided between boys and girls?

2. There are 1,750 freshwater and saltwater fish at a pet store. How many of each type of fish might the pet store have?

3. **WRITING IN MATH** Describe how different combinations of numbers can have the same sum.

Algebra Copy and complete each number sentence. Identify the property or rule. (Lesson 2-1)

1. $136 + 0 = $ ■

2. $(4 + $ ■$) + 7 = 4 + (2 + 7)$

3. $58 + 98 = $ ■ $+ 58$

Algebra Write a number sentence. Identify the property or rule used. (Lesson 2-1)

4. Andrea's pencil box has 3 pencils, 2 pencil-top erasers, and 1 red pen. Max's pencil box has 2 pencils, 1 pencil-top eraser, and 3 red pens. Whose pencil box contains more items? Explain.

5. **MULTIPLE CHOICE** What number completes the number sentence below? (Lesson 2-1)

$$(21 + ■) + 12 = 21 + (17 + 12)$$

A 11   **C** 17

B 12   **D** 21

Estimate. Round to the indicated place value. (Lesson 2-2)

6. $22 + $63; tens

7. $567 - 203$; hundreds

8. $5,825 - 551$; hundreds

9. **MULTIPLE CHOICE** About how many miles did a soccer team travel during the weekend? (Lesson 2-2)

Distance Traveled	
Day	**Distance (miles)**
Friday	146
Saturday	175
Sunday	206

F 400 miles   **H** 600 miles

G 500 miles   **J** 700 miles

Tell whether an estimate or exact answer is needed. Then solve. (Lesson 2-3)

10. Celia needs to make a fence in her yard for her puppy. She wants it to be square. One side measures 20 feet. How much fence should she buy?

Find each sum. Check your work by estimating. (Lesson 2-4)

11. $\begin{array}{r} 28{,}180 \\ + 7{,}233 \\ \hline \end{array}$ 12. $\begin{array}{r} 63{,}456 \\ + 37{,}425 \\ \hline \end{array}$

13. Gina's brother is starting college in the fall. The cost of tuition for one year will be $5,491. All the other expenses for the year will cost $10,065. What will the total cost of one year of college be for Gina's brother? (Lesson 2-4)

14. **WRITING IN ►MATH** Explain how you could add $175 + 139 + 225$ mentally. (Lesson 2-1)

Subtract Whole Numbers

When subtracting whole numbers, you may need to regroup.

MAIN IDEA

I will explore how to subtract whole numbers.

SC Academic Standards

Reinforcement of 3-2.3 Apply an algorithm to add and **subtract whole numbers fluently.**

You Will Need
base-ten blocks

New Vocabulary

minuend

subtrahend

difference

SC Math Online

macmillanmh.com
• Concepts in Motion

ACTIVITY   Use models to find 421 − 241.

Step 1   Model 421.
Use base-ten blocks to model 421.

Hundreds	Tens	Ones

Step 2   Subtract the ones.
Subtract.

$$\begin{array}{r} 42\mathbf{1} \\ -\ 24\mathbf{1} \\ \hline 0 \end{array}$$

Step 3   Subtract the tens.
Since you cannot take 4 tens from 2 tens, you need to regroup. Regroup one hundreds flat as 10 tens. You now have 12 tens.

$$\begin{array}{r} \overset{3\ 12}{4\cancel{2}1} \\ -\ 241 \\ \hline 80 \end{array}$$

Hundreds	Tens	Ones

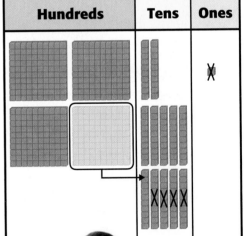

Step 4 Subtract the hundreds.

Take 2 hundreds flats away from the 3 hundreds flats.

$$
\begin{array}{r}
{}^{3}\;{}^{12} \\
\cancel{4}\cancel{2}1 \quad \leftarrow \textbf{minuend} \\
-\;241 \quad \leftarrow \textbf{subtrahend} \\
\hline
180 \quad \leftarrow \textbf{difference}
\end{array}
$$

Check
You can use addition to check your subtraction.

$$
\begin{array}{r}
421 \\
-\;241 \\
\hline
180
\end{array}
\quad
\begin{array}{r}
180 \\
+\;241 \\
\hline
421
\end{array}
$$

So, the answer is correct. ✔

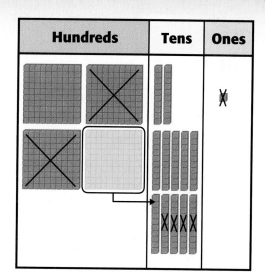

Hundreds	Tens	Ones

Think About It

1. How did you subtract 241 from 421 using base-ten blocks?

2. Describe how you regrouped the tens place.

CHECK What You Know

Subtract. Check by adding.

3. 357 − 98

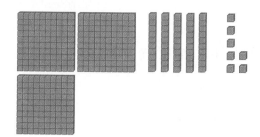

4. 679 − 345

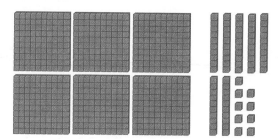

5. 287 − 195

6. 525 − 385

7. 632 − 248

8. 727 − 469

9. 861 − 593

10. 948 − 729

11. **WRITING IN MATH** Why is it important to line up the digits in each place-value position when subtracting?

GET READY to Learn

The Trevino family is moving to a new city. They have driven 957 miles out of the 3,214 miles that they need to drive. How many more miles do they need to drive?

MAIN IDEA

I will subtract multi-digit numbers.

SC Academic Standards

Reinforcement of 3-2.3 Apply an algorithm to add and **subtract whole numbers fluently.**

SC Math Online

macmillanmh.com

• Extra Examples
• Personal Tutor
• Self-Check Quiz

Subtraction of whole numbers is similar to addition of whole numbers in that you may need to regroup.

Real-World EXAMPLE   Subtract Whole Numbers

① **MEASUREMENT** **Find 3,214 − 957 to find how many miles the Trevino family needs to drive.**

Estimate
$$
\begin{array}{r}
3,214 \\
-\ 957 \\
\end{array}
\longrightarrow
\begin{array}{r}
3,200 \\
-\ 1,000 \\
\hline
2,200 \\
\end{array}
$$

Step 1 Subtract ones.

$$
\begin{array}{r}
^{0}\!\!\not{1}4 \\
3,2\not{1}\not{4} \\
-\ 957 \\
\hline
7 \\
\end{array}
$$

← Regroup a ten as 10 ones.

Step 2 Subtract tens.

$$
\begin{array}{r}
10 \\
1\not{0}\ 14 \\
3,2\not{1}\not{4} \\
-\ 957 \\
\hline
57 \\
\end{array}
$$

← Regroup a hundred as 10 tens.

Step 3 Subtract hundreds.

$$
\begin{array}{r}
11\ 10 \\
2\not{1}\not{0}14 \\
3,2\not{1}\not{4} \\
-\ 957 \\
\hline
257 \\
\end{array}
$$

← Regroup a thousand as 10 hundreds.

Step 4 Subtract thousands.

$$
\begin{array}{r}
11\ 10 \\
2\not{1}\not{0}14 \\
3,\not{2}\not{1}\not{4} \\
-\ 957 \\
\hline
2,257 \\
\end{array}
$$

So, the Trevino family needs to drive 2,257 more miles.

Check You can use addition to check your subtraction.

$$
\begin{array}{r}
3,214 \\
-\ 957 \\
\hline
2,257 \\
\end{array}
\longrightarrow
\begin{array}{r}
2,257 \\
+\ 957 \\
\hline
3,214\ ✓ \\
\end{array}
$$

Real-World EXAMPLE Subtract Money

2 **MONEY** The parent-teacher organization at an elementary school has raised $1,345 toward new playground equipment. If the goal is to raise $4,275, how much money must still be raised?

Estimate

$$\begin{array}{r} \$4,275 \rightarrow \$4,300 \\ - \$1,345 \rightarrow - \$1,300 \\ \hline \$3,000 \end{array}$$

Step 1 Subtract ones.

$$\begin{array}{r} \$4,275 \\ - \$1,345 \\ \hline 0 \end{array}$$

Step 2 Subtract tens.

$$\begin{array}{r} \$4,275 \\ - \$1,345 \\ \hline 30 \end{array}$$

Step 3 Subtract hundreds.

$$\begin{array}{r} \overset{3\;12}{\$4,\cancel{2}75} \\ - \$1,345 \\ \hline 930 \end{array}$$

> Regroup a thousand as 10 hundreds.

Step 4 Subtract thousands.

$$\begin{array}{r} \overset{3\;12}{\$4,\cancel{2}75} \\ - \$1,345 \\ \hline \$2,930 \end{array}$$

So, the amount of money that must still be raised is $2,930.

Check

$$\begin{array}{r} \$4,275 \\ - \$1,345 \\ \hline \$2,930 \end{array} \qquad \begin{array}{r} \$2,930 \\ + \$1,345 \\ \hline \$4,275 \end{array}$$

The answer is correct and close to the estimate. ✔

CHECK What You Know

Subtract. Use addition or estimation to check. See Examples 1 and 2 (pp. 72–73)

1.
$$\begin{array}{r} 526 \\ - 403 \end{array}$$

2.
$$\begin{array}{r} \$937 \\ - \$729 \end{array}$$

3.
$$\begin{array}{r} 2,962 \\ - 845 \end{array}$$

4.
$$\begin{array}{r} \$4,785 \\ - \$2,293 \end{array}$$

5. Kerri had $95 in her bank account. She bought her mom a bottle of perfume for her birthday for $25. How much money does she have left?

6. **Talk About It** Explain how to check the answer to a subtraction problem by using addition.

Subtract. Use addition or estimation to check. See Examples 1 and 2 (pp. 72–73)

7. 479
   − 292

8. $924
   − $837

9. $524
   − $246

10. $986
   − $339

11. 4,273
   − 365

12. 8,845
   − 627

13. $5,751
   − $4,824

14. $8,327
   − $5,709

15. 39,536 − 18,698

16. $64,779 − $42,788

17. Ramon is buying a DVD that costs $14, a book that costs $15, and pays $2 in tax. If he hands the cashier $40, how much change will he get back?

18. Mount Everest is 29,035 feet tall. From base camp at 17,600 feet, a climber hiked 2,300 feet. How much farther does the climber have before reaching the top of the mountain?

Real-World PROBLEM SOLVING

History This table shows information about former Presidents of the United States.

19. Who was older when he became President, John Adams or Harry S. Truman?

20. Who was the youngest person on this list to become President? How old was he?

21. How old was Ronald Reagan when John F. Kennedy died?

United States Presidents			
President	Born	Year became President	Death
John Adams	1732	1797	1801
James K. Polk	1795	1845	1849
Harry S. Truman	1884	1945	1972
John F. Kennedy	1917	1961	1963
Ronald Reagan	1911	1981	2004

Source: The White House

H.O.T. Problems

22. **WHICH ONE DOESN'T BELONG?** Which subtraction problem does not require regrouping? Explain.

67,457
− 40,724

70,639
− 39,607

89,584
− 57,372

95,947
− 26,377

23. **WRITING IN ►MATH** Write a real-world problem that involves subtraction and regrouping to solve. The numbers used in the problem must have at least three digits.

Make a Big Difference
Subtract Multi-Digit Numbers

Get Ready!
Players: 2 players

You will need: paper and pencil, 0–9 spinner

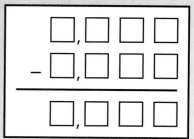

Get Set!
Make a game sheet like the one shown. Divide a spinner into ten equal sections. Label 0–9.

Go!
- Player 1 spins the spinner. Both players write that digit in a box of their choice on their game sheets.
- Continue until all eight boxes are filled. Then find the difference.
- Compare the differences. The player with the greatest difference scores 1 point.
- If the differences are equal, both players score 1 point.
- Continue playing until one player scores 5 points.

Problem-Solving Investigation

MAIN IDEA I will choose the best strategy to solve a problem.

SCAS 4-1.1 Analyze information to solve increasingly more sophisticated problems.

P.S.I. TEAM +

MARCO: I am downloading music. So far, I have downloaded 4 CDs. Each CD has 14 songs.

YOUR MISSION: Find how many songs Marco has downloaded.

Understand	Marco has downloaded 4 CDs, and each CD has 14 songs. Find how many songs Marco has downloaded.
Plan	You can organize the information in a table and use repeated addition to find how many songs Marco has downloaded.
Solve	Start with 14, the number of songs on the first CD. Then continue to add 14 for each additional CD.

$$\begin{array}{r} 14 \\ +\,14 \\ \hline 28 \end{array}$$ ← first CD, second CD

$$\begin{array}{r} \overset{1}{28} \\ +\,14 \\ \hline 42 \end{array}$$ ← third CD

$$\begin{array}{r} 42 \\ +\,14 \\ \hline 56 \end{array}$$ ← fourth CD

CDs	Songs
1	14
2	28
3	42
4	56

So, he downloaded a total of 56 songs.

Check	Look back. 56 − 14 = 42, 42 − 14 = 28, 28 − 14 = 14, and 14 − 14 = 0. The answer is correct.

Use any strategy to solve each problem.

1. Mrs. Thomas had $85. She bought a toaster. She now has $43. How much was the toaster?

2. **Measurement** The Nile River is 4,145 miles long. The Mississippi–Missouri River is 405 miles shorter than the Nile River. How long is the Mississippi–Missouri River?

3. Rosana has $9 left over after buying a movie ticket. If she buys a soft pretzel, what other item can she buy?

Movie Palace	
Item	Cost
Small soda	$4
Large soda	$6
Soft pretzel	$5
Medium popcorn	$6

4. Alonso has 139 comic books. Maggie has 72 comic books. Do they have a total of about 225 comic books? Explain.

5. A piñata is $36, and party decorations are $18. A gift is $28. About how much is spent altogether?

6. There are 58 third graders and 62 fourth graders going on a field trip. Each bus can carry 40 people. How many buses are needed?

7. Marcel earns $5 a week for doing his chores. About how many weeks will he have to save his money in order to buy the sports equipment below?

$79

8. Greta earns $5 each week walking dogs. Her portion of the family cell phone bill each month is $15. How much does she have left after paying her cell phone bill for a month that has four weeks?

9. Prem is thinking of three numbers from 1 to 10. The sum of the numbers is 14. Find the numbers.

10. **Measurement** About how much farther does the willow warbler migrate than the barn swallow?

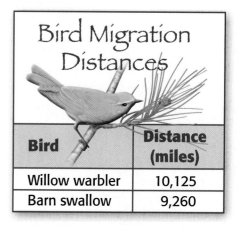

Bird Migration Distances	
Bird	Distance (miles)
Willow warbler	10,125
Barn swallow	9,260

11. **WRITING IN ►MATH** Juan bowls 133 in his first game. He bowls 148 in his second game. The answer is 280. What is the question?

Problem Solving in Science

Ready, Set, Click!

The first photographers had difficult jobs. They carried separate pieces of film in large metal containers. Each container was 12 inches wide and 16 inches long.

Taking a picture was first a chemical process. Today, taking a picture is a digital process, too. Digital cameras take pictures like a television records images.

There are now many different types of cameras that are affordable. Some cameras that scientists have invented are used only once. There are many different kinds of these cameras, including digital disposable cameras.

Did You Know?

The digital camera revolution started in 1981.

Real-World Math

Use the information on pages 78 and 79 to solve each problem.

1. Hanna paid $35 for 4 disposable cameras. Which ones did she buy?

2. Coty buys two digital cameras, three outdoor cameras, and three flash cameras. How much money does Coty spend?

3. Suppose you buy an outdoor disposable camera and a flash disposable camera. If you pay with $30, how much change will you get?

4. Which two cameras cost the same as one underwater camera?

5. If you buy 2 underwater cameras, you get a $3 discount. How much money will you spend?

6. What two cameras can you buy with $9?

7. Emily has $30. Identify two ways she can spend her money on individual cameras without having any change.

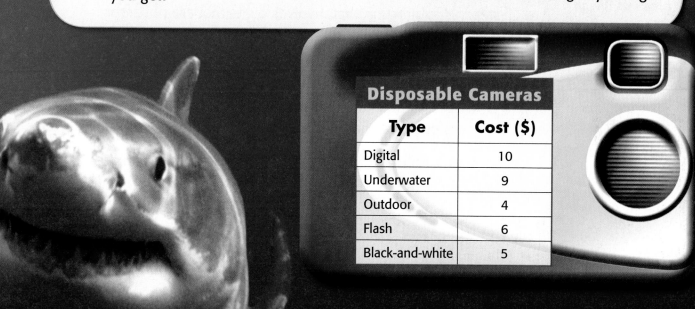

Disposable Cameras

Type	Cost ($)
Digital	10
Underwater	9
Outdoor	4
Flash	6
Black-and-white	5

Subtract Across Zeros

GET READY to Learn

The bar graph shows the number of movies produced by five countries. What is the difference in the greatest and least number of movies produced?

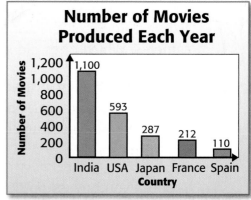

Number of Movies Produced Each Year

Source: *The Top 10 of Everything*

Subtraction that involves digits that are zeros uses the same steps as subtraction that involves digits that are not zeros.

Real-World EXAMPLE   Subtract Across Zeros

① **MOVIES Refer to the graph. How many more movies does India produce than Spain?**

Step 1 Subtract ones.

$$\begin{array}{r} 1{,}100 \\ -110 \\ \hline 0 \end{array}$$ ← $0 - 0 = 0$

Step 2 Subtract tens.

$$\begin{array}{r} 010 \\ 1{,}100 \\ -110 \\ \hline 90 \end{array}$$ ← Regroup 1 hundred as 10 tens. $10 - 1 = 9$

Step 3 Subtract hundreds.

$$\begin{array}{r} 10 \\ 0\ 10 \\ 1{,}100 \\ -110 \\ \hline 990 \end{array}$$ ← Regroup 1 thousand as 10 hundreds. $10 - 1 = 9$

Step 4 Subtract thousands.

$$\begin{array}{r} 10 \\ 0\ 10 \\ 1{,}100 \\ -110 \\ \hline 990 \end{array}$$ ← $0 - 0 = 0$

So, India produces 990 more movies a year than Spain.

Check $990 + 110 = 1{,}100$. So, the answer is correct. ✔

2 **MONEY** A school bought music equipment for $5,004. The drums cost $2,815. How much money was spent on music equipment other than the drums?

Remember

When you subtract, start at the place farthest to the right.

Step 1 Subtract ones.

```
      9 9
   4 10 10 14
  $5,0 0 4
 − $2,8 1 5
          9
```

Regroup 1 thousand as 10 hundreds. Regroup 1 hundred as 10 tens. Regroup 1 ten as 10 ones. $14 - 9 = 5$

Step 2 Subtract tens.

```
      9 9
   4 10 10 14
  $5,0 0 4
 − $2,8 1 5
         8 9
```

$9 - 8 = 1$

Step 3 Subtract hundreds.

```
      9 9
   4 10 10 14
  $5,0 0 4
 − $2,8 1 5
       1 8 9
```

$9 - 8 = 1$

Step 4 Subtract thousands.

```
      9 9
   4 10 10 14
  $5,0 0 4
 − $2,8 1 5
  $2,1 8 9
```

$4 - 2 = 2$

So, $2,189 was spent on music equipment other than drums.

✓ CHECK What You Know

Subtract. Use addition to check. See Examples 1 and 2 (pp. 80–81)

1. 309
      − 57

2. 608
      − 45

3. $707
      − $535

4. 903
      − 791

5. 2,006
      − 536

6. $8,005
      − $4,423

7. On Saturday, there were 1,000 balloons at a hot air balloon festival. On Sunday, there were 350 balloons. How many more balloons were there on Saturday than on Sunday?

8. **Talk About It** Explain where you would start regrouping to find the difference in the problem below.

66,000
− 23,475

Subtract. Use addition to check. See Examples 1 and 2 (pp. 80–81)

9. 408
    − 36

10. 805
    − 75

11. 604
    − 492

12. $502
    − $130

13. $708
    − $222

14. 809
    − 566

15. $8,001
    − $6,930

16. 9,006
    − 7,474

17. 8,007 − 4,836

18. $9,003 − $5,295

19. 30,070 − 14,021

20. Ava guessed that there were 1,007 marbles in a jar for a contest. There were actually 972 marbles in the jar. How far off was Ava's guess?

21. **Measurement** Dillan hiked one and a half miles or 7,920 feet. If Sato hiked two miles or 10,560 feet, how many more feet did Sato hike?

Real-World PROBLEM SOLVING

Travel The length of paved and unpaved roads in four countries is shown.

22. How many more miles of road does Australia have than Spain?

23. Which two countries have the greatest difference in miles of roads? France and Australia, Australia and Spain, or Spain and Russia?

Countries' Roads	
Country	**Length (miles)**
France	555,506
Australia	504,307
Spain	412,463
Russia	330,814

Source: The Top 10 of Everything

H.O.T. Problems

24. **OPEN ENDED** Identify a number that results in a 3-digit number when 35,475 is subtracted from it.

25. **FIND THE ERROR** Jim and Sabrina are solving the subtraction problem shown. Who is correct? Explain.

Jim
530,000
− 304,547
235,453

Sabrina
530,000
− 304,547
225,453

26. **WRITING IN ►MATH** Explain how you would regroup to subtract 3,406 from 5,000.

27. There were 4,668 people at the fair on Saturday and 3,816 people on Sunday. How many more people were at the fair on Saturday?
(Lesson 2-5)

A 842   **C** 942

B 852   **D** 952

28. There were 34,007 visitors at the amusement park last week. There were 21,829 visitors this week. How many fewer visitors were there this week?
(Lesson 2-7)

F 12,178   **H** 13,108

G 12,912   **J** 13,112

Spiral Review

Solve. (Lesson 2-6)

29. Measurement On Friday, Nida drove 178 miles. On Saturday, she drove 129 miles. On Sunday, she drove 205 miles. How many miles did she drive in the three days?

30. Henri is going to buy a football that costs $10, a shirt that costs $8, and a hat that costs $6. If he has $30, about how much change can he expect to get back?

Subtract. Use addition or estimation to check. (Lesson 2-5)

31.   952
        − 624

32. $8,961
        − $1,258

33.   19,034
        − 1,617

Find each sum. Check your work by estimating. (Lesson 2-4)

34.   6,922
        + 24,367

35. $8,738
        + $2,253

36.   36,640
        + 14,255

Measurement For Exercises 37–39, use the table shown.
(Lesson 1-3)

37. What is the difference between the lakes with the greatest and least area?

38. Which two lakes have the least difference in area?

39. Is the combined area of Lake Erie and Lake Michigan greater than the area of Lake Superior? Explain.

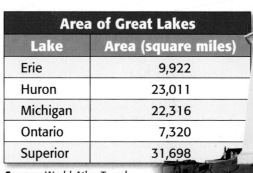

Area of Great Lakes	
Lake	**Area (square miles)**
Erie	9,922
Huron	23,011
Michigan	22,316
Ontario	7,320
Superior	31,698

Source: World Atlas Travel

SC Math Online macmillanmh.com
• STUDY *TO GO*
• Vocabulary Review

FOLDABLES
Study Organizer GET READY to Study

Be sure the following Key Vocabulary words and Key Concepts are written in your Foldable.

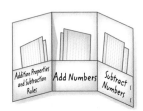

Key Concepts

Addition Properties and Subtraction Rules (p. 55)

• Addition properties and subtraction rules can help you to add and subtract.

Estimate Sums and Differences (p. 58)

3,678	rounds to →	4,000
+ 1,295	rounds to →	+ 1,000
		5,000

7,418	rounds to →	7,000
− 2,557	rounds to →	− 3,000
		4,000

Add and Subtract Whole Numbers (pp. 64, 72)

• To add or subtract whole numbers, add or subtract each place, starting with the place farthest to the right. Regroup when needed.

```
  1 1                8 13
3,752              9,368
+  481             −  827
4,233              8,541
```

 Key Vocabulary

Associative Property of Addition (p. 55)

Commutative Property of Addition (p. 55)

estimate (p. 58)

Vocabulary Check
Complete each sentence with the correct vocabulary word.

1. The number sentence $3 + 7 = 7 + 3$ represents the _____?_____ .

2. If you do not need an exact answer, you can _____?_____ .

3. The _____?_____ says you can change the grouping without changing the sum.

4. The _____?_____ says the order in which numbers are added does not change the sum.

5. When the word *about* is used in a problem, you should find a(n) _____?_____ .

Lesson-by-Lesson Review

2-1 **Algebra: Addition Properties and Subtraction Rules** (pp. 55–57)

4-1.3,
4-1.2

Example 1
Complete 4 + ■ = 6 + 4. Identify the property or rule.

The right side of the sentence shows 6 + 4. The left side shows a 4. So, the missing number is 6.

$$4 + 6 = 6 + 4$$

This is the Commutative Property of Addition.

Copy and complete each number sentence. Identify the property or rule used.

6. ■ + 0 = 11   7. 12 − ■ = 12

8. (■ + 9) + 2 = 9 + (9 + 2)

9. 5 + 4 + 3 = 4 + 3 + ■

10. Lamont has 3 red pencils and 2 yellow pencils. Aida has 2 yellow pencils and 3 red pencils. Who has more pencils? Identify the property used.

2-2 **Estimate Sums and Differences** (pp. 58–61)

3-2.3

Example 2
Estimate 1,352 + 487. Round to the hundreds place.

Round. Then add.

1,352	rounds to →	1,400
+ 487	rounds to →	+ 500
		1,900

So, 1,352 + 487 is about 1,900.

Example 3
Estimate $53 − $27. Round to the tens place.

Round. Then subtract.

$53	rounds to →	$50
− $27	rounds to →	− $30
		$20

So, $53 − $27 is about $20.

Estimate. Round to the indicated place value.

11. $519 + $368; tens

12. 3,436 + 597; hundreds

13. 8,728 − 6,493; thousands

14. $17 − $12; tens

15. Neka wants to buy a book that costs $32 and a bookmark that costs $3. Approximately how much will these items cost?

16. **Measurement** Derek is 3,285 days old. Tionna is 4,015 days old. About how much older is Tionna?

2-3 **Problem-Solving Skill:** Estimate or Exact Answer (pp. 62–63)

4-1.1

Example 4
Jenelle and her sister are going to build a bookcase. They will need $9 for nails, $18 for tools, and $38 for wood. About how much money do they need to build the bookcase?

Understand

What facts do you know?
- Nails cost $9.
- Tools cost $18.
- Wood costs $38.

What do you need to find?
- Find about how much money they need to build the bookcase.

Plan Since the question asks *about* how much money is needed, you can estimate the sum.

Solve
$$
\begin{array}{rcl}
\$ 9 & \rightarrow & \$10 \\
\$18 & \rightarrow & \$20 \\
+ \$38 & \rightarrow & + \$40 \\
\hline
 & & \$70
\end{array}
$$

So, about $70 is needed to build the bookcase.

Check Look back at the problem. If the question asked for an exact answer, the result would be $9 + $18 + $38 or $65. Since $70 is close to $65, you know that an estimate of $70 makes sense.

17. Measurement There are 365 days in a year. Tess's younger brother is 3 years old. About how many days old is he?

18. Benton needs to buy the items shown. He has $20. Does Benton have enough money?

$5 $3 $13

19. Admission to a water park is $21 for adults and $14 for children. How much will admission cost for two adults and three children?

20. Measurement Rebeca will go to the park when her chores are complete. How many minutes before she will go to the park?

List of Chores

Chore	Time (min)
Clean room	45
Dust	15
Sweep	25

21. Chet has $7 after buying skates for $62 and a helmet for $22. How much money did he have?

2-4 Add Whole Numbers (pp. 64–67)

3-2.3

Example 5
Find 714 + 249.

Step 1   Add ones.

```
  1
  714
+ 249
    3
```

> 4 + 9 = 13
> Regroup 13 ones as
> 1 ten and 3 ones.

Step 2   Add tens.

```
  1
  714
+ 249
   63
```

> 1 + 1 + 4 = 6

Step 3   Add hundreds.

```
  1
  714
+ 249
  963
```

> 7 + 2 = 9

Find each sum. Check your work by estimating.

22. 564
    + 308

23. 2,875
    + 496

24. $4,691
    + $ 872

25. $6,467
    + $5,237

26. 61,248
    + 47,229

27. 82,267
    + 21,037

28. **Measurement** Rick drove 12,363 miles in his new car the first year he owned it. He drove 15,934 miles in his car the second year. How many miles did Rick drive these two years?

2-5 Subtract Whole Numbers (pp. 72–74)

3-2.3

Example 6
Find 4,274 – 857.

Step 1   Subtract ones.

```
     6 14
4, 2 7̸ 4̸
 − 8 5 7
        7
```

> Regroup 1 ten
> as 10 ones.

Step 2   Subtract each place.

```
3 12 6 14
4̸ 2̸ 7̸ 4̸
 − 8 5 7
3, 4 1 7
```

> Regroup if necessary.

Subtract. Use addition or estimation to check.

29. 478
    − 293

30. 872
    − 694

31. 5,524
    − 2,346

32. $54,751
    − $43,226

33. 7,367
    − 2,128

34. 73,979
    − 63,485

35. **Measurement** A moose weighs 1,820 pounds. A camel weighs 1,521 pounds. How much more does a moose weigh than a camel?

2-6 **Problem-Solving Investigation: Choose a Strategy** (pp. 76–77)

4-1.1

Example 7
Naomi had $125. She bought rollerblades. She now has $19. How much were the rollerblades?

Understand Naomi had $125. She now has $19. You need to find the cost of the rollerblades.

Plan Solve $125 − $19 to find the cost of the rollerblades.

Solve
$$\begin{array}{r} 115 \\ \$1\cancel{25} \\ -\ \$\ 19 \\ \hline \$106 \end{array}$$

So, the cost was $106.

Check $19 + $106 = $125. So, the answer is correct.

Use any strategy to solve.

36. Jase earned $125 last month for delivering newspapers. He will earn $185 this month. How much money will Jase earn from delivering newspapers for the two months?

37. **Measurement** A cheetah can run up to 71 miles per hour. A horse can run up to 45 miles per hour. Suppose both animals ran at these speeds for two hours. How much farther would a cheetah have run?

38. **Measurement** The highest elevation in the United States is 20,320 feet. The second highest elevation is 14,494. What is the difference in these heights?

2-7 **Subtract Across Zeros** (pp. 80–83)

3-2.3

Example 8
Find 2,005 − 593.

Step 1 Subtract ones.

$$\begin{array}{r} 2,005 \\ -\ 593 \\ \hline 2 \end{array}$$ ← 5 − 3 = 2

Step 2 Subtract each place.

$$\begin{array}{r} 9 \\ 1\ \cancel{1\!0}\ 10 \\ \cancel{2},\cancel{0}\cancel{0}5 \\ -\ 593 \\ \hline 1,412 \end{array}$$ ← Regroup.

Subtract. Use addition to check.

39. $$\begin{array}{r} 300 \\ -\ 206 \end{array}$$

40. $$\begin{array}{r} \$800 \\ -\ \$392 \end{array}$$

41. $$\begin{array}{r} 4,008 \\ -\ 642 \end{array}$$

42. $$\begin{array}{r} \$9,004 \\ -\ \$\ 531 \end{array}$$

43. 8,000 − 3,836

44. $1,300 − $1,195

45. Mr. Acosta had $2,003 in his bank account. He bought a laptop computer for $1,299. How much money does he have left?

Chapter Test

For Exercises 1–3, tell whether each statement is *true* or *false*.

1. Always start with the ones place when subtracting.

2. When asked to find the sum, you are to subtract.

3. To regroup means to add again.

Algebra Copy and complete each number sentence. Identify the property or rule used.

4. ■ + 73 + 79 = 73 + 79 + 65

5. ■ − 389 = 0

6. 2 + (3 + 9) = (2 + ■) + 9

7. **MULTIPLE CHOICE** What number completes this number sentence?

$$23 + ■ = 17 + 23$$

   A 17   **C** 36

   B 23   **D** 38

Estimate. Round to the indicated place value.

8. 5,364 + 482; hundreds

9. 89,325 − 80,236; ten thousands

Tell whether an estimate or exact answer is needed. Then solve.

10. Mr. Murphy had $92. He bought a watch. Now he has $36. How much was the watch?

11. **MULTIPLE CHOICE** What is the sum of 212,048 and 37,251?

   F 249,299

   G 289,299

   H 289,399

   J 299,289

Subtract. Use addition or estimation to check.

12. 612
   − 430

13. 8,547
   −6,391

14. 4,005
   − 273

15. 6,007
   − 317

16. Vickie had $87 in her bank account. She bought her sister a doll for her birthday for $15. How much money does she have left in her account?

17. **Measurement** The lengths of the longest rivers in the world are shown in the table.

World's Longest Rivers	
River	**Length (miles)**
Nile	4,145
Amazon	4,000
Mississippi-Missouri	3,740

Source: *The Top 10 of Everything*

Find the difference in the lengths of the Nile and the Mississippi-Missouri Rivers.

18. **WRITING IN ►MATH** Explain how you would regroup to subtract 2,317 from 4,000.

PART 1   Multiple Choice

Read each question. Then fill in the correct answer on the answer sheet provided by your teacher or on a sheet of paper.

1. On Saturday, a store had 218 customers. On Sunday, the store had 24 fewer customers. How many customers did the store have on Sunday?

   A 188   **C** 236

   B 194   **D** 242

2. Which point on the number line represents 8?

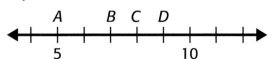

   F point *A*   **H** point *C*

   G point *B*   **J** point *D*

3. Which number is 10,000 more than 312,884?

   A 302,884   **C** 322,884

   B 319,884   **D** 324,882

4. Which symbol makes the following true?

   76,153 ● 76,149

   F >   **H** =

   G <   **J** +

5. Which of the following is another way to write *nine million, three hundred thirty-one thousand, one-hundred eight*?

   A 9,313,180   **C** 9,331,180

   B 9,331,108   **D** 90,331,108

6. Silvio says his street address has a 3 in the hundreds place. Which of the following could be his address?

   F 1368   **H** 2437

   G 1483   **J** 3865

7. Kayla used a catalog to make a list of the clothes she wants to buy. Her list is shown below.

Kayla's Wish List	
Item	Cost
Shorts	$20
T-shirt	$15
Hooded sweatshirt	$35
Sneakers	$43

   If Kayla orders all the clothing items, about how much will she spend?

   A $70   **C** $110

   B $100   **D** $120

8. What is the difference in height of Angel Falls and Yosemite Falls?

Highest Waterfalls	
Waterfall	**Height (feet)**
Angel	3,212
Yosemite	2,425

Source: *Scholastic Book of World Records*

F 1,000 ft	**H** 887 ft
G 900 ft	**J** 787 ft

9. Which is the value of the digit 5 in 1,853,742?

A 50	**C** 50,000
B 500	**D** 500,000

10. A hobby store has sold 15,871 kites since the store opened 25 years ago. What is the number rounded to the nearest thousand?

F 15,000	**H** 15,900
G 15,800	**J** 16,000

11. What is $7,959 rounded to the nearest hundred?

A $700	**C** $8,000
B $7,900	**D** $9,000

PART 2   Short Response

Record your answers on the answer sheet provided by your teacher or on a sheet of paper.

12. What is the value of the digit 3 in 805,312?

13. What is the difference in width of Earth's moon and Jupiter's moon?

Largest Moons	
Moon	**Width (miles)**
Jupiter's moon	3,270
Saturn's moon	3,200
Earth's moon	2,160

Source: *Scholastic Book of World Records*

PART 3   Extended Response

Record your answers on the answer sheet provided by your teacher or on a sheet of paper.

14. What number is 1,000 more than 456,987? Explain your reasoning.

15. What is the standard form for twelve million, two hundred thirty-five thousand, one hundred twelve? Explain your reasoning.

NEED EXTRA HELP?															
If You Missed Question...	1	2	3	4	5	6	7	8	9	10	11	12	13	14	15
Go to Lesson...	2-5	1-4	2-4	1-4	1-2	1-1	2-4	2-5	1-2	1-6	1-6	1-1	2-5	2-5	1-2
SC Academic Standards	3-2.3	3-2.1	3-2.3	3-2.1	4-2.6	4-2.6	3-2.3	3-2.3	4-2.6	3-2.4	3-2.4	4-2.6	3-2.3	3-2.3	4-2.6

CHAPTER 3 Organize, Display, and Interpret Data

BIG Idea What are data and graphs?

Data is a set of information. When data is displayed in a **graph**, it may be easier to read and interpret.

Example The graph shows the number of children in the United States. About 35 million children are 5 to 13 years old.

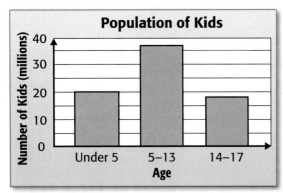

Source: U.S. Census Bureau

What will I learn in this chapter?

- Collect and represent data on a number line, and in graphs, tables, and charts.
- Read and interpret data.
- Determine all possible outcomes of a situation.
- Solve problems by making a table.

Key Vocabulary

data

survey

bar graph

probability

tree diagram

> **SC Math Online** **Student Study Tools**
> at **macmillanmh.com**

FOLDABLES®
Study Organizer

Make this Foldable to help you organize information about data and graphs. Begin with three sheets of $8\frac{1}{2}$" × 11" paper.

① Stack the paper about 3 inches apart.

② Roll up the bottom so all tabs are the same size.

③ Crease and staple along the fold as shown.

④ Label. Take notes as you move through the chapter.

> Organize, Display, and Interpret Data
> Collect and Organize Data
> Find Mode, Median, and Outliers
> Line Plots
> Bar and Double Bar Graphs
> Probability

You have two ways to check prerequisite skills for this chapter.

Option 2

SC Math Online > Take the Chapter Readiness Quiz at macmillanmh.com.

Option 1

Complete the Quick Check below.

QUICK Check

Make a tally chart for each situation. (Prior Grade)

1. Alexi took a survey to find out her friends' favorite colors.

Favorite Colors		
red	yellow	green
blue	pink	red
green	blue	pink
red	blue	blue

2. Mr. Bailey recorded the ages of the students on the basketball team.

Ages of Basketball Players		
10	11	9
9	10	11
10	9	10
10	10	10

Order from least to greatest. (Lesson 1-5)

3. 12, 17, 19, 15, 13

4. 87, 56, 72, 34, 94

5. 31, 60, 23, 87, 91

Use the graph to answer each question. (Prior Grade)

6. How many more students like art than gym?

7. How do the number of students who like music and gym compare to the number of students who like art?

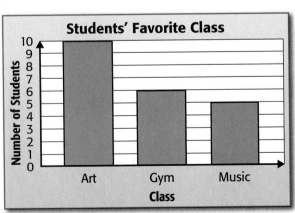

Collect and Organize Data

GET READY to Learn

Ms. Alvarez asked each of her students, "What is your favorite after school activity?" The results are shown.

Playing a Sport	Reading	Watching T.V.
Staci	Alita	Julian
Eric	Sue	Chen
Melisa	Omar	Sarita
Kensey	Nicolas	
Alano		

Ms. Alvarez took a survey. A **survey** is a way to collect **data** or information that answers a question. You can use a **tally chart** or a **frequency table** to record data.

Real-World EXAMPLE   Organize Data

1 SCHOOL Look at the data Ms. Alvarez collected. Organize the data in a tally chart and a frequency table.

Step 1 Draw a table with two columns. Include a title.

Step 2 List each activity in the first column.

Step 3 Use tally marks or numbers to record the results.

Tally Chart

Favorite After School Activities	
Activity	**Tally**
Playing a sport	|||||
Reading	||||
Watching T.V.	|||

Each tally mark represents a student.

Frequency Table

Favorite After School Activities	
Activity	**Frequency**
Playing a sport	5
Reading	4
Watching T.V.	3

Numbers are used to record the results.

How would the results change if Ms. Alvarez asked a kindergarten class?

You can take a survey and collect and represent data on charts and tables.

 Hands-On Mini Activity

Step 1 Write a survey question. An example is shown.

What type of pet is your favorite?

a) Dog   b) Cat

c) Fish   d) I do not like pets.

Step 2 Create a tally chart to record your results.

Step 3 Ask the question to each of your classmates. Organize the data as you collect it.

Step 4 Use the information on your tally chart to create a frequency table.

Analyze the data.

1. Write two sentences that describe your survey results.

2. Do you think the results would be different if you surveyed a group or met with each person individually? Explain.

3. Do you think the results of your survey would have changed if you had asked people attending a dog show? Explain.

> **Remember**
>
> The tally marks used to represent a value of 5 are ||||, not ||||||.

CHECK What You Know

1. The data shows the ways Mrs. Jackson's students travel to school. Organize the data in a tally chart. See Example 1 (p. 95)

How Do You Travel to School?	
Method	**Frequency**
Bicycle	3
Bus	6
Car	9
Walk	5

2. Mary lists all of the fish in her fish tank. Organize the data below in a frequency table. See Example 1 (p. 95)

Mary's Fish Tank	
angelfish	damsel
angelfish	damsel
angelfish	damsel
clown fish	eel
clown fish	eel

3. Refer to Exercise 1. What is the most popular way to travel to school? What is the least popular? See Example 1 (p. 95)

4. **Talk About It** Would the data in Exercise 1 change if teachers were asked the question? Explain.

Organize each set of data in a tally chart. See Example 1 (p. 95)

5. Mr. Ortega records the type of pizza that his science club members like.

Favorite Type of Pizza		
cheese	cheese	sausage
cheese	pepperoni	sausage
cheese	pepperoni	
cheese	pepperoni	

6. Elisa took a survey to find out which movie to rent for her party.

Type of Movie	
action	comedy
action	comedy
action	comedy
animated	comedy

Organize each set of data in a frequency table. See Example 1 (p. 95)

7. Measurement Damián recorded the temperatures in one week.

Weekly Temperatures	
Temperature (°F)	Days
70–75	‖
76–80	‖‖
81–85	‖
86–90	‖

8. A survey was taken to see how students spend their time at recess.

Recess Activities		
kickball	drawing	swing
kickball	drawing	swing
kickball	swing	tag
kickball	swing	tag
drawing	swing	tag

For Exercises 9–12, use the tally chart that shows items sold at a school store.

9. Which item was the top seller? How many were sold?

10. Which item sold once?

11. How many items were sold altogether?

12. Organize the data in a frequency table.

Items Sold at School Store	
Item	Tally
Eraser	‖‖‖
Bottle of glue	
Pencil	‖‖‖ ‖‖
Scissors	‖

H.O.T. Problems

13. OPEN ENDED Identify a way that the data collected in Exercise 6 would be different if the data-collection method changes.

14. **WRITING IN ►MATH** Suppose you are collecting and organizing data about the population of your city. Would it be better to use a frequency table or a tally chart? Explain.

Find Mode, Median, and Outliers

GET READY to Learn

The largest spider in the world is almost one foot long. Look at the table. Which spider's length appears most often? Which length is in the middle?

World's Largest Spiders	
Spider	**Length (in.)**
Goliath birdeater	11
Slate red ornamental	9
King baboon	8
Salmon pink birdeater	10
Colombian giant redleg	8

Source: *Scholastic Book of World Records*

The **mode** of a set of data is the number or numbers that occur(s) most often. If no number occurs more than once, there is no mode. The **median** is the number in the middle when the numbers have been arranged from least to greatest.

Real-World EXAMPLE

Identify Mode and Median

1 **SCIENCE** Use the spider data above. What are the mode and the median of the data?

To find the mode, find the number that occurs most often.

11, 9, **8**, 10, **8** ← 8 appears twice.

So, the mode is 8.

To find the median, first arrange the numbers in order from least to greatest. Then, find the middle number.

8, 8, **9**, 10, 11 ← 9 is the middle number.

So, the median is 9.

An **outlier** is an item of data that is either much larger or much smaller than the rest of the data. A data set may not have outliers.

2 **MOVIES** **What is the outlier of the data?**

Movie Tickets Sold							
Day	Sun.	Mon.	Tues.	Wed.	Thurs.	Fri.	Sat.
Tickets	285	110	232	236	235	252	306

Look for the number that is either much larger or much smaller than the rest of the data items.

The number of tickets sold on Monday was 110. The number 110 is an outlier because it is much less than the other data items, which were between 235 and 306.

Remember

In some cases, when no numbers repeat in a data set, there is no mode. There can also be more than one mode.

CHECK **What You Know**

Find the mode and median of the set of data. Identify any outliers. See Examples 1 and 2 (pp. 98–99)

1.

Shells Found on a Beach	
Name	**Shells Found**
Margo	9
Eva	7
Dani	9
Sondra	8
Louis	7

2.

Fish Caught While Camping	
Day	**Fish Caught**
Monday	3
Tuesday	6
Wednesday	2
Thursday	4
Friday	7

3.

Tall Mammals							
Mammal	Antelope	Camel	Gorilla	Giraffe	Okapi	Wallaby	Takin
Height (ft)	6	7	5	18	5	3	4

The table shows the time spent studying by 4th grade students each day.

Time Spent Studying					
Day	Mon.	Tues.	Wed.	Thurs.	Fri.
Time (min)	15	20	18	40	10

4. Identify the outlier.

5. **Talk About It** Give a possible explanation for an outlier in this situation.

Find the mode and median of the set of data. Identify any outliers. See Examples 1 and 2 (pp. 98–99)

6.

Pints of Strawberries Sold	
Day	Pints Sold
Monday	18
Tuesday	14
Wednesday	11
Thursday	16
Friday	3

7.

Faces Painted at a Fair	
Day	Faces Painted
Wednesday	8
Thursday	23
Friday	25
Saturday	24
Sunday	28

8.

Scores in Golf Tournament	
Player	Scores
Trisha	58
Marita	42
Aashi	64
Ted	49
Ciro	56

9.

Arts Festival Visitors	
Day	Visitors
Wednesday	46
Thursday	40
Friday	35
Saturday	12
Sunday	40

10.

Theme Park Ticket Prices							
Theme Park	A	B	C	D	E	F	G
Adult Ticket	$39	$59	$49	$45	$20	$50	$35

11.

Average High Temperatures for Each Month (°F)							
Month	August	September	October	November	December	January	February
Temp. (°F)	85	78	68	50	45	42	45

12. Look at Exercise 10. What is the difference in cost of one adult ticket for parks C and G?

13. **Measurement** Look at Exercise 11. How much warmer was it in August than in September?

Real-World PROBLEM SOLVING

Science The table at the right shows the number of rings for five planets.

14. Identify the mode and median of the data.

15. Identify the outlier.

16. How many more rings does Saturn have than Uranus? Neptune?

Planets with Rings	
Planet	Rings
Uranus	11
Jupiter	1
Saturn	1,000
Neptune	6
Earth	0

Source: The Nine Planets

H.O.T. Problems

17. FIND THE ERROR Jasmine and Grady are finding the median of the data set 34, 51, 49, 27, and 38. Who is correct? Explain.

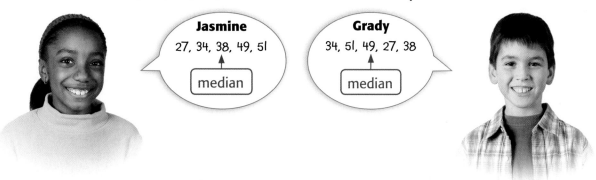

Jasmine

27, 34, 38, 49, 5l
↑
median

Grady

34, 5l, 49, 27, 38
↑
median

18. ✏️ **WRITING IN ►MATH** Explain a way that you can remember the difference between median and mode.

PASS Practice 4-6.3, 4-6.2

19. Which sentence best descibes the data? (Lesson 3-1)

Favorite Animals	
Animal	**Number of Students**
Dolphin	||||
Elephant	||
Lion	ＨＴ
Snake	|||

A Thirteen students were surveyed.

B Lions are the least popular.

C Elephants are the most popular.

D Three students like snakes.

20. What is the median of the data set? (Lesson 3-2)

Math Test Scores	
Student	**Score**
Angela	89
Carmen	93
Edgardo	85
Rafiq	78
Justin	89

F 78

G 85

H 89

J 93

Spiral Review

21. Miss Moore recorded the jersey sizes for the girls' volleyball team. Organize the information in a frequency table. (Lesson 3-1)

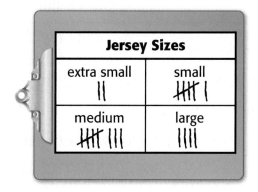

Jersey Sizes	
extra small ||	small ＨＴ |
medium ＨＴ |||	large ||||

22. Find the missing number in the equation
$5{,}007 - 3{,}746 = $ ▪. (Lesson 2-7)

Problem-Solving Strategy

<u>MAIN IDEA</u> I will solve problems by making a table.

 SCAS **4-6.3 Organize data in tables,** line graphs, and bar graphs whose scale increments are greater than or equal to 1.

The music club at Steven's school is going to a concert. There are 2 teachers going to the concert for every 9 students going. If there are 16 teachers going, how many students are going to the concert?

Understand	**What facts do you know?**
	• There are 2 teachers going for every 9 students going to the concert.
	• The total number of teachers going is 16.
	What do you need to find?
	• Find how many students are going to the concert.
Plan	You can make a table to solve the problem.
Solve	Make a table to show that there are 2 teachers going for every 9 students going.

+2 +2 +2 +2 +2 +2 +2

Teachers	2	4	6	8	10	12	14	16
Students	9	18	27	36	45	54	63	72

+9 +9 +9 +9 +9 +9 +9

So, 72 students are going to the concert.

Check	Divide the total number of teachers by the number of teachers per group.
	16 ÷ 2 = 8
	There are 8 groups. There are 9 students in each group. So, there are 8 × 9 = 72 students going altogether. The answer is correct. ✔

Refer to the problem on the previous page.

1. Explain how a table was used to find the number of students going to the concert.

2. What pattern is shown on the table?

3. Suppose 1 teacher was going for every 3 students. How many teachers would be going on the trip? Make a table.

4. Refer to Exercise 3. Check your answer. How do you know that it is correct?

▶ PRACTICE the Strategy

SCAS • PASS
Extra Practice, p. R7

Solve. Use the make a table strategy.

5. **Algebra** Kenya's school day is 6 hours long. Copy and complete the table to find if her school day is more or less than 300 minutes.

Hours	1	2	3	4	5	6
Minutes	60	120	■	■	■	■

6. Malik buys a $2 lunch every day at school. How many lunches can Malik purchase for $17?

7. Martín sold some of his old toys on the Internet. The cost of shipping each item is shown. If he paid $32 in shipping, how many of his toys did he ship?

Shipping Cost: $4

8. Jenna scored 24 points in her last basketball game. She made 2 baskets for every 5 shots she took. If one basket is equal to 2 points, how many shots did she take for the entire game?

9. Elki received her first paycheck from a job. She earns $150 every 2 weeks. How many weeks will it take her to earn more than $1,000?

10. The state sales tax is $7 for every $100 spent on certain items. Takara's mother is charged $21 in tax at the store. What was the total cost of all the items she purchased?

11. **Algebra** Don spends 40 minutes on homework every night. How many minutes of homework does he complete in 5 days?

Day	Total Homework Time (min)
Monday	40
Tuesday	80
Wednesday	120
Thursday	■
Friday	■

12. **WRITING IN ▶MATH** Explain why the make a table strategy is a good problem-solving strategy to use for Exercise 10.

Line Plots

MAIN IDEA

I will represent and interpret data in a line plot.

SC Academic Standards

Reinforcement of 3-6.2 Organize data in tables, bar graphs, **and dot plots.**

Reinforcement of 3-6.3 Interpret data in tables, bar graphs, pictographs, **and dot plots.**

New Vocabulary

line plot

SC Math Online

macmillanmh.com

• Extra Examples
• Personal Tutor
• Self-Check Quiz

GET READY to Learn

Vijay went camping in Pennsylvania Wilds. He recorded the number of elk he saw in a tally chart.

Elk Observed	
Day	**Tally**
Monday	‖
Tuesday	卌
Wednesday	‖‖
Thursday	‖
Friday	‖‖
Saturday	卌 ‖
Sunday	‖

You have used tally charts and frequency tables to show data. A **line plot** is a way to show data using Xs above a number line.

 **Real-World EXAMPLE**   Make a Line Plot

① **SCIENCE Represent Vijay's elk data in a line plot.**

Step 1 Draw and label a number line.

```
  ◄──┼──┼──┼──┼──┼──┼──┼──┼──►
     1  2  3  4  5  6  7  8
```

Step 2 Mark an X above the number line to show each data item. Add a title.

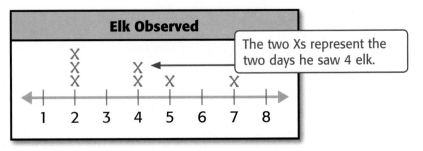

The two Xs represent the two days he saw 4 elk.

You can also read a line plot to answer questions about the data.

Real-World EXAMPLE   Read a Line Plot

2 **READING** Bianca's class took part in a reading competition. The results are shown below. Identify the mode, median, and any outliers for the data set.

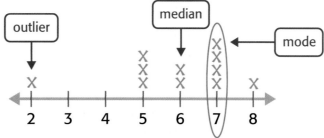

So, the mode is 7, the median is 6, and 2 is an outlier.

Remember

The least and greatest numbers included in the line plot should fit the data being displayed.

CHECK What You Know

Organize each set of data in a line plot. See Example 1 (p. 104)

1.

Ages of Students			
11	11	10	12
10	11	11	11
10	11	11	10

2.

Time Spent on Chores	
Student	**Time (hr)**
Mac	3
Julio	1
Tala	2
Peyton	3

Identify the mode, median, and any outliers for each data set. See Example 2 (p. 105)

3.

Distance Live From School (miles)

4.

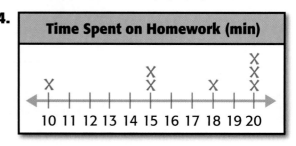

The line plot shows weekly allowances.

5. What is the most money a person receives?

6. Sumi's weekly allowance is $4. Should she use the line plot to convince her parents to increase her allowance? Explain.

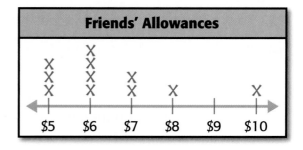

Organize each set of data in a line plot. See Example 1 (p. 104)

7.

Crickets Caught	
Day	Crickets
Monday	6
Tuesday	3
Wednesday	8
Thursday	6
Friday	6

8.

Test Scores	
Student	Score
Darin	95
Janna	91
Grace	90
Arnoldo	95
Lali	86

9.

Points Scored per Game			
4	4	6	10
8	3	4	5
6	5	2	4

10.

Magazine Subscriptions Sold			
12	15	9	16
11	10	12	8
15	11	10	11

Identify the mode, median, and any outliers for each data set. See Example 2 (p. 105)

11.

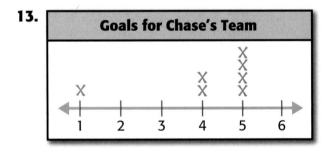

12.

13.

14.

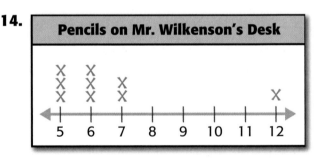

Real-World PROBLEM SOLVING

Measurement Mr. Simmons recorded the height of each player on his basketball team.

15. How many players are 58 inches tall?

16. The median height of the Los Angeles Clippers is 80 inches. Compare this height to the median height of the players on Mr. Simmons's team.

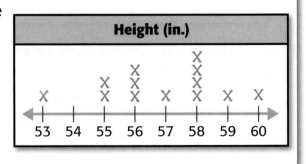

H.O.T. Problems

17. OPEN ENDED Create a survey question to ask your classmates. Ask your question. Collect and represent the data on a line plot.

18. **WRITING IN** ►**MATH** How would the median change if the lowest score in Exercise 8 was replaced with 93?

19. What is the median of the data shown in the frequency table below? (Lesson 3-2)

Garden Vegetables	
Vegetable	**Frequency**
Carrots	49
Celery	25
Cucumbers	28
Lettuce	32
Onions	44

A 49   **C** 32

B 44   **D** 28

20. What is the mode of the data shown on the line plot? (Lesson 3-4)

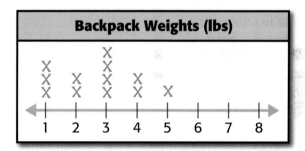

F 2   **H** 4

G 3   **J** 8

Spiral Review

21. There are eight hamburger buns in a package. How many packages of hamburger buns should Mr. Green buy to make 43 hamburgers? (Lesson 3-3)

For Exercises 22–24, use the table to the right. It lists the items in Ella's school supply box. (Lesson 3-2)

22. Find the mode of the set of data.

23. Find the median of the set of data.

24. Identify any outliers in the set of data.

Ella's School Supply Box	
Supply	**Frequency**
Crayons	36
Erasers	5
Glue	1
Pencils	7
Scissors	1

GET READY to Learn

MAIN IDEA

I will interpret a bar graph.

SC Academic Standards

4-6.2 Interpret data in tables, line graphs, **bar graphs,** and double bar graphs **whose scale increments are greater than or equal to 1.**

New Vocabulary

bar graph

SC Math Online

macmillanmh.com
• Extra Examples
• Personal Tutor
• Self-Check Quiz

The students in Mrs. Smith's class measured their heights in inches. What was the most common height?

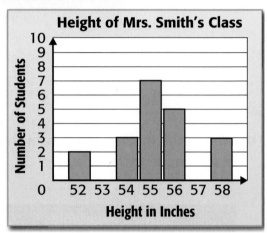

A **bar graph** is used to compare data by using bars of different heights to represent values. You can interpret data that is displayed in a bar graph.

EXAMPLE   Interpret a Bar Graph

① **MEASUREMENT** **What was the most common height?**

The tallest bar represents the height of the most students.

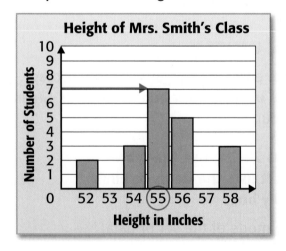

So, the most common height was 55 inches tall.

EXAMPLE Interpret a Bar Graph

Remember

In grade 3, you learned that a scale is a set of numbers that represents data.

② MEASUREMENT
The bar graph shows the land area of four cities in North Carolina. Write a statement that describes the data.

To write a statement that describes the data in a bar graph, you need to compare the lengths of the bars in the graph.

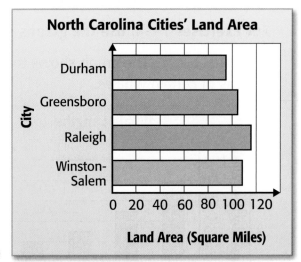

Source: North Carolina Bigger Cities

The bar for Raleigh is the longest. So, you can write that Raleigh has the largest land area of the four cities shown.

CHECK **What You Know**

For Exercises 1–6, use the graph shown. See Examples 1–2 (pp. 108–109)

1. During which grade was Janet absent the most days?

2. What grade was Janet in when she was absent for 3 days?

3. How many more days was Janet absent in second grade than in third grade?

4. How many days has Janet been absent since she finished the first grade?

5. Write a statement that describes the data in the graph.

6. **Talk About It** Refer back to Exercise 4. How did you find the answer?

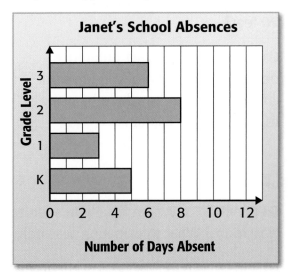

For Exercises 7–14, use the graphs shown. See Examples 1–2 (pp. 108–109)

Measurement The graph shows the lengths of certain whales.

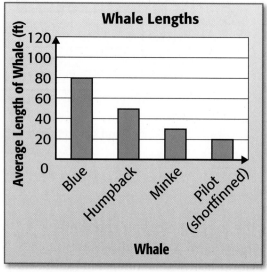

Source: Animal Planet

7. Which type of whale is the shortest?

8. Which whale is about 50 feet long?

9. Why is the scale set in intervals of 20 feet?

10. Can you find the exact difference between the length of a humpback whale and a minke whale by using this bar graph? Explain.

The graph shows the states with the most tornadoes in a recent year.

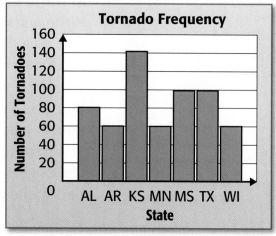

Source: National Weather Service

11. Which states appear to have had the same number of tornadoes?

12. About how many more tornadoes were in Texas than in Alabama?

13. About how many more tornadoes were in Kansas than in Wisconsin?

14. Which two states had a combined total of about 220 tornadoes? Explain how you found your answer.

H.O.T. Problems

15. **OPEN ENDED** Where have you seen bar graphs used outside of the classroom? What information was being described?

16. **NUMBER SENSE** Why is it sometimes necessary to estimate when reading a bar graph?

17. **WRITING IN ►MATH** Refer to the graph used for Exercises 11–14. Would this graph be easier to read if the scale was changed to intervals of 100? Explain.

1. Organize the set of data in a tally chart and in a frequency table. (Lesson 3-1)

Sandwiches for a Picnic		
Peanut butter	Ham	Turkey
Turkey	Turkey	Peanut butter
Ham	Ham	Ham

For Exercises 2 and 3, use the tally chart below. (Lesson 3-1)

Where Do You Read?	
Place	**Tally**
Outside	||||	
Bedroom	|||| ||
Library	||||
Living room	|||

2. Where do most students like to read?

3. How many students read in their bedroom or at the library?

4. **MULTIPLE CHOICE** What is the mode of the data set {4, 5, 8, 8, 4, 3, 4}?
(Lesson 3-2)

   A 3   **C** 5

   B 4   **D** 8

5. Find the mode and median of the data. Identify any outliers. (Lesson 3-2)

Movies Rented During a Week					
Day	1	2	3	4	5
Movies	29	58	62	55	64

Solve. Use the make a table strategy.
(Lesson 3-3)

6. It costs $32 for 2 admissions to a museum. Ebony and her father invite 10 friends for opening night. At this rate, how much would it cost for everyone to go to the museum?

7. Organize the set of data in a line plot. (Lesson 3-4)

Time it Takes to Walk Home (min)			
10	11	12	15
12	15	8	7
10	8	10	9

8. **MULTIPLE CHOICE** About how much farther did Greg travel than Joy? (Lesson 3-5)

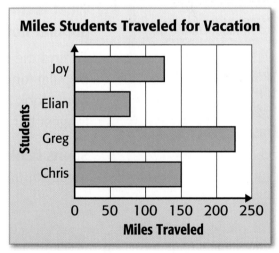

Miles Students Traveled for Vacation

   F 50 miles   **H** 200 miles
   G 100 miles   **J** 300 miles

9. **WRITING IN ▸ MATH** Explain the difference between median and mode. (Lesson 3-2)

Bar and Double Bar Graphs

GET READY to Learn

The graph shows the amount of time four astronauts spent in space during a single mission. You can use the graph to compare the time spent in space.

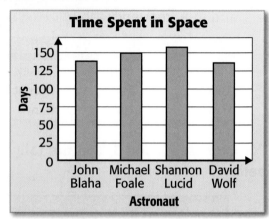

Source: *Time for Kids*

A bar graph allows you to compare data easily.

Real-World EXAMPLES   Read Bar Graphs

BOOKS The bar graph shows the number of books checked out of a school library.

1 **What is the most popular book?**

To find the most popular kind of book, look for the longest bar.

Sports books are most popular.

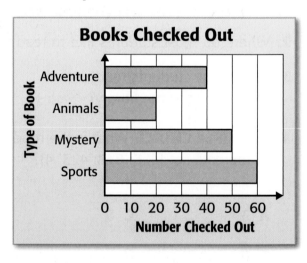

2 **How many sports and animal books were checked out?**

60 sports books and 20 animal books were checked out.

$60 + 20 = 80$

So, there were 80 sports and animal books checked out.

A **double bar graph** displays two sets of related data using bars of different colors and heights.

Remember

When reading a double bar graph, always look at the scale and the key.

Real-World EXAMPLE   Read Double Bar Graphs

3 **SCHOOL** Students are selling magazines for a fundraiser. About how many students will sell magazines in the second grade?

There are about 40 boys and about 45 girls in the second grade.

$40 + 45 = 85$

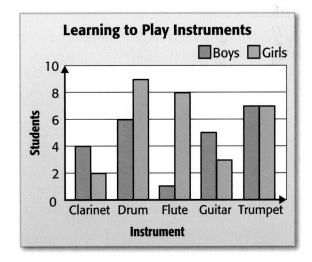

So, about 85 students will sell magazines in second grade.

CHECK What You Know

For Exercises 1–4, use the graphs shown. See Examples 1–3 (pp. 112–113)

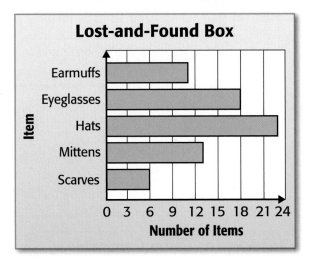

1. What is the most common item in the lost-and-found box?

2. How many more eyeglasses are in the box than scarves?

3. What is the least popular instrument for boys?

4. What is the total number of students surveyed?

5. Describe when you would use a bar graph and a double bar graph to display sets of data.

For Exercises 6–9, use the bar graph that shows the number of Little League Championship wins. See Examples 1–2 (p. 112)

6. Which team has the most wins?

7. Which team has the least wins?

8. How many more wins does the United States have than the team that has the second most wins?

9. If the wins for Japan, Mexico, and Taiwan were added together, would they have as many wins as the United States? Explain.

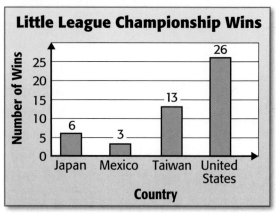

Little League Championship Wins

Source: *Scholastic Book of World Records*

For Exercises 10–13, use the double bar graph that shows the number of tickets sold for a high school play. See Example 3 (p. 113)

10. Which day had the highest total attendance?

11. Did more adults or children attend on Friday?

12. About how many adults attended in all?

13. Suppose adult tickets cost $4 and children tickets cost $2. On which day was more than $100 made in ticket sales?

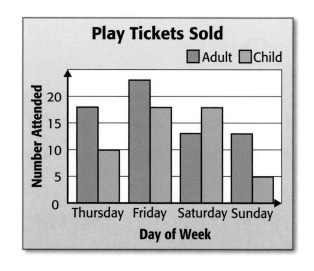

Play Tickets Sold

H.O.T. Problems

14. **WRITING IN MATH** The graph shows the value of stocks for three companies. Write 2 sentences that describe the data.

15. **OPEN ENDED** Describe a set of data that could not be shown in a double bar graph.

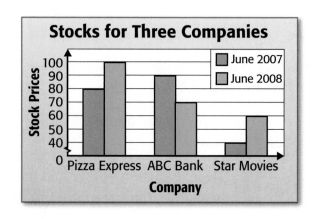

Stocks for Three Companies

Graph Race

Create a Bar Graph

Get Ready!

Players: 2 players

Get Set!

Draw a bar graph on grid paper as shown.

You will need: 0–5 number cube, grid paper

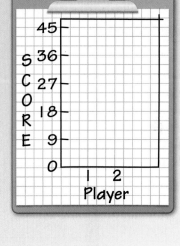

Go!

- Roll. The greater number goes first.

- Player 1 rolls the number cube and graphs the number on the bar graph. If a 0 is rolled, it is Player 2's turn.

- Player 2 rolls the number cube and graphs the number on the bar graph.

- Player 1 rolls the number cube again and adds the result to his or her previous amount.

- Play continues until a player's bar goes over 45. That player wins.

Double bar graphs are used to compare two sets of related data.

ACTIVITY

Step 1 **Collect data.**

Create a frequency table that shows the number of minutes you and a partner spend studying or doing homework each day over the span of a school week.

Time Spent Studying/Homework		
Day	**Student 1**	**Student 2**
Mon.		
Tues.		
Wed.		
Thurs.		
Fri.		

Step 2 **Create a graph.**

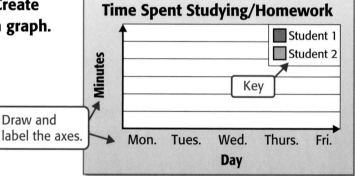

Draw two axes and label them. Write a title at the top. Choose a color for each set of data and make a **key**.

Step 3 Choose a scale.

The scale should include the least and the greatest number from your data.

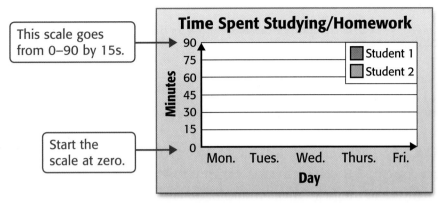

This scale goes from 0–90 by 15s.

Start the scale at zero.

Step 4 Draw bars.

Draw the bars for your data on the graph. Then draw the bars for your partner's data on the graph.

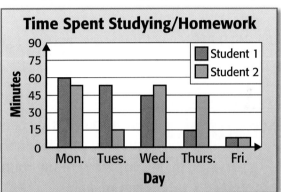

Think About It

1. Tell how you can use a double bar graph to compare data.

2. Explain how you choose a scale and intervals.

CHECK What You Know

Represent each set of data in a double bar graph.

3.

Books Read		
Month	Miki	Alicia
May	3	2
June	5	6
July	4	5
August	6	4

4.

Allowance		
Age	Morgan	Eli
7	$2	$0
8	$3	$1
9	$4	$3
10	$5	$5

5. **WRITING IN ►MATH** Look at Exercises 3 and 4. Write a comparison sentence that describes the data in each table.

3-7 Problem-Solving Investigation

MAIN IDEA I will choose the best strategy to solve a problem.

 SCAS **4-6.2 Interpret data in tables,** line graphs, bar graphs, and double bar graphs whose scale increments are greater than or equal to 1.

P.S.I. TEAM +

SETH: I take the subway to get to school and back. Each round trip costs $2. My subway card has a value of $11.

YOUR MISSION: Find how many round trips Seth can make with $11.

Understand	Each round trip costs $2. Seth's subway card has a value of $11. Find how many round trips he can make.
Plan	Organize the data in a table to solve the problem.
Solve	For each round trip, the total cost increases by $2.

Trips	1	2	3	4	5	6
Cost	$2	$4	$6	$8	$10	$12

+2   +2   +2   +2   +2

Seth's card has a value of $11. He cannot make a sixth trip because after making 5 trips he has only $1 left. This is not enough for another trip. So, he can make 5 trips to school and back.

Check	Use a set of play money that is in piles of $2. Add the money until you have more than $11.

Use any strategy to solve.

1. Algebra Mrs. Vargas is making costumes for a play. She needs 4 buttons for each costume. Copy and complete the table to find how many buttons she will need for 14 costumes.

Costumes	Buttons
1	4
2	8
4	16
6	24
8	32
10	40
12	■
14	■

2. It costs $12 for 2 admissions to miniature golf. Marcus wants to invite 9 friends. At this rate, how much would it cost for 10 people?

3. Paz is making granola bars for her scout meeting. There are 8 girls in her troop, including herself. If she makes 2 dozen granola bars, how many will each girl get?

4. Ricardo has to mail 27 party invitations. The invitations come in packs of 8 that cost $3. How much will he spend on invitations?

5. Measurement Pete spends 30 minutes a night reading. About how many hours does he spend reading each month?

6. Tomas has $49. He wants to buy as many video games as he can. How many can he get at the yard sale?

3 video games for $7

7. A parent-teacher organization sells bottled water at elementary school basketball games. They sold three cases in 20 minutes. If they continue selling bottled water at this rate, how many cases of bottled water would they sell in two hours?

8. Measurement The Castros drove 64 miles to a water park. The Baxters drove 81 miles. The Klines drove 19 miles. How much farther did the Castros have to drive than the Klines?

9. During a basketball game, Faith and Brandy each scored 4 points. Maria and Jo each scored 7 points. Dena scored 12 points. Find the total points scored by this team.

10. WRITING IN ►MATH Explain when to use the make a table strategy to solve a word problem.

Problem Solving in Science

A Head Above the Rest

Objects' Heights

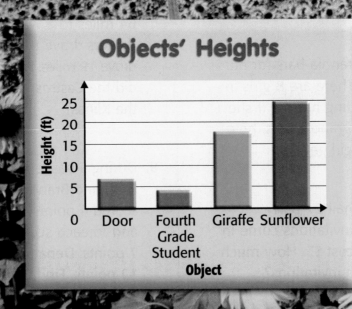

Sunflowers are giants in the plant world. The tallest sunflower grew to a total height of 25 feet 5 inches. The size of the largest sunflower head is 32 inches across. This is almost three feet across!

Sunflowers can be used for decoration, but they are also an important source of food.

Sunflower oil is a valued and healthy vegetable oil. In addition, sunflower seeds are enjoyed as a healthy, tasty snack and nutritious ingredient in many foods.

Did You Know?

The shortest sunflower on record measured just over 2 inches tall.

Real-World Math

Use the information on page 120 to solve each problem.

1. What is the tallest object on the bar graph? How tall is this object?

2. What is the difference in height of a sunflower and a giraffe?

3. What is the shortest object on the bar graph? How tall is this object?

4. Look at Exercise 3. Explain how you found the answer.

5. What is the difference between the tallest and shortest objects on the bar graph?

6. The height of how many fourth grade students equals the height of a sunflower?

Explore

Possible Outcomes

Possible **outcomes** are all of the results that could occur from an experiment. In this activity, you will explore the possible outcomes of an experiment.

MAIN IDEA

I will determine the possible outcomes of an experiment.

SC Academic Standards

4-6.7 Analyze possible outcomes for a simple event.

You Will Need
spinner
labeled 1–4

SC Math Online

macmillanmh.com

ACTIVITY

1 **Use a spinner to create multi-digit numbers.**

Step 1 **Spin a spinner like the one shown two times.**

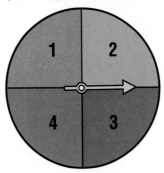

Step 2 **Create two-digit numbers.**

Use each digit once to make as many two-digit numbers as possible. Record the numbers.

Step 3 **Create three-digit numbers.**

Spin the spinner a third time. If it lands on a digit already spun, spin again. Use the two digits spun in step 1 and the digit you just spun to make as many three-digit numbers as possible. Remember to use each digit only once. Record the numbers you made.

Step 4 **Create four-digit numbers.**

Spin a fourth digit to go with the three digits you previously spun. If the spinner lands on a digit you already have, spin again. Use the fourth digit to create as many numbers as possible.

Think About It

1. How many two-digit numbers can be made with two digits, if each digit is used only once?

2. How many three-digit numbers can be made with three digits, if each digit is used only once?

3. How many four-digit numbers can be made with four digits, if each digit is used only once?

4. Describe the strategy you used to find the numbers you made.

CHECK What You Know

Determine all the possible outcomes for each situation.

5. What are all the possible outcomes if the spinner is spun twice?

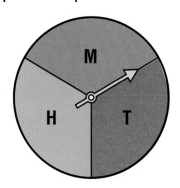

6. Describe an outcome that is not possible if two connecting cubes are chosen from the bag at a time.

7. What are all the possible outcomes if the coin is flipped twice?

8. What are all the possible outcomes if two counters are each flipped once?

9. **WRITING IN ►MATH** Create an experiment using two spinners. What are all the possible outcomes for that experiment? How did you find all the possible outcomes? What predictions can you make?

3-8 Determine Possible Outcomes

MAIN IDEA

I will use pictures to find all the possible outcomes in a problem situation.

SC Academic Standards

4-6.7 Analyze possible outcomes for a simple event.

New Vocabulary

outcome

tree diagram

SC Math Online

macmillanmh.com
• Extra Examples
• Personal Tutor
• Self-Check Quiz

GET READY to Learn

In a basketball game, Samantha went to the free-throw line. She attempted to make a basket twice. What are all the possible combinations of her free throws?

In the previous Explore Activity, you learned that an **outcome** is a result in an experiment. You can use a grid to help you find outcomes.

EXAMPLE Determine Outcomes

1 **SPORTS** How many possible outcomes does Samantha have for her two free throws?

You know that Samantha attempted to make a basket twice.

One way to find the possible outcomes is by making a grid. On a grid, each outcome is shown where each row and column intersect.

		Second Shot	
		Make	**Miss**
First Shot	**Make**	Make, Make	Make, Miss
	Miss	Miss, Make	Miss, Miss

These are Samantha's possible outcomes.

So, there are 4 possible outcomes.

Another way to find the possible outcomes is by using a **tree diagram**. A tree diagram uses "branches" to show all the possible outcomes.

EXAMPLE Possible Outcomes

2 **A student is spinning two spinners. How many possible outcomes are there?**

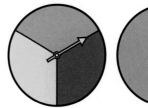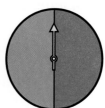

A tree diagram can be used to find all the possible outcomes for spinning both spinners.

First Spinner	Second Spinner	Outcomes
Orange	Red	Orange, Red
	Blue	Orange, Blue
Purple	Red	Purple, Red
	Blue	Purple, Blue
Yellow	Red	Yellow, Red
	Blue	Yellow, Blue

So, there are 6 possible outcomes.

CHECK What You Know

1. Draw a grid to find the number of possible outcomes if the spinner is spun twice. See Example 1 (p. 124)

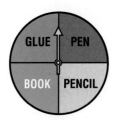

2. Draw a tree diagram to find the number of possible outcomes if the coin is tossed and the spinner is spun.

See Example 2 (p. 125)

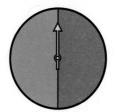

3. **Talk About It** In Exercise 2, what generalization can be made about determining all possible outcomes?

Draw a grid to find the number of possible outcomes for each situation. See Example 1 (p. 124)

4. How many outcomes are possible if the spinner below is spun twice?

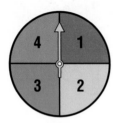

5. How many outcomes are possible if the 5–10 number cube is rolled twice?

Draw a tree diagram to find the number of possible outcomes for each situation. See Example 2 (p. 125)

6. How many outcomes are possible if the spinners are spun?

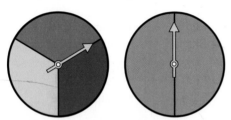

7. How many outcomes are possible if the 0–5 number cube is rolled and the spinner is spun?

South Carolina Data File

The shells in the table are found in South Carolina and other states along the Atlantic Coast.

8. Make a tree diagram to show all of the two-shell combinations that are possible from the shells listed if each shell is used once.

9. After you take out shell combinations that are the same, how many combinations are left?

Shells of the Atlantic Coast
Lettered olive
Auger shell
Channeled whelk
Keyhole sand dollar

Source: Folly Beach USA

H.O.T. Problems

10. OPEN ENDED Create two spinners with at least three different colors on each spinner. The possible combinations of the spinners must include red more often than any other color.

11. WRITING IN ►MATH In Exercise 10, what generalization can you make about determining all possible combinations?

12. About how many more moons does Saturn have than Uranus? (Lesson 3-6)

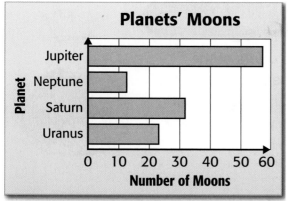

Source: *Scholastic Book of World Records*

  A 2   **C** 10

  B 5   **D** 15

13. If Ellis spins the arrow twice, which of these is **NOT** a possible outcome? (Lesson 3-8)

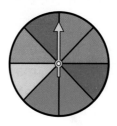

  F Blue, blue

  G Red, purple

  H Yellow, red

  J Green, blue

Spiral Review

14. There were 2,367 students buying lunch on Monday. On Wednesday there were 2,745 buying lunch. If 45 more students bought lunch on Tuesday than Monday, how many lunches were sold on those three days in all? (Lesson 3-7)

For Exercises 15–18, use the graph that shows speeds of land animals. (Lesson 3-6)

15. How fast can an antelope run?

16. Which animal can run 35 miles per hour faster than an elephant?

17. How much faster can a cheetah run than a lion?

18. Which animal can run twice as fast as an elephant?

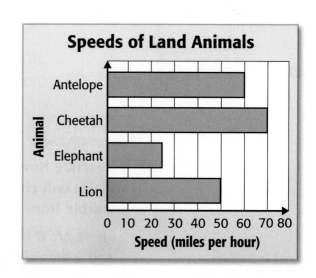

Compare. Use >, <, or =. (Lesson 1-4)

19. 2,483 ● 2,438   **20.** 42,395 ● 42,935   **21.** 739,305 ● 739,305

GET READY to Learn

Only Sophie knew the colors of the marbles in the bag. She asked Marta to reach in and choose a marble without looking. What color do you think Marta will grab?

MAIN IDEA

I will describe probability with words and numbers.

SC Academic Standards

4-6.6 Predict on the basis of data whether events are *likely, unlikely, certain, impossible,* or *equally likely* to occur.

New Vocabulary

probability

SC Math Online

macmillanmh.com
• Extra Examples
• Personal Tutor
• Self-Check Quiz

The chance that an outcome will occur is its **probability**. The words *certain, likely, equally likely, unlikely,* and *impossible* can describe probability.

certain to choose red

likely to choose red

equally likely to choose red or blue

unlikely to choose red

impossible to choose red

EXAMPLE Use Words to Describe Probability

1 **Describe how likely it is that Marta will choose a yellow marble from Sophie's bag.**

There are 8 marbles in the bag, and 2 are yellow.

In the bag, less than half of the marbles are yellow. So, it is *unlikely* that Marta will choose a yellow marble.

Real-World EXAMPLE — Use Words to Describe Probability

2 **MONEY** The table shows the coins Tucker has in his pocket. Suppose he drops a coin on the ground. Describe the probability that the coin he dropped is a dime.

Coin	Frequency
Quarter	1
Dime	5
Penny	2
TOTAL	8

Of the 8 coins in Tucker's pocket, 5 are dimes.

So, it is *likely* that Tucker dropped a dime.

You can also use numbers to describe probability.

EXAMPLE — Use Numbers to Describe Probability

3 The letter tiles below spell out mathematics. Use numbers to describe the probability of choosing a vowel without looking.

Four out of eleven letters are vowels.

So, the probability of choosing a vowel is 4 out of 11.

CHECK What You Know

The spinner is spun. Describe the probability of each outcome. Write *certain, likely, equally likely, unlikely,* or *impossible.*
See Examples 1 and 2 (pp. 128–129)

1. odd number

2. even number

3. number less than 3

4. the number 5, 11, or 13

For Exercises 5 and 6, use the cubes at the right. See Example 3 (p. 129)

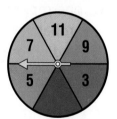

5. Use numbers to describe the probability of choosing a cube that is not yellow without looking.

6. **Talk About It** Omar reaches into the bag and chooses one cube without looking. Are there any colors that are more likely to be chosen? Explain.

A marble is chosen from the bag without looking. Describe the probability of each outcome. Write *certain*, *likely*, *equally likely*, *unlikely*, or *impossible*. See Examples 1 and 2 (pp. 128–129)

7. green

8. yellow

9. red, yellow, or green

10. blue

11. not green

12. red or green

The spinner is spun. Use numbers to describe the probability of each outcome. See Example 3 (p. 129)

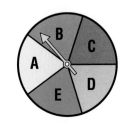

13. A

14. not E

15. consonant

16. vowel

17. not A or B

18. letter in the name LILY

19. Sancho spun a spinner 21 times. The tally chart shows his results.

Color	Results
Blue	卌 ||
Green	卌 卌 ||
Orange	||

Suppose Sancho spins the spinner one more time. Describe the probability that the spinner will land on orange.

20. Erin dropped 32 plastic cups. The frequency table shows how the cups landed.

How Cup Landed	Number
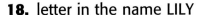	10
	18
	4

Suppose Erin drops one more cup. Describe the probability that the cup will land on its side.

H.O.T. Problems

21. **OPEN ENDED** Make a spinner with 8 equal parts in which green is most *likely* to be landed on and so that red and blue are *unlikely* to occur.

22. **WRITING IN MATH** Describe a probability situation in which an outcome is certain to happen.

Technology Activity for 3-9
Find Probability

Tech Link

You can use the *Math Tool Chest* to explore probability.

ACTIVITY

Angelo is using a spinner with four sections: one green, one red, one yellow, and one blue, to conduct an experiment. He spins the spinner 100 times and draws a bar graph of the results. Try the experiment.

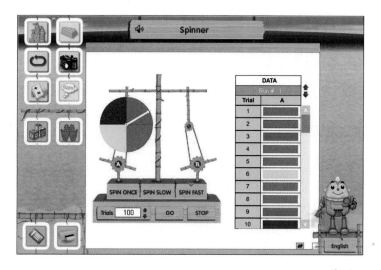

- Click on the spinner toolchest.
- Set the number of trials at 100.
- Click on SPIN FAST.
- Click on the links icon (⬛) below the data table.
- Click on Bar Graph to display the data.
- Use numbers to tell which color the spinner landed on.

✓ CHECK What You Know

For Exercises 1–4, repeat the activity above. Change the number of trials for each exercise. Use numbers to describe the probability of landing on each color, red, yellow, green, and blue.

1. 15 times   **2.** 25 times   **3.** 30 times   **4.** 50 times

5. Spin a spinner with three sections 25 times. Draw a bar graph to display the results. Use numbers to tell what color was spun most.

SC Math Online macmillanmh.com
• STUDY TO GO
• Vocabulary Review

FOLDABLES
Study Organizer
GET READY to Study

Be sure the following Key Vocabulary words and Key Concepts are written in your Foldable.

Organize, Display, and Interpret Data
Collect and Organize Data
Find Mode, Median, and Outliers
Line Plots
Bar and Double Bar Graphs
Probability

Key Concepts

Displaying Data

• A **survey** is a way to collect data. **Data** can be organized in different ways, such as a tally chart and a frequency table. (p. 95)

• A **bar graph** is used to compare data by using bars of different heights to represent data. (p. 108)

Probability describes the likelihood of an event taking place. (p. 128)

The probability of two coins landing on heads after being tossed can be found by using the grid.

		Second Coin	
		Heads	**Tails**
First Coin	**Heads**	heads, heads	heads, tails
	Tails	tails, heads	tails, tails

The probability of two coins landing on heads is unlikely, or 1 out of 4.

Key Vocabulary

bar graph (p. 108)

data (p. 95)

probability (p. 128)

survey (p. 95)

tree diagram (p. 125)

Vocabulary Check

Match each phrase with the correct vocabulary word above.

1. A survey is a way to collect ____?____ .

2. ____?____ describes the likelihood of an event taking place.

3. A ____?____ is used to compare data by using bars of different heights to represent values.

4. A ____?____ is a way to collect information that answers a question.

5. A ____?____ uses "branches" to show all possible combinations of a probability situation.

6. A grid can be used to find the ____?____ of a situation.

Lesson-by-Lesson Review

3-1 **Collect and Organize Data** (pp. 95–97)

4-6.3

Example 1
Organize the data shown in a tally chart and frequency table.

Favorite Sports		
basketball	basketball	track
basketball	softball	volleyball
basketball	softball	volleyball
basketball	softball	volleyball
basketball	track	volleyball

Favorite Sports	
Sport	**Tally**
Softball	|||
Track	||
Basketball	卌 |
Volleyball	||||

Favorite Sports	
Sport	**Frequency**
Softball	3
Track	2
Basketball	6
Volleyball	4

Organize the data shown in a tally chart and frequency table.

7. Family members were asked what they wanted to do after dinner.

After Dinner Activity		
nap	read	game
game	nap	read
game	game	read
read	game	game

8. Fourth graders voted for Student Council President.

Votes for President		
Tom	Monica	Lamar
Monica	Tom	Tom
Tom	Monica	Monica
Lamar	Monica	Lamar

3-2 **Find Mode, Median, and Outliers** (pp. 98–101)

4-6.2

Example 2
Find the mode and median for the data set 50, 50, 51, 53, 95. Identify any outliers.

Order from least to greatest.

50, 50, 51, 53, 95

The mode occurs most often: 50. The median is the number in the middle: 51. The outlier is the number that lies outside of the data: 95.

Find the mode and median of the set of data. Identify any outliers.

9. Hours of practice each week: 3, 8, 2, 4, 3

10. Wild birds seen at a state park: 54, 17, 15, 16, 15

11. The number of students in Mr. Parker's class who brought lunches this week: 8, 6, 5, 7, 17

3-3 **Problem-Solving Strategy: Make a Table** (pp. 102–103)

4-6.3

Example 3

Students are going on a class trip. There are 140 students going, and 28 students fit on each bus. How many buses are needed?

Understand

You know that 140 students are going, and each bus holds 28 students. Find the number of buses needed.

Plan You can make a table.

Solve

Bus	Students	
1	28	+28
2	56	+28
3	84	+28
4	112	+28
5	140	

So, 5 buses are needed.

Check Use subtraction to check.

$$\begin{array}{r} 140 \\ -\ 28 \end{array}$$ one bus

$$\begin{array}{r} 112 \\ -\ 28 \end{array}$$ one bus

$$\begin{array}{r} 84 \\ -\ 28 \end{array}$$ one bus

$$\begin{array}{r} 56 \\ -\ 28 \end{array}$$ one bus

$$\begin{array}{r} 28 \\ -\ 28 \\ \hline 0 \end{array}$$ one bus

Subtracting 28 from 140 five times equals 0. So, the answer makes sense.

Solve the problems using a table.

12. **Algebra** Jordan has to read a 125-page book by Friday. It is Sunday, and Jordan plans to read 25 pages each night. Will he finish reading the book by Friday? Explain.

Day	Pages Read
Sunday	25
Monday	50
Tuesday	75
Wednesday	■
Thursday	■

13. There are 26 cars waiting on the on-ramp to the freeway. A green light lets 2 cars on at a time. How many lights will it take before all the cars enter the freeway?

14. At Riverside Elementary, there are 346 students in the school who take the bus each day.

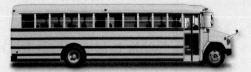

1 bus = 40 students

What is the least number of buses the school will need to transport children to and from the school?

15. Thirty-six students are going rafting. Each raft holds 7 students. How many more students are needed to fill each raft with 7 people?

3-4 **Line Plots** (pp. 104–107)

3-6.2,
3-6.3

Example 4
Organize the information from the frequency table in a line plot.

Children at the Park				
1	5	6	6	3
3	2	3	4	2
2	4	5	2	
6	3	6	7	
7	2	1	6	
5	6	6	5	

Children at the Park

```
                                    X
                                    X
          X                         X
          X       X         X       X
     X    X       X         X       X
     X    X       X    X    X       X    X
     X    X       X    X    X       X    X
    ←——+——+——+——+——+——+——+——→
        1    2    3    4    5    6    7
```

Organize each set of data in a line plot.

16.
Phone Calls Made Each Day	
Day	**Calls**
Monday	3
Tuesday	2
Wednesday	5
Thursday	7
Friday	4

17.
Canned Goods Collected Each Month			
27	26	24	24
30	33	28	26
25	29	30	28

3-5 **Bar Graphs** (pp. 108–110)

4-6.2

Example 5
Which sport was played twice as long as another sport?

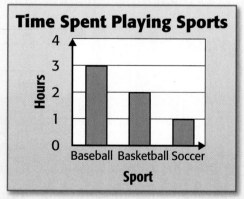

Time Spent Playing Sports

Basketball was played for 2 hours. Soccer was played for one hour. So, basketball was played twice as long as soccer. $1 \times 2 = 2$.

For Exercises 18 and 19, use the graph.

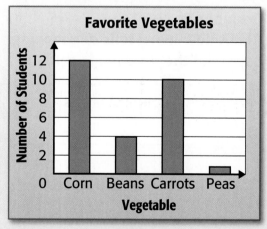

Favorite Vegetables

18. Which vegetable is the class's least favorite?

19. What is the sum of students who liked beans and corn?

3-6 Bar and Double Bar Graphs (pp. 112–114)

4-6.2

Example 6

About how many new members joined the school choir in 2007?

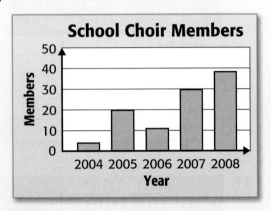

To find the answer, subtract the number of 2006 choir members from the number of 2007 choir members.

$$30 - 10 = 20$$

2007 choir members   2006 choir members   new members

So, about 20 members joined the school choir in 2007.

Example 7

About how many rolls of wrapping paper did the third grade sell?

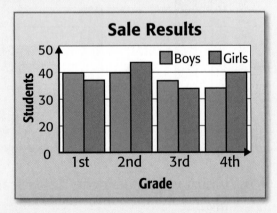

$35 + 40 = 75$. So, about 75 rolls of wrapping paper were sold.

For Exercises 20 and 21, use the graph that shows the type of music dog owners play for their dogs while they are not home.

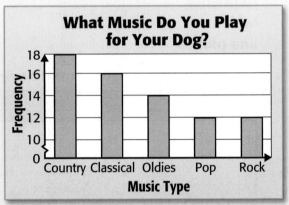

Source: *USA Today*

20. How many dogs listened to oldies?

21. What is the total number of dogs that listened to pop and rock music?

For Exercises 22 and 23, use the graph.

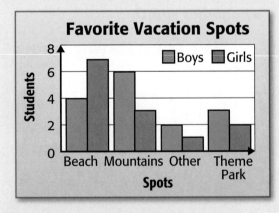

22. What is the most popular spot?

23. What is the difference in number of students who liked the most popular and least popular vacation spots?

Problem-Solving Investigation: Choose a Strategy (pp. 118–119)

Example 8

4-6.2

Pia wants to earn $75. If she earns $15 each time she babysits, how many times will she have to babysit in order to earn $75?

Understand

Pia earns $15 each time she babysits. She wants to earn $75. Find the number of days Pia needs to babysit to earn $75.

Plan Organize the data in a table to solve the problem.

Solve

Day	Money Earned
1	$15
2	$30
3	$45
4	$60
5	$75

Pia will have to babysit 5 times to earn $75.

Check $75 − $15 = $60
$60 − $15 = $45
$45 − $15 = $30
$30 − $15 = $15
$15 − $15 = $0

Subtracting $15 from $75 five times equals 0. So, the answer makes sense.

Use any strategy to solve.

24. Bruce has 19 baseball hats. Rashid has 5 more than Bruce. Shelly has 2 less than Rashid. How many baseball hats does Shelly have?

25. **Algebra** What four shapes come next in the pattern if it continues?

26. The sum of two numbers is 14. The difference between those same two numbers is 0. What are the two numbers?

27. **Algebra** What shape will be tenth in the pattern if it continues?

28. **Measurement** Grant's favorite video game takes him 132 minutes to win. Each level takes Grant about 22 minutes to clear. About how many levels does his video game have?

29. Doria works at a sandwich shop. There are 3 different kinds of bread and 5 different kinds of meat to choose from. How many different sandwiches can be made using one bread and one meat?

3-8 Determine Possible Outcomes (pp. 124–127)

4-6.7

Example 9
Angie can use clay or paper for an art project. Her project can be blue or yellow. What are all the outcomes of the art project?

Use a tree diagram.

Material	Color	Outcome
clay	blue	clay, blue
	yellow	clay, yellow
paper	blue	paper, blue
	yellow	paper, yellow

There are four possible outcomes.

Draw a tree diagram to find the number of possible outcomes for the situation.

30. How many outcomes are possible if the coin is tossed and the spinner is spun?

 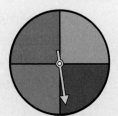

3-9 Probability (pp. 128–130)

4-6.6

Example 10
A marble is chosen without looking. Describe the probability that the chosen marble will be red.

There are 10 marbles in the bag, and 6 are red.

In the bag, more than half of the marbles are red. So, it is likely that a red marble will be chosen.

The spinner is spun. Describe the probability of each outcome. Write *certain, likely, equally likely, unlikely,* or *impossible*.

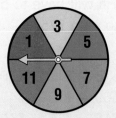

31. 3 or 5   **32.** even number

33. a number greater than 7

34. prime number

35. Identify an outcome that is certain to take place when the spinner is spun.

For Exercises 1–2, tell whether each statement is *true* or *false*.

1. A double bar graph displays two sets of related data using bars of different colors.

2. A tree diagram uses "branches" to show all possible combinations of a probability situation.

3. **MULTIPLE CHOICE** Reggie will spin the arrow on a spinner like the one shown below.

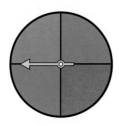

 If the spinner lands on two different sections, which of the following is NOT a possible outcome?

 A Red, Blue

 B Green, Green

 C Red, Red

 D Green, Red

Make a table to solve each problem.

4. A car needs an oil change every 3 months. Joe's car has had 4 oil changes so far. How many months have passed?

5. How much money will Kendall save if he saves $35 a month for a year?

One piece of fruit is chosen without looking. Use words and a number to describe the probability of each outcome.

6. orange

7. apple or peach

8. **MULTIPLE CHOICE** The graph below shows the number of touchdowns made in four different games.

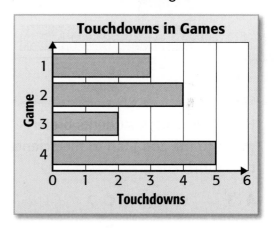

 According to the graph, how many more touchdowns were made in game 4 than in game 1?

 F 2   **H** 4

 G 3   **J** 5

9. **WRITING IN ▶MATH** Write two sentences to describe the graph in Exercise 8.

PART 1   Multiple Choice

Read each question. Then fill in the correct answer on the answer sheet provided by your teacher or on a sheet of paper.

1. Marla asked her class about their favorite class trip. She made a bar graph to show the results.

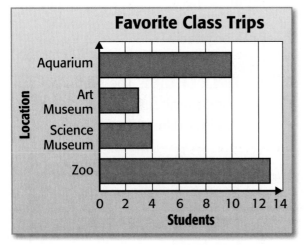

How many more students prefer going to the zoo than to the science museum?

   A 3   **C** 7

   B 6   **D** 9

2. What is the median of the shoe sizes shown in the data set shown below?

       {6, 4, 5, 7, 8, 5, 6}

   F 3

   G 4

   H 5

   J 6

3. Which number is 1,000 more than 82,753?

   A 82,853   **C** 92,735

   B 83,753   **D** 92,753

4. A mountain is 9,485 feet tall. A climber has hiked 6,208 feet. How many more feet does the climber need to hike to reach the top of the mountain?

   F 15,693   **H** 3,277

   G 15,267   **J** 3,183

5. What is the mode of the data set {3, 5, 7, 2, 2, 4, 6}?

   A 2   **C** 4

   B 3   **D** 5

6. What is the value of the digit 9 in 169,328,457?

   F 900,000   **H** 90,000,000

   G 9,000,000   **J** 900,000,000

7. Kari has a bag of 20 blocks. Six are blue, 4 are red, 7 are green, and 3 are yellow. If Kari chooses a block without looking, which color is most likely to be chosen?

   A green   **C** red

   B blue   **D** yellow

8. What is 736,249 rounded to the nearest hundred?

F 736,000   **H** 736,250

G 736,200   **J** 740,000

---

9. Ron sold lemonade at soccer practice. On which two days did he sell the least amount of lemonade?

Lemonade Sales	
Day	**Tally**
Monday	卌 IIII
Tuesday	IIII
Wednesday	卌 I
Thursday	IIII
Friday	卌 III

A Monday and Friday

B Wednesday and Friday

C Tuesday and Thursday

D Thursday and Friday

---

10. Nadia tossed a number cube labeled 0–5. What is the probability that she will toss an even number?

F 2 out of 6   **H** 4 out of 6

G 3 out of 6   **J** 5 out of 6

PART 2   Short Response

Record your answers on the answer sheet provided by your teacher or on a sheet of paper.

11. A piggy bank contains the coins shown below. If a coin is selected at random, what is the probability in numbers that the coin will be a penny?

PART 3   Extended Response

Record your answers on the answer sheet provided by your teacher or on a sheet of paper.

12. Larisa has three pairs of pants and two sweaters.

Larisa's Outfits	
Pants	tan, black, navy
Sweaters	red, stripe, white

a. Draw a tree diagram to show the possible outfits Larisa can wear if she chooses one pair of pants and one sweater.

b. How many different outfits can Larisa wear?

NEED EXTRA HELP?												
If You Missed Question...	1	2	3	4	5	6	7	8	9	10	11	12
Go to Lesson...	3-5	3-2	2-4	2-5	3-2	1-2	3-9	1-6	3-1	3-9	3-9	3-8
SC Academic Standards	4-6.2	4-6.2	3-2.3	3-2.3	4-6.2	4-2.6	4-6.6	3-2.4	4-6.3	4-6.6	4-6.6	4-6.7

Apply Multiplication and Division Facts

BIG Idea   What are multiplication and division?

Multiplication means to find the total of equal groups.
Division means to separate an amount into equal groups.

Example Two years on Earth is about one year on Mars. Andrés is 10 years old. If he lived on Mars, he would be $10 \div 2$ or 5 years old.

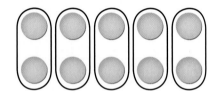

$10 \div 2$ means to separate 10 into equal groups of 2.

$10 \div 2 = 5$

What will I learn in this chapter?

- Understand how multiplication and division are related.
- Use multiplication properties and division rules.
- Multiply and divide facts through 12.
- Identify factors and multiples.
- Choose an operation to solve problems.

Key Vocabulary

Commutative Property of Multiplication

Associative Property of Multiplication

factor

multiple

Distributive Property of Multiplication

 **SC Math Online**   **Student Study Tools** at **macmillanmh.com**

FOLDABLES®
Study Organizer

Make this Foldable to help you organize information about multiplication and division. Begin with four sheets of $8\frac{1}{2}" \times 11"$ paper.

1 **Stack** 4 sheets of paper. Place each sheet $\frac{3}{4}$ inch apart.

2 **Roll** up the edges, so all tabs are the same size.

3 **Crease** and staple along the fold.

4 **Label** the tabs with the topics from the chapter.

Relate × and ÷
Properties and Rules
Facts Through 5
Facts Through 10
Multiply with 11 and 12
Multiply Three Numbers
Factors & Multiples

You have two ways to check prerequisite skills for this chapter.

Option 2

SC Math Online ⟩ Take the Chapter Readiness Quiz at macmillanmh.com.

Option 1

Complete the Quick Check below.

QUICK Check

Algebra Complete each number sentence. (Prior Grade)

1. $4 + 4 + 4 = \blacksquare$

2. $6 + 6 + \blacksquare + 6 = 24$

3. $9 + 9 + 9 = 3 \times \blacksquare$

4. $11 + 11 + 11 + 11 = \blacksquare \times 11$

5. Write the multiplication fact modeled by the array at the right.

Copy each array. Then circle equal groups of 3. (Prior Grade)

6. ★ ★ ★ ★
★ ★ ★ ★
★ ★ ★ ★

7. ((((((
((((((
((((((
((((((

8. Marcia has 15 action figures. If Marcia places the figures in 3 equal rows, how many figures will be in each row?

Algebra The number patterns below are formed by skip counting. Copy and complete each pattern. (Prior Grade)

9. 2, 4, 6, $\blacksquare$, 10, $\blacksquare$, 14

10. 4, 8, 12, $\blacksquare$, 20, 24, $\blacksquare$

11. 5, $\blacksquare$, 15, 20, $\blacksquare$, 30, $\blacksquare$

12. $\blacksquare$, 18, 27, $\blacksquare$, 45, 54, $\blacksquare$

13. Write a number pattern that involves skip counting forward by 25.

14. Write a number pattern that involves skip counting backward by 4.

Meaning of Multiplication and Division

You can use models to represent multiplication and division.

MAIN IDEA

I will use models to represent multiplication and division.

SC Academic Standards

4-2.3 Apply an algorithm to multiply whole numbers fluently.

4-2.5 Generate strategies to divide whole numbers by single-digit divisors.

You Will Need
counters
cups

SC Math Online

macmillanmh.com
• Concepts in Motion

ACTIVITY

1) Find 3 × 4.

Step 1 **Model 3 × 4.**

To model 3 × 4, arrange counters in an array with 3 rows and 4 columns.

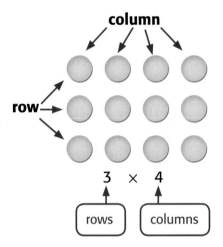

$$3 \times 4$$
rows   columns

Step 2 **Use repeated addition to find 3 × 4.**

Add 3 rows of 4 counters.

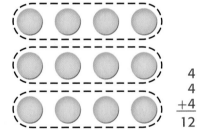

$$\begin{array}{r} 4 \\ 4 \\ +4 \\ \hline 12 \end{array}$$

Step 3 **Make the connection.**

Multiplication and repeated addition result in the same answer.

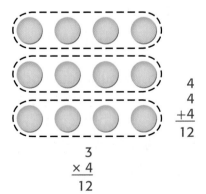

$$\begin{array}{r} 4 \\ 4 \\ +4 \\ \hline 12 \end{array}$$

$$\begin{array}{r} 3 \\ \times 4 \\ \hline 12 \end{array}$$

So, 3 × 4 = 12.

factor   factor   product

2 Find 15 ÷ 3.

Step 1 **Model 15 ÷ 3.**

Use 15 counters.
Put the counters
in 3 rows since
the divisor is 3.

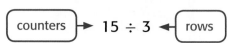

counters → 15 ÷ 3 ← rows

Step 2 **Place the counters
in the cups.**

Divide the counters
equally one by one
into the cups until all
15 counters are gone.

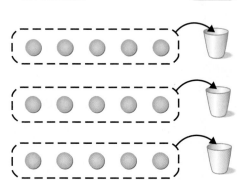

Step 3 **Find 15 ÷ 3.**

There are 5 counters
in each cup.

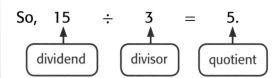

So, 15 ÷ 3 = 5.

dividend   divisor   quotient

Think About It

1. How would you model 2 × 8?   **2.** How would you model 10 ÷ 5?

CHECK What You Know

Draw pictures to model. Then multiply or divide.

3. 3 × 7   **4.** 6 ÷ 3   **5.** 6 × 8   **6.** 24 ÷ 6

7. **WRITING IN ►MATH** Explain how to model 4 groups of 9. Write a
number sentence to show the total amount in 4 groups of 9.

Relate Multiplication and Division

GET READY to Learn

Latanya and her father are baking a cake. Her father asks her how many eggs they have. The eggs in the carton are arranged in an array.

You can write related multiplication and division sentences to describe the array of eggs. You can think of this array as 2 rows and 3 columns or 3 rows and 2 columns.

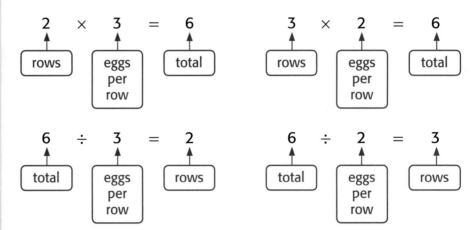

$2 \times 3 = 6$

rows — eggs per row — total

$3 \times 2 = 6$

rows — eggs per row — total

$6 \div 3 = 2$

total — eggs per row — rows

$6 \div 2 = 3$

total — eggs per row — rows

The number sentences above show a fact family. A **fact family** is a set of four related multiplication and division facts that use the same three numbers. The fact family follows a pattern.

EXAMPLE Write a Fact Family

① **Write a fact family for the array.**

There are 3 rows, 4 columns, and a total of 12 objects.

$3 \times 4 = 12$ $4 \times 3 = 12$

$12 \div 3 = 4$ $12 \div 4 = 3$

Lesson 4-1 Relate Multiplication and Division **147**

You can use a related multiplication fact to help you divide.

Remember

Multiplication and division are opposite, or *inverse*, operations.

2 **BOOKS** Vanesa has 36 books to put on 4 shelves. The same number of books will be placed on each shelf. How many books will be on each shelf?

Find 36 ÷ 4. You can use a related multiplication fact to help you divide.

36 ÷ 4 = ■

What number times 4 is 36?

36 ÷ 4 = 9

So, Vanesa will place 9 books on each shelf.

CHECK What You Know

Write a fact family for each array or set of numbers. See Example 1 (p. 147)

1.

2.

3. 6, 8, 48

4. 3, 12, 4

Algebra **Copy and complete each fact family.** See Example 1 (p. 147)

5. 3 × 6 = ■   6 × ■ = 18

18 ÷ ■ = 3   18 ÷ 3 = ■

6. 5 × 7 = ■   ■ × 5 = 35

35 ÷ ■ = 7   35 ÷ 7 = ■

Algebra **Divide. Use a related multiplication fact.** See Example 2 (p. 148)

7. 22 ÷ 2 = ■

8. 81 ÷ 9 = ■

9. Ed wants to share 18 grapes equally among himself and two friends. How many grapes will each get?

10. **Talk About It** How are multiplication and division related? Use examples to support your answer.

Write a fact family for each array or set of numbers. See Example 1 (p. 147)

11.

12.

13.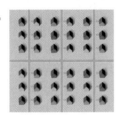

14.

15. 6, 9, 54   **16.** 7, 8, 56   **17.** 9, 11, 99   **18.** 11, 12, 132

Algebra Copy and complete each fact family. See Example 1 (p. 147)

19. $4 \times 8 = \blacksquare$ $\blacksquare \times 4 = 32$ **20.** $\blacksquare \times 9 = 72$ $9 \times 8 = \blacksquare$

$32 \div \blacksquare = 8$ $32 \div 8 = \blacksquare$ $72 \div \blacksquare = 8$ $72 \div 8 = \blacksquare$

Algebra Divide. Use a related multiplication fact. See Example 2 (p. 148)

21. $18 \div 2 = \blacksquare$ **22.** $36 \div 6 = \blacksquare$ **23.** $63 \div 7 = \blacksquare$ **24.** $64 \div 8 = \blacksquare$

South Carolina Data File

The Carolina wren is the state bird of South Carolina. It became the state bird in 1939.

25. Carolina wrens can grow up to 6 inches in length. Suppose a flock of Carolina wrens, lined up end-to-end, has a total length of 60 inches. How many Carolina wrens are there in this flock?

26. A Carolina wren lays 3 to 7 eggs in each clutch (a set of eggs laid at one time). Suppose 24 eggs are found in nests throughout a park. There are four eggs in each nest. How many nests contained eggs?

H.O.T. Problem

27. **WRITING IN ►MATH** Explain how fact families and multiplication facts can help you solve division problems.

Algebra: Multiplication Properties and Division Rules

MAIN IDEA

I will use multiplication properties and division rules.

SC Academic Standards

4-1.3 Explain and justify answers to problems on the basis of mathematical properties, structures, and relationships. *Also addresses 4-1.2.*

New Vocabulary

Commutative Property of Multiplication

Associative Property of Multiplication

Identity Property of Multiplication

Zero Property of Multiplication

SC Math Online

macmillanmh.com

• Extra Examples
• Personal Tutor
• Self-Check Quiz

GET READY to Learn

The table shows Jenny and Cliff's chores. Jenny earns $3 for each chore and Cliff earns $2 for each chore. How much does each person earn for completing chores?

Jenny	Cliff
Pack lunches	Set table
Take out trash	Clean room
Laundry	Walk dog
Clean room	Wash dishes
	Sweep floor

Multiplication has properties similar to addition. You can use the patterns and relationships in these properties.

Multiplication Properties   Key Concepts

Commutative Property of Multiplication

When multiplying, the order of the factors does not change the product.

$3 \times 2 = 6$
$2 \times 3 = 6$

Associative Property of Multiplication

The way in which the factors are grouped does not change the product.

$(5 \times 2) \times 3 = 30$
$5 \times (2 \times 3) = 30$

Identity Property of Multiplication

When any number is multiplied by 1, the product is that number.

$4 \times 1 = 4$

Zero Property of Multiplication

When any number is multiplied by 0, the product is 0.

$3 \times 0 = 0$

EXAMPLE   Identify Properties

1 **Identify the property shown by $8 \times 1 = 8$.**

A number is multiplied by 1, and the product is that number. This is the Identity Property of Multiplication.

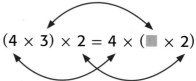

EXAMPLE Use Properties

2 **Complete $(4 \times 3) \times 2 = 4 \times (\blacksquare \times 2)$. Identify the property used.**

$$(4 \times 3) \times 2 = 4 \times (\blacksquare \times 2)$$

A 3 completes the number sentence. The way in which the factors are grouped does not change the product. This is the Associative Property of Multiplication.

The following facts can help you with division.

Remember

Quotient is the name of the answer for division problems.

Division Rules	Key Concepts
Zeros in Division	
When you divide 0 by any number other than 0, the quotient is 0.	$0 \div 5 = 0$
It is not possible to divide a number by 0.	$7 \div 0$
Ones in Division	
When you divide any number by 1, the quotient is always the dividend.	$8 \div 1 = 8$
When you divide any number by itself, the quotient is always 1. This is true for all numbers except 0.	$9 \div 9 = 1$

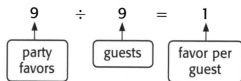

Real-World EXAMPLE Use a Division Rule

3 **PARTIES** There are 9 party favors and 9 guests. How many party favors will each guest get?

$$\underset{\substack{\uparrow \\ \text{party} \\ \text{favors}}}{9} \div \underset{\substack{\uparrow \\ \text{guests}}}{9} = \underset{\substack{\uparrow \\ \text{favor per} \\ \text{guest}}}{1}$$

A non-zero number divided by the same number is 1. So, each guest will get 1 party favor.

Identify the property or rule shown by each number sentence.

See Examples 1–3 (pp. 150–151)

1. $12 \times 0 = 0$

2. $8 \times 5 = 5 \times 8$

3. $6 \div 1 = 6$

Algebra Copy and complete each number sentence. Identify the property or rule used. See Example 2 (p. 151)

4. $7 \times \blacksquare = 7$

5. $5 \div \blacksquare = 1$

6. $(7 \times 2) \times 3 = 7 \times (\blacksquare \times 3)$

7. Brenda has 4 rows of 6 stickers. What is another way she can arrange the stickers? Write a number sentence.

8. **Talk About It** Explain why the Identity Property of Multiplication uses 1 while the Identity Property of Addition uses 0.

Practice and Problem Solving

SCAS • PASS

Extra Practice, p. R10

Identify the property or rule shown by each number sentence.

See Examples 1–3 (pp. 150–151)

9. $10 \div 10 = 1$

10. $6 \times (3 \times 4) = (6 \times 3) \times 4$

11. $8 \times 0 = 0$

12. $0 \div 12 = 0$

13. $(6 \times 3) \times 4 = 6 \times (3 \times 4)$

14. $22 \times 1 = 22$

Algebra Copy and complete each number sentence. Identify the property or rule used. See Example 2 (p. 151)

15. $3 \div \blacksquare = 1$

16. $\blacksquare \times 8 = 8 \times 4$

17. $\blacksquare \div 11 = 0$

18. $3 \times (\blacksquare \times 6) = (3 \times 3) \times 6$

19. $15 \times \blacksquare = 15$

20. $28 \times \blacksquare = 0$

Real-World PROBLEM SOLVING

Hiking Write a number sentence for each situation. Then solve.

21. On their first hiking trip, Tamika and Brian hiked 7 miles a day. They hiked for 5 days. Kurt and Suki hiked 5 miles a day. How many days did it take Kurt and Suki to hike the same distance as Tamika and Brian?

22. On their second trip, Tamika and Brian hiked twice as long as they did on their first trip. How many days will Kurt and Suki need to hike to go the same distance as Tamika and Brian?

H.O.T. Problems

23. OPEN ENDED Using the same three numbers, write two different multiplication expressions with a product of 60.

24. NUMBER SENSE When finding the value of $(2 \times 9) \times 5$, is it easier to find 2×9 or 2×5 first? Explain.

25. **WRITING IN ►MATH** Marcie thinks it is easier to find $(7 \times 6) \times 2$ than to find $7 \times (6 \times 2)$. What property tells her that the number sentences are equal? Why might Marcie think it is easier to find the answer to the first number sentence?

PASS Practice 4-2.3, 4-1.3

26. Which number sentence is in the same fact family as $42 \div 7 = \blacksquare$?
(Lesson 4-1)

A $7 + \blacksquare = 42$

B $\blacksquare - 7 = 42$

C $7 \times \blacksquare = 42$

D $42 \times 7 = 42$

27. Luther's photo album has 6 pages with 8 photos on each page. Identify the number sentence that describes this situation. (Lesson 4-2)

F $8 \times 6 = 6 \times 8$

G $8 \times 6 > 6 \times 8$

H $8 \times 6 < 6 \times 8$

J $8 \times 8 > 6 \times 6$

Spiral Review

Algebra Divide. Use a related multiplication fact. (Lesson 4-1)

28. $12 \div 3 = \blacksquare$

29. $16 \div 4 = \blacksquare$

30. $20 \div 5 = \blacksquare$

For Exercises 31 and 32, use the graph.
(Lesson 3-6)

31. What is the most and least favorite place to visit?

32. Identify which two places to visit received a difference in votes of 5.

33. Fernando's two dogs eat 3 cups of food each day. How much food do his dogs eat in a week? (Lesson 3-3)

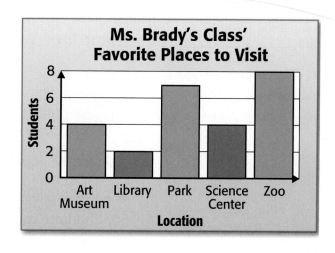

Ms. Brady's Class' Favorite Places to Visit

Multiply and Divide Facts Through 5

MAIN IDEA

I will recall multiplication and division facts 0 through 5.

SC Academic Standards

4-2.3 Apply an algorithm to multiply whole numbers fluently.

4-2.5 Generate strategies to divide whole numbers by single-digit divisors.

SC Math Online

macmillanmh.com

• Extra Examples
• Personal Tutor
• Self-Check Quiz

GET READY to Learn

Charlotte is competing in a 3-mile race. Every 4 laps equals 1 mile. How many laps does she need to complete to finish the race?

To find the number of laps that Charlotte needs to complete, multiply. There are different strategies that can be used to multiply.

Real-World EXAMPLE   Multiply

1 RACING How many laps does Charlotte need to complete in order to travel 3 miles?

You need to find 3×4.

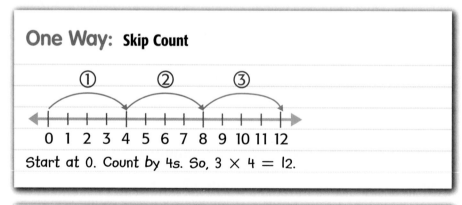

One Way: Skip Count

① ② ③

0 1 2 3 4 5 6 7 8 9 10 11 12

Start at 0. Count by 4s. So, $3 \times 4 = 12$.

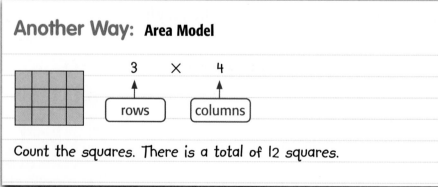

Another Way: Area Model

3 × 4

rows   columns

Count the squares. There is a total of 12 squares.

So, Charlotte must complete 12 laps to travel 3 miles.

There are different strategies to use when finding division facts.

2 **Omari has football practice 3 days a week. He drinks a sports drink during each practice. Suppose 12 sports drinks come in a package. How many weeks will a package of sports drinks last?**

You need to find 12 ÷ 3.

One Way: Related Facts

12 ÷ 3 = ■

THINK 3 × ■ = 12?

12 ÷ 3 = 4

Another Way: Array

Use an array to find 12 ÷ 3.
Separate an array of 12 counters into 3 equal groups.

There are 4 counters in each group. So, 12 ÷ 3 = 4.

So, one package of sports drinks will last 4 weeks.

Remember

You can also draw pictures, use a times table, or use models to help divide.

CHECK What You Know

Multiply or divide. Use arrays or area models if needed. See Examples 1 and 2 (pp. 154–155)

1. 5 × 3	**2.** 9 × 0	**3.** 1 × 5	**4.** 2 × 8

5. 6 ÷ 2   **6.** 24 ÷ 3   **7.** 5)‾10‾   **8.** 4)‾28‾

9. Nancy's dog gets 3 treats each day. There are 36 treats in a box. How many days will the treats last?

10. **Talk About It** What multiplication fact can help you find 9 ÷ 3? Explain.

Multiply or divide. Use arrays or area models if needed. See Examples 1 and 2 (pp. 154–155)

11.
  5
× 6

12.
  2
× 3

13.
  9
× 2

14.
  8
× 4

15. 7 × 1

16. 3 × 7

17. 9 × 5

18. 4 × 11

19. 8 ÷ 1

20. 10 ÷ 2

21. 12 ÷ 3

22. 32 ÷ 4

23. 2)‾24‾

24. 3)‾33‾

25. 4)‾40‾

26. 5)‾60‾

Algebra Complete each number sentence.

27. 2 × ▇ = 2

28. ▇ × 5 = 35

29. 33 ÷ ▇ = 11

30. ▇ ÷ 5 = 10

Algebra Solve.

31. If ☆ = 3, then what is ☆ + ☆ + ☆ + ☆ + ☆ + ☆ + ☆ ?

32. If ☺ + ☺ + ☺ + ☺ + ☺ + ☺ + ☺ + ☺ + ☺ = 45, then what is ☺ ?

33. There are 5 sets of paint in an art class. There are 25 students in the art class. How many students share each set of paint?

34. Jared has 6 packs of baseball cards. There are 5 cards in each pack. How many baseball cards does Jared have?

Real-World PROBLEM SOLVING

Technology The number of computers in classrooms is increasing. The results of a recent study are shown to the right.

35. There are 5 computers in a fourth grade classroom. The number of students per computer matches the results of the study. How many students are in this classroom?

One computer for every 4 students in a classroom.

Source: *USA Today*

36. There are 24 students in Mr. Montoya's class. The number of computers per student matches the results of the study. How many computers are in Mr. Montoya's class?

H.O.T. Problems

37. OPEN ENDED Write three 2-digit numbers that are divisible by 2.

38. WHICH ONE DOESN'T BELONG? Identify the expression that does not belong with the other three. Explain.

2×4	$24 \div 3$	3×4	$8 \div 1$

39. **WRITING IN ►MATH** Write a real-world problem that can be represented by $55 \div 5$.

PASS Practice   4-2.4, 4-2.5

40. George has 3 rows of 5 stamps. Which number sentence shows another way he can arrange the stamps? (Lesson 4-2)

  A $3 + 3 + 3$

  B $3 + 5$

  C $5 + 5$

  D 5×3

41. Which number is missing from the number sentence? (Lesson 4-3)

$$45 \div \blacksquare = 9$$

  F 2

  G 3

  H 4

  J 5

Spiral Review

Algebra Copy and complete each number sentence. Identify the property or rule used. (Lesson 4-2)

42. $8 \div \blacksquare = 1$ **43.** $\blacksquare \times 5 = 5 \times 4$ **44.** $\blacksquare \div 12 = 0$

Algebra Copy and complete each fact family. (Lesson 4-1)

45. $4 \times 7 = \blacksquare$ $7 \times \blacksquare = 28$ **46.** $8 \times 9 = \blacksquare$ $\blacksquare \times 8 = 72$

    $28 \div \blacksquare = 7$ $28 \div 7 = \blacksquare$ $72 \div \blacksquare = 8$ $72 \div 9 = \blacksquare$

47. The number of children who visited a science museum is shown. About how many children visited the museum during the weekend? (Lesson 2-4)

Museum Visitors							
Day	Mon.	Tues.	Wed.	Thur.	Fri.	Sat.	Sun.
Visitors	325	279	312	348	441	519	495

4-4 Problem-Solving Skill

MAIN IDEA I will choose an operation to solve a problem.

 SCAS 4-2.3 Apply an algorithm to multiply whole numbers fluently.

There are 9 rows on the Twisted Zipper roller coaster. Each row has 4 seats. Choose an operation to find how many people can ride the roller coaster at a time.

Understand	**What facts do you know?** • There are 9 rows. • There are 4 seats per row. **What do you need to find?** • The operation you should use to find how many people can ride the roller coaster at a time.
Plan	There are groups with the same number in each group. So, multiply the number of rows by the number of seats per row.
Solve	Multiply to find the answer. 4 × 9 = 36 seats per row rows So, 36 people can ride the roller coaster at a time.
Check	Look back. Find 4 × 9 another way to see if you get the same answer. You can use an array. 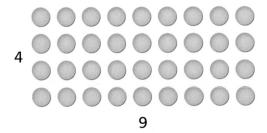 Since 4 × 9 = 36, the answer is correct.

Refer to the problem on the previous page.

1. Explain why you multiplied 9 and 4 to find the answer.

2. What operation can be used to check the answer?

3. If 6 people can sit in each row, how many people could ride in all?

4. Refer to Exercise 3. How do you know the answer is correct?

PRACTICE the Skill

SCAS • PASS
Extra Practice, p. R10

Tell which operation you would use to solve each problem. Then solve.

5. Jocelyn completed 28 problems for her math homework on Tuesday. She completed 17 more on Thursday than on Tuesday. How many problems did she complete on Thursday?

6. There are three jugglers in a circus. Each juggler can juggle 5 balls at a time. How many balls will they need for their act if they all perform at the same time?

7. A page from Dana's album is shown. Dana puts the same number of stickers on each page. She has 11 pages of stickers. How many stickers does she have in all?

8. Park Street School has 98 students who have perfect attendance. West Glenn School has 64 students. How many more students have perfect attendance at Park Street School?

9. **Measurement** The graph shows how long some animals sleep. The koala sleeps 6 hours more than which animal?

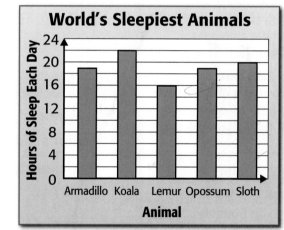

Source: *Scholastic Book of World Records*

10. Use the graph above. How many more hours does a sloth sleep than a lemur?

11. Corey and his 2 friends earned $12 for doing yard work. How much money will each person get paid if they share the money evenly?

12. A lizard eats 6 crickets each day. How many crickets does it eat in one week?

13. **WRITING IN ►MATH** Explain how you chose an operation for Exercise 12.

Multiply and Divide Facts Through 10

GET READY to Learn

Lorenzo is storing his friends' phone numbers in his cell phone. Each number has 7 digits. How many number buttons did Lorenzo press if he has 9 friends?

MAIN IDEA

I will recall multiplication and division facts through 10.

SC Academic Standards

4-2.3 Apply an algorithm to multiply whole numbers fluently.

4-2.5 Generate strategies to divide whole numbers by single-digit divisors.

SC Math Online

macmillanmh.com
• Extra Examples
• Personal Tutor
• Self-Check Quiz

You can find how many number buttons Lorenzo pressed by multiplying. Two multiplication strategies that you can use are area models and related facts.

Real-World EXAMPLE   Multiply

① **PHONES Each number has 7 digits. How many number buttons did Lorenzo press if he has 9 friends?**

You need to find 7×9.

One Way: Area Model	Another Way: Related Fact
Make an area model.	Think of a related fact.
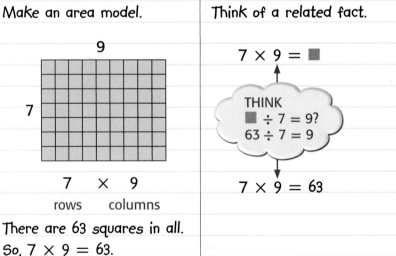 9 7 7 × 9 rows columns There are 63 squares in all. So, $7 \times 9 = 63$.	$7 \times 9 = \blacksquare$ THINK $\blacksquare \div 7 = 9?$ $63 \div 7 = 9$ $7 \times 9 = 63$

So, Lorenzo must press 63 number buttons.

2 **TELEVISION** Carolyn noticed that 9 minutes of commercials play during a 30-minute television program. How many 30-minute shows did Carolyn watch during a weekend if she watched 54 minutes of commercials?

Remember

The factors in a multiplication problem become the divisor and quotient in the related division problem.

Each program has 9 minutes of commercials. Divide 54 by 9 to find how many 30-minute shows Carolyn watched.

Separate an array of 54 counters into 9 equal groups.

There are 6 counters in each group.

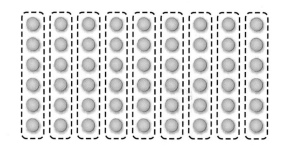

So, Carolyn watched 6 thirty-minute shows.

Check Use a related fact to check your answer. Since $9 \times 6 = 54$, the answer is correct.

So, $54 \div 9 = 6.$ ✔

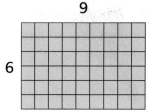

CHECK **What You Know**

Multiply or divide. Use arrays or area models if needed. See Examples 1 and 2 (pp. 160–161)

1. 9
   $\times 8$

2. 10
   $\times 7$

3. 6×4

4. 8×8

5. $49 \div 7$

6. $60 \div 6$

7. $8\overline{)48}$

8. $10\overline{)100}$

9. Linda sold 8 magazine subscriptions to make money for her school. Each magazine subscription costs $9. How much money did Linda collect?

10. **Talk About It** What do you notice when you multiply 10 and a number? Explain an easy method for finding a product when 10 is one of the factors.

Multiply or divide. Use arrays or area models if needed. See Examples 1 and 2 (pp. 160–161)

11. 6
 × 6

12. 10
 × 8

13. 7
 × 7

14. 6
 × 7

15. 9×4

16. 10×5

17. 6×8

18. 10×10

19. $30 \div 6$

20. $42 \div 7$

21. $72 \div 8$

22. $90 \div 10$

23. $7\overline{)70}$

24. $9\overline{)63}$

25. $8\overline{)56}$

26. $10\overline{)80}$

27. Juliana played 9 holes of miniature golf. Her total score was 54. Suppose she got the same score on each hole. What was Juliana's score per hole?

28. While on vacation, Felipe sent 42 postcards to his friends. How many friends did he send to if he sent 7 postcards to each person?

Real-World PROBLEM SOLVING

Fruit Oranges are the fruit of a citrus tree originally from southeast Asia. Oranges grow in different sizes and colors. Most oranges have 10 sections inside.

29. Nadia bought 2 oranges for each member of her family. Nadia has 4 family members. Each orange has 10 sections. How many sections will there be in all?

30. Suppose Nadia cuts 6 oranges in half. She finds that there are 54 sections in all. If there are the same number of sections in each orange, how many sections are in each orange?

H.O.T. Problems

31. **OPEN ENDED** Write three number sentences that each contain the number 6 and have a product greater than 40.

32. **NUMBER SENSE** Explain why the fact family of 7 and 49 has only two number sentences.

33. **CHALLENGE** The product of two numbers is 24. The sum of the numbers is 11. What are the two numbers?

34. **WRITING IN ►MATH** Is the quotient of $135 \div 9$ greater than or less than the quotient of $153 \div 9$? Explain how you know without finding the quotients.

Write a fact family for each set of numbers. (Lesson 4-1)

1. 7, 28, 4

2. 3, 24, 8

Algebra Divide. Use a related multiplication fact. (Lesson 4-1)

3. $18 \div 2$

4. $20 \div 5$

5. $33 \div 3$

6. $36 \div 4$

7. MULTIPLE CHOICE Which number sentence is in the same fact family as $63 \div 7 = \blacksquare$? (Lesson 4-1)

A $7 + \blacksquare = 63$

C $7 \times \blacksquare = 63$

B $\blacksquare - 7 = 63$

D $63 \times 7 = \blacksquare$

Identify the property or rule shown by each number sentence. (Lesson 4-2)

8. $15 \times 0 = 0$

9. $9 \times 3 = 3 \times 9$

Algebra Copy and complete each number sentence. Identify the property or rule used. (Lesson 4-2)

10. $5 \div \blacksquare = 1$

11. $7 \times \blacksquare = 0$

Multiply or divide. (Lesson 4-3)

12. $20 \div 5$

13. 4×3

14. Emmett brushes his teeth 3 times a day. How many times does Emmett brush his teeth in one week? (Lesson 4-3)

Algebra Complete each number sentence. (Lesson 4-3)

15. $\blacksquare \times 5 = 45$

16. $3 \times \blacksquare = 3$

17. MULTIPLE CHOICE Which number is missing from the number sentence? (Lesson 4-3)

$$27 \div \blacksquare = 9$$

F 2

H 4

G 3

J 5

Tell which operation you would use to solve each problem. Then solve. (Lesson 4-4)

18. Lance walked 4 dogs on Monday. He walked twice that many on Tuesday. How many dogs did he walk on Tuesday?

19. Each row of the stadium can hold 9 people. Diana reserved 3 rows for her family. How many people in Diana's family will be at the stadium?

Multiply or divide. (Lesson 4-5)

20. 10×6

21. $56 \div 7$

22. **WRITING IN** ►**MATH** Does the Associative Property work with division? Explain how you know. (Lesson 4-2)

Problem Solving in History

Pop Culture

Did you know that pop was invented by doctors? Many people thought that the mineral water in natural springs had healing powers. In 1767, a doctor invented the first glass of carbonated water, which came to be known as "soda water."

About 80 years later, pharmacy owners and scientists began to add flavors to soda water. It was renamed "soda pop" in 1861. Soon, Americans could buy soda in bottles from grocery stores and vending machines. These drinks are still very popular.

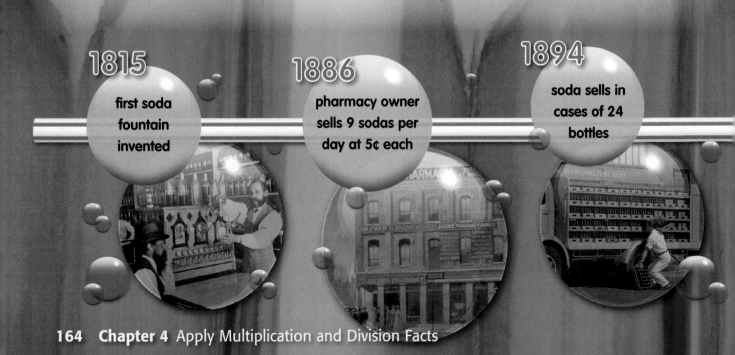

1815

first soda fountain invented

1886

pharmacy owner sells 9 sodas per day at 5¢ each

1894

soda sells in cases of 24 bottles

Real-World Math

Use the information on pages 164 and 165 to solve each problem.

Did You Know?

In 1929, there were more than 600 lemon-lime soda flavors to choose from!

1. In 1886, how much money would a pharmacy owner make each day from selling soda?

2. How much money in cents would the pharmacy owner make in a week?

3. Suppose the same pharmacy owner decreased the price of soda to 3¢ per bottle. How many sodas needed to be sold each day to make the same amount?

4. A 2-liter bottle of soda costs $3. How much will 16 liters of soda pop cost?

5. Soda was once sold in 8-ounce bottles. If you bought 96 ounces of soda, how many 8-ounce bottles did you buy? How many home-packs did you buy?

6. Suppose a customer buys $15 worth of 2-liter bottles, which cost $3 each. How many 2-liter bottles can the customer buy?

7. In 1894, a soda fountain owner sold 1 case of soda. How many different ways can you arrange the bottles in the case so that there are the same number of bottles in each row and column?

1923

soda is packaged in convenient six-bottle cartons, called "home-packs"

1977

soda is packaged in 2-liter bottles

Catch the Fun
2 LITERS

4-6 Multiply with 11 and 12

MAIN IDEA

I will recall and apply multiplication facts for 11 and 12.

SC Academic Standards

4-2.3 Apply an algorithm to multiply whole numbers fluently.

4-2.5 Generate strategies to divide whole numbers by single-digit divisors.

New Vocabulary

Distributive Property of Multiplication

SC Math Online

macmillanmh.com
• Extra Examples
• Personal Tutor
• Self-Check Quiz

> ## GET READY to Learn
>
> One day, a florist receives 7 orders for a dozen roses. How many roses does the florist need to make the 7 bouquets?

To multiply larger numbers, the Distributive Property of Multiplication is helpful. The **Distributive Property of Multiplication** says that you can multiply the addends of a number and then add the products.

Real-World EXAMPLE   Multiply

1 How many roses does the florist need to make 7 bouquets?

There are 12 roses in one dozen. So, you need to find 7×12.

Think of 7×12 as $(7 \times 10) + (7 \times 2)$.

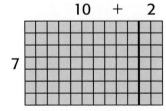

$$7 \times 12 = (7 \times 10) + (7 \times 2)$$
$$= \quad 70 \quad + \quad 14$$
$$= \quad 84$$

So, 84 roses are needed to make 7 bouquets.

You can use a related multiplication fact to find the quotient in a division problem.

 **Real-World EXAMPLE** Divide

2 MOVIES Shaun and 10 of his friends went to a movie. The total cost for the 11 movie tickets was $66. How much did each ticket cost?

You know that 11 tickets cost $66.
Use a related multiplication fact to help you find $66 ÷ 11.

Shaun + 10 friends

$66 ÷ 11 = ▪

THINK $11 \times ▪ = 66?
$11 \times $6 = 66

$66 ÷ 11 = $6

So, each ticket cost $6.

Check The area model shows that $6 \times 11 = 66.

So, $66 ÷ 11 = $6 is correct. ✔

$$10 \quad + \quad 1$$

| $6 | $60 | | $6 |

$60 + $6 = $66

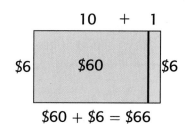

CHECK What You Know

Multiply or divide. Use arrays or area models if needed.

See Examples 1 and 2 (pp. 166–167)

1. $\begin{array}{r} 11 \\ \times\ 9 \\ \hline \end{array}$

2. $\begin{array}{r} 10 \\ \times\ 12 \\ \hline \end{array}$

3. 4×11

4. 6×12

5. $88 \div 11$

6. $108 \div 9$

7. $11\overline{)121}$

8. $12\overline{)132}$

9. There are 8 cartons of eggs on a grocery store shelf. Each carton contains one dozen eggs. How many eggs are on the shelf?

10. **Talk About It** How would you use two smaller area models to find 9×12? Draw the area models.

Multiply or divide. Use arrays or area models if needed. See Examples 1 and 2 (pp. 166–167)

11.
11
× 5

12.
12
× 5

13.
11
× 7

14.
12
× 8

15.
2
× 11

16.
12
× 7

17.
11
× 10

18.
12
× 12

19. 44 ÷ 11

20. 72 ÷ 6

21. 99 ÷ 11

22. 120 ÷ 10

23. 12)‾48‾

24. 11)‾66‾

25. 12)‾84‾

26. 11)‾110‾

Algebra Find the value of each number sentence if = 12 and = 11.

27. × 6

28. 8 × 😊

29. 132 ÷ 😊

30. 144 ÷ ♥

Compare. Use >, <, or =.

31. 11 × 8 ● 6 × 12

32. 132 ÷ 12 ● 99 ÷ 9

33. 12 × 10 ● 11 × 11

34. A group of notes on a piano, has 7 white and 5 black keys. How many keys are in 5 groups?

35. Mrs. Hanson has 12 grandchildren. She gives each grandchild $10. How much money does she give in all?

Real-World PROBLEM SOLVING

Animals The table gives expected life spans for some animals when they live in the wild.

36. Identify the two animals that have life spans of 60 months.

37. What is the life span of a Tasmanian devil in months?

38. How many more months is a platypus expected to live than a koala?

39. A mongoose is 7 years old. How many months longer is it expected to live?

40. Find the difference between a mongoose's life span and a toucan's life span in months.

Animal Life Spans	
Animal	**Years**
Bat	5 years
Gerbil	5 years
Koala	8 years
Mongoose	12 years
Platypus	10 years
Toucan	6 years
Tasmanian devil	8 years

Source: Zoological Society of San Diego

H.O.T. Problems

41. OPEN ENDED Write three number sentences. Each should contain the number 12, a one-digit number as the other factor, and a product less than 60.

42. WHICH ONE DOESN'T BELONG? Identify the number sentence that does not belong with the other three. Explain.

$$9 \times 11 \qquad 99 \div 9 \qquad 11 \times 9 \qquad 88 \div 11$$

43. **WRITING IN ►MATH** Write a problem about a real-world situation that involves finding the product of 6 and 12.

PASS Practice 4-2.5, 4-2.3

44. In which number sentence does 8 make the number sentence true? (Lesson 4-5)

A $36 \div \blacksquare = 4$

B $42 \div \blacksquare = 6$

C $56 \div \blacksquare = 7$

D $81 \div \blacksquare = 9$

45. Look at the problem below.

$$\square = \triangle \times 12$$

If $\triangle = 10$, what is $\square$? (Lesson 4-6)

F 120

G 121

H 132

J 143

Spiral Review

Multiply or divide. Use arrays or area models if needed. (Lesson 4-5)

46. 7×5

47. $\begin{array}{r} 8 \\ \times\ 9 \\ \hline \end{array}$

48. $64 \div 8$

49. $10\overline{)90}$

**Tell which operation you would use to solve each problem.
Then solve.** (Lesson 4-4)

50. There are 108 cotton balls in a bag. Each student needs 9 cotton balls for an art project. How many students will get the cotton balls?

51. There are 24 rocks in Hatsu's rock collection. She wants to display her rocks in an array. Identify 3 possible ways to display the rocks.

Algebra Complete each number sentence. (Lesson 4-3)

52. $3 \times \blacksquare = 3$

53. $\blacksquare \times 4 = 28$

54. $22 \div \blacksquare = 11$

55. $\blacksquare \div 4 = 10$

Problem-Solving Investigation

MAIN IDEA I will choose the best strategy to solve a problem.

 SCAS 4-2.3 Apply an algorithm to multiply whole numbers fluently.
4-2.5 Generate strategies to divide whole numbers by single-digit divisors.

P.S.I. TEAM ✛

KASA: I go to ballet lessons every week. I dance 2 hours during every lesson. I dance a total of 6 hours each week.

YOUR MISSION: Find how many ballet lessons Kasa has in 4 weeks.

Understand	Kasa dances 2 hours during each lesson. She dances a total of 6 hours each week. Find how many lessons she has in 4 weeks.
Plan	Divide the number of hours Kasa practices each week by the number of hours each lesson lasts. Then multiply by 4, the number of weeks..

Solve	hours per week hours per lesson lessons per week
	
	  6 ÷ 2 = 3
	
	So, Kasa has 3 ballet lessons each week.
	
	lessons per week weeks lessons in 4 weeks
	
	  3 × 4 = 12
	
	So, Kasa has 12 ballet lessons in 4 weeks.

Check	Look back. Check your answer by dividing the number of lessons in 4 weeks by the number of weeks. 12 ÷ 4 = 3. Then, multiply the number of hours per lesson by the number of lessons each week. 2 × 3 = 6. So, the answer is correct.

Use the make a table strategy or choose an operation to solve each problem.

PROBLEM-SOLVING STRATEGY
• Make a table.

1. **Geometry** Mr. and Mrs. Lopez are putting square tiles on the floor in their bathroom. They can fit 6 rows of 4 tiles in the bathroom. How many tiles do they need to buy?

2. **Algebra** A teacher gives quizzes that are each worth 15 points. If the teacher gives 5 quizzes, how many points are all of the quizzes worth?

3. Marisol has 7 books from the library. She gets 5 new books and returns 3 books. How many library books does she have now?

4. Raheem is playing a game at a carnival. He needs to earn 400 points to win a large stuffed animal. The dart board below shows the 4 out of 5 darts he has thrown. Is it possible for him to win the large stuffed animal? If so, how many points does he still need?

5. **Measurement** A scout troop went hiking on the trail shown below. They hiked 4 miles an hour. How long did they hike?

12 miles

6. Wesley needs to finish reading a book before Monday. He started reading the 44-page book on Thursday. How many pages will he need to read each day if he reads an equal number of pages each day?

7. Twenty students want to raise money for new playground equipment. They need $2,200. Copy and complete the table to find out how much money each student needs to raise.

New Playground Equipment	
Money per Student	**Total Raised**
$90	$1,800
$95	$1,900
$100	$2,000
$105	■
■	■

8. **WRITING IN ►MATH** Tell which problem-solving strategy you used to solve Exercise 7. Explain how you used this strategy when solving Exercise 7.

Algebra: Multiply Three Numbers

GET READY to Learn

There are 2 baseball cards in each pack. There are 6 packs in each box. If Raul buys 3 boxes for his collection, how many cards will he have?

MAIN IDEA

I will multiply 3 factors.

SC Academic Standards

4-2.3 Apply an algorithm to multiply whole numbers fluently.

SC Math Online

macmillanmh.com

• Extra Examples
• Personal Tutor
• Self-Check Quiz

In Lesson 2-1, you learned to use the Associative Property of Addition to add more than two numbers. You can use the Associative Property of Multiplication to multiply more than two numbers.

 Real-World EXAMPLE   **Associative Property**

① **TRADING CARDS How many baseball cards will Raul have?**

You need to find 2 × 6 × 3. There are two ways to group the numbers.

One Way	Another Way
Multiply 2 × 6 first.	Multiply 6 × 3 first.
2 × 6 × 3	2 × 6 × 3
(2 × 6) × 3	2 × (6 × 3)
12 × 3	2 × 18
36	36

So, Raul will have 36 baseball cards.

Multiply. See Example 1 (p. 172)

1. 3 × 1 × 5

2. 2 × 2 × 3

3. 3 × 5 × 3

4. 6 × 2 × 3

5. 4 × 2 × 7

6. 3 × 4 × 8

7. Art supply paint comes in a box that contains 3 sets of 8 bottles of paint. An art teacher ordered 2 boxes. How many bottles of paint were ordered?

8. **Talk About It** Identify the order that makes it easiest to multiply the factors in the expression 9 × 6 × 2. Explain.

Practice and Problem Solving

SCAS • PASS
Extra Practice, p. R12

Multiply. See Example 1 (p. 172)

9. 6 × 1 × 5

10. 2 × 2 × 7

11. 5 × 7 × 2

12. 10 × 2 × 5

13. 3 × 9 × 3

14. 2 × 6 × 7

15. 4 × 3 × 7

16. 2 × 9 × 4

17. 5 × 1 × 12

Algebra Copy and complete each number sentence.

18. 4 × ▓ × 1 = 12

19. 2 × 6 × ▓ = 60

20. ▓ × 3 × 4 = 24

Algebra Compare. Use >, <, or =.

21. 4 × 2 × 9 ● 7 × 4 × 2

22. 5 × 2 × 8 ● 6 × 2 × 6

Algebra Find the value of each number sentence if ☼ = 2, ☺ = 3, and ☆ = 4.

23. 5 × 1 × ☆

24. 6 × ☼ × 9

25. ☺ × 12 × ☆

26. **Measurement** Gabriel is training for a race. He jogs 2 miles a day. He jogs this distance 4 days a week. How many miles will he jog in 6 weeks?

27. **Measurement** Blanca bikes 2 miles to her grandfather's house and 2 miles back to her house 5 times each month. How many miles does she bike?

28. **Measurement** For one week, 4 inches of snow fell every morning, and 3 inches fell every night. Was this enough snow to cover a bench that is 4 feet tall? Explain.

29. Helen borrowed 12 books from the library. The books are due in 4 weeks. If she reads 2 books 2 days a week, will she have enough time to read all of the books? Explain.

Animals Did you know that pigs are very intelligent animals? They are considered to be smarter than dogs. More information about farm animals is shown to the right.

30. There are 4 chickens on a farm. How many eggs will they lay in 4 weeks?

31. Use the number sentence $2 \times 5 \times \blacksquare = 30$ to find how many weeks it will take 2 chickens to lay 30 eggs.

32. On a farm there are 4 sows that have had 2 litters of 8 piglets. How many piglets have the sows had?

Source: U.S. Poultry & Egg Association, Ontario Pork

33. How many weeks would it take 2 chickens to have more eggs than the number of piglets that were mentioned in Exercise 32?

H.O.T. Problems

34. OPEN ENDED Copy and complete $2 \times 11 \times \blacksquare > 4 \times 9 \times 3$ to make a true sentence.

35. FIND THE ERROR Lucas and Denise are finding $4 \times \blacksquare \times 7 = 56$. Who is correct? Explain.

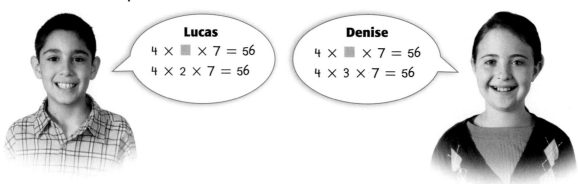

Lucas
$4 \times \blacksquare \times 7 = 56$
$4 \times 2 \times 7 = 56$

Denise
$4 \times \blacksquare \times 7 = 56$
$4 \times 3 \times 7 = 56$

36. CHALLENGE Identify four factors that result in a product of 24.

37. WRITING IN MATH Manuel has 24 marbles in his collection. He wants to store his marbles in 2 cases. If the marbles are displayed in even rows and columns, what arrays could the marbles be displayed in?

Multiplication Bingo

Multiplication Facts

Get Ready!

Players: 3 or more players

You will need: 6 index cards

Get Set!

Make a game board like the one shown. Label each square with a number that can be found on a multiplication table. Cut each index card in half, and label each card with a number from 1 to 12.

6	27	12	9
36	18	10	45
8	54	32	15
72	144	16	81

Go!

- Shuffle the cards. Place them facedown in a stack on the table.

- Player 1 chooses a card.

- Players look at the game board to find a number that results from multiplying the number on the card times any other number. Color 1 square if it contains a product of the number.

- Player 2 chooses a card.

- Play continues the same way.

- The first player that colors 4 squares in a row, column, or diagonally wins.

Factors and Multiples

4-9

GET READY to Learn

Mrs. Navarro is arranging desks in her classroom. There are 24 desks. How many ways can she arrange the desks so that the number of desks in each row is the same?

Two or more numbers that are multiplied together to form a product are called **factors**. To find the different arrangements of desks, break down or decompose 24 into its factors.

Real-World EXAMPLE   Identify Factors

1 **SCHOOL** **How many ways can Mrs. Navarro arrange the desks in her classroom?**

Think of number pairs that result in a product of 24.

$1 \times 24 = 24$

$2 \times 12 = 24$

$3 \times 8 = 24$

$4 \times 6 = 24$

THINK There are 4 more arrays:
| 24 × 1 | 8 × 3 |
| 12 × 2 | 6 × 4 |

The factors of 24 are 1, 2, 3, 4, 6, 8, 12, and 24. So, the desks can be arranged in eight ways.

A **multiple** of a number is the product of that number and any whole number. For example, 15 is a multiple of 5 because it is composed or made up of 3 groups of 5.

EXAMPLE Identify Multiples

2 **Identify the first five multiples of 7.**

On a multiplication table, look across the row for 7, or down the column for 7. All of the numbers listed in the row or the column are multiples of 7.

×	0	1	2	3	4	5	6	7	8	9	10	11	12
0	0	0	0	0	0	0	0	0	0	0	0	0	0
1	0	1	2	3	4	5	6	7	8	9	10	11	12
2	0	2	4	6	8	10	12	14	16	18	20	22	24
3	0	3	6	9	12	15	18	21	24	27	30	33	36
4	0	4	8	12	16	20	24	28	32	36	40	44	48
5	0	5	10	15	20	25	30	35	40	45	50	55	60
6	0	6	12	18	24	30	36	42	48	54	60	66	72
7	0	7	14	21	28	35	42	49	56	63	70	77	84
8	0	8	16	24	32	40	48	56	64	72	80	88	96
9	0	9	18	27	36	45	54	63	72	81	90	99	108
10	0	10	20	30	40	50	60	70	80	90	100	110	120
11	0	11	22	33	44	55	66	77	88	99	110	121	132
12	0	12	24	36	48	60	72	84	96	108	120	132	144

So, the first five multiples of 7 are 0, 7, 14, 21, and 28.

CHECK What You Know

Find all of the factors of each number. See Example 1 (p. 176)

1. 6   **2.** 10   **3.** 12   **4.** 36

Identify the first five multiples for each number. See Example 2 (p. 177)

5. 2   **6.** 4   **7.** 9   **8.** 12

9. Elena is baking muffins in the pan shown at the right. How many muffins will Elena make if she uses 1, 2, 3, or 4 pans?

10. Explain the relationship between factors and multiples.

Find all of the factors of each number. See Example 1 (p. 176)

11. 4	**12.** 7	**13.** 14	**14.** 20
15. 28	**16.** 30	**17.** 35	**18.** 42

Identify the first five multiples for each number. See Example 2 (p. 177)

19. 1	**20.** 3	**21.** 5	**22.** 6
23. 7	**24.** 8	**25.** 9	**26.** 11

Identify all of the factors that are related to each array.

27.

28.

29. A chameleon eats 6 crickets a day. How many crickets does a chameleon eat in one week? in 8, 9, 10, and 11 days?

30. Pedro walks his dog 3 times a day. How many times does Pedro walk his dog in one week? in 10, 11, or 12 days?

31. There are 50 stars on the American flag. One way the stars can be arranged is a 5 × 10 array. Identify two more ways to arrange the stars.

32. There are 24 cans of soup on a shelf. One way the cans can be displayed is in a 4 × 6 array. Identify two more ways the cans can be displayed.

Real-World PROBLEM SOLVING

Science A comet named Kohoutek can be seen every 6 years.

33. How old is a person who has seen the comet 4, 5, 6, or 7 times if they first saw the comet when they were 6 years old?

34. Warren is 10 years old. His dad is 38 years old, and his mom is 36 years old. Find the total number of times Warren and his parents could have seen the comet.

35. Suppose the comet can be seen every 4 years. Would your answer to Exercise 34 change? Explain.

H.O.T. Problems

36. OPEN ENDED List three numbers that have 2 and 3 as factors.

37. CHALLENGE Identify the number less than 144 with the most factors.

38. WRITING IN ►MATH A fourth grade class is having a class picture taken for the yearbook. There are 24 students in the class. Explain why standing in 1 row of 24 is not the best way for the students to be arranged for the picture.

PASS Practice 4-2.3, 5-2.7

39. In which number sentence does 9 make the equation true? (Lesson 4-8)

  A $3 \times \blacksquare \times 4 = 108$

  B $3 \times \blacksquare \times 7 = 108$

  C $3 \times \blacksquare \times 9 = 108$

  D $4 \times \blacksquare \times 7 = 108$

40. Which number has more than 6 factors? (Lesson 4-9)

  F 6

  G 12

  H 15

  J 360

Spiral Review

Multiply. (Lesson 4-8)

41. $2 \times 7 \times 3$

42. $3 \times 5 \times 4$

43. $11 \times 5 \times 2$

For Exercises 44 and 45, use the picture at the right. Identify the operation you used. (Lesson 4-7)

44. The number of marbles each player gets is shown. There are 5 people who want to play the game. How many marbles do they need in all?

45. There are 30 marbles on the game board at the start of a game. How many players are there?

Algebra Find the value of each if ⭐ = 11 and ☀ = 12. (Lesson 4-6)

46. ⭐ × 6

47. 132 ÷ ☀

48. ☀ × ⭐

SC Math Online macmillanmh.com
- STUDY TO GO
- Vocabulary Review

FOLDABLES Study Organizer — GET READY to Study

Be sure the following Key Vocabulary words and Key Concepts are written in your Foldable.

Relate × and ÷
Properties and Rules
Facts Through 5
Facts Through 10
Multiply with 11 and 12
Multiply Three Numbers
Factors & Multiples

BIG Ideas

Relate Multiplication and Division (p. 147)

- A **fact family** is a set of four related multiplication and division facts.

$$3 \times 4 = 12 \qquad 4 \times 3 = 12$$
$$12 \div 4 = 3 \qquad 12 \div 3 = 4$$

Multiplication Properties (pp. 150–151)

$3 \times 4 = 4 \times 3$ — Commutative Property

$3 \times 0 = 0$ — Zero Property

$3 \times 1 = 3$ — Identity Property

$3 \times (4 \times 2) = (3 \times 4) \times 2$ — Associative Property

Factors and Multiples (pp. 176–177)

- Two or more numbers that are multiplied together to form a product are called **factors**.

  factors of 6: 1, 2, 3, and 6

- A **multiple** of a number is the product of that number and any whole number.

  multiples of 7: 0, 7, 14, 21, …

Key Vocabulary

Associative Property of Multiplication (p. 150)

Commutative Property of Multiplication (p. 150)

Distributive Property of Multiplication (p. 166)

factor (p. 176)

multiple (p. 177)

Vocabulary Check

Complete each sentence with the correct vocabulary word.

1. Two or more numbers that are multiplied together to form a product are called ____?____ .

2. The ____?____ says that the order of the factors does not change the product when multiplying.

3. The ____?____ says that you can multiply the addends of a sum by a number and then add the products.

4. A(n) ____?____ of a number is the product of that number and any whole number.

Lesson-by-Lesson Review

4-1 **Relate Multiplication and Division** (pp. 147–149)

4-2.3,
4-2.5

Example 1
Write a fact family for the array.

$2 \times 4 = 8$
$4 \times 2 = 8$
$8 \div 4 = 2$
$8 \div 2 = 4$

Example 2
Write a fact family for the numbers 3, 5, and 15.

$3 \times 5 = 15$ $5 \times 3 = 15$
$15 \div 3 = 5$ $15 \div 5 = 3$

Example 3
Stefanie and Eva want to share the shells that they collected on their trip to the beach. They have 18 shells in all. Use related facts and draw an array that will help them decide how they can divide their shells evenly.

$2 \times 9 = 18$
$9 \times 2 = 18$
$18 \div 2 = 9$
$18 \div 9 = 2$

So, each girl will have 9 shells.

Write a fact family for each array or set of numbers.

5. 3, 7, 21   **6.** 9, 5, 45

7.

8.

Algebra Solve. Use a related multiplication or division fact.

9. $4 \times 3 = $ ■   **10.** $5 \times 6 = $ ■

11. $36 \div 4 = $ ■   **12.** $40 \div 8 = $ ■

13. Lonzo bought four packs of trading cards. If there are eight cards in each pack, how many trading cards did Lonzo buy?

14. Andrea needs to read a book with 25 chapters. How many chapters will she need to read each day to finish the book in 5 days?

4-2 Algebra: Multiplication Properties and Division Rules (pp. 150–153)

4-1.3,
4-1.2

Example 4
Identify the property shown by
$9 \times 1 = 9$.

A number is multiplied by 1, and the product is the number. This is the Identity Property of Multiplication.

Example 5
Complete $(5 \times 2) \times 3 = 5 \times (\blacksquare \times 3)$. Identify the property used.

$(5 \times 2) \times 3 = 5 \times (2 \times 3)$

The way in which the factors are grouped does not change the product.

This is the Associative Property of Multiplication.

Identify the property or rule shown by each number sentence.

15. $12 \div 12 = 1$ **16.** $3 \times 6 = 6 \times 3$

Algebra Copy and complete each number sentence. Identify the property or rule used.

17. $5 \div \blacksquare = 1$ **18.** $\blacksquare \div 14 = 0$

19. David has soccer practice for 3 hours each night. Sofia has softball practice for 2 hours each night. Will David and Sofia practice for the same amount of time in 5 nights? Use a multiplication property to justify your answer.

4-3 Multiply and Divide Facts Through 5 (pp. 154–157)

4-2.3,
4-2.5

Example 6
Find 4×5.

You can use an area model to find 4×5.

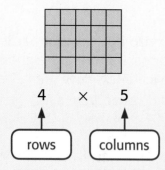

4   ×   5

↑   ↑

rows   columns

Count the squares. There is a total of 20 squares.

Multiply or divide.

20. 4×4 **21.** 5×3

22. $6 \div 3$ **23.** $9\overline{)18}$

Algebra Complete each number sentence.

24. $\blacksquare \times 3 = 6$ **25.** $4 \times \blacksquare = 32$

26. $56 \div \blacksquare = 8$ **27.** $44 \div \blacksquare = 11$

28. Algebra If ☆ = 2, then what is

☆ + ☆ + ☆ + ☆ + ☆ ?

4-4 **Problem-Solving Skill:** **Choose an Operation** (pp. 158–159)

Example 7
There are 9 rows on the bleachers. Each row holds 10 people. How many people can sit in the bleachers at once?

Understand

What facts do you know?
- There are 9 rows.
- There are 10 seats per row.

What do you need to find?
- The number of people that can sit in the bleachers at a time.

Plan There are groups with the same number in each group. So, multiply the number of rows by the number of seats per row.

Solve Multiply to find the answer.

$$9 \times 10 = 90$$

rows — seats per row

So, 90 people can sit on the bleachers at a time.

Check Look back. Use division to check the answer. Since $90 \div 10 = 9$, the answer is correct.

Tell which operation you would use to solve each problem. Then solve.

29. Lyn spent $80 on 10 concert tickets. Two tickets were for the front row. How many tickets did she buy for each of the other sections?

Smooth Jazz Concert	
Front row seats	$15
Center section	$10
Side sections	$5

30. Measurement Mike's vacation is 2 weeks long. Nina's vacation is 3 weeks longer than Mike's. How long is Nina's vacation?

31. Gavin purchased one bus ticket. He paid with a $10 bill. How much change did he get back?

Bus Tickets
1 for $5
2 for $10
3 for $15

32. There are 5 members in the band who play the drums. Three times as many members play the flute. How many members play the flute?

33. West Elementary has 5 fourth grade classes. Each glass made 12 posters. If 10 posters were destroyed before they could be put up on the wall, how many posters are there in all on the wall?

Chapter 4 Study Guide and Review **183**

4-2.3,
4-2.5

Example 8
Find 4 × 7.

Make an area model to represent 4 × 7.

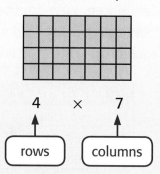

4   ×   7

↑   ↑

rows   columns

There are 28 squares in all.

So, 4 × 7 = 28.

Multiply or divide.

34. 4 × 8   **35.** 9 × 6

36. 10 ÷ 2   **37.** 90 ÷ 9

38. Spencer sold 9 magazine subscriptions to make money for his club. Each magazine subscription costs $7. How much money did Spencer collect?

39. Mr. Dunn has 6 rows of desks in his classroom. There are 5 desks in each row. How many desks are in Mr. Dunn's classroom?

4-2.3,
4-2.5

Example 9
Marina has scored 9 points on each of 11 quizzes. How many points has she scored in all?

Think of 9 × 11 as (9 × 10) + (9 × 1).

10   +   1

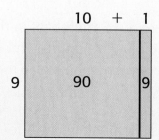

9   90   9

9 × 11 = (9 × 10) + (9 × 1)
   =   90   +   9
   =   99

So, Marina has scored 99 points.

Multiply or divide.

40. 72 ÷ 8   **41.**   12
                              × 6

42. 12)‾84   **43.** 12 × 9

Compare. Use >, <, or =.

44. 108 ÷ 12 ● 88 ÷ 8

45. 12 × 6 ● 8 × 10

46. 36 ÷ 3 ● 6 × 2

47. Kirsten's parents go to the grocery store once a week. How many times do they go to the grocery store in one year?

4-7 **Problem-Solving Investigation: Choose a Strategy** (pp. 170–171)

4-2.3,
4-2.5

Example 10
Carlo wants to buy a frozen yogurt. The flavors of yogurt are vanilla, chocolate, or strawberry. The yogurt comes in a dish or on a cone. How many choices does he have?

Understand

What facts do you know?

• The yogurt flavors are vanilla, chocolate, and strawberry.

• Yogurt comes in a dish or on a cone.

What do you need to find?

• How many yogurt choices Carlo has.

Plan Make a table.

Solve

Flavor	Cone	Dish
Vanilla	X	X
Chocolate	X	X
Strawberry	X	X

Carlo has 6 choices for his yogurt.

Check There are 3 flavors and two choices for each flavor. So, Carlo has 6 choices. The answer is correct.

Use the make a table strategy or choose an operation to solve each problem.

48. Amy wants to buy two dolls. Each doll costs $16. What is the total cost of the dolls?

49. Mr. Sullivan bought pizza for the reading club. Each pizza had 10 slices. How many pizzas did he buy if there were 120 slices?

50. Twyla worked five days in one week. She worked 40 hours during that week. She worked the same number of hours each day. How many hours did she work each day?

51. Conchita has 25 math problems for homework each day. Use the table to find how many problems she completes in five days.

Day	Problems Completed
1	25
2	50
3	75
4	▓
5	▓

52. **Measurement** Bradley has 3 tap dancing lessons each week. Each lesson is 2 hours long. How many hours of lessons will Bradley have completed in 4 weeks?

4-8 **Algebra: Multiply Three Numbers** (pp. 172–174)

4-2.3

Example 11
Find 3 × 5 × 4.

There are two ways to group the numbers.

One Way	Another Way
Multiply 3 × 5 first.	Multiply 5 × 4 first.
3 × **5** × 4	3 × **5** × 4
(3 × 5) × 4	3 × (5 × 4)
15 × 4	3 × 20
60	60

So, 3 × 5 × 4 = 60.

Multiply.

53. 6 × 2 × 3   **54.** 2 × 4 × 9

55. 2 × 8 × 4   **56.** 5 × 1 × 11

Algebra Copy and complete each number sentence.

57. ■ × 7 × 3 = 42

58. 4 × ■ × 3 = 108

59. Jason goes to the park for 2 hours a day, 5 days a week. How many hours will he spend in the park in a four-week month?

4-9 **Factors and Multiples** (pp. 176–179)

5-2.7

Example 12
Find all of the factors of 6.

Think of number pairs that result in a product of 6.

1 × 6

2 × 3

So, the factors of 6 are 1, 2, 3, and 6.

Example 13
Identify the first five multiples of 4.

Multiples of 4: 0, 4, 8, 12, 16, 20, 24, ...

The first five multiples of 4 are 0, 4, 8, 12, and 16.

Find all of the factors of each number.

60. 8   **61.** 12

62. 16   **63.** 28

Identify the first five multiples for each number.

64. 3   **65.** 5

66. 8   **67.** 10

68. Lora is arranging her 18 snow globes on a shelf. Write the different ways she can arrange the snow globes.

69. Glenn reads 11 pages in his book each day. How many pages will he read in one week? in 9, 10, or 11 days?

For Exercises 1–3, tell whether each statement is *true* or *false*.

1. Two or more numbers that are multiplied together to form a product are called multiples.

2. Factors are numbers that do not divide into a whole number evenly.

Algebra Compare. Use >, <, or =.

3. $2 \times 7 \times 3$ ■ $8 \times 3 \times 4$

4. $5 \times 3 \times 9$ ■ $4 \times 2 \times 5$

5. There are 5 boxes of paints on an art store shelf. Each box contains one dozen colors. How many paint colors are on the shelf?

Find all of the factors of each number.

6. 27   7. 36

8. **MULTIPLE CHOICE** Which of the following numbers will make the number sentence true?

$$4 \times ■ \times 5 = 180$$

A 7   **C** 9

B 8   **D** 10

9. Write a fact family for the array.

Algebra Find the value of each number sentence if ♥ **= 5 and** ☺ **= 10.**

10. ♥ $\times 8$ 11. ☺ $\div 5$

Algebra Copy and complete each number sentence. Identify the property or rule used.

12. ■ $\times 7 = 7 \times 4$ 13. ■ $\div 12 = 0$

14. Identify all of the factors related to the array.

Identify the first five multiples for each number.

15. 7   16. 9

Multiply.

17. $6 \times 3 \times 12$ 18. $4 \times 2 \times 7$

Divide.

19. $33 \div 11$ 20. $36 \div 6$

21. **MULTIPLE CHOICE** Which number has more than six factors?

F 6   **H** 15

G 12   **J** 64

22. **WRITING IN ►MATH** Explain how multiplication and division are related.

PART 1 — **Multiple Choice**

Read each question. Then fill in the correct answer on the answer sheet provided by your teacher or on a sheet of paper.

1. Mrs. Park has 35 students. She puts 7 students in each group. How many groups are there?

   A 4   **C** 6

   B 5   **D** 7

2. The table below shows the number of miles Neil biked during June. About how many miles did he bike in all?

Neil's Biking Distance for June	
Week	**Number of Miles**
1	39
2	52
3	46
4	53

   F 150 miles   **H** 190 miles

   G 175 miles   **J** 210 miles

3. Which of the following statements is true?

   A The only factors of 3 are 1 and 3.

   B The only factors of 4 are 1 and 4.

   C The only factors of 6 are 1 and 6.

   D The only factors of 10 are 1 and 10.

4. Which of these is another way to write the number 3,003,013?

   F three million, 3 hundred, thirteen

   G three million, 3 thousand, thirteen

   H three hundred thousand, thirteen

   J thirty million, thirty thousand, thirteen

5. Which of the following has the greatest value?

   A 297,503   **C** 457,650

   B 329,450   **D** 479,350

6. A drawer has 6 white, 2 blue, and 4 brown socks. If a sock is picked at random, what is the probability it will be brown?

   F certain   **H** unlikely

   G likely   **J** impossible

7. Which pair of numbers correctly completes this equation?

   $$\bigcirc \times 10 = \square$$

   A $\bigcirc$ 5 and $\boxed{50}$

   B $\bigcirc$ 6 and $\boxed{9}$

   C $\bigcirc$ 2 and $\boxed{200}$

   D $\bigcirc$ 3 and $\boxed{15}$

8. Ajay wants to use one color pencil and one color crayon to make a drawing.

Pencil Colors	Crayon Colors
red	brown
blue	black
green	

Which of the following is possible if Ajay chooses one color pencil and one color crayon?

F red and green

G blue and purple

H green and brown

J blue and green

9. Which number is 10,000 less than 78,305?

A 68,305   **C** 78,205

B 77,305   **D** 88,305

10. Which of these is another way to write the product of 12 × 5?

F 1 × 6 × 5

G 2 × 6 × 5

H 3 × 6 × 5

J 6 × 6 × 5

PART 2 Short Response

Record your answers on the answer sheet provided by your teacher or on a sheet of paper.

11. Kyra bought 72 eggs at the grocery store for the school breakfast. The eggs come in cartons of 12. How many cartons of eggs did Kyra buy?

12. Write a fact family for the array.

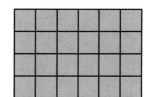

PART 3 Extended Response

Record your answers on the answer sheet provided by your teacher or on a sheet of paper.

13. How many more students prefer football and baseball than basketball and soccer? Explain your reasoning.

Favorite Sport	
Sport	**Number of Students**
Baseball	9
Basketball	8
Football	12
Soccer	6

NEED EXTRA HELP?													
If You Missed Question...	1	2	3	4	5	6	7	8	9	10	11	12	13
Go to Lesson...	4-5	2-2	4-9	1-2	1-4	3-9	4-5	3-8	2-5	4-8	4-6	4-1	2-5
SC Academic Standards	4-2.5	3-2.3	5-2.7	4-2.6	3-2.1	4-6.6	4-2.3	4-6.7	3-2.3	4-2.3	4-2.5	4-2.3	3-2.3

Describe Algebraic Patterns

BIG Idea **What are expressions and equations?**

An **expression** is a combination of variables, numbers, and at least one operation. An **equation** is a number sentence that contains an equals sign (=), showing that two expressions are equal.

Example A tiger can live x years in the wild and 5 years longer than that in a zoo. The equation below can be used to find how long a tiger could live in the wild if it could live 20 years in a zoo.

$$x \quad + \quad 5 \quad = \quad 20$$

years in wild   years in zoo

What will I learn in this chapter?

- Identify, describe, and extend patterns.
- Write and find the value of expressions.
- Write and solve equations.
- Find and use a rule to write an equation.
- Identify extra or missing information.

Key Vocabulary

expression

parentheses

equation

pattern

 **SC Math Online**   **Student Study Tools**
at macmillanmh.com

FOLDABLES®
Study Organizer

Make this Foldable to help you organize information about describing algebraic patterns. Begin with a piece of 11″ × 17″ paper.

① **Fold** lengthwise 3″ from the bottom.

② **Fold** the paper in half.

③ **Open** and staple on either side to form pockets.

④ **Label** as shown. Take notes on index cards.

Expressions | Equations

ARE YOU READY for Chapter 5?

You have two ways to check prerequisite skills for this chapter.

Option 2

SC Math Online › Take the Chapter Readiness Quiz at macmillanmh.com.

Option 1

Complete the Quick Check below.

QUICK Check

Find the missing number. (Prior Grade)

1. $8 + \blacksquare = 11$

2. $\blacksquare + 5 = 9$

3. $6 + \blacksquare = 15$

4. $13 - \blacksquare = 7$

5. $\blacksquare - 4 = 8$

6. $18 - \blacksquare = 16$

7. Use the number sentence $12 + 15 + \blacksquare = 36$ to find how many books Tony read in August.

8. What property is illustrated by $6 + 5 = 5 + 6$?

Summer Reading Club	
Month	**Number of Books Read**
June	12
July	15
August	$\blacksquare$

Find the value of each expression. (Prior Grade)

9. $8 + 1 + 6$

10. $7 + 2 - 3$

11. $2 + 10 - 6$

12. $11 + 6 - 6$

13. $12 - 3 + 4$

14. $16 + 4 - 10$

Identify each pattern. Then find the next number in the pattern. (Prior Grade)

15. 3, 6, 9, 12, 15

16. 7, 12, 17, 22, 27

17. 23, 19, 15, 11, 7

18. Each baseball uniform needs 3 buttons. Copy and complete the table to find how many buttons are needed for 12 uniforms.

Uniforms	3	6	9	12
Buttons	9	18	27	$\blacksquare$

Addition and Subtraction Expressions

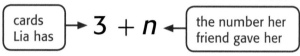
GET READY to Learn

Lia has 3 baseball cards. Her friend gave her some more. You can show the number of cards Lia now has by using the expression below.

cards Lia has → $3 + n$ ← the number her friend gave her

An **expression** like $3 + n$ is a statement with numbers and/or variables, and at least one operation. A variable can represent the unknown value. You can find the value of an expression if you know the value of the variable.

Real-World EXAMPLE   Find Value of an Expression

① **ALGEBRA If Lia's friend gives her 5 baseball cards, how many cards will she have?**

You need to find the value of $3 + n$ when $n = 5$.

$3 + n$ Write the expression.

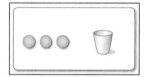

$3 + 5$ Replace n with 5.

8 Add 3 and 5.

So, the value of $3 + n$ when $n = 5$ is 8.

Lia will have 8 baseball cards.

Some expressions contain parentheses, ( ). The **parentheses** tell you which operation to perform first.

EXAMPLE Find the Value of an Expression

2 Find the value of 12 − (r + 2) if r = 7.

12 − (**r** + 2)   Write the expression.

12 − (**7** + 2)   Replace r with 7.

12 −   9   Find (7 + 2) first.

3   Next, find 12 − 9.

Real-World EXAMPLE Write an Expression

3 **ALGEBRA Latisha made 3 fewer baskets than Felisa. Write an expression for the number of baskets Latisha made.**

Words	3 fewer baskets than Felisa
Symbol	Define a variable. Let k represent the baskets Felisa made.
Expression	k − 3

So, Latisha made k − 3 baskets.

✓ CHECK What You Know

Find the value of each expression if x = 4 and m = 8. See Examples 1 and 2 (pp. 193–194)

1. x + 2

2. 19 − m

3. 8 − (x + 1)

Write an expression for each situation. See Example 3 (p. 194)

4. two more than k

5. 44 minus y

6. the sum of 17 and z

Measurement The length of a condor is 7 inches more than the length of a bald eagle.

7. If a bald eagle is 12 inches, what is the length of a condor?

8. Talk About It   Describe a situation that could be represented by x − 6.

Find the value of each expression if $y = 9$ and $b = 5$. See Examples 1 and 2 (pp. 193–194)

9. $y + 2$ **10.** $b + 9$ **11.** $y - 4$ **12.** $11 - b$

13. $y + 20$ **14.** $14 + b$ **15.** $8 - b$ **16.** $12 - y$

17. $(y - 3) + 7$ **18.** $15 - (b + 1)$ **19.** $(y + 8) - 5$ **20.** $b + (17 - 9)$

21. $(y - 5) + 23$ **22.** $(b - 2) + 8$ **23.** $36 + (y - 1)$ **24.** $(25 - 5) + y$

Write an expression for each situation. See Example 3 (p. 194)

25. three more than t

26. the sum of d and six

27. ten subtracted from m

28. the difference of x and fifty-six

29. the sum of a and seven

30. thirteen more than n

31. the sum of w and 5 subtracted from 16

32. the sum of c and 23 subtracted from 100

Brock had 3 cats. One of the cats had kittens. See Example 3 (p. 194)

33. Define a variable. Then write an expression for the number of cats and kittens Brock has now.

34. Using the expression above, if the one cat has 4 kittens, how many cats will Brock have?

Cole has 5 fewer soccer cards than his brother. See Example 3 (p. 194)

35. Define a variable. Then write an expression for the number of cards Cole has.

36. Using the expression above, if Cole's brother has 15 cards, how many cards does Cole have?

H.O.T. Problems

37. OPEN ENDED Describe a real-world situation for $12 - a$.

38. WHICH ONE DOESN'T BELONG? Identify the expression that does not belong with the other three. Explain your reasoning.

$$3 - x \qquad 2 + 5 \qquad 4 - y \qquad z + 1$$

39. WRITING IN ►MATH Explain what a variable means in an expression.

Algebra Activity for 5-2
Addition and Subtraction Equations

An **equation** is a sentence like $4 + 5 = 9$ that contains an equals sign ($=$). The equals sign shows that the expressions on each side of it are equal. Equations sometimes have a missing number.

$$4 + x = 9 \qquad 10 - m = 6 \qquad k - 1 = 7$$

When you find the value of the missing number that makes the equation true, you **solve** the equation.

MAIN IDEA

I will explore addition and subtraction equations.

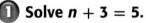

SC Academic Standards

4-3.5 Apply procedures to find the value of an unknown letter or symbol **in a whole-number equation.**

You Will Need
counters
cups

ACTIVITY

1 **Solve $n + 3 = 5$.**

Step 1 **Model the expression on the left side.**

To model $n + 3$, use a cup to show n and 3 counters.

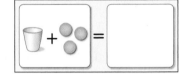

Step 2 **Model the expression on the right side.**

Place 5 counters on the right to show 5. An equals sign shows that both sides are the same.

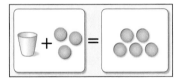

Step 3 **Find the value of n.**

Put enough counters in the cup so that the number of counters on each side of the equals sign is the same.

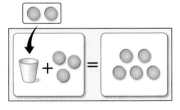

The value of n that makes $n + 3 = 5$ true is 2. So, $n = 2$.

You can also use counters to model equations involving subtraction.

ACTIVITY

2 Solve $x - 4 = 2$.

Step 1 **Model $x - 4 = 2$.**

Use a cup and counters to show $x - 4 = 2$.

Step 2 **Find the value of x.**

Think how many counters need to be placed in the cup so that when 4 are taken away, 2 will be left.

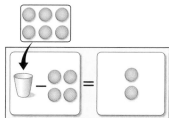

The number of counters in the cup is the missing number. So, the value of x that makes this equation true is 6. So, $x = 6$.

Think About It

1. How would you model $k + 2 = 9$?

2. What is the value of k in $k + 2 = 9$?

3. Explain how to check your answer.

CHECK What You Know

Write an equation for each model. Then find the value of n.

4.

5.

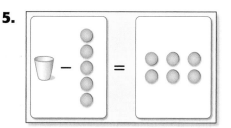

Solve each equation. Use models if needed.

6. $b + 3 = 8$ **7.** $14 - f = 8$ **8.** $17 - h = 12$ **9.** $k + 9 = 19$

10. **WRITING IN ►MATH** Explain the difference between an expression and an equation. Give an example of each.

Wendy downloaded 4 songs on Monday. After she downloaded some more songs on Tuesday, she had a total of 9 songs. How many songs did she download on Tuesday?

MAIN IDEA

I will solve addition and subtraction equations.

SC Academic Standards

4-3.5 Apply procedures to find the value of an unknown letter or symbol **in a whole-number equation.**

New Vocabulary

equation

solve

SC Math Online

macmillanmh.com
• Extra Examples
• Personal Tutor
• Self-Check Quiz

In the previous Explore Activity, you **solved equations** using models. Equations can also be solved mentally.

Real-World EXAMPLE   Solve Addition Equations

1. **MUSIC** How many songs did Wendy download on Tuesday?

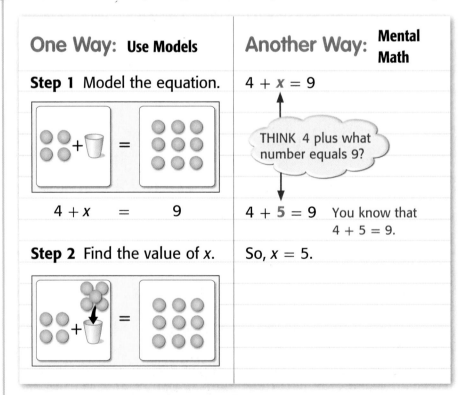

One Way: Use Models	Another Way: Mental Math
Step 1 Model the equation.	$4 + x = 9$
	THINK 4 plus what number equals 9?
$4 + x = 9$	$4 + 5 = 9$ You know that $4 + 5 = 9$.
Step 2 Find the value of x.	So, $x = 5$.

So, $x = 5$. Wendy downloaded 5 songs on Tuesday.

EXAMPLE Solve Subtraction Equations

2 **Solve $18 - y = 13$.**

$18 - y = 13$	18 minus what number equals 13?
$18 - \mathbf{5} = 13$	You know that $18 - 5 = 13$.
$y = 5$	

So, the value of y is 5.

Real-World EXAMPLE Write and Solve Equations

3 **ALGEBRA Garcia had 9 video games. He bought some more video games and now has a total of 12. How many video games did he buy?**

Write and solve an equation.

Words	9 video games plus some more equals 12.
Symbol	Let v represent the additional video games.
Expression	$9 \quad + \quad v \quad = \quad 12$

$9 + v = 12$	9 plus what number equals 12?
$9 + 3 = 12$	You know that $9 + 3 = 12$.
$v = 3$	

So, $v = 3$. Garcia bought 3 more video games.

CHECK What You Know

Solve each equation. See Examples 1 and 2 (pp. 198–199)

1. $5 + c = 11$ **2.** $k + 9 = 17$ **3.** $13 + n = 20$

4. $8 - h = 4$ **5.** $14 - f = 9$ **6.** $m - 12 = 12$

7. Keisha scored 14 points in the first half of a basketball game. At the end of the game, she had a total of 36 points. Write and solve an equation to find how many points she scored in the second half of the game. See Example 3 (p. 199)

8. Talk About It   Explain how to solve $k - 3 = 12$.

Solve each equation. See Examples 1 and 2 (pp. 198–199)

9. $1 + a = 4$

10. $d + 4 = 6$

11. $6 + f = 10$

12. $h + 8 = 15$

13. $k + 10 = 17$

14. $9 + n = 20$

15. $4 - b = 2$

16. $m - 5 = 6$

17. $7 - r = 2$

18. $w - 8 = 12$

19. $9 = 15 - y$

20. $11 = z - 12$

Write and solve an equation for each situation. See Example 3 (p. 199)

21. A number plus 8 equals 19.

22. The sum of 11 and a number is 35.

23. Nine subtracted from a number equals 12.

24. Fifteen less than a number is 15.

Real-World PROBLEM SOLVING

Science Some mammals live as long as humans. The table shows the average number of years some mammals can live.

25. Write an equation to represent a killer whale's life span minus x years equals the African elephant's life span. Find x.

26. Write an equation to represent a human's life span plus another mammal's life span (y) equals 111. What is the value of y? Which animal's life span does the y stand for?

Mammals with Longest Lives	
Mammal	**Years Lived**
Killer whale	90
Blue whale	80
Human	76
African elephant	70
Gorilla	35

Source: *Scholastic Book of World Records*

H.O.T. Problems

27. FIND THE ERROR Caleb and Adriana say that the two equations have the same solution for *n*. Are they correct? Explain.

Caleb

$9 - n = 5$

Adriana

$5 + n = 9$

28. **WRITING IN ►MATH** Write one or two sentences explaining how to solve an equation.

29. What is the value of the expression $16 - (8 + x)$ if $x = 2$? (Lesson 5-1)

A 6

B 10

C 20

D 22

30. What is the value of the expression below if $y = 5$? (Lesson 5-2)

$$y + (22 - 7)$$

F 20

G 21

H 22

J 24

31. Ann sweeps the floor every third day. If she sweeps the floor on September 10, on which of the following days will she NOT have to sweep the floor? (Lesson 5-2)

		September				
Sunday	Monday	Tuesday	Wednesday	Thursday	Friday	Saturday
	1	2	3	4	5	6
7	8	9	10	11	12	13
14	15	16	17	18	19	20
21	22	23	24	25	26	27
28	29	30				

A September 13

B September 19

C September 23

D September 28

Spiral Review

32. Write an expression for *three less than n*. (Lesson 5-1)

Find all the factors of each number. (Lesson 4-9)

33. 36

34. 45

35. 100

36. A giant panda bear eats 84 pounds of bamboo a day. Copy and complete the table to find out the total amount of bamboo the bear will eat in a week. (Lesson 3-3)

Day	1	2	▨	4	5	▨	7
Bamboo	84	▨	252	336	▨	504	▨

37. Measurement The longest airport runway in the world is 5,000 meters. The shortest airport runway is 533 meters. What is the difference in the lengths of these two runways? (Lesson 2-5)

Compare. Use $>$, $<$, or $=$. (Lesson 1-4)

38. 4,714 ● 4,741

39. 64,962 ● 64,926

Problem-Solving Skill

MAIN IDEA I will identify extra or missing information.

 SCAS 4-3.5 **Apply procedures to find the value of an unknown letter** or symbol **in a whole-number equation.**

Trina is making friendship bracelets to sell for $2 each. Last week, she sold 63 bracelets. Two weeks ago, she sold 21 bracelets. How many more bracelets did Trina sell last week than two weeks ago?

Understand	**What facts do you know?** • Trina sells friendship bracelets for $2 each. • She sold 63 bracelets last week. • She sold 21 bracelets two weeks ago. **What do you need to find?** • Find how many more bracelets Trina sold last week than two weeks ago.
Plan	Once you identify the information needed to solve the problem, you can write an equation. Look for any extra information.
Solve	Subtract 21 from 63. You do not need to know how much the bracelets cost. This is extra information. last week two weeks ago $$63 - 21 = n$$ $$42 = n$$ So, Trina sold 42 more bracelets last week than the week before.
Check	Look back. Check the subtraction with addition. Since $21 + 42 = 63$, the answer is correct.

Refer to the problem on the previous page.

1. Explain why you do not need to know the cost of the bracelets.

2. Suppose the problem did not include how many bracelets were sold last week. Could you solve it? Explain.

3. If you need to find the difference in profit between the two weeks, is there enough information to solve the problem?

4. Find the difference in profit between the two weeks.

▶ PRACTICE the Skill

SCAS • PASS
Extra Practice, p. R13

Identify any missing or extra information. Then solve if possible.

5. Chango the monkey eats 4 apples and 3 bananas every day at 12:30 P.M. How much fruit does he eat in a week?

6. Nidia asked her classmates to name their favorite flavor of ice cream. Chocolate received 14 votes, which is 5 more votes than vanilla. How many students liked vanilla?

7. Sheri and two friends want to go to a movie. The movie starts at 2 P.M. How much will it cost for these 3 students to go to the movie?

MOVIE THEATER

Adult Ticket	$6
Student Ticket	$4
Movie Times 10 A.M., 12 P.M., 2 P.M.	

8. **Measurement** Each day, Zoe trains each of her horses for 30 minutes and then rides them for 20 minutes. How much time does Zoe spend with her horses in one day?

9. Candace wants to buy the fish aquarium supplies shown. How much change will she get back?

Scuba Diver

$5

ROCKS

$2

10. Three fourth-grade classes are going on a field trip. How many students are going on a field trip?

11. James and Donna have $18. Each pack of baseball cards costs $3. There are 8 cards in each pack. How many packs can they buy?

12. The Video Depot is having a sale on DVDs. The cost is $27 for 3. How many DVDs can Edgar buy?

13. **WRITING IN ▶ MATH** Explain how you identified any extra or missing information in Exercise 12.

Identify, Describe, and Extend Patterns

MAIN IDEA

I will identify, describe, and extend numeric and nonnumeric patterns.

SC Academic Standards

4-3.1 Analyze numeric, nonnumeric, and repeating patterns involving all operations and decimal patterns through hundredths. *Also addresses 4-3.2.*

New Vocabulary

pattern

rule

SC Math Online

macmillanmh.com

• Extra Examples
• Personal Tutor
• Self-Check Quiz

> **GET READY to Learn**

Carla sells 3 picture frames for $15 and 4 picture frames for $20. If the pattern for the price of the frames remains the same, how much will Carla make if she sells 6 frames?

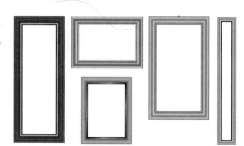

In this situation, there is a pattern in the cost of the frames. A **pattern** is a sequence of numbers, figures, or symbols that follow a **rule**. You can find and extend a pattern.

> **Real-World EXAMPLE**   Complete a Pattern

1. **MONEY How much will Carla make if she sells 6 frames?**
Identify and describe the pattern by dividing the total cost by the number of frames.

Carla sells 3 picture frames for $15, and 4 picture frames for $20.

$15 ÷ 3 = $5
$20 ÷ 4 = $5

So, one picture frame costs $5. The rule is to multiply the number of frames by $5.

Use the rule to extend the pattern.

Number of Frames	1	2	3	4	5	6
Cost	$5	$10	$15	$20	$25	$30

+$5 +$5 +$5 +$5 +$5

So, Carla will make $5 × 6 or $30 if she sells 6 picture frames.

Sometimes, patterns are not easily identified.

Real-World EXAMPLES   Find the Rule

2 **READING** **The chapters in Daniel's book follow a pattern. Identify, describe, and extend the pattern to find how many pages are in the sixth chapter.**

Look at the table to identify and describe the pattern.

The table shows that the odd numbered chapters have 16 pages and the even numbered chapters have 12 pages.

Remember

A pattern can be identified by looking at the relationship among the numbers in the pattern.

Daniel's Book	
Chapter	Ending Page
1	16
2	28
3	44
4	56
5	72
6	▪

+12
+16
+12
+16
+12

3 **What is the page number of the last page in chapter 6?**

Extend the pattern to find the page number of the last page in chapter 6.

The sixth chapter will have 12 pages. So, the last page is 72 + 12, or 84.

Real-World EXAMPLE   Examples and Non-examples

4 **ART** **Alyssa is drawing the figures to the right. If the pattern continues, which of the figures shown below will she draw next?**

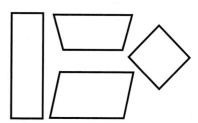

figure A   figure B   figure C   figure D

Identify and describe what the figures Alyssa is drawing have in common.

The figures Alyssa is drawing all have 4 sides. So, she will draw figure C next.

Identify, describe, and extend each pattern. See Examples 1–3 (pp. 204–205)

1. 9, 12, 15, 18, 21, ■   **2.** 5, 6, 4, 5, 3, ■   **3.** 3, 5, 7, 9, 11, ■

4. Marcos reads each day. What is the rule for the pattern shown in his reading log? See Example 3 (p. 205)

Reading Log					
Day	1	2	3	4	5
Time (min)	30	60	90	120	150

5. Talk About It   These are Inexes.

Explain why these are not Inexes.
See Example 4 (p. 205)

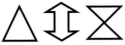

SCAS • PASS
Extra Practice, p. R13

Practice and Problem Solving

Identify, describe, and extend each pattern. See Examples 1–3 (pp. 204–205)

6. 26, 30, 34, 38, 42, ■   **7.** 13, 18, 23, 28, 33, ■   **8.** 8, 8, 6, 6, 4, ■

9. 10, 20, 30, 40, 50, ■   **10.** 28, 24, 28, 24, 28, ■   **11.** 3, 6, 12, 15, 21, ■

12. Explain why 75 is not an example of a number that would be in the number pattern in Exercise 9.

13. Bob swims 10 laps on even numbered dates. He swims 15 laps on odd numbered dates. How many laps has he swum during a month by the sixth?

14. It is recommended to drink 64 fluid ounces of water each day. Below is a pattern to show how many days it would take to drink 448 fluid ounces. Explain how another pattern could be used to find the same answer.

Recommended Water in a Week							
Day	1	2	3	4	5	6	7
Amount (fl oz)	64	128	192	256	320	384	448

+64 +64 +64 +64 +64 +64

H.O.T. Problems

15. OPEN ENDED Create a number pattern involving two operations. Explain your pattern.

16. WRITING IN ►MATH Describe the pattern. What figure comes next?

△ ▷ ▽ ◁ △ ▷ ▽ ◁

Mid-Chapter Check
Lessons 5-1 through 5-4

Find the value of each expression if $x = 2$ and $m = 8$. (Lesson 5-1)

1. $x + 3$

2. $18 - m$

3. $m - (1 + 4)$

4. $(m - 2) + x$

Write an expression for each situation. (Lesson 5-1)

5. three more than k

6. the sum of 27 and z

Amado has 13 more books than Sara. (Lesson 5-1)

7. Define a variable. Then write an expression for the number of books Amado has.

8. If Sara has 8 books, how many does Amado have?

Solve each equation. (Lesson 5-2)

9. $7 + a = 11$

10. $m - 4 = 12$

11. MULTIPLE CHOICE Which number makes the equation true?
(Lesson 5-2)

$$67 + y = 121$$

A 54

C 64

B 56

D 68

Write and solve the equation for the situation. (Lesson 5-2)

12. A number plus 7 equals 19. What is the number?

Identify any missing or extra information. Then solve. (Lesson 5-3)

13. Raekwon bought his lunch every day this week. How much did he spend on lunches this week?

14. Dakota is buying a basketball for $12 and an air pump for $5. She wants to buy a baseball for $6. After purchasing the basketball and pump the cashier gives Dakota $3. How much money did Dakota give the cashier?

15. MULTIPLE CHOICE Extend the pattern in the table. (Lesson 5-4)

Party Supplies						
Tables	2	4	6	8	10	12
Chairs	12	24	36	48	60	▨

F 68

H 72

G 70

J 74

Identify, describe, and extend each pattern. (Lesson 5-4)

16. 4, 9, 14, 19, 24, ▨

17. 41, 34, 27, 20, 13, ▨

18. 12, 10, 13, 11, 14, ▨

19. WRITING IN ►MATH Explain how to extend the pattern below. (Lesson 5-4)

6, 10, 14, 18, 22, ▨

Function Tables: Find a Rule (+, −)

Mr. Mathis put an input number into his *function* machine. The function machine took the input number and performed one or more operations on it to get an output number.

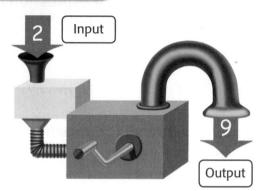

Input 2

Output 9

MAIN IDEA

I will find and use rules to write addition and subtraction equations.

SC Academic Standards

4-3.3 Use a rule to complete a sequence or a table.

4-3.4 Translate among, letters, symbols, and words to represent quantities in simple mathematical expressions or **equations.**

New Vocabulary

function

SC Math Online

macmillanmh.com
• Extra Examples
• Personal Tutor
• Self-Check Quiz

A relationship where one quantity depends upon another quantity is called a **function**. You can use a rule to write an equation that describes a pattern between input and output numbers.

EXAMPLES Find an Addition Rule

1. **Write an equation that describes the pattern in the table.**

Input (x)	Output (y)
2	9
4	11
6	13
8	■
10	■
12	■

Pattern: $2 + 7 = 9$
$4 + 7 = 11$
$6 + 7 = 13$

Rule: Add 7.

Equation: $x + 7 = y$

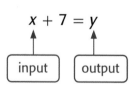

input   output

2. **Use the equation to find the next three numbers.**

Find the next three numbers when the input (x) is 8, 10, and 12.

$x + 7 = y$ $x + 7 = y$ $x + 7 = y$
$8 + 7 = 15$ $10 + 7 = 17$ $12 + 7 = 19$

So, the next three numbers in the pattern are 15, 17, and 19.

Remember

Always check to make sure the equation works for each pair of numbers in the table.

③ ALGEBRA A pizza shop offers $3 off any order over $10. Write an equation that describes the pattern. Then use the equation to find the next three costs.

Input (c)	Output (d)
$11	$8
$12	$9
$14	$11
$16	▦
$18	▦
$20	▦

Identify the rule and write it as an equation.

Rule: Subtract 3.

Equation: $c - \$3 = d$

                     ↑ input   ↑ output

Find the next three numbers when the input (c) is $16, $18, and $20.

$c - \$3 = d$ $c - \$3 = d$ $c - \$3 = d$
$\$16 - \$3 = \$13$ $\$18 - \$3 = \$15$ $\$20 - \$3 = \$17$

So, the next three amounts are $13, $15, and $17.

CHECK What You Know

Write an equation that describes each pattern. Then use the equation to find the next three numbers.

See Examples 1–3 (pp. 208–209)

1.

Input (a)	5	9	13	17	21	25
Output (b)	9	13	17	▦	▦	▦

2.

Input (m)	11	16	21	26	31	36
Output (n)	2	7	12	▦	▦	▦

3. The amounts a bus company charges to take students on a field trip are shown at the right. How much would it cost for 30, 40, and 50 students to go on a field trip?

Students	Cost ($)
10	$60
20	$70
30	▦
40	▦
50	▦

4. **Talk About It** Explain what you should do if you test a number in an equation and it does not work.

Write an equation that describes each pattern. Then use the equation to find the next three numbers. See Examples 1–3 (pp. 208–209)

5.

Input (f)	3	6	9	12	15	18
Output (h)	6	9	12	■	■	■

6.

Input (s)	2	6	10	14	18	22
Output (t)	15	19	23	■	■	■

7.

Input (v)	16	22	28	34	40	46
Output (w)	5	11	17	■	■	■

8.

Input (g)	14	19	24	29	34	39
Output (h)	9	14	19	■	■	■

Create an input/output table for each equation.

9. $y + 4 = z$ **10.** $t + 11 = v$ **11.** $a - 7 = c$ **12.** $g - 10 = h$

Real-World PROBLEM SOLVING

Money The table shows what a taxi company charges c for every m miles traveled.

13. Use the table to write an equation for this situation.

14. Find the costs of a 20-mile, 25-mile, and 30-mile trip.

15. Use the equation you wrote for Exercise 13 to find the cost of a 60-mile trip.

16. Write an equation for the number of miles traveled and $4 charged for each trip.

17. How much would a 40-mile trip cost?

Taxi Rates	
Input (m)	Output (c)
10	$12
15	$17
20	■
25	■
30	■

H.O.T. Problems

18. OPEN ENDED Write a real-world situation that can be represented by the table.

Input (h)	1	2	3	4	5
Output (m)	$10	$20	■	■	■

19. **WRITING IN ►MATH** Explain how the pattern of the input numbers is related to the pattern of the output numbers.

20. Which of the following describes the rule for this pattern? (Lesson 5-4)

Input (*a*)	Output (*b*)
16	15
18	17
20	19
22	21
24	23
26	25

A Add 4, subtract 3.

B Subtract 4, add 3.

C Subtract 3, add 4.

D Add 3, subtract 5.

21. Each number in Set R is paired with a number in Set S. (Lesson 5-5)

Set R	Set S
2	10
5	13
6	14

The relationship for each pair of numbers is the same. If the number in Set R is 12, how will you find its paired number in Set S?

F Add 8 to 8.

G Subtract 8 from 12.

H Add 8 to 12.

J Subtract 12 from 12.

Spiral Review

Identify, describe, and extend each pattern. (Lesson 5-4)

22. 28, 25, 22, 19, 16, 13

23. 9, 12, 15, 18, 21, 24

Identify any missing or extra information. Then solve if possible. (Lesson 5-3)

24. Callie the cat is two years old. Callie eats treats twice a day. If there are 365 days in a year, how many days old is Callie?

25. Camille scored 12 points in the first half of a basketball game. She scored a total of 26 points at the end of the game. How many points did she score during the second half of the game?

Solve each equation. (Lesson 5-2)

26. $a + 15 = 25$

27. $b - 36 = 4$

28. $12 + c = 26$

Round each number to the given place value. (Lesson 1-6)

29. 16,543; hundreds

30. 2,345; tens

31. 67,343; thousands

Do Flying Squirrels Really Fly?

There are 36 types of flying squirrels. Southern flying squirrels and northern flying squirrels are found in the United States. These squirrels do not actually fly. They glide from tree to tree. These animals climb as high as 30 feet into trees. Then they use their hind legs to push off from branches.

Flying squirrels build their nests in trees, where they collect nuts and berries. They store up to 15,000 nuts in a season. What an appetite.

Southern Flying Squirrel Facts

Length of Body,
including Tail . . . . .14 inches
Length of Tail . . . . .6 inches
Weight of Adult. . . . . .3 ounces
Life Span . . . . .5 years

How Far Flying Squirrels Glide

Height of Squirrel in Tree (ft)	5	10	15	20
Distance of Glide (ft)	11	16	21	26

Did You Know?

Some flying squirrels can glide as far as 1,500 feet!

Real-World Math

Use the information on page 212 to solve each problem.

1. What is the length of a southern flying squirrel's body? Write and find the value of an expression.

2. The length of a northern squirrel's body, including the tail, is 16 inches. Its tail is the same length as a southern squirrel's tail. Write and find the value of an equation to find the length of the northern squirrel's body.

3. A southern flying squirrel lives to be 8 years old. How many years did this squirrel live beyond its average life span?

4. Write a rule that describes how far a flying squirrel will glide when it jumps from a given height.

5. Suppose a squirrel jumps from a tree that is 25 feet tall. How far will the squirrel glide?

6. A squirrel jumps from a tree that is 30 feet tall. Will it glide farther than 40 feet? Explain.

7. What is the difference in gliding distances of a squirrel that jumps from a 40-foot tree and a squirrel that jumps from a 50-foot tree?

Multiplication and Division Expressions

MAIN IDEA

I will write and find the value of multiplication and division expressions.

SC Academic Standards

4-3.4 Translate among, letters, symbols, **and words to represent quantities in simple mathematical expressions** or equations.

SC Math Online

macmillanmh.com

• Extra Examples
• Personal Tutor
• Self-Check Quiz

GET READY to Learn

Liza has 4 cans of tennis balls. The total number of balls can be represented by the expression below.

$$\boxed{\text{cans}} \rightarrow 4 \times n \leftarrow \boxed{\text{balls per can}}$$

Finding the value of multiplication and division expressions is similar to finding the value of addition and subtraction expressions.

Real-World EXAMPLE   Find Value of an Expression

1 TENNIS BALLS If there are 3 balls in each can, what is the total number of tennis balls? Find the value of $4 \times n$ if $n = 3$.

$4 \times n$ Write the expression.

4×3 Replace n with 3.

12 Multiply 4 and 3.

The value of the expression is 12. Liza has 12 tennis balls.

Recall that you perform the operations inside parentheses first.

EXAMPLE   Find the Value of an Expression

2 Find the value of $2 \times (15 \div x)$ if $x = 5$.

$2 \times (15 \div x)$ Write the expression.

$2 \times (15 \div 5)$ Replace x with 5.

$2 \times \quad 3$ Find $(15 \div 5)$ first.

6 Next, find 2×3.

You can write expressions for real-world situations.

Real-World EXAMPLE   Write an Expression

3 MONEY Jorge has *d* dollars to buy airplane models. Write an expression for the number of models Jorge can buy with his money.

Write an expression. You know that Jorge has *d* dollars and that the cost of one model plane is $7.

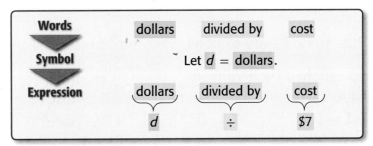

Words	dollars	divided by	cost
Symbol		Let *d* = dollars.	
Expression	dollars	divided by	cost
	d	÷	$7

So, the number of airplane models Jorge can buy is $d \div \$7$.

CHECK What You Know

Find the value of each expression if $a = 3$ and $c = 6$. See Examples 1 and 2 (p. 214)

1. $2 \times a$ **2.** $c \div a$ **3.** $(15 \div a) \times 6$

Write an expression for each situation. See Example 3 (p. 215)

4. 9 times *n*

5. *n* multiplied by 12

6. a number divided by 8

7. 24 divided by a number

For Exercises 8 and 9, use the following information. See Example 3 (p. 215)
Luis has four times as much money as Kyle.

8. Define a variable. Then write an expression for the amount of money Luis has.

9. If Kyle has $8, how much money does Luis have?

10. *Talk About It*   How do you find the value of $9 \times (y \div 4)$ when $y = 20$?

Find the value of each expression if $f = 10$ and $g = 5$.

See Examples 1 and 2 (p. 214)

11. $6 \times g$

12. $f \times 7$

13. $f \div 5$

14. $g \div 5$

15. $g \times f$

16. $f \div g$

17. $4 \times (f \div 2)$

18. $(f \div g) \times 9$

19. $(f \times g) \div 5$

Write an expression for each situation. See Example 3 (p. 215)

20. n multiplied by 5

21. the product of 2 and a number

22. 8 divided by n

23. 18 divided by a number

A teacher has some boxes of pens. Each box contains 8 pens. See Example 3 (p. 215)

24. Define a variable. Then write an expression for the number of pens the teacher has.

25. If the teacher has 9 boxes of pens, how many pens will the teacher have?

Eduardo has some CDs with 9 songs on each of them. See Example 3 (p. 215)

26. Define a variable. Then write an expression for the number of songs that are on the CDs.

27. Eduardo has 5 CDs and lets a friend borrow 2 of his CDs. How many songs will be on the CDs he has left?

South Carolina Data File

The state reptile of South Carolina is the loggerhead sea turtle. This turtle can dive for up to 20 minutes while looking for prey.

28. Write an expression for the total length of n loggerhead sea turtles.

29. **Measurement** Find the total length of 6 loggerhead sea turtles that are laid head to tail.

Loggerhead Sea Turtle Facts	
Maximum length	7 feet
Maximum weight	1,200 pounds

Source: University of Michigan

H.O.T. Problems

30. OPEN ENDED Write a division expression that has a value of 3 if $n = 7$.

31. WRITING IN ►MATH Write a problem that uses the expression $(4 \times n) \div 7$.

Expression Race

Evaluate Expressions

Get Ready!

Players: 2 players

Get Set!

Label 16 index cards as shown.

Go!

- Shuffle the cards. Then spread out the cards facedown. Keep the expression and the variable cards separate.

- Player 1 turns over one expression and one variable card.

- Both players use mental math to find the value of the expression.

- The first player to correctly find the value of the expression gets 1 point.

- Player 2 turns over another expression card. Repeat steps until all of the cards have been used.

- The player with more points wins.

You will need: 16 index cards

$n = 2$	$n = 3$	
$n = 4$	$n = 6$	$n = 12$
$n + 5$	$7 + n$	$n + 11$
$14 - n$	$17 - n$	$20 - n$
$n \times 3$	$7 \times n$	$n \times 9$
$12 \div n$	$24 \div n$	

Problem-Solving Investigation

MAIN IDEA I will choose the best strategy to solve a problem.

SCAS **4-6.3 Organize data in tables,** line graphs, and bar graphs whose scale increments are greater than or equal to 1.

P.S.I. TEAM +

TASHA: My soccer team is raising money by having a car wash. We earn $36 each hour of washing cars.

YOUR MISSION: Find how much money Tasha's soccer team will make in 5 hours.

Understand	The soccer team earns $36 each hour. You need to find how much money the team will make in 5 hours.
Plan	You can make a table that shows how much the team will earn in 1, 2, 3, 4, and 5 hours.
Solve	The table shows how much money the team earns in 1, 2, 3, 4, and 5 hours.

Hours	1	2	3	4	5
Money	$36	$72	$108	$144	$180

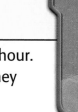

+36   +36   +36   +36

So, Tasha's soccer team will make $180 in 5 hours.

Check	Look back. Start with $180. Subtract $36 five times.

$180 − $36 = $144
$144 − $36 = $108
$108 − $36 = $72
$72 − $36 = $36
$36 − $36 = $0

So, you know the answer is correct.

Use any strategy shown below to solve. Tell what strategy you used.

PROBLEM-SOLVING STRATEGIES
• Make a table.

1. **Algebra** Gigi is planting flowers in her garden in the pattern shown. How many daisies will she have if she plants 24 flowers in one row?

2. Julio is setting up square tables for a party. One person can sit at each side of a table. He connects the tables together to form one long table. He invited 9 friends. How many tables does he need for everyone, including himself?

3. Victor wants to buy CDs that cost $12 each. He has $40. How many CDs can he buy?

4. Russell wants to buy juice, a fruit cup, and a salad for lunch. He has $5. How much change will he get back?

LUNCH MENU

Juice.......$1   Salad........$2
Milk.......50¢   Spaghetti..$2
Fruit cup..50¢

5. **Measurement** Kirk rode his bike to school, which is 2 miles away. After school, he rode to his friend's house, which is 1 mile from school. Then he rode home. If he rode a total of 4 miles, how far does he live from his friend?

6. Della made 2 bowls of fruit punch for a family reunion. Each bowl fills 24 glasses. There are 12 family members at the reunion. How many glasses of punch can each person get?

7. **Algebra** What are the next two figures in the pattern?

8. Polly is making a scrapbook. She is making the pattern shown as a border for one of the pages. How many bones will she need to glue to the page if she uses 36 shapes in all?

9. Darnell has baseball practice four days a week. Practice lasts for two hours each day. How many hours does he practice in four weeks?

10. **WRITING IN ►MATH** Niles's bedtime was 8:00 P.M. in first grade. It was 8:30 P.M. in second grade and 9:00 P.M. in third grade. The answer is 10:00 P.M. What is the question?

Function Tables: Find a Rule (×, ÷)

MAIN IDEA

I will find and use rules to write multiplication and division equations.

SC Academic Standards

4-3.3 Use a rule to complete a sequence or a table.

4-3.4 Translate among, letters, symbols, **and words to represent quantities in simple** mathematical expressions or **equations.**

SC Math Online

macmillanmh.com
• Extra Examples
• Personal Tutor
• Self-Check Quiz

GET READY to Learn

Tracy rakes yards to earn money. If she rakes 2 yards a day, she earns $12. If she rakes 4 yards, she earns $24. If she rakes 6 yards, she earns $36. How much money will she earn if she rakes 8, 10, or 12 yards?

You can write an equation to describe and extend a pattern.

Real-World EXAMPLES   Find a Multiplication Rule

① **MONEY Write an equation that describes the amount of money Tracy earns.**

Show the information in a table. Then look for the pattern that describes the rule.

Yards Raked	Amount Earned ($)
Input (*a*)	Output (*b*)
2	12
4	24
6	36
8	■
10	■
12	■

Pattern: $2 \times 6 = 12$
$4 \times 6 = 24$
$6 \times 6 = 36$

Rule: Multiply by 6.

Equation: $a \times 6 = b$
input   output

② **Use the equation to find how much money Tracy will earn if she rakes 8, 10, and 12 yards.**

$a \times \$6 = b$ $a \times \$6 = b$ $a \times \$6 = b$
$8 \times \$6 = \$48$ $10 \times \$6 = \$60$ $12 \times \$6 = \$72$

So, Tracy will earn $48, $60, and $72.

Real-World EXAMPLES Find a Division Rule

3 **MONEY** The cost of crackers is shown. Write an equation that describes the pattern.

Total Cost ($)	Boxes of Crackers
Input (g)	Output (h)
4	1
8	2
12	3
16	■
20	■
24	■

Look for the pattern that describes the rule.

Pattern: $4 \div 4 = 1$
$8 \div 4 = 2$
$12 \div 4 = 3$

Rule: Divide by 4.

Equation: $g \div 4 = h$
↑ input ↑ output

Remember

Always check to make sure the rule works for each number in the table.

4 Use the equation to find how many boxes you get for $16, $20, or $24.

$g \div 4 = h$ $g \div 4 = h$ $g \div 4 = h$
$16 \div 4 = 4$ $20 \div 4 = 5$ $24 \div 4 = 6$

So, $16, $20, or $24 will buy 4, 5, or 6 boxes of crackers.

CHECK What You Know

Write an equation that describes each pattern. Then use the equation to find the next three numbers. See Examples 1–4 (pp. 220–221)

1.

Input (w)	2	4	6	8	10	12
Output (v)	12	24	36	■	■	■

2.

Input (x)	16	24	32	40	48	56
Output (y)	2	3	4	■	■	■

3. The table shows the cost of movie tickets. How many tickets will you get for $72? See Examples 1–4 (pp. 220–221)

Total Cost	Input (c)	$12	$24	$36	$48	$60	$72
Tickets	Output (t)	2	4	6	■	■	■

4. **Talk About It** How are a rule and an equation alike? How are they different?

Write an equation that describes each pattern. Then use the equation to find the next three numbers. See Examples 1–4 (pp. 220–221)

5.

Input (m)	1	3	5	7	9	11
Output (n)	5	15	25	■	■	■

6.

Input (b)	2	4	6	8	10	12
Output (c)	14	28	42	■	■	■

7.

Input (j)	4	8	12	16	20	24
Output (k)	1	2	3	■	■	■

8.

Input (e)	10	20	30	40	50	60
Output (f)	2	4	6	■	■	■

9. A local sports team sells $6 tickets for $3, $8 tickets for $4, and $10 tickets for $5. Write a rule and equation to find the cost of a $20 ticket.

10. The admission for an art museum costs $5 per person. Make a table to find how much it would cost for 2, 3, 4, 5, and 6 people to attend the exhibit.

Real-World PROBLEM SOLVING

Art Sari makes bead necklaces. The table shows the number of blue beads and green beads Sari uses.

11. Write an equation that describes the relationship between green beads and blue beads.

12. How many green beads does Sari need if she is using 36 blue beads?

13. How many beads does Sari have in all if she has 9 green beads?

Blue Beads	Green Beads
Input (j)	Output (k)
3	1
9	3
15	5
21	■
27	■
33	■

H.O.T. Problems

14. OPEN ENDED Create a table that shows inputs and outputs. Choose a multiplication or division rule for the table. Then choose six input numbers and find the output numbers.

15. CHALLENGE Can both an addition equation and a multiplication equation be written for the number pattern in the table to the right? Explain.

16. **WRITING IN ►MATH** Write a real-world problem that involves a pattern. What equation describes the pattern?

Input (m)	Output (n)
1	2
2	4
3	6

17. What is the value of the expression below if $n = 6$? (Lesson 5-6)

$$9 \times n + 3$$

A 18

B 27

C 57

D 81

18. What is the value of the expression below? (Lesson 5-6)

$$8 \times (9 - 6)$$

F 11   **H** 48

G 24   **J** 66

19. Which equation can be used to describe the pattern in the table? (Lesson 5-8)

Input (a)	Output (b)
1	■
3	9
5	15
7	21
9	27

A $a + 3 = b$

B $a + 6 = b$

C $a \times 3 = b$

D $b \times 3 = a$

Spiral Review

For Exercises 20 and 21, copy and complete each number pattern. (Lesson 5-7)

20. 2, 4, 8, 16, ■, ■, ■

21. 5, 17, 29, 41, ■, ■, ■

Find the value of each expression if $a = 12$ and $b = 3$. (Lesson 5-6)

22. $b \times 6$ **23.** $a \div 4$ **24.** $a \div b$

Write an equation that describes each pattern. Then use the equation to find the next two numbers. (Lesson 5-5)

25.

Input (a)	Output (b)
30	20
24	14
18	8
15	■
16	■

26.

Input (m)	Output (n)
3	15
5	17
7	19
9	■
11	■

Study Guide and Review

SC Math Online > macmillanmh.com
- STUDY TO GO
- Vocabulary Review

FOLDABLES
Study Organizer

GET READY to Study

Be sure the following Key Vocabulary words and Key Concepts are written in your Foldable.

Key Concepts

Expressions

- An **expression** is a combination of variables, numbers, and at least one operation. (p. 193)

$$n - 3$$

Equations

- An **equation** is a number sentence with an equals sign (=), showing that two expressions are equal. (p. 198)

$$n + 8 = 17$$

- An equation can be used to describe the pattern in a table. (p. 208)

Input (*a*)	8	10	15	26	28
Output (*b*)	12	14	19	▪	▪

Rule: Add 4.

Equation: $a + 4 = b$

Key Vocabulary

equation (p. 198)

expression (p. 193)

parentheses (p. 194)

pattern (p. 204)

Vocabulary Check

Choose the vocabulary word that completes each sentence.

1. A(n) ____?____ is a statement with numbers and/or variables and at least one operation.

2. $9 + n = 19$ is a(n) ____?____ .

3. In an expression or an equation, the operation in the ____?____ should be performed first.

4. A(n) ____?____ is a sequence of numbers, figures, or symbols that follow a rule.

5. $6 - 2 = 4$ is a(n) ____?____ .

6. In the expression $2 + (7 - 3)$ you should do what is in the ____?____ first.

7. $n + 18$ is a(n) ____?____ .

Lesson-by-Lesson Review

5-1 Addition and Subtraction Expressions (pp. 193–195)

4-3.4

Example 1
What is the value of 5 + n if n = 2?

5 + n   Write the expression.

5 + 2   Replace n with 2.

  7   Add 5 and 2.

Example 2
Find the value of 13 − (x + 3) if x = 8.

13 − (x + 3)   Write the expression.

13 − (8 + 3)   Replace x with 8.

13 −   11   Add (8 + 3) first.

      2   Subtract 13 − 11.

Find the value of each expression if f = 9 and g = 5.

8. f + 3   **9.** 12 + g

10. (f − 2) + 6   **11.** 14 − (g + 2)

Write an expression for each situation.

12. five more than n

13. the sum of n and four

14. seven subtracted from n

Hayden's score was 15 more than Mario's.

15. Define a variable. Then write an expression for Hayden's score.

16. If Mario's score was 60, what was Hayden's score?

5-2 Solve Equations (pp. 198–201)

4-3.5

Example 3
Solve 4 + x = 10.

4 + x = 10   4 plus what equals 10?

4 + 6 = 10   4 + 6 = 10

   x = 6

Example 4
Solve 18 − n = 12.

18 − n = 12   18 minus what equals 12?

18 − 6 = 12   18 − 6 = 12

   n = 6

Solve each equation.

17. k + 10 = 18   **18.** c − 8 = 11

19. 7 − z = 3   **20.** m + 9 = 15

Write and solve an equation for each situation.

21. A number plus 7 equals 19. What is the number?

22. Five subtracted from a number equals 12. What is the number?

Problem-Solving Skill: Extra or Missing Information

(pp. 202–203)

4-3.5

Example 5

Troy's family went to the zoo. Admission to the local zoo is $12 for adults and $5 for children. How much did it cost for Troy's family to go to the zoo?

Understand

What facts do you know?

Troy's family went to the zoo.

Zoo admission is $12 for adults and $5 for children.

What do you need to find?

Find the cost for Troy's family to go to the zoo.

Plan Identify the information needed to solve the problem. Look for any extra or missing information.

Solve To find the cost of admission, add the cost of each family member.

This information is missing, so the problem can not be solved.

Check Since no answer was found, there is no answer to check.

Identify any missing or extra information. Then solve if possible.

23. The table shows the points Yoshi scored in a basketball game. How many points did she score in the second half of the game?

Points Yoshi Scored		
first half	second half	total
12 points	■	26 points

24. The Cougars scored 36 points and defeated the Falcons by 12 points. How many points did the Falcons score?

25. A pet frog is two years old. It eats four times a week. If there are 365 days in a year, how many days old is the frog?

26. Kendra's parents drove 269 miles to Seattle. Kendra's aunt flew 457 miles to Seattle. What is the round-trip distance Kendra's parents will drive to Seattle and back?

27. **Measurement** Malia bikes one mile in five minutes. How many miles did Malia bike?

4-3.1,
4-3.2

Example 6
Harry plays ball with his friends. The table shows how long he plays each day. Identify, describe, and extend the pattern to find how many minutes he will play ball on Friday.

Day	Time	
Monday	15 minutes	+15
Tuesday	30 minutes	+15
Wednesday	45 minutes	+15
Thursday	60 minutes	+15
Friday	■ minutes	+15

Look at the table to identify and describe the pattern.

The table shows that Harry played ball for 15 minutes on Monday, and that he plays 15 minutes more each day than the previous day.

Extending the pattern, you find that Harry will play ball for 60 + 15, or 75 minutes on Friday.

Example 7
Genni drew these figures.

Which of the following is like the figures she drew? Explain.

Since she has drawn triangles, the triangle is most like the others.

Identify, describe, and extend each pattern.

28. 26, 23, 20, 17, ■, ■

29. 200, 175, 150, ■, ■

30. Tomás is making a pattern with shells from his family vacation. In the first row, there are 4 shells. In the second row, there are 10 shells, and in the third row, there are 16 shells. How many shells will be in the fourth and fifth rows?

31. Cynthia sold oatmeal bars at 4 for $1. How much would 10 oatmeal bars cost?

32. The table shows the cost of admission to an outdoor theater. How much will it cost for 5 people to go to the theater?

People	Cost ($)
1	8
2	16
3	24
4	32
5	■

33. Look at the figures below.

Which of the following would not belong in this group of figures? Explain.

5-5 **Function Tables: Find a Rule (+, −)** (pp. 208–211)

4-3.3,
4-3.4

Example 8

Write an equation that describes the pattern in the table. Then use the equation to find the next two numbers in the pattern.

Input (a)	Output (b)
12	2
17	7
22	12
27	■
32	■
37	■

First, write an equation.

Pattern:
$$12 - 10 = 2$$
$$17 - 10 = 7$$
$$22 - 10 = 12$$

Rule: Subtract 10.

Equation: $a - 10 = b$

Then use the equation to find the next three numbers.

Find the next three numbers when the input (a) is 27, 32, and 37.

$a - 10 = b$

$27 - 10 = 17$

$32 - 10 = 22$

$37 - 10 = 27$

So, the next three numbers in the pattern are 17, 22, and 27.

Write an equation to describe the pattern. Then use the equation to find the next two numbers.

34.

Input (x)	Output (y)
14	5
21	12
27	18
33	■
39	■
45	■

35.

Input (a)	Output (b)
15	21
20	26
25	31
30	■
35	■
40	■

36.

Input (m)	Output (n)
11	7
13	9
15	11
17	■
19	■
21	■

5-6 Multiplication and Division Expressions (pp. 214–216)

4-3.4

Example 9
Find the value of 5 × n if n = 3.

5 × n   Write the expression.

5 × 3   Replace n with 3.

15   Multiply 5 and 3.

So, the value of the expression is 15.

Example 10
Maggie has some money to buy kites for her club. Write an expression for the number of kites Maggie can buy with her money.

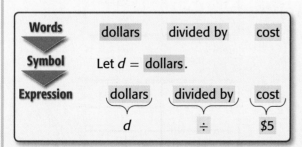

$5

Write an expression.

Words	dollars	divided by	cost
Symbol	Let d = dollars.		
Expression	dollars	divided by	cost
	d	÷	$5

So, the number of kites Maggie can buy is d ÷ $5.

Find the value of each expression if a = 4 and b = 6.

37. $a \times 3$ **38.** $b \div 2$

39. $24 \div (b \times 2)$

40. $(16 \div a) \times b$

Write an expression for each situation.

41. a number divided by 7

42. 32 divided by a number

43. Terri has 4 times as many coins as Kuni. Write an expression for the numbers of coins Terri has.

44. Jason wants to buy five toy cars. Write an expression to show how much he will pay for the cars.

$d

45. Brenden has 3 times as much paper as Clark. If Clark has 10 sheets of paper, how many sheets does Brenden have? Write an expression. Then solve.

5-7 **Problem-Solving Investigation:** **Choose a Strategy** (pp. 218–219)

4-6.3

Example 11

Sonia's bank account increases with each paycheck. Use the table to find how much her account increased after her fourth and fifth paychecks.

Number of Paychecks	Account Total
1	$25
2	$75
3	$125
4	▪
5	▪

Use the table to find a pattern. Each paycheck shows a rule of +$50. So, the missing outputs are $175 and $225.

Use any strategy to solve.

46. Lucas is collecting coupons to raise funds for his school. The first week he collects 525. The second week he collects 600. He collects 675 in the third week. If this pattern continues, how many should he collect the 7th week?

47. Karina has $27 and Jessica has $48. Do they have enough money to buy the $82 concert tickets they want? Explain.

5-8 **Function Tables: Find a Rule** ($\times$, $\div$) (pp. 220–223)

4-3.3, 4-3.4

Example 12
Write an equation that describes the pattern in the table.

Input (a)	Output (b)
5	1
10	2
15	3

Each input is divided by 5 to result in each output.

So, $a \div 5 = b$ is the equation.

input ↑   output ↑

Write an equation that describes the pattern. Then use the equation to find the next number.

48.

Input (x)	Output (y)
1	7
3	21
5	35
7	▪

49.

Input (m)	Output (n)
9	3
18	6
27	9
36	▪

Chapter Test

For Exercises 1–3, tell whether each statement is *true* or *false*.

1. The parentheses tell you which operation to perform first.

2. An expression is a math statement without numbers and symbols.

3. A pattern is a series of numbers or figures that follow a rule.

Write an expression for each situation.

4. thirty subtracted from a

5. the difference of m and twenty-six

6. the sum of x and 13

7. eight more than c

Solve each equation.

8. $13 + b = 25$

9. $n - 12 = 22$

10. Justice rode his bike for 35 minutes on Monday, 20 minutes on Tuesday, and 44 minutes on Saturday. Did he spend more than an hour riding his bike on Monday and Tuesday? Identify any missing or extra information.

11. **MULTIPLE CHOICE** Which number would make the equation true?

$$17 + x = 20$$

A 2 **C** 37

B 3 **D** 33

Solve each equation.

12. $f \div 10 = 12$ 13. $6 \times z = 54$

14. The product of a number and 12 is 84. Write an equation to find the number.

15. **MULTIPLE CHOICE** Which equation describes the pattern?

Input (*a*)	Output (*b*)
8	1
24	3
40	5
56	7
72	9

F $a - 7 = b$ **H** $a \div 8 = b$

G $a \div 7 = b$ **J** $b + 7 = b$

16. The ski club is having a car wash. They make \$5 for each car they wash. Write a rule and an equation to find how much money they will make if they wash 4 cars.

Find the value of each expression if $a = 2$ and $b = 6$.

17. $b \times 4$ 18. $16 \div a$

19. **WRITING IN ▸MATH** Explain how to find the missing number in the equation $(9 \times 4) \div n = 60 \div 10$.

PART 1 Multiple Choice

Read each question. Then fill in the correct answer on the answer sheet provided by your teacher or on a sheet of paper.

1. What expression is shown?

   A 2×9 **C** 3×10

   B 3×8 **D** 3×9

2. Find $24 + (n - 8)$ if $n = 12$.

   F 4   **H** 28

   G 12   **J** 44

3. Find the value of y in the equation.

   $$y + 27 = 48$$

   A 20   **C** 32

   B 21   **D** 75

4. Which equation can be used to describe the pattern in the table?

Input (x)	1	2	3	4	5	6
Output (y)	5	10	15	20	25	30

   F $y = 3x$ **H** $y = x \div 3$

   G $y = 5x$ **J** $y = x \div 5$

5. There are 48 students traveling on a field trip. Each van holds 8 students. How many vans are needed in all?

   A 6   **C** 8

   B 7   **D** 9

6. The graph shows the number of points scored by Mark and Kim during the first 4 games of the basketball season.

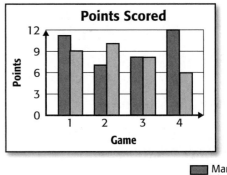

Mark
Kim

   How many more points did Kim score than Mark in Game 2?

   F 2 points   **H** 4 points

   G 3 points   **J** 5 points

7. Tonisha's family has 2 newspapers delivered to their house each day. When they came back from a trip, there were 14 newspapers. Which equation can be used to find the number of days they were gone?

   A $14 \div 2 = d$ **C** $14 - d = 2$

   B $14 + d = 2$ **D** $14 \times 2 = d$

Preparing for PASS

For test-taking strategies and practice, see pages R42–R55.

8. Which rule describes the pattern?

Input (c)	Output (d)
12	19
19	26
28	35
37	44

F Add 5.   **H** Add 8.

G Add 7.   **J** Add 9.

9. Darin bought four books. Each book cost $6. Darin has $16 left. Which equation can be used to find how much money he had before he went shopping? Let m = money.

A $m - (4 \times \$6) = \$16$

B $(4 \times \$6) - m = \$16$

C $(4 \times \$6) - \$16 = m$

D $\$16 - (4 \times m) = \$6$

10. What number goes in the box to make this number sentence true?

$$(8 - 5) \times 9 = 3 \times \blacksquare$$

F 3   **H** 8

G 5   **J** 9

Record your answers on the answer sheet provided by your teacher or on a sheet of paper.

11. Write an equation to describe the pattern below.

Input (x)	Output (y)
2	7
4	9
6	11
8	13

12. Steve added 5 coins to his collection. Now he has 62 coins. Write an equation to show how many coins he had before.

Record your answers on the answer sheet provided by your teacher or on a sheet of paper.

13. Which rule describes the pattern in the table below? Explain.

Input (x)	Output (y)
1	4
2	8
3	12
4	16

NEED EXTRA HELP?													
If You Missed Question...	1	2	3	4	5	6	7	8	9	10	11	12	13
Go to Lesson...	4-3	5-1	5-2	5-8	4-5	3-6	5-8	5-5	5-8	4-2	5-5	5-8	5-8
SC Academic Standards	4-2.3	4-3.4	4-3.5	4-3.3	4-2.5	4-6.2	4-3.4	4-3.3	4-3.4	4-1.3	4-3.4	4-3.4	4-3.3

CHAPTER 6 Multiply by One-Digit Numbers

BIG Idea How do you multiply by one-digit numbers?

Multiply each digit by the one-digit number, starting with the ones place. Regroup when necessary.

Example A great white shark can swim 2,900 miles on a single meal. If a great white shark eats 3 meals a day, it could swim 2,900 × 3 or 8,700 miles.

$$
\begin{array}{r}
2{,}900 \\
\times\quad 3 \\
\hline
6{,}000 \\
+\ 2{,}700 \\
\hline
8{,}700
\end{array}
$$

Multiply 3 × 2,000.
Multiply 3 × 900.
Add the partial products.

What will I learn in this chapter?

- Multiply multiples of 10, 100, and 1,000.
- Estimate products using rounding.
- Multiply a multi-digit number by a one-digit number.
- Determine reasonable answers.

Key Vocabulary

multiply

estimate

product

Distributive Property of Multiplication

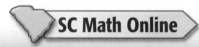 **SC Math Online** **Student Study Tools** at macmillanmh.com

FOLDABLES®
Study Organizer

Make this Foldable to help you organize information about multiplying by one-digit numbers. Begin with one sheet of 11″ × 17″ paper.

1 **Fold** the short sides so they meet in the middle.

2 **Fold** the top to the bottom.

3 **Unfold** and cut to make four tabs.

4 **Label** each tab as shown.

Estimate Products

Multiply Two-Digit Numbers

Multiply Multi-Digit Numbers

Multiply Across Zeros

You have two ways to check prerequisite skills for this chapter.

Option 2

SC Math Online › Take the Chapter Readiness Quiz at macmillanmh.com.

Option 1

Complete the Quick Check below.

QUICK Check

Multiply. Use models if needed. (Lessons 4-3 and 4-5)

1. 2×3 **2.** $4 \times \$4$ **3.** 5×6 **4.** $7 \times \$8$

5. $\begin{array}{r} 9 \\ \times 4 \\ \hline \end{array}$ **6.** $\begin{array}{r} 8 \\ \times 3 \\ \hline \end{array}$ **7.** $\begin{array}{r} \$7 \\ \times 5 \\ \hline \end{array}$ **8.** $\begin{array}{r} 9 \\ \times 9 \\ \hline \end{array}$

9. Evan's photo album has 8 pages of pictures. How many photos are in Evan's album if the same number of photos are on each page?

Identify the place value of the underlined digit. (Lesson 1-1)

10. 1,6̲30   **11.** $5̲,367   **12.** 20,49̲5   **13.** $8̲9,196

14. Measurement Mount Everest's tallest peak is 29,035 feet. It is the highest point on Earth. Identify the place value of each digit in 29,035.

Round each number to its greatest place value. (Lesson 1-6)

15. 26   **16.** $251   **17.** 4,499   **18.** $33,103

19. There are 1,366 students at Sunrise Elementary School. Approximately how many students attend the school?

6-1

Multiples of 10, 100, and 1,000

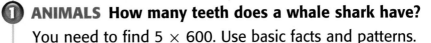

GET READY to Learn

The whale shark is the world's largest fish. Its mouth is 5 feet long, and each foot contains 600 teeth. How many teeth does a whale shark have?

MAIN IDEA

I will multiply multiples of 10, 100, and 1,000 using basic facts and patterns.

SC Academic Standards

4-2.3 Apply an algorithm to multiply whole numbers fluently.

4-2.4 Explain the effect on the product when one of the factors is changed.

SC Math Online

macmillanmh.com
• Extra Examples
• Personal Tutor
• Self-Check Quiz

You can use basic facts and number patterns to multiply.

Real-World EXAMPLE Multiples of 100

1 **ANIMALS How many teeth does a whale shark have?**
You need to find 5×600. Use basic facts and patterns.

$5 \times 6 = 30$	5×6 ones $= 30$ ones $= 30$
$5 \times 60 = 300$	5×6 tens $= 30$ tens $= 300$
$5 \times 600 = 3,000$	5×6 hundreds $= 30$ hundreds $= 3,000$

So, a whale shark has 3,000 teeth. Notice that this answer is 5×6 with two zeros at the end.

EXAMPLE Multiples of 1,000

2 **Find $3 \times 7,000$.**

$3 \times 7 = 21$	3×7 ones $= 21$ ones $= 21$
$3 \times 70 = 210$	3×7 tens $= 21$ tens $= 210$
$3 \times 700 = 2,100$	3×7 hundreds $= 21$ hundreds $= 2,100$
$3 \times 7,000 = 21,000$	3×7 thousands $= 21$ thousands $= 21,000$

So, $3 \times 7,000$ is 21,000. Notice that this answer is 3×7 with three zeros at the end.

When you know basic facts and number patterns, you can multiply mentally.

Real-World EXAMPLE   Multiply Mentally

③ **MEASUREMENT The weight of a fire truck is 8 × 4,000 pounds. What is its weight in pounds?**

To find its weight, you need to find 8 × 4,000.

8 × 4,**000**

THINK You know that 8 × 4 = 32. There are 3 zeros.

32,**000**

Since 8 × 4,000 = 32,000, the weight of the fire truck is 32,000 pounds.

✓CHECK **What You Know**

Multiply. Use basic facts and patterns. See Examples 1 and 2 (p. 237)

1. 2 × 1
2 × 10
2 × 100
2 × 1,000

2. 6 × 8
6 × 80
6 × 800
6 × 8,000

3. 7 × 9
7 × 90
7 × 900
7 × 9,000

Multiply. Use mental math. See Example 3 (p. 238)

4. 3 × 20

5. 8 × 600

6. 9 × 9,000

7. A zookeeper is in charge of feeding an anteater. Each day the anteater eats 5 × 6,000 ants. How many ants must the zookeeper give the anteater each day?

8. **Talk About It** What is the product of 4 and 5,000? Explain why there are more zeros in the product than in the factors in the problem.

Multiply. Use basic facts and patterns. See Examples 1 and 2 (p. 237)

9. 5 × 3
5 × 30
5 × 300
5 × 3,000

10. 3 × 4
3 × 40
3 × 400
3 × 4,000

11. 2 × 9
2 × 90
2 × 900
2 × 9,000

12. 6 × 7
6 × 70
6 × 700
6 × 7,000

13. 9 × 1
9 × 10
9 × 100
9 × 1,000

14. 8 × 5
8 × 50
8 × 500
8 × 5,000

Multiply. Use mental math. See Example 3 (p. 238)

15. 4 × 30

16. 6 × 40

17. 7 × 200

18. 4 × 500

19. 3 × 9,000

20. 9 × 6,000

Algebra Copy and complete.

21. If 6 × ■ = 42,
then 60 × ■ = 4,200.

22. If 5 × 7 = ■,
then 50 × ■ = 3,500.

23. Mr. Singh's car payments are $300 a month. How much money will he pay in 6 months?

24. Mia's cell phone plan includes 2,000 monthly minutes. How many minutes does she get over 6 months?

Real-World PROBLEM SOLVING

Travel The Williams family is going to a theme park.

25. Admission tickets cost $30 for each person. What is the total cost for the 5 family members for one day?

26. The cost for each person to eat for one week is $100. Find the total cost for the family to eat for one week.

27. Suppose each family member goes on 70 rides during the week. How many rides will they go on altogether?

H.O.T. Problems

28. OPEN ENDED Write two multiplication expressions that have a product of 20,000.

29. WRITING IN ►MATH How would you find 1 × 10,000? What is 1 × 10,000?

Problem-Solving Skill

MAIN IDEA I will decide whether an answer to a problem is reasonable.

 SCAS **4-2.3 Apply an algorithm to multiply whole numbers fluently.**

Odell donated 3 cases of dog treats to a dog shelter. Each case has 900 treats. The dogs eat 2,500 treats each month. Odell says he has donated enough treats for more than one month. Is his claim reasonable?

Understand	**What facts do you know?** • 3 cases of treats were donated. • Each case has 900 treats. • The animals eat 2,500 treats each month. **What do you need to find?** • Is it reasonable to say that the 3 cases of treats will last longer than one month?
Plan	Find 3 × 900. Then determine if the amount is reasonable.
Solve	3 × 900 THINK 3 × 9 = 27 Place 2 zeros in the product. 2,700 Since 2,700 > 2,500, it is reasonable to say that the three cases will last longer than one month.
Check	You can add to check the multiplication. 900 + 900 + 900 = 2,700 So, the answer is correct.

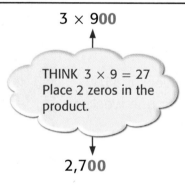

ANALYZE the Skill

Refer to the problem on the previous page.

1. Explain why 3 is multiplied by 900 to decide if Odell's claim was reasonable.

2. Explain why there are 2 zeros at the end of the product of 3 and 900.

3. Look back at the example. What would make Odell's claim *not* reasonable?

4. Suppose Odell donates 5 cases of treats. Is it reasonable to believe the treats will last 2 months? Explain.

PRACTICE the Skill

SCAS • PASS

Extra Practice, p. R15

Decide whether each answer is reasonable. Explain your reasoning.

5. **Measurement** The calendar shows the number of days each month Olivia rides her bike.

September						
Sun	Mon	Tues	Wed	Thurs	Fri	Sat
					1	2 (B)
3 (B)	4	5	6	7	8 (B)	9
10 (B)	11	12	13 (B)	14	15	16 (B)
17	18	19	20	21	22 (B)	23
24 (B)	25	26	27	28 (B)	29	30 (B)

Each time she rides her bike, she travels 10 miles. Is it reasonable to say that Olivia will bike more than 500 miles in 6 months?

6. Ben delivers 40 newspapers each day. Is 400 a reasonable estimate for the number of newspapers Ben delivers each week?

7. Jay makes $40 a week doing yard work. He is saving his money to buy a computer that costs $400. He has already saved $120. Is it reasonable to say that Jay will save enough money to buy the computer in 6 weeks?

8. **Measurement** The distance from Ian's home to the museum is 2,640 yards. Is it reasonable to say that Ian's home is more than 9,000 feet away from the museum? (3 feet = 1 yard)

9. Kiri spends 60 minutes a week walking to school. Is it reasonable to say that she spends 240 minutes walking to school in four weeks?

10. The table below shows the number of pennies collected by four children.

Pennies Collected	
Child	Number of Pennies
Myron	48
Teresa	52
Veronica	47
Warren	53

Is it reasonable to say that the children collected about 200 pennies in all?

11. **WRITING IN ▸MATH** Write a problem where $180 would be a reasonable answer.

Use Rounding to Estimate Products

GET READY to Learn

The fastest passenger train in the world actually floats above its track. This train in China can travel up to 267 miles per hour. About how far can the train travel in 3 hours?

To **estimate** products, round factors to their greatest place.

Real-World EXAMPLE   Estimate Products

1 TRAVEL **About how far can the train travel in 3 hours?**

Estimate 3×267. Round the larger factor to its greatest place. Then use basic facts and patterns to multiply.

3×267

THINK 267 rounds to 300.

$3 \times 300 = 900$

So, the train can travel about 900 miles in 3 hours. Since 267 was rounded up, the estimated product is greater than the actual product.

EXAMPLE   Estimate Greater Products

2 **Estimate $8 \times 2{,}496$.**

First round, then multiply using basic facts and patterns.

$8 \times 2{,}496$

THINK 2,496 rounds to 2,000.

$8 \times 2{,}000 = 16{,}000$

So, $8 \times 2{,}496$ is about 16,000.
Since 2,496 was rounded down, the estimated product is less than the actual product.

You can also estimate products involving money.

Remember

- When you round up, the estimated product is greater than the actual product.

- When you round down, the estimated product is less than the actual product.

Real-World EXAMPLE — Estimate Money

3 **MONEY** Lacey's older brother is going to a four-year college. The cost of his tuition is $8,562 each year. About how much will 4 years of college tuition cost?

You need to estimate 4 × $8,562.

First round, then multiply.

4 × $8,562

↓

> THINK
> 8,562 rounds to 9,000.

4 × $9,000 = $36,000

So, tuition will cost about $36,000.

College Tuition

Cost per Year

$8,562

✓ CHECK What You Know

Estimate each product. Then tell if the estimate is *greater than* or *less than* the actual product. See Examples 1–3 (pp. 242–243)

1. 449
    × 5

2. $870
    ×   9

3. 3,293
    ×   3

4. 7 × $1,395

5. 6 × 5,500

6. 9 × $7,420

For Exercises 7 and 8, use the data at the right.

7. Mr. and Mrs. Rivera are planning to go on an African safari. They have saved $1,125 a year for 8 years. If the trip costs $9,830, do they have enough money saved for the trip? Explain.

8. **Talk About It** Suppose Mr. and Mrs. Rivera saved $1,499 a year for 8 years. Why would an estimated answer be misleading for the amount saved?

African Safari
$ 9,830

Estimate each product. Then tell if the estimate is *greater than* or *less than* the actual product. See Examples 1–3 (pp. 242–243)

9. 562
× 6

10. 896
× 2

11. 729
× 8

12. 949
× 4

13. 2 × $438

14. 8 × $647

15. 5 × $355

16. 7 × $450

17. 7 × 1,125

18. 3 × 5,489

19. 9 × 3,500

20. 6 × 8,816

21. 4 × $6,502

22. 7 × $8,856

23. 9 × $9,498

24. 7 × $9,310

25. There are 24 students in each class at Watson Elementary School. About how many students are there if there are 8 classes?

26. The round-trip distance from Woodward to Oklahoma City is 139 miles. Ms. Hodges travels this distance 6 days a week. About how many miles does she travel each week?

Real-World PROBLEM SOLVING

Entertainment Toby and Lena like to go to the arcade. They earn points toward prizes.

27. Toby went to the arcade 2 times. He earned 5,150 points each time. What is the biggest prize Toby can get?

28. How many toy cars could Toby get with his points?

2,000   10,000   50,000   500

29. Lena went to the arcade 7 times. She earned 9,050 points each time. What are the two largest prizes she can get?

H.O.T. Problems

30. **NUMBER SENSE** Explain how you can tell if your estimated answer is more or less than the exact answer to a multiplication problem.

31. **WRITING IN ►MATH** Suppose you need to find the exact answer to 4 × $189. How can you use estimation to check the reasonableness of your answer?

Estimation Station

Estimate Products

Get Ready!

Players: 2 players
You will need: spinner, 1 number cube,
2 whiteboards

Get Set!

Each player makes a spinner and a
game board as shown.

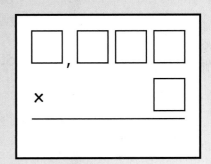

Go!

- Player 1 rolls the number cube to find a
  one-digit factor. Record the number in the
  second row on the game board.

- Player 1 then spins to find how many
  digits will be in the second factor.

- Player 1 rolls the number cube to find the
  digits in the second factor. Record each digit.

- Player 1 estimates the product and
  gets 1 point if the estimate is
  correct.

- Player 2 takes a turn.

- Continue playing. The
  player who earns
  10 points first wins.

Multiply Two-Digit Numbers

MAIN IDEA

I will multiply a two-digit number by a one-digit number.

SC Academic Standards

4-2.3 Apply an algorithm to multiply whole numbers fluently.

SC Math Online

macmillanmh.com

- Extra Examples
- Personal Tutor
- Self-Check Quiz
- Concepts in Motion

Hands-On Mini Activity

Materials: base-ten blocks

Base-ten blocks can be used to explore multiplying two-digit numbers. In this activity, you will find 4×13.

Step 1 Model 4 groups of 13.

Step 2 Combine the tens and ones. Regroup 12 ones as 1 ten and 2 ones.

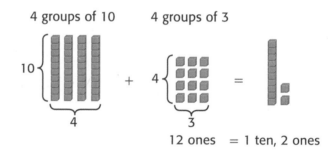

Step 3 Add the partial products.

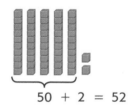

$$50 + 2 = 52$$

So, $4 \times 13 = 52$.

Find each product. Use base-ten blocks.

1. 3×18 **2.** 4×19 **3.** 3×21

4. Multiplication can be a shortcut for which operation?

5. When is it necessary to regroup in a multiplication problem? When is regrouping not needed?

Using place-value models is not the only way to multiply a two-digit number by a one-digit number.

EXAMPLE Multiply with Regrouping

① **Find 6 × 38. Estimate** $6 \times 38 \longrightarrow 6 \times 40 = 240$

Remember
To review the Distributive Property of Multiplication, see Lesson 4-6 (p. 166).

One Way: Distributive Property

$6 \times 38 = (6 \times 30) + (6 \times 8)$
$ = 180 + 48$
$ = 228$

Another Way: Partial Products

$$\begin{array}{r} 38 \\ \times\ 6 \\ \hline 48 \\ +\ 180 \\ \hline 228 \end{array}$$

Multiply 6 × 8.
Multiply 6 × 30.
Add the partial products.

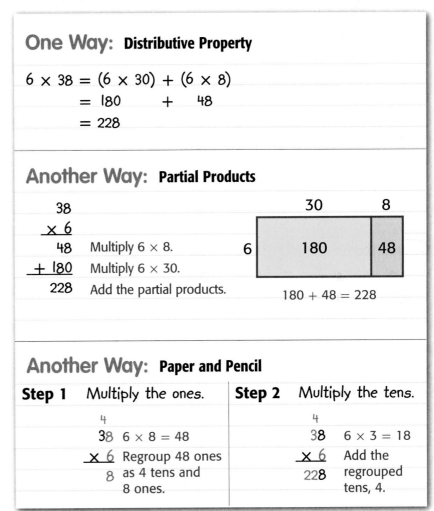

$180 + 48 = 228$

Another Way: Paper and Pencil

Step 1 Multiply the ones.	**Step 2** Multiply the tens.
$\overset{4}{3}8 \quad 6 \times 8 = 48$ $\underline{\times\ 6}$ Regroup 48 ones 8 as 4 tens and 8 ones.	$\overset{4}{3}8 \quad 6 \times 3 = 18$ $\underline{\times\ 6}$ Add the 228 regrouped tens, 4.

Check for Reasonableness
The product, 228, is close to the estimate, 240. ✔

✓ CHECK What You Know

Multiply. Check for reasonableness. See Example 1 (p. 247)

1. $\begin{array}{r} 23 \\ \underline{\times\ 2} \end{array}$

2. $\begin{array}{r} 42 \\ \underline{\times\ 2} \end{array}$

3. $8 \times \$98$

4. Haley can fit 25 books on each of 5 shelves. How many books will fit in all?

5. **Talk About It** Explain how to find 6×37.

Multiply. Check for reasonableness. See Example 1 (p. 247)

6. 33
     × 2

7. $24
     × 2

8. 11
     × 7

9. 13
     × 3

10. 2 × $27

11. 4 × 29

12. 5 × 18

13. 7 × $36

14. 6 × 52

15. 8 × 75

16. 4 × $83

17. 9 × 99

18. Will makes $4 an hour shampooing dogs at a pet shop. Last month he worked 26 hours. How much money did Will earn?

19. Suppose the sales tax is 7 cents for each dollar that is spent on any item. How much sales tax is charged for a badminton set that costs $35?

South Carolina Data File

Letterboxing is an outdoor hobby. It involves hiking and following clues to find a hidden box.

20. Ross's first letterbox clue tells him to take 39 paces west. How many steps should Ross take if 1 pace = 2 steps?

21. Ross's second clue tells him to walk 65 yards north. How many feet will Ross walk if 1 yard = 3 feet?

22. Ross is letterboxing with two friends. How many steps did they take altogether for the first clue?

• There are about 244 letterboxes hidden in South Carolina.

Source: Letterboxing North America

H.O.T. Problems

23. OPEN ENDED Write two problems that result in a product of 120.

24. WHICH ONE DOESN'T BELONG? Which multiplication problem does not belong with the other three? Explain.

  12
  ×8

  22
  ×4

  52
  ×2

  33
  ×3

25. **WRITING IN** ►**MATH** How do you use partial products to find 6 × 42?

Multiply. Use basic facts and patterns.

(Lesson 6-1)

1. 3×4
3×40
3×400
$3 \times 4,000$

2. 12×5
12×50
12×500
$12 \times 5,000$

3. A Triceratops weighs $2 \times 7,000$ pounds. How much does a Triceratops weigh?

4. Kyra needs 292 toothpicks for a project. A box holds 150 toothpicks. Is it reasonable to buy 2 boxes? Explain. (Lesson 6-2)

5. Mara and Billy have 6 bags of 12 balloons. Is it reasonable to say they have more than 75 balloons? (Lesson 6-2)

Estimate each product. (Lesson 6-3)

6. 3×252

7. $5 \times 7,493$

8. MULTIPLE CHOICE Jada pays $1,875 a year in car payments. About how much money will she pay in 5 years? (Lesson 6-3)

A $5,000

C $9,375

B $7,500

D $10,000

9. Juan plans to read 264 pages a month to complete his book in 6 months. About how many pages are in his book? (Lesson 6-3)

10. Measurement Each gallon of paint covers about 350 square feet. Ann estimated that 3 gallons of paint would be enough to cover 1,400 square feet. Will Ann have enough paint? Explain. (Lesson 6-3)

Multiply. Check for reasonableness.

(Lesson 6-4)

11. $\begin{array}{r} 43 \\ \times\ 2 \\ \hline \end{array}$

12. $\begin{array}{r} \$51 \\ \times\ 3 \\ \hline \end{array}$

13. 9×62

14. 8×47

15. MULTIPLE CHOICE There are 27 boxes of markers in the art room. If each box holds 8 markers, how many markers are in the art room? (Lesson 6-4)

F 106

H 216

G 166

J 226

16. WRITING IN ►MATH Cassie got the following problem wrong on her math test. Explain what she did wrong. (Lesson 6-4)

$\begin{array}{r} 5 \\ 47 \\ \times\ 8 \\ \hline 326 \end{array}$

Problem-Solving Investigation

MAIN IDEA I will choose the best strategy to solve a problem.

SCAS 4-2.3 Apply an algorithm to multiply whole numbers fluently.

P.S.I. TEAM +

ISABEL: I am making punch for a party. One bowl of punch serves 35 guests. I am going to make four bowls of punch.

YOUR MISSION: Find how many guests four bowls of punch serve.

Understand	One bowl of punch serves 35 guests. Isabel is making four bowls of punch. Find how many guests will be served by four bowls of punch.
Plan	Use the four-step plan and write a number sentence. Multiply the number of guests served by one bowl of punch by the number of bowls being made.
Solve	You need to find $35 \times 4 = $ ∎.

$$\begin{array}{r} 35 \\ \times 4 \\ \hline 20 \\ +120 \\ \hline 140 \end{array}$$

20 Multiply 4×5.
+120 Multiply 4×30.
140 Add.

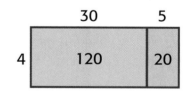

$120 + 20 = 140$

So, four bowls of punch will serve 140 guests.

Check	Look back. You can use repeated addition to check your answer. $35 + 35 + 35 + 35 = 140$. So, the answer is correct.

Use any strategy shown below to solve. Tell what strategy you used.

PROBLEM-SOLVING STRATEGIES
• Make a table.

1. **Algebra** There are 12 members in each scout troop. Make a table to find out how many members will attend a meeting if there are 10, 11, 12, or 13 scout troops attending.

2. Nate is trying to choose 3 items from the menu below. What are 3 possible combinations Nate could choose?

DINNER
Steak   Chicken
Spaghetti   Hamburger

SIDES
Potatoes
Vegetables
Corn
Salad

Water
Soda
Milk
Juice

3. Kishi is choosing an outfit to wear to school. She has 3 shirts, 2 pairs of pants, and 3 pairs of shoes to choose from. How many different outfits does she have to choose from?

4. While on a class field trip, Hally learned that four bears eat 2,000 ants per day. How many ants will 2 bears eat in one day?

5. There are 18 stickers on each sheet. There are five sheets in one pack. How many stickers are in one pack?

6. **Algebra** Copy and complete the pattern below. Describe the pattern.

    100, 200, 400, ■, 1,600, ■, 6,400

7. **Geometry** If this pattern is repeated, identify the 18th shape in the pattern.

8. A wall has an animal poster to the right of a car poster. A space poster is last. A music poster is to the left of the space poster. What is the order of the 4 posters?

9. Emma now has $32. She earned $12 babysitting and she received $5 for her allowance. How much money did she have originally?

10. The Turner family played miniature golf. What is the total cost if 2 adults and 3 children played 18 holes of golf?

Goofy Golf

9 holes
Adult............ $4
Child............ $3
18 holes
Adult............ $7
Child............ $5

11. **WRITING IN ▶MATH** Look at Exercise 9. Identify the strategy you used. Explain how you used this strategy to solve the problem.

6-6 Multiply Multi-Digit Numbers

MAIN IDEA

I will multiply a multi-digit number by a one-digit number.

SC Academic Standards

4-2.3 Apply an algorithm to multiply whole numbers fluently.

SC Math Online

macmillanmh.com
• Extra Examples
• Personal Tutor
• Self-Check Quiz

GET READY to Learn

Today is Laura's birthday, and she is nine years old. Except for leap years, there are 365 days in one year. How many days old is Laura?

You multiply multi-digit numbers the same way you multiply a two-digit number by a one-digit number.

Real-World EXAMPLE   Partial Products

1 TIME How many days old is Laura?

To find how old Laura is in days, multiply the number of days in a year by the number of years. That is, find 365 × 9. You can use partial products.

Estimate 9 × 365 ⟶ 9 × 400 = 3,600

$$
\begin{array}{r}
365 \\
\times\ 9 \\
\hline
45 \\
540 \\
+\ 2,700 \\
\hline
3,285 \\
\end{array}
$$

  45   Multiply 9 × 5.
  540   Multiply 9 × 60.
+ 2,700 Multiply 9 × 300.
  3,285 Add the partial products.

	300	+	60	+ 5
9	2,700		540	45

$$
\begin{array}{r}
2,700 \\
540 \\
+\ \ \ 45 \\
\hline
3,285 \\
\end{array}
$$

So, Laura is 3,285 days old.

Check for Reasonableness

The product, 3,285, is close to the estimate, 3,600. ✔

You can also use paper and pencil to multiply.

EXAMPLE Multiply Money

2 Find 3 × $1,175.

Step 1 Multiply the ones.

$$\begin{array}{r} 1 \\ \$1,175 \\ \times\ \ 3 \\ \hline 5 \end{array}$$

3 × 5 ones = 15
Regroup 15 ones as 1 ten and 5 ones.

Step 2 Multiply the tens.

$$\begin{array}{r} 21 \\ \$1,175 \\ \times\ \ 3 \\ \hline 25 \end{array}$$

3 × 7 tens = 21 tens
Add the regrouped tens.
21 tens + 1 ten = 22 tens
Regroup 22 tens as 2 hundreds and 2 tens.

Step 3 Multiply the hundreds.

$$\begin{array}{r} 21 \\ \$1,175 \\ \times\ \ 3 \\ \hline 525 \end{array}$$

3 × 1 hundred = 3 hundreds
Add the regrouped hundreds.
3 hundreds + 2 hundreds = 5 hundreds

Step 4 Multiply the thousands.

$$\begin{array}{r} 21 \\ \$1,175 \\ \times\ \ 3 \\ \hline \$3,525 \end{array}$$

3 × 1 thousand = 3 thousands

	$1,000	+ $100	+ $70	+ $5
3	$3,000	$300	$210	$15

$$\begin{array}{r} \$3,000 \\ \$300 \\ \$210 \\ +\ \ \$15 \\ \hline \$3,525 \end{array}$$

Remember

Always check for reasonableness.

3 × $1,175
↓
3 × $1,000 = $3,000

Since $3,525 is close to $3,000, the answer is reasonable.

CHECK What You Know

Multiply. Check for reasonableness. See Examples 1 and 2 (pp. 252–253)

1. $\begin{array}{r} 135 \\ \times\ 2 \\ \hline \end{array}$

2. $\begin{array}{r} 532 \\ \times\ 6 \\ \hline \end{array}$

3. 2 × $2,957

4. 7 × 7,832

5. A vacation costs $1,389 for one person. What is the total cost of this vacation for a family of four?

6. **Talk About It** Explain why it is a good idea to estimate answers to multiplication problems.

Practice and Problem Solving

Multiply. Check for reasonableness. See Examples 1 and 2 (pp. 252–253)

7. $168
   × 2

8. 313
   × 3

9. 252
   × 2

10. $338
   × 3

11. 238
   × 4

12. 819
   × 5

13. $781
   × 5

14. 340
   × 6

15. 7 × $4,160

16. 7 × 5,611

17. 8 × 6,328

18. 9 × $5,679

19. 8 × 7,338

20. 7 × 8,469

21. 9 × $9,927

22. 9 × 8,586

Algebra Find the value of each expression if $n = 8$.

23. $n \times 295$

24. $737 \times n$

25. $n \times \$2,735$

26. $7,372 \times n$

Compare. Replace each ● with >, <, or =.

27. 4 × 198 ● 3 × 248

28. 7 × 385 ● 6 × 457

29. Ms. Gibbons buys 8 cases of seeds at the school plant sale. If there are 144 packages of seeds in each case, how many packages of seeds has she bought?

30. Measurement On average 1,668 gallons of water are used by each person in the United States daily. How much water is used by one person in a week?

Real-World PROBLEM SOLVING

Science The rainforests are the richest, oldest, and most productive ecosystems on Earth. Animals such as anacondas, iguanas, monkeys, and parrots live in rainforests.

31. A four-square-mile section of rainforest has 125 mammals. How many mammals would live in an area 3 times that size?

32. Rainforest land that is used to raise cattle is worth $60 an acre. Rainforest land that is used for its plants is worth $2,400 an acre. Find the difference in the worth of 5 acres used to raise cattle compared to 5 acres used for plants.

H.O.T. Problems

33. OPEN ENDED Write a four-digit number and a one-digit number whose product is greater than 6,000 and less than 6,200.

34. FIND THE ERROR Roberta and Camden are finding 362 × 2. Who is correct? Explain.

Roberta
```
 362
×  2
─────
 724
```

Camden
```
 362
×  2
─────
 624
```

35. WRITING IN ►MATH   Write a real-world problem that involves multiplying a three-digit by a one-digit number, and regrouping.

PASS Practice   4-2.3

36. How long would 6 train cars be? (Lesson 6-4)

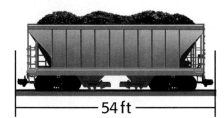

54 ft

A 300 ft   **C** 330 ft

B 324 ft   **D** 360 ft

37. There are 1,440 minutes in a day. How many minutes are in 7 days? (Lesson 6-6)

F 7,880 minutes

G 9,880 minutes

H 10,080 minutes

J 11,080 minutes

Spiral Review

Multiply. Check for reasonableness. (Lesson 6-4)

38. 3 × 21   **39.** 5 × 34   **40.** 8 × $72

Estimate each product. (Lesson 6-3)

41. 2 × 265   **42.** 3 × 849   **43.** 7 × 5,513

44. One teacher, 24 students, and 7 parents are going on a field trip. Each car can hold 4 people. Is it reasonable to say that 7 cars will allow every person to go on the field trip? Explain. (Lesson 6-2)

EMPERORS OF THE ICE

There are 17 different types of penguins. Emperor penguins are the tallest and heaviest penguins. An Emperor penguin is over 3 feet tall and can weigh from 42 to 101 pounds. The average Emperor penguin weighs 66 pounds and can swim 15 miles per hour.

About 200,000 pairs of Emperor penguins live in 40 different groups in Antarctica. Penguins huddle together to share their body heat during the cold winter temperatures and bitter winds.

Did You Know?

Emperor penguins usually dive 60 to 70 feet. An average dive lasts 3 to 6 minutes.

Real-World Math

Use the information on pages 256 and 257 to solve each problem.

1. Suppose that eight average-sized Emperor penguins are standing together. What is their total weight?

2. Six penguins of varying weights are standing together. What is the least they can weigh? the most?

3. Suppose a penguin's dive lasts 4 minutes. How many times did its heart beat during the dive?

4. How many miles can a penguin swim in 3 hours?

5. Suppose it takes a penguin 3 minutes to walk from its resting place to the place where it dives. What is a reasonable number of times its heart beats in these three minutes before it dives?

6. Based on the following table, estimate how many times a penguin's heart beats after completing all of the activities listed for two minutes each.

PENGUIN HEARTBEAT	
Activity	Heartbeat (beats per minute)
Resting	65
Before a dive	180–200
Hitting the water	100
Diving	20
Returning to surface	200

MAIN IDEA

I will multiply multi-digit numbers with zeros by a one-digit number.

SC Academic Standards

4-2.3 Apply an algorithm to multiply whole numbers fluently.

SC Math Online

macmillanmh.com

• Extra Examples
• Personal Tutor
• Self-Check Quiz

GET READY to Learn

The cost of Iván's braces is about $108 each month for 4 years. How much money will his parents pay in 6 months?

You can use partial products or the Distributive Property to multiply across zeros.

Real-World EXAMPLE Multiply Across Zeros

1 **MONEY** **How much will Iván's parents pay in 6 months for his braces?**

Multiply the cost of each month by 6. That is, find 6 × $108.

Estimate 6 × $108 ⟶ 6 × $100 = $600

$100 + $8

	$100	$8
6	6 × $100	6 × $8

6 × 0 = 0, so there is no space in the rectangle for that product.

One Way: Distributive Property	**Another Way:** Partial Products
6 × $108 = (6 × $100) + (6 × $8) = $600 + $0 + $48 = $648	$108 × 6 $ 48 6 × $8 $ 0 6 × $0 $600 6 × $100 $648 Add the partial products.

So, Iván's parents will pay $648 in 6 months.

Check for Reasonableness

The answer, $648, is close to the estimate, $600. ✔

You can also use an algorithm to multiply.

Real-World EXAMPLE Multiply Across Zeros

2 TREES If three trees are each 2,025 years old, what is the total age of the trees?

Estimate 3 × 2,025 → 3 × 2,000 = 6,000

Step 1 Multiply the ones.

```
      1
   2,025        3 × 5 ones = 15 ones
 ×    3         Regroup 15 ones as 1 ten and 5 ones.
      5
```

Step 2 Multiply the tens.

```
      1
   2,025        3 × 2 tens = 6 tens
 ×    3         Add the regrouped tens.
     75         6 tens + 1 ten = 7 tens
```

Step 3 Multiply the hundreds.

```
      1
   2,025        3 × 0 hundreds = 0 hundreds
 ×    3
    075
```

Step 4 Multiply the thousands.

```
      1
   2,025        3 × 2 thousands = 6 thousands
 ×    3
  6,075
```

So, the total age of the trees is 6,075 years.

Check for Reasonableness
The answer, 6,075, is close to the estimate, 6,000. ✔

CHECK What You Know

Multiply. Check for reasonableness. See Examples 1 and 2 (pp. 258–259)

1. 303
 × 3

2. $507
 × 6

3. 908
 × 8

4. 2 × 1,073

5. 7 × $3,102

6. 9 × 7,004

7. Valerie jogs 3 miles every day. If there are 5,280 feet in a mile, how many feet does she run in one day?

8. Explain how to find the product of 4 and 2,008.

Multiply. Check for reasonableness. See Examples 1 and 2 (pp. 258–259)

9. 201
× 2

10. $402
× 3

11. 709
× 5

12. 904
× 9

13. 2 × $1,108

14. 4 × 6,037

15. 3 × 8,504

16. 5 × $9,082

17. 6 × 4,005

18. 6 × 6,007

19. 7 × $8,009

20. 9 × 9,002

Algebra Copy and complete each table.

21.

Rule: Multiply by 4.	
Input	Output
607	■
1,085	■
3,009	■
5,104	■
8,006	■

22.

Rule: Multiply by 6,008.	
Input	Output
2	■
3	■
5	■
7	■
8	■

23. Measurement A city in Africa is one of the wettest places in the world. It receives 405 inches of rain each year. How many inches of rain would it receive in 5 years?

24. Diller Elementary is collecting money to donate to the Special Olympics. About $103 is collected each month. How much money is collected over the 9 months of the school year?

Real-World PROBLEM SOLVING

Health The bar graph shows the time people spend on certain activities in one year.

25. How many times will a person laugh in 3 years?

26. How many dreams does a person have in five years?

27. How many telephone calls does a family of 4 make in one year?

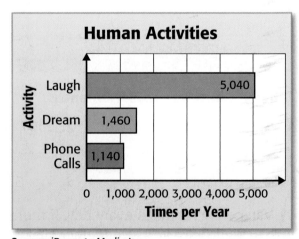

Source: iPromote Media Inc.

H.O.T. Problems

28. OPEN ENDED Copy and complete ■,005 × ■ = ■,0 ■5.

29. FIND THE ERROR Silvia and Dexter are finding 3 × 6,005. Who is correct? Explain.

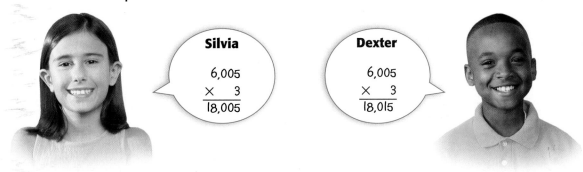

Silvia

$$\begin{array}{r} 6{,}005 \\ \times\quad 3 \\ \hline 18{,}005 \end{array}$$

Dexter

$$\begin{array}{r} 6{,}005 \\ \times\quad 3 \\ \hline 18{,}0l5 \end{array}$$

30. WRITING IN ►MATH Write a real-world problem that involves multiplying a 4-digit number with a zero in the hundreds place by a 1-digit number.

PASS Practice   4-2.3

31. There are 245 boxes of canned juice in a warehouse. If there are 6 cans of juice in each box, how many cans of juice are in the warehouse? (Lesson 6-6)

A 1,240

B 1,440

C 1,470

D 1,480

32. The weights of animals are shown. What is the total weight of 6 bison? (Lesson 6-7)

Animals' Weights	
Animal	**Weight (lb)**
African elephant	14,432
White rhinoceros	7,937
Hippopotamus	5,512
Giraffe	3,527
American bison	2,205

Source: *Scholastic Book of World Records*

F 12,200 lb   H 13,200 lb

G 12,230 lb   J 13,230 lb

Spiral Review

Multiply. Check for reasonableness. (Lessons 6-6 and 6-4)

33. 4 × 65

34. 7 × $327

35. 9 × 1,948

36. Suppose the pattern 7, 12, 17, 22, 27, … continues until there is a total of 12 numbers. Find the sum of the last two numbers. (Lesson 6-5)

FOLDABLES
Study Organizer

GET READY to Study

Be sure the following Key Vocabulary words and Key Concepts are written in your Foldable.

Estimate Products | Multiply Two-Digit Numbers
Multiply Multi-Digit Numbers | Multiply Across Zeros

Key Concepts

Multiply Multiples of 10, 100, and 1,000

Use basic facts and patterns. (p. 237)

$3 \times 7 = 21$	3×7 ones
$3 \times 70 = 210$	3×7 tens
$3 \times 700 = 2,100$	3×7 hundreds
$3 \times 7,000 = 21,000$	3×7 thousands

Estimate Products (p. 242)

$4 \times 192 \rightarrow 4 \times 200 = 800$

Multiply by Multi-Digit Numbers (p. 252)

There are many ways you can multiply.

	3,000 +	500 +	0 +	2	18,000
6	18,000	3,000	0	12	3,000 0 + 12

21,012

$$
\begin{array}{r}
\overset{3\ \ 1}{3,502} \\
\times\ \ \ \ 6 \\
\hline
21,012
\end{array}
$$

Multiply the ones, tens, hundreds, and thousands. Regroup as needed.

Key Vocabulary

Distributive Property of Multiplication (pp. 166, 247)

estimate (pp. 58, 242)

multiply (pp. 142, 237)

product (p. 242)

Vocabulary Check

Choose the vocabulary word that completes the sentence.

1. When you do not need an exact answer, you can _____?_____.

2. Finding the product means you need to _____?_____.

3. The _____?_____ says that you can multiply the addends of a number and then add the products.

4. To _____?_____ products, round factors to their greatest place.

5. When two factors are multiplied together, the result is a(n) _____?_____ .

6. You need to _____?_____ to find the total of equal groups.

Lesson-by-Lesson Review

6-1 **Multiples of 10, 100, and 1,000** (pp. 237–239)

4-2.3,
4-2.4

Example 1
Find 7 × 6,000.

Use basic facts and patterns to
find 7 × 6,000.

7 × 6 = 42	7 × 6 ones
7 × 6**0** = 42**0**	7 × 6 tens
7 × 6**00** = 4,2**00**	7 × 6 hundreds
7 × 6,**000** = 42,**000**	7 × 6 thousands

So, 7 × 6,000 = 42,000.
Notice that this answer is 7 × 6 with
three zeros added to the end.

Multiply. Use basic facts and patterns.

7. 2 × 50   **8.** 4 × 90

9. 5 × 400   **10.** 8 × 600

11. 6 × 3,000   **12.** 9 × 7,000

13. Measurement One ton is equal
to 2,000 pounds. How many
pounds are equal to 7 tons?

6-2 **Problem-Solving Skill: Reasonable Answers** (pp. 240–241)

4-2.3

Example 2
**Andrés walks 40 miles each month.
Is it reasonable to say that he
will walk more than 300 miles in
6 months? Explain.**

Andrés walks 40 miles each month.
Find if it is reasonable to say he will
walk more than 300 miles in 6 months.
Find 6 × 40 and then compare.

6 × 4 = 24

6 × 4**0** = 24**0**

240 < 300. So, it is not reasonable to
say Andrés will walk more than 300
miles in 6 months.

14. Edmund's family eats 12 fruit cups
each week. Is 200 a reasonable
number of fruit cups they will eat
in four weeks? Explain.

15. There are
8 party bags.
Each bag
contains the
items shown.
Is it reasonable to
say that the bags will
have 75 items in all? Explain.

16. Ahmik donates $200 each month
to the local homeless shelter. Is it
reasonable to say that he will give
more than $3,000 a year? Explain.

6-3 Use Rounding to Estimate Products (pp. 242–244)

4-2.3

Example 3
Estimate 4 × 8,596.

First round. Then use basic facts and patterns to multiply.

4 × 8,596

THINK 8,596 rounds to 9,000.

4 × 9,000 = 36,000

So, 4 × 8,596 is about 36,000.

Estimate each product. Then tell if the estimate is *greater than* or *less than* the actual product.

17. 5 × 248
18. 7 × 584

19. 1,478
    × 4
20. 9,385
    × 8

21. About how many children play football if there are 9 teams of 18 children?

22. Rob can read a 240-page book in a week. About how many pages can he read in 6 weeks?

6-4 Multiply Two-Digit Numbers (pp. 246–248)

4-2.3

Example 4
Tania has four decks of 52 cards. How many cards does Tania have?

Find 4 × 52.

Step 1 Multiply the ones.
52
× 4
8   4 × 2 = 8

Step 2 Multiply the tens.
52
× 4
208   4 × 5 = 20

	50	+	2
4	200		8

200
+ 8
208

So, Tania has 208 cards.

Multiply. Check for resonableness.

23. 62
    × 7
24. 77
    × 9

25. 35
    × 3
26. 88
    × 5

27. **Measurement** A kangaroo can jump as far as 44 feet in a single jump. What distance would three jumps of this size cover?

28. Paulo watched 7 movies in one month. Each movie was 120 minutes long. How many minutes did Paulo watch movies during this month?

6-5 Problem-Solving Investigation: Choose a Strategy (pp. 250–251)

4-2.3

Example 5
Dominic is making dinner. Setting the table and preparing a salad will take 15 minutes each. Making the entree will take 1 hour. If dinner is to be served at 6:00 P.M., what time does he need to start preparing dinner?

Use the work backward strategy.

6 P.M.	end result
− 1 hour	entree
5 P.M.	
−15 minutes	salad
4:45 P.M.	
−15 minutes	set table
4:30 P.M.	

So, Dominic needs to start at 4:30 P.M.

Use any strategy to solve.

29. There are 11 fish in an aquarium. Three of the fish are yellow. There are twice as many blue fish as yellow fish. The rest of the fish are red. How many red fish are there?

30. Adelina earns $35 a day for babysitting. She earns a total of $315 for babysitting. How many days did she babysit?

31. Katelyn is going to rent a movie last. She is going to the post office second. She is going to the pet store before the post office. She is going to the library before she rents a movie. In what order is she completing her errands?

6-6 Multiply Multi-Digit Numbers (pp. 252–255)

4-2.3

Example 6
Find $1,276 × 4.

Step 1
Multiply ones.

$$\begin{array}{r} 2 \\ \$1{,}276 \\ \times \quad 4 \\ \hline 4 \end{array}$$

Step 2
Multiply tens.

$$\begin{array}{r} 3\,2 \\ \$1{,}276 \\ \times \quad 4 \\ \hline 04 \end{array}$$

Step 3
Multiply hundreds.

$$\begin{array}{r} 1\ 3\,2 \\ \$1{,}276 \\ \times \quad 4 \\ \hline 104 \end{array}$$

Step 4
Multiply thousands.

$$\begin{array}{r} 1\ 3\,2 \\ \$1{,}276 \\ \times \quad 4 \\ \hline \$5{,}104 \end{array}$$

Multiply. Check for reasonableness.

32. 6 × 109   **33.** 8 × 854

34. $\begin{array}{r} 4{,}355 \\ \times \quad 3 \\ \hline \end{array}$ **35.** $\begin{array}{r} 5{,}820 \\ \times \quad 7 \\ \hline \end{array}$

36. A hen lays an average of 228 eggs in one year. How many eggs does a hen lay in four years?

37. Measurement Except for leap years, there are 365 days in one year. Kevin is 8 years old. How many days old is Kevin?

6-7 Multiply Across Zeros (pp. 258–261)

4-2.3

Example 7

The cost for one person to go skiing for two days is $109. What is the cost for a family of five to go skiing for two days?

You need to find the product of $109 × 5.

Step 1 Multiply the ones.

```
    4
 $109      5 × 9 ones = 45 ones
 ×  5      Regroup 45 ones as 4 tens
    5      and 5 ones.
```

Step 2 Multiply the tens.

```
    4
 $109      5 × 0 tens = 0 tens
 ×  5      Add the regrouped tens.
   45      0 tens + 4 tens = 4 tens
```

Step 3 Multiply the hundreds.

```
    4
 $109
 ×  5      5 × 1 hundred = 5 hundreds
 $545
```

	$100 +	$9
5	$500	$45

```
  $500
+  $45
  $545
```

So, the cost is $545.

Multiply. Check for reasonableness.

38. 107
   × 2

39. 205
   × 4

40. 409
   × 6

41. 603
   × 7

42. 8 × 906

43. 5 × 6,009

Algebra Find the value of *y*.

44. 3 × 207 = *y*

45. *y* = 7 × 4,081

46. Copy and complete the table.

Rule: Multiply by 6.	
Input	Output
307	■
1,009	■
4,708	■
6,003	■
9,002	■

47. **Measurement** A truck driver covered the distance shown in the table below. How many miles did he cover in 5 weeks?

Distance Covered	
Week	Distance (miles)
1	3,008
2	3,008
3	2,805
4	2,805
5	2,805

Multiply. Use basic facts and patterns.

1. 5 × 4
5 × 40
5 × 400
5 × 4,000

2. 9 × 6
9 × 60
9 × 600
9 × 6,000

Multiply. Use mental math.

3. 2 × 60

4. 4 × 50

5. 6 × 800

6. 8 × 9,000

7. School supplies cost $30. Is it reasonable for 9 students to purchase supplies with $300? Explain.

8. MULTIPLE CHOICE Which pair of numbers best completes the equation?

$$\boxed{} \times 100 = \bigcirc$$

A 65 and 650

B 65 and 6,500

C 605 and 6,500

D 650 and 6,500

9. Fiona makes $25 a day babysitting. Is it reasonable to say she will have more than $200 at the end of a week? Explain.

Estimate each product.

10. 4 × 657

11. 7 × 9,431

Multiply.

12. 5 × 604

13. 9 × 7,005

14. Hakeem takes 60-minute tennis lessons twice a week. How many minutes of tennis lessons does Hakeem take in four weeks?

Algebra Find the value of each expression if *n* = 6.

15. $n \times 827$

16. $\$3{,}285 \times n$

Multiply.

17. 4 × 226

18. 8 × 591

Algebra Copy and complete.

19. If 3 × ■ = 21,
then 30 × ■ = 2,100.

20. If 8 × ■ = 48,
then 80 × ■ = 4,800.

21. MULTIPLE CHOICE A plane carries 234 passengers. If the plane makes 4 trips a day, how many passengers does the plane transport a day?

F 826

H 936

G 926

J 981

22. **WRITING IN ►MATH** Joshua does not understand why 4,200 is not a reasonable estimate for 681 × 7. Explain.

PART 1   Multiple Choice

Read each question. Then fill in the correct answer on the answer sheet provided by your teacher or on a sheet of paper.

1. Cora has 9 rolls of pennies. Suppose 50 pennies are in each roll. How many pennies does she have?

   A 360   **C** 450

   B 400   **D** 500

2. Find n if $38 + n = 107$.

   F 68   **H** 79

   G 69   **J** 145

3. The bar graph shows Connor's savings for the month of April.

   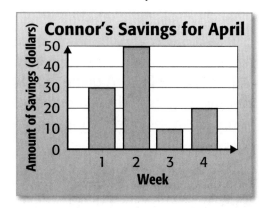

   Which week did Connor save more than $30?

   A Week 1   **C** Week 3

   B Week 2   **D** Week 4

4. How many sheets of paper are there in 6 packages?

   F 3,000   **H** 3,500

   G 3,200   **J** 4,000

5. Which is the value of the digit 3 in 564,327?

   A 30   **C** 3,000

   B 300   **D** 30,000

6. Hugh practices the piano 30 minutes per day 6 days per week. Which expression shows how many minutes he practices in 10 weeks?

   F $6 \times 10 + 30$ **H** $6 \times 10 \times 30$

   G $6 + 10 + 30$ **J** $30 \div 10 \times 6$

7. Joel is going on a three-day biking trip. The daily cost is $46. How much will the trip cost?

   A $92   **C** $138

   B $128   **D** $460

8. Shandra has 3 red crayons, 2 blue crayons, and 4 green crayons. Suppose a crayon is selected at random. Describe the probability that it will be blue.

   F certain   **H** unlikely

   G likely   **J** impossible

9. Samir earns $22 each week mowing lawns. How much will he earn in 4 weeks?

   A $75   **C** $88

   B $80   **D** $125

10. The table shows the number of miles the Lin family drove over three days.

Day	Miles
Tuesday	176
Wednesday	228
Thursday	132

Approximately how many miles did the Lin family drive in the three days?

   F 300 miles

   G 400 miles

   H 500 miles

   J 600 miles

PART 2   Short Response

Record your answers on the answer sheet provided by your teacher or on a sheet of paper.

11. How many CDs are there in 8 packages?

12. Adult admission to the aquarium is $9. On Tuesday, 345 adults visited the aquarium. How much money did the aquarium collect on Tuesday?

PART 3   Extended Response

Record your answers on the answer sheet provided by your teacher or on a sheet of paper.

13. The Marshall School has 8 classrooms. Each classroom has 22 desks. How many desks does the school have? Explain.

14. A male tortoise can weigh up to 573 pounds. What is the greatest amount seven male tortoises can weigh? Explain.

NEED EXTRA HELP?														
If You Missed Question...	1	2	3	4	5	6	7	8	9	10	11	12	13	14
Go to Lesson...	6-1	5-2	3-5	6-1	1-1	5-6	6-4	3-9	6-4	2-2	6-1	6-6	6-4	6-6
SC Academic Standards	4-2.3	4-3.5	4-6.2	4-2.3	4-2.6	4-3.4	4-2.3	4-6.6	4-2.3	3-2.3	4-2.3	4-2.3	4-2.3	4-2.3

CHAPTER 7
Multiply by Two-Digit Numbers

 **BIG Idea** How do you multiply by a two-digit number?

You can use area models and partial products.

Example During recycling week, 15 students collected 12 pounds of recyclable items each. The model shows that 15 × 12 or 180 pounds of recyclable items were collected.

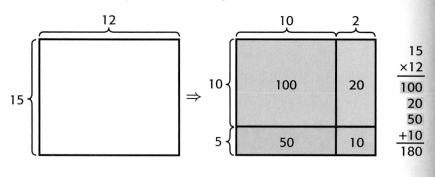

What will I learn in this chapter?

- Multiply by multiples of ten.
- Estimate products by rounding.
- Multiply by two-digit numbers.
- Determine when to estimate or find an exact answer.

Key Vocabulary

Distributive Property of Multiplication

estimate

factor

multiple

product

 **SC Math Online**   **Student Study Tools** at macmillanmh.com

FOLDABLES®
Study Organizer

Make this Foldable to help you organize information about multiplying by two-digit numbers. Begin with 3 sheets of $8\frac{1}{2}$" × 11" paper.

1 **Stack** the paper so that the sheets are $\frac{3}{4}$ inch apart.

2 **Roll** up the edges so tabs are the same size.

3 **Crease** and staple along the fold as shown.

4 **Label** the tabs as shown.

Multiply by Two-Digit Numbers
Estimate Products
Multiply Two-Digit Numbers
Multiply Three-Digit Numbers by Two-Digit Numbers
Multiply Greater Numbers
Vocabulary

You have two ways to check prerequisite skills for this chapter.

Option 2

SC Math Online > Take the Chapter Readiness Quiz at macmillanmh.com.

Option 1

Complete the Quick Check below.

QUICK Check

Round to the given place. (Lesson 1-6)

1. 604; nearest hundred

2. 2,188; nearest thousand

3. 85,888; nearest ten-thousand

4. 681,002; nearest hundred thousand

5. The students raised $6,784 for a new playground. To the nearest thousand, about how much money did the students raise?

Add. (Lesson 2-4)

6.   759
       + 307

7. 5,138
       + 507

8. 9,290
       + 812

9. 6,005
       + 8,204

10. 34,068
        + 6,055

11.   242,607
        + 480,196

Write the multiplication expression for each model. Then multiply. (Lesson 6-4)

12.

13.

Multiply.

14. 36 × 7

15. 40 × 9

16. 86 × 5

7-1 Multiply by Tens

Rita took 20 pictures at her family reunion. She printed the pictures so that each of her 25 family members could have them. How many pictures did Rita print?

MAIN IDEA

I will multiply a whole number by a multiple of ten.

SC Academic Standards

4-2.3 Apply an algorithm to multiply whole numbers fluently.

SC Math Online

macmillanmh.com
• Extra Examples
• Personal Tutor
• Self-Check Quiz

When you multiply a two-digit number by a multiple of ten such as 20, 30, 40, …, the digit in the ones place is always a zero.

Real-World EXAMPLE Multiply by Tens

1 PHOTOGRAPHS How many pictures did Rita print?

You need to find 25×20.

One Way: Use Properties

25×20	Write the problem.
$25 \times (10 \times 2)$	Think of 20 as 10×2.
$25 \times (2 \times 10)$	Commutative Property of Multiplication
$(25 \times 2) \times 10$	Associative Property of Multiplication
50×10	Multiply. $25 \times 2 = 50$
500	Mental Math

Another Way: Use Paper and Pencil

Step 1 Multiply the ones.	**Step 2** Multiply the tens.
$\begin{array}{r} 25 \\ \times\ 20 \\ \hline 0 \end{array}$ ← 0 ones × 25 = 0	$\begin{array}{r} 25 \\ \times\ 20 \\ \hline 500 \end{array}$ ← 2 tens × 25 = 50 tens

So, Rita printed 500 pictures.

② **MUSIC** An electronics store has 30 digital music players in stock that cost $125 each. How much do the digital music players cost altogether?

Step 1 Multiply the ones.

$$\begin{array}{r} \$125 \\ \times\ 30 \\ \hline 0 \end{array}$$ ← 0 ones × 125 = 0

Step 2 Multiply the tens.

$$\begin{array}{r} \$125 \\ \times\ 30 \\ \hline \$3,750 \end{array}$$ ← 3 tens × 125 = 375 tens

So, the music players cost a total of $3,750.

Check

Think of 30 × 125 as 3 × 10 × 125.

30 × $125	Write the problem.
(3 × 10) × $125	Think of 30 as 3 × 10.
(10 × 3) × $125	Commutative Property
10 × (3 × $125)	Associative Property
10 × $375	Multiply. 3 × $125 = $375
$3,750	Mental Math

So, the answer is correct. ✓

Remember

When you multiply a number by a multiple of ten, the digit in the ones place is always zero.

CHECK What You Know

Multiply. See Examples 1 and 2 (pp. 273–274)

1. $\begin{array}{r} 36 \\ \times\ 10 \\ \hline \end{array}$

2. $\begin{array}{r} 53 \\ \times\ 30 \\ \hline \end{array}$

3. $\begin{array}{r} 79 \\ \times\ 80 \\ \hline \end{array}$

4. $255 × 20

5. $389 × 40

6. $518 × 70

7. Measurement Latasha bikes 20 miles every week. There are 52 weeks in a year. How many miles does she bike in a year?

8. (Talk About It) Joey is finding 40 × 67. Explain why he can think of 40 × 67 as 4 × 10 × 67.

Multiply. See Examples 1 and 2 (pp. 273–274)

9. 15
    × 20

10. 27
    × 30

11. 46
    × 40

12. 53
    × 60

13. 80 × 80

14. 94 × 90

15. $275 × 10

16. $312 × 30

17. $381 × 50

18. $457 × 50

19. $564 × 70

20. $698 × 80

21. If 7 × 29 = 203, then what is 70 × 29?

22. If 3 × 52 = 156, then what is 30 × 52?

23. Baby robins eat 14 feet of earthworms each day. How many feet of worms does a baby robin eat in 20 days?

24. Mozart could learn a piece of music in 30 minutes. How long would it take him to learn 15 pieces of music?

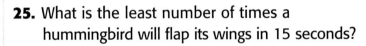

Real-World PROBLEM SOLVING

Birds Hummingbirds feed every 10 minutes. They fly about 25 miles per hour and flap their wings 60 to 80 times each second.

25. What is the least number of times a hummingbird will flap its wings in 15 seconds?

26. What is the greatest number of times it will flap its wing in 15 seconds?

27. How many minutes have passed if a hummingbird has eaten 45 times?

28. If a hummingbird flies a total of 20 hours, how far did it fly?

H.O.T. Problems

29. **OPEN ENDED** Create a number sentence with two 2-digit factors whose product has 3 zeros.

30. **WHICH ONE DOESN'T BELONG?** Identify the multiplication problem that does not belong with the other three. Explain.

| 15 × 30 | 28 × 20 | 41 × 21 | 67 × 40 |

31. **WRITING IN ►MATH** How many zeros would be in the product of 50 and 60? Explain.

Estimate Products

GET READY to Learn

Did you know that a hamster sleeps more than half the day? It sleeps about 14 hours each day. About how many hours does it sleep in 3 weeks?

The word *about* tells you to estimate. When you estimate the product of two two-digit factors, it is helpful to round them both.

Real-World EXAMPLE   Estimate Products

1   **ANIMALS A hamster sleeps 14 hours each day. About how many hours does a hamster sleep in 3 weeks?**

There are 21 days in 3 weeks. So, estimate 21 × 14.

Step 1 Round each factor to the nearest ten.

$$\begin{array}{r} 21 \\ \times\ 14 \end{array} \longrightarrow \begin{array}{r} 20 \\ \times\ 10 \end{array}$$

21 rounds to 20.
14 rounds to 10.

Step 2 Multiply.

$$\begin{array}{r} 20 \\ \times\ 10 \\ \hline 200 \end{array}$$

0 ones × 20 = 0
1 ten × 20 = 20 tens

So, a hamster sleeps about 200 hours in 21 days or 3 weeks. Since both factors were rounded down, the estimate is less than the actual product.

	21
14	Actual Product

	20
10	Estimate
	Part Not Included

② MEASUREMENT Tonya spends 35 minutes playing at the park each day. About how many minutes does she play at the park in a year?

There are approximately 365 days in a year. So, you need to estimate 365 × 35.

Step 1 Round each factor to its greatest place.

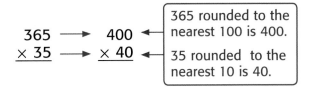

$$365 \longrightarrow 400$$
$$\times\ 35 \longrightarrow \times\ 40$$

365 rounded to the nearest 100 is 400.

35 rounded to the nearest 10 is 40.

Step 2 Multiply.

$$\begin{array}{r} 400 \\ \times\ 40 \\ \hline 16{,}000 \end{array}$$

So, Tonya spends about 16,000 minutes playing at the park in a year. Since both factors were rounded up, the estimate is greater than the actual product.

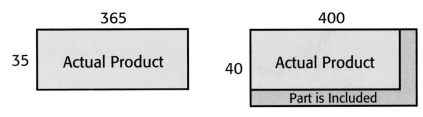

Remember

If one factor is rounded up and one factor is rounded down, it will not be obvious whether the estimate is greater or less than the actual product.

CHECK What You Know

Estimate. Tell whether the estimate is *greater than* or *less than* the actual product. See Examples 1 and 2 (pp. 276–277)

1. $\begin{array}{r} 34 \\ \times\ 12 \end{array}$

2. $\begin{array}{r} 57 \\ \times\ 25 \end{array}$

3. $376 × 17

4. 525 × 43

5. The average person makes about 22 phone calls each week. About how many phone calls is this each year?

6. **Talk About It** Explain how you know if an estimated product is more or less than the actual product.

Estimate. Tell whether the estimate is *greater than* or *less than* the actual product. See Examples 1 and 2 (pp. 276–277)

7. 28
    × 25

8. 43
    × 14

9. $56
    × 37

10. 58
    × 29

11. 64
    × 41

12. 79
    × 55

13. $91
    × 64

14. 94
    × 82

15. $234 × 11

16. 352 × 37

17. 489 × 86

18. 535 × 42

19. 678 × 56

20. 739 × 84

21. 891 × 78

22. 919 × 92

23. An antelope can run 55 miles per hour. About how many miles would it travel if it ran a total of 12 hours?

24. Gabe averages 16 points in each basketball game. About how many points will he score in 14 games?

25. A certain type of millipede has 750 legs. About how many legs would 12 of these millipedes have?

26. **Measurement** About how many pounds of fruit would the average American eat in 11 years?

Food Eaten Each Year	
Type of Food	Amount (lb)
Fresh fruit	127
Fresh vegetables	148
Milk and cream	205

Source: *The Top 100 of Everything*

South Carolina Data File

Adventure Carolina offers fun trips down the Saluda, Congaree, and Edisto Rivers in South Carolina.

27. What would be the approximate cost of 14 Edisto River Canoe and Kayak Trips?

28. What would be the approximate cost for 26 people to participate in a Tube Launch?

Adventure Carolina Activities	
Activity	Fee
Full Moon Canoe and Kayak Trip	$75
Tube Launch	$25
Edisto River Canoe and Kayak Trip	$45

Source: Adventure Carolina

H.O.T. Problems

29. OPEN ENDED Identify two factors that have an estimated product of 2,000.

30. NUMBER SENSE Estimate 51 × 39 and 84 × 45. Which is closer to its actual product? Explain your reasoning.

31. **WRITING IN ►MATH** Write a real-world problem that involves estimating the product of two 2-digit numbers.

PASS Practice   4-2.3

32. What is the total length of 35 anacondas? (Lesson 7-1)

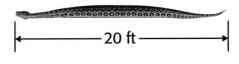

|← 20 ft →|

A 600 feet **C** 800 feet

B 700 feet **D** 900 feet

33. There are 365 days in a year. Which is the best estimate of the number of days in 12 years? (Lesson 7-2)

F 7,000

G 6,000

H 5,000

J 4,000

Spiral Review

Multiply. (Lesson 7-1)

34. 27
× 10

35. 43
× 50

36. $96
× 70

Multiply. Check for reasonableness. (Lesson 6-7)

37. 1,006 × 3

38. 4,065 × 6

39. 7,040 × 9

40. Write an equation that describes the pattern in the table. Then use the equation to find the next three numbers. (Lesson 5-8)

Input (w)	1	3	5	7	9	11
Output (v)	4	12	20	▨	▨	▨

41. Arthur earns $20 for every lawn he mows. He mows 12 lawns twice a month. He has been mowing for 3 months. How much money does he make in 1 month? Identify any extra or missing information. Then solve. (Lesson 5-3)

Write the value of the underlined digit. (Lesson 1-2)

42. 189,3<u>9</u>7

43. <u>2</u>,670,830

44. 34,7<u>9</u>1,028

Problem-Solving Strategy

MAIN IDEA I will solve a problem by acting it out.

 SCAS **4-1.1 Analyze information to solve increasingly more sophisticated problems.**

Sonoda has 6 coins in his bank. The coins equal 65¢. What combination of coins does he have in his bank?

Understand	**What facts do you know?** • Sonoda has 6 coins. • The value of the 6 coins is 65¢. **What do you need to find?** • Find the coins Sonoda has in his bank.
Plan	You can use play money to act out different combinations of 65¢.
Solve	One way to make 65¢ is with 2 quarters, 1 dime, and 1 nickel. But, that is only 4 coins. You need 2 more coins.  Take 1 quarter and exchange it for 2 dimes and 1 nickel. The value stays the same, and the number of coins increases to 6.  So, Sonoda has 1 quarter, 3 dimes, and 2 nickels.
Check	Look back at the problem.

$$
\begin{array}{llll}
& 1 \text{ quarter} + & 3 \text{ dimes} & + \ 2 \text{ nickels} \\
= & 25¢ \ + & 10¢ + 10¢ + 10¢ & + \ 5¢ + 5¢ \\
= & 25¢ \ + & 30¢ & + \ 10¢ \\
= & & 65¢ &
\end{array}
$$

So, the answer is correct.

Refer to the problem on the previous page.

1. If Sonoda has a few coins that total 55¢, what is the least amount of coins he can have?

2. Suppose Sonoda had 60¢ in his bank. What 5 coins would he have?

3. Suppose Sonoda found 3 coins on the sidewalk. The coins total $1. What coins did Sonoda find? Explain.

4. Describe another strategy you could use to solve this problem.

▶ PRACTICE the Strategy

SCAS • PASS
Extra Practice, p. R18

Solve. Use the act it out strategy.

5. Angelo's father is 30 years old. This is 10 years older than twice Angelo's age. How old is Angelo?

6. Ellen needs to visit 3 Web sites for her homework. In how many different ways can she visit the Web sites?

7. There are five people at a party, and each person has shaken hands with every other person. How many handshakes took place among the five people?

8. **Geometry** Can 12 toothpicks be used to form 4 squares that are the same size and same shape?

9. Berta, Maya, and Zach are in different checkout lines at a store. Berta has 3 more people in front of her than are in front of Maya. There are 2 times as many people in front of Zach as there are in front of Maya. The total number of people in front of the girls is 11. How many people are in front of each person?

10. **Geometry** How many different rectangles can you make using all of the squares shown below?

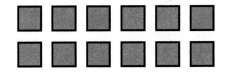

11. List five different money combinations that equal 34¢.

12. Jamaica has 8 coins with a value of $1. What coins does she have?

13. Dane needs to set up tables for his nine family members and himself to eat dinner. The square tables will seat one person on each side. Explain how Dane can arrange six square tables in a rectangle so that there is one seat for each person with no extra seats.

14. **WRITING IN ▶MATH** When should the act it out strategy be used to solve a problem? Explain.

Multiply Two-Digit Numbers

In Lesson 4-6, you learned that the **Distributive Property of Multiplication** allows you to break apart factors to find a product. You can use the Distributive Property to multiply two-digit numbers.

Distributive Property   Key Concept

To multiply a sum by a number, multiply each addend by the number and add the products.

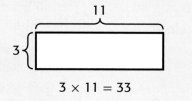
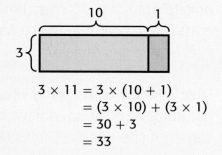

$3 \times 11 = 33$

$3 \times 11 = 3 \times (10 + 1)$
$= (3 \times 10) + (3 \times 1)$
$= 30 + 3$
$= 33$

ACTIVITY   Find 12×15.

Step 1 **Draw a rectangle.**

Draw a rectangle on graph paper. Use 12 and 15 as the dimensions.

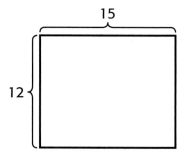

Step 2 **Separate the tens and ones.**

First, break up the 15 as 10 and 5. Next, break up the 12 as 10 and 2.

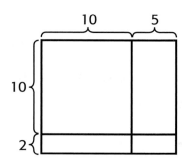

Step 3 **Find each product. Then add.**

10 × 10	=	100
10 × 5	=	50
2 × 10	=	20
2 × 5	=	+ 10
		180

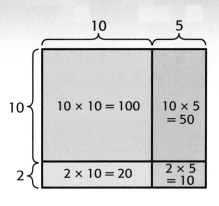

Step 4 **Make the connection.**

Distributive Property

$$12 \times 15 = (10 \times 15) + (2 \times 15)$$
$$= (10 \times 10) + (10 \times 5) + (2 \times 10) + (2 \times 5)$$
$$= 100 + 50 + 20 + 10$$
$$= 180$$

Partial Products

	15	
	× 12	
	10	2 × 5
	20	2 × 10
	50	10 × 5
	+ 100	10 × 10
	180	Add partial products.

Think About It

1. How would you use the Distributive Property to find 12 × 18?

 CHECK What You Know

Write the multiplication sentence for each area model. Multiply.

2.

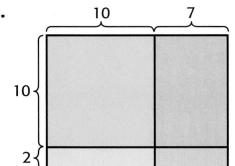

3.

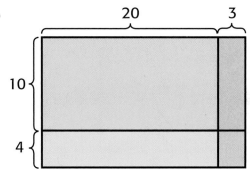

Multiply. Use an area model and the Distributive Property.

4. 12 × 10

5. 14 × 18

6. 25 × 28

7. **WRITING IN ►MATH** Explain how to find 16 × 19.

Multiply Two-Digit Numbers

GET READY to Learn

A coyote travels 27 miles per hour. How far would a coyote travel in 12 hours?

MAIN IDEA

I will multiply two-digit numbers.

SC Academic Standards

4-2.3 Apply an algorithm to multiply whole numbers fluently.

SC Math Online

macmillanmh.com
• Extra Examples
• Personal Tutor
• Self-Check Quiz

There is more than one way to multiply two-digit numbers.

Real-World EXAMPLE

1 **MEASUREMENT** A coyote travels 27 miles each hour. Multiply 27×12 to find how far a coyote can travel in 12 hours.

One Way: Partial Products	Another Way: Paper and Pencil
$\begin{array}{r} 27 \\ \times\ 12 \\ \hline 14 \\ 40 \\ 70 \\ +\ 200 \\ \hline 324 \end{array}$ Multiply 2×7. Multiply 2×20. Multiply 10×7. Multiply 10×20. Add partial products.	**Step 1** Multiply the ones. $\begin{array}{r} 1 \\ 27 \\ \times\ 12 \\ \hline 54 \end{array}$ ← 2×27

One Way partial products area model:

	20	7
10	200	70
2	40	14

Step 2 Multiply the tens.

$\begin{array}{r} 1 \\ 27 \\ \times\ 12 \\ \hline 54 \\ 270 \end{array}$ ← 2×27 ← 10×27

Step 3 Add the products.

$\begin{array}{r} 1 \\ 27 \\ \times\ 12 \\ \hline 54 \\ +\ 270 \\ \hline 324 \end{array}$ ← Add.

So, a coyote can travel 324 miles in 12 hours.

Real-World EXAMPLE **Multiply Money**

2 EXPENSES Heidi's monthly bills are shown. How much does she spend on her cell phone service in 2 years?

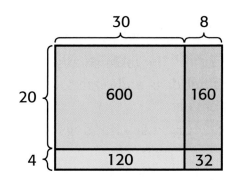

Monthly Bills	
Cable	$55
Cell phone	$38
Movie club	$21
Water	$93

Heidi's cell phone bill is $38. There are 24 months in 2 years. So multiply $38 by 24 to find how much she spends in 2 years.

Estimate $40 \times 20 = 800$

Step 1 Multiply the ones.

$$\begin{array}{r} \$38 \\ \times\ 24 \\ \hline 152 \end{array}$$ ← 4×38

Step 2 Multiply the tens.

$$\begin{array}{r} \$38 \\ \times\ 24 \\ \hline 152 \\ +\ 760 \end{array}$$ ← 20×38

Remember

Make an estimate to check the reasonableness of the answer.

Step 3 Add the products.

$$\begin{array}{r} \$38 \\ \times\ 24 \\ \hline 152 \\ +760 \\ \hline 912 \end{array}$$ ← Add.

	30	8
20	600	160
4	120	32

So, the cost of cell phone service for 2 years is $912.

Check for Reasonableness
912 is close to the estimate of 800. The answer is reasonable. ✔

CHECK What You Know

Multiply. See Examples 1 and 2 (pp. 284–285)

1.
$$\begin{array}{r} 35 \\ \times\ 24 \end{array}$$

2.
$$\begin{array}{r} \$57 \\ \times\ 42 \end{array}$$

3. 92×81

4. A farmer plants 35 rows of tomatoes. There are 25 plants in each row. How many plants are there altogether?

5. **Talk About It** Explain the steps needed to find the product of 23 and 56.

Practice and Problem Solving

Multiply. See Examples 1 and 2 (pp. 284–285)

6. 19
× 15

7. 36
× 24

8. 42
× 38

9. 52
× 47

10. $54
× 51

11. $68
× 46

12. $74
× 63

13. $82
× 49

14. 47 × 24

15. 64 × 46

16. 83 × 67

17. 91 × 78

18. Bamboo plants can grow up to 36 inches in a day. How many inches could they grow in 3 weeks?

19. Josie earns about 28 points on each quiz she takes. How many points will Josie earn on 12 quizzes?

20. Measurement A greyhound dog can jump a distance of 27 feet. How many feet will a greyhound travel if it jumps 12 times?

21. Measurement Each day, enough paper is recycled in the U.S. to fill 15 miles of train boxcars. How many miles of boxcars could be filled over 25 days?

Real-World PROBLEM SOLVING

Food The table shows the average amount of hot dogs and pizza slices each person eats per year.

22. How many hot dogs will a person eat in 11 years?

23. How many slices of pizza will a person eat in 12 years?

24. How many more hot dogs than pizza slices will a person eat in 15 years?

Amount of Food Eaten Each Year	
Food	Number
Hot dog	60
Slice of pizza	46

Source: National Association of Pizza Operators

H.O.T. Problems

25. OPEN ENDED Copy and complete the multiplication problem to make a true sentence.

20
× ■■
■00

26. WHICH ONE DOESN'T BELONG? Identify the multiplication problem that does not belong with the other three. Explain.

22
× 15

$45
× 28

37
× 18

$66
× 25

27. **WRITING IN ►MATH** Explain why the product of two 2-digit numbers can never be two digits.

Multiply. (Lesson 7-1)

1. 38
× 30

2. 52
× 20

3. Measurement John jogs 30 miles every week. There are 52 weeks in a year. How many miles does John jog in a year? (Lesson 7-1)

4. MULTIPLE CHOICE What is the total length of 30 newborn Florida alligators? (Lesson 7-1)

|← 10 in. →|

A 200 inches   **C** 400 inches

B 300 inches   **D** 500 inches

Estimate. Tell whether the estimate is *greater than* or *less than* the actual product. (Lesson 7-2)

5. 24
× 14

6. $37
× 21

7. MULTIPLE CHOICE There are 365 days in a year. Which is the best estimate of the number of days in 23 years? (Lesson 7-2)

F 4,000 days   **H** 7,000 days

G 5,000 days   **J** 8,000 days

8. The average person sends about 25 E-mails a month. About how many E-mails is this each year? (Lesson 7-2)

For Exercises 9 and 10, use the act it out strategy. (Lesson 7-3)

9. Talia's mother is 40 years old. This is 13 years older than three times Talia's age. How old is Talia?

10. Emil has 4 coins in his pocket equaling 41¢. What combination of coins does he have in his pocket?

Multiply. (Lesson 7-4)

11. 27
× 13

12. 45
× 14

13. $67 × 42

14. 77 × 53

15. Measurement A person breathes 95 gallons of air every hour. How many gallons of air does a person breathe in one day? (Lesson 7-4)

16. **WRITING IN ►MATH** Mae is finding the product to the multiplication problem shown below. How many zeros will the product have? Explain. (Lesson 7-1)

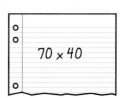

70 × 40

Multiply Three-Digit Numbers by Two-Digit Numbers

MAIN IDEA

I will multiply a three-digit number by a two-digit number.

SC Academic Standards

4-2.3 Apply an algorithm to multiply whole numbers fluently.

SC Math Online

macmillanmh.com

• Extra Examples
• Personal Tutor
• Self-Check Quiz

GET READY to Learn

Rose uses about 275 minutes on her cell phone each month. How many minutes does she use in a year?

You can multiply 3-digit numbers by 2-digit numbers.

Real-World EXAMPLE

1 PHONES How many minutes does Rose use in a year?

There are 12 months in 1 year. So, multiply the number of minutes each month by 12. Find 275×12.

Estimate $300 \times 10 = 3,000$

Step 1 Multiply 275 by 2.

$$
\begin{array}{r}
{\scriptstyle 1\ 1} \\
275 \\
\times\ 12 \\
\hline
550
\end{array}
$$
← 2×275

Step 2 Multiply 275 by 1 ten.

$$
\begin{array}{r}
{\scriptstyle 1\ 1} \\
275 \\
\times\ 12 \\
\hline
550 \\
2,750
\end{array}
$$
← 10×275

Step 3 Add the products.

$$
\begin{array}{r}
{\scriptstyle 1\ 1} \\
275 \\
\times\ 12 \\
\hline
550 \\
+2,750 \\
\hline
3,300
\end{array}
$$
← Add.

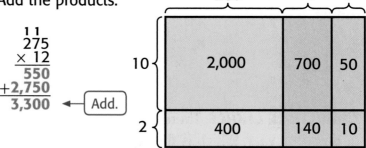

	200	70	5
10	2,000	700	50
2	400	140	10

So, Rose uses 3,300 minutes in a year.

Check for Reasonableness

Since 3,300 is close to the estimate, the answer is reasonable. ✔

2 **MONEY A school bought 25 of the computers shown. What was the total cost?**

You need to multiply $749 by 25.

Estimate $700 × 30 = $21,000

Step 1 Multiply $749 by 5.

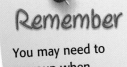

Remember

You may need to regroup when multiplying the ones, tens, and hundreds.

$$\begin{array}{r} \overset{4}{} \\ \$749 \\ \times\ 25 \\ \hline \$3{,}745 \end{array}$$ ◄── $749 × 5

Step 2 Multiply $749 by 20.

$$\begin{array}{r} \overset{1}{\overset{4}{}} \\ \$749 \\ \times\ 25 \\ \hline \$3{,}745 \\ \$14{,}980 \end{array}$$ ◄── $749 × 20

Step 3 Add the partial products.

$$\begin{array}{r} \overset{1}{\overset{4}{}} \\ \$749 \\ \times\ 25 \\ \hline \$3{,}745 \\ +\$14{,}980 \\ \hline \$18{,}725 \end{array}$$ ◄── Add.

So, the product of $749 and 25 is $18,725.

Check for Reasonableness
Since $18,725 is close to the estimate, the answer is reasonable. ✓

CHECK What You Know

Multiply. See Examples 1 and 2 (pp. 288–289)

1. 135
× 18

2. 340
× 32

3. $703 × 89

4. A herd of elephants can travel 50 miles a day. At this rate, how far could a herd travel in a year?

5. **Talk About It** Explain how to find the product of 56 and 945.

Multiply. See Examples 1 and 2 (pp. 288–289)

6. 106
    × 12

7. 248
    × 24

8. 283
    × 33

9. 362
    × 35

10. 467
    × 41

11. 489
    × 53

12. $508
    × 59

13. $632
    × 66

14. $770 × 71

15. $862 × 87

16. $901 × 96

17. $934 × 97

18. Every second, 630 steel cans are recycled. How many cans are recycled in 1 minute?

19. **Measurement** If a city receives 451 inches of rainfall each year, how much rainfall will the city receive in 35 years?

20. **Measurement** Aiden's pet cat is 13 years old. How many days old is Aiden's cat?

21. Suppose a city has 206 days of fog each year. How many days of fog will occur in 12 years?

Real-World PROBLEM SOLVING

Sports The table shows facts about balls used in sports.

22. How many dimples are on a dozen golf balls?

23. How many stitches do 75 baseballs have?

24. Find the difference in the number of dimples on 25 golf balls and the number of stitches on 25 baseballs.

Sports Ball Facts	
Ball	**Fact**
Golf ball	450 dimples
Baseball	108 stitches
Soccer ball	32 panels

H.O.T. Problems

25. **FIND THE ERROR** Michelle and Alberto are finding 351 × 26. Who is correct? Explain.

Michelle
351
× 26
9,126

Alberto
351
× 26
3,106

26. **WRITING IN MATH** Write a real-world problem that involves multiplying a 3-digit number by a 2-digit number.

27. While riding in a car, Denzel counted 17 blue cars on a highway in 1 minute. At this rate, how many blue cars will Denzel see in 45 minutes? (Lesson 7-4)

A 360

B 400

C 765

D 775

28. There are 24 hours in a day and 365 days in a year. How many hours are in a year? (Lesson 7-5)

F 2,190

G 7,440

H 8,000

J 8,760

Spiral Review

Multiply. (Lesson 7-4)

29.
$$\begin{array}{r} 34 \\ \times\ 10 \\ \hline \end{array}$$

30.
$$\begin{array}{r} 55 \\ \times\ 49 \\ \hline \end{array}$$

31.
$$\begin{array}{r} \$72 \\ \times\ 66 \\ \hline \end{array}$$

32. The tables shown need to be joined together so that 20 students can sit down for a student council meeting. Two people can sit on each side of a table. Draw a picture to show how the tables should be arranged. (Lesson 7-3)

Estimate. Tell whether the estimate is *greater than* or *less than* the actual product. (Lesson 7-2)

33.
$$\begin{array}{r} 26 \\ \times\ 17 \\ \hline \end{array}$$

34.
$$\begin{array}{r} 61 \\ \times\ 33 \\ \hline \end{array}$$

35.
$$\begin{array}{r} \$87 \\ \times\ 75 \\ \hline \end{array}$$

Find the value of each expression if $a = 2$ and $b = 5$. (Lesson 5-6)

36. $24 \div (a \times 4)$

37. $6 \times (11 - b)$

38. $b \times (23 - 15)$

Find all of the factors of each number. (Lesson 4-9)

39. 8

40. 11

41. 24

42. 36

43. For every 4 magazines Avery sells, his school receives $2. Use the table to find how much money he will raise if he sells 20 magazines. (Lesson 3-3)

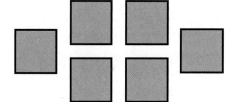

Magazines Sold	4	8	12	16	20
Money	$2	$4	$6		

WALLS
WITH HISTORY

Humans have built forts all over the world for thousands of years. There are more than 136 forts in the United States. Some forts can hold hundreds to thousands of people, while others hold less than 100. Fort Sumter, a fort in South Carolina, could house 650 soldiers. This fort is where the shots starting the Civil War were fired.

Some forts like Sutter's Fort are now museums or state parks. However, other forts like Fort Knox in Kentucky are still used by the military today.

Famous Forts

Fort	Size of Main Building
Fort McIntosh (Georgia)	33 yd by 33 yd
The Alamo (Texas)	148 ft by 159 ft
Stone Fort at Harper's Ferry (West Virginia)	40 ft by 100 ft
Sutter's Fort (California)	64 ft by 35 ft
Fort Clatsop (Oregon)	50 ft by 50 ft

Did You Know?

Cannons at Fort Sumter could shoot one and a quarter miles.

🌐 Real-World Math

Use the information on pages 292 and 293 to solve each problem.

1. What is the area, or amount of space, that Stone Fort at Harper's Ferry covers? (*Hint:* Multiply the length and width to find its area.)

2. The Alamo's main building is divided into 2 rooms. One room is 148 feet × 74 feet. What is the area of this room?

3. How much larger is the area of the Stone Fort at Harper's Ferry than the area of Fort Clatsop?

4. Fort Sumter has 5 walls. Each wall is between 170 and 190 feet long. What is the total estimated distance around Fort Sumter?

5. What is the area of Sutter's Fort?

6. What is the distance around The Alamo?

7. Which fort is larger, the Stone Fort at Harper's Ferry or Fort McIntosh? Explain.

Problem-Solving Investigation

<u>MAIN IDEA</u> I will choose the best strategy to solve a problem.

 SCAS 4-1.1 Analyze information to solve increasingly more sophisticated problems.

P.S.I. TEAM +

GREGORY: I spent 4 hours at a carnival. I spent 45 minutes eating and 55 minutes playing games. I also rode 12 rides, which took about 15 minutes each.

YOUR MISSION: Determine if Gregory is correct in saying that he spent 4 hours at the carnival.

Understand	You know the amount of time Gregory spent at the carnival and on each activity. Find if he is correct.
Plan	Solve a multi-step problem. Find the total number of minutes spent on activities and compare to 4 hours.
Solve	First, change hours to minutes. Then compare.

$$
\begin{array}{r}
60 \text{ minutes} \\
60 \text{ minutes} \\
60 \text{ minutes} \\
+ \ 60 \text{ minutes} \\
\hline
240 \text{ minutes}
\end{array}
\qquad
\begin{array}{r}
15 \\
\times \ 12 \\
\hline
30 \\
+ \ 150 \\
\hline
180
\end{array}
\qquad
\begin{array}{r}
45 \text{ minutes} \\
55 \text{ minutes} \\
+ \ 180 \text{ minutes} \\
\hline
280 \text{ minutes}
\end{array}
$$

time Gregory said he spent at carnival	time spent riding rides	time spent on carnival activities

Since 240 minutes does not equal 280 minutes, Gregory is not correct.

Check	Look back. Use subtraction to check amount of time spent on carnival activities. $280 - 180 - 55 - 45 = 0$. So, Gregory was not correct.

Use any strategy shown below to solve. Tell what strategy you used.

PROBLEM-SOLVING STRATEGIES
• Make a table.
• Act it out.

1. A coach bought 5 pizzas. Each pizza has 12 slices. There are 18 players on the team. Is it reasonable to say that each player can eat 3 slices? Explain.

2. Betty has 12 vases to make gifts for her family. Each vase will need ribbon that costs 30¢ and beads that cost $1. She estimates she will spend $15. Is her estimate reasonable? Explain.

3. **Measurement** Javon hikes the trail shown below 3 times a week. Is it reasonable to say that he hikes more than 20 miles in one month? Explain.

Hiking Trail 2 Miles

4. Two numbers have a sum of 16 and a product of 48. What are the numbers?

5. Carson has 57¢. He has 3 kinds of coins and 9 coins in all. What coins does Carson have?

6. Ashanti has 13 trophies. Three of the trophies are for swimming. She has two times as many soccer trophies as swimming trophies. The rest of the trophies are for tennis. How many tennis trophies does she have?

7. Edmundo has $36 saved and needs to buy the items below. Does he have enough money? Explain.

8. **Measurement** At 6:00 A.M. the temperature was 45°F. At 12:00 P.M. the temperature was 55°F. At 8:00 P.M. the temperature was 49°F. Create a number sentence to show the changes in temperatures.

9. Every teacher at Elmwood Elementary is provided with 3,000 sheets of paper. How many sheets of paper do the 40 teachers have altogether?

10. **WRITING IN MATH** Isaac is baking four batches of bran muffins. There are 12 muffins in each batch. The answer is 144 muffins. What is the question?

Multiply Greater Numbers

GET READY to Learn

Suppose 7,275 visitors go to a certain zoo every week. How many visitors go to the zoo in a year?

You can multiply multi-digit numbers by two-digit numbers.

Real-World EXAMPLE

① **ZOOS** If 7,275 visitors go to a zoo every week, how many visitors go to the zoo in a year? Find 7,275 × 52.

Estimate 7,000 × 50 = 350,000

Step 1 Multiply the ones. Regroup if necessary.

```
    1 1
  7,275
×    52
─────────
 14,550  ◄── 7,275 × 2
```

Step 2 Multiply the tens.

```
    1 3 2
    1 1
  7,275
×    52
─────────
 14,550
363,750  ◄── 7,275 × 50
```

Step 3 Add the partial products. Check for reasonableness.

```
    1 3 2
    1 1
  7,275
×    52
─────────
 14,550
+363,750
─────────
378,300  ◄── Add.
```

So, the zoo gets 378,300 visitors in a year.

Check for Reasonableness

Since 378,300 is close to the estimate, the answer is reasonable. ✔

2 **SPORTS** Suppose a stadium can seat 45,050 fans. There are 81 home games in a season. What is the greatest number of fans that can attend the home games in one season?

You need to find 45,050 × 81.

Estimate 50,000 × 80 = 4,000,000

Remember

Write a zero in the ones place when you multiply the tens.

Step 1 Multiply the ones.

$$
\begin{array}{r}
45{,}050 \\
\times\quad 81 \\
\hline
45{,}050
\end{array}
$$
← 45,050 × 1

Step 2 Multiply the tens.

$$
\begin{array}{r}
\overset{4\ \ 4}{45{,}050} \\
\times\quad 81 \\
\hline
45{,}050 \\
3{,}604{,}000
\end{array}
$$
← 45,050 × 80

Step 3 Add the partial products.

$$
\begin{array}{r}
\overset{4\ \ 4}{45{,}050} \\
\times\quad 81 \\
\hline
45{,}050 \\
+\ 3{,}604{,}000 \\
\hline
3{,}649{,}050
\end{array}
$$
← Add.

So, 3,649,050 fans can attend all of the home games.

Check for Reasonableness

3,649,050 is close to the estimate. The answer is reasonable. ✓

CHECK What You Know

Multiply. See Examples 1 and 2 (pp. 296–297)

1.
$$
\begin{array}{r}
1{,}360 \\
\times\quad 29 \\
\end{array}
$$

2.
$$
\begin{array}{r}
7{,}251 \\
\times\quad 58 \\
\end{array}
$$

3. $23,973 × 41

4. An average professional baseball player earns $15,750 per game. How much money does a player earn in a month in which 23 games are played?

5. **Talk About It** How is multiplying a 3-digit number by a 2-digit number like multiplying a 5-digit number by a 2-digit number?

Multiply. See Examples 1 and 2 (pp. 296–297)

6. 1,418
    × 12

7. 2,983
    × 24

8. 4,166
    × 35

9. 6,873
    × 39

10. 8,316
    × 14

11. 9,809
    × 67

12. $13,820
    × 21

13. $17,846
    × 26

14. $25,067 × 30

15. $29,452 × 38

16. $30,824 × 43

17. $37,525 × 48

18. **Measurement** Gabrielle rides her bike 2 miles a day. In one mile there are 5,280 feet. How many feet does she ride her bike in 2 weeks?

19. **Measurement** If a cow produces 2,305 gallons of milk each year, how many gallons of milk do 75 cows produce in a year?

Real-World PROBLEM SOLVING

Measurement The map shows distances between some cities in the United States.

20. Meliah traveled round trip from Sacramento to Boston 6 times during the summer months. How many miles did she travel altogether?

21. Marcos traveled round trip from Miami to Seattle 8 times. How many miles did he travel altogether?

H.O.T. Problems

22. **OPEN ENDED** Create a multiplication exercise that has a product greater than 1,000,000.

23. **NUMBER SENSE** Is the product of 11 and 1,000 greater or less than 10,000? How can you tell without multiplying?

24. **WRITING IN ►MATH** What is the greatest number of digits a product could have if a 2-digit factor is multiplied by a 5-digit number? Explain.

Greatest Products

Multiply Multi-Digit Numbers

Get Ready!

Players: 2

Get Set!

Each player should have a sheet of notebook paper.

Go!

- Player 1 rolls all 6 number cubes.

- Player 1 uses the number cubes to create a problem that involves multiplying a 4-digit number by a 2-digit number.

- Player 1 can arrange the digits in any place value and then find the product of the 2 factors.

- Player 2 takes a turn.

- The player who creates the greatest product earns 1 point.

- The player to earn 5 points first wins.

You will need: 6 number cubes labeled 0–5, paper and pencil

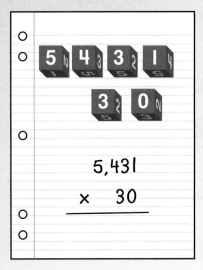

Study Guide and Review

FOLDABLES Study Organizer **GET READY to Study**

Be sure the following Key Vocabulary words and Key Concepts are written in your Foldable.

Key Concepts

Estimate Products (p. 276)
Round each factor, then multiply.

$$\begin{array}{r} 36 \\ \times\ 28 \\ \end{array} \longrightarrow \begin{array}{r} 40 \\ \times\ 30 \\ \hline 1,200 \end{array}$$

36 rounds to 40.
28 rounds to 30.

Multiply by Two-Digit Numbers (p. 284)

$$\begin{array}{r} 178 \\ \times\ \ \ 34 \\ \hline 712 \\ +5,340 \\ \hline 6,052 \end{array}$$

Multiply the ones, tens, and hundreds. Regroup as needed.

Add the partial products.

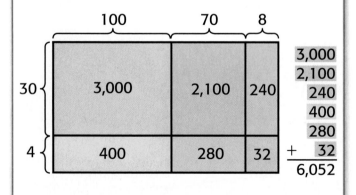

Key Vocabulary

Distributive Property of Multiplication (p. 282)

estimate (p. 276)

factor (p. 276)

multiple (p. 273)

product (p. 276)

Vocabulary Check

1. A number that is close to an exact value is a(n) _____?_____.

2. The numbers 1, 2, 3, and 6 are _____?_____ of the number 6.

3. A(n) _____?_____ of a number is the product of that number and any whole number.

4. The _____?_____ allows you to multiply a sum by a number by multiplying each addend by the number and adding the products.

5. A(n) _____?_____ is a number that divides into a whole number evenly.

6. A number is a(n) _____?_____ of its factors.

Lesson-by-Lesson Review

7-1 **Multiply by Tens** (pp. 273–275)

4-2.3

Example 1

A football coach is ordering 30 jerseys for his football team. The jerseys cost $29 each. What will the total cost of the jerseys be?

Step 1 Multiply the ones.

$$
\begin{array}{r}
29 \\
\times\ 30 \\
\hline
0
\end{array}
$$
← 0 ones × 29 = 0

Step 2 Multiply the tens.

$$
\begin{array}{r}
29 \\
\times\ 30 \\
\hline
870
\end{array}
$$
← 3 tens × 29 = 87 tens

So, the total cost will be $870.

Multiply.

7.
$$
\begin{array}{r}
90 \\
\times\ 90 \\
\hline
\end{array}
$$

8.
$$
\begin{array}{r}
34 \\
\times\ 80 \\
\hline
\end{array}
$$

9. $28 × 40

10. $45 × 30

11. Jeremy reads the number of books shown in a month. How many books will he read in 2 years?

12. There are 30 students in each class. There are 27 classrooms. How many students are there?

7-2 **Estimate Products** (pp. 276–279)

4-2.3

Example 2

Estimate 33 × 18.

Step 1 Round each factor to the nearest ten.

$$
\begin{array}{r}
33 \\
\times 18
\end{array}
\rightarrow
\begin{array}{r}
30 \\
\times 20
\end{array}
$$
← Round 33 to 30.
  Round 18 to 20.

Step 2 Multiply.

$$
\begin{array}{r}
30 \\
\times\ 20 \\
\hline
600
\end{array}
$$
← 0 ones × 30 = 0
  2 tens × 30 = 60 tens

So, 33 × 18 is about 600.

Estimate. Tell whether the estimate is *greater than* or *less than* the actual product.

13.
$$
\begin{array}{r}
82 \\
\times 38 \\
\hline
\end{array}
$$

14.
$$
\begin{array}{r}
\$76 \\
\times 24 \\
\hline
\end{array}
$$

15. $244 × 31

16. 482 × 49

17. 371 × 66

18. 527 × 84

19. Tamara makes $12 an hour. She worked 28 hours this week. About how much money will she make?

7-3 **Problem-Solving Strategy: Act It Out** (pp. 280–281)

4-1.1

Example 3

Elvio has 6 coins in his pocket equaling 72¢. What combination of coins does he have in his pocket?

Understand

What facts do you know?
- Elvio has 6 coins in his pocket.
- The value of the coins is 72¢.

What do you need to find?
- The coins Elvio has.

Plan   Act out the problem.

Solve   One way to make 72¢ is with 1 fifty-cent piece, 2 dimes, and 2 pennies. You need one more coin.

Take the fifty-cent piece and exchange it for 2 quarters.

The value of the coins stays the same, and the number of coins increases to six.

So, Elvio has 2 quarters, 2 dimes, and 2 pennies.

Check   The answer makes sense for the facts given in the problem. You have 6 coins that have a total value of 72¢.

20. There are cartons of milk in 10 rows of 8. You remove 4 cartons from each of 5 rows. How many cartons are left?

21. Jewel is painting a pattern on a bowl in art class. She is using the shapes below to form the pattern. How many ways can Jewel arrange the shapes to form a repeating pattern if she uses each shape once?

22. Joan saved $8 the first week, three times that the second week, and $15 the third week. How much did she save in three weeks?

23. **Geometry** Look at the pattern below. How many squares are needed to make the 6th figure in the pattern shown?

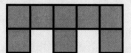

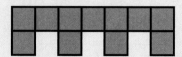

24. Can nine toothpicks be used to make four triangles that are the same size and same shape?

7-4 Multiply Two-Digit Numbers (pp. 284–286)

4-2.3

Example 4

Julio scores 18 points in each basketball game. If there are 14 games in a season, how many points will Julio score?

Multiply the number of games by the number of points scored in each game.

```
    3
   18
 ×14
   72  ← Multiply the ones.
+ 180  ← Multiply the tens.
  252  ← Add.
```

So, Julio will score 252 points.

Multiply.

25.
```
   63
 × 46
```

26.
```
   26
 ×34
```

27.
```
  $72
 × 49
```

28.
```
  $55
 × 41
```

29. 37 × 68

30. 89 × 53

31. $19 × 72

32. 95 × 84

33. **Measurement** Kittens can run up to 31 miles per hour. At this rate, how much distance would a kitten cover in a day?

7-5 Multiply Three-Digit Numbers by Two-Digit Numbers (pp. 288–291)

4-2.3

Example 5

Find 803 × 42.

Estimate $800 × 40 = $32,000

```
      1
  $803
 × 42
  1,606  ← Multiply the ones.
+32,120  ← Multiply the tens.
 $33,726 ← Add.
```

Check for Reasonableness
Since $33,726 is close to the estimate, the answer is reasonable. ✔

Multiply.

34.
```
   712
 × 87
```

35.
```
   841
 × 96
```

36.
```
   367
 × 71
```

37.
```
   670
 × 87
```

38. $705 × 88

39. $234 × 45

40. 103 × 33

41. 632 × 35

42. A school bought 35 microscopes at $125 each for the science lab. What was the total cost?

43. If a person makes $625 each week, how much will that person have made after one year?

Chapter 7 Study Guide and Review **303**

7-6 Problem-Solving Investigation: Choose a Strategy (pp. 294–295)

4-1.1

Example 6
A theater can seat 785 people. There are 23 performances in a month. Is it reasonable to say that more than 20,000 people can attend the performances in a month?

Multiply 785 by 23. Then compare.

```
   11
   21
   785
 × 23
  2,355  ← Multiply the ones.
+15,700  ← Multiply the tens.
 18,055  ← Add the products.
```

Since 18,055 < 20,000, it is not reasonable to say that more than 20,000 people can attend the performances in a month.

Use any strategy to solve.

44. By the end of the school year, Lolita wants to read 50 books. If she reads 3 books each month for the 9 months she is in school, will she reach her goal?

45. Elan has a $20 bill. He wants to buy a ball cap that costs $16. What will his change be?

46. Toni wants to save enough money to buy a tennis racquet for $75. She earns $5 a week for doing chores. Is it reasonable to say that Toni will have enough money to buy the tennis racquet in 3 months? Explain.

7-7 Multiply Greater Numbers (pp. 296–298)

4-2.3

Example 7
One of the fastest planes in the world can fly up to 5,329 miles per hour. At this rate, how far would this plane fly in 24 hours?

```
    1
   113
   5,329
 ×    24
  21,316
+106,580
 127,896  ← Add.
```

So, this plane would fly 127,896 miles in 24 hours.

Multiply.

47. 1,418 × 14

48. 2,983 × 21

49. 13,720 × 31

50. 17,946 × 25

51. $24,017 × 30

52. $39,402 × 48

53. **Measurement** Jena's grandparents live 35 miles away. There are 5,280 feet in one mile. How many feet away do Jena's grandparents live?

Multiply.

1.   26
     ×10

2.   43
     ×30

3. 89 × 33

4. 82 × 91

5. Measurement Elio jogs for 30 minutes each time he exercises. If he exercises 18 times in a month, how many minutes will he jog?

Estimate.

6. 152 × 47

7. 439 × 81

8. Shannon is reading a book that has about 18 pages in each chapter. The book has 12 chapters. About how many pages does the book have?

9. Lina buys groceries for $14 at the store. She gives the cashier a $20 bill. List two combinations of bills she could receive as change.

10. MULTIPLE CHOICE A school needs to buy 475 math books for its fourth grade students. Each book costs $85. What will the total cost be?

    A $40,000   **C** $45,000

    B $40,375   **D** $53,150

11. Roxana brought 6 dozen snacks for her birthday party at school. Each person got 3 snacks. How many people are in her class? Explain your answer.

Multiply.

12. 107 × 12

13. 258 × 24

14.   1,324
     ×   12

15.   2,831
     ×   24

16. Measurement The table shows how many miles Ari biked each week of a month. If Ari bikes the same number of miles each month, how many miles will Ari bike in a year?

Distance Biked	
Week	**Miles**
1	12
2	14
3	8
4	10

17. A store has 275 boxes of oranges. Each box costs $12. Find the total cost.

18. MULTIPLE CHOICE There are 24 hours in a day. There are 365 days in a year. How many hours are there in a year?

    F 9,560

    G 8,760

    H 8,670

    J 8,000

19. **WRITING IN ►MATH** What is the greatest number of digits a product could have if a 4-digit number is multiplied by a 3-digit number? Explain.

PART 1   Multiple Choice

Read each question. Then fill in the correct answer on the answer sheet provided by your teacher or on a sheet of paper.

1. Blake planted 12 rows of corn. Each row had 15 corn plants. How many corn plants will he have in all?

   A 170   **C** 225

   B 180   **D** 240

2. What number should come next in the pattern?

   4, 7, 10, 13, 16, 19, ▦

   F 20   **H** 22

   G 21   **J** 23

3. If Sean buys all the items, about how much will he spend?

Baseball Equipment	
Item	Cost
mitt	$39
bat	$34
ball	$19
T-shirt	$12

   A $80   **C** $100

   B $90   **D** $120

4. Leslie surveyed 30 students about their favorite kinds of books.

Favorite Kinds of Books	
Kind	**Tally**
Adventure	⊕⊕ ⊕⊕
Science fiction	⊕⊕ |||
Mystery	⊕⊕ ||||
Poetry	|||

   Which 2 kinds of books do 19 students enjoy reading most?

   F Adventure and science fiction

   G Science fiction and mystery

   H Mystery and adventure

   J Poetry and science fiction

5. Miguela mowed 54 lawns over the summer. She charged $23 a lawn. How much money did she earn over the summer?

   A $1,242   **C** $1,132

   B $1,232   **D** $124

6. While playing a board game, Vera scored 10 points on her first turn. At the end of the game, she had a total of 38 points. Which equation describes her points?

   F $p - 10 = 38$ **H** $10 + 38 = p$

   G $10 + p = 38$ **J** $10 - p = 38$

Preparing for PASS

For test-taking strategies and practice, see pages R42–R55.

7. Which number is 100,000 more than 873,496?

A 773,496   **C** 883,496

B 874,496   **D** 973,496

8. Emanuel has 72 photos. His photo album holds 6 pictures on a page. How many pages will he use?

F 12   **H** 9

G 10   **J** 8

9. Which number is represented by c in the equation $12 \times c = 108$?

A 5   **C** 8

B 6   **D** 9

10. Which statement best describes the relationship between a and b?

Input (a)	1	2	3	4	5
Output (b)	3	6	9	12	15

F b is 3 more than a

G b is 3 times a

H b is 3 less than a

J b is 2 times a

PART 2   Short Response

Record your answers on the answer sheet provided by your teacher or on a sheet of paper.

11. Kamilah read 38 pages in a book each day for 11 days. About how many pages did she read in all?

12. How many total visitors came to Wyatt Park in May and July?

Wyatt Park	
Month	**Visitors**
May	6,453
June	7,782
July	8,134
August	7,996

PART 3   Extended Response

Record your answers on the answer sheet provided by your teacher or on a sheet of paper.

13. Mr. Cook has 32 students in his homeroom. He makes groups with 8 students in each group. How many groups are there? Explain.

14. Fran baked 15 trays of muffins for a bake sale. Each tray has 6 muffins. How many muffins did Fran bake in all? Explain.

NEED EXTRA HELP?														
If You Missed Question...	1	2	3	4	5	6	7	8	9	10	11	12	13	14
Go to Lesson...	7-4	5-4	2-2	3-1	7-4	5-2	2-4	4-6	5-8	5-8	7-3	2-4	4-5	7-4
SC Academic Standards	4-2.3	4-3.1	3-2.3	4-6.3	4-2.3	4-3.5	3-2.3	4-2.5	4-3.4	4-3.3	4-1.1	3-2.3	4-2.5	4-2.3

CHAPTER 8
Divide by One-Digit Numbers

 **BIG Idea** **How do you divide by a one-digit number?**

Divide each digit of the dividend by the divisor.

Example A toll worker on the Mackinac Bridge in Michigan collected $75 in tolls. How many cars passed through the toll booth if the toll cost is $3 per car?

```
      25
   3)75
    −6↓      For each place, divide, multiply, subtract, and compare.
     15      Then bring down the next digit in the dividend.
    −15
      0
```

So, 25 cars passed through the toll booth.

What will I learn in this chapter?

- Divide two-, three-, or multi-digit numbers by a one-digit number.
- Estimate quotients.
- Solve problems by using the guess and check strategy.

Key Vocabulary

dividend   remainder

divisor   compatible numbers

quotient

 **SC Math Online** **Student Study Tools** at macmillanmh.com

FOLDABLES®
Study Organizer

Make this Foldable to help you organize information about dividing by one-digit numbers. Begin with 5 sheets of 11″ × 17″ paper.

① **Fold** one sheet in half widthwise.

② **Open** and fold the bottom to form a pocket. Glue.

③ **Repeat** Steps 1 and 2 four times. Glue the back of one folder to the front of another.

④ **Label** the pockets as shown. Place an index card in each pocket.

Lesson 1 Lesson 2

ARE YOU READY for Chapter 8?

You have two ways to check prerequisite skills for this chapter.

Option 2

SC Math Online Take the Chapter Readiness Quiz at macmillanmh.com.

Option 1

Complete the Quick Check below.

QUICK Check

Subtract. (Prior Grade)

1. $25 - 6$ **2.** $42 - 8$ **3.** $67 - 29$ **4.** $93 - 54$

5. 24 – 15 **6.** 31 – 17 **7.** 50 – 23 **8.** 86 – 49

9. There are 81 pages in Gerardo's book. He has read 38 pages. How many pages are left to read?

Divide. (Lesson 4-5)

10. $2\overline{)3}$ **11.** $4\overline{)5}$ **12.** $6\overline{)7}$ **13.** $8\overline{)9}$

14. 4 ÷ 3 **15.** 7 ÷ 5 **16.** 9 ÷ 6 **17.** 9 ÷ 7

18. Sharon has $32. She wants to buy CDs that cost $8 each. How many can she buy?

Round each number to its greatest place value. (Lesson 1-6)

19. 269 **20.** $2,513 **21.** 14,895 **22.** 56,071

23. A zoo has 2,515 mammals and 3,496 animals that are not mammals. About how many animals are at the zoo?

Model Division

In division, the **dividend** is the number that is being divided. The **divisor** is the number that divides the dividend. The **quotient** is the result.

$$\text{divisor} \overline{)\text{dividend}}^{\text{quotient}}$$

MAIN IDEA

I will explore dividing by one-digit numbers.

SC Academic Standards

4-2.5 Generate strategies to divide whole numbers by single-digit divisors.

You Will Need
base-ten blocks

New Vocabulary

dividend
divisor
quotient
remainder

ACTIVITY

1 Find 39 ÷ 3.

Step 1 **Model the dividend, 39.**

Use 3 tens and 9 ones to show 39.

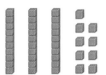

Step 2 **Divide the tens.**

The divisor is 3. So, divide the tens into 3 equal groups. There is a ten in each group.

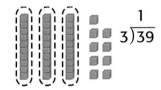

$$3\overline{)39}^{\,1}$$

Step 3 **Divide the ones.**

Divide the ones into 3 equal groups. There are 1 ten and 3 ones in each group.
So, 39 ÷ 3 = 13.

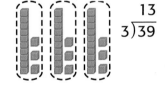

$$3\overline{)39}^{\,13}$$

2 Find 68 ÷ 5.

Step 1 **Model the dividend, 68.**

Use 6 tens and 8 ones to show 68.

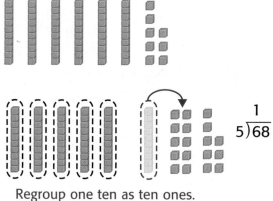

Step 2 **Divide the tens.**

The divisor is 5. So, divide the tens into 5 equal groups. There is a ten in each group.

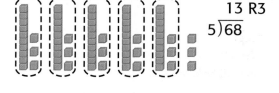

$$5\overline{)68}$$ with 1 above

Regroup one ten as ten ones.

Step 3 **Divide the ones.**

Divide the ones into 5 equal groups. There is 1 ten and 3 ones in each group. There are 3 ones left over. The 3 is the **remainder**.

So, 68 ÷ 5 = 13 R3.

$$\begin{array}{r} 13\ R3 \\ 5\overline{)68} \end{array}$$

Think About It

1. How would you use base-ten blocks to find 58 ÷ 4?

2. Explain what it means to have a remainder when dividing.

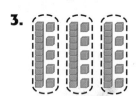 **CHECK What You Know**

Write the division expression shown by each model. Then divide.

3.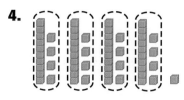

4.

Use models to find each quotient.

5. 36 ÷ 2   **6.** 48 ÷ 3   **7.** 57 ÷ 4   **8.** 77 ÷ 5

9. **WRITING IN ►MATH** Explain how to use models to find 79 ÷ 6.

8-1 Division with Remainders

GET READY to Learn

Mr. Hein's class is going to a natural history museum. Each seat on the bus can hold 2 people. There are 28 students and 8 adults. How many seats are needed?

MAIN IDEA

I will carry out division with and without remainders.

SC Academic Standards

4-2.5 Generate strategies to divide whole numbers by single-digit divisors.

SC Math Online

macmillanmh.com
• Extra Examples
• Personal Tutor
• Self-Check Quiz

You have used models to divide. You can also use paper and pencil.

Real-World EXAMPLE

1 SCHOOL How many bus seats are needed for the field trip?

There are 36 people. Each seat holds 2 people. Find $36 \div 2$.

Step 1 Divide the tens.

$2\overline{)36}$ Can 3 tens be divided equally into groups of 2?

$\begin{array}{r} 1 \\ 2\overline{)36} \end{array}$ There is one ten in each group. Put 1 in the quotient over the tens place.

Step 2 Multiply, subtract, and compare.

$\begin{array}{r} 1 \\ 2\overline{)36} \\ -2 \\ \hline 1 \end{array}$

Multiply. $2 \times 1 = 2$
Subtract. $3 - 2 = 1$
Compare. $1 < 2$

Step 3 Bring down the ones.

$\begin{array}{r} 1 \\ 2\overline{)36} \\ -2\downarrow \\ \hline 16 \end{array}$

Bring down 6 ones.
16 ones in all.

Step 4 Divide the ones.

$\begin{array}{r} 18 \\ 2\overline{)36} \\ -2\downarrow \\ \hline 16 \\ -16 \\ \hline 0 \end{array}$

Divide. $16 \div 2 = 8$
Put 8 in the quotient over the ones place.
Multiply. $2 \times 8 = 16$
Subtract. $16 - 16 = 0$
Compare. $0 < 2$

So, 18 seats are needed.

Lesson 8-1 Division with Remainders **313**

When a remainder occurs, there is an amount left over that cannot be divided equally into the number of groups set by the divisor. You can interpret the remainder in division problems.

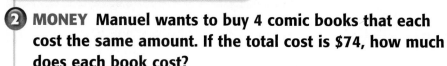

Real-World EXAMPLE Division with Remainders

② **MONEY** Manuel wants to buy 4 comic books that each cost the same amount. If the total cost is $74, how much does each book cost?

Manuel has $74. Each comic book costs the same amount. So, divide $74 by 4 to find how much each book will cost.

Step 1 Divide the tens.

$$\begin{array}{r} 1 \\ 4\overline{)\$74} \\ -4 \\ \hline 3 \end{array}$$

Divide. $7 \div 4 = 1$
So, put 1 in the quotient over the tens place.
Multiply. $4 \times 1 = 4$
Subtract. $7 - 4 = 3$
Compare. $3 < 4$

Step 2 Divide the ones.

$$\begin{array}{r} 18\ \text{R2} \\ 4\overline{)\$74} \\ -4\downarrow \\ \hline 34 \\ -32 \\ \hline 2 \end{array}$$

Bring down the ones.
Divide. $34 \div 4 = 8$
Put 8 over the ones place.
Multiply. $4 \times 8 = 32$
Subtract. $34 - 32 = 2$
Compare. $2 < 4$
Remainder $= 2$

So, each comic book will cost a little more than $18.

Check The model shows that $\$74 \div 4$ is a little more than $18.

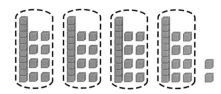

Remember

To check a division answer, multiply the quotient by the divisor.

$$\begin{array}{r} 18 \\ \times\ 4 \\ \hline 72 \\ +\ 2 \\ \hline 74 \end{array}$$ ← Add the remainder.

✓ CHECK What You Know

Divide. Check each answer. See Examples 1 and 2 (pp. 313–314)

1. $2\overline{)26}$

2. $3\overline{)36}$

3. $5\overline{)59}$

4. $8\overline{)84}$

5. $93 \div 3$

6. $84 \div 4$

7. $61 \div 2$

8. $86 \div 3$

9. There are 4 zookeepers to feed 85 animals. If each zookeeper feeds the same number of animals, will all of the animals be fed by the 4 zookeepers? Explain.

10. **Talk About It** Why is the remainder always less than the divisor?

Divide. Check each answer. See Examples 1 and 2 (pp. 313–314)

11. $2\overline{)28}$ **12.** $4\overline{)48}$ **13.** $3\overline{)33}$ **14.** $2\overline{)26}$

15. $5\overline{)53}$ **16.** $6\overline{)67}$ **17.** $7\overline{)73}$ **18.** $9\overline{)96}$

19. $93 \div 3$ **20.** $84 \div 4$ **21.** $64 \div 2$ **22.** $69 \div 3$

23. $79 \div 2$ **24.** $91 \div 4$ **25.** $77 \div 3$ **26.** $99 \div 4$

27. Marlene makes $4 an hour babysitting. If she earned $48, how many hours did she babysit?

28. Seven scouts need to sell 75 boxes of cookies. Each scout gets the same number of boxes. How many boxes will be left to sell?

Real-World PROBLEM SOLVING

Science There are many different insects on Earth.

29. Measurement The lifespan of a firefly is 7 days. How many fireflies have a total lifespan of 77 days?

30. Measurement A cockroach can travel 3 miles per hour. How long would it take the cockroach to travel 32 miles?

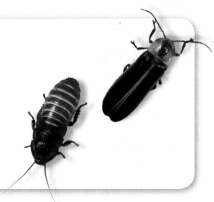

H.O.T. Problems

31. OPEN ENDED Identify a two-digit dividend that will result in a quotient with a remainder of 1 when the divisor is 4.

32. FIND THE ERROR Kate and Yutaka found $46 \div 4$. Who is correct? Explain.

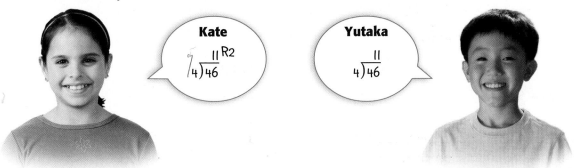

Kate

$4\overline{)46}^{\,11\ R2}$

Yutaka

$4\overline{)46}^{\,11}$

33. **WRITING IN MATH** When you divide a number by 6, can the remainder be 6? Explain.

Divide Multiples of 10, 100, and 1,000

GET READY to Learn

A certain amusement park has 5 entrances. If 1,500 people entered the amusement park and separated into equal lines, how many people are in each line?

MAIN IDEA

I will use basic facts and patterns to divide mentally.

SC Academic Standards

4-2.5 Generate strategies to divide whole numbers by single-digit divisors.

SC Math Online

macmillanmh.com
• Extra Examples
• Personal Tutor
• Self-Check Quiz

You can find and use patterns to divide multiples of 10, 100, and 1,000. Using patterns makes it easy to divide.

Real-World EXAMPLE Divide Multiples of 10, 100, and 1,000

1 AMUSEMENT PARKS How many people are in each line at the amusement park?

You need to divide 1,500 people into 5 equal groups. Find 1,500 ÷ 5.

One Way: Use a Multiplication Pattern

$5 \times 3 = 15$	⟶	$15 \div 5 = 3$
$5 \times 30 = 150$	⟶	$150 \div 5 = 30$
$5 \times 300 = 1,500$	⟶	$1,500 \div 5 = 300$

Another Way: Use a Basic Fact

The basic fact for 1,500 ÷ 5 is 15 ÷ 5.

$15 \div 5 = 3$ ⟵ basic fact
$150 \div 5 = 30$
$1,500 \div 5 = 300$

So, there are 300 people in each line.

Remember

Multiplication can be used to check division.

EXAMPLE Divide Multiples of 10, 100, and 1,000

2 Find the quotient of 2,400 and 4.

One Way: Use a Multiplication Pattern

$4 \times 6 = 24$ $\longrightarrow$ $24 \div 4 = 6$
$4 \times 60 = 240$ $\longrightarrow$ $240 \div 4 = 60$
$4 \times 600 = 2,400$ $\longrightarrow$ $2,400 \div 4 = 600$

Another Way: Use a Basic Fact

The basic fact for $2,400 \div 4$ is $24 \div 4$.

$24 \div 4 = 6$ $\longleftarrow$ (basic fact)
$240 \div 4 = 60$
$2,400 \div 4 = 600$

So, $2,400 \div 4$ is 600.

Check
You know that $2,400 \div 4 = 600$ because $4 \times 600 = 2,400$. ✔

CHECK What You Know

Copy and complete each set of patterns. See Examples 1 and 2 (pp. 316–317)

1. $12 \div 4 = \blacksquare$
$120 \div 4 = \blacksquare$
$1,200 \div 4 = \blacksquare$

2. $\$36 \div 6 = \blacksquare$
$\$360 \div 6 = \blacksquare$
$\$3,600 \div 6 = \blacksquare$

3. $45 \div 9 = \blacksquare$
$450 \div 9 = \blacksquare$
$4,500 \div 9 = \blacksquare$

Divide. Use patterns. See Examples 1 and 2 (pp. 316–317)

4. $\$400 \div 2$

5. $1,600 \div 4$

6. $\$3,200 \div 8$

For Exercise 7, use the information at the right.

7. There are 4 members of a family planning a weekend camping trip. How much will the trip cost for each person?

8. (Talk About It) What basic fact will help you find the quotient of 4,200 and 7?

Family Vacation

Item	Total Cost
Campsite rental cost	$50
Camping supplies	$75
Food	$75

Copy and complete each set of patterns. See Examples 1 and 2 (pp. 316–317)

9.
$12 \div 2 = \blacksquare$
$120 \div 2 = \blacksquare$
$1,200 \div 2 = \blacksquare$

10.
$\$28 \div 7 = \blacksquare$
$\$280 \div 7 = \blacksquare$
$\$2,800 \div 7 = \blacksquare$

11.
$54 \div 9 = \blacksquare$
$540 \div 9 = \blacksquare$
$5,400 \div 9 = \blacksquare$

12.
$\$36 \div 4 = \blacksquare$
$\$360 \div 4 = \blacksquare$
$\$3,600 \div 4 = \blacksquare$

13.
$42 \div 6 = \blacksquare$
$420 \div 6 = \blacksquare$
$4,200 \div 6 = \blacksquare$

14.
$\$72 \div 8 = \blacksquare$
$\$720 \div 8 = \blacksquare$
$\$7,200 \div 8 = \blacksquare$

Divide. Use patterns. See Examples 1 and 2 (pp. 316–317)

15. $200 \div 5$

16. $\$600 \div 3$

17. $800 \div 2$

18. $900 \div 3$

19. $\$1,400 \div 7$

20. $4,500 \div 5$

21. $6,300 \div 9$

22. $\$6,400 \div 8$

23. $\$3,500 \div 5$

24. $1,600 \div 8$

25. $5,400 \div 6$

26. $\$8,100 \div 9$

27. The cost of a used car is $3,200. If the payments are spread over 8 months, what is the payment each month?

28. The Nair family collected 2,400 pennies. The pennies will be divided evenly among the 4 children. How many dollars will each child get?

Real-World PROBLEM SOLVING

Measurement Animals migrate due to factors such as climate and food availability. The table shows a few migration distances.

29. Suppose a group of green sea turtles travels 7 miles a day. How many days will the migration take?

30. Suppose a swarm of desert locusts travels 7 miles per hour. They travel 10 hours per day. How many days will the migration take?

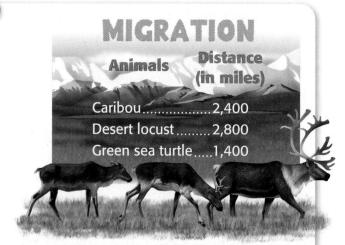

MIGRATION

Animals	Distance (in miles)
Caribou	2,400
Desert locust	2,800
Green sea turtle	1,400

Source: U.S. Fish and Wildlife Service

31. A herd of caribou migrated the distance shown in 8 months. If they traveled the same distance each month, how many miles did the herd travel each month?

H.O.T. Problems

32. NUMBER SENSE Without actually dividing, tell which has the greater quotient, 1,500 ÷ 3 or 2,400 ÷ 6? Explain.

33. **WRITING IN ►MATH** Explain how you would know that the quotient of 600 ÷ 2 is a 3-digit number.

PASS Practice 4-2.5

34. Rosita read a 75-page book in 5 days. She read the same number of pages each day. How many pages did she read each day? (Lesson 8-1)

A 5

B 10

C 15

D 150

35. Antoine went to his sister's college graduation. There were 1,200 students graduating. They were separated equally into 4 sections of the auditorium. How many students were seated in each section? (Lesson 8-2)

F 3   **H** 300

G 30   **J** 3,000

Spiral Review

Divide. Check each answer. (Lesson 8-1)

36. 2)37   **37.** 5)49   **38.** 7)81

Multiply. (Lesson 7-7)

39. 1,672
   × 18

40. 4,061
   × 39

41. 9,544
   × 65

Measurement For Exercises 42–44, use the table. It shows the life spans of reptiles. Choose the best operation. Then solve. (Lesson 4-4)

42. How many years will three generations of Galapagos turtles live?

43. How much longer can an American alligator live than a komodo dragon?

44. Which animal lives 90 years longer than the boa constrictor?

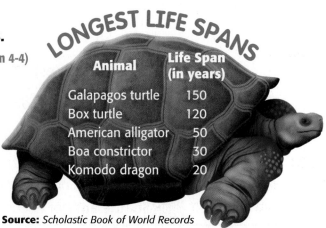

LONGEST LIFE SPANS

Animal	Life Span (in years)
Galapagos turtle	150
Box turtle	120
American alligator	50
Boa constrictor	30
Komodo dragon	20

Source: *Scholastic Book of World Records*

8-3

Problem-Solving Strategy

 SCAS > 4-1.1 Analyze information to solve increasingly more sophisticated problems.

Ruben bought 3 gifts for his sisters. Two of the gifts cost the same. The other gift costs $3 more than the other two. If the total amount of money spent was $27, how much did each gift cost?

Understand	**What facts do you know?** • There are 3 gifts, and two gifts cost the same. • One gift is $3 more than the other two. • Ruben spent $27 on all 3 gifts. **What do you need to find?** • The cost of each gift.
Plan	You can guess and check to solve the problem.
Solve	Use gift + gift + (gift + $3) = $27 and make logical guesses. Start with numbers smaller than $10 because $10 × 3 = $30 and the total is less than $30. Try $9. $9 + $9 + ($9 + $3) = $30 No, too large. Try $8. $8 + $8 + ($8 + $3) = $27 Yes So, two gifts cost $8 each and the third gift costs $8 + $3, or $11.
Check	Subtract the cost of each gift from the total cost. First gift: $27 − $8 = $19 Second gift: $19 − $8 = $11 Third gift: $11 − $11 = $0 So, the answer is correct.

Refer to the problem on the previous page.

1. Explain why gift + gift + (gift + $3) is used to solve the equation.

2. Explain why the first guess was $9 instead of a smaller number.

3. Suppose Ruben spent $39 on the gifts. How much does each gift cost?

4. Explain how you found the answer to Exercise 3.

▶ PRACTICE the Strategy

SCAS • PASS
Extra Practice, p. R20

Solve. Use the guess and check strategy.

5. Kendra took photographs at the park. She photographed 20 dogs and owners in all. If there was a total of 64 legs, how many dogs and owners were there?

6. **Measurement** Corrine is making twice as much fruit punch as lemonade. She is making 12 gallons total. How many gallons will be fruit punch and how many will be lemonade?

7. **Measurement** Theo lives twice as far from Cassidy as Jarvis. How far do Theo and Jarvis live from Cassidy?

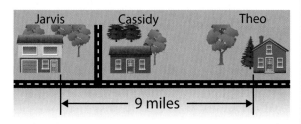

Jarvis   Cassidy   Theo

◀—— 9 miles ——▶

8. The total number of tickets sold for a play was 450. On Friday, 150 tickets were sold. Fifty more tickets sold on Saturday than on Sunday. How many tickets sold on Saturday and Sunday?

9. At a zoo gift shop, Jeffrey bought two of the items shown. He gave the cashier $20, and received $4 in change. Which two items did he buy?

$12
$4
$16
$2

10. **Algebra** Denzell and Marco collect miniature cars. Marco has 37 fewer cars than Denzell. They have 249 cars altogether. How many cars does each boy have?

11. Mirna's basketball team has played 14 games. They have lost and tied an equal number of times. They have won 5 times as many games as they have lost. How many games have they won, lost, and tied?

12. **WRITING IN ▶MATH** Explain what it means to solve a problem by guess and check.

Estimate Quotients

GET READY to Learn

Circuses have been around for more than 200 years. They sometimes travel by train. Suppose a circus travels 642 miles in 8 hours. *About* how many miles per hour did the train travel?

There are different ways to estimate quotients. One way is to use compatible numbers. **Compatible numbers** are numbers that are easy to divide mentally.

Real-World EXAMPLE   Estimate Quotients

1 **MEASUREMENT** **Estimate the quotient of 642 and 8 to find how fast the train is traveling.**

One Way: Compatible Numbers	Another Way: Basic Facts
$642 \div 8$	$642 \div 8$
642 is close to 640. 640 and 8 are compatible numbers because they are easy to divide mentally.	What basic multiplication fact is close to the numbers in the problem?
$640 \div 8 = 80$ $8 \times 8 = 64$	$8 \times 8 = 64$ $8 \times 80 = 640$ So, $640 \div 8 = 80$.

So, the circus train is traveling about 80 miles per hour.

Check

You know that $640 \div 8 = 80$ because $8 \times 80 = 640$. ✔

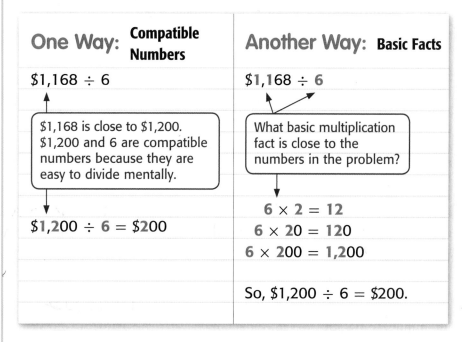

Real-World EXAMPLE   **Estimate Quotients**

2 **DOLLS** Isabella has 6 dolls in her doll collection. The collection is worth $1,168. Each doll is worth the same amount of money. About how much is each doll worth?

You need to estimate $1,168 ÷ 6.

One Way: Compatible Numbers	**Another Way:** Basic Facts
$1,168 ÷ 6	$1,168 ÷ 6
$1,168 is close to $1,200. $1,200 and 6 are compatible numbers because they are easy to divide mentally.	What basic multiplication fact is close to the numbers in the problem?
$1,200 ÷ 6 = $200	6 × 2 = 12 6 × 20 = 120 6 × 200 = 1,200 So, $1,200 ÷ 6 = $200.

So, each doll is worth about $200.

Check
You know that $1,200 ÷ 6 = $200 because
6 × $200 = $1,200. ✔

CHECK What You Know

Estimate. Check your estimate. See Examples 1 and 2 (pp. 322–323)

1. 161 ÷ 4   **2.** $424 ÷ 6   **3.** 715 ÷ 8

4. 2,660 ÷ 9   **5.** $5,643 ÷ 8   **6.** 8,099 ÷ 9

7. On Saturday, 1,164 people saw a movie at Upcity Theater. There were a total of 4 movie screens with the same number of people in each audience. About how many people watched each screen?

8. **Talk About It** Explain how to estimate $4,782 ÷ 6.

Estimate. Check your estimate. See Examples 1 and 2 (pp. 322–323)

9. 123 ÷ 3

10. $244 ÷ 6

11. 162 ÷ 2

12. 345 ÷ 7

13. $538 ÷ 6

14. 415 ÷ 6

15. $1,406 ÷ 7

16. 2,431 ÷ 8

17. $2,719 ÷ 9

18. 4,187 ÷ 7

19. $7,160 ÷ 9

20. 8,052 ÷ 9

21. Terrence earned 806 points on 9 tests. If he earned about the same number of points on each test, about how many points did he earn on each test?

22. Measurement Gloria ran 1,575 miles in 8 months. If she runs the same number of miles each month, about how many miles does she run each month?

South Carolina Data File

Patriots Point is located in Mount Pleasant, South Carolina. It is a museum that houses ships and airplanes from wars fought by the United States.

23. The USS Laffey, an American destroyer from World War II, is about 376 feet long. About how many yards long is the USS Laffey? (Hint: 3 feet = 1 yard)

24. The USS Clamagore, a submarine from World War II, is about 312 feet long. What is the approximate length of this submarine in yards?

Source: Patriots Point Naval and Maritime Museum

H.O.T. Problems

25. OPEN ENDED The estimated quotient of a division sentence is 200. What could the division sentence be?

26. WRITING IN MATH Estimate 5,425 ÷ 6 using 5,400 ÷ 6. Is the estimate greater than or less than the actual quotient? Explain.

Divide. Check each answer. (Lesson 8-1)

1. 92 ÷ 3   **2.** 37 ÷ 2

3. Gwen earns $5 an hour delivering newspapers. If she earned $35 this week, how many hours did she spend delivering newspapers? (Lesson 8-1)

4. MULTIPLE CHOICE Gabriel solved the problem below. Which expression could be used to check his answer? (Lesson 8-1)

$$136 \div 5 = 27 \text{ R}1$$

A $(27 \times 1) + 5$ **C** $(27 + 5) \times 1$

B $(27 \times 5) + 1$ **D** $(27 + 1) \times 5$

Copy and complete each set of patterns. (Lesson 8-2)

5. $42 \div 7 = \blacksquare$ **6.** $25 \div 5 = \blacksquare$
  $420 \div 7 = \blacksquare$ $250 \div 5 = \blacksquare$
  $4{,}200 \div 7 = \blacksquare$ $2{,}500 \div 5 = \blacksquare$

Divide. Use patterns. (Lesson 8-2)

7. 150 ÷ 5   **8.** 600 ÷ 2

9. Measurement Cheri has 200 minutes left on her cell phone plan for the last five days of the month. If Cheri uses the same number of minutes each day, how many minutes can Cheri use her cell phone each day? (Lesson 8-2)

Solve. Use the guess and check strategy. (Lesson 8-3)

10. Patricia and Ashley collect stamps. Patricia has 13 more stamps than Ashley. Together they have 229 stamps. How many stamps do Patricia and Ashley each have?

11. Dion bought three of the items shown below. He gave the cashier $10 and received $1 in change. Which three items did he buy?

Estimate. Check your estimate. (Lesson 8-4)

12. 156 ÷ 3   **13.** 182 ÷ 9

14. MULTIPLE CHOICE Vikas drove 325 miles in five hours. Approximately how many miles did Vikas drive each hour? (Lesson 8-4)

F 60   **H** 68

G 64   **J** 70

15. **WRITING IN ►MATH** If you estimate $4{,}225 \div 6$ using $4{,}200 \div 6$, is the estimate greater than or less than the actual quotient? Explain. (Lesson 8-4)

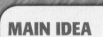

8-5 Two-Digit Quotients

> ## GET READY to Learn
>
> More than 75% of the world's geysers are found in Yellowstone National Park. Suppose one of Yellowstone's geysers erupts every 7 minutes, how many times does it erupt in 95 minutes?

Recall that to divide a two-digit number by a one-digit number, you need to divide the tens, then divide the ones.

Real-World EXAMPLE   Two-Digit Quotients

1 **How many times does the geyser erupt in 95 minutes?**

The geyser erupts every 7 minutes. You need to find the number of times it erupts in 95 minutes. So, find $95 \div 7$.

Estimate $95 \div 7 \longrightarrow 100 \div 10 = 10$

Step 1 Divide the tens.

$$
\begin{array}{r}
1 \\
7\overline{)95} \\
-7 \\
\hline
2
\end{array}
$$

Divide. $9 \div 7 = 1$
Put 1 in the quotient over the tens place.
Multiply. $7 \times 1 = 7$
Subtract. $9 - 7 = 2$
Compare. $2 < 7$

Step 2 Divide the ones.

$$
\begin{array}{r}
13 \text{ R4} \\
7\overline{)95} \\
-7\downarrow \\
\hline
25 \\
-21 \\
\hline
4
\end{array}
$$

Bring down the ones.
Divide. $25 \div 7 = 3$
Put 3 in the quotient over the ones place.
Multiply. $7 \times 3 = 21$
Subtract. $25 - 21 = 4$
Compare. $4 < 7$
Remainder = 4

So, the geyser will erupt about 13 times in 95 minutes.

Check for Reasonableness

13 is close to the estimate. The answer is reasonable. ✔

Sometimes it is not possible to divide the first digit of the dividend by the divisor.

Real-World EXAMPLE   **Divide with Remainders**

2 **SPORTS** A tennis coach has 125 tennis balls. There are 4 members on the team. How many balls does each player get for practice if each player gets the same number of balls?

There are 125 tennis balls and 4 team members.
Divide 125 by 4 to find how many balls each player gets.

Estimate $125 \div 4 \longrightarrow 120 \div 4 = 30$, so about 30 balls per person

Step 1 Estimate to place the first digit.

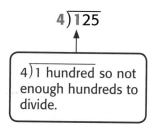

$4\overline{)125}$

$4\overline{)1}$ hundred so not enough hundreds to divide.

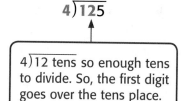

$\overset{x}{4\overline{)125}}$

$4\overline{)12}$ tens so enough tens to divide. So, the first digit goes over the tens place.

Step 2 Divide the tens.

$$\begin{array}{r} 3 \\ 4\overline{)125} \\ -12 \\ \hline 0 \end{array}$$

Divide. $12 \div 4 = 3$
Put 3 in the quotient over the tens place.
Multiply. $4 \times 3 = 12$
Subtract. $12 - 12 = 0$
Compare. $0 < 4$

Step 3 Divide the ones.

$$\begin{array}{r} 31 \text{ R1} \\ 4\overline{)125} \\ -12\downarrow \\ \hline 05 \\ -4 \\ \hline 1 \end{array}$$

Bring down the ones.
Divide. $5 \div 4 = 1$
Put 1 in the quotient over the ones place.
Multiply. $4 \times 1 = 4$
Subtract. $5 - 4 = 1$
Compare. $1 < 4$
Remainder $= 1$

So, each team member gets 31 balls.

Check for Reasonableness
The answer is close to the estimate. So, it is reasonable. ✔

Remember
When a real-world problem has a remainder, you have to interpret the remainder.

✓ CHECK What You Know

Divide. Use estimation to check. See Examples 1 and 2 (pp. 326–327)

1. $2\overline{)33}$

2. $4\overline{)56}$

3. $5\overline{)71}$

4. $179 \div 3$

5. $387 \div 4$

6. $697 \div 7$

7. Holden and Alma earned $32 by doing yard work in their neighborhood. They will share their money equally. How much money will each person get?

8. **Talk About It** Estimation is one method that can be used to check division answers. Identify another method.

▶ Practice and Problem Solving

SCAS • PASS
Extra Practice, p. R21

Divide. Use estimation to check. See Examples 1 and 2 (pp. 326–327)

9. $2\overline{)37}$

10. $3\overline{)64}$

11. $4\overline{)79}$

12. $5\overline{)82}$

13. $7\overline{)74}$

14. $6\overline{)91}$

15. $2\overline{)151}$

16. $3\overline{)286}$

17. $387 \div 5$

18. $493 \div 5$

19. $567 \div 6$

20. $682 \div 7$

21. $694 \div 7$

22. $783 \div 8$

23. $795 \div 8$

24. $883 \div 9$

25. There are 78 campers at a summer camp. There are 6 campers per cabin. How many cabins are there?

26. Carlo has $46 to spend on trading cards. If each pack of cards costs $3, how many packages can he buy?

🌐 Real-World PROBLEM SOLVING

Recycling Every month, Americans throw out enough bottles and jars to fill up a giant skyscraper. All of these jars are recyclable.

27. When one aluminum can is recycled, enough energy is saved to run a television for 3 hours. How many cans need to be recycled to run a television for 75 hours?

28. Most Americans use 7 trees a year in products that are made from trees. How old is a person who has used 85 trees?

H.O.T. Problems

29. OPEN-ENDED When Kira's father's age is divided by Kira's age, you get a quotient of 13 R1. Identify one possibility for their ages.

30. FIND THE ERROR Amber and Paul are finding 53 ÷ 3. Who is correct? Explain.

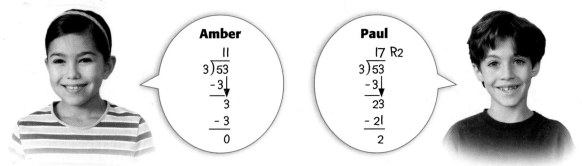

31. **WRITING IN** ▶**MATH** Write a division problem that requires regrouping and has a remainder in the quotient. Give to a classmate to solve.

PASS Practice 4-2.5

32. Cailin biked 78 miles in 5 days. About how many miles did she bike each day? (Lesson 8-4)

 A 14   **C** 18

 B 16   **D** 20

33. Tyrone ran 54 feet during a football game. If there are 3 feet in one yard, how many yards did he run?
(Lesson 8-5)

 F 17   **H** 19

 G 18   **J** 20

Spiral Review

Estimate. Check your estimate. (Lesson 8-4)

34. 139 ÷ 2   **35.** $449 ÷ 5   **36.** 562 ÷ 7   **37.** $805 ÷ 9

38. Pablo works at an animal hospital. Last week he took care of 49 birds and snakes. He took care of four birds for every three snakes. How many of each animal did he take care of? (Lesson 8-3)

Divide. Use patterns. (Lesson 8-2)

39. $600 ÷ 3   **40.** 2,400 ÷ 4   **41.** 4,900 ÷ 7   **42.** 4,800 ÷ 8

43. Jerry was given 3 CDs from his friends, 4 from his parents, and 1 from his sister. He now has 38. How many did he have originally? (Lesson 4-4)

8-6 Problem-Solving Investigation

MAIN IDEA I will choose the best strategy to solve a problem.

SCAS 4-1.1 Analyze information to solve increasingly more sophisticated problems.

P.S.I. TEAM +

CINDY: I had some stamps. I bought 6 more stamps. I traded 4 of my stamps for 8 of my friend's stamps. I now have 32 stamps.

YOUR MISSION: Find how many stamps Cindy started with.

Understand	You know that Cindy bought 6 stamps. She traded 4 stamps for 8 stamps. She now has 32 stamps. You need to find the number of stamps Cindy started with.
Plan	You need to find how many stamps Cindy started with. So, the work backward strategy is a good choice.
Solve	Start with the end result, then work backward.

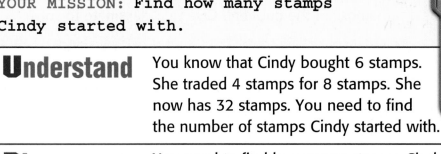

End result →
32 — stamps Cindy has now
− 8 — stamps Cindy received from a friend
24

24
+ 4 — stamps Cindy gave to a friend
28

28
− 6 — stamps Cindy bought
22

Check	Look back. Cindy gained 14 stamps and lost 4. This means she has 10 more stamps then she started with. If she now has 32 stamps, then she started with 22 stamps. The answer is correct.

Use any strategy shown below to solve. Tell what strategy you used.

PROBLEM-SOLVING STRATEGIES
• Make a table.
• Act it out.
• Guess and check.

1. Ellis rode his bike to and from his cousin's home over the weekend. His cousin lives 5 miles away. If Ellis rode a total of 20 miles, how many times did he visit his cousin?

2. Algebra What is the next number in the pattern 2, 5, 11, 23, ▮?

3. Judie and her dad caught 63 fish over the summer. The license allowed them to keep fish longer than 8 inches. Only 2 out of every 5 fish were long enough to keep. About how many did they keep?

4. Alvin buys 2 pairs of jeans, 2 pairs of shoes, 3 T-shirts, and 2 dress shirts for school. How much did he spend?

$8 $15 $23 $16

5. There are 24 cars in a parking lot. There are twice as many 4-door cars as 2-door. How many of each are there?

6. Measurement Lucy the Great Dane eats the amount of dog food shown each day. Roscoe the Pug eats 1 cup for every 2 that Lucy eats each day. How much food does Roscoe eat in a week?

1 CUP   1 CUP   1 CUP   1 CUP

7. A worker at an arcade is handing out 30 tokens for a party. There are more than 6 people at the party. The tokens are shared equally among the people. After the tokens are handed out, 6 are left. How many people are at the party? How many tokens does each person get?

8. Darin has 5 coins that total 62¢. What are the coins?

9. Measurement Selena is going to a birthday party at 12 P.M. She needs to complete the activities shown before the party starts. What time should Selena start to get ready?

Activity	Time
Shower/get ready	30 minutes
Eat breakfast	30 minutes
Chores	2 hours
Pick up Felix and go	30 minutes

10. **WRITING IN ►MATH** Identify the problem-solving strategy you used to solve Exercise 9. Explain how you used the strategy to solve the problem.

Three-Digit Quotients

GET READY to Learn

There are 678 people in line to ride a roller coaster. Each coaster car holds 6 people. How many coaster cars are needed so that everyone in line rides the coaster once?

MAIN IDEA

I will solve division problems that result in three-digit quotients.

SC Academic Standards

4-2.5 Generate strategies to divide whole numbers by single-digit divisors.

SC Math Online

macmillanmh.com
• Extra Examples
• Personal Tutor
• Self-Check Quiz

Finding a quotient like 678 ÷ 6 is similar to dividing a two-digit number by a one-digit number.

Real-World EXAMPLE   Three-Digit Quotients

① **ROLLER COASTERS How many coaster cars are needed?**

Divide 678 by 6 to find the number of coaster cars needed.

Estimate 678 ÷ 6 ⟶ 700 ÷ 7 = 100

Step 1 Divide the hundreds.

```
    1        Divide. 6 ÷ 6 = 1
6)678        Put 1 in hundreds place.
 −6          Multiply. 6 × 1 = 6
  0          Subtract. 6 − 6 = 0
             Compare. 0 < 6
```

Step 2 Divide the tens.

```
   11        Bring down the tens.
6)678        Divide. 7 ÷ 6 = 1
 −6↓         Put 1 in the tens place.
  07
  −6         Multiply. 6 × 1 = 6
   1         Subtract. 7 − 6 = 1
             Compare. 1 < 6
```

Step 3 Divide the ones.

```
  113        Bring down the ones.
6)678        Divide.
 −6↓
  07
  −6↓
   18        Divide. 18 ÷ 6 = 3
  −18        Put 3 in ones place.
    0        Multiply. 6 × 3 = 18
             Subtract. 18 − 18 = 0
             Compare. 0 < 6
```

Check
Since 113 × 6 = 678, the answer is correct. ✓

So, 113 coaster cars are needed.

When dividing three-digit numbers, you can have a remainder like you sometimes have when dividing two-digit numbers.

Remember

Always start a division problem by dividing the greatest place value.

Real-World EXAMPLE Three-Digit Quotients with Remainders

2 MEASUREMENT A roller coaster takes about 2 minutes to travel its 985-foot track. How many feet does the coaster travel in one minute?

The coaster travels 985 feet in 2 minutes. To find how far it travels in 1 minute, divide 985 by 2.

Estimate 985 ÷ 2 ⟶ 1,000 ÷ 2 = 500

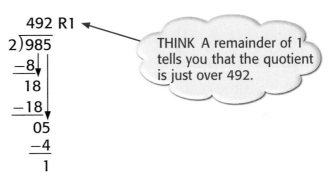

THINK A remainder of 1 tells you that the quotient is just over 492.

So, the roller coaster travels a little more than 492 feet each minute.

Check for Reasonableness
The answer, a little more than 492, is close to the estimate. So, it is reasonable. ✓

CHECK What You Know

Divide. Use estimation to check. See Examples 1 and 2 (pp. 332–333)

1. 2)286

2. 3)345

3. 4)492

4. 745 ÷ 2

5. 679 ÷ 3

6. 917 ÷ 4

7. Measurement A tug-of-war team weighs a total of 774 pounds. The 6 members on the team weigh the same amount. How much does each person weigh?

8. **Talk About It** How would you mentally figure out how many digits the quotient of 795 ÷ 5 will have? Explain your reasoning.

Lesson 8-7 Three-Digit Quotients **333**

Divide. Use estimation to check. See Examples 1 and 2 (pp. 332–333)

9. $2\overline{)324}$ **10.** $3\overline{)585}$ **11.** $5\overline{)775}$ **12.** $6\overline{)696}$

13. $7\overline{)847}$ **14.** $7\overline{)973}$ **15.** $2\overline{)573}$ **16.** $3\overline{)787}$

17. $849 \div 2$ **18.** $994 \div 4$ **19.** $1,863 \div 3$ **20.** $3,974 \div 4$

21. A coach ordered 6 soccer goals for $678. How much did each goal cost?

22. Britney needs to finish reading a book in 3 days. If the book is 348 pages long, how many pages does she need to read each day?

Real-World PROBLEM SOLVING

Architecture The White House is the official home and workplace of the President of the United States. President Theodore Roosevelt gave the White House its name, based on its color.

23. Measurement It takes 570 gallons of paint to paint the outside of the White House. If the number of gallons used to paint each of its 4 sides is equal, how many gallons of paint are used on each side?

24. There are 132 rooms and 6 floors in the White House. If each floor had the same number of rooms, how many rooms would each floor have?

H.O.T. Problems

25. OPEN ENDED Write a division problem that results in a quotient that is greater than 200 and less than 250.

26. **WRITING IN ►MATH** Write a real-world division problem that involves dividing a 3-digit number by a 1-digit number that results in a 2-digit quotient with a remainder.

Extend

Technology Activity for 8-7
Division

Elizabeth downloads many CDs throughout the year. The total cost of downloaded CDs for last year was $324. If she paid this in 6 payments, how much would each payment be?

You can use the *Math Tool Chest* to show $324 divided by 6.

MAIN IDEA

I will use technology to divide three-digit dividends.

SC Academic Standards

4-2.5 Generate strategies to divide whole numbers by single-digit divisors.

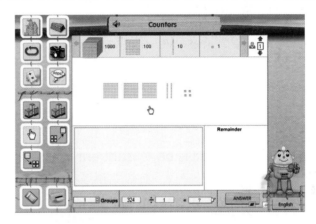

- Click on the counters tool box.
- Click on level 2. Then click on mat type.
- Choose base ten. Then click on OK.
- Stamp out 3 hundreds, 2 tens, and 4 ones.
- Choose to divide this number into 6 groups.
- Click on answer to find the amount each payment will be.

CHECK What You Know

Model each division problem. Then solve.

1. $155 \div 7$ **2.** $225 \div 8$ **3.** $352 \div 4$

Use technology to solve.

4. A group of 9 friends bought tickets to a baseball game. The total cost of the tickets was $153. What was the cost of each ticket?

5. A case of trading cards has 5 boxes. The total cost of the case is $130. What is the cost of each box of trading cards?

6. Analyze How can modeling help you find the solution to a division problem?

SC Math Online

macmillanmh.com
• Extra Examples
• Personal Tutor
• Self-Check Quiz

MAIN IDEA

I will solve division problems that result in quotients that have zeros.

SC Academic Standards

4-2.5 Generate strategies to divide whole numbers by single-digit divisors.

 **GET READY to Learn**

The Ramos family is going on a behind-the-scenes tour of a wildlife reserve in a park. How much will it cost for each person?

Cost of Tour	
Number of People	Cost ($)
3	$327

In division, a quotient will sometimes contain zeros.

Real-World EXAMPLE   Divide Greater Numbers

① **ANIMALS How much it will cost for each family member to go on the tour?**

You need to find $327 ÷ 3.

Step 1 Divide the hundreds.

$$
\begin{array}{r}
\$1 \\
3\overline{)\$327} \\
-3 \\
\hline
0
\end{array}
$$

Divide. 3 ÷ 3 = 1
Put 1 in hundreds place.
Multiply. 3 × 1 = 3
Subtract. 3 − 3 = 0
Compare. 0 < 3

Step 2 Divide the tens.

$$
\begin{array}{r}
\$10 \\
3\overline{)\$327} \\
-3\!\downarrow \\
\hline
02 \\
-0 \\
\hline
2
\end{array}
$$

Bring down the tens.
Divide. Since 2 < 3, there is not enough to divide. So, put 0 in the tens place.
Multiply. 3 × 0 = 0
Subtract. 2 − 0 = 0
Compare. 2 < 3

Step 3 Divide the ones.

$$
\begin{array}{r}
\$109 \\
3\overline{)\$327} \\
-3\!\downarrow \\
\hline
02 \\
-0\!\downarrow \\
\hline
27 \\
-27 \\
\hline
0
\end{array}
$$

Bring down the ones.
Divide. 27 ÷ 3 = 9
Put 9 in the ones place.
Multiply. 3 × 9 = 27
Subtract. 27 − 27 = 0
Compare. 0 < 3

So, it will cost each family member $109.

Real-World EXAMPLE **Divide with Remainders**

2 **VACATIONS** The Kincaid family is going on vacation. They have to drive 415 miles to get to and from Dolphin Cove. How far is it to Dolphin Cove?

415 miles

The total distance the Kincaids will travel is 415 miles. To find the distance to Dolphin Cove, divide 415 by 2.

Estimate $415 \div 2 \longrightarrow 400 \div 2 = 200$

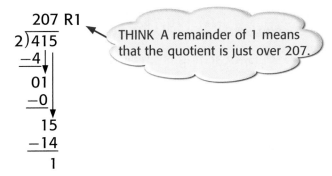

```
       207 R1
   2)415
    -4
      01
     -0
      15
     -14
       1
```

THINK A remainder of 1 means that the quotient is just over 207.

Remember

Remember to divide, multiply, subtract, and compare. Then bring down the next number in the dividend.

So, the distance to Dolphin Cove is a little more than 207 miles.

Check for Reasonableness
The quotient, 207 R1, is close to the estimate. So, the answer is reasonable. ✓

CHECK What You Know

Divide. Use estimation to check. See Examples 1 and 2 (pp. 336–337)

1. 2)212

2. 3)$627

3. 4)416

4. $617 \div 2$

5. $913 \div 3$

6. $825 \div 4$

7. Clara's total score for 3 games of bowling is 312. If Clara earned the same score for each game, what was her score for each game?

8. **Talk About It** Explain how to find the quotient of $624 \div 3$.

Divide. Use estimation to check. See Examples 1 and 2 (pp. 336–337)

9. $2\overline{)214}$ **10.** $3\overline{)327}$ **11.** $5\overline{)\$545}$ **12.** $6\overline{)648}$

13. $7\overline{)742}$ **14.** $8\overline{)\$824}$ **15.** $2\overline{)417}$ **16.** $3\overline{)622}$

17. $\$613 \div 3$ **18.** $837 \div 4$ **19.** $1{,}819 \div 2$ **20.** $\$2{,}429 \div 3$

21. There are 412 toys to be put on 4 shelves at a toy store. If the same number of toys fit on each shelf, how many toys fit on each shelf?

22. There are 408 students at a school. There are 4 lunch periods. If there are the same number of students in each lunch period, how many students are in each period?

Real-World PROBLEM SOLVING

Treasure Geocaching is an outdoor treasure hunting game in which participants use a Global Positioning System to hide and seek "treasures" all over the world. The "treasures" are usually toys or trinkets.

23. Chad is saving his money to buy a Global Positioning System receiver so that he can go geocaching. He has 2 months to save $215. How much money does he need to save each month?

24. **Measurement** Some of the treasures have been hidden on mountains. If the treasure is 325 feet away, how many yards away is it? (*Remember:* 3 feet = 1 yard)

H.O.T. Problems

25. **OPEN ENDED** Identify a 3-digit dividend that will result in a 3-digit quotient that has a zero in the tens place when the divisor is 6.

26. **WRITING IN ▶MATH** Explain how an estimate could help you remember to write a zero in a quotient that results in a 2-digit quotient with a remainder.

Division Shuffle

Division of Multi-Digit Numbers

Get Ready!

Players: 2 players

Get Set!

- Cut each index card in half. Label each card with one number so that the cards are labeled 0 through 9.

You will need: 5 index cards, 2 white boards, 2 dry erase markers

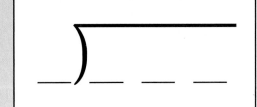

Go!

- Shuffle and then place the cards facedown on the table.

- Both players draw a division symbol on their white boards.

- Player 1 draws four cards, and then turns them over one at a time. After each card is turned over, Players 1 and 2 write each number in any blank on their white boards.

- After all of the numbers are recorded, Players 1 and 2 find and check the quotients.

- The player that has the greatest quotient gets 1 point.

- Continue playing until a player earns 5 points. Reshuffle the cards if needed.

A DESERT SAFARI!

The Sahara desert in Africa is 800 to 1,200 miles wide and 3,000 miles long. Animals like elephants, giraffes, lions, and chimpanzees live in or near this desert. Many African desert animals can also be found in zoos, where they are protected and fed.

Some animals, such as the elephant, are very large. An average elephant weighs 12,250 pounds, and its trunk weighs 400 pounds!

FOOD EATEN BY ZOO ANIMALS

Animal	Number of Animals	Daily Food (lb)
Hippopotamus	6	900
Elephant	10	1,600
Giraffe	6	360
Lion	7	218
Camel	5	94
Hyena	8	144
Chimpanzee	9	117
Flamingo	8	1

Real-World Math

Use the information on page 340 to solve each problem.

1. Suppose each camel eats the same amount of food. About how much food would one camel eat in one week?

2. A visitor travels the length of the Sahara desert in 10 days and travels the same amount each day. How many miles does the visitor travel each day?

3. Suppose each elephant eats the same amount of food. How much food do four elephants eat in a day?

4. How many ounces of food does each flamingo eat per day? (*Hint*: 1 pound = 16 ounces)

5. Does a hyena or a chimpanzee eat more each day? Explain.

6. How much more do three elephants eat than three hippopotamus?

7. How much food is eaten each day by one giraffe, one hyena, and one lion? Order these animals in order from greatest to least with respect to the amount of food each eats.

Did You Know?

The African elephant is the largest land mammal.

Divide Greater Numbers

GET READY to Learn

One of the largest holes in the world is a copper mine in Utah. It is 5,808 feet wide. How many yards wide is the hole?

You can use the same process to divide greater numbers that you use with smaller numbers.

Real-World EXAMPLE   Divide Greater Numbers

 MEASUREMENT How many yards wide is the copper mine?

The mine is 5,808 feet wide. There are 3 feet in 1 yard. So, to find the width in yards, divide 5,808 by 3.

Step 1 Divide the thousands.

$$\begin{array}{r} 1 \\ 3\overline{)5,808} \\ \underline{-3} \\ 2 \end{array}$$

Divide. $5 \div 3 = 1$
Put 1 in thousands place.
Multiply. $3 \times 1 = 3$
Subtract. $5 - 3 = 2$
Compare. $2 < 3$

Step 2 Divide the hundreds.

$$\begin{array}{r} 1\ 9 \\ 3\overline{)5,808} \\ \underline{-3}\downarrow \\ 2\ 8 \\ \underline{-2\ 7} \\ 1 \end{array}$$

Bring down the hundreds.
Divide. $28 \div 3 = 9$
Multiply. $3 \times 9 = 27$
Put 9 in hundreds place.
Subtract. $28 - 27 = 1$
Compare. $1 < 3$

Step 3 Divide each place.

$$\begin{array}{r} 1,936 \\ 3\overline{)5,808} \\ \underline{-3}\downarrow \\ 28 \\ \underline{-27}\downarrow \\ 10 \\ \underline{-9}\downarrow \\ 18 \\ \underline{-18} \\ 0 \end{array}$$

For each place, divide, multiply, subtract, compare, and bring down the next digit to form a new number to be divided.

So, the copper mine is 1,936 yards wide.

2 **MONEY** Crater of Diamonds State Park in Arkansas allows visitors to mine for diamonds and keep any that are found. If a person finds a 2-carat diamond that is worth $7,585, how much is each carat worth?

Divide $7,585 by 2 to find how much each carat is worth.

Estimate $7,585 ÷ 2 ⟶ $8,000 ÷ 2 = $4,000

Step 1 Divide the thousands.

$$\begin{array}{r} \$3 \\ 2\overline{)\$7,585} \\ -6 \\ \hline 1 \end{array}$$

Divide. 7 ÷ 2 = 3
Put 3 in the quotient over the thousands place.

Multiply. 2 × 3 = 6
Subtract. 7 − 6 = 1
Compare. 1 < 2

Step 2 Divide the hundreds.

$$\begin{array}{r} \$3\textbf{7} \\ 2\overline{)\$7,\!585} \\ -6\downarrow \\ \hline 15 \\ -14 \\ \hline 1 \end{array}$$

Bring down the hundreds.
Divide. 15 ÷ 2 = 7
Put 7 in the quotient over the hundreds place.

Multiply. 2 × 7 = 14
Subtract. 15 − 14 = 1
Compare. 1 < 2

Step 3 Divide each place.

$$\begin{array}{r} \$3,\!792 \text{ R1} \\ 2\overline{)\$7,\!585} \\ -6\downarrow \\ \hline 15 \\ -14\downarrow \\ \hline 18 \\ -18\downarrow \\ \hline 05 \\ -04 \\ \hline 1 \end{array}$$

For each place, divide, multiply, subtract, and compare. Then bring down the next digit in the dividend.

So, each carat is worth a little more than $3,792.

Check for Reasonableness
The answer is close to the estimate. So, it is reasonable. ✓

Remember
For each place, divide, multiply, subtract, compare, and bring the next digit in the dividend directly down to form a new number to be divided.

Divide. Use estimation to check. See Examples 1 and 2 (pp. 342–343)

1. $2\overline{)2{,}764}$ **2.** $3\overline{)\$6{,}163}$ **3.** $5\overline{)8{,}045}$

4. $8{,}436 \div 4$ **5.** $\$6{,}197 \div 6$ **6.** $7{,}893 \div 8$

7. An art museum hosted an exhibit. One day, 6,414 people attended the exhibit during the 6 hours it was open. If the same number of people attended each hour, how many people attended each hour?

8. **Talk About It** Explain how dividing a 4-digit dividend by a 1-digit divisor is similar to dividing a 3-digit dividend by a 1-digit divisor. How is it different?

Practice and Problem Solving

SCAS • PASS
Extra Practice, p. R22

Divide. Use estimation to check. See Examples 1 and 2 (pp. 342–343)

9. $2\overline{)2{,}418}$ **10.** $3\overline{)3{,}428}$ **11.** $4\overline{)\$4{,}228}$ **12.** $5\overline{)7{,}465}$

13. $6\overline{)8{,}802}$ **14.** $8\overline{)\$9{,}597}$ **15.** $7\overline{)7{,}248}$ **16.** $8\overline{)8{,}072}$

17. $\$7{,}621 \div 4$ **18.** $6{,}417 \div 6$ **19.** $84{,}932 \div 2$ **20.** $\$91{,}387 \div 3$

21. Kirby bought a used car for $3,626. He plans on paying for it in two years. How much will he pay each year?

22. **Measurement** The farthest distance a pumpkin has ever been thrown is 4,434 feet. How many yards is this?

Real-World PROBLEM SOLVING

Measurement The map shows distances between cities in the United States.

23. The Regan family is driving cross country for a vacation. They are driving from San Francisco to Boston. If they drive an equal distance each day, how many miles will they travel each day if they make the trip in 6 days?

24. The Collins family is moving to Miami from Anchorage. If they drive an equal distance each day, about how many miles would they travel each day if they make the trip in 8 days?

Distance Between U.S. Cities

From	To	Distance (miles)
Boston, MA	San Francisco, CA	3,102
Anchorage, AL	Miami, FL	4,999

C08-01A-105733

H.O.T. Problems

25. OPEN ENDED Write a division problem that involves dividing a 4-digit number by a 1-digit number. The quotient must be between 1,000 and 1,200.

26. CHALLENGE Divide 218,376 by 2.

27. **WRITING IN ►MATH** How many digits would be in the quotient of 12,495 ÷ 5? Explain how you know.

28. The map shows the distance in feet to the treasure.

C09-25A-105711

Find 318 ÷ 3 to find how many yards it is from X to the treasure. (Lesson 8-8)

A 104   **C** 106

B 105   **D** 107

29. Derrick's horse ate 3,150 pounds of food in 3 months. How many pounds of food did it eat each month if it ate the same amount each month? (Lesson 8-9)

F 1,025 pounds

G 1,050 pounds

H 1,500 pounds

J 1,550 pounds

Spiral Review

Divide. Use estimation to check. (Lesson 8-8)

30. 3)$\overline{624}$

31. 4)$\overline{\$824}$

32. 5)$\overline{537}$

Divide. Use estimation to check. (Lesson 8-7)

33. 2)$\overline{468}$

34. 3)$\overline{\$645}$

35. 4)$\overline{872}$

36. Janise bought the items shown to the right. If the shirts are equal in price and the total cost was $80, how much did each item cost? (Lesson 8-6)

C09-26A-105711

37. Algebra Find the value of $n \times 317$ if $n = 4$. (Lesson 5-6)

Study Guide and Review

SC Math Online > macmillanmh.com
• STUDY*TO GO*
• Vocabulary Review

FOLDABLES Study Organizer GET READY to Study

Be sure the following Key Vocabulary words and Key Concepts are written in your Foldable.

Lesson 1   Lesson 2

Key Concepts

Estimate Quotients (p. 322)

• You can use **compatible numbers** to estimate quotients.

$722 \div 9$

THINK 722 is close to 720. 720 and 9 are compatible numbers because they are easy to divide mentally.

$720 \div 9 = 80 \qquad 9 \times 8 = 72$

Division of Multi-Digit Numbers (p. 332)

• Divide a multi-digit number by a one-digit number.

```
      $234
   2)$468
     -4↓|
      06|
    - 6↓
       08
     - 8
        0
```

For each place, divide, multiply, subtract, and compare. Then bring down the next digit in the dividend.

Key Vocabulary

compatible numbers (p. 322)

dividend (p. 311)

divisor (p. 311)

quotient (p. 311)

remainder (p. 312)

Vocabulary Check

Complete each sentence with the correct vocabulary word.

1. The number that is left over in a division problem is the ___?___ .

2. The number that divides the dividend is the ___?___ .

3. The number you are dividing is the ___?___ .

4. ___?___ are numbers that are easy to divide mentally.

5. The result of a division problem is the ___?___ .

6. In the division problem $4\overline{)136}$, the number 136 is the ___?___ .

Lesson-by-Lesson Review

  8-1 **Division with Remainders** (pp. 313–315)

4-2.5

Example 1
Find 59 ÷ 3.

$$
\begin{array}{r}
19 \text{ R2} \\
3\overline{)59} \\
-3\downarrow \\
\overline{29} \\
-27 \\
\overline{2}
\end{array}
$$

For each place, divide, multiply, subtract, and compare.

Then bring down the next digit in the dividend.

Check
$$
\begin{array}{r}
19 \\
\times\ 3 \\
\hline
57 \\
+\ 2 \\
\hline
59
\end{array}
$$

So, the answer is correct. ✔

Divide.

7. $5\overline{)53}$ **8.** $6\overline{)67}$

9. $91 \div 4$ **10.** $77 \div 3$

11. Christy has 37 books. She wants to put them evenly on her 4 shelves. How many books will she not be able to fit?

12. Rafael wants to earn $40 for a new pair of skates. If he earns $6 an hour for yard work, how many hours will he have to work to have the money for the skates?

 8-2 **Divide Multiples of 10, 100, and 1,000** (pp. 316–319)

4-2.5

Example 2
Find 1,600 ÷ 4.

Use patterns to divide.

$16 \div 4 = 4$
$160 \div 4 = 40$
$1,600 \div 4 = 400$

So, $1,600 \div 4 = 400$.

Check
Use addition to check.

$$
\begin{array}{r}
400 \\
400 \\
400 \\
+\ 400 \\
\hline
1,600
\end{array}
$$

So, the answer is correct. ✔

Divide. Use patterns.

13. $27 \div 9 = \blacksquare$ **14.** $49 \div 7 = \blacksquare$
$\ 270 \div 9 = \blacksquare$ $\ 490 \div 7 = \blacksquare$
$\ 2,700 \div 9 = \blacksquare$ $\ 4,900 \div 7 = \blacksquare$

15. $900 \div 3$ **16.** $1,800 \div 9$

17. $3,600 \div 4$ **18.** $4,900 \div 7$

19. $6,400 \div 8$ **20.** $7,200 \div 9$

21. Chuck collected 150 shells during his five days of vacation. If Chuck collected the same number of shells each day, how many shells did he collect each day?

8-3 **Problem-Solving Strategy:** **Guess and Check** (pp. 320–321)

4-1.1

Example 3

Opal and Steve collect coins. Opal has 32 more coins than Steve. They have 146 coins altogether. How many coins does each person have?

Understand

What facts do you know?

• Opal has 32 more coins than Steve.

• They have 146 coins altogether.

What do you need to find?

• The number of coins each person has.

Plan   You can guess and check to solve the problem.

Solve   Make logical guesses.

Think of two addends that have a difference of about 30, and a sum of about 150.

Try 90 + 60. 90 + 60 = 150

The sum is too high. Try smaller numbers until you find the correct answer.

The correct answers are 89 and 57 because 89 + 57 = 146.

Check   The answers are correct because 89 − 57 = 32 and 89 + 57 = 146.

Solve. Use the guess and check strategy.

22. Juanita made a vegetable tray. There are 2 times more cucumber slices than tomato slices and 4 times more carrot slices than cucumber slices. If there are 5 tomato slices, how many slices of carrots and cucumbers are there on the tray?

23. Toru bought a CD and a DVD. The CD cost $5 less than the DVD, and the total was $29. How much was each item?

24. There are rabbits, ponies, and goats at a petting zoo. There are eight times as many goats as ponies. There are six more rabbits than ponies. The number of ponies is shown. Find how many rabbits and goats there are.

25. Etta is buying a sweater and a pair of pants. The sweater cost $12 more than the pants. The total cost will be $84. What is the cost of each clothing item?

8-4 Estimate Quotients (pp. 322–324)

4-2.5

Example 4
Find 273 ÷ 9.

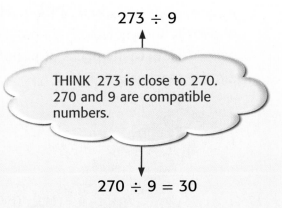

$273 \div 9$

THINK 273 is close to 270. 270 and 9 are compatible numbers.

$270 \div 9 = 30$

So, $273 \div 9$ is about 30.

Estimate.

26. $254 \div 5$ **27.** $634 \div 7$

28. $5{,}571 \div 8$ **29.** $7{,}218 \div 9$

30. Measurement A roller coaster car made it to the bottom of a 318-foot hill in 5 seconds. About how many feet did the car travel each second?

31. A skate park has $3,225 to spend on 8 new ramps. About how much can be spent on each ramp?

8-5 Two-Digit Quotients (pp. 326–329)

4-2.5

Example 5
Find 95 ÷ 4.

Step 1 Divide the tens.

$$\begin{array}{r} 2 \\ 4\overline{)95} \\ -8 \\ \hline 1 \end{array}$$

Divide. $9 \div 4 = 2$
Put 2 in the quotient.
Multiply. $4 \times 2 = 8$
Subtract. $9 - 8 = 1$
Compare. $1 < 4$

Step 2 Divide the ones.

$$\begin{array}{r} 23 \text{ R3} \\ 4\overline{)95} \\ -8\downarrow \\ \hline 15 \\ -12 \\ \hline 3 \end{array}$$

Bring down the ones.
Divide. $15 \div 4 = 3$
Put 3 in the quotient.
Multiply. $4 \times 3 = 12$
Subtract. $15 - 12 = 3$
Compare. $3 < 4$
Remainder = 3

So, $95 \div 4 = 23$ R3.

Divide.

32. $3\overline{)86}$ **33.** $6\overline{)96}$

34. $87 \div 4$ **35.** $95 \div 3$

36. Miranda has 85 crayons. She wants to share them equally with two of her friends. How many crayons will Miranda and her friends each get? How many will be left?

37. Garcia placed his baseball cards into 3 envelopes. He ended up with 17 cards in each envelope and 2 left over. How many cards did Garcia have to begin with?

8-6 **Problem-Solving Investigation: Choose a Strategy** (pp. 330–331)

4-1.1

Example 6
There are 1,323 students trying out for basketball teams. Is it reasonable to say that more than 150 teams will be formed if there are nine players on each team?

Understand

There are 1,323 students trying out for basketball teams. Nine players will be on each team.

Will there be more than 150 teams formed?

Plan

Divide the number of students trying out by the number of players per team.

Solve

Divide 1,323 by 9.

$$
\begin{array}{r}
147 \\
9\overline{)1{,}323} \\
-9\downarrow \\
\hline
42 \\
-36\downarrow \\
\hline
63 \\
-63 \\
\hline
0
\end{array}
$$

There will be 147 teams. So, it is not reasonable to say there will be more than 150 teams.

Check

Use multiplication to check.

$90 \times 147 = 1,323$

So, the answer is correct. ✔

Use any strategy to solve.

38. Frida had 3 pencils. Then her teacher gave her some of the packs of pencils shown. Now Frida has 11 pencils. How many packs of pencils did the teacher give Frida?

39. Each hand in the human body has 27 bones. There are 6 more bones in the fingers than in the wrist. There are 3 fewer bones in the palm than in the wrist. How many bones are in the fingers and wrist?

40. One banner is made using three sheets of paper. How many different banners can be made using red, yellow, and black paper one time each if the paper is placed in a row?

41. Algebra What number is missing from the pattern 2, 7, 12, 17, ▪?

42. A number is divided by 5. Next, 4 is subtracted from the quotient. Then, 6 is added to the difference. The result is 10. What is the number?

Three-Digit Quotients (pp. 332–334)

4-2.5

Example 7
Find 426 ÷ 4.

Estimate 426 ÷ 4 ⟶ 400 ÷ 4 = 100

$$
\begin{array}{r}
106 \text{ R2} \\
4\overline{)426} \\
\underline{-4} \\
02 \\
\underline{-\ 0} \\
26 \\
\underline{-24} \\
2
\end{array}
$$

For each place, divide, multiply, subtract, and compare.

Then bring down the next digit in the dividend.

So, 426 ÷ 4 = 106 R2.

Check for Reasonableness

The quotient, 106 R2, is close to the estimate. So, the answer is reasonable. ✔

Divide.

43. $3\overline{)787}$ **44.** 994 ÷ 4

45. There are 7 teachers and 147 students in the 4th grade. If the same number of students are in each class, how many students will be in each class?

46. There are 1,035 cars in the airport parking lot. The lot has 9 rows of parked cars. How many cars are in each row if the same number of cars are in each row?

47. Explain how to check Exercise 46 to be sure your answer is correct.

Quotients with Zeros (pp. 336–338)

4-2.5

Example 8
Find $416 ÷ 2.

$$
\begin{array}{r}
\$208 \\
2\overline{)\$416} \\
\underline{-4} \\
01 \\
\underline{-0} \\
16 \\
\underline{-16} \\
0
\end{array}
$$

For each place, divide, multiply, subtract, and compare.

Then bring down the next digit in the dividend.

So, $416 ÷ 2 = $208.

Divide.

48. $2\overline{)217}$ **49.** $3\overline{)621}$

50. 817 ÷ 4   **51.** 925 ÷ 3

52. The number of students who ride the bus home each day is 432. The students are divided evenly into 8 buses. How many students fit on each bus?

53. Tamera wants to fit all of her 749 marbles into 7 jars. How many should she put in each jar?

8-9 **Divide Greater Numbers** (pp. 342–345)

4-2.5

Example 9
Find 6,213 ÷ 3.

Estimate 6,213 ÷ 3 ➞ 6,000 ÷ 3 = 2,000

Step 1 Divide the thousands.

```
      2
3)6,213
 −6
  0
```

Step 2 Divide the hundreds.

```
    2 0
3)6,213
 −6↓
  02
 − 0
   2
```

Step 3 Divide each place.

```
   2,071
3)6,213     For each place, divide, multiply,
 −6          subtract, and compare.
  02
 − 0         Then bring down the next digit in
  21         the dividend.
 −21
  03
 − 3
   0
```

So, 6,213 ÷ 3 = 2,071.

Check for Reasonableness
The quotient, 2,071, is close to the estimate.
So the answer is correct ✓

Divide.

54. 3)$6,597

55. 5)8,802

56. 7,561 ÷ 6

57. $9,387 ÷ 8

58. Measurement Candice is making bows. She uses a 8-inch piece of ribbon for each bow. How many bows can she make with 1,827 inches of ribbon?

59. A total of 3,915 people attended three orchestra concerts. How many people attended each concert if the same number of people attended each concert?

60. There are 1,440 students who attend a school. There are four lunch periods. If the same number of students eat during each lunch period, how many students eat during each lunch period?

61. Measurement A 3-kilometer race is about 9,842 feet long. How many yards long is the race? (*Remember*: 3 feet = 1 yard)

For Exercises 1 and 2, decide whether each statement is *true* or *false*.

1. A quotient is the number being divided.

2. In the problem 62 ÷ 2, the number 2 is the divisor.

Divide. Check each answer.

3. 2)‾4‾5‾

4. 73 ÷ 4

5. MULTIPLE CHOICE There are 5,280 feet in a mile. Since 1 yard equals 3 feet, how many yards are in one mile?

A 1,760 yd   **C** 1,780 yd

B 1,770 yd   **D** 1,790 yd

Copy and complete each set of patterns.

6. 24 ÷ 4 = ▦
    240 ÷ 4 = ▦
    2,400 ÷ 4 = ▦

7. 18 ÷ 2 = ▦
    180 ÷ 2 = ▦
    1,800 ÷ 2 = ▦

Divide. Use patterns.

8. $3,200 ÷ 4

9. 5,400 ÷ 6

10. Three members of the Cotter family are flying to Washington, D.C., for vacation. The total cost of the tickets is $1,250. About how much was each person's ticket?

Divide. Use estimation to check.

11. 5)‾4‾1‾0‾

12. 863 ÷ 3

13. Sara earned the same score on her last 2 tests. Her total score was 184. What was her score on each of the 2 tests?

Divide. Use estimation to check.

14. 2)‾4‾1‾7‾

15. $929 ÷ 3

16. Measurement The Toshiro family is moving across the country. They will drive a total of 2,835 miles over 7 days. If they drive the same distance each day, how far will they drive each day?

Divide. Use estimation to check.

17. 2)‾4‾,‾3‾0‾2‾

18. 6,932 ÷ 7

19. A family is buying a boat. They hope to have it paid off in 3 years. How much do they have to pay each year to reach their goal?

Boat for Sale
$6,129

Call 555-5555

20. MULTIPLE CHOICE Jed hiked a trail that is 7,920 feet long. Since there are 3 feet in a yard, how many yards did Jed hike?

F 2,540   **H** 2,630

G 2,580   **J** 2,640

21. WRITING IN ►MATH How many digits would be in the quotient of 2,795 ÷ 5? Explain how you know.

PART 1 Multiple Choice

Read each question. Then fill in the correct answer on the answer sheet provided by your teacher or on a sheet of paper.

1. What is the mode of {2, 3, 3, 3, 5, 5}?

A 2   **C** 5

B 3   **D** 7

2. Which number is represented by n in the equation $n + 938 = 1,456$?

F 518   **H** 528

G 522   **J** 594

3. Which of the following has the least value?

A 45,034,653   **C** 45,689,236

B 45,073,542   **D** 45,856,494

4. How many students live 8 or more miles from school?

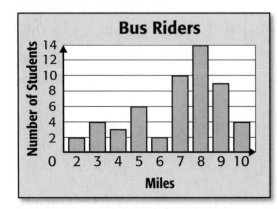

F 25   **H** 27

G 26   **J** 28

5. Which number makes each equation true?

$$54 \div 6 = \blacksquare$$
$$540 \div 60 = \blacksquare$$
$$5,400 \div 600 = \blacksquare$$

A 6   **C** 60

B 9   **D** 90

6. What multiplication expression does this model represent?

F 3×6 **H** 3×7

G 4×6 **J** 4×7

7. Josh has 84 toy cars to share equally among himself and 3 friends. How many toy cars will each person receive?

A 18   **C** 28

B 21   **D** 30

8. There are 8,000 fans at a sold out baseball game. Each section of the stadium holds 100 people. How many sections are there in the stadium?

F 8   **H** 80

G 40   **J** 800

9. The soccer team has 144 water bottles in 6 boxes. How many water bottles are in each box?

A 20   **C** 24

B 22   **D** 25

10. Which number is 100,000 more than 7,186,335?

F 7,086,335   **H** 7,286,335

G 7,196,335   **J** 8,186,335

11. Use the graph. Which two students collected a sum of cans fewer than 750?

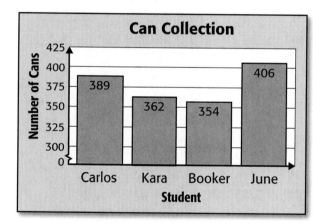

Can Collection

A Carlos and Kara

B Kara and June

C June and Booker

D Booker and Carlos

PART 2   Short Response

Record your answers on the answer sheet provided by your teacher or on a sheet of paper.

12. Write a rule to describe the pattern below.

Input (x)	Output (y)
3	9
5	15
7	21
9	27
11	33

13. Which number makes this equation true?

$$88 \div \blacksquare = 11$$

PART 3   Extended Response

Record your answers on the answer sheet provided by your teacher or on a sheet of paper.

14. Rosa has 150 goldfish. She wants to put about the same number of fish into each of 8 ponds. About how many fish will be in each pond? Explain.

15. What is a good estimate for $351 \div 5$? Explain your reasoning.

NEED EXTRA HELP?															
If You Missed Question...	1	2	3	4	5	6	7	8	9	10	11	12	13	14	15
Go to Lesson...	3-2	5-2	1-4	3-5	8-2	4-3	8-5	8-2	8-5	2-4	3-5	5-8	4-6	8-4	8-4
SC Academic Standards	4-6.2	4-3.5	3-2.1	4-6.2	4-2.5	4-2.3	4-2.5	4-2.5	4-2.5	3-2.3	4-6.2	4-3.3	4-2.5	4-2.5	4-2.5

Identify and Describe Geometric Figures

 **BIG Idea** What are two-dimensional and three-dimensional figures?

A **two-dimensional figure** has length and width.
A **three-dimensional figure** has length, width, and height.

Example Two-dimensional and three-dimensional figures are often found in traffic signs.

  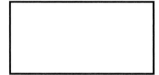

What will I learn in this chapter?

- Identify, describe, and classify two- and three-dimensional figures.
- Identify angles.
- Identify and make nets.
- Solve problems by looking for a pattern.

Key Vocabulary

three-dimensional figure

two-dimensional figure

polygon

angle

 **SC Math Online**   **Student Study Tools** at macmillanmh.com

Make this Foldable to help you organize information about geometric figures. Begin with 8 sheets of notebook paper.

1 **Staple** the sheets of notebook paper together to form a booklet.

2 **Cut** a tab as shown. On the third page, make the tab longer, and so on.

3 **Write** the chapter title on the cover. Label each tab with a lesson number.

Chapter 9 Identify and Describe Geometric Figures **357**

You have two ways to check prerequisite skills for this chapter.

Option 2

SC Math Online > Take the Chapter Readiness Quiz at macmillanmh.com.

Option 1

Complete the Quick Check below.

QUICK Check

Identify each figure. (Prior Grade)

1.

2.

3.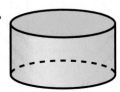

4. Identify the three-dimensional figure that represents the objects at the right.

How many sides does each figure have? (Prior Grade)

5.

6.

7.

8. The musical instrument at the right resembles a triangle. How many sides does the instrument have?

Identify each figure. (Prior Grade)

9.

10.

11.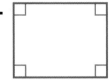

Three-Dimensional Figures

GET READY to Learn

The dog crate shown resembles a three-dimensional figure. A **three-dimensional figure** is a solid figure. It has length, width, and height.

- A **face** is a flat side.
- Two faces meet at an **edge**.
- A **vertex** is where three or more faces meet.

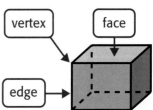

Three-Dimensional Figures   Key Concepts

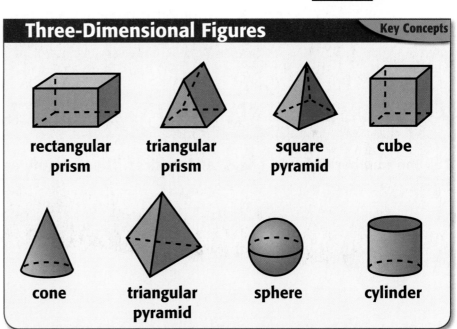

rectangular prism   triangular prism   square pyramid   cube

cone   triangular pyramid   sphere   cylinder

Real-World EXAMPLE   Identify Three-Dimensional Objects

1 **GIFTS** Tell the number of faces, edges, and vertices. Then identify the shape of the gift box.

It has 6 faces, 12 edges, and 8 vertices. The gift box is a rectangular prism.

A **net** is a two-dimensional figure that can be folded to make a three-dimensional figure.

Hands-On Mini Activity

Step 1 Using grid paper, draw and cut out the net shown.

Step 2 Fold along the dotted lines. Tape the edges.

Step 3 Identify the three-dimensional figure.

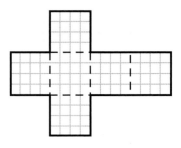

1. Draw another net that could be used to form a cube.

2. Identify the three-dimensional figure the net shown at the right makes.

3. Explain how to identify a three-dimensional figure from its net without folding the paper.

CHECK What You Know

Tell the number of faces, edges, and vertices. Then identify each figure. See Example 1 (p. 359)

1.

2.
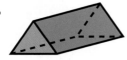

3.

Identify the three-dimensional figure each net makes.

4.
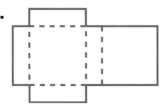

5.
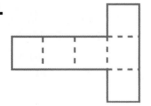

6.
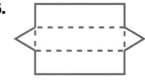

7. Name two three-dimensional figures that have 6 faces.

8. **Talk About It** Compare a triangular prism and a triangular pyramid.

Tell the number of faces, edges, and vertices. Then identify each figure.

See Example 1 (p. 359)

9.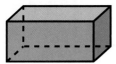

10.

11.

12.

13.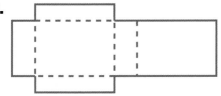

14.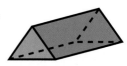

Identify the three-dimensional figure each net makes.

15.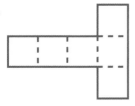

16.

17.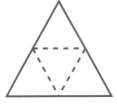

18.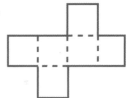

19.

20.

21. This three-dimensional figure has 4 faces, 6 edges, and 4 vertices. What figure is it?

22. This three-dimensional figure can be made using 2 circles and 1 large rectangle. What figure is it?

H.O.T. Problems

23. OPEN ENDED Draw a three-dimensional figure. Then describe its faces, edges, and vertices.

24. WHICH ONE DOESN'T BELONG? Identify the figure that does not belong with the other three. Explain.

25. **WRITING IN ▶MATH** Compare a cone and cylinder.

GET READY to Learn

These are traffic signs that you may see every day. What shapes are the signs?

MAIN IDEA

I will identify, describe, and classify two-dimensional figures.

SC Academic Standards

4-4.6 Represent points, lines, line segments, rays, angles, and **polygons.** *Also addresses 4-4.4.*

New Vocabulary

two-dimensional figure

polygon   sides

triangle

quadrilateral

pentagon

hexagon   octagon

SC Math Online

macmillanmh.com
• Extra Examples
• Personal Tutor
• Self-Check Quiz

The shapes of the signs are two-dimensional figures. A **two-dimensional figure** is a plane figure. It has length and width. **Polygons** are closed plane figures that have three or more line segments called **sides**.

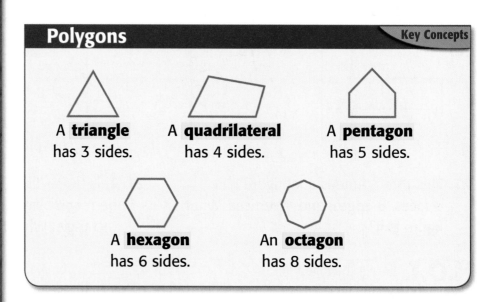

Polygons   Key Concepts

A **triangle** has 3 sides.

A **quadrilateral** has 4 sides.

A **pentagon** has 5 sides.

A **hexagon** has 6 sides.

An **octagon** has 8 sides.

Real-World EXAMPLE   Identify a Polygon

1 SPORTS Identify the shape of home plate.

Look at the shape of the home plate. It has 5 sides.

So, this figure is a pentagon.

A circle is not a polygon because it does not have straight sides. Other shapes are not polygons as well.

Remember
Polygons have straight sides only, not curved sides.

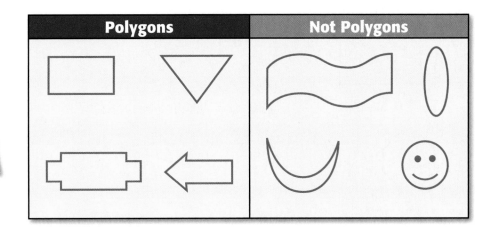

Polygons	Not Polygons

EXAMPLES Identify a Polygon

Tell whether each shape is a polygon.

2

The figure has curved sides. It is not a polygon.

3

The figure has 6 straight sides. It is a polygon.

CHECK **What You Know**

Identify each polygon. See Example 1 (p. 362)

1.

2. (hexagon)

3. (four-pointed star)

Tell whether each shape is a polygon. See Examples 2 and 3 (p. 363)

4.

5.  (burst shape)

6. (star)

7. Identify the shape of the nut.

8. Talk About It If we take a quadrilateral and cut it into two pieces, what shapes could the pieces be?

Lesson 9-2 Two-Dimensional Figures **363**

Identify each polygon. See Example 1 (p. 362)

9.

10.

11.

12.

13.

14.

Tell whether each shape is a polygon. See Examples 2 and 3 (p. 363)

15.

16.

17.

18.

19.

20.

Identify two polygons on each real-world object.

21.

22.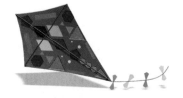

🌐 Real-World **PROBLEM SOLVING**

Art Polygons and other shapes are used in the painting *Castle and Sun*.

23. Name two polygons in the painting.

24. Is the sun a polygon? Explain.

25. What polygon is in the painting most often?

26. What polygon in the painting has the most sides?

H.O.T. Problems

27. OPEN ENDED Draw and identify a polygon.

28. FIND THE ERROR Carlota and Gabe are drawing a polygon. Who is correct? Explain.

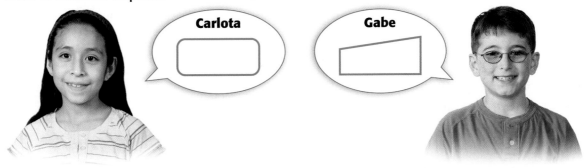

Carlota   Gabe

29. WRITING IN ►MATH Write about a real-world object that is made of polygons.

PASS Practice   4-4.2, 4-4.4

30. Which figure can form a cube when folded on the dotted lines without overlapping? (Lesson 9-1)

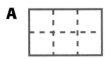

A

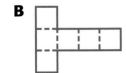

B

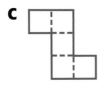

C

D

31. Which statement about these figures is true? (Lesson 9-2)

F There is one polygon.

G These are all polygons.

H There are two polygons.

J None of these are polygons.

Spiral Review

Identify each figure. Then tell the number of faces, edges, and vertices. (Lesson 9-1)

32.

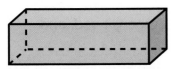

33.

Divide. Use estimation to check. (Lesson 8-9)

34. $6{,}204 \div 3$

35. $\$7{,}816 \div 8$

36. $5\overline{)9{,}675}$

37. $7\overline{)\$7{,}371}$

Problem-Solving Strategy

MAIN IDEA I will solve problems by looking for a pattern.

 4-3.1 Analyze numeric, nonnumeric, and repeating patterns involving all operations and decimal patterns through hundredths.

Amado is helping his dad put tile on a table top. They are laying the tiles in a pattern. They have run out of tiles and need to buy more. What color of tiles need to be purchased to complete the table?

Understand	**What facts do you know?** • You know the tiles form a pattern. • You know they need to buy more tiles. **What do you need to find?** • Find the tile colors that need to be purchased.
Plan	Look for a pattern. Then continue the pattern to find the missing tiles.
Solve	There are two rows of tile, and the tiles repeat red, green, blue, and yellow.  In the first row, the missing tiles are blue and green. In the second row, the missing tiles are red, blue, and yellow. So, Amado and his father need 2 blue, 1 green, 1 red, and 1 yellow tile.
Check	Look back. The answer makes sense for the facts given. So, the answer is correct. ✔

366   Chapter 9 Identify and Describe Geometric Figures

Refer to the problem on the previous page.

1. How do you identify a pattern in a problem-solving situation?

2. If Amado and his dad used 36 tiles, how many tiles would they use of each color?

3. Suppose Amado and his dad laid 3 more rows of tiles. How many green tiles would they need in all?

4. Look back at Exercise 3. Check your answer. Explain how you know the answer is correct.

PRACTICE the Strategy

SCAS • PASS

Extra Practice, p. R23

Solve. Use the look for a pattern strategy.

5. Draw the next three figures in the pattern below. Explain.

6. **Algebra** Copy and complete the table. What is the pattern?

Input (g)	Output (h)
6	24
8	32
5	20
3	■
■	36

7. Claudia will arrive at the airport on the first plane after 9 A.M. Planes arrive every 45 minutes after 6 A.M. When will Claudia's plane arrive?

8. Ming found 8 seashells on the first day, 20 on the second day, and 32 on the third day. If the pattern continues, how many shells will she find on the fifth day?

9. Describe the pattern below. Then find the missing number.

    2, 4, 8, ■, 32

10. Two hikers take turns carrying a backpack. The first hiker carries the pack. They change every 3 miles. They have hiked 14 miles so far. How many times have they changed? Who has the pack now?

11. **Algebra** A pattern of figures is shown below. Draw the next two figures. Explain your pattern.

12. **Geometry** A border on a scrapbook page has a repeating design that shows a triangle, a pentagon, and a hexagon. Draw the first eight figures in the pattern.

13. **WRITING IN ►MATH** Create a pattern with geometric figures. Give it to a classmate and see if he or she can continue it.

> **GET READY to Learn**

Brent's teacher assigned ten problems for homework. Brent started his homework at 4:00 P.M. He completed it at the time shown. How far has the minute hand turned?

An **angle** is a figure made from two rays that have the same endpoint. Angles are measured in degrees (°).

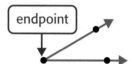

Turns and Angles   Key Concepts

$45° = \frac{1}{8}$ turn

$90° = \frac{1}{4}$ turn

$180° = \frac{1}{2}$ turn

$270° = \frac{3}{4}$ turn $360° = $ full turn

> **Real-World EXAMPLE**   Turns and Angles

1) **MEASUREMENT Refer to the clock above. Write how far the minute hand has turned in degrees and as a fraction.**

Compare the angle shown on the clock to the angles shown in the Key Concepts box.

So, the angle shown on the clock is 90° or a $\frac{1}{4}$ turn.

Types of Angles

A **right angle** measures 90°.
A right angle is formed by
perpendicular lines.

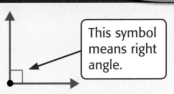

This symbol means right angle.

An **acute angle** measures greater
than 0° and less than 90°.

An **obtuse angle** measures greater
than 90°, but less than 180°.

Remember

A corner, like the corners on a desk, is a right angle.

EXAMPLES   Classify an Angle

Classify each angle as *right*, *acute*, or *obtuse*.

2

The angle is 90°.
So, it is a right angle.

3

The angle is greater than 90°
and less than than 180°.
It is an obtuse angle.

CHECK What You Know

Write the measure of each angle in degrees and as a fraction. See Example 1 (p. 368)

1.
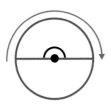

2.

3.
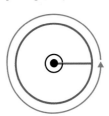

Classify each angle as *right*, *acute*, or *obtuse*. See Examples 2 and 3 (p. 369)

4.

5.
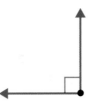

6.

7. **Talk About It** Describe what makes each type of angle an *acute*, *obtuse*,
or *right* angle.

Write the measure of the angle in degrees and as a fraction. See Example 1

8.

9.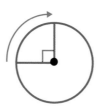

10.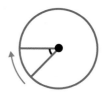

Classify each angle as *right*, *acute*, or *obtuse*. See Examples 2 and 3

11.

12.

13.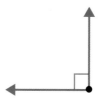

14.

15.

16.

17. The timer is set to 30 minutes. How many degrees will the dial have turned when the timer goes off?

18. Classify the angle shown on the gas gauge below.

Real-World PROBLEM SOLVING

Geography A compass can be used to find direction. The arrow on a compass always faces north.

19. If you are facing north and turn west, what angle could be drawn to represent your movement?

20. You are facing east and are told to turn 180°. What direction will you be facing? Write the angle your body has turned as a fraction.

H.O.T. Problems

21. OPEN ENDED Draw three different acute angles.

22. WRITING IN ►MATH Choose three objects in your classroom that have angles. Describe how to classify each angle as *acute*, *obtuse*, or *right*.

Tell the number of faces, edges, and vertices. Identify each figure. (Lesson 9-1)

1.

2.

3. Identify the three-dimensional figure the net would make.
(Lesson 9-1)

Identify each polygon. (Lesson 9-2)

4.

5.

6. **MULTIPLE CHOICE** Look at the figures below. Which statement is true? (Lesson 9-2)

A There is one polygon.

B These are all polygons.

C There are two polygons.

D None of these are polygons.

7. Identify two polygons on the bird house.
(Lesson 9-2)

8. **MULTIPLE CHOICE** What is this figure called? (Lesson 9-2)

F hexagon

G triangle

H octagon

J pentagon

For Exercises 9 and 10, solve. Use the look for a pattern strategy. (Lesson 9-3)

9. Describe the pattern in 3, 9, 27, ▨, 243. Then find the missing number.

10. A ferry leaves a harbor every 35 minutes starting at 6:30 A.M. Davion plans to take the first ferry after 8 A.M. When will his ferry leave?

Write the measure of each angle in degrees and as a fraction. (Lesson 9-4)

11.

12.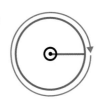

Classify each angle as *right, acute,* or *obtuse.* (Lesson 9-4)

13.

14.

15. WRITING IN ▶MATH Can a figure be a polygon and three-dimensional? Explain. (Lesson 9-2)

9-5 Triangles

MAIN IDEA

I will identify, describe, and classify triangles.

SC Academic Standards

4-4.6 Represent points, lines, line segments, rays, angles, and **polygons.**

New Vocabulary

right triangle

acute triangle

obtuse triangle

isosceles triangle

equilateral triangle

scalene triangle

SC Math Online

macmillanmh.com

• Extra Examples
• Personal Tutor
• Self-Check Quiz

▷ GET READY to Learn

This sandwich is cut in half. What figure does each half resemble?

There are many different types of triangles. You can classify triangles by the measure of their angles

Classify Triangles by Angles   Key Concepts

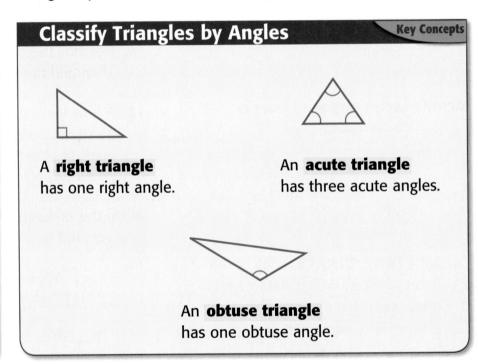

A **right triangle** has one right angle.

An **acute triangle** has three acute angles.

An **obtuse triangle** has one obtuse angle.

EXAMPLE   Classify by Angles

1 Classify the triangle. Use *right, acute,* or *obtuse*.

Since there is one obtuse angle, the triangle is obtuse.

Triangles can also be classified by the measure of their angles.

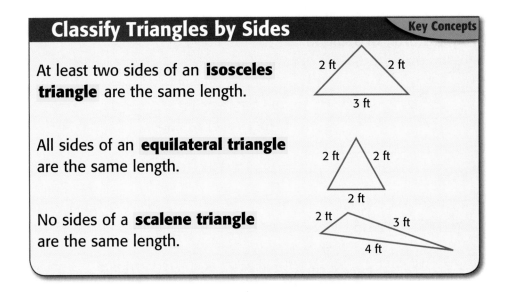

Classify Triangles by Sides

Key Concepts

At least two sides of an **isosceles triangle** are the same length.

All sides of an **equilateral triangle** are the same length.

No sides of a **scalene triangle** are the same length.

EXAMPLE Classify by Angles and Sides

2 **Classify the triangle. Use** *acute,* *right,* **or** *obtuse* **and** *isosceles,* *equilateral,* **or** *scalene.* **The triangle has three angles that are less than 90°. The triangle is acute. All of the sides are the same length, so it is also equilateral.**

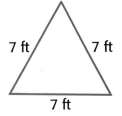

CHECK What You Know

Classify each triangle. Use *acute, right,* or *obtuse* and *isosceles, equilateral,* or *scalene.* See Examples 1 and 2 (pp. 372–373)

1.
3 cm
3 cm
5 cm

2.
7 ft   7 ft
7 ft

3.
4 in.   5 in.

4. What type of triangle is the pennant?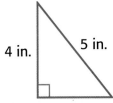

5. **Talk About It** Two sides of an equilateral triangle measure 3 feet. What is the measure of the third side? Explain.

Classify each triangle. Use *acute, right,* or *obtuse* and *isosceles, equilateral,* or *scalene.* See Examples 1 and 2 (pp. 372–373)

6.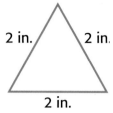
2 in.   2 in.
2 in.

7.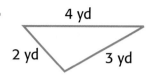
4 yd
2 yd   3 yd

8.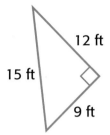
12 ft
15 ft
9 ft

9.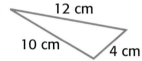
12 cm
10 cm   4 cm

10.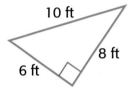
10 ft
8 ft
6 ft

11.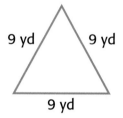
9 yd   9 yd
9 yd

12. Describe the triangle formed by the ladder and the wall.

13. Classify the triangle on the wedge of cheese.

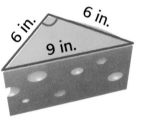
6 in.   6 in.
9 in.

14. Measurement Shonda draws an equilateral triangle with 2 sides whose sum equals 12 inches. What is the length of the third side?

15. Measurement Ross draws an isosceles triangle with sides 5 centimeters and 3 centimeters. What could the measure of the third side be?

South Carolina Data File

Columbia is the capital and the largest city in South Carolina. The city is named after Christopher Columbus.

16. Classify the triangle formed by Columbia, Sumter, and Charleston.

17. Explain how you classified the triangle in Exercise 16.

Rock Hill ●
Greenville ●

South Carolina

Columbia ●   ● Sumter

Charleston ● ●
Mount Pleasant

H.O.T. Problems

OPEN ENDED Draw an example of each triangle.

18. right scalene triangle

19. obtuse isosceles triangle

20. WHICH ONE DOESN'T BELONG? Identify the term that does not belong with the other three. Explain.

| right | obtuse | scalene | acute |

21. WRITING IN ►MATH Can an equilateral triangle be obtuse? Explain your answer.

PASS Practice   4-4.6

22. In the figure, which two angles appear to be obtuse? *(Lesson 9-4)*

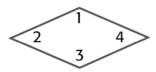

A Angles 1 and 2

B Angles 1 and 3

C Angles 1 and 4

D Angles 2 and 4

23. What kind of triangle always has 3 acute angles and 3 sides the same length? *(Lesson 9-5)*

F isosceles

G right

H equilateral

J scalene

Spiral Review

Classify each angle as *right, acute,* or *obtuse.* *(Lesson 9-4)*

24.

25.

26.

27. Suppose the pattern at the right was extended to 30 figures in all. How many pentagons and octagons would there be? *(Lesson 9-3)*

Identify the first five multiples for each number. *(Lesson 4-9)*

28. 3   **29.** 5   **30.** 8   **31.** 11

Quadrilaterals

MAIN IDEA

I will identify, describe, and classify quadrilaterals.

SC Academic Standards

4-4.1 Analyze the quadrilaterals squares, rectangles, trapezoids, rhombuses, and parallelograms according to their properties. *Also addresses 4-4.4, 4-1.4.*

New Vocabulary

rectangle

square

rhombus

parallelogram

trapezoid

SC Math Online

macmillanmh.com

• Extra Examples
• Personal Tutor
• Self-Check Quiz

GET READY to Learn

There are many quadrilaterals in these fields. How can you describe some of the different figures?

All quadrilaterals have 4 sides and 4 angles.

Quadrilaterals   Key Concepts

A **rectangle** has 4 right angles with opposite sides equal and parallel.

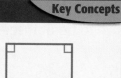

A **square** has 4 right angles with opposite sides parallel. All sides are equal in length.

A **rhombus** has 4 equal sides with opposite sides parallel.

These marks show equal sides. →

A **parallelogram** has opposite sides equal in length and parallel.

A **trapezoid** has exactly 1 pair of parallel sides.

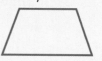

EXAMPLE   Classify a Quadrilateral

① **Classify the quadrilateral in as many ways as possible.**

It can be classified as a parallelogram, rectangle, square, and rhombus.

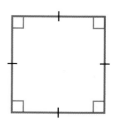

Many real-world objects have the shapes of quadrilaterals.

2 **VIDEO GAMES** Write the type of quadrilateral that best describes the shape around the game controller.

The shape has one pair of parallel sides. So, it is a trapezoid.

3 Identify the red shape in as many ways as possible.

The shape has 4 right angles, with opposite sides equal and parallel. So, it is a rectangle and a parallelogram.

CHECK What You Know

Classify each quadrilateral in as many ways as possible.

See Example 1 (p. 376)

1.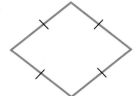

2.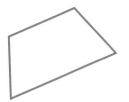

3.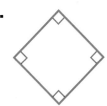

Write the type of quadrilateral that best describes the shape.

See Examples 2–3 (p. 377)

4.

5.

6.

7. **Talk About It** How are a square and a rhombus alike? How are they different?

Classify each quadrilateral in as many ways as possible.

See Example 1 (p. 376)

8.

9.

10.

11.

12.

13.

Write the type of quadrilateral that best describes the shape.

See Examples 2 and 3 (p. 377)

14.

15.

16.

17.

18.

19.

20. A quadrilateral has 4 sides with opposite sides parallel and 4 right angles. Two sides are longer than the others. What is the quadrilateral?

21. Phillip draws a quadrilateral. All 4 sides are the same length. Its opposite sides are parallel. What figure did he draw?

H.O.T. Problems

22. OPEN ENDED Draw two quadrilaterals that can be classified as parallelograms.

REASONING Tell whether each statement is *true* or *false*. If the statement is false, draw a counterexample.

23. A rhombus is a square.

24. A rectangle is a parallelogram.

25. **WRITING IN ▶MATH** True or false: All squares are rectangles, but not all rectangles are squares. Explain.

Art is Shaping Up

Draw Figures

You will need: 10 index cards

Get Ready!

Players: 2

Get Set!

Cut the cards in half. Then label the cards with the terms shown.

Go!

- Shuffle the cards. Then spread the cards facedown on the table.

- Player 1 turns over a card and draws the figure. If the drawing is correct, Player 1 keeps the card.

- If Player 1 cannot draw the figure, Player 2 is given a chance to draw the figure.

- Player 2 keeps the card if he or she can draw the figure. If he or she cannot, the card is put back.

- Player 2 selects a card.

- Continue playing until all cards are gone. The player who collects more cards wins.

○ polygon	right angle
○ quadrilateral	acute angle
triangle	obtuse angle
pentagon	rectangle
hexagon	square
○ parallelogram	rhombus
trapezoid	
○	
○	

Problem-Solving Investigation

MAIN IDEA I will choose the best strategy to solve a problem.

 SCAS **4-1.7** Use flexibility in mathematical representations. **4-1.8** Recognize the limitations of various forms of mathematical representations.

P.S.I. TEAM +

ARTURO: I have the five puzzle pieces shown. I need to form a square using all of the pieces.

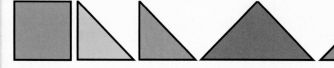

YOUR MISSION: Arrange the five puzzle pieces to form a square.

Understand	You know there are five puzzle pieces. Find how to arrange the pieces to form a square.
Plan	Use the act it out strategy. Trace the pieces and cut them out of paper. Then arrange the polygons in different ways to figure out how they will form a square.
Solve	Arrange the pieces in different ways until you form a square. 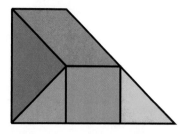 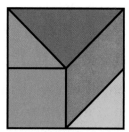
Check	Look back. The figure formed by the pieces is a square because it is a rectangle that has four equal sides. So, the answer is correct. ✔

Use any strategy shown below to solve. Tell what strategy you used.

PROBLEM-SOLVING STRATEGIES
• Make a table.
• Act it out.
• Guess and check.

1. **Measurement** Keli can run 3 miles in 36 minutes. She plans to run each mile one minute faster every 2 weeks. Is it reasonable to say that Keli will be able to run 3 miles in 25 minutes in 3 weeks? Explain.

2. Identify a combination of four bills which are worth a total of $50.

3. **Algebra** Draw the next three figures in the pattern below.

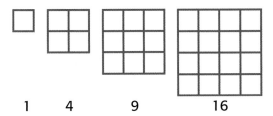

1   4   9   16

4. Audrey had 8 trading cards. She then bought some packs with 6 cards in each pack. Audrey now has 44 cards. How many packs did she buy?

5. Kareem has $20. He wants to buy the items shown. Will he have enough money? Explain.

6. **Measurement** Kala wants to download 12 songs on her digital music player. She only has 5 minutes to download the songs. If it takes 30 seconds for Kala to download one song, will she have enough time to download all of the songs? Explain.

7. **Algebra** The polygons below form a pattern. How many sides will the ninth polygon have? Explain.

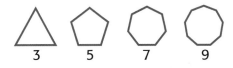

3   5   7   9

8. Mason has $12. He earns $5 every week for doing chores. Is it reasonable to say that Mason will be able to buy a skateboard that costs $60 in 10 weeks? Explain.

9. A number is multiplied by 2. Then 4 is subtracted from the product. The result is 8. What was the original number?

10. **Measurement** During football practice, Tyrell is running drills. He runs 20 yards forward and then 10 yards backward starting at the goal line. How many sets will it take him to reach the other goal line 100 yards away?

11. **WRITING IN ►MATH** Look at Exercise 7. Which problem-solving strategy did you use to find the answer? Explain how you used this strategy to solve the problem.

Problem Solving in Art

Garden Art

The Sculpture Garden in Washington, D.C., is filled with many figures. It has 17 large sculptures. Many of these sculptures are made of different three-dimensional figures. For example, the *Four-Sided Pyramid* is made of concrete cubes. It is about 32 feet tall and 33 feet wide.

Another sculpture in this garden, *Cluster of Four Cubes,* is made of four metal cubes that spin in the breeze. These cubes are about 9 feet high in the air. *Moondog* is a metal sculpture that has triangles, hexagons, and pentagons in its shape. It is so large you can walk under it!

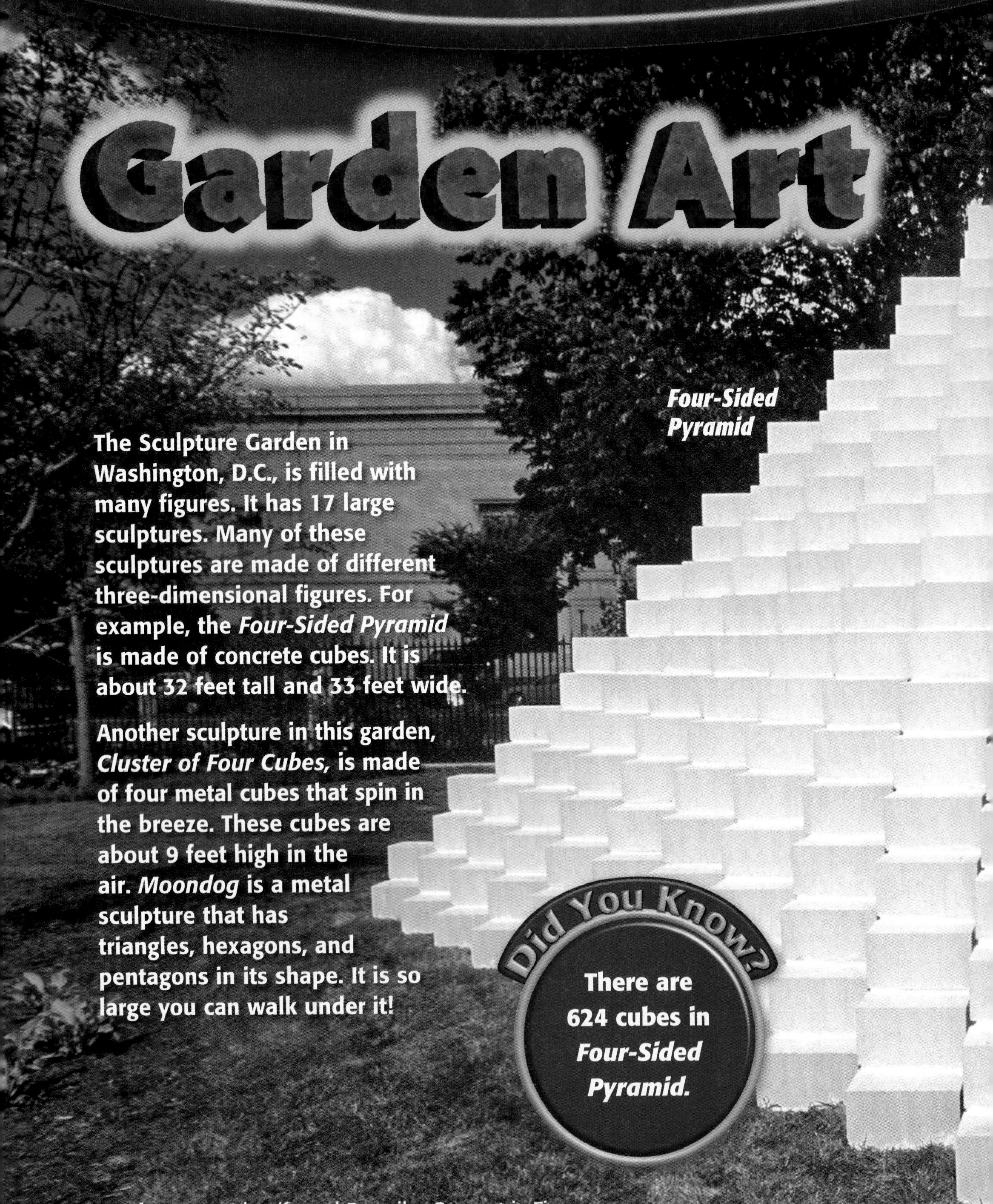

Four-Sided Pyramid

Did You Know?

There are 624 cubes in *Four-Sided Pyramid.*

Cluster of Four Cubes

Moondog

Real-World Math

Use the sculptures *Moondog*, *Four-Sided Pyramid,* and *Cluster of Four Cubes* to solve each problem.

1. What geometric figure does *Four-Sided Pyramid* resemble?

2. How many faces, edges, and vertices does *Four-Sided Pyramid* have?

3. How many edges does one cube in *Cluster of Four Cubes* have?

4. Can you see a rectangle in the picture of *Moondog*? Explain.

5. How many equilateral triangles do you see in the picture of the *Moondog*?

6. All the edges of the *Four-Sided Pyramid* are equal. What kind of triangles make up the faces? How many triangles are there?

7. Suppose one face of a cube on *Cluster of Four Cubes* is cut diagonally. What kind of triangle will it make?

Study Guide and Review

SC Math Online > macmillanmh.com
• STUDY TO GO
• Vocabulary Review

FOLDABLES®
Study Organizer

GET READY to Study

Be sure the following Key Vocabulary words and Key Concepts are written in your Foldable.

Identify and Describe Geometric Figures

Key Concepts

- A **three-dimensional figure** is a solid figure with length, width, and height. (p. 359)

- A **two-dimensional figure** is a plane figure with length and width. (p. 362)

- An **angle** is a figure made from two rays that have the same endpoint. (p. 368)

Key Vocabulary

angle (p. 368)

polygon (p. 362)

three-dimensional figure (p. 359)

two-dimensional figure (p. 362)

Vocabulary Check

Decide which vocabulary word best completes each sentence.

1. A(n) _____?_____ is a solid figure.

2. A(n) _____?_____ is a figure made from two rays that have the same endpoint.

3. A(n) _____?_____ is a closed plane figure that has three or more line segments.

4. A(n) _____?_____ has length, width, and height.

5. A(n) _____?_____ is a plane figure that has length and width.

6. A(n) _____?_____ is measured in degrees (°).

Lesson-by-Lesson Review

9-1 **Three-Dimensional Figures** (pp. 359–361)

4-4.2,
4-4.4

Example 1
Identify the shape of the cooking pot. Then tell the number of faces, edges, and vertices.

The cooking pot is a cylinder.

It has 2 faces, 0 edges, and 0 vertices.

Identify each figure. Then tell how many faces, edges, and vertices it has.

7.   8.

9. Identify the two-dimensional figure the net would make.

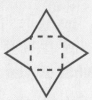

9-2 **Two-Dimensional Figures** (pp. 362–365)

4-4.6,
4-4.4

Tell whether each shape is a polygon.
Example 2

The moon has curved sides. So, it is not a polygon.

Example 3

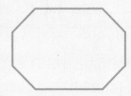
This figure has 8 sides. The sides are straight. So, it is a polygon.

Identify each polygon.

10.   11.

12.    13.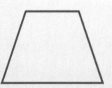

Tell whether the shape is a polygon.

14.   15.

9-3 **Problem-Solving Strategy:** Look for a Pattern (pp. 366–367)

4-3.1

Example 4

Bruce is creating the pattern below on a bowl in art class. There is enough space on the bowl for the pattern below to repeat three times. How many stars will he make?

Understand

What facts do you know?

- The figures form a pattern that repeats three times.

What do you need to find?

- The number of stars Bruce will make.

Plan Look for a pattern to solve.

Solve The pattern is sun, star, moon, moon, star, sun. There are 2 stars in the pattern before it repeats.

So, the number of stars Bruce will make after the pattern repeats three times is 2 × 3 or 6.

Check The answer makes sense for the facts given. The answer is correct.

16. Describe the pattern below. Then find the missing number.

45, 36, 27, ■, 9

17. Copy and complete the pattern. What are the next two figures in this pattern?

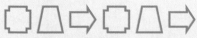

18. **Algebra** Copy and complete the table. What is the pattern?

8	40
4	20
9	45
7	■
■	15

19. Nell jogged for 8 minutes on Monday, 13 minutes on Tuesday, and 18 minutes on Wednesday. If this pattern continues, how many minutes will Nell jog on Sunday?

20. The pattern below can also be shown as 1, 4, 7, 10. Draw the next two figures. What are the next two numbers?

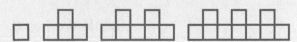

21. Describe the pattern below. Then find the missing number.

1, 3, 7, 15, ■

386 Chapter 9 Identify and Describe Geometric Figures

9-4 Angles (pp. 368–370)

4-5.2,
4-4.6

Example 5
Write the measure of the angle shown below in degrees and as a fraction of a full turn.

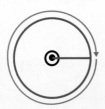

The angle shown is 360° or a full turn.

Write the measure of each angle in degrees and as a fraction of a full turn.

22. 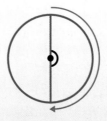   23.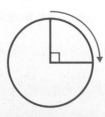

Classify each angle as *right, acute,* or *obtuse.*

24.

25.

9-5 Triangles (pp. 372–375)

4-4.6

Example 6
Classify the triangle. Use *acute, right,* or *obtuse* and *isosceles, equilateral* or *scalene.*

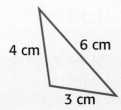

4 cm   6 cm

3 cm

The triangle has one obtuse angle, so it is obtuse.

Since no sides are the same length, the triangle is scalene.

Classify each triangle. Use *acute, right,* or *obtuse* and *isosceles, equilateral,* and *scalene.*

26.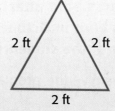

2 ft   2 ft

2 ft

27.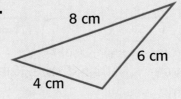

8 cm

6 cm

4 cm

9-6 Quadrilaterals (pp. 376–378)

4-4.1,
4-4.4,
4-1.4

Example 7
Classify the quadrilateral in as many ways as possible.

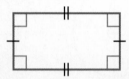

The figure has parallel sides. So, it is a parallelogram.

It has 4 right angles. So, it is a rectangle.

So, the quadrilateral can be classified as a parallelogram and rectangle.

Classify each quadrilateral in as many ways as possible.

28.

29.

30.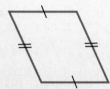

31.

32.

33.

9-7 Problem-Solving Investigation: Choose a Strategy (pp. 380–381)

4-1.7,
4-1.8

Example 8
Students are lining up by birthdays. Nathan is first in line. His birthday is in September. Beatriz was born in December. Ruby was born after Carlie. Carlie was born in October. What is the order of the students?

Work backward to solve the problem.

So, the order is Nathan, Carlie, Ruby, and Beatriz.

Use any strategy to solve.

34. Draw the next two figures in the pattern.

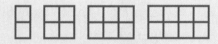

35. Liana rounds a number to the nearest hundred and gets 200. What is the least number it could be? the greatest number?

36. **Algebra** Logan has 7 jars of coins. Each jar has 35 coins. How many coins does he have?

For Exercises 1–3, decide whether each statement is *true* or *false*.

1. A square is a two-dimensional figure in which all the sides are the same length.

2. A trapezoid has two pairs of parallel sides.

3. An obtuse triangle has two obtuse angles.

4. Identify the three-dimensional figure the net would make.

Classify each quadrilateral in as many ways as possible.

5.

6.

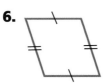

7. **MULTIPLE CHOICE** How many faces does this figure have?

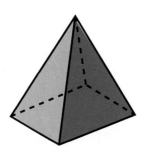

 A 3   **C** 5

 B 4   **D** 6

Classify each triangle. Use *acute, right,* or *obtuse* and *isosceles, equilateral,* or *scalene*.

8.

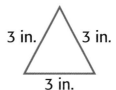

3 in.   3 in.

3 in.

9.

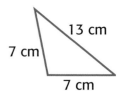

13 cm

7 cm

7 cm

Classify each angle as *right, acute,* or *obtuse*.

10.

11.

12. Draw the next two figures in the pattern below.

13. **MULTIPLE CHOICE** In the figure below, which angles appear to be acute?

1   2

3   4

 F Angles 1 and 2   **H** Angles 2 and 4

 G Angles 1 and 3   **J** Angles 3 and 4

14. **WRITING IN ►MATH** Is it possible to draw an isosceles triangle that is acute? Explain. Draw a picture to support your answer.

PART 1 — Multiple Choice

Read each question. Then fill in the correct answer on the answer sheet provided by your teacher or on a sheet of paper.

1. Nara is wrapping a gift in a box shaped like a rectangular prism. How many faces does a rectangular prism have?

A 4   **C** 8

B 6   **D** 12

2. Which number makes this equation true?

$$126 \div \blacksquare = 9$$

F 10   **H** 12

G 11   **J** 14

3. What kind of triangle is shown below?

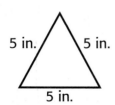
5 in.   5 in.   5 in.

A scalene   **C** isosceles

B right   **D** equilateral

4. What number comes next in the pattern below?

20, 17, 14, 11, 8, ___

F 5   **H** 3

G 4   **J** 2

5. Which of the following angles appears to be right?

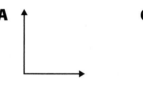

A   **C**   **B**   **D**

6. Tyrell has 162 pennies. He wants to put about the same number of pennies into each of 8 jars. About how many pennies will be in each jar?

F 18   **H** 22

G 20   **J** 24

7. What solid figure has one circular face and one vertex?

A cone

B cylinder

C prism

D sphere

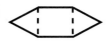

Preparing for PASS

For test-taking strategies and practice, see pages R42–R55.

8. Which figure can form a square pyramid when folded on the dotted lines without overlapping?

F

H

G

J

---

9. Gigi has 4 boxes filled with books. Each box can hold 24 books. How many books does she have?

A 68   **C** 96

B 88   **D** 120

---

10. Which is the best estimate for 423 ÷ 7?

F 50   **H** 70
G 60   **J** 80

---

11. A zoo had 1,295 visitors on Tuesday and 1,523 visitors on Wednesday. How many visitors in all on the two days?

A 228   **C** 2,818

B 2,808   **D** 2,908

PART 2   Short Response

Record your answers on the answer sheet provided by your teacher or on a sheet of paper.

12. How many vertices does a cube have?

_____

13. Which quadrilateral has exactly one pair of parallel sides?

_____

14. Tell whether the angle shown below is *acute, obtuse,* or *right*.

PART 3   Extended Response

Record your answers on the answer sheet provided by your teacher or on a sheet of paper.

15a. What is the name of the figure for the net shown below? Explain.

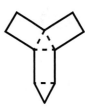

15b. How many vertices will the figure have after it is formed? Explain.

NEED EXTRA HELP?																
If You Missed Question...	1	2	3	4	5	6	7	8	9	10	11	12	13	14	15a	15b
Go to Lesson...	9-1	5-8	9-5	9-3	9-4	8-4	9-1	9-1	6-4	8-4	2-4	9-1	9-6	9-4	9-1	9-1
SC Academic Standards	4-4.4	4-3.4	4-4.6	4-3.1	4-4.6	4-2.5	4-4.4	4-4.2	4-2.3	4-2.5	3-2.3	4-4.4	4-4.1	4-4.6	4-4.2	4-4.2

Understand and Develop Spatial Reasoning

BIG Idea **What is a transformation?**

A **transformation** is a movement of a figure. The three types of transformations are **translation** (slide), **reflection** (flip), and **rotation** (turn).

Example Beth and Daniel are playing chess. Beth is moving the chess piece as shown. This movement is an example of a slide or translation.

What will I learn in this chapter?

- Find points on number lines and coordinate planes.
- Identify and describe lines, line segments, and rays.
- Explore and identify rotations, reflections, and translations.
- Use rotations, reflections, and translations to identify congruent figures and symmetry in figures.
- Solve problems by making an organized list.

Key Vocabulary

number line	**transformation**
point	**congruent**
coordinate plane	

SC Math Online

Student Study Tools
at **macmillanmh.com**

FOLDABLES®
Study Organizer

Make this Foldable to help you organize information about spatial reasoning. Begin with one sheet of notebook paper.

1 **Fold** the sheet of paper in half as shown.

2 **Cut** every sixth line on one side. The result is five tabs.

3 **Label** each tab as shown.

Number Lines

Lines, Line Segments, Rays

Coordinate Plane

Transformations

Congruence and Symmetry

Chapter 10 Understand and Develop Spatial Reasoning **393**

ARE YOU READY for Chapter 10?

You have two ways to check prerequisite skills for this chapter.

Option 2

SC Math Online Take the Chapter Readiness Quiz at macmillanmh.com.

Option 1

Complete the Quick Check below.

QUICK Check

Tell whether the dashed line divides the figure in half.
Write *yes* or *no*. (Prior Grade)

1.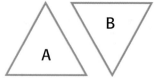

2.

3.

4. Jon is sharing his sandwich with his brother. Is the sandwich divided in half?

Identify the figure that is different. (Prior Grade)

5.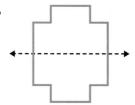

6.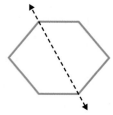

Identify each polygon. (Lesson 9-2)

7.

8.

9.

10. Peyton is looking in a kaleidoscope. Identify two of the polygons that can be seen.

Locate Points on a Number Line

GET READY to Learn

Andrés is trying to find what whole number is represented by point *T* on the number line.

<table>
<tr><td></td><td>T</td></tr>
</table>

| 1,021 | 1,023 | 1,025 | 1,027 |

MAIN IDEA

I will locate points on a number line.

SC Academic Standards

4-4.6 Represent points, lines, line segments, rays, angles, and polygons.
Also addresses 4-2.1.

New Vocabulary

number line

point

SC Math Online

macmillanmh.com
• Extra Examples
• Personal Tutor
• Self-Check Quiz

A **number line** is a line with numbers on it in order at regular intervals. A **point** is an exact location in space. You can locate points on a number line.

EXAMPLES   Locate Points on a Number Line

1 **What number is represented by point *T*?**

To find what number point *T* represents, use the number line.

The scale for the number line is in one-unit intervals. Count to find what number point *T* represents.

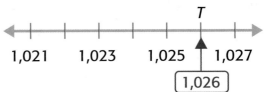

T

| 1,021 | 1,023 | 1,025 | 1,027 |

1,026

So, point *T* represents 1,026.

2 **What number does point *Z* represent on the number line?**

Locate *Z* on the number line. The scale is in intervals of 5. Count by fives to find what number point *Z* represents.

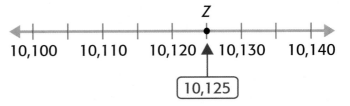

Z

| 10,100 | 10,110 | 10,120 | 10,130 | 10,140 |

10,125

So, point *Z* represents 10,125.

3 **What number does point *Z* represent on the number line?**
Locate *Z* on the number line. The scale is in intervals of 1,000. Count by thousands to find what point *Z* represents.

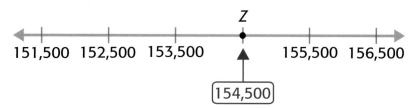

So, point *Z* represents 154,500.

CHECK What You Know

Tell what number each letter on the number line represents.
See Examples 1–3 (pp. 395–396)

1.
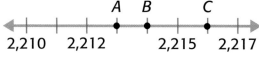

2.

Tell what number point *Z* represents on each number line. See Examples 1–3 (pp. 395–396)

3.

4.
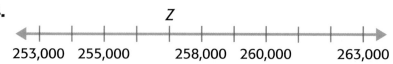

5. In 1787, Delaware became the first state in the United States. In 1803, Ohio became a state. Indiana became a state 13 years after Ohio. Create a number line that has intervals of 10. Locate these points on your number line.

6. **Talk About It** Why do most number lines have intervals greater than one?

Tell what number each letter on the number line represents. See Examples 1–3 (pp. 395–396)

7.

8.
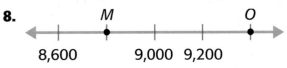

9.
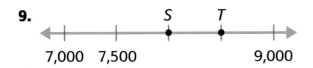

10.
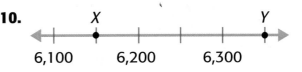

Tell what number point Z represents on each number line. See Examples 1–3 (pp. 395–396)

11.
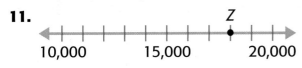

12.
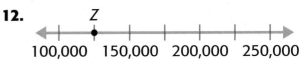

13.
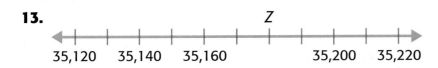

14.
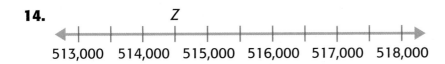

15. A number line starts with 4,250 and ends on 4,500. It is marked with intervals of 50. The letter X is on the third tick mark from the beginning. What is the value for X?

16. A number line starts with 30,405 and ends on 30,415. It is marked with intervals of 1. The letter N is halfway between 30,405 and 30,415. What is the value for N?

H.O.T. Problems

17. CHALLENGE Estimate the number that each letter on the number line represents.

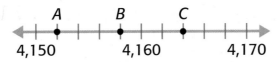

18. **WRITING IN ►MATH** Explain how to locate points on a number line.

Parallel and Intersecting Lines

In this activity, you will use pattern blocks to explore parallel and intersecting lines. You will also decide if the intersecting lines are perpendicular.

MAIN IDEA

I will identify and describe parallel and intersecting lines.

SC Academic Standards

Reinforcement of 3-4.3 Classify lines and line segments as either parallel, perpendicular, or intersecting.

You Will Need
pattern blocks
paper and pencil
ruler

ACTIVITY **Parallel and Intersecting Lines**

① **Use a pattern block to explore parallel and intersecting lines.**

Step 1 **Observe.**

Look at the pattern block shown. There are four corners. At each corner there is a point of intersection, where two lines meet.

Step 2 **Trace the shape.**

Place the pattern block on a piece of paper. Trace the shape.

Step 3 **Extend the lines.**

Extend the lines with a ruler. Notice how the sides intersect above the pattern block.

The top and bottom lines appear to be parallel. That is, they do not intersect and the distance between them is always the same.

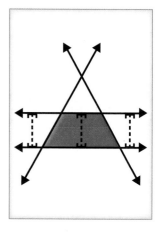

ACTIVITY Perpendicular Lines

Hands-On Activity

2 Model intersecting lines.

Step 1 Label the cards.
Label the index cards A and B.

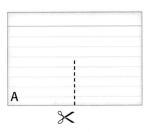

Step 2 Cut the cards.
Hold the cards together. Cut a slit halfway through both cards as shown.

Step 3 Form perpendicular lines.
Insert one card into the slit of the other. Use tape to hold the cards together at right angles. These cards are now perpendicular.

Step 4 Identify perpendicular lines.
Use the cards to identify objects in your classroom that illustrate perpendicular lines.

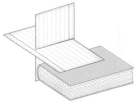

Think About It

1. Are any of the intersecting lines perpendicular on the trapezoid?

2. Name two other shapes that have parallel lines.

3. Name two shapes that have perpendicular lines of intersection.

✓ CHECK What You Know

Identify and describe lines as *parallel*, *intersecting*, or *perpendicular*.

4.
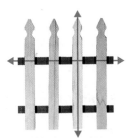

5.

6.

7. **WRITING IN** ►**MATH** How would you determine if two lines are parallel?

Lines, Line Segments, and Rays

GET READY to Learn

Farmers often plant crops like corn in rows. The rows resemble line segments.

Lines, Rays, Line Segments

Key Concepts

Words
A **line** is a straight set of points that extend in opposite directions without ending.

Model

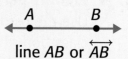

line *AB* or $\overleftrightarrow{AB}$

Words
A **ray** is a part of a line that has one **endpoint** and extends in one direction without ending.

Model endpoint

ray *AB* or $\overrightarrow{AB}$

Words
A **line segment** is a part of a line between two endpoints.

Model endpoint

segment *AB* or $\overline{AB}$

EXAMPLES Identify Lines, Rays, or Line Segments

Identify each figure.

1

The figure extends in opposite directions without ending. Line *XY* or $\overleftrightarrow{XY}$.

2

The figure has one endpoint and extends in one direction without ending. Ray *AB* or $\overrightarrow{AB}$.

You can describe lines, rays, and line segments by the way they meet or cross each other. In the previous Explore Activity, you learned how to identify parallel and intersecting lines.

Types of Lines   Key Concepts

Words **Parallel** lines are always the same distance apart. They do not meet.

Model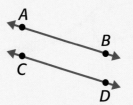

line AB is parallel to line CD

$$\overleftrightarrow{AB} \parallel \overleftrightarrow{CD}$$

Words Lines that meet or cross each other are called **intersecting** lines.

Model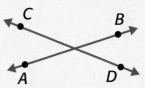

line AB intersects line CD

$$\overleftrightarrow{AB} \text{ intersects } \overleftrightarrow{CD}$$

Words Lines that meet or cross each other to form right angles are called **perpendicular** lines.

Model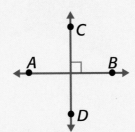

line segment AB is perpendicular to line segment CD

$$\overleftrightarrow{AB} \perp \overleftrightarrow{CD}$$

EXAMPLE   Describe Lines, Rays, or Line Segments

3 **Describe the figure.**

The figure shows ray AB and line segment CD. Notice that ray AB intersects line segment CD.

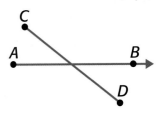

$\overrightarrow{AB}$ intersects $\overline{CD}$.

Identify each figure. See Examples 1 and 2 (p. 400)

1.
Q   R

2.
F
       B

3.
                    C
A

4. Describe the line segments formed on a tennis racquet.

See Example 3 (p. 401)

5.  List a real-world example for a line segment, parallel lines, and intersecting lines.

Practice and Problem Solving

SCAS • PASS
Extra Practice, p. R25

Identify each figure. See Examples 1 and 2 (p. 400)

6.
        F
  D

7.
F
        G

8.
                    K
H

Describe each figure. See Example 3 (p. 401)

9.
        K
L
  J   M

10.

11.

Real-World PROBLEM SOLVING

Geography On a map, streets resemble line segments. Use the map to answer Exercises 12–15.

12. Identify two streets that are parallel to Oak Street.

13. Tell whether Center Street and Johnston Street are parallel, intersecting, or perpendicular lines. Explain.

14. Identify two streets that are parallel.

15. Are there any streets that are intersecting? Explain.

H.O.T. Problems

OPEN ENDED Draw an example of each figure described.

16. ray CD

17. $\overleftrightarrow{DE} \parallel \overleftrightarrow{FG}$

18. $\overline{RS}$ intersecting $\overline{TU}$

REASONING Tell whether each statement is *true* or *false*.

19. If two lines are parallel, they are the same distance apart.

20. If two lines are parallel, they are also perpendicular.

21. **WRITING IN** ►**MATH** Can you draw two lines on a sheet of paper that are both parallel and perpendicular? Explain.

PASS Practice 4-4.6, 3-4.3

22. What number does point B best represent? (Lesson 10-1)

A 900

B 950

C 970

D 1,000

23. Which figure shows parallel lines? (Lesson 10-2)

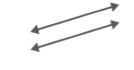
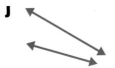

Spiral Review

Tell what number each letter on the number line represents. (Lesson 10-1)

24.

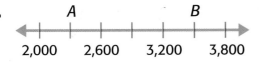

25.

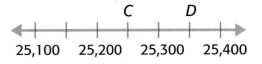

Algebra For Exercises 26 and 27, use the table.
(Lesson 9-7)

26. Mr. Larson's class is playing a game. The table shows how many playing pieces are needed. Copy and complete the table.

27. Explain how to find the number of pieces needed if you know the number of students playing.

Game Pieces Needed	
Students	**Number of Pieces**
4	36
7	63
▢	72
9	▢
10	90

Problem-Solving Strategy

MAIN IDEA I will make an organized list to solve problems.

 SCAS **4-6.7 Analyze possible outcomes for a simple event.**

The Burke family is going camping for the weekend. There are four children in the Burke family, Devon, Nikki, Jade, and Terrell. They will sleep in two tents, with two children in each tent. How many different combinations are possible?

Understand	**What facts do you know?** • There are 4 children going camping. • Two children will sleep in each tent. **What do you need to find?** • Find how many combinations are possible.
Plan	You can make a list of all the possible combinations. Then count the total number of different combinations.
Solve	First, write the name of one of the children. Then, write the name of another child by the first child's name. Continue to do this with each child. Do not repeat pairs. Nikki–Jade Jade–Terrell Terrell–Devon Nikki–Terrell Jade–Devon Nikki–Devon There are 6 different combinations that can be in each tent.
Check	Look back. There are 4 children. They can each pair up with three other children. Each child's name does appear 3 times on the list. So, the answer is correct. ✓

Refer to the problem on the previous page.

1. Suppose one of the children brings a friend camping. How does the additional child affect the possible combinations?

2. Identify another way to organize all of the possible outcomes.

3. Suppose Nikki, Jade, and Terrell go for a hike in a single file line. Make a list to show all the possible ways they can line up.

4. What is the probability that Nikki will be first in line if the children line up in random order?

PRACTICE the Strategy

SCAS • PASS
Extra Practice, p. R26

Solve. Make an organized list.

5. Richard has one blue shirt and one red shirt. He has gray pants and navy pants. How many different outfits can he wear?

6. Sadie put four slips of paper into a hat. Each slip of paper has a number written on it as shown. Sadie chooses two slips of paper. How many different sums could she have?

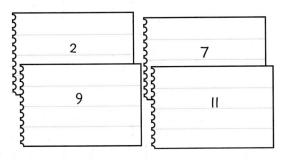

7. Yogi's mom is hanging three photographs side-by-side on a wall. How many different ways can the photographs be arranged?

8. Pari, Montana, Katie, and Dominic are in line for lunch. Montana is first. How many ways could the other people be arranged behind her?

9. Jimmy put the coins shown into a piggy bank. If he chooses 2 coins at a time, what possible combinations might he choose?

10. Sandra is arranging three animal-shaped pillows. One is a dog, another is a cat, and the third is a fish. How many different ways can she arrange her pillows in a row?

11. Alexa needs to read a mystery, biography, or fantasy book. Then she must write a report, give a speech, or act out a scene from the book. How many different options are there?

12. **WRITING IN** ►**MATH** Explain how you used the make an organized list strategy to solve Exercise 11.

Find Points on a Grid

MAIN IDEA

I will use ordered pairs to find and name points on a grid

SC Academic Standards

4-4.7 Represent with ordered pairs of whole numbers the location of points in the first quadrant of a coordinate grid.

4-4.8 Illustrate possible paths from one point to another along vertical and horizontal grid lines in the first quadrant of the coordinate plane.

Review

Vocabulary

coordinate plane

origin

x-axis

y-axis

ordered pair

coordinates

SC Math Online

macmillanmh.com

GET READY to Learn

The map gives the locations of several students' homes and their school. From the location of the school at (0, 0), Dave lives 5 units right and 3 units up. This can be written as (5, 3).

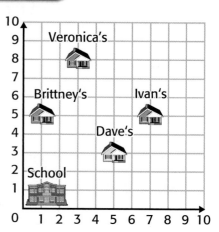

The map shown above is an example of a coordinate plane. A **coordinate plane** is formed when two number lines intersect at their zero points.

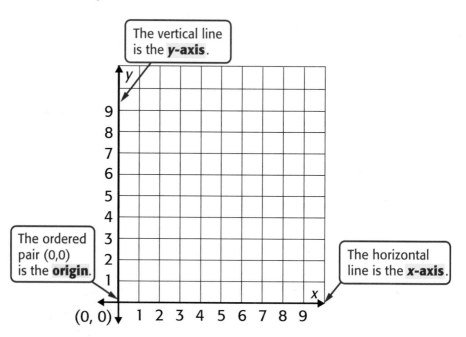

The point (5, 3) is an example of an **ordered pair**. The numbers in an ordered pair are called **coordinates**. The coordinates give the location of the point.

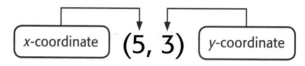

x-coordinate (5, 3) y-coordinate

Real-World EXAMPLE   **Find Ordered Pairs**

① **ZOO** A map of a zoo is shown. Identify the animal that is located at (5, 4).

To find (5, 4), start at (0, 0). Move right 5 units. Then, move up 4 units. The ordered pair (5, 4) locates the lions.

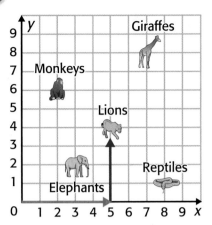

CHECK What You Know

Identify the building that is located at each ordered pair. See Example 1 (p. 407)

1. (6, 8)

2. (3, 7)

3. (2, 4)

4. (8, 6)

Identify the ordered pair for each building.

See Example 1 (p. 407)

5. grocery store

6. hospital

7. bus station

8. town hall

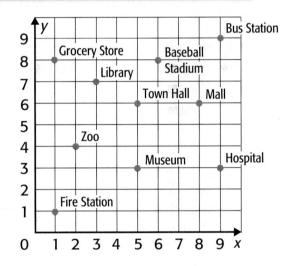

Use the grid to write the path you would follow. The starting point is the museum.

9. go to the bus station

10. go to the fire station

11. go to the grocery store

12. go to the hospital

For Exercises 13–16, use the coordinate plane above.

13. Describe the path from the library to the grocery store.

14. Describe the path from the zoo to the museum.

15. Jameson is at the bus station. He needs to go to the town hall. How does he get there on the grid?

16. Jill is at the museum. She lives near the library. How will she get there on the grid?

17. **Talk About It** How does an ordered pair name a location?

Identify the object that is located at each ordered pair. See Example 1 (p. 407)

18. (9, 6)   **19.** (2, 8)

20. (5, 1)   **21.** (1, 2)

Identify the ordered pair for each object.

See Example 1 (p. 407)

22. coat rack   **23.** bulletin board

24. door   **25.** chalkboard

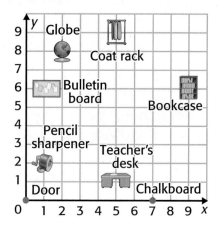

For Exercises 26 and 27, use the coordinate plane above.

26. Describe the path from the ordered pair for the pencil sharpener to the ordered pair for the coat rack.

27. Describe the path from the ordered pair for the teacher's desk to the ordered pair for the globe.

South Carolina Data File

Latitude and longitude lines can be used to find locations on a map. These lines form a coordinate plane.

28. What city can be found at 33°N and 80°W?

29. What latitude and longitude lines are near Spartanburg?

30. Name two other cities on this map and their lines of latitude and longitude.

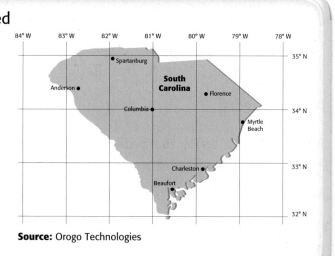

Source: Orogo Technologies

H.O.T. Problems

31. OPEN ENDED Draw a picture of your classroom on grid paper. Draw the location of your desk on the grid. What is the ordered pair for your location?

32. **WRITING IN** ►**MATH** How is the location of (2, 4) different from the location of (4, 2)? Explain.

Tell what number each letter on the number line represents. (Lesson 10-1)

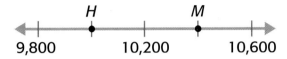

1. point *H*   **2.** point *M*

3. MULTIPLE CHOICE Which number does point *K* represent? (Lesson 10-1)

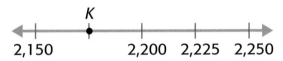

    A 2,075   **C** 2,155

    B 2,125   **D** 2,175

4. Describe the line segments formed by the top of the step stool. (Lesson 10-2)

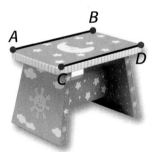

Identify each figure. (Lesson 10-2)

5.

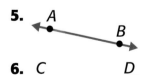

6. *C*   *D*

7. Serena has one red shirt and one white shirt. She has one blue skirt and one black skirt. How many different shirt-skirt outfits can she wear? (Lesson 10-3)

8. MULTIPLE CHOICE Which ordered pair is graphed? (Lesson 10-4)

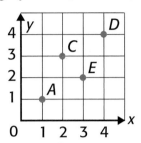

  F (3, 4)   **H** (3, 1)

  G (2, 3)   **J** (5, 2)

Identify the letter that is located at each ordered pair. (Lesson 10-4)

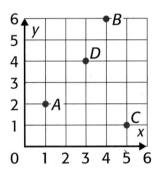

9. (1, 2)   **10.** (4, 6)

11. (3, 4)   **12.** (5, 1)

13. Refer to the coordinate plane above. Describe how to get from the ordered pair for point *A* to the ordered pair for point *B*. (Lesson 10-4)

14. **WRITING IN** ►**MATH** Do the ordered pairs (2, 3) and (3, 2) give the location of the same point? Explain. (Lesson 10-4)

A **transformation** is a movement of a figure. The three types of transformations are **translation** (slide), **reflection** (flip), and **rotation** (turn).

MAIN IDEA

I will explore rotations, reflections, and translations.

SC Academic Standards

4-4.3 Predict the results of multiple transformations of the same type—translation, reflection, or rotation—on a two-dimensional geometric shape.

You Will Need
pattern blocks

ACTIVITY   Explore Rotations, Reflections, and Translations

Step 1 **Trace a figure.**

Trace a square pattern block onto a piece of paper.

Step 2 **Rotate (turn) a figure.**

Take the figure and turn or rotate it $\frac{1}{2}$ a turn.

Then trace it again.

This is called a rotation.

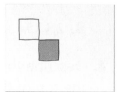

Step 3 **Show a reflection (flip).**

Now trace the square again. Next, draw a mirror image of the square. This is called a reflection.

Step 4 **Show a translation (slide).**

Trace the square one last time. Now move the square to the right (horizontally) and draw it again. Remember, do not turn it. This is called a translation.

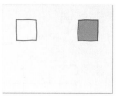

Think About It

1. What did you do to the square to demonstrate a rotation?

2. What is the difference between a rotation and a reflection?

3. Name two shapes that will look exactly the same after being reflected.

4. Describe the transformation that would move figure *A* to the location of figure *B*.

A ◣   B ◣

CHECK What You Know

Use each pattern block to demonstrate and draw all three transformations.

5.

6.

7.

8.

9.

10.

11. Choose 3 objects from your classroom. Demonstrate one transformation with each object. Copy and complete the table.

Object	Transformation
Crayon	Rotation
▦	Reflection
▦	Translation

12. **WRITING IN ▶MATH** In your own words, define the terms *rotation*, *reflection*, and *translation*.

Rotations, Reflections, and Translations

> ## GET READY to Learn

In this picture, the square pattern block has been moved. Demonstrate the movement of the square. What type of movement is shown?

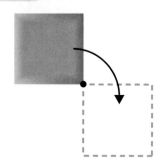

MAIN IDEA

I will identify rotations, reflections, and translations.

SC Academic Standards

4-4.3 Predict the results of multiple transformations of the same type—translation, reflection, or rotation—on a two-dimensional geometric shape.

New Vocabulary

transformation
translation
reflection
rotation

SC Math Online
macmillanmh.com
• Extra Examples
• Personal Tutor
• Self-Check Quiz

In the picture above, the square pattern block was moved or transformed. A **transformation** is a movement of a figure. The three types of transformations are **translation** (slide), **reflection** (flip), and **rotation** (turn).

> **EXAMPLE**   Identify Transformations

① **Identify the transformation of the square pattern block.**

Look at the square pattern block. Notice where the pattern block started.

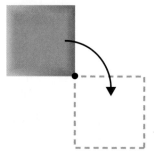

Now look at where the square pattern block ended.

The bottom right corner has not moved. It stayed on the same point. The square pattern block has been turned.

So, this is an example of rotation.

Vocabulary Link

transformation

Everyday Use a complete change

Math Use a movement of a figure

rotation	reflection	translation
		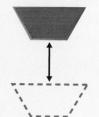
A rotation is a transformation in which a figure is rotated or turned around a point.	A reflection is a transformation that flips a figure across a line to make a mirror image of that figure.	A translation is moving a figure in a vertical, horizontal, or diagonal direction.

Real-World EXAMPLE   Identify Transformations

2️⃣ **CLOTHING The T-shirt has a design of geometric shapes in a pattern. Identify the transformation of the shapes that has created this pattern.**

Notice the geometric shapes on the T-shirt.

If we fold the shirt down the middle we see that the shapes are the same, mirror images.

The shapes have been flipped. They are examples of reflections.

EXAMPLE   Identify Transformations

3️⃣ **Identify the transformation. Write *rotation*, *reflection*, or *translation*.**

The triangle above moved sideways. It has not turned or flipped.

So, the transformation of the triangle is a translation.

Identify each transformation. Write *rotation*, *reflection*, or *translation*.

See Examples 1–3 (pp. 412–413)

1.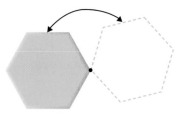

2.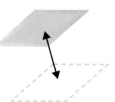

3. Miguel is designing a mosaic picture of a tree. He is using geometric shapes to create the picture. At the right, what transformation are the triangles an example of?

4. *Talk About It* Suppose a game piece moves forward two spaces. What kind of transformation is this? Explain your reasoning.

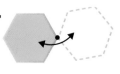

Practice and Problem Solving

SCAS • PASS
Extra Practice, p. R26

Identify each transformation. Write *rotation*, *reflection*, or *translation*.

See Examples 1–3 (pp. 412–413)

5.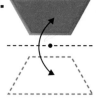

6.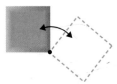

7.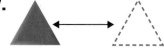

8.

9.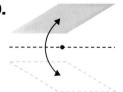

10.

11. Eliza and Joey drew the picture to the right on the sidewalk with chalk. What transformations can be seen in the picture?

12. Explain how the squares on a checkerboard demonstrate each transformation.

H.O.T. Problems

13. OPEN ENDED Draw a picture. Then draw the picture again using a transformation. Explain what transformation you demonstrated.

OPEN ENDED Using pattern blocks, draw examples of the following transformations.

14. translation   **15.** rotation   **16.** reflection

17. **WRITING IN ►MATH** Describe how a translation can also be a reflection.

PASS Practice 4-4.7, 4-4.3

18. Which of the following describes where point *J* is located? (Lesson 10-4)

   A (1, 5)

   B (2, 7)

   C (5, 8)

   D (8, 5)

19. Which pair of figures does **NOT** show a rotation? (Lesson 10-5)

 F

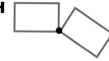 H

 G

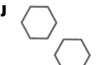 J

Spiral Review

Identify the place that is located at each ordered pair. (Lesson 10-4)

20. (5, 8)

21. (8, 3)

22. (3, 2)

Identify the ordered pair for each building.
(Lesson 10-4)

23. hospital

24. police station

25. mall

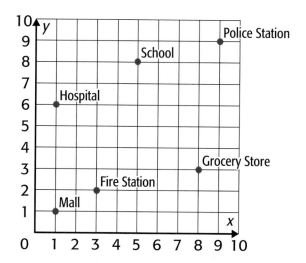

26. Dan has 85 cents. Name one combination of coins that could make up this amount. (Lesson 10-3)

27. Sarah purchased 5 items. If each item was the same price and she spent $45, how much did each item cost? (Lesson 4-3)

Problem-Solving Investigation

MAIN IDEA I will choose the best strategy to solve a problem.

 SCAS **4-1.1** Analyze information to solve increasingly more sophisticated problems.

P.S.I. TEAM +

CARMEN: My family ate at a restaurant. We ordered salads for $6 each, steaks for $15 each, and sandwiches for $8 each. The total cost was $43.

YOUR MISSION: Find how many of each item was ordered.

Understand	You know the cost of each item and the total cost of the meal. Find how many of each item was ordered.
Plan	Use logical reasoning to solve the problem.
Solve	At least one of each item was ordered. Add the costs.

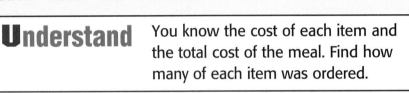

	$15 1 steak
	$ 6 1 salad
	+ $ 8 1 sandwich
	$29

So, the cost of the other items ordered must be $43 − $29, or $14.

Since $8 + $6 is the only combination of costs that equal $14, you know that another salad and another sandwich were ordered.

So, they ordered 1 steak, 2 salads, and 2 sandwiches.

Check	Look back. Check your answer with addition.
	$6 + $6 + $8 + $8 + $15 = $43
	So, the answer is correct. ✔

Use any strategy shown below to solve. Tell what strategy you used.

PROBLEM-SOLVING STRATEGIES
- Use logical reasoning.
- Make a model.
- Make an organized list.
- Draw a picture.
- Work backward.

1. There are 6 wagons for the fall hayride. Each wagon needs 4 horses to pull it. How many horses will it take to pull all 6 wagons?

2. There are four boys and six girls in line at a movie theater. Each is carrying two food items purchased at the concession stand. How many food items do they have in all?

3. Curtis bought the meal shown below. He paid with a $20 bill and his change was $13. If the fruit juice cost $1, how much did each taco cost?

4. Macie made 70 bracelets in 3 colors. She made 22 red bracelets and 18 blue bracelets. How many bracelets were yellow?

5. Carol, Irina, Yori, and Nora are on a relay team. The fastest girl will run last. The slowest girl will run second. Irina runs faster than Carol. Nora runs first. Irina runs slower than Yori. In what order does the team run?

6. Algebra Julie sold roses at a bike club fundraiser. Use the pattern in the table below to find how many roses she had left on Friday.

Day	Started with	Ended with
Monday	96	48
Tuesday	48	24
Wednesday	24	12
Thursday	12	6
Friday	6	▪

7. Malik's baseball team needs $2,500 to pay for camp. They raised $310 in April and $477 in May. They already had $1,203 saved. How much do they still need to pay for camp?

8. Measurement An object on Earth weighs 6 times its weight on the Moon. An astronaut weighs 210 pounds on Earth. How much would he or she weigh on the Moon?

9. WRITING IN MATH There are three rock, five country, and two oldies CDs in Mrs. Link's car. The answer is $\frac{5}{10}$. What is the question?

MAIN IDEA

I will identify congruent figures.

 SC Academic Standards

4-4.5 Use transformation(s) to prove congruency.

4-4.3 Predict the results of multiple transformations of the same type—translation, reflection, or rotation—on a two-dimensional geometric shape.

New Vocabulary

congruent

 SC Math Online

macmillanmh.com

• Extra Examples
• Personal Tutor
• Self-Check Quiz

GET READY to Learn

Hands-On Mini Activity

Materials: graph paper

Step 1 Copy figures A, B, and C on graph paper.

Step 2 Cut out figures A, B, and C.

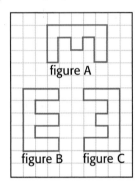

Step 3 Place the figures on top of each other, one at a time. Use transformations if needed until one fits exactly on top of another one.

1. What transformation(s) took place to find the two figures that are the same?

2. Which two figures are the same? Explain.

When figures have the same size and shape, they are **congruent**.

EXAMPLES   Identify Congruent Figures

Tell whether the figures appear to be congruent. Write *yes* or *no*. If they are, describe the movements that show their congruence.

1

The hexagons appear to have the same size and shape. So, they are congruent. A translation took place.

2

The triangles appear to have the same shape, but have a different size. So, they are not congruent.

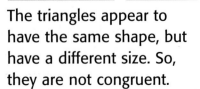

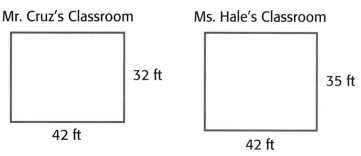

3 **SCHOOL** The diagrams show the shapes and sizes of two classrooms. Do the two classrooms appear to be congruent? Explain.

Mr. Cruz's Classroom

32 ft

42 ft

Ms. Hale's Classroom

35 ft

42 ft

Both classrooms have the same shape. They are rectangles.

Both classrooms have the same length, but Ms. Hale's classroom has a greater width. So, they are not the same size.

Since the classrooms have different sizes, they are not congruent.

CHECK What You Know

Tell whether the figures appear to be congruent. Write *yes* or *no*. If they are, describe the movements that show the congruence. See Examples 1–3 (pp. 418–419)

1.

2.

3. A ceramic tile design is shown. How many of the blue kitchen tiles appear to be congruent to the tile labeled *E*?

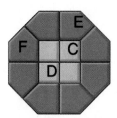

4. In the birdhouse, do the windows and door appear to be congruent? Explain.

5. **Talk About It** Describe the movements that can be used to check if two figures appear to be congruent.

Tell whether the figures appear to be congruent. Write *yes* or *no*. If they are, describe the movements that show the congruence. See Examples 1–3 (pp. 418–419)

6.

7.

8.

9.

10. Tell whether the cells on a honeycomb appear to be congruent.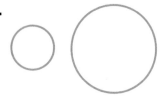

11. Which figures on a soccer ball appear to be congruent?

12. Measurement The television in Lin's room is 30 inches wide and 24 inches long. His friend has the same television. If the television is 30 inches wide, how long is it?

13. Measurement One of Paloma's picture frames is 5 inches wide and 7 inches long. She has another picture frame that is the same size. If it is 7 inches long, how wide is it?

H.O.T. Problems

14. OPEN ENDED Create two rectangles. Tell whether they are congruent or not congruent. Explain.

15. FIND THE ERROR Tammy and Jacinto are comparing their slices of pizza. Who is correct? Explain.

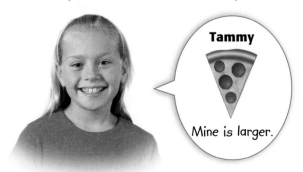

Tammy

Mine is larger.

Jacinto

They are congruent.

16. WRITING IN ►MATH Are all squares with one side measuring 5 inches congruent? Explain your reasoning.

MAIN IDEA

I will use technology to explore congruent figures.

SC Academic Standards

4-4.5 Use transformation(s) to prove congruency.

The *Math Tool Chest* can be used to create congruent figures.

Stamp a trapezoid. Then stamp a congruent trapezoid. Use transformations to prove both figures are congruent.

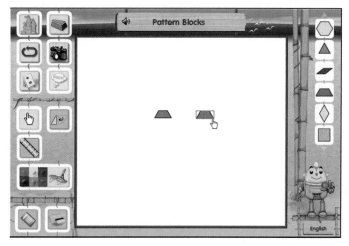

- Click on the pattern blocks tool chest.
- Click on the trapezoid pattern block.
- Stamp two trapezoids on the mat.
- Click on the move button.
- Click on one trapezoid and drag it until it is on top of the other trapezoid.

What transformation shows that the two figures are congruent?

CHECK What You Know

Use *Math Tool Chest* to stamp each figure. Then stamp a congruent figure.

1. triangle

2. square

3. hexagon

For Exercises 4–6, use *Math Tool Chest* to solve.

4. Kurt wants to create a design for a book cover. He draws congruent octagons to use in his design. Draw an example of what his design could look like.

5. Two pictures in a magazine are to be outlined with congruent rectangles. Draw two rectangles that could be used to outline the pictures. Explain how you know your figures are congruent.

GET READY to Learn

A butterfly uses its wings to fly. Look at the left side and the right side of the butterfly. When a butterfly folds its wings in half, will the two parts match?

A figure has **line symmetry** or **bilateral symmetry** if it can be folded so that the two parts of the figure match, or are congruent. The fold line is a **line of symmetry**.

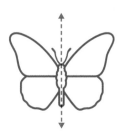 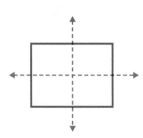 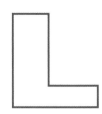

1 line of symmetry   2 lines of symmetry   no lines of
line symmetry   symmetry

EXAMPLES Identify Line Symmetry

Tell whether each figure has line symmetry. Write *yes* or *no*. Then tell how many lines of symmetry the figure has.

❶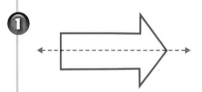

❷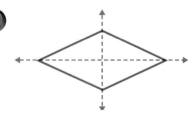

Yes; the figure has 1 line of symmetry.

Yes; the figure has 2 lines of symmetry.

When a figure fits exactly over itself after being rotated 180° or less, it has **rotational symmetry**.

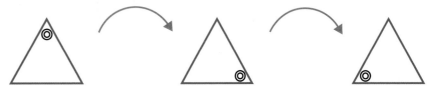

An equilateral triangle has rotational symmetry because it is the same after each rotation.

EXAMPLE Identify Rotational Symmetry

③ Tell whether the figure has rotational symmetry.

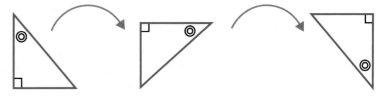

The right triangle does not look like it did before the turn. So, it does not have rotational symmetry.

✓ CHECK What You Know

Tell whether each figure has line symmetry. Write *yes* or *no*. Then tell how many lines of symmetry the figure has.

See Examples 1 and 2 (p. 422)

1.

2.

Tell whether the figure has rotational symmetry. Write *yes* or *no*. See Example 3 (p. 423)

3.

4.

5. Tell whether the snowflake shown at the right has rotational symmetry. Explain.

6. Talk About It Do you think that a figure with bilateral symmetry can also have rotational symmetry? Draw a picture to explain your reasoning.

Tell whether each figure has line symmetry. Write *yes* or *no*.
Then tell how many lines of symmetry the figure has.

See Examples 1 and 2 (p. 422)

7.

8.

9.

10.

Tell whether the figure has rotational symmetry.
Write *yes* or *no*. See Example 3 (p. 423)

11.

12.

13.

14.

15. Does the letter C have symmetry? If it does, tell how many lines of symmetry the letter has.

16. Does a square have symmetry? If is does, tell how many lines of symmetry the shape has.

 Real-World PROBLEM SOLVING

Art Lines of symmetry can be seen in many pieces of art work such as cultural masks.

17. Sketch the mask shown and show the line of symmetry.

18. Using a sheet of grid paper, create half of a cultural mask. Then, switch papers with another student. Complete the image of the cultural mask you now have.

19. Does the cultural mask you created have rotational symmetry?

H.O.T. Problems

20. **OPEN ENDED** Design a two-dimensional figure that has more than 3 lines of symmetry.

21. **WRITING IN ►MATH** How many lines of symmetry do you think a circle has? Explain.

Reflections and Symmetry

Get Ready!

Players: 2 or 3 players

Get Set!

Draw 2-dimensional shapes on the index cards. They can be regular geometric shapes, unusual shapes (like a moon), or real objects such as a house. Make sure not all of the shapes have symmetry.

Go!

- Begin with all cards facedown in a stack.

- Player 1 picks a card from the stack.

- Player 1 can use the mirror to decide if the shape is symmetrical.

- If the shape is symmetrical he or she receives a point.

- If the shape is not symmetrical the player can draw a shape symmetrical to the one picked to receive a point.

- The player with the highest score when all the cards have been used wins.

You will need: 30 index cards, paper and pencil, mirror

Problem Solving in Science

Symmetry in Nature

Symmetry can be seen in different habitats in nature. The next time you walk near a pond, you may find symmetry. A calm lake can act as a mirror and show the reflection of surrounding trees. This is an example of line symmetry.

Many animals have symmetrical bodies to help them survive. If an animal had an odd number of wings or legs, it might have a difficult time flying or walking because it would not be balanced. Think about the different parts of a plant. The petals of some flowers show rotational symmetry.

The next time you take a walk outside, take a closer look at your environment. You may discover symmetry all around you.

Did You Know?

A mirror that is curved will not show a true reflection.

Real-World Math

Use the photos below to solve each problem.

 1. Identify which plants or animals above show line symmetry.

2. Does the leaf have symmetry? If it does, tell how many lines of symmetry it has.

3. Draw a picture of something in nature that shows line symmetry. Label the line of symmetry.

4. Explain how you could test an object in nature to see if it has symmetry.

5. Explain the difference between line symmetry and rotational symmetry.

6. What could affect the symmetry shown in the picture of the lake and trees?

FOLDABLES Study Organizer GET READY to Study

Be sure the following Key Vocabulary words and Key Concepts are written in your Foldable.

Number Lines
Lines, Line Segments, Rays
Coordinate Plane
Transformations
Congruence and Symmetry

Key Concepts

- A **number line** is a line with numbers on it in order at regular intervals. (p. 395)

P

100   300   500   700

$P = 600$

- Transformations are movements of figures such as: (p. 412)

Translation

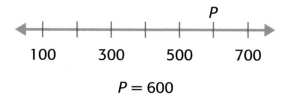

Rotation

Reflection

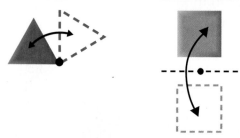

Key Vocabulary

coordinate plane (p. 406)

congruent (p. 418)

number line (p. 395)

point (p. 395)

transformation (p. 412)

Vocabulary Check

Decide which vocabulary word best completes each sentence.

1. A _____?_____ is formed when two number lines intersect at their zero points.

2. A _____?_____ is a movement of a figure.

3. A _____?_____ is an exact location in space.

4. A _____?_____ is a line with numbers on it in order at regular intervals.

5. Figures that are the same size and shape are _____?_____.

Lesson-by-Lesson Review

10-1 Locate Points on a Number Line (pp. 395–397)

4-4.6,
4-2.1

Example 1
What number is represented by point B?

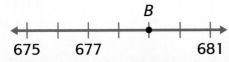

675   677   681

So, point B represents 679.

Example 2
What number does point Z represent on the number line?

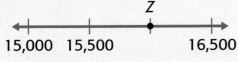

15,000 15,500   16,500

So, point Z represents 16,000.

Tell what number each letter on the number line represents.

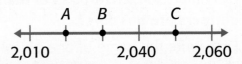

6. point A

7. point B

8. point C

9. Tell what number point W represents on the number line.

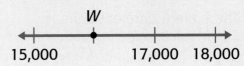

10-2 Lines, Line Segments, and Rays (pp. 400–403)

3-4.3,
4-4.6

Example 3
Describe the figure.

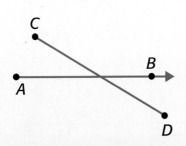

The figure shows ray AB and line segment CD. Notice that ray AB intersects line CD.

$\overrightarrow{AB}$ intersects $\overline{CD}$.

Identify each figure.

10.   H 11. I

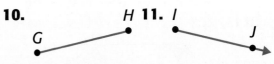

Describe each figure.

12. Q   13.

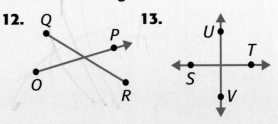

14. W   Z 15.   B

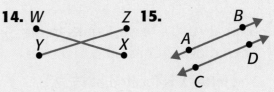

10-3 Problem-Solving Strategy: Make an Organized List (pp. 404–405)

4-6.7

Example 4
Alfonso, Erik, Owen, and Alek are going hiking. They will hike in pairs. How many different pairs of hiking partners are possible?

First, write the name of one person. Then, write the name of another person by the first person's name. Continue to do this without repeating pairs.

Alfonso – Erik   Erik – Owen

Alfonso – Owen   Erik – Alek

Alfonso – Alek   Owen – Alek

There are 6 different pairs.

Solve. Use the make an organized list strategy.

16. Sergio has to find a combination for his lock. It has 2, 4, and 6 written on it. How many possible combinations could he choose?

17. The four toys are to be placed on a shelf. How many different ways can the toys be arranged?

10-4 Find Points on a Grid (pp. 406–408)

4-4.7,
4-4.8

Example 5
Identify the letter that is located at (3, 2).

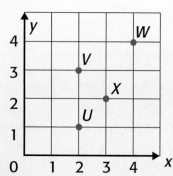

Start at (0, 0). Move 3 units to the right. Then move 2 units up.

The letter *X* is located at (3, 2).

Identify the letter that is located at each ordered pair.

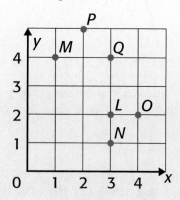

18. (3, 2)   **19.** (1, 4)   **20.** (2, 5)

21. Describe how to get from *L* to *Q*.

10-5 Rotations, Reflections, and Translations (pp. 412–415)

4-4.3

Example 6
Identify the transformation. Write *rotation*, *reflection*, or *translation*.

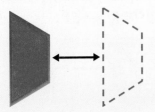

The trapezoid above has moved sideways. It has not turned or flipped.

So, the transformation of the trapezoid is a translation.

Identify each transformation. Write *rotation*, *reflection*, or *translation*.

22.   **23.**

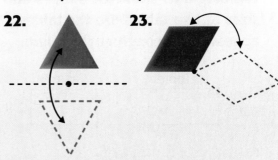

Using pattern blocks, demonstrate the following transformations by tracing.

24. reflection   **25.** rotation

10-6 Problem-Solving Investigation: Choose a Strategy (pp. 416–417)

4-1.1

Example 7
Alberto has $5 left after buying skates for $62 and a helmet for $24. How much did he have originally?

You can find an exact answer by using addition.

    $ 5   change
  + $62   amount for skates
    $67
  + $24   amount for helmet
    $91

So, Alberto had $91 originally.

Use any strategy to solve.

26. A teacher is arranging 24 desks. If she wants to group the desks in groups of 4, how many groups will she have?

27. Peter can choose a ham or turkey sandwich. He can choose an apple or orange. How many different sandwich and fruit combinations can Peter choose?

28. A house has 15 rooms. One room is the kitchen, 4 rooms are bedrooms, and 2 rooms are bathrooms. How many other rooms are there?

10-7 Congruent Figures (pp. 418–420)

4-4.5,
4-4.3

Example 8
The diagrams show the shapes and sizes of two tables. Do the tables appear to be congruent? Explain.

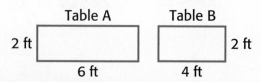

Table A   Table B

2 ft   2 ft

6 ft   4 ft

Both tables are rectangular in shape. They have the same width but do not have the same length.

Since the tables have different sizes, they do not appear to be congruent.

Tell whether the figures appear to be congruent. Write *yes* or *no*. If they are, describe the movements that show the congruence.

29.

30.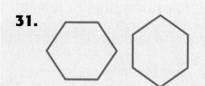

31.

10-8 Symmetry (pp. 422–424)

Example 9
Tell whether each figure has line symmetry. Then tell how many lines of symmetry the figure has.

5-4.6

The figure has 0 lines of symmetry.

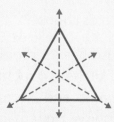

The figure has 3 lines of symmetry.

Tell whether each figure has line symmetry. Write *yes* or *no*. Then tell how many lines of symmetry the figure has.

32.   33.

34.   35.

Chapter Test

Identify each transformation. Write *rotation, reflection,* **or** *translation.*

1.

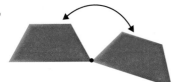

2.

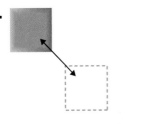

3. MULTIPLE CHOICE Which number does point *C* represent?

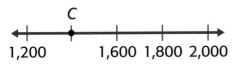

A 2,000   **C** 1,300

B 1,400   **D** 1,000

Tell what number each letter on the number line represents.

4. point *H*   **5.** point *M*

Identify each figure.

6.

7.

Tell whether the figures appear to be congruent. Write *yes* **or** *no.*

8.

9.

10. Measurement Tanika's swimming pool is 8 feet wide and 12 feet long. Tanika's neighbor has the same pool. If the pool is 12 feet long, how wide is it?

Tell whether each figure has line symmetry. Write *yes* **or** *no.* **Then tell how many lines of symmetry the figure has.**

11.   **12.**

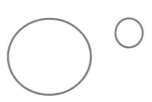

13. MULTIPLE CHOICE How many lines of symmetry does this figure have?

F 0   **H** 2

G 1   **J** 3

14. **WRITING IN ►MATH** Do all squares have the same number of lines of symmetry? Explain.

PART 1   Multiple Choice

Read each question. Then fill in the correct answer on the answer sheet provided by your teacher or on a sheet of paper.

1. Which streets appear to be parallel to each other on the map below?

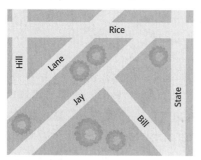

A Rice and Bill   **C** Lane and Jay

B State and Lane   **D** Hill and Rice

2. Justin practices the piano 30 minutes per day, 6 days per week. How many minutes does he practice in 10 weeks?

F $6 \times 10 + 30$ **H** $6 \times 10 \times 30$

G $6 + 10 + 30$ **J** $30 \div 10 \times 6$

3. Which line, line segment, or ray is perpendicular to line *d*?

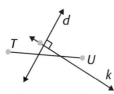

A Ray *Q*   **C** Line *s*

B Line segment *TU*   **D** Line *k*

4. Jen has 24 swimming trophies. She wants to arrange an equal number on 4 shelves of a bookcase. How many trophies will she place on each shelf?

F 8   **H** 4

G 6   **J** 3

5. In the figure below, which angle appears to be obtuse?

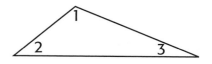

A 1   **C** 3

B 2   **D** none

6. Valerie has 84 beads. She wants to arrange them into 12 equal groups. How many beads will be in each group?

F 5   **H** 7

G 6   **J** 8

7. A total of 8,297 visitors attended a museum on Saturday and Sunday. If 5,129 visitors attended on Saturday, how many visitors attended on Sunday?

A 3,086   **C** 3,618

B 3,168   **D** 3,816

8. What number on the number line does point *J* best represent?

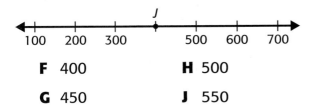

F 400 **H** 500

G 450 **J** 550

9. Which of these represents 9 × 7?

A 1 × 3 × 7 **C** 2 × 9 × 7

B 2 × 7 × 7 **D** 3 × 3 × 7

10. Mira made a map of her neighborhood. Identify the building located at (7, 2).

Mira's Neighborhood

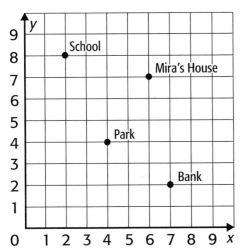

F Mira's house **H** Park

G Bank **J** School

PART 2 **Short Response**

Record your answers on the answer sheet provided by your teacher or on a sheet of paper.

11. What is the value of the digit 3 in 564,327?

12. How many lines of symmetry does this shape have?

13. Identify two numbers that have at least one line of symmetry.

PART 3 **Extended Response**

Record your answers on the answer sheet provided by your teacher or on a sheet of paper.

14. Identify the transformation shown below. Explain.

15. Draw two triangles to show a rotation of figures. Explain.

NEED EXTRA HELP?															
If You Missed Question...	1	2	3	4	5	6	7	8	9	10	11	12	13	14	15
Go to Lesson...	10-2	5-6	10-2	4-3	9-4	4-6	2-5	10-1	4-2	10-4	1-1	10-8	10-8	10-5	10-5
SC Academic Standards	3-4.3	4-3.4	3-4.3	4-2.5	4-4.6	4-2.5	3-2.3	4-4.6	4-1.3	4-4.7	4-2.6	5-4.6	5-4.6	4-4.3	4-4.3

CHAPTER 11
Measure Length, Area, and Temperature

BIG Idea What is perimeter?

Perimeter is the distance around a closed figure.

Example Pennsylvania is home to 560,000 dairy cows. A cow pasture is a field of grass where dairy cows often graze, or eat. You can find the perimeter of the cow pasture shown by adding the lengths of the sides of the fence.

```
  225 yd
  150 yd
  225 yd
+ 150 yd
  750 yd
```

225 yd

150 yd

150 yd

225 yd

So, the perimeter of the pasture is 750 yards.

What will I learn in this chapter?

- Measure lengths in customary and metric units.
- Estimate and determine perimeters and areas.
- Relate perimeter and area.
- Measure temperatures and changes in temperature.
- Solve problems by working simpler problems.

Key Vocabulary

perimeter

area

SC Math Online

Student Study Tools
at macmillanmh.com

FOLDABLES®
Study Organizer

Make this Foldable to help you organize information about measurement. Begin with a sheet of notebook paper.

① **Fold** a sheet of paper in half.

② **Cut** every third line on one side. Ten tabs will result.

③ **Label** each tab as shown.

Customary Units
Metric Units
Length
Convert
Perimeter
Area
Square Units
Temperature
Celsius
Fahrenheit

You have two ways to check prerequisite skills for this chapter.

Option 2

SC Math Online   Take the Chapter Readiness Quiz at macmillanmh.com.

Option 1

Complete the Quick Check below.

QUICK Check

Identify which figure is longer. (Prior Grade)

1. |————————— Figure A —————————|

|———— Figure B ————|

2.

Figure A

Figure B

3. Ted is comparing his shoe to his mom's shoe. Which is longer?

Ted's shoe   Mom's shoe

Find the value of each expression. (Lessons 5-1 and 5-6)

4. $8 + 14 + 8 + 14$ **5.** $9 + 16 + 9 + 16$ **6.** 15×7

7. 12×6 **8.** $(2 \times 7) + (2 \times 14)$ **9.** $(2 \times 13) + (2 \times 9)$

Identify which sides are the same length. (Prior Grade)

10.   **11.**   **12.**

13. Geometry Mercedes is making a picture frame. It will be a square. How many sides are the same length?

Estimate and Measure Lengths

In this activity, you will use a ruler to measure lengths to the nearest inch, $\frac{1}{2}$ inch, and $\frac{1}{4}$ inch.

MAIN IDEA

I will estimate and measure lengths to the nearest inch, $\frac{1}{2}$ inch, and $\frac{1}{4}$ inch.

SC Academic Standards

4-5.1 Use appropriate tools to measure objects to the nearest unit: measuring length in quarter inches, centimeters, and millimeters; measuring liquid volume in cups, quarts, and liters; and measuring weight and mass in pounds, milligrams, and kilograms.

You Will Need
ruler

ACTIVITY

1. **Find the length of the pencil to the nearest inch, $\frac{1}{2}$ inch, and $\frac{1}{4}$ inch.**

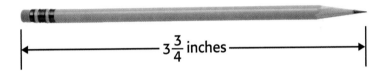

$3\frac{3}{4}$ inches

Step 1   Copy the table.

Object	Estimate	Whole Inch	$\frac{1}{2}$ Inch	$\frac{1}{4}$ Inch
Pencil				

Step 2   Estimate.

Estimate the length of the pencil. Record your estimate in the table.

Step 3   Measure.

Place the ruler against a side of the pencil so that the 0 on the ruler lines up with one end. Measure the length to the nearest inch, $\frac{1}{2}$ inch, and $\frac{1}{4}$ inch. Record the measurements in your table.

ACTIVITY

2 **Find four items in your classroom to measure to the nearest inch, $\frac{1}{2}$ inch, and $\frac{1}{4}$ inch.**

Step 1 **Select the items.**

Find four items from your classroom that are less than 12 inches long.

Step 2 **Estimate.**

Estimate their length in inches. Record your estimates in a table similar to the one in Activity 1.

Step 3 **Measure.**

Measure each object's length to the nearest inch, $\frac{1}{2}$ inch, and $\frac{1}{4}$ inch. Record the measurements in your table.

Think About It

1. Which is more accurate, measuring to the nearest inch or measuring to the nearest $\frac{1}{4}$ inch? Explain.

2. How could the length around a round object, such as a globe, be measured?

CHECK What You Know

Estimate. Then measure each to the nearest inch, $\frac{1}{2}$ inch, and $\frac{1}{4}$ inch.

3.

4.

5. **WRITING IN ►MATH** Describe a situation in which measuring to the nearest $\frac{1}{4}$ inch is necessary.

Customary Units of Length

GET READY to Learn

The actual size of a neon damsel marine fish is shown. How long is this fish?

MAIN IDEA

I will estimate and measure customary units of length.

SC Academic Standards

4-5.1 Use appropriate tools to measure objects to the nearest unit: measuring length in quarter inches, centimeters, and millimeters; measuring liquid volume in cups, quarts, and liters; and measuring weight and mass in pounds, milligrams, and kilograms.

4-5.10 Exemplify situations in which highly accurate measurements are required.

Review Vocabulary

length   foot
customary   yard
inch

SC Math Online
macmillanmh.com

Length is the measurement of a line between two points. Inch, foot, and yard are all **customary** units of measure for length.

Customary Measurements   Key Concepts

An **inch** is about the length of one paper clip.	A **foot** is about the length of a textbook.	A **yard** is about the height of a chair.
	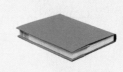	

Real-World EXAMPLE   Estimate and Measure

① **FISH** Estimate. Then measure the length of the neon damsel fish to the nearest inch, $\frac{1}{2}$ inch and $\frac{1}{4}$ inch.

Step 1
Estimate.
Compare the length to what you know about inches.

Step 2
Measure.
Using a ruler, measure the length of the fish to the nearest $\frac{1}{2}$ inch.

Step 3
Measure.
Measure the length of the fish to the nearest $\frac{1}{4}$ inch.

So, the fish is about 2, $1\frac{1}{2}$, or $1\frac{2}{4}$ inches long.

2 Josh is building shelves to fit inside his closet. He measures the space and decides the shelves should be about 12 inches deep.

This situation requires a very accurate measurement. Which measurement would be the most accurate?

A $12\frac{1}{4}$ inches   **B** 12 inches   **C** $12\frac{1}{2}$ inches

Since $\frac{1}{4}$ of an inch is the smallest unit of measurement given, the answer is A, $12\frac{1}{4}$ inches. It is the most accurate measurement.

Remember

Certain situations call for highly accurate measurement.

Estimate. Then measure each to the nearest inch, $\frac{1}{2}$ inch, and $\frac{1}{4}$ inch. See Example 1 (p. 441)

1.

2.

Choose the best estimate for each length. See Example 2 (p. 442)

3. length of a bicycle

A 12 inches   **C** 12 feet

B 4 feet   **D** 4 yards

4. length of a paintbrush

F 3 inches   **H** 3 feet

G 8 inches   **J** 8 feet

5. **Talk About It** Why do you think there is more than one unit of measure for length?

Estimate. Then measure each to the nearest inch, $\frac{1}{2}$ inch, and $\frac{1}{4}$ inch. See Example 1 (p. 441)

6.

7.

8.

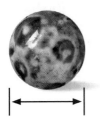

9.

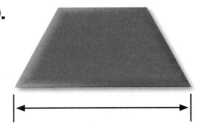

10. Patrice found a book that was $2\frac{1}{4}$ inches thick. She stacked it with another book that was the same thickness. How tall was the stack?

11. Helki found a stick that was $5\frac{3}{4}$ feet long. He needed one that was about 5 feet long. Is it reasonable to say that this stick will work? Explain.

Choose the best estimate for each length. See Example 2 (p. 442)

12. length of a whistle

   A 2 yards

   B 2 feet

   C 12 inches

   D 2 inches

13. width of a chalkboard

   F 1 foot

   G 2 feet

   H 1 yard

   J 2 yards

H.O.T. Problems

14. OPEN ENDED Find two objects in your home that are longer than 2 inches and shorter than 4 inches. How did you use estimation in selecting objects?

15. WRITING IN ►MATH List two tools used to measure length and provide a situation in which that tool would be useful.

Convert Customary Units of Length

Marla's dog, Cory, competes in big air competitions. Each dog jumps into water. Cory's longest jump is 21 feet. How many yards are in 21 feet?

MAIN IDEA

I will convert customary units of length.

SC Academic Standards

4-5.3 Use equivalencies to convert units of measure within the U.S. Customary System: converting length in inches, feet, yards, and miles; converting weight in ounces, pounds, and tons; converting liquid volume in cups, pints, quarts, and gallons; and converting time in years, months, weeks, days, hours, minutes, and seconds. *Also addresses 4-5.8.*

New Vocabulary

convert

SC Math Online

macmillanmh.com
• Extra Examples
• Personal Tutor
• Self-Check Quiz

To **convert** between units of measurement means to change the unit. When converting measurements, think about two things:

• The unit you are starting with and the unit you are ending with.

• Are you converting from a smaller unit to a larger unit or a larger unit to a smaller unit?

Real-World EXAMPLE   Convert to Larger Units

① **SPORTS Cory's longest jump is 21 feet. How many yards are in 21 feet?**

You know the number of feet and want to find the number of yards. Feet are a smaller unit than yards. So use division.

To convert 21 feet to yards, divide by 3.

21 ft = ■ yd

21 ÷ 3 = ■   ← Divide by 3 because 3 feet = 1 yard.

21 ÷ 3 = 7

So, there are 7 yards in 21 feet.

EXAMPLE   Convert to Smaller Units

② **Complete. 6 yds = ■ ft**

To convert 6 yards to feet, multiply by 3.

6 × 3 = ■

6 × 3 = 18   ← Multiply by 3 because 3 feet = 1 yard.

So, there are 18 feet in 6 yards.

Complete. See Examples 1 and 2 (p. 444)

1. 36 in. = ■ ft

2. 12 ft = ■ yd

3. 4 yd = ■ in.

4. 2 yd = ■ ft

5. ■ in. = 7 ft

6. 24 in. = ■ ft

7. The Costa family hiked a trail that was 2 miles in one direction. How many feet was the hike round-trip?

8. **Talk About It** Explain how to convert a smaller unit of measure to a larger unit of measure.

Practice and Problem Solving

SCAS • PASS
Extra Practice, p. R28

Complete. See Examples 1 and 2 (p. 444)

9. 2 ft = ■ in.

10. 6 ft = ■ in.

11. ■ in. = 2 yd

12. 6 ft = ■ yd

13. ■ ft = 132 in.

14. ■ in. = 12 ft

15. 18 ft = ■ in.

16. 18 yd = ■ in.

17. ■ in. = 4 ft

18. 16 ft = ■ in.

19. 216 in. = ■ yd

20. 84 ft = ■ yd

21. Darin is 4 feet 10 inches tall. His brother is 68 inches tall. How many more inches taller is Darin's brother than Darin?

22. Sumi lives 2 miles from school. Valerie lives 10,542 feet from school. Who lives closer to school? Explain your answer.

23. Cassie's mom bought 16 yards of yarn. She needs 580 inches of yarn for her art project. Does she have enough? Explain.

24. Mr. Shank used 15 feet of tape. He bought a container of tape that was 5 yards long. Did he buy enough? Explain.

H.O.T. Problems

25. **OPEN ENDED** Measure two objects that are at least one foot long. Convert the measurement to a smaller unit.

26. **CHALLENGE** Ramiro sits 5 feet from the bookshelf. Michelle sits 64 inches from the bookshelf. Who sits closer to the bookshelf?

27. **WRITING IN ►MATH** Write a real-world problem involving the conversion of customary lengths. Give your problem to a classmate to solve.

Problem-Solving Strategy

MAIN IDEA I will solve problems by solving a simpler problem.

 SCAS 4-1.1 Analyze information to solve increasingly more sophisticated problems.

It takes Pearl 2 minutes to ride her bike one block in her neighborhood. How long does it takes Pearl to ride the route shown in her neighborhood three times?

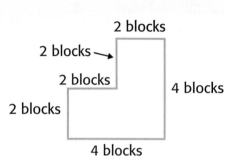

2 blocks

2 blocks →

2 blocks

4 blocks

2 blocks

4 blocks

Understand	**What facts do you know?**
	• The length of each block in her neighborhood.
	• It takes Pearl 2 minutes to ride her bike 1 block.
	What do you need to find?
	• Find how long it will take to ride the route three times.
Plan	You can solve a simpler problem to find the answer.
Solve	First, find the number of blocks Pearl rides one time around.
	$$2 + 2 + 2 + 2 + 4 + 4 = 16$$
	Add the distances. Total blocks
	Using the result, you find that Pearl rides $16 + 16 + 16$ or 48 blocks when she rides three times around.
	Now, find how many minutes it takes her to ride three times around.
	$$2 \times 48 = 96$$
	Minutes per block Total blocks Total minutes
	So, it takes Pearl 96 minutes to ride three times around.
Check	Look back. Estimate the total number of blocks times 2.
	$48 \times 2 \rightarrow 50 \times 2$ or 100.
	Since 96 is close to 100, the answer is correct. ✓

Refer to the problem on the previous page.

1. Explain why $2 + 2 + 2 + 2 + 4 + 4$ was the first step in finding the answer to the problem.

2. Could you have used multiplication to find the number of blocks it takes Pearl to ride the route three times? Explain.

3. Suppose it takes Pearl 1 minute to ride her bike one block. Would it take her less than 1 hour to ride three times around her neighborhood? Explain.

4. Look back at Exercise 3. Explain how you found the answer.

► PRACTICE the Strategy

SCAS • PASS
Extra Practice, p. R28

Solve. Use the solve a simpler problem strategy.

5. Marcos is making three tile pictures. He uses 310 green tiles to make each picture. He uses 50 less red tiles than green tiles for each picture. How many red and green tiles does he use in all?

6. **Measurement** Ling is putting up a wallpaper border on three walls that are 14 feet long and 12 feet tall. How many feet of wallpaper border will she use if she puts the border only at the top of the wall?

7. Darius sells twice as much orange juice as lemonade. He charges $2 for each. He sold 10 cups of lemonade. How much did he earn in all?

8. A basketball coach is going to buy 16 basketballs. What will be the total cost of the basketballs?

9. Jerome's CD has 16 songs, and each song is 3 minutes long. Ana's CD has 14 songs, and each song is 4 minutes. Whose CD plays longer and by how much?

10. Five gardeners spent 260 hours in all planting trees. One of the gardeners spent 40 hours. The rest spent the same amount of time. How many hours did each spend on planting trees?

11. Marian is placing 72 photographs in an album. She will put the same number of photos on each of 6 pages. She can put 4 pictures in each row. How many rows will be on each page?

12. **WRITING IN ►MATH** Explain how you solved Exercise 11.

Centimeters are **metric** units of measure for length. Each side of a base-ten unit is equal to 1 centimeter (cm).

1 cm

MAIN IDEA

I will estimate and measure objects to the nearest centimeter.

SC Academic Standards

4-5.1 Use appropriate tools to measure objects to the nearest unit: measuring length in quarter inches, **centimeters,** and millimeters; measuring liquid volume in cups, quarts, and liters; and measuring weight and mass in pounds, milligrams, and kilograms.

You Will Need
metric ruler

ACTIVITY

1 **Estimate and measure lengths.**

Step 1 **Copy the table.**

Copy the table shown.

Object	Estimate	Length

Step 2 **Choose four items.**

Choose four items in your classroom that can be measured in centimeters.

Step 3 **Estimate length.**

Estimate the length of each object you selected in centimeters. Record the estimates in your table.

Step 4 **Measure length.**

Place the ruler against a side of one of the objects so that 0 on the ruler lines up with the edge. Measure the object's length to the nearest centimeter.

Think About It

1. Which of the objects you measured was the longest?

2. Which of the objects you measured was the shortest?

3. How did you estimate the length of each object?

4. Name two things in the room that would be about 100 centimeters long.

CHECK What You Know

Estimate. Then measure each line segment to the nearest centimeter.

5.

6.

7.

8.

9.

10.

11. **WRITING IN ►MATH** Describe the steps in measuring the length of an object using a metric ruler.

MAIN IDEA

I will estimate and measure lengths within the metric system.

SC Academic Standards

4-5.1 Use appropriate tools to measure objects to the nearest unit: measuring length in quarter inches, **centimeters, and millimeters;** measuring liquid volume in cups, quarts, and liters; and measuring weight and mass in pounds, milligrams, and kilograms.

New Vocabulary

metric

millimeter

centimeter

meter

kilometer

SC Math Online

macmillanmh.com

• Extra Examples
• Personal Tutor
• Self-Check Quiz

GET READY to Learn

Doug is growing carrots in his garden. He pulled out a carrot to see if it was growing. Measure the carrot to the nearest centimeter.

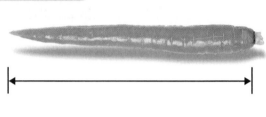

A metric ruler is used to measure metric lengths. The **metric** units of length are the millimeter, centimeter, meter, and kilometer.

Metric Measurements				Key Concepts
A **millimeter** is about as thick as 6 sheets of notebook paper.	A **centimeter** is about the length of a ladybug.	A **meter** is about the height of a chair.	A **kilometer** is about six city blocks.	

Real-World EXAMPLE Measure Length

1 **FOOD** Measure the carrot to the nearest centimeter.

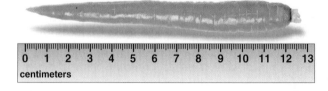

Align the 0 on the ruler with the left side of the carrot. The carrot ends before the 13-centimeter mark. So, the carrot is almost 13 centimeters long.

Before measuring any object, always estimate the length to decide which unit of measurement is best to use.

Real-World EXAMPLE   Estimate Length

2 SCHOOL Which is the best estimate of the length of a student's desk?

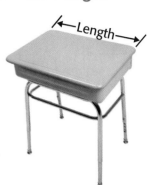
←Length→

A 5 centimeters

B 5 millimeters

C 50 centimeters

D 50 millimeters

A desk has to be long enough to do work. 5 centimeters, 5 millimeters, and 50 millimeters are all too small. So, the answer must be C, 50 centimeters.

 CHECK What You Know

Measure each object to the nearest centimeter. See Example 1 (p. 450)

1.

2.

Choose the best estimate. See Example 2 (p. 451)

3. length of a kayak

   A 6 centimeters

   B 2 meters

   C 6 meters

   D 2 kilometers

4. width of a piece of yarn

   F 1 millimeter   **H** 1 meter

   G 1 centimeter   **J** 1 kilometer

5. Patty said to Lina, "I'm about 150 millimeters tall." Is Patty correct? Explain why or why not.

6. **Talk About It** Describe a situation when it would be appropriate to measure an object using millimeters.

Measure each object to the nearest centimeter. See Example 1 (p. 450)

7.

8.

9.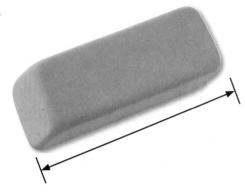

Choose the best estimate. See Example 2 (p. 451)

10. height of a cornstalk

A 2 millimeters	**C** 2 meters
B 2 centimeters	**D** 2 kilometers

11. length of an airport runway

F 5 millimeters	**H** 5 meters
G 50 centimeters	**J** 5 kilometer

12. A giraffe at the zoo is 5 meters tall. Name something else that is about 5 meters tall.

13. Is the distance from Boston, Massachusetts, to Phoenix, Arizona, about 4,000 kilometers? Explain.

H.O.T. Problems

14. OPEN ENDED Find three things in the classroom that are longer than 10 centimeters and smaller than 100 centimeters. Estimate and determine the actual measurements.

15. WRITING IN ►MATH Explain why it would be better to measure the length of your classroom with a meter stick instead of a centimeter ruler.

Estimate. Then measure each to the nearest inch, $\frac{1}{2}$ inch, and $\frac{1}{4}$ inch. (Lesson 11-1)

1.

2.

3. MULTIPLE CHOICE Choose the best estimate for the height of a giraffe. (Lesson 11-1)

A 19 inches   C 19 yards

B 19 feet   D 19 miles

Complete. (Lesson 11-2)

4. 3 feet = ■ inches

5. 2 yards = ■ feet

6. MULTIPLE CHOICE Kenyi's family wants to fence in their yard. They need 80 yards of fence. How many feet of fence should they buy? (Lesson 11-2)

F 79 feet   H 240 feet

G 96 feet   J 960 feet

7. Which measurement best describes the length of a couch, 6 feet or 6 inches? (Lesson 11-2)

8. What is the width of the rectangle below if the length of one side of each square is 1 centimeter long? (Lesson 11-3)

9. MULTIPLE CHOICE What is the length of one side of the square shown? (Lesson 11-3)

A 2 mm   C 2 m

B 2 cm   D 2 km

10. Dexter went on a hiking trip. Which measurement best describes how far he hiked, 10 kilometers or 10 meters? (Lesson 11-4)

11. **WRITING IN ►MATH** Explain why 3 yards is equal to 108 inches. (Lesson 11-2)

CORAL REEFS

Coral reefs are among the most diverse communities on Earth. Coral reefs can include up to 800 kinds of coral. Coral reefs can be a variety of colors, such as white, red, pink, green, blue, orange, and purple. They also provide food and shelter for about 4,000 kinds of fish and hundreds of other marine animals and plants.

Some of the marine animals that live in this habitat are sponges, fish, jellyfish, starfish, crabs, lobsters, turtles, and sea snakes.

Did You Know? Millions of plants and animals living near coral reefs have not been discovered.

SCAS

4-5.3 Use equivalencies to convert units of measure within the U.S. Customary System: converting length in inches, feet, yards, and miles; converting weight in ounces, pounds, and tons; converting liquid volume in cups, pints, quarts, and gallons; and converting time in years, months, weeks, days, hours, minutes, and seconds.

Animals of the Coral Reef

Animal	Range of Length
Anemone	1 cm–50 cm
Dolphin	1 m–11 m
Hard coral	1 mm–50 cm
Jellyfish	1 cm–2 m
Sea cucumber	1 cm–60 cm
Sea snake	500 cm–2 m
Sea turtle	5 cm–3 m
Sea urchin	1 cm–20 cm
Soft coral	1 mm–1 m
Whale shark	9 m–20 m

Source: Reef Education Network

 Real-World Math

Use the information in the table to solve each problem.

1. Identify the two shortest animals.

2. Identify the two longest animals.

3. What animal can be as short as 1 centimeter and as long as 60 centimeters?

4. A sea snake can be as long as 2 meters. What other animals can be that same length?

5. Identify the animal that can grow to be 2,000 centimeters long. (*Hint:* 1 meter = 100 centimeters)

6. Suppose a dolphin is 2 meters long. What is the dolphin's length in millimeters? (*Hint:* 1 meter = 1,000 millimeters)

7. Draw a sea turtle that is 8 centimeters long.

Measure Perimeters

MAIN IDEA

I will find the perimeter of a figure.

SC Academic Standards

4-5.4 Analyze the perimeter of a polygon.

New Vocabulary

perimeter

SC Math Online

macmillanmh.com
• Extra Examples
• Personal Tutor
• Self-Check Quiz

GET READY to Learn

Berto is walking around a park on the path shown. How far did Berto walk?

12 yd

6 yd

The distance around a closed figure is called the **perimeter**.

Perimeter of a Rectangle　　　　　　　**Key Concept**

Words　　To find the perimeter of a rectangle, add the lengths of the sides. The perimeter of a rectangle also equals 2 times its length plus 2 times its width.

Symbols　$P = \ell + w + \ell + w$
　　　　　　$P = 2 \times \ell + 2 \times w$
　　　　　　$P = (2\ell) + (2w)$

ℓ

w ⬚ w

ℓ

Real-World EXAMPLE　Find Perimeter

1 **DISTANCE** How far did Berto walk?

One Way: Use Addition	Another Way: Use a Formula
Add the measures of all of the sides of the figure.	Multiply the length and the width each by 2. Then add.
$P = 12 + 6 + 12 + 6$ $P = 36$	$P = (2\ell) + (2w)$ $P = (2 \times 12) + (2 \times 6)$ $P = 24 + 12$ or 36

So, Berto walked 36 yards.

You can estimate perimeter before finding the exact perimeter.

EXAMPLE Estimate and Find Perimeter

2 **Find the perimeter of a square with side lengths of 6 inches.**

Estimate: $5 + 5 + 5 + 5 = 20$

6 in.

6 in.   6 in.

6 in.

One Way: Use Addition	**Another Way:** Use a Formula
Add the measures of all of the sides of the figure.	Multiply the length of one side by 4 because there are 4 sides of equal length.
$P = 6 + 6 + 6 + 6$ $P = 24$	$P = 4 \times$ side length $P = 4 \times 6$ $P = 24$

So, the perimeter of the square is 24 inches.

Check for Reasonableness
The answer, 24, is close to the estimate, 20. ✔

CHECK What You Know

Estimate the perimeter. Then find the exact perimeter.

See Examples 1 and 2 (pp. 456–457)

1.
8 cm

8 cm   8 cm

8 cm

2.
7 in.

4 in.   4 in.

7 in.

3.
5 cm

5 cm   5 cm

5 cm

4. Byron made a drawing of his room. His drawing is shown. What is the perimeter of Byron's room?

5. What is the perimeter of a square with side lengths of 4 inches?

6. **Talk About It** Explain the two ways to find the perimeter of a rectangle. What are the two ways to find the perimeter of a square?

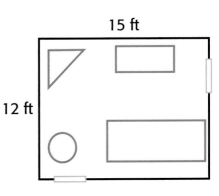

15 ft

12 ft

Practice and Problem Solving

SCAS • PASS

Extra Practice, p. R29

Estimate the perimeter. Then find the exact perimeter.

See Examples 1 and 2 (pp. 456–457)

7.

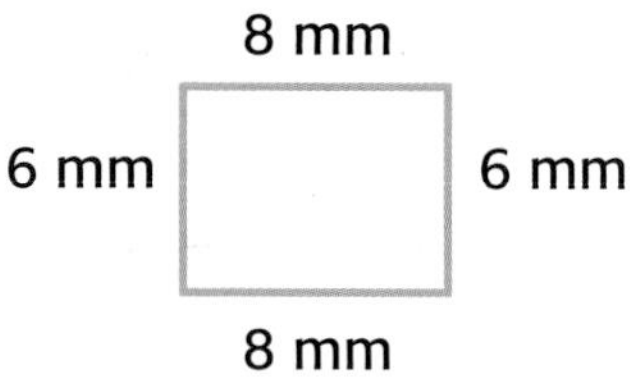

8 mm
6 mm
6 mm
8 mm

8.

12 ft
12 ft
12 ft
12 ft

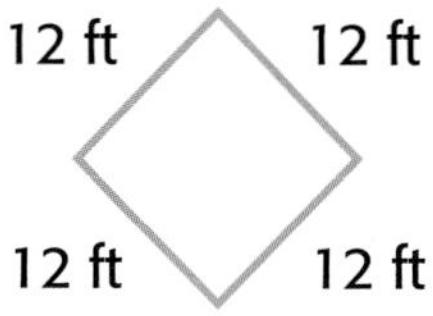

9.

15 cm
3 cm
3 cm
15 cm

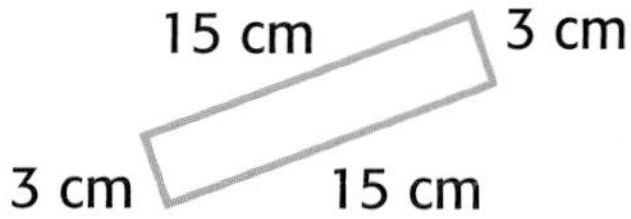

10.

8 m
3 m
3 m
8 m

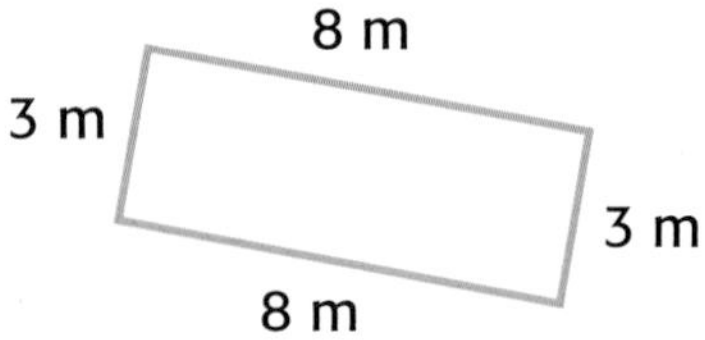

11.

10 yd
6 yd
6 yd
10 yd

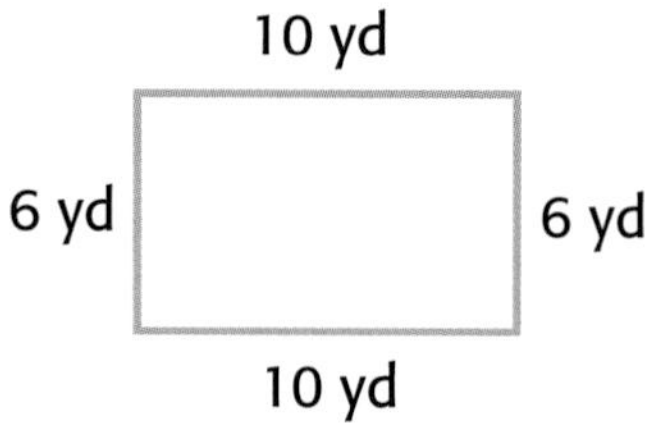

12.

4 in.
4 in.
4 in.
4 in.

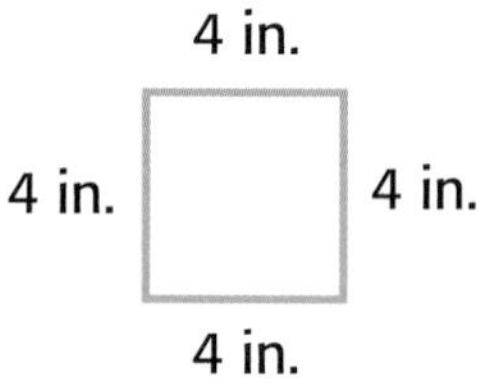

Estimate. Then find the perimeter of each rectangle in units.

13.

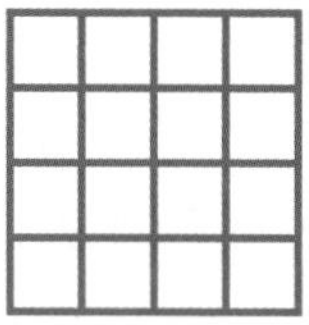

14.

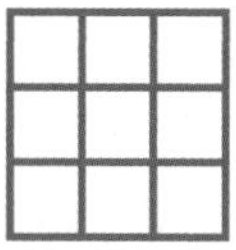

15.

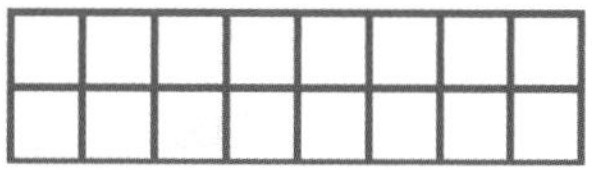

16. A baseball diamond is shaped like a square. Each side is 90 feet long. What is its perimeter?

17. A yard is 82 feet long and 45 feet wide. What is the perimeter of the yard?

Real-World PROBLEM SOLVING

Social Studies The Parthenon is an ancient building in Athens, Greece. It has a rectangular base measuring about 228 feet by 101 feet.

18. What is the perimeter of the base of the Parthenon?

19. If you doubled the length of each side of the base, is the perimeter doubled? Show your work.

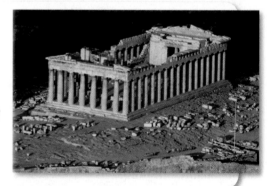

H.O.T. Problems

20. OPEN ENDED Explain how to find the perimeter of the figure shown to the right.

8 ft
10 ft
4 ft
4 ft

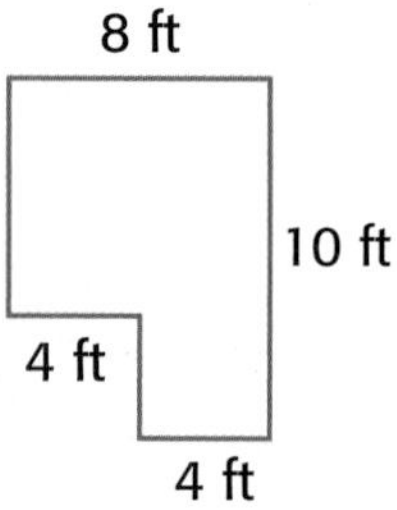

21. WRITING IN ▸MATH Suppose you double the side length of a square. Will the perimeter also double? Explain.

22. Choose the best unit for measuring distance across the United States. (Lesson 11-4)

 A centimeter

 B meter

 C millimeter

 D kilometer

23. What is the perimeter of the figure below if the side of each block represents 1 centimeter? (Lesson 11-5)

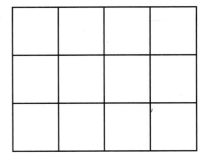

 F 7 centimeters

 G 12 centimeters

 H 14 centimeters

 J 20 centimeters

Spiral Review

Measure each object to the nearest centimeter. (Lesson 11-4)

24.

25.

26. There are 15 girls in class and 13 boys in class. If 7 more girls came to class, how many students will there be in the class? (Lesson 11-3)

Complete. (Lesson 11-2)

27. 36 in. = ▇ ft

28. 12 ft = ▇ yd

29. 4 yd = ▇ in.

30. **Algebra** Write an equation that describes the pattern. Then use the equation to find the next three numbers. (Lesson 5-5)

Input (x)	3	7	11	15	19	23
Output (y)	8	12	16	▇	▇	▇

11-6 Measure Areas

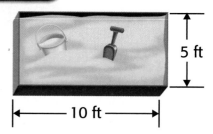

GET READY to Learn

The Perez family wants to put the sandbox shown in their backyard. What is the area of the sandbox?

5 ft

10 ft

MAIN IDEA

I will find the area of rectangles and squares.

SC Academic Standards

4-5.5 Generate strategies to determine the area of rectangles and triangles.

New Vocabulary

area

square units

SC Math Online

macmillanmh.com

• Extra Examples
• Personal Tutor
• Self-Check Quiz

Area is the number of square units needed to cover a region or figure without any overlap. It is measured in **square units**.

Real-World EXAMPLE   Area of a Rectangle

① **SANDBOX** Find the area of the sandbox.

One Way: Count	Another Way: Multiply
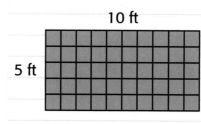 10 ft 5 ft There are 50 square feet.	Multiply the length times the width to find the area. A = length × width $A = \ell \times w$ A = 10 feet × 5 feet A = 50 square feet

So, the area of the sandbox is 50 square feet.

Area of a Rectangle   Key Concept

Words	To find the area of a rectangle, multiply the length by the width.
Formula	$A = \ell \times w$

ℓ

w w

ℓ

460 Chapter 11 Measure Length, Area, and Temperature

You can also find the area of a square.

Area of a Square

Words	To find the area of a square, multiply the length of one side s by itself.
Formula	$A = s \times s$

Real-World EXAMPLE   Area of a Square

2 **PHOTOS** Find the area of the photo if its sides are 9 centimeters in length.

Estimate 9 cm × 9 cm ⟶ 10 cm × 10 cm = 100 sq cm

$A = \text{side} \times \text{side}$ Formula

$A = 9 \text{ cm} \times 9 \text{ cm}$ $s = 9$

$A = 81$ square centimeters   Multiply.

The area of the photo is 81 square centimeters.

9 cm

9 cm

Check for Reasonableness
81 square centimeters is close to 100 square centimeters. ✓

 CHECK What You Know

Estimate the area. Then find the exact area of each square or rectangle.

See Examples 1 and 2 (pp. 460–461)

1.

2.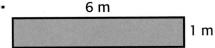
6 m
1 m

3. 3 yd

3 yd

4. Mr. Hart is hanging a picture on a wall. The picture frame has a length of 12 inches and a width of 9 inches. How much wall space will the picture need?

5. **Talk About It** Explain two ways to find the area of a rectangle. What are two ways to find the area of a square?

Estimate the area. Then find the exact area of each square or rectangle. See Examples 1 and 2 (pp. 460–461)

6.

7.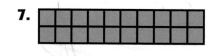

8.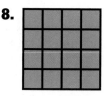

9. 6 m
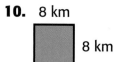 2 m

10. 8 km
8 km

11. 10 yd
2 yd

12. Each child in Mrs. Dixon's class has a rectangular desk that is 15 inches long and 32 inches wide. What is the area of the top of each student's desk?

13. Ricky's computer monitor is a rectangle. The length is 15 inches and the width is 12 inches. Estimate the area of the monitor.

14. A car is 15 feet long and 6 feet wide. It is parked on a rectangular driveway with an area of 112 square feet. How much of the driveway is *not* covered by the car?

15. A rectangular playground is 40 meters by 10 meters. Its area will be covered with shredded tires. Each bag of shredded tires covers 200 square meters and costs $30. Find the total cost for this project.

H.O.T. Problems

16. OPEN ENDED Draw three rectangles that each have an area of 36 square inches, but have different perimeters.

NUMBER SENSE The area and the measure of one side of each square or rectangle is given. Find the missing sides.

17.
6 in.
Area = 36 sq in.

18.
4 m
Area = 36 sq m

19. 1 cm
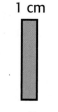
Area = 5 sq cm

20. **WRITING IN** ►**MATH** A square has sides measuring 3 feet. If the sides of a square are doubled, will the area also double? Explain.

Area Guess

Find Area of Rectangles

Get Ready!

Players: 2 players

Get Set!

Each player makes a copy of the table shown.

Go!

- Each player selects four objects in the classroom that have a rectangular surface.

- Each player estimates the area of the objects selected to the nearest square centimeter.

- Find the exact areas of the objects.

- Find the differences between the estimated areas and the actual areas of the objects.

- Find the sum of the four differences.

- The player who has the least difference between the estimated and actual areas wins.

You will need: ruler, paper and pencil

Object	Area		Difference
Player _____			
	Estimated	Actual	

In this activity, you will explore whether rectangles with the same area can have different perimeters.

ACTIVITY   Relate Perimeter and Area

Step 1   **Draw rectangles.**

Draw the following rectangles on grid paper.

- 1 unit by 24 units
- 2 units by 12 units
- 3 units by 8 units
- 4 units by 6 units

Step 2   **Copy and complete the table.**

Find the perimeter and area of the rectangles. Record the information on your table.

Figure	Perimeter	Area
Rectangle 1	■ units	■ square units
Rectangle 2	■ units	■ square units
Rectangle 3	■ units	■ square units
Rectangle 4	■ units	■ square units

Step 3   **Examine your table.**

What similarities and differences do you notice among the rectangles?

Is it possible for rectangles with the same area to have different perimeters?

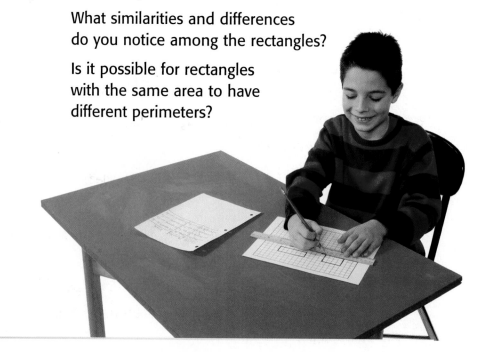

MAIN IDEA

I will explore perimeter and area.

SC Academic Standards

4-1.2 Construct arguments that lead to conclusions about general mathematical properties and relationships.

You Will Need
grid paper

SC Math Online
macmillanmh.com
• Concepts in Motion

Think About It

1. Explain the difference between area and perimeter.

2. Is it possible to draw a rectangle that has an area of 24 square units and a perimeter of 24 units? Explain.

3. Is there a relationship between the area and the perimeter of a rectangle? Explain.

4. Look at the rectangles that you drew. What do you notice about the shape of the rectangle that has the greatest perimeter?

✓ CHECK What You Know

Find the perimeter and area for each square or rectangle.

5.
6.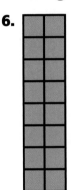

7.

8. What do the figures in Exercises 5–7 have in common? How do these figures differ?

9. Draw two rectangles that have the same areas and the same perimeters.

10. Can rectangles that have the same perimeter have different areas? Explain.

11. **WRITING IN ►MATH** If a figure has a greater perimeter than another, does it also have a greater area? Explain your thinking.

MAIN IDEA I will choose the best strategy to solve a problem.

SCAS 4-5.5 Generate strategies to determine the area of rectangles and triangles. 4-5.9 Exemplify situations in which highly accurate measurements are required.

P.S.I. TEAM +

LYNN: I am painting a backdrop that is 30 feet long and 12 feet wide for the school play. The backdrop needs two coats of paint. I have two cans of paint and each covers 400 square feet.

YOUR MISSION: Determine if Lynn has enough paint to paint the backdrop.

Understand	You know the size of the backdrop and the amount of paint Lynn has. Find if she has enough paint to paint the backdrop twice.
Plan	Use a model and solve a simpler problem.
Solve	The model shows the backdrop. Find the area of one section of the backdrop.

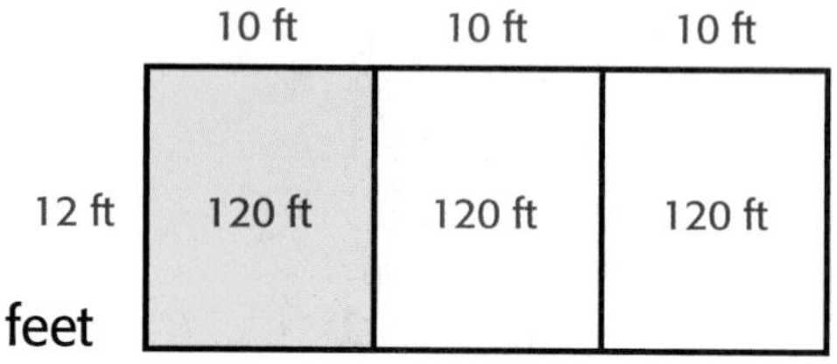

$10 \times 12 = 120$ square feet

Now multiply by 3 to find the area of the entire backdrop.

$120 \times 3 = 360$ square feet

Since the backdrop needs to be painted twice, you need enough paint to cover $360 + 360$ or 720 square feet. Since $720 < 800$, there is enough paint. |
| **Check** | The area of the backdrop is $30 \times 12 = 360$ square feet. Two coats of paint would need to cover 720 square feet. Since Lynn has enough paint to cover 800 square feet, the answer is correct. ✔ |

Model diagram: sections labeled 10 ft, 10 ft, 10 ft across the top; 12 ft on the left side; each section labeled 120 ft. Labeled "Backdrop".

Use any of the strategies shown below to solve. Tell what strategy you used.

PROBLEM-SOLVING STRATEGIES
• Act it out.
• Guess and check.
• Look for a pattern.
• Work a simpler problem.

1. Measurement One seal weighs 328 pounds. The second seal weighs 79 pounds less. How much does the second seal weigh?

2. Measurement A lion cub's weight is shown. An older lion weighs three times as much as the cub. How much do the lions weigh altogether?

26 lbs

3. Four numbers between 1 and 9 have a sum of 23. Each number is used once. What are the numbers?

4. A movie theater has 18 screens. About 212 people see a movie on each screen at the same time on Friday. About how many people are seeing movies in the theater at that time?

5. The table shows the amount of vegetables sold at a grocery store every four weeks. Is it reasonable to say that the store sells about 300 vegetables every week?

Vegetable	Amount
Corn	396
Onions	316
Tomatoes	489

6. Heath brought 25 trading cards to a hobby show. He received three cards for one card in three trades. Then he gave 2 cards for one card in two trades. How many cards does Heath have now?

7. Pedro bought 3 pencils for 15¢. How much would 10 pencils cost?

8. Algebra Describe the pattern below. Then find the missing number.

20, 200, 2,000, ■, 200,000

9. Measurement Clarissa has 4 pictures that are the size of the one shown. How much space will they take up in her photo album?

5 in.

3 in.

10. WRITING IN ▶MATH Explain how you solved Exercise 9.

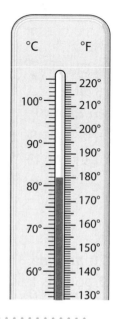

GET READY to Learn

Ashton's teacher is measuring the temperature of the liquid being used in a science experiment. What is the temperature?

MAIN IDEA

I will measure temperature and calculate changes in temperature.

SC Academic Standards

4-5.7 Use Celsius and Fahrenheit thermometers to determine temperature changes during time intervals.

New Vocabulary

degrees

Fahrenheit (°F)

Celsius (°C)

SC Math Online

macmillanmh.com
• Extra Examples
• Personal Tutor
• Self-Check Quiz

Degrees are the units of measurement used to describe temperature. Temperature can be measured in degrees **Celsius (°C)** or degrees **Fahrenheit (°F)**.

Real-World EXAMPLE   Read a Thermometer

① **SCIENCE Find the temperature of the liquid being used in the experiment in degrees Celsius and Fahrenheit.**

Find the numbers next to the top of the red line.

The °C shows the temperature in degrees Celsius, and the °F shows the temperature in degrees Fahrenheit.

So, the temperature is about 82°C or 180°F.

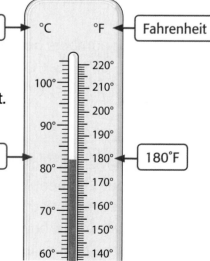

Hands-On Mini Activity

In this activity, you will measure and calculate changes in temperature.

1. Set a thermometer in the back of the classroom and another one outside.

2. At the end of math class, find the temperature indoors and outdoors.

3. How much warmer was one thermometer than the other in degrees Fahrenheit? How did you find the difference?

4. How much warmer was one thermometer than the other in degrees Celsius? How did you find the difference?

Use addition or subtraction to find changes in temperatures.

EXAMPLE   Temperature Change

Remember
When subtracting, you may need to regroup.

2 **Find the change in the inside and outside temperatures.**

inside thermometer

outside thermometer

$84° - 68° =$ change in temperature

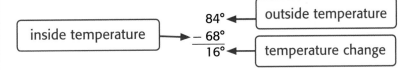

inside temperature

84° ← outside temperature
$-$ 68°
16° ← temperature change

So, it is 16°F warmer outside than inside.

Write the approximate temperature in degrees Fahrenheit and Celsius. See Example 1 (p. 468)

1.

2.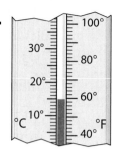

Find the change in temperature. See Example 2 (p. 469)

3. 16°C to 5°C

4. 34°F to 21°F

5. The thermometer reads 15°C. Vickie decides to wear her mittens and hat. Is this a good idea? Explain.

6. **Talk About It** The temperature outside is 16°F warmer than in the classroom temperature of 67°F. Write a number sentence for the outside temperature.

Practice and Problem Solving

SCAS • PASS
Extra Practice, p. R30

Write the approximate temperature in degrees Fahrenheit and Celsius. See Example 1 (p. 468)

7.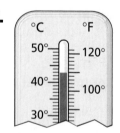

8.

9.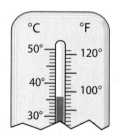

10.

11.

12.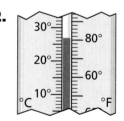

Find the change in the temperature. See Example 2 (p. 469)

13. 0°F to 26°F

14. 18°F to 6°F

15. 15°C to 8°C

16. 15°C to 31°C

17. 6°F to 38°F

18. 94°F to 59°F

19. 42°C to 78°C

20. 81°C to 13°C

21. 114°F to 67°F

22. Which is greater, a temperature change from 47°F to 79°F, or a temperature change from 28°F to 63°F?

23. Which is less, a temperature change from 17°C to 55°C, or a temperature change from 112°C to 71°C?

24. Two hamburgers are cooking on a grill. The grill's flame is 187°F. The flame needs to be 163°F hotter. At what temperature should the burgers cook?

25. When Neva woke up, the temperature was 20°C. By lunchtime, the temperature went up 6°C. The high temperature for the day was 31°C. How much higher did the temperature get after Neva had lunch?

 South Carolina Data File

South Carolina temperatures can vary greatly between cities and during different times of day.

26. Identify the city and month(s) that show the least change in temperature.

27. Identify the city and month(s) that show a change in temperature equal to 25°F.

South Carolina Temperatures			
	August	**September**	**October**
Clemson Average	High 88°F	High 82°F	High 73°F
	Low 66°F	Low 60°F	Low 48°F
Port Royal Average	High 89°F	High 85°F	High 78°F
	Low 72°F	Low 68°F	Low 58°F

Source: Canty and Associates

H.O.T. Problems

28. OPEN ENDED Research the high and low temperatures from last week. Which day experienced the greatest change in temperature?

29. FIND THE ERROR Abbie and Sashi each found the change in the temperature for today. Who is correct? Prove it.

Abbie
"The high was 55°F and the low was 42°F. The change in temperature was 13°F."

Sashi
"The high was 55°F and the low was 42°F. The change in temperature was 97°F."

30. **WRITING IN ►MATH** Write a real-world problem involving temperature. Have a classmate solve your problem.

SC Math Online macmillanmh.com
• STUDY *TO GO*
• Vocabulary Review

FOLDABLES
Study Organizer **GET READY to Study**

Be sure the following Key Vocabulary words and Key Concepts are written in your Foldable.

Customary Units
Metric Units
Length
Convert
Perimeter
Area
Square Units
Temperature
Celsius
Fahrenheit

Key Concepts

Measure Length (pp. 439–443 and 448–452)

- Common customary units of length are **inch**, **foot**, and **yard**.

- Metric units of length are **millimeter**, **centimeter**, **meter**, and **kilometer**.

- To measure the distance between two cities, you would use kilometers.

Perimeter and Area (pp. 456 and 460)

Perimeter is the distance around a figure.

- To find perimeter, add the lengths of the sides. $P = \ell + \ell + w + w$

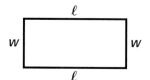

$$\ell$$
w w
ℓ

Area is the number of square units needed to cover a region or figure without any overlap.

- Area of a Rectangle = length × width

Key Vocabulary

area (p. 460)

convert (p. 444)

customary (p. 441)

metric (p. 448)

perimeter (p. 456)

Vocabulary Check

Choose the vocabulary word that completes each sentence.

1. The distance around a figure is the ____?____.

2. To find the ____?____ of a rectangle, you can multiply the length of the rectangle by its width.

3. When you change the unit of measure, you ____?____ measurements.

4. ____?____ is the number of square units needed to cover a region or figure.

5. Inch, foot, and yard are all ____?____ units of measure for length.

Lesson-by-Lesson Review

11-1 Customary Units of Length (pp. 441–443)

4-5.1

Example 1
Estimate. Then measure the height of the seahorse below to the nearest inch, $\frac{1}{2}$ inch and $\frac{1}{4}$ inch.

The seahorse is about 2, $1\frac{1}{2}$, or $1\frac{3}{4}$ inches long.

Estimate. Then measure to the nearest inch, $\frac{1}{2}$ inch, and $\frac{1}{4}$ inch.

6.

7. The school supply store has index cards that are $2\frac{1}{2}$ inches wide and 3 inches long. How many inches long will four index cards be that are placed end to end?

11-2 Convert Customary Units of Length (pp. 444–445)

4-5.3, 4-5.8

Example 2
How many feet are in 3 yards?

You need to find the number of feet in 3 yards. Since a yard is a larger unit than a foot, use multiplication to convert.

To convert 3 yards to feet, multiply by 3.

3 yards = ■ feet

3 yards × 3 = ■ feet

> Multiply by 3 since there are 3 feet in each yard.

3 × 3 = 9

So, 3 yards = 9 feet

Complete.
8. 2 ft = ■ in.

9. 6 ft = ■ in.

10. ■ in. = 2 yd

11. How many inches long is this wagon?

3 ft

12. John's mom needs 15 feet of fabric. She buys 4 yards of fabric. Did she buy enough? Explain.

11-3 **Problem-Solving Strategy: Solve a Simpler Problem** (pp. 446–447)

4-1.1

Example 3
Find the perimeter of the first floor of the house shown below.

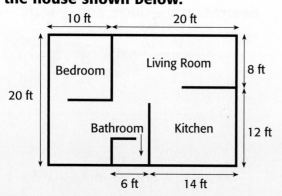

Understand

What facts do you know?

- One side measures 20 feet.
- Another side measures the sum of 10 feet and 20 feet.

What do you need to find?

- The perimeter of the house.

Plan Solve a simpler problem.

Solve Multiply the width by 2.

$20 \times 2 = 40$

Next, add 10 and 20. Then multiply the sum by 2.

$10 + 20 = 30$

$30 \times 2 = 60$

So, the perimeter is $40 + 60$ or 100 feet.

Check Add all the measures
$20 + 10 + 6 + 14 + 12 + 8 + 20 + 10 = 100$

So, our answer is correct. ✔

13. Measurement Mr. and Mrs. Lobo are building a fence around their rectangular yard that is 16 feet long and 14 feet wide. How much fence will they need?

14. Heidi ran two laps around the track. How many feet did she run?

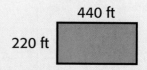

15. Measurement Oliver is buying a border for a poster. How many inches of border will Oliver need for a poster that is 44 inches long and 28 inches wide?

16. Look at this figure. What is the length of the dashed line?

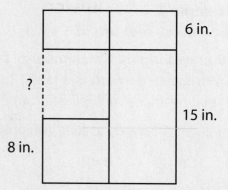

17. Martell had boxes he was stacking. Each was 2 feet high. If he stacks 3 boxes on top of a table that is 3 feet high, what will be the total height?

11-4 Metric Units of Length (pp. 450–452)

4-5.1

Example 4
Measure the flower to the nearest centimeter.

Align the 0 mark on the ruler to the left side of the flower. The flower ends at the 4-centimeter mark on the ruler.

So, the flower is 4 centimeters long.

Measure the object to the nearest centimeter.

18.

19.

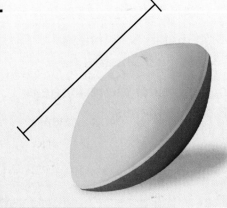

11-5 Measure Perimeters (pp. 456–459)

4-5.4

Example 5
Find the perimeter of the rectangle.

12 in.
8 in. ☐ 8 in.
12 in.

$P = \ell + w + \ell + w$
$P = 12 + 8 + 12 + 8$
$P = 24 + 16$
$P = 40$ inches

Example 6
Find the perimeter of the square.

3 cm ☐

$P = 4 \times s$
$P = 4 \times 3$
$P = 12$ centimeters

Estimate the perimeter. Then find the exact perimeter.

20.
15 cm
3 cm

21. 6 yd
☐ 6 yd

22. **Measurement** A poster has a length of 24 inches, and its width is 12 inches. What is the perimeter of the poster?

11-6 **Measure Areas** (pp. 460–462)

4-5.5

Example 7
Find the area of a rectangle that is 7 meters long and 4 meters wide.

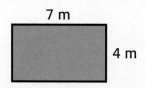

7 m

4 m

To find the area, multiply the length and the width.

$A = \ell \times w$
$A = 7$ meters $\times$ 4 meters
$A = 28$ square meters

So, the area of the rectangle is 28 square meters.

Example 8
What is the area of a square with sides that are 5 inches long?

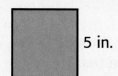

5 in.

To find the area, multiply the side length by itself.

$A = s \times s$
$A = 5$ inches $\times$ 5 inches
$A = 25$ square inches

So, the area of the square is 25 square inches.

Find the area of each square or rectangle.

23.

24.

30 ft

10 ft

25. 12 in.

12 in.

Algebra **The area and the measure of one side of each square or rectangle is given. Find the measure of the missing side.**

26. 6 in.

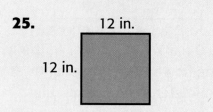

Area = 24 sq in.

27.

8 ft

Area = 64 sq ft

28. Rodolfo's table tennis table has an area of 45 square feet. The length is 9 feet. What is the perimeter of the table tennis table?

11-7 Problem-Solving Investigation: Choose a Strategy (pp. 466–467)

4-5.5,
4-5.9

Example 9

Mr. Palmer is buying a cover for his pool table. Is it reasonable to say that a cover with an area of 30 square feet will be large enough to cover his pool table?

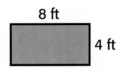

Understand

What facts do you know?

- The pool table is 8 feet by 4 feet.
- The area of the cover is 30 square feet.

What do you need to find?

- Is 30 square feet reasonable?

Plan Solve a simpler problem.

Solve $A = \ell \times w$

$A = 8 \text{ feet} \times 4 \text{ feet}$

$A = 32 \text{ square feet}$

The pool table has an area of 32 square feet. Since $30 < 32$, it is not reasonable to say that the cover is large enough.

Check $32 - 30 = 2$

So, the area of the pool table is 2 square feet larger than the cover. It is not large enough.

Use any strategy to solve.

29. Mindy is mowing the lawn. What area does she have to mow?

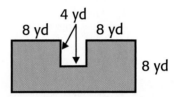

30. Measurement What is the total area of the three squares below?

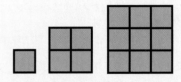

31. Measurement There are six tables that measure 3 feet by 6 feet. If a room measures 25 feet by 10 feet, will the tables fit in the room?

32. A sandbox measures 12 feet by 8 feet. The area of the playground is 200 square feet. How many square feet are not used by the sandbox?

33. James bought lunch for $3. Then he paid his club $1. He earned $5 for mowing grass. He now has $25. How much did he start with?

11-8 **Measure Temperatures** (pp. 468–471)

4-5.7

Example 10
Write the approximate temperature in degrees Fahrenheit and Celsius.

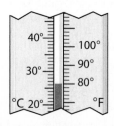

The red shows 80°F. So, it is approximately 25°C and 80°F.

Example 11
Find the change in the temperatures.

A thermometer inside reads:

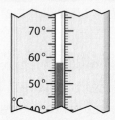

A thermometer outside reads:

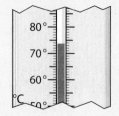

74° − 58° = change in temperature

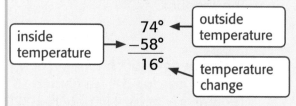

It is 16°C warmer outside than inside.

34. Write the approximate temperature in degrees Fahrenheit and Celsius.

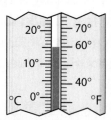

35. The thermometer reads 10°C. What type of clothing should be worn outside?

Find the change in temperature.

36.
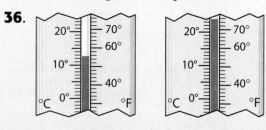

37.
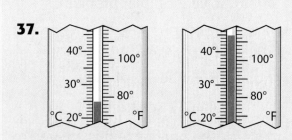

38. 2°F to 37°F   **39.** 95°C to 41°C

40. Elton's class is taking a field trip to the zoo. When the students arrived at school, the temperature was 80°F. When they left for the zoo, it was 95°F. How much warmer was it when they left for the zoo?

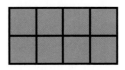
For Exercises 1 and 2, tell whether each statement is *true* or *false*.

1. Area is the distance around a figure.

2. To change units of measurement is to convert.

Choose the best estimate for each length.

3. length of a green bean, 2 inches or 2 feet

4. length of a sheep, 3 yards or 3 feet

5. Tessa's swimming pool is 13 feet long. How many inches is this?

6. A bottle of glue is about 15 centimeters tall. Name something else that has a height or width of about 15 centimeters.

7. **MULTIPLE CHOICE** Which statement about the rectangle is true?

4 cm
6 cm

A The area is equal to the perimeter.

B The area is less than the perimeter.

C The perimeter is 20 centimeters.

D The area is 10 square centimeters.

8. Find the area of the rectangle.

9. Brett painted 3 walls. Each wall was 9 feet tall and 12 feet long. How much wall area did he paint?

10. Which figure has the greater perimeter?

7 m
4 m
Figure A

2 m
8 m
Figure B

11. **Algebra** Three numbers between 1 and 8 have a sum of 20. Each number is used once. What are the numbers?

Find the change in temperature.

12. 25°C to 38°C

13. 70°F to 52°F

14. **MULTIPLE CHOICE** Which equation represents the area (A) of the square in square inches?

5 in.

F $5 = A \times 5$

H $A = 5 + 5$

G $A = 5 \times 5$

J $A = 5 \times 4$

15. **WRITING IN ➤ MATH** Do all squares with one side of 3 inches have the same area? Explain.

PART 1   Multiple Choice

Read each question. Then fill in the correct answer on the answer sheet provided by your teacher or on a sheet of paper.

1. Which shape has bilateral symmetry?

A

B

C

D

2. The numbers in the pattern decrease by the same amount each time. What are the next three numbers?

32, 28, 24, 20, 16, ■, ■, ■

F 14, 10, 6   **H** 10, 6, 2

G 12, 8, 4   **J** 9, 5, 1

3. Hannah plans to put a fence around her yard.

5 yd

12 yd

What is the perimeter of the yard?

A 28 yards   **C** 34 yards

B 32 yards   **D** 46 yards

4. The map shows the distance from Lora's house to school. Use a ruler to measure the line segment. What is the distance from Lora's house to school?

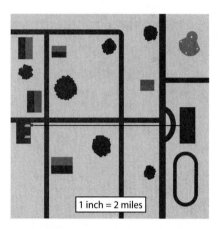

1 inch = 2 miles

F 2 miles   **H** 3 miles

G 2.5 miles   **J** 4.5 miles

5. Nate hiked two miles. If one mile equals 5,280 feet, how many feet did he hike?

A 10,056 feet   **C** 10,506 feet

B 10,065 feet   **D** 10,560 feet

6. What is the value of the expression below if $n = 4$?

$$42 \div (n + 2)$$

F 7   **H** 5

G 6   **J** 4

7. How many tiles that are 1 foot long and 1 foot wide are needed to tile the floor shown?

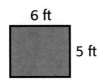

6 ft

5 ft

A 11 tiles   **C** 26 tiles

B 25 tiles   **D** 30 tiles

8. A rectangle has an area of 28 square units. Which of the following could not be its length and width?

F 7×4 **H** 14×2

G 9×3 **J** 28×1

9. Which triangle appears to be congruent to the one shown at the right?

A   **C**

B    **D**

PART 2   Short Response

Record your answers on the answer sheet provided by your teacher or on a sheet of paper.

10. Rina's bedroom is shaped like a rectangle. It is 12 feet long and 10 feet wide. What is the area, in square feet, of the room?

11. What is the perimeter of a square that has an area of 49 square centimeters?

PART 3   Extended Response

Record your answers on the answer sheet provided by your teacher or on a sheet of paper.

12. Suppose the temperature on the thermometer shown below increases by 12°F. Explain how to find the new temperature.

NEED EXTRA HELP?												
If You Missed Question...	1	2	3	4	5	6	7	8	9	10	11	12
Go to Lesson...	10-8	5-4	11-5	11-1	2-4	5-6	11-6	11-6	10-7	11-6	11-6	11-8
SC Academic Standards	5-4.6	4-3.1	4-5.4	4-5.1	3-2.3	4-3.4	4-5.5	4-5.5	4-4.5	4-5.5	4-5.5	4-5.7

Measure Capacity, Weight, and Volume

BIG Idea How do you convert units of weight?

To convert a larger unit to a smaller unit, you multiply. To convert a smaller unit to a larger unit, you divide.

Example Suppose the total birth weight of eight pandas is 32 ounces. To find the total birth weight in pounds, divide 32 by 16 since there are 16 ounces in 1 pound.

$$16\overline{)32} \quad \begin{array}{r} 2 \\ -32 \\ \hline 0 \end{array}$$

16 ounces = 1 pound
Divide 32 by 16 to find the birth weight in pounds.

So, the total birth weight of 8 pandas is 2 pounds.

What will I learn in this chapter?

- Use customary units of capacity and weight.
- Use metric units of capacity and mass.
- Solve problems using logical reasoning.
- Measure and estimate volume.
- Solve problems about elapsed time.

Key Vocabulary

capacity

weight

mass

weight

elapsed time

SC Math Online **Student Study Tools** at macmillanmh.com

FOLDABLES®
Study Organizer

Make this Foldable to help you organize information about capacity, weight, and volume. Begin with 5 sheets of $8\frac{1}{2}$ " × 11" paper.

① **Stack** 5 sheets of paper so they are $\frac{3}{4}$ inch apart.

② **Roll** up the edge, so all tabs are the same size.

③ **Crease** and staple along the fold.

④ **Label** the tabs with the topics from each lesson.

Measure Capacity, Weight, and Volume
Customary Units of Capacity
Convert Customary Units of Capacity
Metric Units of Capacity
Customary Units of Weight
Convert Customary Units of Weight
Metric Units of Mass
Estimate and Measure Volume
Elapsed Time

You have two ways to check prerequisite skills for this chapter.

Option 2

SC Math Online ▷ Take the Chapter Readiness Quiz at macmillanmh.com.

Option 1

Complete the Quick Check below.

QUICK Check

Multiply or divide. (Lesson 4-5)

1. 2×8 **2.** 4×16 **3.** 8×24 **4.** 9×36

5. $4 \div 2$ **6.** $12 \div 4$ **7.** $36 \div 6$ **8.** $64 \div 8$

9. Dan shared his markers equally with three friends. How many markers did each person get?

Compare. Use >, <, or =. (Lesson 1-4)

10. 12 ● 21   **11.** 64 ● 36   **12.** 128 ● 182

13. The table shows the number of cans collected by two fourth grade classes at Franklin Elementary School. Which class collected more cans?

Cans Collected	
Class	**Number of Cans Collected**
Mr. Santos	236
Miss Davis	263

Write the time shown on each clock. (Prior Grade)

14.

15.

16.

Measurement Activity for 12-1

Estimate and Measure Capacity

MAIN IDEA

I will estimate and measure capacity.

SC Academic Standards

4-5.1 Use appropriate tools to measure objects to the nearest unit: measuring length in quarter inches, centimeters, and millimeters; **measuring liquid volume in cups, quarts,** and liters; and measuring weight and mass in pounds, milligrams, and kilograms.

Capacity is the amount of liquid a container can hold.

 1 cup

 1 pint

 1 quart

 **1 gallon**

ACTIVITY Measure Capacity

Step 1 Measure.

Fill the cup with water and pour its contents into the pint. Repeat until the pint is full. It takes 2 cups to fill the pint. So, there are 2 cups in a pint.

Step 2 Copy and complete the table.

Estimate. Then use water to find the exact measures.

Container	Estimate	Actual
Pint	■ cups	■ cups
Quart	■ pints	■ pints
Gallon	■ quarts	■ quarts

Think About It

1. How many cups are in one pint?

2. How many quarts are in one gallon?

 **CHECK What You Know**

3. ■ cups = 3 pints   **4.** ■ pints = 4 gallons

5. **WRITING IN ►MATH** Is it faster to water two large flower pots using a one-cup pitcher or a one-quart pitcher? Explain.

Customary Units of Capacity

12-1

GET READY to Learn

Jorge is filling an aquarium. He went to the kitchen to find a container to fill the aquarium. Which container should Jorge use to fill his aquarium most quickly?

1 cup   1 quart   1 gallon

MAIN IDEA

I will estimate and measure customary capacities.

SC Academic Standards

4-5.1 Use appropriate tools to measure objects to the nearest unit:...measuring liquid volume in cups, quarts, and liters; and measuring weight and mass in pounds, milligrams, and kilograms.

New Vocabulary

capacity
fluid ounce
cup
pint
quart
gallon

SC Math Online

macmillanmh.com
• Extra Examples
• Personal Tutor
• Self-Check Quiz

The amount a container can hold is its **capacity**. Different containers measure different capacities. A cup contains 8 **fluid ounces**.

1 **fl oz**   1 **cup**   1 **pint**   1 **quart**   1 **gallon**

Real-World EXAMPLE   Estimate Capacity

1 AQUARIUMS Which container should Jorge use to fill the aquarium most quickly?

To fill the aquarium most quickly, Jorge should use the container that will hold the most liquid. The gallon is the largest unit. It will fill the aquarium most quickly.

2 **FOOD** Nita is pouring salsa into a small bowl. Is the most reasonable estimate for the capacity of the bowl 8 fluid ounces, 8 cups, 8 quarts, or 8 gallons?

The salsa is a small amount. So, 8 gallons, 8 quarts, and 8 cups are too much. The most reasonable estimate for the capacity of the bowl is 8 fluid ounces.

3 Is the most reasonable estimate for the capacity of the bathtub 20 fluid ounces, 20 cups, 20 quarts, or 20 gallons?

The bathtub can hold a large amount of water. So, 20 fluid ounces, 20 cups, and 20 quarts are too small. The most reasonable estimate for the capacity of the bathtub is 20 gallons.

CHECK What You Know

Choose the most reasonable estimate for each capacity. See Examples 1–3 (pp. 486–487)

1.

A 1 fluid ounce
B 1 pint
C 1 quart
D 100 quarts

2.

F 4 fluid ounces
G 4 cups
H 40 cups
J 4 gallons

3.

A 1 fluid ounce
B 1 cup
C 1 pint
D 1 gallon

4. **Talk About It** Is it possible for both of the containers shown to have a capacity of 1 pint? Explain why or why not.

Choose the most reasonable estimate for each capacity. See Examples 1–3 (pp. 486–487)

5.

F 12,000 fluid ounces
G 12,000 pints
H 12,000 quarts
J 12,000 gallons

6.

A 2 fluid ounces
B 2 cups
C 2 pints
D 2 gallons

7.

F 1 fluid ounce
G 1 cup
H 1 quart
J 1 gallon

8.

A 8 fluid ounces
B 8 cups
C 8 pints
D 8 gallons

9.

F 1 quart
G 10 quarts
H 100 quarts
J 1,000 quarts

10.

A 16 gallons
B 16 quarts
C 16 fluid ounces
D 16 cups

Estimate and then measure the capacity of each object.

11. water bottle

12. juice box

13. sink

Real-World PROBLEM SOLVING

Water Some household activities and the amount of water they consume are listed in the table.

14. If Callie takes one shower each day, is it reasonable to say that she could use 210 gallons of water in one week? Explain.

15. Callie brushes her teeth three times each day. Is it reasonable to say that she uses 2 cups of water in one day? Explain.

16. Callie washes dishes three times each week. Is it reasonable to say that she could save 30 gallons of water in a week by washing the dishes in a dishwasher instead of by hand? Explain.

Water Consumption	
Activity	**Water Used (gallons)**
Take shower	15–30
Brush teeth (water running)	1–2
Wash dishes (by hand)	20
Wash dishes (in dishwasher)	9–12
Flush toilet	5–7

Source: California Urban Water Conservation Council

H.O.T. Problems

17. OPEN ENDED Name two things in your classroom that would hold more than one cup.

18.  **MATH** A set of twins is equally sharing 1 pint of ice cream. Their friend, Shannon, is eating 1 cup of ice cream. Who is eating the most ice cream? Explain.

PASS Practice 4-5.7, 4-5.1

19. At bedtime the temperature was 45°F. In the morning it was 15°F cooler. What was the temperature in the morning? (Lesson 11-8)

A 75°F

B 60°F

C 30°F

D 15°F

20. Which of the following holds about 1 quart of water? (Lesson 12-1)

F   H

G   J

Spiral Review

Find the change in the temperatures. (Lesson 11-8)

21. 75°F to 34°F
22. 35°C to 50°C
23. 85°F to 68°F

Write the approximate temperature in degrees Fahrenheit and Celsius. (Lesson 11-8)

24.

25.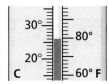

26. Tonya got money for her birthday. She got $8 from her friends, $16 from her parents, and $5 from her sister. She now has $48. How much did she have originally? (Lesson 11-7)

Estimate. Then measure each to the nearest inch, $\frac{1}{2}$ inch, and $\frac{1}{4}$ inch. (Lesson 11-1)

27.

28.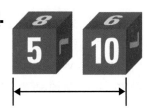

GET READY to Learn

Marcus has a 2-gallon container of laundry detergent. How many quarts of laundry detergent does he have?

MAIN IDEA

I will convert customary units of capacity.

SC Academic Standards

4-5.8 Recall equivalencies associated with liquid volume, time, weight, and length: **8 liquid ounces = 1 cup, 2 cups = 1 pint, 2 pints = 1 quart, 4 quarts = 1 gallon;** 365 days = 1 year, 52 weeks = 1 year; 16 ounces = 1 pound, 2,000 pounds = 1 ton; and 5,280 feet = 1 mile. *Also addresses 4-5.3.*

SC Math Online

macmillanmh.com
• Extra Examples
• Personal Tutor
• Self-Check Quiz

You can use multiplication and division to convert units.

- To change from a larger unit to a smaller unit, multiply.
- To change from a smaller unit to a larger unit, divide.

Customary Units of Capacity   Key Concepts

$$1 \text{ cup} = 8 \text{ fluid ounces (fl oz)}$$
$$2 \text{ cups (c)} = 1 \text{ pint}$$
$$2 \text{ pints (pt)} = 1 \text{ quart}$$
$$4 \text{ quarts (qt)} = 1 \text{ gallon (gal)}$$
$$1 \text{ gallon} = 128 \text{ fluid ounces}$$

Real-World EXAMPLE   Convert Capacity

1 **MEASUREMENT If Marcus has 2 gallons of laundry detergent, how many quarts does he have?**

Complete 2 gallons = ■ quarts. Since quarts are smaller than gallons, multiply.

2 gallons × 4 quarts = ■ quarts

> Multiply by 4 because there are 4 quarts in each gallon.

2 gallons × 4 quarts = 8 quarts

So, there are 8 quarts in 2 gallons.

2 Complete 8 pints = ▨ quarts.

Since quarts are larger than pints, divide.

8 pints ÷ 2 quarts = ▨ quarts

> Divide by 2 because there are 2 pints in each quart.

8 pints ÷ 2 quarts = 4 quarts

So, 8 pints = 4 quarts.

✓ CHECK What You Know

Complete. See Examples 1 and 2 (pp. 490–491)

1. 20 pt = ▨ qt

2. 3 c = ▨ fl oz

3. 4 qt = ▨ pt

4. Gwenith has 3 gallons of milk. How many quarts of milk does she have?

5. (Talk About It) Explain how to convert 6 pints to cups.

Practice and Problem Solving

SCAS • PASS
Extra Practice, p. R31

Complete. See Examples 1 and 2 (pp. 490–491)

6. 64 fl oz = ▨ c

7. 6 gal = ▨ qt

8. ▨ gal = 20 qt

9. 5 c = ▨ fl oz

10. ▨ pt = 30 c

11. ▨ c = 128 fl oz

Compare. Use >, <, or =.

12. 4 qt ● 10 pt

13. 10 gal ● 1,280 fl oz

14. 1 qt ● 2 c

15. Tomas is buying a 16-fluid ounce container of liquid dish soap. How many cups of dish soap is he buying?

16. Karen is buying 4 gallons of orange juice. How many quarts of orange juice is she buying?

H.O.T. Problem

17. WRITING IN ►MATH Write a rule for converting capacities measured in customary units.

GET READY to Learn

Hands-On Mini Activity

A liter is a metric unit of capacity. This container holds a liter.

Materials: 3 different containers, liter measuring tool

Step 1 Copy the table.

Object	Estimate	Actual

Step 2 Estimate.

Select three containers. Choose one and estimate whether it has a capacity that is greater than, less than, or equal to 1 liter. Record the estimate.

Step 3 Measure.

Fill a liter measuring tool with water. Pour the water into each of the containers. Tell whether each container is greater than, less than, or equal to 1 liter. Record the results.

In the metric system, the **liter** and **milliliter** are often used as units of measurement for capacity.

liter (L)

A bottle about this size can hold a liter.

milliliter (mL)

A milliliter is less than half of an eyedropper.

 SC Academic Standards

4-5.1 Use appropriate tools to measure objects to the nearest unit: …measuring liquid volume in cups, quarts, and **liters;** and measuring weight and mass in pounds, milligrams, and kilograms.

New Vocabulary

liter

milliliter

SC Math Online

macmillanmh.com

• Extra Examples
• Personal Tutor
• Self-Check Quiz

1 **MUGS** Decide whether 300 milliliters or 300 liters is the more reasonable estimate for the capacity of the mug.

Use logic to estimate the capacity.

300 mL

300 L

THINK 300 eye drops are reasonable.

THINK 300 bottles are too much.

So, 300 milliliters is the more reasonable estimate.

2 **POOLS** Decide whether 600 milliliters or 600 liters is the more reasonable estimate for the capacity of the swimming pool.

Use logic to estimate the capacity.

600 mL

600 L

THINK 600 eye drops is too small.

THINK 600 bottles are reasonable.

So, 600 milliliters is the more reasonable estimate.

CHECK What You Know

Choose the more reasonable estimate for each capacity. See Examples 1 and 2 (p. 493)

1.

1 mL or 1 L

2.

hand soap

220 mL or 220 L

3.

135 mL or 135 L

4. Jonah said he drank 3 liters of water after his soccer game. Is this a reasonable statement? Explain.

5. **Talk About It** Describe the unit of capacity you would use to measure the capacity of a bottle of medicine.

Choose the more reasonable estimate for each capacity.

See Examples 1 and 2 (p. 493)

6.

150 mL or 150 L

7.

120 mL or 120 L

8.

500 mL or 500 L

9.

700 mL or 700 L

10.

1 mL or 1 L

11.

30 mL or 30 L

12. Jenna said that she took 4 milliliters of medicine for her cold. Is this a reasonable statement? Explain.

13. Select three containers. Estimate and then measure whether each container has a capacity that is greater than, less than, or equal to 1 liter.

Object	Estimate	Actual

H.O.T. Problems

14. OPEN ENDED Identify four objects in your house that can hold more than 1 liter.

15. CHALLENGE Suppose you have a 4-liter bucket and a 7-liter bucket. You need 3 liters of water for an aquarium. Explain how to get 3 liters of water if neither bucket is marked.

16. WRITING IN ▶MATH How many milliliters are in 15 liters? Explain.

17. Theo drank 64 fluid ounces of water in one day. Which of the following is equal to the amount of water Theo drank? (Lesson 12-2)

A 4 cups   **C** 4 quarts

B 4 pints   **D** 4 gallons

18. Which is the best estimate of the capacity of a glass of iced tea? (Lesson 12-3)

F 250 L   **H** 250 lb

G 250 mL   **J** 250 fl oz

Spiral Review

Complete. (Lesson 12-2)

19. 12 gal = ▨ qt

20. 32 fl oz = ▨ c

21. ▨ pt = 18 c

Choose the most reasonable estimate for each capacity. (Lesson 12-1)

22.

A 2 fl oz   **C** 2 qt

B 2 c   **D** 2 gal

23.

F 78 fl oz   **H** 78 qt

G 78 c   **J** 78 gal

Tell whether the figures appear to be congruent. Write *yes* or *no*. If they are, describe the movements that show the congruence. (Lesson 10-7)

24.
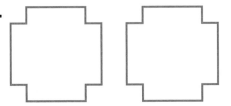

25.

Multiply. Check for reasonableness. (Lesson 6-6)

26. $\begin{array}{r} 218 \\ \times\ 3 \\ \hline \end{array}$

27. $\begin{array}{r} 896 \\ \times\ 5 \\ \hline \end{array}$

28. $\begin{array}{r} 2{,}731 \\ \times\ \ \ \ 7 \\ \hline \end{array}$

29. Matt drank 22 fluid ounces of grape juice in one day. Is it reasonable to say that he drank more than 3 cups of grape juice that day? Explain. (Lesson 6-2)

Explore

In this activity, you will measure the weight of objects. The **weight** of an object is how heavy it is.

MAIN IDEA

I will estimate and measure weight.

SC Academic Standards

4-5.1 Use appropriate tools to measure objects to the nearest unit: measuring length in quarter inches, centimeters, and millimeters; measuring liquid volume in cups, quarts, and liters; and **measuring weight** and mass **in pounds,** milligrams, and kilograms.

You Will Need
chalkboard eraser
balance scale
glue bottle

ACTIVITY — Measure Weight

Step 1 Copy the table.

Object	Estimate	Actual
Eraser		
Glue bottle		
Math book		
Object of your choice		

Step 2 Estimate.

Estimate the weight of a chalkboard eraser. Record the estimate.

Step 3 Measure.

Place the eraser on one side of a balance scale. Set ounce or pound weights on the other side until the sides are balanced. Record the actual weight. Repeat Steps 2 and 3 for the other objects.

Think About It

1. Order the four objects you weighed in the activity from greatest to least weight.

2. Use the weights of the objects you found to estimate the weight of two other objects in your classroom. Weigh the objects. Were your estimations close?

3. Is the total weight of the four objects you measured greater than 2 pounds? Explain.

 CHECK **What You Know**

4. How many 1-ounce weights are needed to balance the scale when a 1-pound weight is in the other pan?

5. How many ounces are in two pounds?

6. How many ounces are in four pounds?

Compare. Use >, <, or =.

7. 46 ounces ● 3 pounds

8. 5 pounds ● 78 ounces

9. 96 ounces ● 6 pounds

10. 7 pounds ● 110 ounces

11. 130 ounces ● 8 pounds

12. 9 pounds ● 145 ounces

13. Identify three objects in your classroom that weigh more than an eraser and less than your math book. Estimate each object's weight. Then weigh each object and record the exact weight in a table like the one shown below.

Object	Estimate	Actual

14. **WRITING IN ►MATH** Write a sentence that describes the relationship that is usually found between an object's size and weight.

GET READY to Learn

Suzie's father went to the store to buy some sugar for their favorite recipe. Suzie wondered how much the bag of sugar weighed.

MAIN IDEA

I will estimate and measure customary units of weight.

SC Academic Standards

4-5.1 Use appropriate tools to measure objects to the nearest unit: ...measuring weight and mass **in pounds,** milligrams, and kilograms.

New Vocabulary

weight
ounce
pound
ton

SC Math Online

macmillanmh.com
• Extra Examples
• Personal Tutor
• Self-Check Quiz

The **weight** of an object is how heavy it is. The customary units of weight are **ounce (oz)**, **pound (lb)**, and **ton (T)**.

1 ounce   1 pound   1 ton

Real-World EXAMPLE   Estimate Weight

1 FOOD Which is a more reasonable unit to use for the weight of a bag of sugar, ounces or pounds?

A small packet of sugar would be weighed in ounces.

A bag of sugar is much larger and would be weighed in pounds.

Real-World EXAMPLE Estimate Weight

2) PLANTS Which is the most reasonable estimate for the weight of a leaf: 1 ounce, 1 pound, 1 ton, or 10 tons?

Compare the weight of a leaf to the weight of objects that you know. A leaf weighs less than a pineapple or one pound.

Objects that weigh less than one pound are weighed in ounces. The only option that contains ounces is **1 ounce**.

CHECK What You Know

Choose the most reasonable estimate for the weight of each object.

See Examples 1 and 2 (pp. 498–499)

1. paper airplane

   A 4 ounces   **C** 4 pounds

   B 40 ounces   **D** 4 tons

2. helicopter

   F 5 ounces   **H** 5 tons

   G 500 ounces   **J** 500 tons

3. rabbit

   A 4 ounces   **C** 40 pounds

   B 4 pounds   **D** 4 tons

4. chair

   F 5 ounces   **H** 50 tons

   G 50 pounds   **J** 500 tons

5. Is it more reasonable to say that a fourth grade student weighs 56 ounces, 56 pounds, or 5 tons? Explain.

6. **Talk About It** Does an object that is small always weigh less than an object that is large? Explain.

Lesson 12-4 Customary Units of Weight **499**

Choose the most reasonable estimate for the weight of each object.

See Examples 1 and 2 (pp. 498–499)

7. acorn

A 1 ounce

B 11 ounces

C 1 pound

D 1 ton

8. bed

F 20 ounces

G 20 pounds

H 200 pounds

J 20 tons

9. shell

A 4 ounces

B 4 pounds

C 400 pounds

D 4 tons

10. camper

F 3 ounces

G 3 pounds

H 300 pounds

J 3 tons

11. goldfish

A 2 ounces

B 2 pounds

C 20 pounds

D 2 tons

12. desk

F 18 ounces

G 18 pounds

H 180 pounds

J 1 ton

South Carolina Data File

Kings Mountain State Park has a horseback riding trail loop over 15 miles long.

13. Is it reasonable to say that two adult horses weigh one ton? Explain.

14. Is it reasonable to say that a herd of eight adult horses weighs 3 tons? Explain.

Source: South Carolina State Parks

H.O.T. Problem

15. **NUMBER SENSE** Estimate the weight of three objects in your desk. Then weigh. Order the objects from greatest to least weight.

Choose the most reasonable estimate for each capacity. (Lesson 12-1)

1.

A 5 pints
B 5 gallons
C 5 fluid ounces
D 5 cups

2.

F 16 fluid ounces
G 16 cups
H 16 pints
J 16 gallons

3. Wendy is washing her mother's car. Is it reasonable to say that she will need about 16 pints of water? Explain.

4. Adamo is filling his cat's water bowl. Is it reasonable to say that he will need about 8 fluid ounces of water? Explain.

Complete. (Lesson 12-2)

5. 6 c = ▧ fl oz

6. ▧ gal = 8 qt

7. ▧ pt = 30 c

8. 20 pt = ▧ qt

Compare. Use >, <, or =. (Lesson 12-2)

9. 5 pt ● 3 qt

10. 1 c ● 7 fl oz

11. MULTIPLE CHOICE Which of the comparisons is true? (Lesson 12-2)

A 4 qt > 10 pt
B 6 pt < 11 c
C 1 gal > 5 qt
D 16 oz < 2 gal

12. MULTIPLE CHOICE Which of the following is a reasonable estimate? (Lesson 12-3)

F A glass of water can hold about 10 milliliters of water.

G A swimming pool can hold about 15 liters of water.

H A bottle of juice has a capacity of 100 milliliters.

J A bucket can hold about 5 liters of water.

Choose the more reasonable estimate for each capacity. (Lesson 12-3)

13.

600 L or 600 mL

14.

3 mL or 3 L

15. Choose the most reasonable estimate for the weight of a guinea pig. (Lesson 12-4)

A 2 pounds
B 12 pounds
C 120 pounds
D 2 tons

16. **WRITING IN ►MATH** Explain how metric units of capacity are related. (Lesson 12-3)

Problem-Solving Strategy

MAIN IDEA I will solve problems using logical reasoning.

 SCAS **4-1.1 Analyze information to solve increasingly more sophisticated problems.**

Adina, Tonisha, and Carl are each writing a report. The reports are about elephants, lions, and monkeys. Adina is writing about an animal whose weight is measured in tons. Carl is writing about an animal whose average weight is 375 pounds. Which animal is each student writing a report about?

Understand	**What facts do you know?** • Adina is writing about an animal whose weight is in tons. • Carl is writing about an animal whose weight is 375 pounds. **What do you need to find?** • The animal each student is writing about.
Plan	You can make a table and use logical reasoning to solve.
Solve	Place an X in the boxes that you know cannot be correct. • Adina must be writing about elephants because the other two animals' weights are in pounds. • Carl must be writing about lions because monkeys weigh much less than 300 pounds.

	Elephant	Lion	Monkey
Adina	yes	X	X
Tonisha	X	X	yes
Carl	X	yes	X

	So, Adina is writing about elephants, Tonisha is writing about monkeys, and Carl is writing about lions.
Check	Look back. The answer makes sense for the facts given in the problem. So, the answer is correct. ✔

ANALYZE the Strategy

Refer to the problem on the previous page.

1. Explain how logical reasoning helped to solve the problem.

2. Why do you think a table was used in solving the problem?

3. Suppose a rhinoceros is being written about instead of a monkey. Would it be possible to determine which animal each person is writing about?

PRACTICE the Strategy

SCAS • PASS

Extra Practice, p. R32

Solve. Use logical reasoning.

4. Three dogs are named Max, Sam, and Rufus. One is a collie, one is a spaniel, and one is a pug. Sam is not the collie. The spaniel's name is the longest. What are the names of each dog?

5. Hector arranges the cards in a row. The 2 is between the two odd numbered cards. The 4 has no card to its left. The 3 has cards on both sides. What is the order?

6. There are 4 people in a line. Tiernon is at the end. Juan is second in line. Moses is in front of Tiernon. Amy is first. What is the order of the people?

7. Manuella, Danny, and Tyson are wearing red, blue, and yellow T-shirts. Manuella is wearing red, and Danny is not wearing blue. What color T-shirt is each person wearing?

8. Jesse, Kata, Romeo, and Sheldon play basketball. Their numbers are 5, 7, 9, and 12. Jesse's number equals the number of letters in his name. Kata's is a two-digit number, while Romeo's number is not a prime number. What is Sheldon's number?

9. Lizzy has dogs, birds, and fish. She has twice as many dogs as birds. She has three more fish than dogs. She has two birds. How many dogs and fish does she have?

10. Copy and complete the table below. Use the digits 1, 2, 3, and 4 so that each row and column has each digit listed one time.

2	3	■	1
1	4	■	2
3	■	2	4
4	■	■	3

11. **WRITING IN ►MATH** Explain what it means to use logical reasoning.

12-6 Convert Customary Units of Weight

SC Academic Standards

4-5.8 Recall equivalencies associated with liquid volume, time, **weight,** and length: 8 liquid ounces = 1 cup, 2 cups = 1 pint, 2 pints = 1 quart, 4 quarts = 1 gallon; 365 days = 1 year, 52 weeks = 1 year; **16 ounces = 1 pound, 2,000 pounds = 1 ton;** and 5,280 feet = 1 mile. *Also addresses 4-5.3.*

GET READY to Learn

Leigh needs to buy 2 pounds of hamburger for dinner. The package she found was 32 ounces. Does 32 ounces equal 2 pounds?

Recall that to convert from a larger unit to a smaller unit, multiply. To convert from a smaller unit to a larger unit, divide.

Units of Weight   Key Concepts

16 ounces (oz) = 1 pound (lb)

2,000 pounds (lb) = 1 ton (T)

Real-World EXAMPLE   Convert Customary Weights

1 **FOOD Is 32 ounces of hamburger equal to 2 pounds of hamburger?**

One Way: Divide	Another Way: Multiply
Convert 32 ounces to pounds. Ounces are smaller than pounds. Divide.	Convert 2 pounds to ounces. Pounds are larger than ounces. Multiply.
32 ÷ 16 = ■	2 × 16 = ■
Divide by 16 because there are 16 ounces in a pound.	Multiply by 16 because there are 16 ounces in a pound.
So, 32 ounces = 2 pounds.	So, 2 pounds = 32 ounces.

So, 32 ounces of hamburger equals 2 pounds of hamburger.

A ton is a very heavy unit of measurement. Recall that there are 2,000 pounds in one ton.

Real-World **EXAMPLE**   **Convert Customary Weights**

② **DINOSAURS** Use the table to find how many pounds a Stegosaurus weighed.

Dinosaur Weights	
Dinosaur	**Weight (tons)**
Allosaurus	2
Megalosaurus	1
Stegasaurus	3
Supersaurus	60
Tyrannosaurus	8

Source: Arts & Letters Corporation

To find the weight of a Stegosaurus in pounds, multiply the number of tons by 2,000.

$3 \times 2,000 = \blacksquare$
$3 \times 2,000 = 6,000$

THINK $3 \times 2 = 6$
$3 \times 20 = 60$
$3 \times 200 = 600$
So, $3 \times 2,000 = 6,000$.

So, a Stegosaurus weighed 6,000 pounds.

CHECK **What You Know**

Complete. See Examples 1 and 2 (pp. 504–505)

1. 4 lb = $\blacksquare$ oz

2. 48 oz = $\blacksquare$ lb

3. 4,000 lb = $\blacksquare$ T

4. $\blacksquare$ T = 6,000 lb

5. $\blacksquare$ oz = 1 lb 4 oz

6. $\blacksquare$ lb = 4 T and 100 lb

7. A hippopotamus eats 100 pounds of food a day. How many days would it take the hippo to eat one ton of food?

8. An ostrich egg weighs 64 ounces. Is the weight of the ostrich egg greater than 5 pounds? Explain.

9. **Talk About It** Explain why you multiply to convert a larger unit of measure to a smaller unit of measure.

Complete. See Examples 1 and 2 (pp. 504–505)

10. 1 lb = ▪ oz

11. 160 oz = ▪ lb

12. ▪ T = 8,000 lb

13. 5 lb = ▪ oz

14. ▪ lb = 3 T and 600 lb

15. ▪ oz = 3 lb and 6 oz

16. Algebra Copy and complete the table below.

Pounds	6	▪	8	▪
Ounces	▪	112	▪	144

17. A baby blue whale weighs about 3,000 pounds and can gain about 200 pounds each day. About how many days would it take a baby blue whale to gain 1 ton of weight?

18. The weight capacity of a bridge is 3 tons. Three trucks need to cross the bridge at the same time. If each truck weighs 1,800 pounds, can they safely cross at the same time? Explain.

Real-World PROBLEM SOLVING

Animals Baby animals weigh different amounts at birth.

19. What is the fewest number of baby walruses whose weight would equal about 1 ton?

20. What is the greatest number of giant pandas whose weight would equal about 3 pounds?

21. An alligator nest usually contains about 30 eggs. What will the total weight of the babies be in pounds after all 30 eggs hatch?

Animal	Birth Weight
Alligator	2 ounces
Giraffe	100–150 pounds
Giant panda	3 to 5 ounces
Walrus	100–160 pounds

Source: San Diego Zoo

H.O.T. Problems

22. OPEN ENDED Give two examples of objects that can be measured in tons and two examples of objects that cannot be measured in tons.

23. CHALLENGE Tiffany weighed 7 pounds 12 ounces when she was born. Her weight doubled after four months. How much did Tiffany weigh after four months?

24. WRITING IN ►MATH Explain how to convert 2 tons 1,265 pounds to pounds.

25. Which is the most reasonable measurement for a can of green beans? (Lesson 12-4)

A 13 ounces **C** 13 pounds

B 130 ounces **D** 13 tons

26. Russ paid $10 for dog food that costs $1.25 per pound. Which is the most reasonable estimate for the amount of dog food Russ bought? (Lesson 12-4)

F 8 ounces **H** 80 pounds

G 8 pounds **J** 8 tons

27. Which table represents the relationship between pounds and ounces? (Lesson 12-6)

A

Pounds	1	2	3	4
Ounces	16	32	48	64

B

Pounds	1	2	3	4
Ounces	8	16	24	32

C

Pounds	1	2	3	4
Ounces	16	24	32	40

D

Pounds	16	32	48	64
Ounces	1	2	3	4

Spiral Review

28. Greg, Liza, Erina, and Julius each play a sport. The sports they play are baseball, soccer, tennis, and volleyball. Liza uses a racquet. Julius does not play volleyball. Greg uses a mitt. Which sport does each student play? (Lesson 12-5)

Choose the more reasonable estimate for the weight of each object. (Lesson 12-4)

29.

10 ounces or 10 pounds

30.

50 ounces or 50 pounds

Choose the more reasonable estimate for each capacity. (Lesson 12-3)

31.

225 mL or 225L

32.

2 mL or 2L

Lesson 12-6 Convert Customary Units of Weight **507**

Metric Units of Mass

MAIN IDEA

I will estimate and measure mass and learn the difference between weight and mass.

SC Academic Standards

4-5.1 Use appropriate tools to measure objects to the nearest unit: measuring length in quarter inches, centimeters and millimeters; measuring liquid volume in cups, quarts, and liters; and **measuring** weight and **mass in** pounds, **milligrams, and kilograms.**

New Vocabulary

mass
gram
kilogram
milligram

SC Math Online

macmillanmh.com

GET READY to Learn

Hands-On Mini Activity

You can use a balance scale to find the mass of objects.

Materials: balance scale, four different objects, gram weights

Step 1 Copy the table.

Object	Estimate	Mass (grams)

Step 2 Estimate.

Select four objects that will fit on one side of the balance scale. Choose one and estimate its mass in grams. Record the estimate.

Step 3 Measure.

Set the object on one side of the balance scale. On the other side, set gram weights until both sides are balanced. Record the actual mass. Repeat Steps 2 and 3 for the other objects.

1. Did the larger objects have a greater mass than the smaller objects?

2. Explain how a larger object can have less mass than a smaller object.

3. How many milligrams does each object weigh if 1 gram = 1,000 milligrams?

Mass is the amount of matter an object has. The mass of an object is not affected by gravity. In contrast, an object's weight differs depending on gravity.

Units of Mass		
Milligram (mg)	**Gram (g)**	**Kilogram (kg)**
The mass of about 25 grains of sugar is about 1 milligram.	The mass of a penny is about 1 gram.	The mass of six medium apples is about 1 kilogram.

You can use what you know about the gram and kilogram to estimate mass in milligrams.

Real-World EXAMPLE   Estimate Mass

① **TECHNOLOGY** **Which is the more reasonable estimate for the mass of the laptop, 2 milligrams, 2 grams, or 2 kilograms?**

If the laptop has a mass of 2 grams, it would have the same mass as 2 pennies. This is not a reasonable estimate.
So, a reasonable estimate is 2 kilograms.

 CHECK What You Know

Choose the more reasonable estimate for the mass of each object.

See Example 1 (p. 509)

1. ball cap

25 mg or 25 g

2. polar bear

450 g or 450 kg

3. Is it more reasonable to say that Cheryl lifts dumbbells that have a mass of 30 grams or 30 kilograms? Explain.

4. **Talk About It** Explain the difference between weight and mass.
Look back at Explore 11-4 if needed.

Choose the more reasonable estimate for the mass of each object.

See Example 1 (p. 509)

5. ant

3 mg or 3 g

6. box of crayons

100 g or 100 kg

7. cooler

25 g or 25 kg

8. kidney bean

410 mg or 410 g

9. tool box

30 g or 30 kg

10. trampoline

50 mg or 50 kg

11. The table lists items that can be found in a classroom. Estimate and then measure the mass of each object. Copy and complete the table.

Mass of Classroom Objects		
Object	Estimate	Actual
Glue bottle	■	■
Paper clip	■	■
Pencil	■	■
Stapler	■	■

12. Tyler bought a large bag of peanuts at a baseball game. Is it more reasonable to say that the mass of the peanuts is 1 gram or 1 kilogram?

13. Alicia is buying 6 oranges that cost $1 per kilogram. Is it reasonable to say that the cost of the oranges will be greater than $6? Explain.

H.O.T. Problems

14. OPEN ENDED Name five classroom objects that have a mass greater than 1 kilogram.

15. CHALLENGE Which weighs more, an astronaut on Earth or the same astronaut on the Moon? Explain.

16. WRITING IN ►MATH Write about a real-world situation in which you would have to decide which metric unit to use to measure an object's mass.

Massive Estimates

Estimate and Measure Mass

You will need: 10 index cards, pencils

Get Ready!

Players: 2 players

Get Set!

Label each index card as shown. Then label the back of each index card with the correct unit of measurement that would be used to find each object's mass.

Go!

- Shuffle the cards. Lay the stack of cards faceup on the table.

- Player 1 shows the object on the first card to Player 2.

- Player 2 decides whether the mass of the object would be measured in grams or kilograms.

- Player 2 keeps the card if his or her answer is correct. If Player 2 is incorrect, Player 1 keeps the card.

- Players take turns showing each other cards.

- Continue playing until all of the cards are used. The player with more cards wins.

| bookshelf | computer |

| desk | eraser | globe |

| glue bottle | pencil |

| pencil sharpener | stapler | scissors |

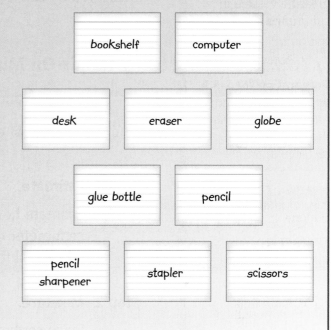

Estimate and Measure Volume

GET READY to Learn

Volume is the amount of space a three-dimensional figure contains. It is measured in **cubic units**. Each side of a centimeter cube has a length of 1 centimeter. So, the volume for a rectangular prism is measured in **cubic centimeters**.

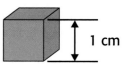

1 cm

 ## Hands-On Mini Activity

Materials: cube and rectangular prism, centimeter cubes

Find the volume of each three-dimensional figure.

Step 1 Estimate.

Estimate how many centimeter cubes it will take to fill the cube.

Step 2 Measure.

Place centimeter cubes inside the cube. When it is full, count the centimeter cubes. The number of centimeter cubes that the cube will hold is the volume of the cube. Compare this with your estimate.

Step 3 Apply.

Repeat Steps 1 and 2 for the rectangular prism.

1. What is the volume of the rectangular prism?

2. Which has a greater volume, the prism or the cube? how much greater?

To find the volume of a figure, count the number of cubic units needed to fill the figure.

> ## Volume
>
> Volume is the number of cubic units needed to fill a three-dimensional figure.

EXAMPLE Find Volume

Remember

To help you determine volume, you can build a model using base-ten blocks.

1 **Find the volume of the cube shown.**

Count the number of cubes it takes to make the object.

The cube shown has 4 layers. Each layer has 16 cubes.

one layer   four layers

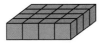

16 cubes $4 \times 16 = 64$ cubes

So, the volume of the cube is 64 cubic units.

You can estimate to find the volume of a three-dimensional figure that has different numbers of cubes in each layer.

EXAMPLE Estimate Volume

2 **Estimate the volume of the figure shown.**

Estimate the volume by counting the cubes that can be seen. Then add the number of cubes that cannot be seen.

Four cubes can be seen in the top layer.   Five cubes can be seen in the bottom layer and three cubes are hidden.

So, the volume of the figure is $4 + 8$ or 12 cubic units.

Find the volume of each figure. See Example 1 (p. 513)

1.

2.

Estimate the volume of each figure. See Example 2 (p. 513)

3.

4.

5. Rona has 12 cubes. Model and describe a rectangular prism she could create that has a volume of 12 cubic units.

6. Talk About It — The volume of a cube is 8 cubic units. What is the height of the cube? Explain.

Practice and Problem Solving

SCAS • PASS
Extra Practice, p. R33

Find the volume of each figure. See Example 1 (p. 513)

7.

8.

9.

Estimate the volume of each figure. See Example 2 (p. 513)

10.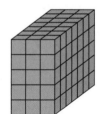

11.

12.

13. A book is 9 units long, 5 units wide, and 2 units high. Use models to find the volume.

14. A shoe box is 10 units long, 6 units wide, and 4 units high. Use models to find the volume.

15. Toby and Lena each have a box. Toby's box is 8 units long, 4 units wide, and 1 unit tall. Lena's box is 5 units long, 7 units wide, and 1 unit tall. Whose box has a volume of 32 cubic units? Explain.

16. Vijay is making a tower 3 units long, 4 units wide, and 5 units tall. So far, the tower is 3 units long, 3 units wide, and 3 units tall. Find the volume that is left to be added to the tower. Explain.

H.O.T. Problems

17. OPEN ENDED Give the dimensions of a rectangular prism that has a volume greater than 50 cubic units.

18. WHICH ONE DOESN'T BELONG? Identify the figure that does not belong with the other three. Explain.

figure A

figure B

figure C

figure D

19. WRITING IN ►MATH Explain the difference between area and volume.

PASS Practice 4-5.1, 5-5.5

20. Which of these units would best measure the mass of a watermelon? (Lesson 12-7)

 A cups

 B grams

 C kilograms

 D meters

21. Which is the best estimate for the volume of the prism? (Lesson 12-8)

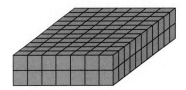

 F 14 cubic units   **H** 77 cubic units

 G 22 cubic units   **J** 154 cubic units

Spiral Review

Choose the more reasonable estimate for the mass of each object. (Lesson 12-7)

22. cherry

5 g or 5 kg

23. wagon

15 g or 15 kg

Complete. (Lesson 12-6)

24. 1 lb = ■ oz   **25.** 80 oz = ■ lb   **26.** 8,000 lb = ■ T

27. Alex's smoothie is 32 ounces. Minda's smoothie is half the size of Alex's smoothie. Tyrell's smoothie is 8 ounces less than Alex's smoothie. How many ounces is each person's smoothie? (Lesson 12-5)

Problem Solving in Science

Tide Pool Ecosystems

Tide pools are rocky areas on the edge of an ocean that are filled with sea water. Many plants and animals live there. Some animals that can be found in tide pools are starfish, mussels, and crabs. Kelp and other sea plants are also found in tide pools.

Life is tough for plants and animals that live in tide pools.

Parts of the shore are covered and then uncovered as tides go in and out. The plants and animals that live in tide pools must avoid being washed away by waves, keep from drying out in the sun, and avoid predators. The tide pool ecosystem is the hardest ecosystem to recreate in an aquarium.

mussel

crab

starfish

SCAS 4-5.3 Use equivalencies to convert units of measure within the U.S. Customary System:
...**converting weight in** ounces, **pounds,** and tons; **converting liquid volume in** cups, pints,
quarts, and gallons; and converting time in years, months, weeks, days, hours, minutes, and seconds.

A starfish can grow back an arm if it loses one.

Aquariums

Capacity (gal)	Length (in.)	Width (in.)
20	24	12
25	30	12
30	36	18
40	48	12

Real-World Math

Use the information above to solve each problem.

1. Elias has decided to buy a 20-gallon aquarium. He will use a one-quart container to fill the aquarium. How many times will Elias use the one-quart container to fill the 20-gallon aquarium?

2. Suppose Elias has decided to get the 25-gallon aquarium. How many times will he need to use his one-quart container to fill the aquarium?

3. How many more times would Elias have to use a quart container to fill a 30-gallon aquarium than you would for a 40-gallon aquarium?

4. If Elias buys the 20-gallon aquarium, what would the length and width of the aquarium be in feet?

5. If Elias buys the 40-gallon aquarium, what would the length and width of the aquarium be in feet?

6. Elias is also buying the gravel to place in the bottom of his 20-gallon aquarium. He needs one pound of gravel for every gallon of water. How many ounces of gravel will he need for the 20-gallon aquarium?

7. If Elias buys the 25-gallon aquarium, how many ounces of gravel will he need?

<u>MAIN IDEA</u> I will solve problems by choosing the best strategy.

 **SCAS** 4-3.3 Use a rule to complete a sequence or a table.

P.S.I. TEAM +

AIDEN: I have a video game system. Games cost $20. Felice has a different video game system. Her games cost $15. How many video games can we each buy if we each have $60?

YOUR MISSION: Find how many games each person can buy.

Understand	Games for Aiden's game system cost $20. Games for Felice's game system cost $15. Each has $60 to spend on video games. Find how many games each person can buy.
Plan	Organize the data to show the number of games and the total amount of money spent.

Solve

Aiden	
Rule: $t = 20g$	
Games	Total ($)
1	20
2	40
3	60

Felice	
Rule: $t = 15g$	
Games	Total ($)
1	15
2	30
3	45
4	60

Since Aiden's games cost more, he can buy only 3. Felice can buy 4.

Check	Look back. Since $20 \times 3 = 60$ and $15 \times 4 = 60$, you know that the answer is correct. ✔

Use any strategy shown below to solve. Tell what strategy you used.

PROBLEM-SOLVING STRATEGIES
- Act it out.
- Guess and check.
- Look for a pattern.
- Work a simpler problem.
- Use logical reasoning.

1. **Measurement** Keisha and Andy went hiking from 9:30 A.M. until 12:00 P.M. After lunch, they hiked for another hour and 40 minutes. How many minutes did they spend hiking?

2. For every day at school that no students are absent, a teacher put 3 marbles in a jar. If the jar holds 426 marbles, how many days of no absences will it take to fill the jar?

3. A family spends $22 on tickets for a community play. If there are two adults, how many children are with them?

Community Play
-TICKETS-
CHILDREN $3   ADULTS $5

4. **Measurement** A roller coaster car carries 32 people every 10 minutes. There are 572 people in line in front of Ruben. About how long will it take for him to ride the roller coaster?

5. Dora took 8 photos with her camera. She takes 2 more photos each day for a week. How many more days does she need to take photos to have 30?

6. Sally gave a cashier $25 for two CDs. They cost the same amount. She got $3 back. How much did each CD cost?

7. **Algebra** April's party is being held at an arcade. Each guest will be given 16 tokens to play games. Copy and complete the table to find how many tokens are needed for 12 guests.

Guests	Tokens
2	32
4	64
6	96
8	128
10	▦
12	▦

8. A concert hall has 13 rows of seats. The hall has a total of 221 seats. Write a number sentence that could be used to find the number of seats in each row.

9. Myron has 2 red marbles for every one green marble. He has three times as many blue marbles as red marbles. Myron has four red marbles. How many green and blue marbles does he have?

10. **WRITING IN ►MATH** Identify the problem-solving strategy you used to find the answer to Exercise 9. Explain how you found the answer.

GET READY to Learn

Hands-On Mini Activity

Materials: stopwatch

You can use a stopwatch to find elapsed time.

Step 1 **Copy the table.**

Activity	Start Time	End Time	Elapsed Time
Write alphabet	■	■	■
Name 10 states	■	■	■
Jump 20 times	■	■	■

Step 2 **Measure.**

Write the alphabet while your partner uses a stopwatch to time you. Record the start and end times. Complete the next two activities while your partner times you. Do not reset the stopwatch between the activities. Record the start and end times.

Step 3 **Copy and complete the table.**

To find the elapsed times, subtract the start times from the end times. Find the elapsed time between each event. Record the results.

1. Which event took the longest time? the shortest time?

2. Select one of the elapsed times. List two more activities that might take that long.

The last column of your table gives examples of elapsed time. **Elapsed time** is the amount of time between the beginning and ending of an activity.

Remember

60 minutes = 1 hour

1 **TRAVEL** It takes Louisa one hour and 30 minutes to travel to her aunt's house. If she leaves at 4:00 P.M., what time will she get to her aunt's house?

Add 1 hour and 30 minutes to 4:00 p.m

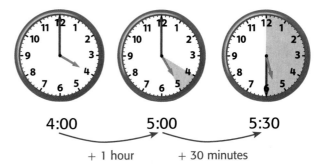

4:00   5:00   5:30

     + 1 hour   + 30 minutes

So, Louisa will get to her aunt's house at 5:30 p.m

2 The clock shows the time Justin's soccer practice started. It ends at 5:30 P.M. Find the elapsed time.

Find the elapsed time between 3:15 p.m and 5:30 p.m

3:15   4:15   5:15   5:30

   1 hour   1 hour   15 minutes

1 HOUR + 1 hour + 15 minutes = 2 hours 15 minutes

So, the elapsed time is 2 hours 15 minutes.

CHECK What You Know

The following are movie times. Find the length of each movie. See Examples 1 and 2 (p. 521)

1. Start Time   End Time

2. Start Time   End Time

3. Julian's family went to the library at the time shown at the right. How much time elapsed if they stayed until 4:00?

See Example 1 (p. 521)

4. Kayla went to sleep at the time shown at the right and awoke at 6:30 A.M. Explain how to find how long Kayla slept.

See Example 2 (p. 521)

The following are times of baseball games. Find the length of each game. See Examples 1 and 2 (p. 521)

5. Start Time  End Time

6. Start Time  End Time

7. Start Time   End Time
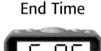

8. Start Time   End Time

Find each elapsed time. See Examples 1 and 2 (p. 521)

9. The clock shows when Helen began reading her book. It is 12:50 when she stops.

10. The clock shows when Chris went to the park. He stays until 5:15 P.M.

Real-World PROBLEM SOLVING

Science The table shows the schedule of an aquarium's daily presentations.

11. Albert attended the Amazon Creature Feature, which ended at 2:45 P.M. How long did it last?

12. Next, Albert attended the Reptile Report. It ended at 3:45 P.M. How long was this presentation?

13. Albert attended You "Otter" Know This last. It lasted 1 hour and 30 minutes. If it takes Albert 20 minutes to get home, did he make it home in time to eat at 6 P.M.? Explain.

Daily Presentations Schedule	
Presentation	**Time**
Amazon Creature Feature	1:30 P.M.
Diver in the Water	11:30 A.M. and 1:30 P.M.
Dolphin Training Lesson	11 A.M. and 1 P.M.
Reptile Report	3 P.M.
You "Otter" Know This	10 A.M. and 4 P.M.

H.O.T. Problems

14. CHALLENGE Dennis earns $5 for each hour he works. One day he worked from 8:00 A.M. until 12:00 P.M., had lunch, and then worked for 3 more hours. How much money did he earn that day?

15. FIND THE ERROR Haley and Hidalgo are finding elapsed time. Who is correct? Explain your reasoning.

Haley

It's 10:30 a.m. In 1 hour and 45 minutes, it will be 12:15 p.m.

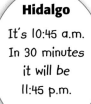

Hidalgo

It's 10:45 a.m. In 30 minutes it will be 11:45 p.m.

PASS Practice   5-5.5, 4-5.6

16. A pencil box is 6 units long, 3 units wide and 2 units high. What is its volume? (Lesson 12-8)

   A 32 cubic units   **C** 36 cubic units

   B 34 cubic units   **D** 38 cubic units

17. Gretchen downloaded music for 45 minutes. She began at 11:45 A.M. What time did she finish? (Lesson 12-10)

   F 11:00 A.M.   **H** 11:00 P.M.

   G 12:30 P.M.   **J** 12:30 A.M.

Spiral Review

18. Airports have limits on luggage weight. Is it more reasonable to say that an airport's weight limit is 35 grams or 35 kilograms? Explain. (Lesson 12-9)

Find the volume of each figure. (Lesson 12-8)

19.

20.

Choose the more reasonable estimate for the mass of each object. (Lesson 12-7)

21. dog

40g or 40 kg

22. hamster

500 g or 500 kg

 **FOLDABLES**
Study Organizer **GET READY to Study**

Be sure the following Key Vocabulary words and Key Concepts are written in your Foldable.

Measure Capacity, Weight, and Volume

Customary Units of Capacity
Convert Customary Units of Capacity
Metric Units of Capacity
Customary Units of Weight
Convert Customary Units of Weight
Metric Units of Mass
Estimate and Measure Volume
Elapsed Time

Key Concepts

• **Capacity** is the amount of liquid a container holds. The customary units of capacity are fluid ounces, cups, pints, gallons, and quarts. The metric units of capacity are liter and milliliter. (p. 486)

• The **weight** of an object is how heavy it is. Weight is measured in ounces, pounds, and tons. (p. 498)

• The **mass** of an object is the amount of matter it has. Mass is measured in grams and kilograms. (p. 509)

• **Volume** is the amount of space a three-dimensional figure contains. It is measured in cubic units. (p. 512)

• **Elapsed time** is the amount of time between the beginning and ending of an activity. (p. 520)

 Key Vocabulary

capacity (p. 486)
elapsed time (p. 520)
mass (p. 509)
volume (p. 512)
weight (p. 498)

 Vocabulary Check

Complete each sentence with the correct vocabulary word.

1. ____?____ is the amount of matter an object has.

2. The ____?____ of an object is how heavy it is.

3. ____?____ is the amount of time between the beginning and end of an activity.

4. ____?____ is measured in grams and kilograms.

5. ____?____ is the amount of space that a three-dimensional figure contains.

6. ____?____ is measured in ounces, pounds, and tons.

7. The amount of liquid a container holds is its ____?____.

Lesson-by-Lesson Review

4-5.1

12-1 Customary Units of Capacity (pp. 486–489)

Example 1

Carrie is pouring fruit juice into a punch bowl. Is the most reasonable estimate for the capacity of the bowl 2 fluid ounces, 2 cups, 2 quarts, or 2 gallons?

The punch is a large amount. So, 2 fluid ounces, 2 cups, and 2 quarts are too small. The most reasonable estimate for the capacity of the punch bowl is 2 gallons.

Choose the most reasonable estimate for each capacity.

8. **A** 4 fluid ounces
   B 4 cups
   C 4 quarts
   D 4 gallons

9. **F** 8 fluid ounces
   G 8 cups
   H 8 quarts
   J 8 gallons

10. **A** 3 fluid ounces
    B 3 cups
    C 3 quarts
    D 3 gallons

12-2 Convert Customary Units of Capacity (pp. 490–491)

4-5.8,
4-5.3

Example 2

Complete the conversion 3 c = ■ fl oz.

Since fluid ounces are smaller than cups, multiply.

3 cups × 8 fluid ounces = ■

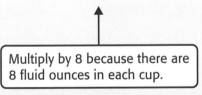
Multiply by 8 because there are 8 fluid ounces in each cup.

3 × 8 = 24

So, there are 24 fluid ounces in 3 cups.

Complete.

11. 16 fl oz = ■ c   **12.** 2 gal = ■ qt

13. ■ pt = 12 qt   **14.** ■ pt = 18 c

Compare. Use >, <, or =.

15. 5 qt ● 10 pt   **16.** 2 cups ● 18 fl oz

17. Chen is buying a 16-fluid ounce container of spaghetti sauce. How many cups of spaghetti sauce is he buying?

12-3 Metric Units of Capacity (pp. 492–495)

Example 3
Decide whether 700 mL or 700 L is the more reasonable estimate for the capacity of a bottle of salad dressing.

Use logic to estimate the capacity of the bottle of salad dressing.

700 mL   700 L

THINK 700 eyedrops is reasonable.

THINK 700 bottles is not reasonable.

So, 700 mL is a more reasonable estimate.

Choose the more reasonable estimate for each capacity.

18.

265 mL or 265 L

19.

6 mL or 6 L

20.

800 mL or 800 L

21. Carina said that her father's car's gas tank holds 200 liters of gas. Is that reasonable? Explain.

12-4 Customary Units of Weight (pp. 498–500)

Example 4
Which is the most reasonable estimate for the weight of a pencil case: 1 ounce, 1 pound, 10 pounds, or 10 tons?

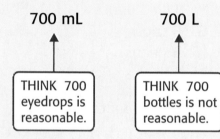

A pencil case weighs more than a strawberry or 1 ounce. A pencil case weighs less than 10 pineapples or 10 pounds. Tons weigh more than pounds, so the answer is 1 pound.

22. Choose the most reasonable estimate for the weight of the table.

A 8 ounces   **C** 800 pounds

B 80 pounds   **D** 8 tons

23. Tristan claimed some dinosaurs weighed 3 tons. Is Tristan's claim reasonable? Explain.

24. Annie claims her basketball weighs 50 lbs. Is Annie's claim reasonable?

Problem-Solving Strategy: Use Logical Reasoning (pp. 502–503)

Example 5

4-1.1

Jed, Sayra, Mark, and Ebony competed in a race. Jed came in third place. Ebony was faster than Mark. Sayra won the race. Which order did they finish the race?

Understand

Jed came in third place. Ebony was faster than Mark. Sayra won the race. Find the order they finished the race.

Plan

Use logical reasoning to solve.

Solve

Since Sayra won the race, she came in first place.

Jed came in third place.

Since Ebony was faster than Mark, she came in second place. Mark came in fourth place.

	1st Place	2nd Place	3rd Place	4th Place
Jed	X	X	yes	X
Sayra	yes	X	X	X
Mark	X	X	X	yes
Ebony	X	yes	X	X

The order was Sayra, Ebony, Jed, and Mark.

Check

Look back. The answer makes sense for the facts given in the problem. ✔

25. The Ruiz family is on a bike ride. Each person is riding either a bicycle or a tricycle. There are 5 members in the family and 11 wheels. The number of bicycles is four times the number of tricycles. How many tricycles and bicycles are there?

26. Felix, Laura, and Suki packed lunches with a peanut butter sandwich, a turkey sandwich, and a bologna sandwich. Laura's sandwich is shown. Suki's sandwich had bologna on it. Which sandwich did each person get in their lunch?

27. Rhonda, Jordan, and Mala were born in September, December, and June. Jordan's birthday is in the winter. The number of letters in Mala's name matches the number of letters in her birth month. In what month was each person born?

28. Bella has a brother named Ricardo and a sister named Rosa. The ages of the three children are 3, 5, and 10. Bella is twice as old as Ricardo. What are the ages of the children?

12-6 Convert Customary Units of Weight (pp. 504–507)

4-5.8,
4-5.3

Example 6
Shawn is holding a 5 pound bag of flour. How many ounces is this?

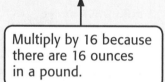

Convert 5 pounds to ounces. Pounds are larger than ounces. Multiply.

$$5 \times 16 = 80$$

Multiply by 16 because there are 16 ounces in a pound.

So, 5 pounds equals 80 ounces.

Complete.

29. 2,000 lb = ■ T

30. 32 oz = ■ lb

31. 16 oz and 1 lb = ■ lb

32. 1 lb = ■ oz

33. ■ lb = 3 T

34. ■ lb = 2 T and 2 lb

35. Benton uses 7 ounces of clay to make a vase. How many pounds of clay will he need to make 4 vases?

36. A sandwich shop uses 2 ounces of ham on a sandwich. If 20 sandwiches are made in one day, how many pounds of ham will be used?

12-7 Metric Units of Mass (pp. 508–510)

4-5.1

Example 7
Which is the more reasonable estimate for the mass of the dog: 20 grams or 20 kilograms?

If the dog has a mass of 20 grams, it would have the same mass as 20 pennies. This is not a reasonable estimate.

So, a reasonable estimate for the mass of the dog is 20 kg.

Choose the more reasonable estimate for the mass of each object.

37. pencil

38. chair

4 g or 4 kg   15 g or 15 kg

39. Is it more reasonable to say that the mass of a pair of scissors is 50 grams or 50 kilograms?

40. Is it more reasonable to say that the mass of a medium tub of popcorn is 1 gram or 1 kilogram?

12-8 Estimate and Measure Volume (pp. 512–515)

5-5.5

Example 8
Use models to find the volume of the cube shown to the right.

The cube shown has 3 layers. Each layer has 9 cubes.

one layer   three layers

9 cubes   9 × 3 = 27 cubes

So, the volume is 27 cubic units.

Find the volume of each figure.

41.   42.

Estimate the volume of each figure.

43.   44.

12-9 Problem-Solving Investigation: Choose a Strategy (pp. 518–519)

4-3.3

Example 9
Jamal's school is going to see a play. There are 230 seats in the theater. If every class has 25 students, how many classes can see the play at the same time?

There are 230 seats in the theater and 25 students in each class. Find how many classes can see the play at the same time.

Divide the number of seats in the theater by the number of students in each class.

seats in theater   students per class

230 ÷ 25 = 9 R5

So, 9 classes can see the play at the same time.

Adding 25 nine times equals 225. So, the answer is correct.

Use any strategy to solve.

45. Kelsey has a week to catch 30 insects for science class. Yesterday she caught 3. The insects she caught today are shown below. If she catches 5 more each day for 4 days, how many more will she need to catch to have 30?

46. Bobby went to the grocery store on Tuesday and tomatoes were $1 each. Jessica went to the store on Wednesday and the price of tomatoes had increased to $2 each. If both spend $12 on tomatoes, how many did each buy?

12-10 **Elapsed Time** (pp. 520–523)

4-5.6

Example 10
Lana started working on her homework at the time shown on the first clock below. She finished her homework at the time shown on the second clock below. How long did it take Lana to complete her homework?

You can find the elapsed time by counting the hours and minutes between 4:45 P.M. and 6:00 P.M.

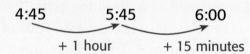

4:45   5:45   6:00

+ 1 hour   + 15 minutes

So, it took Lana 1 hour and 15 minutes to complete her homework.

Example 11
What time will it be in 3 hours and 45 minutes?

Add 3 hours and 45 minutes to 12:15.

12:15   1:15   2:15   3:15   4:00

+ 1 hour + 1 hour + 1 hour + 45 minutes

So, in 3 hours and 45 minutes it will be 4:00.

The following are times of football games. Find the length of each game.

47. Start Time   End Time

48. Start Time   End Time

Find each elapsed time.

49. Franklin walked in the park from 2:10 P.M. until the time shown on the clock.

50. Delia left the store at 7:05 P.M. The clock shows when she arrived home.

51. A school play started at 5:30 P.M. and ended at 7:25 P.M. How long was the play?

For Exercises 1 and 2, tell whether each statement is *true* or *false*.

1. Weight is the amount of matter an object has.

2. You can use a stopwatch to find elapsed time.

Choose the most reasonable estimate for each capacity.

3.

   A 6 fluid ounces
   B 6 cups
   C 6 quarts
   D 6 gallons

4.

   F 1 fluid ounce
   G 1 cup
   H 1 pint
   J 1 quart

Choose the most reasonable estimate for the weight of each object.

5. microscope

   A 7 tons
   B 70 pounds
   C 7 pounds
   D 7 ounces

6. bald eagle

   F 8 ounces
   G 8 pounds
   H 80 pounds
   J 8 tons

7. **MULTIPLE CHOICE** Which of the comparisons is false?

   A 3 qt > 2 pt   C 2 gal > 6 qt
   B 10 pt < 25 c   D 16 oz < 2 c

8. Pete, Tia, and Paz are playing soccer. Their jersey numbers are 4, 7, and 13. Tia's number equals the number of letters in her name. Pete's is a two-digit number. Find Paz's number.

Complete.

9. ■ lb = 4 T   10. 80 oz = ■ lb

Choose the more reasonable estimate for the mass of each object.

11. ruler

12. picture

20 g or 20 kg   10 g or 10 kg

Find the volume of each figure.

13.   14.

15. **MULTIPLE CHOICE** How much time passes from 4:15 p.m. to 5:30 p.m.?

   F 1 hour
   G 1 hour 15 minutes
   H 1 hour 30 minutes
   J 1 hour 45 minutes

16. Find the elapsed time. What time will it be in 4 hours and 40 minutes?

17. **WRITING IN ►MATH**
Explain how to find elapsed time.

PASS Practice
Cumulative, Chapters 1–12

Read each question. Then fill in the correct answer on the answer sheet provided by your teacher or on a sheet of paper.

1. Which unit of measure would be most reasonable to use when finding the capacity of a thermos?

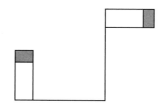

   A fluid ounces   **C** quarts

   B cups   **D** gallons

2. Percy is flying to his grandparents' house. It takes 25 minutes to drive to the airport. He needs to arrive at least 1 hour before his plane leaves. What other information is needed for Percy to arrive at the airport on time?

   F the time the plane leaves

   G how fast he drives

   H the distance he will fly

   J the amount of time he will fly

3. How many lines of symmetry does the figure have?

   A 0

   B 1

   C 2

   D 4

4. Which rule best describes the pattern of numbers below?

   4, 7, 10, 13, 16, 19, 22

   F Subtract 3.   **H** Add 3.

   G Subtract 4.   **J** Add 4.

5. Which term best describes the picture below?

   A dilation   **C** rotation

   B reflection   **D** translation

6. Isabel exercises every three days. If she exercised on Monday and Thursday, what are the next two days she will exercise?

   F Sunday and Tuesday

   G Sunday and Wednesday

   H Friday and Monday

   J Saturday and Monday

7. Rigo has $2,008 in his bank account. If he buys a laptop for $1,299, how much money will he have left?

   A $1,819   **C** $819

   B $1,291   **D** $709

8. Which unit of measure would be most reasonable to use when finding the capacity of cleaning solution a contact lens holds?

F gram   **H** liter

G kilogram   **J** milliliter

9. A vegetable garden is 8 yards long and 55 yards wide. What is the area, in square yards, of the garden?

A 440 square yards

B 430 square yards

C 425 square yards

D 420 square yards

10. The weight of a small puppy is best measured in what units?

F milligrams   **H** pounds

G grams   **J** ounces

PART 2   Short Response

Record your answers on the answer sheet provided by your teacher or on a sheet of paper.

11. How many cups equal 24 fluid ounces?

_____

12. A landscaper orders 3 tons of mulch. How many pounds are there in 3 tons?

_____

13. Compare 4 lb ● 48 oz. Use >, <, or =.

PART 3   Extended Response

Record your answers on the answer sheet provided by your teacher or on a sheet of paper.

14. Which unit of measure would be most reasonable to use when finding the capacity of bubble solution that a bottle of bubbles holds: fluid ounces, cups, pints, or quarts? Explain.

_____

15. Is it reasonable to say that the capacity of the bottle of bubbles shown above is 48 fluid ounces? Explain.

NEED EXTRA HELP?															
If You Missed Question...	1	2	3	4	5	6	7	8	9	10	11	12	13	14	15
Go to Lesson...	12-1	12-10	10-8	5-4	10-5	5-4	2-7	12-3	11-6	12-4	12-2	12-6	12-6	12-1	12-2
SC Academic Standards	4-5.1	4-5.6	5-4.6	4-3.2	4-4.3	4-3.1	3-2.3	4-5.1	4-5.5	4-5.1	4-5.3	4-5.3	4-5.3	4-5.1	4-5.3

CHAPTER 13

Describe and Compare Fractions

 **BIG Idea** What is a fraction?

A **fraction** is a number that names part of a whole or part of a set.

Example If you have a pizza that is cut into eight pieces, each piece would be *one eighth* or *one of eight* pieces.

 or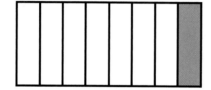

What will I learn in this chapter?

- Identify, read, and write fractions.
- Identify and find equivalent fractions.
- Compare and order fractions.
- Solve problems by drawing a picture.

Key Vocabulary

fraction

numerator

denominator

equivalent fractions

mixed number

 **Student Study Tools** at macmillanmh.com

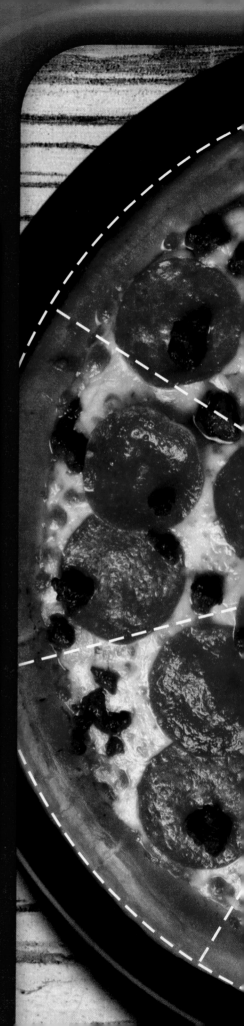

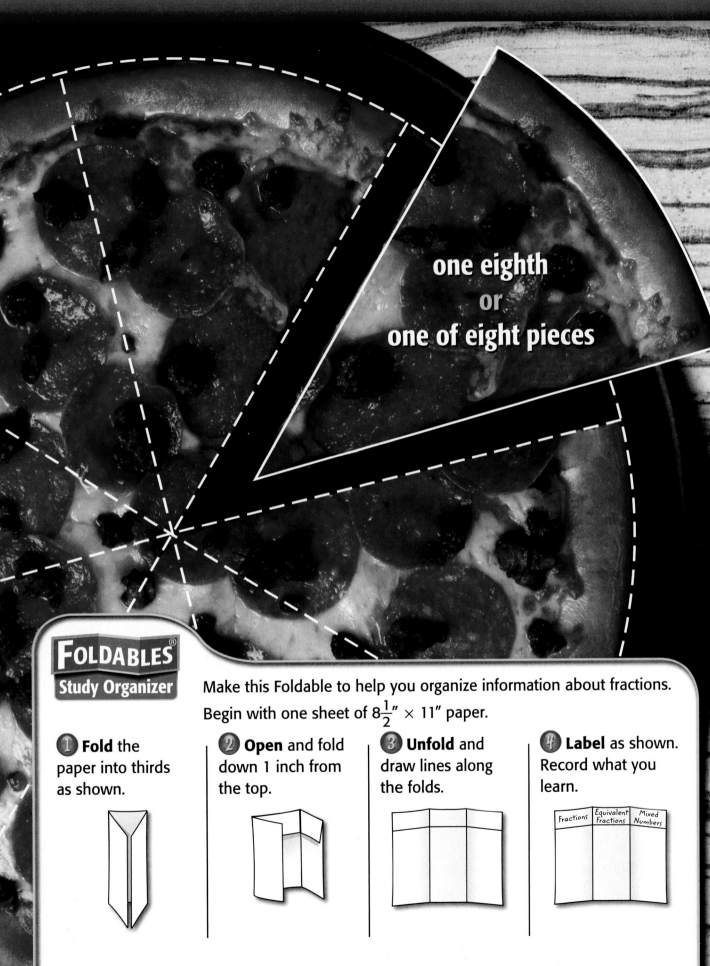

one eighth
or
one of eight pieces

FOLDABLES
Study Organizer

Make this Foldable to help you organize information about fractions. Begin with one sheet of $8\frac{1}{2}'' \times 11''$ paper.

① **Fold** the paper into thirds as shown.

② **Open** and fold down 1 inch from the top.

③ **Unfold** and draw lines along the folds.

④ **Label** as shown. Record what you learn.

Fractions	Equivalent Fractions	Mixed Numbers

You have two ways to check prerequisite skills for this chapter.

Option 2

SC Math Online > Take the Chapter Readiness Quiz at macmillanmh.com.

Option 1

Complete the Quick Check below.

QUICK Check

Write the word that names the equal parts in each whole. Write *halves*, *thirds*, *fourths*, or *fifths*.
(Prior Grade)

1.

2.

3.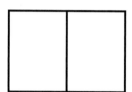

4.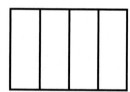

Divide. (Lesson 4-5)

5. $16 \div 4$ **6.** $48 \div 8$ **7.** $24 \div 3$ **8.** $36 \div 6$

9. $72 \div 9$ **10.** $64 \div 8$ **11.** $42 \div 6$ **12.** $56 \div 8$

13. Tyree downloaded 120 songs in 10 days. He downloaded the same number of songs each day. How many songs did he download each day?

List the factors of each number. (Lesson 4-9)

14. 12 **15.** 30 **16.** 45 **17.** 21

18. Write the factor of 36 that is missing from the list
1, 2, 3, 4, 6, ■, 12, 18, 36.

GET READY to Learn

Some of the pieces of pizza have pepperoni. Some have just cheese. You can use a fraction to describe the pizza and the toppings.

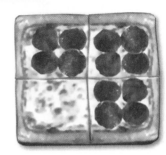

A **fraction** is a number that names part of a whole or part of a set. In a fraction, the **numerator** tells the number of equal parts. The **denominator** tells the number of equal parts in all.

pieces with pepperoni → $\dfrac{3}{4}$ ← numerator ← denominator
total number of pieces →

Real-World EXAMPLE

1 **FOOD** Suppose Molly and her mom made the pizza shown. What fraction of the pizza is pepperoni?

Write   pepperoni slices → $\dfrac{4}{6}$
total slices in all →

Read   *four sixths* or *four divided by six*

So, $\dfrac{4}{6}$ of the whole pizza is pepperoni.

EXAMPLE   Write and Read Fractions

2 **What fraction of the figure is shaded?**

Write   parts shaded → $\dfrac{1}{4}$
total equal parts in all →

Read   *one fourth* or *one divided by four*

So, $\dfrac{1}{4}$ of the whole figure is shaded.

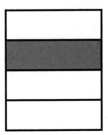

Sidebar

MAIN IDEA

I will identify, write, and read fractions for parts of a whole.

SC Academic Standards

Reinforcement of 3-2.5 Understand fractions as parts of a whole.

New Vocabulary

fraction
numerator
denominator

SC Math Online

macmillanmh.com
• Extra Examples
• Personal Tutor
• Self-Check Quiz

You can use different pictures to show the same part of a whole.

Real-World EXAMPLE   Draw a Fraction Model

3 GARDENS The students at Watson Elementary School are making a garden. They will plant vegetables in $\frac{1}{3}$ of the whole garden. Draw a picture to show this fraction.

One Way: Use a Rectangle	**Another Way:** Use a Circle
vegetables | other | other	vegetables / other | other
Divide a rectangle into 3 equal parts. Shade one part to show one third.	Divide a circle into 3 equal parts. Shade one part to show one third.

CHECK What You Know

Write the fraction that names part of the whole. See Examples 1 and 2 (p. 537)

1.
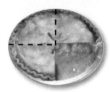
part left

2.
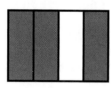
part shaded

3.

part not shaded

Draw a picture and shade part of it to show the fraction. See Example 3 (p. 538)

4. $\frac{1}{4}$ **5.** $\frac{2}{3}$ **6.** $\frac{5}{8}$

7. A birthday cake is cut into 8 equal pieces. Arnaldo ate one piece. The guests ate the remaining pieces. What fraction of the whole cake did the guests eat?

8. **Talk About It** What part of a fraction is the denominator? What does the denominator mean?

Write the fraction that names part of the whole. See Examples 1 and 2 (p. 537)

9.
part left

10.
part filled

11.
part filled

12.
part shaded

13.
part not shaded

14.
part not shaded

Draw a picture and shade part of it to show the fraction. See Example 3 (p. 538)

15. $\frac{3}{5}$ **16.** $\frac{3}{6}$ **17.** $\frac{7}{8}$ **18.** $\frac{4}{10}$

Alphabet flags are used by ships at sea to send short messages. Write the fraction for the part of each flag that is blue.

19.
Letter C

20.
Letter G

21.
Letter N

22.
Letter Z

For Exercises 23–25, use the recipe shown.

23. What is the total number of cups of ingredients needed to make one batch of the party mix?

24. What fraction of the ingredients is pretzels?

25. What fraction of the ingredients is peanuts and raisins?

Recipe for: Party Mix
1 cup peanuts
3 cups rice cereal
2 cups pretzels
2 cups raisins

Makes: one batch

H.O.T. Problems

26. OPEN ENDED Name two different real-world items that can show the fraction $\frac{2}{3}$.

27. **WRITING IN ►MATH** If the denominator of $\frac{2}{5}$ was increased from 5 to 10, would it be greater or less than $\frac{2}{5}$? Explain.

MAIN IDEA

I will identify, write, read, and model fractions for parts of a set.

SC Academic Standards

Reinforcement of 3-2.5 Understand fractions as parts of a whole.

SC Math Online

macmillanmh.com
- Extra Examples
- Personal Tutor
- Self-Check Quiz

GET READY to Learn

A set of toy cars has two red cars, one green car, and one blue car. What fraction of the set of cars is green?

A set is a group of objects. In Lesson 13-1, you learned to use a fraction to name part of a whole. Fractions can also be used to name part of a set.

Real-World EXAMPLE

1 **CARS** What fraction of the set of cars is green?

Write   green cars ⟶ $\dfrac{1}{4}$ ⟵ numerator
total cars ⟶ denominator

Read   *one fourth* or *one divided by four*

So, $\dfrac{1}{4}$ of the set of cars is green.

EXAMPLE   Write and Read Fractions

2 **What fraction of the set of stars is *not* green?**

Write   stars *not* green ⟶ $\dfrac{2}{5}$
total stars ⟶

Read   *two fifths* or *two divided by five*

So, $\dfrac{2}{5}$ of the set of stars are *not* green.

You have learned that fractions can be used to name part of a whole and part of a set. Another way of looking at fractions is as division of whole numbers by whole numbers.

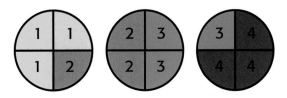
Real-World EXAMPLE   Fraction as a Quotient

③ FOOD Tammy and three friends went to a pancake breakfast. They ordered and shared three pancakes equally. What part of the pancakes did each receive?

Draw a picture to show the division.

Three pancakes are divided among 4 people. So, each person receives 3 divided by 4 or $\frac{3}{4}$ of the pancakes.

CHECK What You Know

Write the fraction for the part of the set that is yellow. Then write the fraction for the part that is *not* yellow. See Examples 1 and 2 (p. 540)

1.

2.

Write the fraction that names the part of the set of vegetables.

See Examples 1 and 2 (p. 540)

3. *not* red peppers

4. *not* corn

5. *not* green peppers

6. Five chimpanzees are sharing four bananas equally. What part of the bananas does each receive?

See Example 3 (p. 541)

7. **Talk About It** Explain what the following sentence means. *Three-fifths of a set of animals are dogs.*

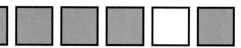
Write the fraction for the part of the set that is blue. Then write the fraction for the part that is *not* blue. See Examples 1 and 2 (p. 540)

8.

9.

10.

11.

Write the fraction that names the part of the set of shapes. See Example 2 (p. 540)

12. circles

13. *not* squares

14. *not* triangles

15. red

16. yellow

17. *not* blue

18. Eight people are sharing five apples equally. What part of an apple does each receive? See Example 3 (p. 541)

19. Twelve elephants are sharing nine bales of hay equally. What part of a bale of hay does each receive?

See Example 3 (p. 541)

South Carolina Data File

Wild boars are commonly found in South Carolina. These animals can grow up to 5 feet long and can weigh up to 300 pounds.

20. Suppose 18 boars are traveling together. If 7 of them are adult females and 5 are piglets, what fraction are adult males?

21. Suppose a boar has 6 piglets. If two of the piglets are male, what fraction of the piglets is female?

H.O.T. Problems

22. OPEN ENDED Draw a set of objects that shows the fraction $\frac{3}{5}$.

23. FIND THE ERROR Three eighths of a set of fruit are oranges. What part is *not* oranges? Who is correct, Sonja or Jairo?

Sonja

$\frac{5}{8}$

Jairo

$\frac{4}{8}$

24. WRITING IN ►MATH Write a problem that involves identifying a fraction that describes part of a group.

---

25. Which figure shows $\frac{2}{5}$? *(Lesson 13-1)*

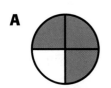

A

C

B

D

26. Stephen walks his dog 4 days each week. His brother walks the dog the other days. What fraction names the part of a week Stephen's brother walks the dog? *(Lesson 13-2)*

F $\frac{3}{7}$ **H** $\frac{4}{7}$

G $\frac{1}{2}$ **J** $\frac{3}{4}$

Spiral Review

Draw a picture and shade part of it to show the fraction. *(Lesson 13-1)*

27. $\frac{2}{5}$ **28.** $\frac{1}{6}$ **29.** $\frac{4}{10}$

30. Measurement Maurice left for school at 8:30 A.M. He arrived at 9:05 A.M. How long did it take him to get to school? Use a clock if needed. *(Lesson 12-10)*

31. Measurement Estimate and measure the weight of two objects in your bookbag. *(Lesson 12-4)*

Problem-Solving Strategy

MAIN IDEA I will solve problems by drawing a picture.

SCAS **4-1.4 Generate descriptions and mathematical statements about relationships between and among classes of objects.**

Brandi and her mom are at a pet store. The pet store has 15 reptiles. One third of the reptiles are turtles. Two are snakes, and the rest are lizards. How many of each reptile are there?

Understand	**What facts do you know?**
	• There are 15 reptiles at the store. • Two are snakes.
	• One third are turtles. • The rest are lizards.
	What do you need to find?
	• Find the number of each reptile.
Plan	Draw a picture to solve the problem.
Solve	• Draw 15 circles. Since the fraction $\frac{1}{3}$ is used, place the circles in 3 equal groups.
	• To show the turtles, shade $\frac{1}{3}$ of the circles. That is, one of the three equal groups. So, there are 5 turtles. There are 2 snakes, so shade 2 circles to show the snakes.
	• There are 8 circles not shaded. This is the number of lizards.
	So, there are 5 turtles, 2 snakes, and 8 lizards at the pet store.
Check	Look back. 5 turtles + 2 snakes + 8 lizards = 15 reptiles. The pet store has 15 reptiles. So, the answer is correct.

turtles

snakes

544 Chapter 13 Describe and Compare Fractions

Refer to the problem on the previous page.

1. Explain why you used 15 circles.

2. You know that $\frac{1}{3}$ of the reptiles are turtles. Explain why 5 circles were shaded to show the number of turtles.

3. If the pet store had 24 reptiles, how many of the reptiles would be lizards?

4. Check your answer to Exercise 3. How do you know that it is correct?

PRACTICE the Strategy

SCAS • PASS
Extra Practice, p. R34

Solve. Use the draw a picture strategy.

5. **Measurement** There are three trees in a backyard. The second tree is half as tall as the first. The third tree is taller than the second tree and shorter than the first tree. The total height of the trees is 24 feet. What is the height of each tree?

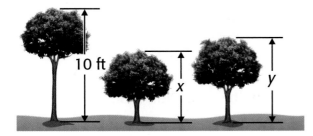

6. Pam and three other students are waiting in a line. Lakita is ahead of Pam. Sanjay is third in line. Rob is behind Sanjay. In what order are the students standing?

7. Emil bought his mom a dozen roses. Some of the roses are shown below. The rest are white. Which color were there the most of? How many roses were that color?

8. There are 22 students in Ms. Lane's class. Half of them packed their lunches. Eight students are buying pizza. The rest are buying salads. How many students are buying salads?

9. **Measurement** The table shows how long Adam and Kenya rode their bikes. Who biked more minutes? How many more minutes?

Biking Schedule	
Name	**Time Spent Biking**
Adam	$\frac{1}{3}$ of an hour
Kenya	15 minutes

10. There are 16 books on a shelf. One-fourth of the books are about animals. Two are adventure. The rest are mystery. How many are mystery books?

11. **WRITING IN MATH** Look back at Exercise 10. Explain how you used the draw a picture strategy to solve the problem.

Explore

Equivalent Fractions

Fractions that represent the same amount are **equivalent fractions.**

MAIN IDEA

I will identify equivalent fractions.

SC Academic Standards

4-2.8 Apply strategies and procedures to find equivalent forms of fractions.

SC Math Online

macmillanmh.com
• Concepts in Motion

ACTIVITY Model Equivalent Fractions

1 **Identify two fractions that are equivalent to $\frac{1}{3}$.**

Step 1 **Model $\frac{1}{3}$.**

Start with 1 whole. Then, use the $\frac{1}{3}$ fraction model to show $\frac{1}{3}$.

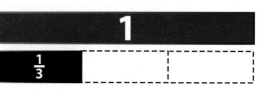

Step 2 **Find a fraction equivalent to $\frac{1}{3}$.**

Using $\frac{1}{6}$ fraction models, place them below the $\frac{1}{3}$ fraction model. How many $\frac{1}{6}$ fraction models are used?

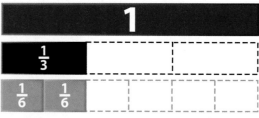

Step 3 **Find another fraction equivalent to $\frac{1}{3}$.**

Use $\frac{1}{12}$ fraction models to equal the length of the $\frac{1}{3}$ fraction model. Count the number of $\frac{1}{12}$ fraction models.

So, $\frac{1}{3}$, $\frac{2}{6}$, and $\frac{4}{12}$ are equivalent fractions.

② **Identify three equivalent fractions.**

Step 1 Draw three identical number lines that show zero and one.

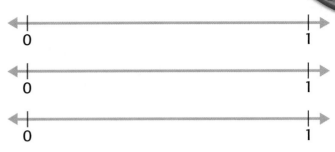

Step 2 Divide the first number line into fourths. Divide the second number line into eighths. Divide the third number line into sixteenths.

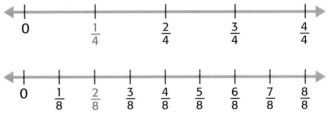

Notice that $\frac{1}{4} = \frac{2}{8} = \frac{4}{16}$.

Think About It

1. **Algebra** Copy and complete $\frac{1}{3} = \frac{\blacksquare}{9} = \frac{\blacksquare}{15}$.

2. Refer to Activity 2. Find two fractions equivalent to $\frac{3}{4}$.

CHECK What You Know

Determine whether each pair of fractions is equivalent. Use fraction models or number lines.

3. $\frac{2}{4}$ and $\frac{6}{12}$ 4. $\frac{6}{8}$ and $\frac{5}{10}$ 5. $\frac{2}{3}$ and $\frac{3}{5}$ 6. $\frac{9}{12}$ and $\frac{3}{4}$

Find two equivalent fractions for each fraction. Use fraction models or number lines.

7. $\frac{1}{5}$ 8. $\frac{2}{6}$ 9. $\frac{4}{8}$ 10. $\frac{2}{12}$

11. **WRITING IN ►MATH** Explain what it means for two fractions to be equivalent.

Equivalent Fractions

MAIN IDEA

I will find equivalent fractions.

SC Academic Standards

4-2.8 Apply strategies and procedures to find equivalent forms of fractions.

New Vocabulary

equivalent fractions

SC Math Online
macmillanmh.com
• Extra Examples
• Personal Tutor
• Self-Check Quiz

GET READY to Learn

Megan has 8 fish in an aquarium. Four fish are green. So, Megan says that $\frac{4}{8}$ of the fish are green. Megan could use another fraction to represent $\frac{4}{8}$.

The fraction models below show that $\frac{4}{8}$ is the same as $\frac{1}{2}$. Fractions that represent the same amount are **equivalent fractions**.

EXAMPLE Find Equivalent Fractions

1 **Find three fractions that are equivalent to $\frac{4}{8}$.**

To find equivalent fractions, you can use multiplication or division.

One Way: **Multiply**		Another Way: **Divide**	
$\dfrac{4 \times \boxed{2}}{8 \times \boxed{2}} = \dfrac{8}{16}$	Multiply the numerator and the denominator by the same number, 2.	$\dfrac{4 \div \boxed{2}}{8 \div \boxed{2}} = \dfrac{2}{4}$ $\dfrac{2 \div \boxed{2}}{4 \div \boxed{2}} = \dfrac{1}{2}$	Divide the numerator and the denominator by the same number, 2.

So, $\frac{8}{16}$, $\frac{2}{4}$, or $\frac{1}{2}$ are equivalent to $\frac{4}{8}$.

You can also use manipulatives, pictures, or a number line to find equivalent fractions.

Remember

You can find many equivalent fractions for any fraction.

EXAMPLE Use Concrete Models

② Dale has $\frac{3}{4}$ of his book completed. Use fraction models to find an equivalent fraction.

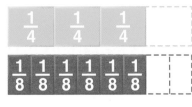

$$\frac{3}{4} = \frac{6}{8}$$

So, $\frac{6}{8}$ is an equivalent fraction to $\frac{3}{4}$.

EXAMPLE Draw a Picture to Model Equivalent Fractions

③ Find an equivalent fraction to $\frac{8}{24}$.
Draw a model.

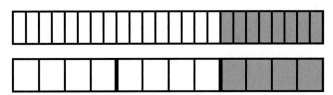

So, $\frac{4}{12}$ is an equivalent fraction.

EXAMPLE Fractions on a Number Line

④ Write the letter on the number line that best represents $\frac{2}{8}$. Find an equivalent fraction.

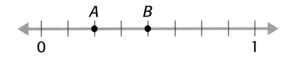

The number line is divided into eighths.

So, $A = \frac{2}{8}$. An equivalent fraction is $\frac{1}{4}$.

Write the fraction for the part that is shaded. Then find an equivalent fraction. See Examples 1–3 (pp. 548–549)

1.

2.

3.

Find an equivalent fraction for each fraction.

See Examples 1–3 (pp. 548–549)

4. $\frac{1}{4}$
5. $\frac{4}{6}$
6. $\frac{1}{5}$
7. $\frac{8}{10}$
8. $\frac{1}{3}$

9. Tell which letter on the number line below best represents $\frac{6}{10}$. Then find an equivalent fraction. See Example 4 (p. 549)

10. Dexter has 4 juice boxes. Three are grape flavored. Write two fractions that describe the part of the juice boxes that is grape.

11. (**Talk About It**) Tell why $\frac{3}{4}$, $\frac{6}{8}$, and $\frac{9}{12}$ are equivalent fractions. Give an example of another set of three equivalent fractions.

> **Practice and Problem Solving**

SCAS • PASS

Extra Practice, p. R35

Write the fraction for the part that is shaded. Then find an equivalent fraction. See Examples 1–3 (pp. 548–549)

12.

13.

14.

15.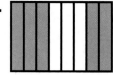

16.

17.

Find an equivalent fraction for each fraction.

See Examples 1–3 (pp. 548–549)

18. $\frac{2}{7}$
19. $\frac{2}{5}$
20. $\frac{6}{10}$
21. $\frac{2}{12}$
22. $\frac{2}{3}$

Tell which letter on the number line best represents the given fraction. Then find an equivalent fraction. See Example 4 (p. 549)

23. $\frac{3}{4}$

```
          C     D     F     J
◄—+—+—●—+—●—+—●—+—●—►
  0                   1
```

24. $\frac{4}{14}$

```
      B  D F  G      J  K
◄—+—●—+—●●—+—●—+—+—●—+—●—+—►
  0                        1
```

25. A roller coaster has 16 cars. Six of the cars are green. Write two fractions for the part of the cars that is green.

26. **Measurement** Lucas ran $\frac{1}{2}$ mile. Candace ran $\frac{4}{6}$ mile. Did they run the same distance? Explain.

Real-World PROBLEM SOLVING

Science Giraffes grow to a height of about 20 feet. Their neck is about $\frac{2}{5}$ their total height. Giraffes spend about $\frac{5}{6}$ of a day eating.

27. What fraction of a day does a giraffe spend eating? Write another fraction that represents this amount.

28. What fraction of the total height is the length of a giraffe's neck? Write a fraction equivalent to this fraction.

H.O.T. Problems

29. **OPEN ENDED** Write a fraction equivalent to $\frac{2}{5}$. Write a fraction equivalent to $\frac{3}{6}$. Which fraction represents a greater amount? Explain.

30. **FIND THE ERROR** Rachel and Miguel are finding a fraction equivalent to $\frac{6}{18}$. Who is correct? Explain.

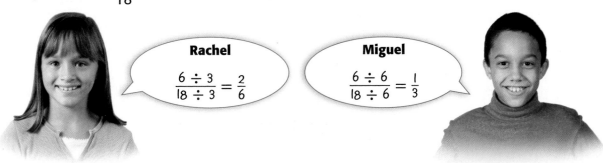

Rachel

$\frac{6 \div 3}{18 \div 3} = \frac{2}{6}$

Miguel

$\frac{6 \div 6}{18 \div 6} = \frac{1}{3}$

31. **WRITING IN ►MATH** Can you always find an equivalent fraction for a fraction? Explain.

Fractions Made Equal

Make Equivalent Fractions

Get Ready!

Players: 2

Get Set!

Cut each index card in half. Then label each card with one fraction as shown.

Go!

- Shuffle the cards. Then spread out the cards facedown on the table.

- Player 1 turns over 1 card and must write an equivalent fraction. If Player 1 is correct, Player 1 keeps the card. If Player 1 is incorrect, the card is put back.

- Player 2 takes a turn.

- Play continues in the same way. The player with the greater number of cards wins.

You will need: 10 index cards

$\frac{2}{4}$ $\frac{3}{6}$ $\frac{5}{10}$ $\frac{7}{14}$

$\frac{2}{6}$ $\frac{3}{9}$ $\frac{5}{15}$ $\frac{7}{21}$

$\frac{3}{12}$ $\frac{4}{16}$ $\frac{6}{24}$ $\frac{8}{32}$

$\frac{2}{10}$ $\frac{3}{15}$ $\frac{5}{25}$ $\frac{7}{35}$

$\frac{2}{12}$ $\frac{3}{18}$ $\frac{5}{30}$ $\frac{6}{36}$

C13-088A-105711

C13-027P-A-105711

Write the fraction that names the shaded part of the whole. (Lesson 13-1)

1.

2.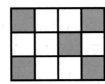

Draw a picture and shade part of it to show the fraction. (Lesson 13-1)

3. $\frac{1}{8}$

4. $\frac{3}{7}$

5. The flag of Italy is shown. What fraction of the flag is green? (Lesson 13-1)

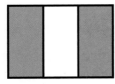

6. MULTIPLE CHOICE What fraction of the hearts is shaded? (Lesson 13-2)

A $\frac{4}{10}$

C $\frac{5}{9}$

B $\frac{1}{2}$

D $\frac{6}{10}$

7. Draw a picture that represents the statement below. (Lesson 13-2)

Three of the five leaves are shaded.

8. There are 3 red apples, 6 green apples, and 1 yellow apple on a table. Of the apples, what fraction is green? (Lesson 13-2)

Write the fraction that names the part of the set of smile faces. (Lesson 13-2)

9. red

10. green

11. Janey is planting 12 trees in her yard. There are 5 maple trees and the rest are oak. What fraction of the trees is oak? (Lesson 13-3)

12. Galeno spent $\frac{1}{2}$ of his money on a movie ticket and $\frac{1}{4}$ of his money on a snack. He had $8 before the movie. How much money does he have now? (Lesson 13-3)

Find an equivalent fraction for each fraction. (Lesson 13-4)

13. $\frac{1}{3}$

14. $\frac{4}{5}$

15. $\frac{1}{2}$

16. $\frac{2}{6}$

17. Jin's mom used 12 of the 20 stamps she had bought. Jin said that she used $\frac{3}{5}$ of the stamps. Is Jin correct? Explain. (Lesson 13-4)

18. WRITING IN ►MATH Is $\frac{1}{4}$ of the rectangle green? Explain why or why not. (Lesson 13-1)

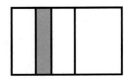

Compare and Order Fractions

GET READY to Learn

Ramon has an insect collection. The table shows the lengths of four insects in his collection. Which is longer, a field cricket or a whirligig beetle?

Insect	Length (in.)
Mosquito	$\frac{1}{4}$
Field cricket	$\frac{5}{8}$
Whirligig beetle	$\frac{3}{8}$
Lightning bug	$\frac{1}{2}$

To compare fractions, you can use models, number lines, and equivalent fractions.

Real-World EXAMPLES Compare Fractions

1 **MEASUREMENT Which insect is longer, a field cricket or a whirligig beetle?**

You can use fraction models to compare $\frac{5}{8}$ and $\frac{3}{8}$.

| $\frac{1}{8}$ | $\frac{1}{8}$ | $\frac{1}{8}$ | $\frac{1}{8}$ | $\frac{1}{8}$ | | |

$\frac{5}{8}$ Field cricket

| $\frac{1}{8}$ | $\frac{1}{8}$ | $\frac{1}{8}$ | | | | |

$\frac{3}{8}$ Whirligig beetle

The models show that $\frac{5}{8} > \frac{3}{8}$.

So, the field cricket is longer than the whirligig beetle.

2 **Which is longer, a mosquito or lightning bug?**

You need to compare $\frac{1}{4}$ and $\frac{1}{2}$.

$\frac{1}{4}$ Mosquito

$\frac{1}{2}$ Lightning bug

So, the lightning bug is longer than the mosquito.

EXAMPLE Order Fractions

3 Order $\frac{2}{3}$, $\frac{1}{2}$, and $\frac{7}{12}$ from least to greatest.

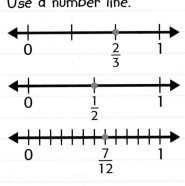

One Way: Number Lines	**Another Way:** Equivalent Fractions
Use a number line.	Find equivalent fractions with the same denominator.
	$\frac{2 \times \boxed{4}}{3 \times \boxed{4}} = \frac{8}{12}$ $\frac{1 \times \boxed{6}}{2 \times \boxed{6}} = \frac{6}{12}$
	Compare the numerators. Order from least to greatest.
$\frac{1}{2} < \frac{7}{12} < \frac{2}{3}$	$\frac{6}{12}$, $\frac{7}{12}$, $\frac{8}{12}$ $\downarrow$ $\downarrow$ $\downarrow$ $\frac{1}{2}$, $\frac{7}{12}$, $\frac{2}{3}$

So, the order from least to greatest is $\frac{1}{2}$, $\frac{7}{12}$, $\frac{2}{3}$.

CHECK What You Know

Compare. Use >, <, or =. See Examples 1 and 2 (p. 554)

1.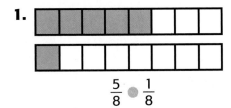

$\frac{5}{8}$ ● $\frac{1}{8}$

2.

(number lines showing 0 to 1 with fourths and sixths)

$\frac{1}{4}$ ● $\frac{1}{6}$

3. $\frac{3}{4}$ ● $\frac{1}{2}$

4. $\frac{3}{6}$ ● $\frac{3}{4}$

Order from least to greatest. See Example 3 (p. 555)

5. $\frac{3}{8}$, $\frac{2}{6}$, $\frac{4}{8}$

6. $\frac{1}{16}$, $\frac{7}{8}$, $\frac{3}{4}$

7. Measurement Griff worked for $\frac{1}{3}$ of an hour. Sasha worked for $\frac{3}{12}$ of an hour. Who worked for a longer time?

8. **Talk About It** Explain how to compare the fractions $\frac{7}{12}$ and $\frac{2}{6}$.

Compare. Use >, <, or =. See Examples 1 and 2 (p. 554)

9.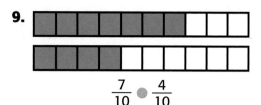

$\dfrac{7}{10}$ ● $\dfrac{4}{10}$

10.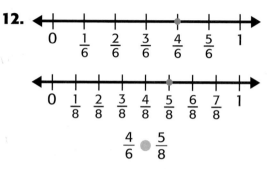

$\dfrac{4}{8}$ ● $\dfrac{1}{4}$

11.

$\dfrac{2}{3}$ ● $\dfrac{5}{6}$

12.

$\dfrac{4}{6}$ ● $\dfrac{5}{8}$

13. $\dfrac{2}{6}$ ● $\dfrac{1}{3}$

14. $\dfrac{3}{5}$ ● $\dfrac{5}{6}$

15. $\dfrac{4}{5}$ ● $\dfrac{8}{10}$

16. $\dfrac{2}{3}$ ● $\dfrac{5}{9}$

17. $\dfrac{4}{10}$ ● $\dfrac{1}{2}$

18. $\dfrac{5}{8}$ ● $\dfrac{2}{3}$

Order from least to greatest. See Example 3 (p. 555)

19. $\dfrac{4}{6}, \dfrac{1}{3}, \dfrac{3}{3}$

20. $\dfrac{3}{4}, \dfrac{2}{3}, \dfrac{7}{8}$

21. $\dfrac{3}{10}, \dfrac{3}{4}, \dfrac{3}{5}$

22. Which meat makes up most of Mr. Collin's sandwich?

23. Allison took a survey. Find the favorite weekend activity.

Favorite Weekend Activities	
Activity	**Fraction of Friends**
Movie	$\dfrac{2}{6}$
Mall	$\dfrac{1}{4}$
Basketball	$\dfrac{5}{12}$

24. Aisha ate $\dfrac{1}{4}$ of the carrots in the bag. Enrique ate $\dfrac{3}{12}$ of the carrots in the bag. Who ate more carrots?

25. Suzanne practiced volleyball for $\dfrac{2}{3}$ hour on Saturday and $\dfrac{1}{6}$ hour on Sunday. Which day did she practice longer?

26. **Measurement** The table shows how much time each student needs to finish an art project. Does Simón need more or less time than Phil? Explain.

Student	Time
Simón	$\dfrac{4}{12}$ hour
Phil	$\dfrac{3}{4}$ hour

H.O.T. Problems

27. OPEN ENDED Write three fractions that are *not* greater than $\frac{1}{2}$.

28. WHICH ONE DOESN'T BELONG? Identify the set of fractions that does not belong with the other three sets. Explain.

$$\frac{1}{4}, \frac{5}{8}, \frac{15}{16} \qquad \frac{2}{9}, \frac{1}{3}, \frac{1}{2} \qquad \frac{2}{5}, \frac{1}{2}, \frac{7}{10} \qquad \frac{3}{4}, \frac{1}{2}, \frac{2}{12}$$

29. CHALLENGE Identify a fraction that is greater than $\frac{150}{300}$.

30. WRITING IN ►MATH Explain how to decide if $\frac{3}{4}$ is greater than or less than $\frac{3}{5}$.

PASS Practice 4-2.8, 4-2.9

31. What fraction is equivalent to the fraction represented by point *M* on the number line? (Lesson 13-4)

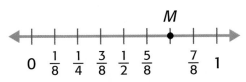

$$M$$

$$0 \quad \frac{1}{8} \quad \frac{1}{4} \quad \frac{3}{8} \quad \frac{1}{2} \quad \frac{5}{8} \quad \frac{7}{8} \quad 1$$

A $\frac{1}{4}$ **C** $\frac{1}{2}$

B $\frac{3}{8}$ **D** $\frac{3}{4}$

32. Which set of fractions is ordered from greatest to least? (Lesson 13-5)

F $\frac{3}{5}, \frac{6}{15}, \frac{2}{10}$

G $\frac{2}{10}, \frac{3}{5}, \frac{6}{15}$

H $\frac{2}{10}, \frac{6}{15}, \frac{3}{5}$

J $\frac{6}{15}, \frac{3}{5}, \frac{2}{10}$

Spiral Review

Find an equivalent fraction for each fraction.

(Lesson 13-4)

33. $\frac{1}{2}$

34. $\frac{2}{3}$

35. $\frac{3}{5}$

36. Toya has 8 coins in her piggy bank. One fourth of the coins are quarters. Three of the coins are dimes. The rest of the coins are pennies. How many pennies does Toya have? (Lesson 13-3)

Find each product. (Lesson 6-4)

37. $\begin{array}{r} 37 \\ \times 4 \\ \hline \end{array}$

38. $\begin{array}{r} 51 \\ \times 7 \\ \hline \end{array}$

39. $\begin{array}{r} 85 \\ \times 9 \\ \hline \end{array}$

Problem Solving in Science

No BONES about it . . .

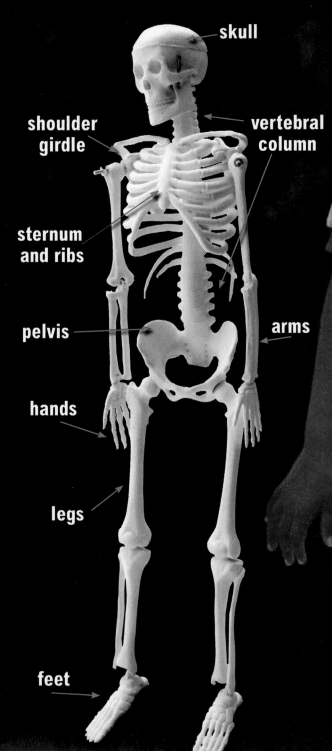

skull

shoulder girdle

vertebral column

sternum and ribs

pelvis

arms

hands

legs

feet

Every human has a skeleton made up of bones. Your skeletal system is very important. Not only does it protect your internal organs, but it also allows you to stand up and walk. Without a skeleton you would be nothing but skin and guts!

Humans are born with 350 bones in their body. But, by the time you are 25, you will have only about 200 bones. This is because some of the bones join together to make a single bone.

The shortest bone is in the ear. It can be as short as $\frac{1}{10}$ of an inch. The longest bone, the femur, is located in the thigh. It is about $\frac{1}{4}$ of your height.

Did You Know?

Of the bones in your skeleton, about $\frac{3}{20}$ are found in your spine.

ADULT HUMAN SKELETON

Body Part	Number of Bones
Skull	22
Middle ears	6
Throat	1
Shoulder girdle	4
Sternum and ribs	25
Vertebral column	24
Arms	6
Hands	54
Pelvis	4
Legs	8
Feet	52

Source: BBC Education

Real-World Math

Use the information on pages 558 and 559 to solve each problem.

1 What fraction of the bones in an adult human is located in the skull?

2 Which two body parts contain $\frac{1}{2}$ of the bones in an adult human? Explain your reasoning.

3 Which body part contains $\frac{8}{206}$ of the bones in an adult human?

4 About what fraction of the bones at birth does a human have when an adult?

5 Are more bones in an adult human located in the skull or in the spine?

6 The backbone is approximately 28 inches. What fraction of a foot is 28 inches?

7 Use your height to determine the length of your femur bone in inches.

MAIN IDEA

I will write mixed numbers and improper fractions.

SC Academic Standards

4-2.11 **Represent improper fractions, mixed numbers,** and decimals.

New Vocabulary

mixed number
improper fraction

SC Math Online

macmillanmh.com
• Extra Examples
• Personal Tutor
• Self-Check Quiz

GET READY to Learn

Nyoko is selling pies at a bake sale. Each pie has 5 slices. Each slice of pie is sold separately. There are 7 slices left. What fraction of the pies is left?

A **mixed number** has a whole number part and a fraction part. An **improper fraction** has a numerator that is greater than or equal to its denominator.

Mixed Numbers	Improper Fractions
$1\frac{1}{2}$ $2\frac{3}{4}$ $3\frac{5}{6}$	$\frac{3}{2}$ $\frac{11}{4}$ $\frac{23}{6}$

Real-World EXAMPLE

1 **FOOD** What fraction of a pie does Nyoko have left?

Each pie has 5 slices. There are 7 slices left.

One Way: Mixed Number	Another Way: Improper Fraction
Count the wholes and the parts.	Count the parts.

 $+$ $\frac{2}{5}$ $=$ $1\frac{2}{5}$

whole   part

$\frac{7}{5}$

So, $1\frac{2}{5}$ or $\frac{7}{5}$ of a pie is left.

You can change from a mixed number to an improper fraction. You can also change from an improper fraction to a mixed number.

② **Write $1\frac{3}{8}$ as an improper fraction.**

$1\frac{3}{8} = 1 + \frac{3}{8}$ Write the mixed number as the sum of a whole and part.

$= \boxed{\frac{8}{8}} + \frac{3}{8}$ Write the whole number as a fraction.

$= \frac{8 + 3}{8}$ Add.

$= \frac{11}{8}$

Remember

The fraction bar stands for *divided by*. So, $\frac{11}{8}$ means *11 divided by 8.*

③ **Write $\frac{11}{8}$ as a mixed number.**

Divide the numerator by the denominator.

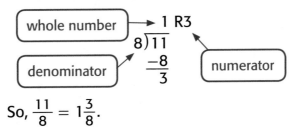

whole number → 1 R3

8)11

denominator

$\frac{-8}{3}$ numerator

So, $\frac{11}{8} = 1\frac{3}{8}$.

You can show improper fractions and mixed numbers on a number line.

④ **Identify point A as a mixed number and improper fraction.**

Each interval on the number line is one third. So, point A is $5\frac{1}{3}$.

$5\frac{1}{3} = \boxed{\frac{3}{3}} + \boxed{\frac{3}{3}} + \boxed{\frac{3}{3}} + \boxed{\frac{3}{3}} + \boxed{\frac{3}{3}} + \frac{1}{3}$

$= \frac{3 + 3 + 3 + 3 + 3 + 1}{3} = \frac{16}{3}$

So, Point A is $5\frac{1}{3}$ or $\frac{16}{3}$.

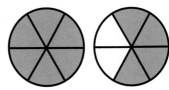
Write a mixed number and an improper fraction for each model.

See Example 1 (p. 560)

1.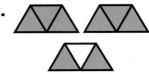

2.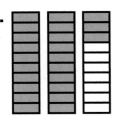

3.

Write each as an improper fraction or a mixed number.
Use models if needed. See Examples 2 and 3 (p. 561)

4. $1\frac{2}{5}$

5. $2\frac{3}{4}$

6. $\frac{9}{4}$

7. $\frac{13}{3}$

Identify each point as a mixed number and an improper fraction. See Example 4 (p. 561)

8.

$$
\begin{array}{ccccccc}
 & & & B & & & \\
7 & & & 8 & & & 9
\end{array}
$$

9.

$$
\begin{array}{cccc}
 & & & G \\
4 & 5 & 6 &
\end{array}
$$

10. Andrew's family ate $1\frac{3}{8}$ pizzas and Sheri's family ate $1\frac{4}{16}$ pizzas. Who ate more pizzas?

11. **Talk About It** Explain how to compare $2\frac{3}{5}$ and $\frac{17}{5}$.

Practice and Problem Solving

SCAS • PASS

Extra Practice, p. R35

Write a mixed number and an improper fraction for each model.

See Example 1 (p. 560)

12.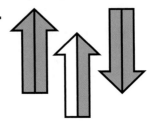

13.

14.

Write each as an improper fraction or a mixed number.
Use models if needed. See Examples 2 and 3 (p. 561)

15. $1\frac{3}{4}$

16. $2\frac{7}{10}$

17. $6\frac{7}{8}$

18. $8\frac{5}{8}$

19. $\frac{7}{3}$

20. $\frac{17}{5}$

21. $\frac{45}{8}$

22. $\frac{50}{6}$

Identify each point as a mixed number and an improper fraction.

See Example 4 (p. 561)

23.

24.

25. Ray needs $1\frac{1}{2}$ cups of flour for pancakes and $1\frac{3}{4}$ cups of sugar for banana bread. Does Ray need more sugar or more flour?

26. Percy drank $2\frac{3}{5}$ cups of water after the first half of the soccer match and $2\frac{4}{6}$ cups of water after the second half. When did he drink more water?

Real-World PROBLEM SOLVING

Travel A diagram of a horseback riding tour is shown. There are resting stops along the trail.

27. Joaquin and his family started at the stables on the left. They are at the covered bridge. How many miles of the trail have they traveled?

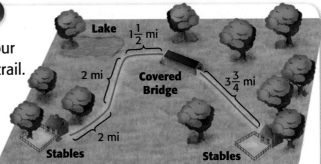

28. Joaquin reached the end of the trail in 2 hours and 15 minutes. Write the amount of time he spent on the trail as an improper fraction.

H.O.T. Problems

29. OPEN ENDED Name an improper fraction that can be written as a whole number.

30. FIND THE ERROR Heather and Wesley are writing $4\frac{3}{5}$ as an improper fraction. Who is correct? Explain.

Heather
$4\frac{3}{5} = \frac{23}{5}$

Wesley
$4\frac{3}{5} = \frac{20}{5}$

31. WRITING IN ►MATH Compare fractions, mixed numbers, and improper fractions.

MAIN IDEA I will choose the best strategy to solve a problem.

 SCAS **4-1.1 Analyze information to solve increasingly more sophisticated problems.**

P.S.I. TEAM +

ANICA: My class visited the zoo. I learned that one sixth of the animals at the zoo are reptiles. There are 420 animals at the zoo. How many animals are reptiles?

YOUR MISSION: Find how many animals are reptiles.

Understand	There are 420 animals at a zoo. One sixth of the animals are reptiles. Find how many animals are reptiles.
Plan	Solve a simpler problem. First, find one sixth of a smaller number. Then multiply to find one sixth of 420.
Solve	First, find one sixth of 42.

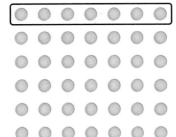

There are 42 counters in 6 equal rows. One of the six equal groups is circled.

So, one sixth of 42 equals 7. Now multiply.

$$\begin{array}{r} 42 \\ \times\ 10 \\ \hline 420 \end{array}$$ THINK What number can you multiply 42 by to equal 420? Then multiply 7 by the same number. $$\begin{array}{r} 7 \\ \times\ 10 \\ \hline 70 \end{array}$$

So, 70 of the animals at the zoo are reptiles.

Check	Since $70 \times 6 = 420$, then 70 is one sixth of 420. The answer is correct.

Use any strategy shown below to solve. Tell what strategy you used.

PROBLEM-SOLVING STRATEGIES
- Use logical reasoning.
- Draw a picture.
- Make a table.
- Act it out.
- Make an organized list.

1. **Measurement** A chef wants to cook an 8-pound turkey. It takes 20 minutes per pound to fully cook. What time should the chef start cooking the turkey for it to be done at 5:00 P.M?

2. After Malcolm buys three packages of stickers like the one shown, the number of stickers in his collection will double. How many stickers will he have?

3. Dario and three of his friends shared the cost of renting a rowboat. It cost $12 an hour, and they used the boat for 3 hours. How much did each friend pay?

4. **Algebra** A geometric pattern is shown. What is the next figure in the pattern?

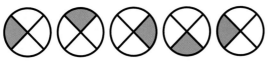

5. Mei has some coins. She has 3 more quarters than nickels and 2 more dimes than quarters. If Mei has 4 nickels, how much money does she have?

6. A customer buys small, medium, and large sweatshirts. The total cost is $68. How many of each size were bought?

SWEATSHIRT SALE

Size	Cost
small	$13
medium	$15
large	$20

7. **Measurement** Daisy exercises for 30 minutes 2 times a day. If she keeps up this schedule for 30 days, how many minutes will she exercise in all?

8. **Measurement** Randall's goal is to run one mile the first week and double the number of miles each week for the next 6 weeks. How many miles will he run the sixth week?

9. **Algebra** Find the area of the fifth figure in the pattern shown.

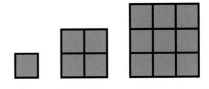

10. **WRITING IN MATH** Write a few sentences to explain what it means to solve a problem by solving a simpler problem.

Study Guide and Review

SC Math Online > macmillanmh.com
• STUDY TO GO
• Vocabulary Review

FOLDABLES Study Organizer GET READY to Study

Be sure the following Key Vocabulary words and Key Concepts are written in your Foldable.

Fractions	Equivalent Fractions	Mixed Numbers

Key Concepts

• A **fraction** names part of a whole or part of a set. (p. 537)

$$\frac{4}{5} \begin{matrix} \leftarrow \text{numerator} \\ \leftarrow \text{denominator} \end{matrix}$$

• **Equivalent fractions** represent the same amount. (p. 548)

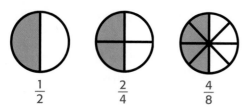

$$\frac{1}{2} \qquad \frac{2}{4} \qquad \frac{4}{8}$$

• **Mixed numbers** have a whole number and a fractional part. (p. 560)

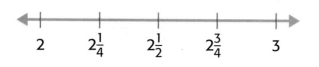

$$2 \qquad 2\frac{1}{4} \qquad 2\frac{1}{2} \qquad 2\frac{3}{4} \qquad 3$$

Key Vocabulary

denominator (p. 537)
equivalent fractions (p. 548)
fraction (p. 537)
mixed number (p. 560)
numerator (p. 537)

Vocabulary Check

Complete each sentence with the correct vocabulary word.

1. In the fraction $\frac{3}{4}$, the 4 is the ___?___.

2. A number that names part of a whole or part of a set is a(n) ___?___.

3. A(n) ___?___ has a whole number part and a fraction part.

4. In the fraction $\frac{3}{4}$, the 3 is the ___?___.

5. Fractions that represent the same amount are ___?___.

6. In a fraction, the ___?___ is the top number and the ___?___ is the bottom number.

Lesson-by-Lesson Review

13-1 Parts of a Whole (pp. 537–539)

3-2.5

Example 1
What fraction of the figure is shaded?

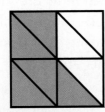

Write   parts shaded $\longrightarrow \dfrac{5}{8}$
         total parts in all $\longrightarrow$

Read   *five eighths* or
         five divided by eight

So, $\dfrac{5}{8}$ of the figure is shaded.

Write the fraction that names part of the whole that is shaded.

7.   8.

Draw a picture and shade part of it to show the fraction.

9. $\dfrac{2}{3}$ 10. $\dfrac{5}{6}$

11. What fraction of the waffle is missing?

13-2 Parts of a Set (pp. 540–543)

3-2.5

Example 2
What fraction of the crayons shown is *not* red?

Write   crayons not red $\longrightarrow \dfrac{3}{5}$
         total crayons $\longrightarrow$

Read   *three fifths* or
         three divided by five

So, $\dfrac{3}{5}$ of the crayons are *not* red.

Write the fraction that names the part of the set of shapes.

12. *not* purple

13. *not* green

14. *not* orange

15. *not* red

16. *not* yellow

17. *not* a sun

18. There are five cars. Two fifths of the cars are blue. Draw a picture to show the set.

13-3 Problem-Solving Strategy: Draw a Picture (pp. 544–545)

4-1.4

Example 3

Marcela has 24 crayons. Of them, $\frac{1}{3}$ are blue. Four are yellow, and the rest are green. How many crayons are green?

Understand

What facts do you know?

- There are 24 crayons.
- $\frac{1}{3}$ are blue.
- 4 are yellow.
- The rest are green.

What do you need to find?

Find how many crayons are green.

Plan   Draw a picture.

Solve   Divide 24 equal parts. Shade $\frac{1}{3}$ to show the blue crayons. Shade 4 to show the yellow crayons.

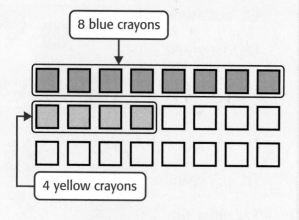

8 blue crayons

4 yellow crayons

There are 12 parts left. So, 12 of the crayons are green.

Check   Since 8 + 4 + 12 = 24 crayons, the answer makes sense.

19. The 24 students in Ms. Cameron's class are working on art projects. One half of them are painting. Eight students are making a clay sculpture. The rest of the students are making sketches. How many students are making sketches?

20. **Measurement** Serefina took part in the activities listed. How long did she eat a snack?

Serefina's Activities	
Activity	**Time Spent**
Read a book	$\frac{1}{2}$ of an hour
Watch TV	20 minutes
Eat a snack	rest of the hour

21. Of 15 cars, 7 are blue and $\frac{1}{5}$ are red. The rest of the cars are black. How many cars are black?

22. Jeff had 28 grapes. He ate $\frac{1}{2}$ of them for lunch. Then he ate 10 more as a snack. How many are left?

23. Marisa has a marble collection. One-fourth of her 16 marbles are blue. Her red marbles are shown below. The rest of the marbles are green. How many are green?

13-4 Equivalent Fractions (pp. 548–551)

4-2.8

Example 4

Find two fractions equivalent to $\frac{4}{6}$.

One Way: Multiply

$$\frac{4 \times \boxed{2}}{6 \times \boxed{2}} = \frac{8}{12}$$ Multiply the numerator and the denominator by the same number, 2.

Another Way: Divide

$$\frac{4 \div \boxed{2}}{6 \div \boxed{2}} = \frac{2}{3}$$ Divide the numerator and the denominator by the same number, 2.

So, $\frac{8}{12}$ and $\frac{2}{3}$ are equivalent to $\frac{4}{6}$.

Find an equivalent fraction for each fraction.

24. $\frac{1}{5}$ **25.** $\frac{1}{3}$ **26.** $\frac{1}{4}$

27. $\frac{6}{8}$ **28.** $\frac{7}{14}$ **29.** $\frac{9}{12}$

Write an equivalent fraction for each amount.

30. Dave hit 4 out of 8 baseballs.

31. Teresa's team won 9 out of 12 tennis matches.

32. Lara ate 4 out of 8 celery sticks.

13-5 Compare and Order Fractions (pp. 554–557)

4-2.9

Example 5

Dakota has a red and a blue pencil. The red pencil is $\frac{1}{2}$ of a foot long. The blue pencil is $\frac{3}{8}$ of a foot long. Which pencil is longer?

You can use number lines to compare the length of the pencils.

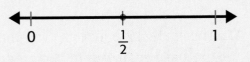

So, the red pencil is longer than the blue pencil.

Compare. Use >, <, or =.

33.

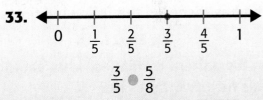

$$\frac{3}{5} \bullet \frac{5}{8}$$

34. $\frac{4}{5} \bullet \frac{8}{10}$ **35.** $\frac{6}{6} \bullet \frac{5}{6}$

Order from least to greatest.

36. $\frac{2}{3}, \frac{3}{7}, \frac{4}{35}$ **37.** $\frac{1}{4}, \frac{3}{16}, \frac{7}{8}$

38. Measurement Patrick took $\frac{3}{4}$ of an hour to finish a test. José took $\frac{3}{8}$ of an hour to finish. Who took more time to finish the test?

13-6 **Mixed Numbers** (pp. 560–563)

4-2.11

Example 6
A fourth grade class had a pizza party. The amount of pizza eaten can be represented as $3\frac{1}{5}$. Write the amout of the pizza eaten as an improper fraction.

$$3\frac{1}{5} = \boxed{\frac{5}{5}} + \boxed{\frac{5}{5}} + \boxed{\frac{5}{5}} + \frac{1}{5}$$

$$= \frac{5 + 5 + 5 + 1}{5}$$

$$= \frac{16}{5}$$

So, $3\frac{1}{5} = \frac{16}{5}$.

Write a mixed number and an improper fraction for each model.

39.

40.

Write each as an improper fraction or a mixed number. Use models if needed.

41. $\frac{18}{4}$ **42.** $\frac{32}{8}$

43. $2\frac{3}{4}$ **44.** $3\frac{7}{8}$

13-7 **Problem-Solving Investigation: Choose a Strategy** (pp. 564–565)

4-1.1

Example 7
Charlie runs track daily and records his time in seconds. In the last four days he has recorded the following times:

27, 24, 21, 18

If his pattern continues, what should his next two times be?

Look for a pattern in the times. Then extend to solve the problem.

Notice that each of Charlie's times goes down by three. So, the pattern is subtract 3.

27, 24, 21, 18, 15, 12
   −3 −3 −3 −3 −3

So, Charlie's next two times will be 15 and 12 seconds.

Use any strategy to solve.

45. Kellie earned $35 a day for chopping wood. If she earned a total of $245, how many days did she chop wood?

46. Draw the next figure in the pattern.

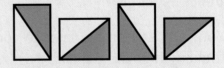

47. There are 12 balloons. One-third of the balloons are red. The green balloons are shown below. The rest of the balloons are yellow. How many of the balloons are yellow?

For Exercises 1 and 2, tell whether each statement is _true_ or _false_.

1. An improper fraction has a numerator that is less than its denominator.

2. To find an equivalent fraction, multiply or divide the numerator and denominator by the same number.

Find an equivalent fraction for each fraction.

3. $\frac{3}{12}$

4. $\frac{24}{40}$

5. $\frac{1}{5}$

6. $\frac{1}{3}$

7. Madison and Alan each ate the amount of apple pie shown. How much of one whole apple pie is left if the shaded parts represent pieces of pie?

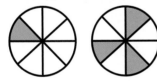

8. **MULTIPLE CHOICE** Which fraction is NOT equivalent to the shaded area of the circle?

A $\frac{1}{2}$

C $\frac{4}{8}$

B $\frac{2}{4}$

D $\frac{7}{12}$

Compare. Use >, <, or =.

9. $\frac{2}{4} \bullet \frac{3}{4}$

10. $\frac{4}{10} \bullet \frac{1}{2}$

Write each mixed number as an improper fraction.

11. $2\frac{3}{4}$

12. $4\frac{5}{12}$

13. There are 12 fish in Nicolas's aquarium. One-half of the fish are goldfish. Four of the fish are tetras. The rest of the fish are rainbow fish. How many of the fish are rainbow fish?

Identify each point as a mixed number and an improper fraction.

14.

15.

16. Abby read $\frac{3}{10}$ of a book on Saturday. Then she read $\frac{4}{10}$ of the book on Sunday. What fraction of the book does Abby still have to read?

17. **MULTIPLE CHOICE** Identify the improper fraction below that is NOT equivalent to $2\frac{4}{5}$.

F $\frac{28}{10}$

H $\frac{15}{5}$

G $\frac{42}{15}$

J $\frac{56}{20}$

18. **WRITING IN** ▸**MATH** Explain how $\frac{2}{7}$ and $\frac{6}{21}$ are equivalent fractions.

PART 1   Multiple Choice

Read each question. Then fill in the correct answer on the answer sheet provided by your teacher or on a sheet of paper.

1. Danielle ate $\frac{1}{3}$ of an orange. Which fraction is equivalent to $\frac{1}{3}$?

   A $\frac{2}{4}$ **C** $\frac{3}{9}$

   B $\frac{5}{12}$ **D** $\frac{2}{8}$

2. Which number is 100,000 more than 32,769,201?

   F 32,769,201   **H** 32,869,201

   G 32,779,201   **J** 42,769,201

3. Kathryn walked $\frac{2}{5}$ of a mile in the morning. Which model shows the fraction of a mile Kathryn walked?

   A   **C**

   B    **D**

4. Which set of fractions is in order from least to greatest?

   F $\frac{6}{10}, \frac{4}{5}, \frac{1}{2}$ **H** $\frac{1}{2}, \frac{4}{5}, \frac{6}{10}$

   G $\frac{4}{5}, \frac{1}{2}, \frac{6}{10}$ **J** $\frac{1}{2}, \frac{6}{10}, \frac{4}{5}$

5. Tionna jogged $2\frac{3}{5}$ miles. Write $2\frac{3}{5}$ as an improper fraction.

   A $\frac{13}{10}$ **C** $\frac{12}{5}$

   B $\frac{10}{5}$ **D** $\frac{13}{5}$

6. Megan's dog is $3\frac{1}{2}$ years old. Which point best represents $3\frac{1}{2}$ on the number line?

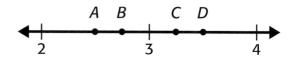

   F point A **H** point C

   G point B **J** point D

7. What is the value of the expression below if $c = 4$?

$$21 - (c + 7)$$

   A 7   **C** 11

   B 10   **D** 32

8. Look at the figures. Which fraction is shown by the shaded part of the figures?

   F $1\frac{1}{4}$ **H** $1\frac{3}{8}$

   G $1\frac{1}{2}$ **J** $1\frac{5}{8}$

9. Which expression is shown below?

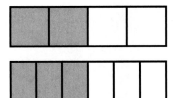

A $\frac{2}{4} = \frac{3}{6}$ **C** $\frac{2}{4} < \frac{3}{6}$

B $\frac{2}{4} > \frac{3}{6}$ **D** $\frac{2}{4} + \frac{3}{6}$

---

10. Which fraction is equivalent to $\frac{8}{12}$?

F $\frac{1}{4}$ **H** $\frac{3}{4}$

G $\frac{2}{3}$ **J** $\frac{3}{5}$

---

11. What fraction does *N* represent?

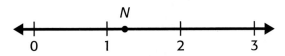

A $\frac{3}{4}$ **C** $1\frac{3}{4}$

B $1\frac{1}{4}$ **D** $2\frac{1}{4}$

---

12. Santos read a 280-page book in 7 days. He read the same number of pages each day. How many pages did he read each day?

F 30   **H** 40

G 36   **J** 42

PART 2   Short Response

Record your answers on the answer sheet provided by your teacher or on a sheet of paper.

13. Malia answered 8 out of 10 questions on a quiz correctly. Write a fraction that is equivalent to $\frac{8}{10}$.

---

14. What fraction does the model represent?

---

15. Amanda swam $3\frac{2}{3}$ laps in a pool. Write $3\frac{2}{3}$ as an improper fraction.

PART 3   Extended Response

Record your answers on the answer sheet provided by your teacher or on a sheet of paper.

16. Draw a model to show $\frac{5}{6}$. Explain how the model shows $\frac{5}{6}$.

---

17. Write a fraction equivalent to $\frac{5}{6}$. Draw a model to explain your reasoning.

NEED EXTRA HELP?																	
If You Missed Question...	1	2	3	4	5	6	7	8	9	10	11	12	13	14	15	16	17
Go to Lesson...	13-4	2-4	13-1	13-5	13-6	13-6	5-1	13-6	13-5	13-4	13-6	8-2	13-4	13-6	13-6	13-1	13-4
SC Academic Standards	4-2.8	3-2.3	3-2.5	4-2.9	4-2.11	4-2.11	4-3.4	4-2.11	4-2.9	4-2.8	4-2.11	4-2.5	4-2.8	4-2.11	4-2.11	3-2.5	4-2.8

Use Place Value to Represent Decimals

What are decimals?

Decimals are numbers that use place value and a decimal point to show part of a whole.

Example There are 10 dimes in a dollar. One dime is $\frac{1}{10}$ of a dollar. There are 100 pennies in a dollar. One penny is $\frac{1}{100}$ of a dollar.

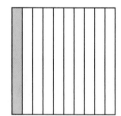

One dime is $\frac{1}{10}$ of a dollar.

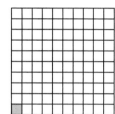

One penny is $\frac{1}{100}$ of a dollar.

What will I learn in this chapter?

- Identify, read, write, and model decimals.
- Relate decimals, fractions, and mixed numbers.
- Compare and order decimals.
- Solve problems by making a model.

Key Vocabulary

decimal

decimal point

tenth

hundredth

SC Math Online ▷ **Student Study Tools** **at** macmillanmh.com

FOLDABLES
Study Organizer

Make this Foldable to help you organize information about decmials. Begin with one sheet of 11″ × 17″ paper.

1 Fold the short sides so they meet in the middle.

2 Fold again so the top meets the bottom.

3 Unfold and cut as shown to make four tabs.

4 Label the outside of each tab as shown.

Fractions and Decimals	Compare and Order Decimals
Relate Mixed Numbers and Decimals	Decimals, Fractions, and Mixed Numbers

You have two ways to check prerequisite skills for this chapter.

Option 2

SC Math Online ▷ Take the Chapter Readiness Quiz at **macmillanmh.com**.

Option 1

Complete the Quick Check below.

QUICK Check

Write a fraction to describe the part that is green. (Lesson 13-1)

1.

2.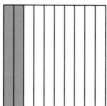

3.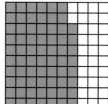

Write each as a fraction. (Lessons 13-1 and 13-2)

4. four tenths

5. eight tenths

6. twenty hundredths

7. Measurement On Tuesday, seven-tenths of an inch of rain fell. Write the amount of rain that fell as a fraction.

Algebra Copy and complete. (Lesson 13-4)

8. $\dfrac{1}{5} = \dfrac{\blacksquare}{10}$

9. $\dfrac{4}{5} = \dfrac{\blacksquare}{10}$

10. $\dfrac{1}{2} = \dfrac{\blacksquare}{10}$

11. $\dfrac{1}{4} = \dfrac{\blacksquare}{100}$

12. $\dfrac{2}{5} = \dfrac{\blacksquare}{100}$

13. $\dfrac{1}{2} = \dfrac{\blacksquare}{100}$

14. In Salvador's aquarium, $\dfrac{4}{10}$ of the fish are yellow and $\dfrac{6}{10}$ are blue. Are there more blue or yellow fish in Salvador's aquarium? Explain how you know.

A fraction shows part of a whole. A decimal also shows a part of a whole. A **decimal** is a number that uses place value, numbers, and a decimal point to show part of a whole.

one whole

$$\frac{1}{1} = 1.0$$

↑ decimal point

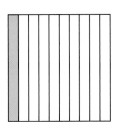

one **tenth**

$$\frac{1}{10} = 0.1$$

↑ decimal point

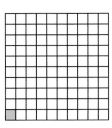

one **hundredth**

$$\frac{1}{100} = 0.01$$

↑ decimal point

ACTIVITY

1 Model 4 tenths using grids.

Step 1 **Use a tenths grid.**

Shade 4 of the 10 parts to show 4 tenths.

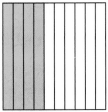

Step 2 **Use a hundredths grid.**

Shade 40 of the 100 parts to show 40 hundredths.

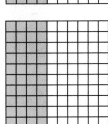

Step 3 **Compare.**

Compare the grids. Write the fraction for each shaded part.

Step 4 **Write decimals.**

How is 4 tenths written as a decimal?
How is 40 hundredths written as a decimal?

ACTIVITY

2 **Model 77 hundredths using coins.**

Step 1 **Use dimes.**

One dime is $\frac{1}{10}$ of a dollar. Count out 7 dimes to represent 7 tenths or $\frac{7}{10}$.

Step 2 **Use pennies.**

One penny is $\frac{1}{100}$ of a dollar. Count out 7 pennies to represent 7 hundredths or $\frac{7}{100}$.

Step 3 **Combine the coins.**

Combine the dimes and pennies to represent $\frac{77}{100}$ or 0.77.

Think About It

1. Do $\frac{4}{10}$, $\frac{40}{100}$, 0.4, and 0.40 represent the same number? Explain.

2. Is 0.02 greater than 0.2? Support your answer with models.

3. Is 0.3 greater than 0.30? Explain.

 CHECK **What You Know**

Write a fraction and a decimal for each shaded part.

4.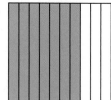

5.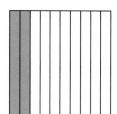

6.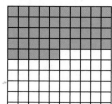

7.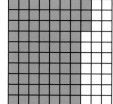

Model each fraction. Then write as a decimal.

8. $\frac{1}{10}$

9. $\frac{3}{10}$

10. $\frac{60}{100}$

11. $\frac{82}{100}$

Model each decimal. Then write as a fraction.

12. 0.5

13. 0.75

14. 0.3

15. 0.25

16. **WRITING IN ►MATH** Explain how to write a fraction with a denominator of 10 as a decimal.

578 **Chapter 14** Use Place Value to Represent Decimals

MAIN IDEA

I will identify, read, and write tenths and hundredths as decimals and fractions.

SC Academic Standards

4-2.10 Identify the common fraction/decimal equivalents $\frac{1}{2} = .5$, $\frac{1}{4} = .25$, $\frac{3}{4} = .75$, $\frac{1}{3} \approx .33$, $\frac{2}{3} \approx .67$, **multiples of** $\frac{1}{10}$, **and multiples of** $\frac{1}{100}$. *Also addresses 4-2.6, 4-2.11.*

New Vocabulary

decimal
decimal point
tenth
hundredth

SC Math Online

macmillanmh.com
• Extra Examples
• Personal Tutor
• Self-Check Quiz

GET READY to Learn

It costs 85 cents for a child to ride the light rail system. Can you write this part of a dollar as a fraction and as a decimal?

A **decimal** is a number that uses place value and a **decimal point** to show part of a whole.

EXAMPLE   Read and Write Decimals

1 MONEY Write 85 cents as a fraction and as a decimal.

The amount 85 cents means 85 pennies out of 1 dollar.

One Way: Use a Model	Another Way: Place Value
Draw a hundreds model. Shade 85 out of 100 parts to show 85 cents. 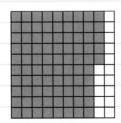	

Place Value table:

Hundreds	Tens	Ones	Tenths	Hundredths
		0	8	5

Read eighty-five hundredths	**Read** eighty-five hundredths
Write $\frac{85}{100}$ or 0.85	**Write** $\frac{85}{100}$ or 0.85

So, 85 cents is $\frac{85}{100}$ as a fraction and 0.85 as a decimal.

Some fractions can be written as **tenths** and **hundredths**.

EXAMPLE   Write Tenths and Hundredths

2 Write $\frac{5}{10}$ as two different decimals.

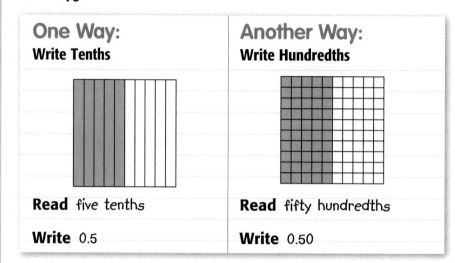

One Way: Write Tenths	Another Way: Write Hundredths
Read five tenths	**Read** fifty hundredths
Write 0.5	**Write** 0.50

The decimals 0.5 and 0.50 are equivalent decimals.

CHECK What You Know

Write a fraction and a decimal for each shaded part. See Example 1 (p. 579)

1. 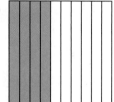   **2.** 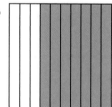   **3.**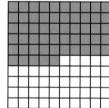

Write as a fraction and as a decimal. See Example 1 (p. 579)

4. one tenth   **5.** twenty-five hundredths   **6.** seven hundredths

Write each fraction as a decimal. See Example 2 (p. 580)

7. $\frac{6}{10}$ **8.** $\frac{9}{10}$ **9.** $\frac{10}{100}$ **10.** $\frac{69}{100}$

11. Measurement A baby owl weighs about twenty-three hundredths of a kilogram. Write this amount as a fraction and decimal.

12. Talk About It   Shade all of the boxes along the outer edge of a hundreds grid. Write a fraction and decimal for the shaded part. Why is it not 0.40?

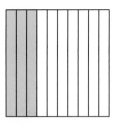
Write a fraction and a decimal for each shaded part. See Example 1 (p. 579)

13.

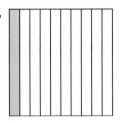

14.

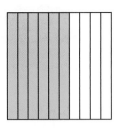

15.

16.

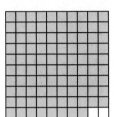

17.

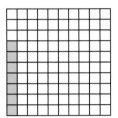

18.

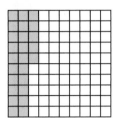

Write as a fraction and as a decimal. See Example 1 (p. 579)

19. sixty-two hundredths

20. two tenths

21. thirty-five hundredths

22. eight tenths

23. fourteen hundredths

24. six tenths

Write each fraction as a decimal. See Example 2 (p. 580)

25. $\frac{22}{100}$

26. $\frac{2}{100}$

27. $\frac{2}{10}$

28. $\frac{50}{100}$

29. $\frac{75}{100}$

30. $\frac{80}{100}$

31. Measurement On Monday, it snowed $\frac{6}{10}$ of an inch.

32. Measurement A car traveled $\frac{3}{10}$ of a mile in 18 seconds.

33. Each state has a representation of $\frac{2}{100}$ in the U.S. Senate.

34. Cody learned that $\frac{4}{10}$ of the students in his class are left handed.

H.O.T. Problems

35. OPEN ENDED Write a fraction whose decimal value is between $\frac{2}{10}$ and $\frac{25}{100}$. Write the fraction and its decimal equivalent.

36. CHALLENGE Decide whether the following sentence is true or false. Explain. *The fraction $\frac{6}{1,000}$ equals 0.006.*

37. **WRITING IN** ►**MATH** Write a summary statement about decimals equivalent to fractions that have denominators of 10 and 100.

Relate Mixed Numbers and Decimals

GET READY to Learn

Giant saguaro (*sah-WAH-ro*) cacti are found in Arizona and Mexico. A saguaro's growth is slow. It takes about 30 years for one to grow $2\frac{5}{10}$ feet tall and start flowering.

A mixed number like $2\frac{5}{10}$ is a fraction greater than one. You can write mixed numbers as decimals.

EXAMPLE Mixed Numbers as Decimals

1. Write $2\frac{5}{10}$ as a decimal.

One Way: Use a Model	Another Way: Place Value
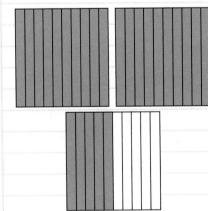		Hundreds	Tens	Ones	Tenths	 			2	5	
Mixed Number $2\frac{5}{10}$ Read two and five tenths Write 2.5	Mixed Number $2\frac{5}{10}$ Read two and five tenths Write 2.5

So, $2\frac{5}{10}$ as a decimal is 2.5.

2 **MEASUREMENT** The length of an iguana is $1\frac{9}{100}$ yards. Write $1\frac{9}{100}$ as a decimal.

You can use a model or a place-value chart.

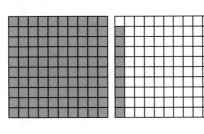

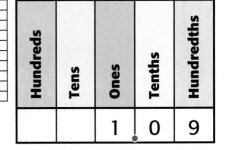

Hundreds	Tens	Ones	Tenths	Hundredths
		1	0	9

Remember

When reading a decimal, the word *and* represents the decimal.

Mixed Number $1\frac{9}{100}$

Read one and nine hundredths

Write 1.09

CHECK What You Know

Write each as a mixed number and decimal. See Examples 1 and 2 (pp. 582–583)

1.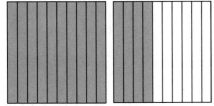

2.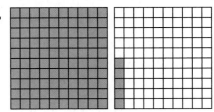

3. twelve and three tenths

4. twelve and three hundredths

5. three and six tenths

6. sixteen and thirty-two hundredths

Write each mixed number as a decimal. See Examples 1 and 2 (pp. 582–583)

7. $5\frac{3}{10}$

8. $12\frac{5}{10}$

9. $6\frac{50}{100}$

10. $24\frac{8}{100}$

11. Measurement Jodi ran the 100-meter dash in 14.6 seconds. Tyra ran the 100-meter dash in 14.64 seconds. Write each girl's time as a mixed number.

12. **Talk About It** Do the numbers $8\frac{5}{10}$, $8\frac{1}{2}$, and 8.5 name the same amount? Explain your reasoning.

Write each as a mixed number and decimal. See Examples 1 and 2 (pp. 582–583)

13.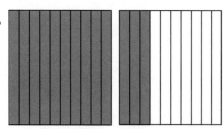

14.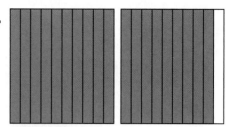

15.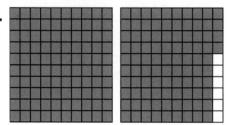

16.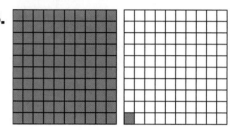

17. one and five tenths

18. sixteen and seven tenths

19. nineteen and one hundred hundredths

20. fifty-six and one hundredth

Write each mixed number as a decimal. See Examples 1 and 2 (pp. 582–583)

21. $2\frac{5}{10}$

22. $6\frac{6}{10}$

23. $50\frac{1}{10}$

24. $78\frac{8}{10}$

25. $10\frac{16}{100}$

26. $60\frac{2}{100}$

27. $5\frac{25}{100}$

28. $22\frac{75}{100}$

29. Measurement Aaron has grown $3\frac{4}{10}$ feet since he was born. Write a decimal to show how many feet Aaron has grown.

30. Measurement Coastal Plains received 5.52 inches of rain. Write a mixed number to show the number of inches Coastal Plains received.

South Carolina Data File

Charles Towne Landing offers tours of the Animal Forest and the History Trail.

31. The History Trail is about $1\frac{5}{10}$ miles long. Write $1\frac{5}{10}$ as a decimal.

32. A fourth grade class visits the Animal Forest from 10:30 to 12:00. Write the number of hours the class spent in the Animal Forest as a fraction and a decimal.

Source: Charles Towne Landing

H.O.T. Problems

33. OPEN ENDED Write a mixed number and decimal that are less than five and eight tenths.

34. FIND THE ERROR Brianna and Nick are writing $2\frac{3}{4}$ as a decimal. Who is correct? Explain your reasoning.

Brianna
$2\frac{3}{4} = 2.75$

Nick
$2\frac{3}{4} = 2.34$

35. **WRITING IN** ➤**MATH** Are $2\frac{4}{8}$ and 2.5 equivalent? Explain.

PASS Practice 4-2.11

36. Which number represents the shaded parts of the figure?
(Lesson 14-1)

   A 0.04

   B 0.4

   C 4.0

   D 4.4

37. Which of the following is seven and seven hundredths? (Lesson 14-2)

   F 0.77

   G 7.07

   H 7.7

   J $7\frac{7}{10}$

Spiral Review

Write as a fraction and as a decimal. (Lesson 14-1)

38. five tenths

39. fifty-six hundredths

40. Justino read $\frac{16}{10}$ books this week. How many books did he read written as a mixed number? (Lesson 13-6)

41. Measurement Select two containers. Estimate and then measure whether each container has a capacity that is greater than, less than, or equal to 2 liters. (Lesson 12-3)

14-3 Problem-Solving Strategy

MAIN IDEA I will solve problems by making a model.

SCAS **4-1.7** Use flexibility in mathematical representations. **4-1.8** Recognize the limitations of various forms of mathematical representations.

Luisa needs to seat 22 guests for her birthday party. They have an oval table that can seat 10 people. They also have square tables that each seat 4 people. How many square tables are needed to seat the guests?

Understand	**What facts do you know?** • An oval table seats 10 people. • There will be 22 guests altogether. • Each square table seats 4 people. **What do you need to find?** • The number of square tables needed to seat the guests.
Plan	You can make a model to see how many tables are needed.
Solve	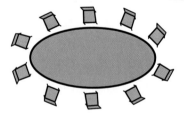 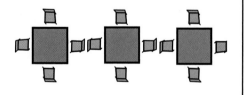 The oval table can seat 10 people. $22 - 10 = 12$ 12 people will sit at square tables. $12 - 12 = 0$ So, three is the fewest number of square tables needed to seat the guests.
Check	Look back. The fewest number of square tables needed is 3. This makes sense because $22 - 10 - (3 \times 4) = 0$. So, the answer is correct. ✓

Refer to the problem on the previous page.

1. Explain how a model was used to find the fewest number of tables.

2. Explain another strategy you could use to solve Luisa's problem.

3. Suppose there were 30 guests. How many square tables would be needed?

4. Look back at Exercise 3. Check your answer. How do you know that it is correct? Show your work.

▶ PRACTICE the Strategy

SCAS • PASS
Extra Practice, p. R36

Solve. Use the make a model strategy.

5. Eileen opened 8 boxes of clay for her project. Each box had 4 sticks of gray clay and half as many sticks of red clay. How many sticks of clay were there in all?

6. Cesar is making a model of the longest bridge in the table for a school project. The scale he is using is one inch equals 200 feet. How many inches long will the model be?

Bridges	
Bridge	**Length (ft)**
Drawbridge	4,200
Suspension Bridge	3,478
Cable-Stayed Bridge	2,310

7. Measurement Katia is painting her living room. The room has 3 walls that are 16 feet long and 9 feet tall. A gallon of paint covers 150 square feet. How many gallons should she buy to cover all 3 walls?

8. Measurement Every day Marvin runs 3,200 meters around the school track. How many times does he run around the track?

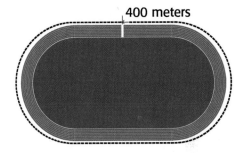
400 meters

9. Mariana rode her bike 5 miles. Then she went back the same route to get her brother. They rode together for 17 miles. How far did Mariana go altogether?

10. A volleyball court measures 18 meters by 9 meters. A basketball court measures 29 meters by 15 meters. How many volleyball courts could be placed in a basketball court?

11. WRITING IN ▶ MATH The bottom layer of a pyramid-shaped display has four boxes. There is one less box in each layer. There are four layers. The answer is 10. What is the question?

Locate Fractions and Decimals on a Number Line

GET READY to Learn

Curtis is trying to find $4\frac{1}{4}$ on the number line. He knows that the point is between 4 and 5.

MAIN IDEA

I will locate fractions and decimals on a number line.

SC Academic Standards

4-2.10 Identify the common fraction/decimal equivalents
$\frac{1}{2} = .5, \frac{1}{4} = .25, \frac{3}{4} = .75,$
$\frac{1}{3} \approx .33, \frac{2}{3} \approx .67,$
multiples of $\frac{1}{10}$, and multiples of $\frac{1}{100}$.
Also addresses 4-2.11.

SC Math Online
macmillanmh.com
• Extra Examples
• Personal Tutor
• Self-Check Quiz

You can locate fractions and decimals on a number line. Use the markings between the whole numbers to determine the fraction or decimal value of a certain point on a number line.

EXAMPLE   Locate Points on a Number Line

1 **Locate $4\frac{1}{4}$ on the number line.**

First find 4. Then, find the $\frac{1}{2}$ mark between 4 and 5.

Finally, find the $\frac{1}{4}$ mark halfway between 4 and $4\frac{1}{2}$.

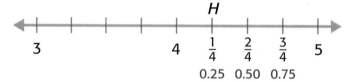

Points on a number line can be represented by a letter.
So, $H = 4\frac{1}{4}$ or 4.25.

EXAMPLE   Name Points on a Number Line

2 **What number does point N represent on the number line?**

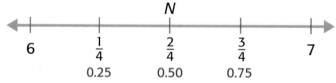

Since N is between 6 and 7, you know N represents a fraction or decimal. The three marks between 6 and 7 let you know the denominator will be 4. Make equivalent fractions to determine the decimal. So, N is $6\frac{2}{4}$ or 6.5

Tell which letter represents each mixed number on the number line. Write as a decimal. See Example 1 (p. 588)

1. $10\frac{7}{10}$

2. $10\frac{2}{10}$

3. Identify the number point *N* represents. See Example 2 (p. 588)

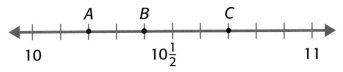

4. Measurement Selma measures a book in centimeters. The book ends at the fourth out of ten marks between 14 and 15. Find the length of the book.

5. **Talk About It** Explain the difference between finding $\frac{1}{2}$ on a number line and finding the halfway point on a number line.

Practice and Problem Solving

SCAS • PASS
Extra Practice, p. R37

Tell which letter represents each mixed number on the number line. Write as a decimal. See Example 1 (p. 588)

6. $12\frac{1}{2}$

7. $12\frac{3}{4}$

8. $2\frac{3}{5}$

9. $2\frac{1}{5}$

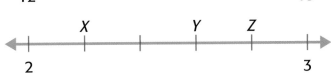

Identify the number point *N* represents. See Example 2 (p. 588)

10.

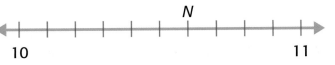

11.

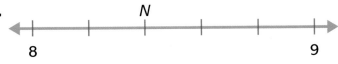

H.O.T. Problems

12. OPEN ENDED Create a number line that shows four points. One point must be $12\frac{3}{4}$.

13. **WRITING IN ►MATH** Explain how to show 2.5 on a number line.

Compare and Order Decimals

GET READY to Learn

The table shows the results from a skateboarding competition. Who has the higher score, Doria or Elise?

Skateboarding Results

Name	Score
Doria	79.7
Lina	79.2
Holly	78.9
Elise	79.5
Jane	78.8

MAIN IDEA

I will compare and order decimals.

SC Academic Standards

4-2.7 Compare decimals through hundredths by using the terms *is less than*, *is greater than*, and *is equal to* and the symbols <, >, and =.

SC Math Online

macmillanmh.com

• Extra Examples
• Personal Tutor
• Self-Check Quiz

To compare decimals, you can use a number line or place value.

Real-World EXAMPLE   Compare Decimals

1 **SCORES** Who has the higher score, Doria or Elise?

Doria has a score of 79.7, while Elise has a score of 79.5.

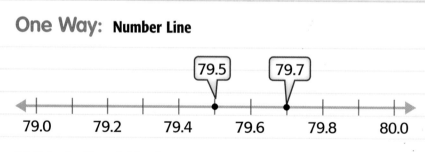

One Way: Number Line

79.7 is to the right of 79.5.
So, 79.7 > 79.5.

Another Way: Place Value
Line up the decimal points. Then compare the digits in each place-value position. In the tenths place, 7 > 5. So, 79.7 is greater than 79.5.

Tens	Ones	Tenths
7	9	7
7	9	5

So, Doria has the higher score.

You can also order decimals.

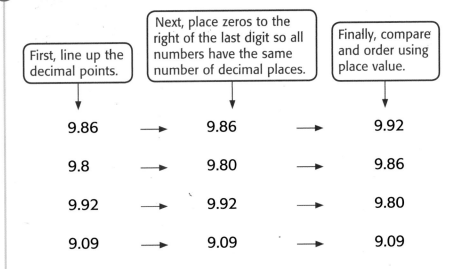

EXAMPLE Order Decimals

Vocabulary Link

order

Everyday Use select desired items

Math Use to arrange in a logical pattern

② Order 9.86, 9.8, 9.92, and 9.09 from greatest to least.

First, line up the decimal points.

Next, place zeros to the right of the last digit so all numbers have the same number of decimal places.

Finally, compare and order using place value.

9.86	→	9.86	→	9.92
9.8	→	9.80	→	9.86
9.92	→	9.92	→	9.80
9.09	→	9.09	→	9.09

The order from greatest to least is 9.92, 9.86, 9.8, and 9.09.

CHECK What You Know

Compare. Use >, <, or =. See Example 1 (p. 590)

1. 0.2 ● 0.6

2. 12.07 ● 1.207

3. 5.60 ● 5.6

Order from greatest to least. See Example 2 (p. 591)

4. 3.2, 4.5, 3.9, 4.1

5. 0.12, 1.2, 1.21, 12.0

6. $6.52, $5.62, $6.50, $5.60

For Exercises 7 and 8, use the number line to compare and order each set of decimals from least to greatest.

7. 5.7, 5.2, 4.7, 4.2

8. 4.2, 4.8, 6.2, 5.8

9. Measurement Four friends are going to different summer camps. The table shows the distance between each camp and their hometown. Order the distances from least to greatest.

| Traveling to Camp | |
Name	Distance (mi)
Bill	64.25
Sami	42.5
Latesha	64.87
Irena	42.35

10. **Talk About It** Tell how to order 5.5, 5.3, 5.4, and 5.0 from greatest to least.

Compare. Use >, <, or =. See Example 1 (p. 590)

11. 0.74 ● 7.4   **12.** 16.33 ● 16.3   **13.** 0.56 ● 0.58   **14.** 0.8 ● 0.80

15. 1 ● 0.09   **16.** 0.90 ● 0.9   **17.** 82.6 ● 82.60   **18.** 1.06 ● 1.05

Order from greatest to least. See Example 2 (p. 591)

19. 0.4, 0.42, 0.54   **20.** 0.08, 0.80, 0.82   **21.** $12.50, $1.25, $12.05

22. $19.62, $19.56, $19.60   **23.** 0.5, 0.55, 0.6   **24.** 68.16, 81.6, 68.1

For Exercises 25–28, use the number line to compare and order each set of decimals from least to greatest.

25. 6.3, 8.1, 7.5, 7.7   **26.** 7.5, 6.2, 7.75, 6.25

27. 6.45, 7.52, 8.01, 6.25   **28.** 8.05, 7.75, 6.8, 7.57

29. Marlon averages 5.6 rebounds per game. Tina averages 5.9 rebounds per game. Bret averages 4.3 rebounds per game. Who averages the most rebounds? Explain.

30. Measurement Rita ran the 100-meter dash four times, which is timed in seconds. Her times were 16.25, 15.36, 16.55, and 15.23. What was her slowest time?

31. Measurement The table at the right shows the distances Seth biked. Did he bike more the first weekend or the last weekend?

Distance Biked in July	
Weekend	**Distance (mi)**
1	3.25
2	3.5
3	3
4	3.6

H.O.T. Problems

32. OPEN ENDED Draw a number line that contains two whole numbers. Divide the number line in tenths. Identify the location of three decimals on the number line.

33. NUMBER SENSE What number is halfway between 4.36 and 4.48 on a number line?

34. WRITING IN ►MATH Write a real-world problem about comparing and ordering decimals.

Write a fraction and a decimal for each shaded part. (Lesson 14-1)

1. 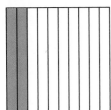   2.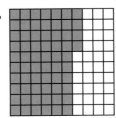

Write each fraction as a decimal. (Lesson 14-1)

3. $\frac{7}{10}$ 4. $\frac{34}{100}$

Write as a fraction and as a decimal. (Lesson 14-1)

5. three fourths   6. one fifth

7. **MULTIPLE CHOICE** Which of the following numbers is *six and six hundredths*? (Lesson 14-1)

A 0.66   C 6.6

B 6.06   D $6\frac{6}{10}$

Write each mixed number as a decimal. (Lesson 14-2)

8. $9\frac{1}{10}$ 9. $10\frac{3}{100}$

10. $7\frac{1}{100}$ 11. $2\frac{3}{10}$

Write each as a mixed number and decimal. (Lesson 14-2)

12. seven and three fourths

13. two and six tenths

14. **MULTIPLE CHOICE** Which number represents the shaded parts of the figure? (Lesson 14-2)

F 0.05   H 5.0

G 0.5   J 5.5

15. Trey has 18 coins. One half are nickels. One third are dimes. The rest are quarters. How much are Trey's coins worth? Use the make a model strategy. (Lesson 14-3)

Identify the numbers points N and P represent. (Lesson 14-4)

16.

N = _____   P = _____

Compare. Use >, <, or =. (Lesson 14-5)

17. 6.4 ● 6.4   18. 13.09 ● 1.309

Order from greatest to least. (Lesson 14-5)

19. 1.2, 2.5, 1.9, 2.1

20. 0.32, 3.2, 1.31, 13.0

21. **WRITING IN MATH** Explain why $\frac{3}{10}$ and $\frac{30}{100}$ are equal.

14-6 Problem-Solving Investigation

MAIN IDEA I will choose the best strategy to solve a problem.

 SCAS 4-1.1 Analyze information to solve increasingly more sophisticated problems.

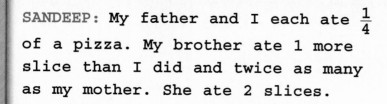

P.S.I. TEAM +

SANDEEP: My father and I each ate $\frac{1}{4}$ of a pizza. My brother ate 1 more slice than I did and twice as many as my mother. She ate 2 slices.

YOUR MISSION: Find the number of slices of pizza Sandeep's family ate.

Understand	You know how much pizza each person ate. Find the total number of slices of pizza the family ate.
Plan	Use logical reasoning to determine the answer.
Solve	Start with what is known. • Mother: 2 slices • Brother: twice as much as his mother or $2 \times 2 = 4$ slices • Sandeep: 1 less slice than his brother or 3 slices • Father: 3 slices So, Sandeep's family ate $2 + 4 + 3 + 3 = 12$ slices of pizza.
Check	Look back. Sandeep and his father ⟶ $\frac{1}{4}$ of $12 = 3$ Sandeep's brother ⟶ $3 + 1 = 4$ Sandeep's mother ⟶ $4 \div 2 = 2$ $3 + 3 + 4 + 2 = 12$. So, the answer is correct. ✓

Use any strategy shown below to solve. Tell what strategy you used.

PROBLEM-SOLVING STRATEGIES
- Look for a pattern.
- Work a simpler problem.
- Use logical reasoning.
- Draw a picture.
- Make a model.

1. Gina cut an apple into 8 slices and ate 3 of them. Rudy cut an apple into 4 slices and ate 2 of them. If the apples were the same size, who ate more?

2. Sarah's dad gave her the money shown. He gave $7 to each of her two brothers. He had $16 left. How much money did Sarah's dad start with?

3. Craig paid $75 for a snowboard that he used 32 times. Owen paid twice as much as Craig but used his board 82 times. Who got a better deal per use? Explain.

4. Measurement Felicia is building a garden. The garden will have an area of 48 square feet. Give three pairs of possible side lengths.

5. Algebra What is the rule for the pattern shown? What number comes next?

5, 13, 10, 18, 15, . . .

6. Measurement Adriano's driveway is rectangular in shape. The area of the driveway is 345 square feet. The length is shown. What is the width of the driveway?

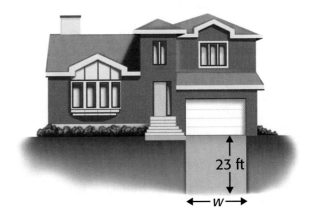

23 ft

←— w —→

7. Paige and Mustafa were in a snow skiing competition. Paige earned a score of 88.6, while Mustafa earned a score of 88.59. Who won? Explain.

8. Measurement Alani started her homework at 4:25 P.M. She stopped at 5:15 P.M. to eat dinner. She started her work again at 5:50 P.M. She then worked another 15 minutes and finished. How many minutes did she do her homework?

9. **WRITING IN** ►**MATH** The sum of Roman and his younger sister's age together equals 24. Roman's age is twice the amount of his sister's. How old is Roman and his sister? Explain.

Fraction and Decimal Equivalents

Nicole and Austin's family is taking a trip. Nicole says that the odometer (mileage tracker) shows they have driven 0.5 mile. Austin says $\frac{1}{2}$ mile. Can they both be correct?

MAIN IDEA

I will find fraction and decimal equivalents.

SC Academic Standards

4-2.10 Identify the common fraction/ decimal equivalents $\frac{1}{2} = .5$, $\frac{1}{4} = .25$, $\frac{3}{4} = .75$, $\frac{1}{3} \approx .33$, $\frac{2}{3} \approx .67$, **multiples of** $\frac{1}{10}$, **and multiples of** $\frac{1}{100}$.

SC Math Online

macmillanmh.com

• Extra Examples
• Personal Tutor
• Self-Check Quiz

When a fraction and a decimal name the same amount, they are fraction and decimal equivalents.

EXAMPLE   Fraction and Decimal Equivalents

1 **Determine whether 0.5 and $\frac{1}{2}$ are equivalent.**

Use tenths and hundredths grids to model that 0.5 and $\frac{1}{2}$ name the same amount.

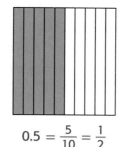

$$0.5 = \frac{5}{10} = \frac{1}{2}$$

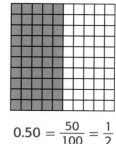

$$0.50 = \frac{50}{100} = \frac{1}{2}$$

The number lines also show that they name the same amount.

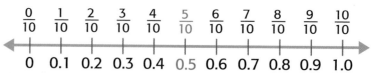

So, 0.5 and $\frac{1}{2}$ are equivalent.

To find a decimal that is equivalent to a fraction, it helps to write the fraction with a denominator of 10 or 100.

EXAMPLE Find Fraction and Decimal Equivalents

2 Write a fraction and decimal to describe the shaded part of the model.

$$\frac{3 \times \boxed{25}}{4 \times \boxed{25}} = \frac{75}{100}$$ ← THINK What number can you multiply the denominator by to get 100?

$$\frac{75}{100} = 0.75$$ Write $\frac{75}{100}$ as a decimal.

So, $\frac{3}{4}$ and 0.75 describe the shaded part of the model.

In Example 2, you found that $\frac{3}{4} = 0.75$ by writing equivalent fractions. Another way to write a fraction as a decimal is to divide.

EXAMPLE Fractions as Decimals

3 Write $\frac{2}{3}$ as a decimal

Divide 2 by 3.

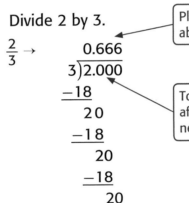

Place the decimal point directly above the decimal point after 2.

To divide 2 by 3, place a decimal point after 2 and annex as many zeros as necessary to complete the devision

This pattern repeats so we use an approximate equivalent decimal.

Therefore, $\frac{2}{3} \approx 0.67$

Remember

≈ means *about* or *approximately*

Here are some common fraction and decimal equivalents.

Fraction-Decimal Equivalents				Key Concept
$\frac{1}{2} = 0.5$	$\frac{1}{4} = 0.25$	$\frac{2}{4} = 0.5$	$\frac{3}{4} = 0.75$	$\frac{1}{3} \approx 0.33$
$\frac{1}{5} = 0.2$	$\frac{2}{5} = 0.4$	$\frac{3}{5} = 0.6$	$\frac{4}{5} = 0.8$	$\frac{2}{3} \approx 0.67$

Write a fraction and decimal to describe the shaded part of each model. See Examples 1 and 2 (pp. 596–597)

1.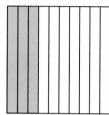

2.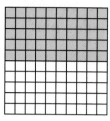

3.

4.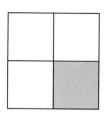

Write each fraction as a decimal. See Example 2 (p. 597)

5. $\frac{6}{10}$

6. $\frac{6}{100}$

7. $\frac{2}{4}$

8. $\frac{2}{3}$

9. Lupe got 20 out of 25 questions correct on a quiz. Write her score as a decimal and a fraction.

10. **Talk About It** What do you notice about $\frac{3}{4}$, $\frac{6}{8}$, and $\frac{12}{16}$?

Practice and Problem Solving

SCAS • PASS
Extra Practice, p. R38

Write a fraction and decimal to describe the shaded part of each model. See Examples 1–3 (pp. 596–597)

11.

12.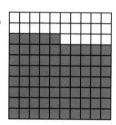

13.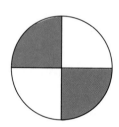

14.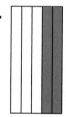

15.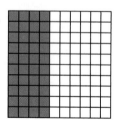

16.

17.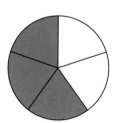

18.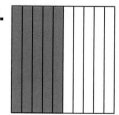

Write each fraction as a decimal. See Example 2 (p. 597)

19. $\frac{1}{3}$

20. $\frac{4}{10}$

21. $\frac{3}{5}$

22. $\frac{35}{100}$

23. $\frac{1}{4}$

24. $\frac{4}{5}$

25. $\frac{7}{25}$

26. $\frac{1}{10}$

H.O.T. Problems

27. OPEN ENDED Create a model and shade in a fraction of it. Write two fractions and a decimal to describe the shaded area of the model.

28. CHALLENGE Talia collects stuffed frogs. She has 25 frogs, and $\frac{2}{25}$ of them are multicolored. The rest are green. How many green frogs are in her collection? Explain how you found your answer.

29. WRITING IN ►MATH Demetri is completing $0.\blacksquare = \frac{5}{50}$. Explain how he can find the correct answer.

PASS Practice 4-2.7, 4-2.10

30. Look at the number line and detemine which order of numbers correctly shows the location of the points. (Lesson 14-5)

$$\longleftarrow \!\!\!\! \underset{3}{\mid} \; \mid \; \bullet \; \mid \; \mid \; \bullet \; \mid \; \mid \; \bullet \; \mid \; \mid \; \underset{4}{\mid} \!\!\!\! \longrightarrow$$

A $3.1,\ 3.3,\ 3\frac{7}{10}$ **C** $3.01,\ 3.04,\ 3\frac{7}{100}$

B $3.1,\ 3\frac{4}{10},\ 3.7$ **D** $3\frac{1}{10},\ 3.1,\ 3\frac{4}{10}$

31. Which of the number sentences is false? (Lesson 14-7)

F $\frac{1}{4} = 0.25$

G $0.5 = \frac{4}{8}$

H $1.2 = 1\frac{1}{4}$

J $0.2 = 0.20$

Spiral Review

32. Elliott's age and his brother's age have a sum of 15. Elliott's age is twice as much as his brother's. How old are the boys? (Lesson 14-6)

Compare. Use >, <, or =. (Lesson 14-5)

33. $0.70 \bullet 0.07$ **34.** $8.75 \bullet 8.7$ **35.** $19.70 \bullet 19.7$

Identify these quadrilaterals as *square, rhombus, rectangle, parallelogram,* **or** *trapezoid.* (Lesson 9-6)

36.
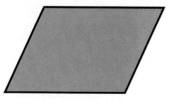

37.
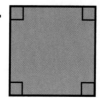

Estimate. Check your estimate. (Lesson 8-4)

38. $153 \div 3$ **39.** $347 \div 5$ **40.** $638 \div 8$

Problem Solving in Music

Decimal Note-ation

Musical notes are a universal language. Musical notes are based on fractions. The most common musical notes include whole, half, quarter, eighth, and sixteenth notes. These values represent the duration of the notes. The durations of the notes are not specific; they are relative to the other notes. For example, a one-eighth note is twice as long as a one-sixteenth note, a one-fourth note is twice as long as a one-eighth note, and so on.

Did You Know?

Beethoven was the first musician to use the one-hundred twenty-eighth note.

Musical Notes Equivalent Fractions		
Note	**Notation**	**Fractional Equivalent**
Whole		$\frac{1}{1}$
Half		$\frac{1}{2}$
Quarter		$\frac{1}{4}$

Real-World Math

Use the table above to solve each problem.

Write the value of each musical note as a decimal.

1.

2.

3.

4. Refer to Exercises 1–3. Draw a number line that shows these values.

Write the value of each musical note as a mixed number. Then write each mixed number as a decimal.

5.

6.

7.

8. Draw three musical notes that represent a value of 2.5.

9. Draw four musical notes that represent a value of $2\frac{1}{4}$.

Decimals, Fractions, and Mixed Numbers

GET READY to Learn

The table shows the number of inches Walter grew each year for four years. At what age did Walter grow the most inches? the fewest inches?

Walter's Change in Growth	
Age	**Growth (in.)**
7	2.5
8	$2\frac{1}{4}$
9	2.0
10	$2\frac{3}{4}$

MAIN IDEA

I will compare and order decimals, fractions, and mixed numbers.

SC Academic Standards

4-2.7 Compare decimals through hundredths by using the terms *is less than, is greater than,* and *is equal to* and the symbols $<$, $>$, and $=$.
Also addresses 4-2.9.

SC Math Online

macmillanmh.com

• Extra Examples
• Personal Tutor
• Self-Check Quiz

To compare fractions and decimals, you can write the fractions as decimals and then compare.

Real-World EXAMPLE

1 **MEASUREMENT** **At what age did Walter grow the most inches? the fewest inches?**

Step 1 Write $2\frac{1}{4}$ and $2\frac{3}{4}$ as decimals.

$$2\frac{1}{4} = 2.25 \qquad 2\frac{3}{4} = 2.75$$

Step 2 Compare 2.5, $2\frac{1}{4}$, 2.0, and $2\frac{3}{4}$.

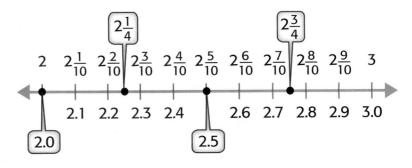

The order from greatest to least is $2\frac{3}{4}$, 2.5, $2\frac{1}{4}$, and 2.0.

So, Walter grew the most when he was 10 and the least when he was 9.

Use a number line to compare. Use >, <, or =. See Example 1 (p. 602)

1. $1.25 \bullet 1\frac{1}{4}$ **2.** $9.2 \bullet 9\frac{2}{10}$ **3.** $3\frac{3}{100} \bullet 3.3$ **4.** 6.6

Use a number line to order from greatest to least. See Example 1 (p. 602)

5. $6.34, 6\frac{1}{4}, 6.5,$ and $6\frac{21}{100}$ **6.** $6\frac{1}{5}, 6.48, 6\frac{4}{10},$ and 6.12

7. Which plant food produced a plant with highest growth? Explain.

Plant Food	Feed Me!	Magic Touch	Feed Booster	Garden Growth
Plant Growth (in.)	$3\frac{7}{10}$	3.1	$3\frac{1}{2}$	3.36

8. **Talk About It** Is the number sentence $5.5 = 5\frac{3}{6} = \frac{44}{8}$ true? Explain.

Practice and Problem Solving

SCAS • PASS

Extra Practice, p. R38

Use a number line to compare. Use >, <, or =. See Example 1 (p. 602)

9. $7 \bullet 6\frac{9}{10}$ **10.** $3.03 \bullet 3\frac{3}{100}$ **11.** $\frac{16}{4} \bullet 4$ **12.** $8.2 \bullet 8$

13. $5.3 \bullet 5.03$ **14.** $4\frac{1}{10} \bullet 4.1$ **15.** $12.5 \bullet 12\frac{2}{5}$ **16.** $15.36 \bullet 15.4$

Use a number line to order from greatest to least. See Example 1 (p. 602)

17. $10\frac{1}{2}, 10.9, 10\frac{36}{100}, 10.75$ **18.** $5.71, 5\frac{67}{100}, 4\frac{5}{10}, 4.75$

19. $\frac{5}{10}, \frac{3}{4}, 0.38, \frac{25}{100}, \frac{1}{1}$ **20.** $\frac{4}{5}, 2.25, 2\frac{3}{4}, 2.77$

Write the letter that represents each mixed number or decimal.

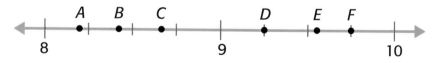

21. $9\frac{6}{10}$ **22.** 8.2 **23.** $8\frac{3}{5}$ **24.** $9\frac{1}{4}$

25. **Measurement** The table at the right shows the amount of rainfall Capitol City received during three months. Order the amounts of rain received from greatest to least.

Month	Rainfall (in.)
March	$2\frac{89}{100}$
April	3.25
May	$3\frac{2}{10}$

Lesson 14-8 Decimals, Fractions, and Mixed Numbers **603**

...ind Chris are identifying the
...ts. Who is correct? Explain.

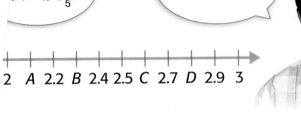

Alicia
...int C is $2\frac{3}{5}$.

Chris
Point C is 2.6.

2 A 2.2 B 2.4 2.5 C 2.7 D 2.9 3

27. WHICH ONE DOESN'T BELONG? Identify the number that does not belong with the others. Explain.

three and five tenths

$3 + 0.5$

$3\frac{1}{2}$

3.05

PASS Practice 4-2.10, 4-2.7

28. Which fraction means the same as 0.25? (Lesson 14-7)

A $\frac{2}{10}$

C $\frac{2}{5}$

B $\frac{1}{4}$

D $\frac{5}{10}$

29. Which letter represents the number closest to 3.6? (Lesson 14-8)

A   B C   D

3.0   3.9

F A   **H** C

G B   **J** D

Spiral Review

Write each fraction as a decimal. (Lesson 14-7)

30. $\frac{4}{10}$

31. $\frac{35}{100}$

32. $\frac{4}{5}$

33. Measurement Trent went to a movie. It started at 3:25 P.M. and lasted 135 minutes. What time was the movie over? (Lesson 14-6)

Order from greatest to least. (Lesson 14-5)

34. 1.5, 1.8, 1.2, 2.1

35. 3.2, 2.3, 3.23, 2.32

36. 7.8, 8.78, 7.88, 8.7

Fraction and Decimal Game

Compare Decimals to Fractions

Get Ready!

Players: 2

Get Set!

On each index card, write a statement using >, <, or =. Write 5 true statements and 5 false statements. A few examples are shown at the right.

You Will Need: 10 index cards

$$0.25 < \frac{1}{3}$$

$$0.5 > \frac{10}{20}$$

$$0.75 = \frac{3}{4}$$

$$0.8 < \frac{75}{100}$$

Go!

- Shuffle the cards.

- Spread out the cards facedown on a desk.

- Player 1 turns over an index card and must say whether the statement is true or false.

- Player 1 keeps the card if the answer is correct, and draws again. If Player 1 is wrong, the index card is put back. Player 2 takes a turn.

- The player who collects the most cards, wins.

SC Math Online ▸ macmillanmh.com
• STUDY *TO GO*
• Vocabulary Review

to Study

Vocabulary
words ... are written in
your Foldable.

Key Concepts

Read, Write, and Model Decimals (p. 579)

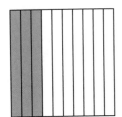

three tenths
$\frac{3}{10}$ or 0.3

twelve hundredths
$\frac{12}{100}$ or 0.12

Compare and Order Decimals (p. 590)

• You can compare and order decimals, fractions, and mixed numbers using a number line.

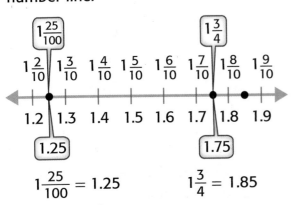

$1\frac{25}{100} = 1.25$ $1\frac{3}{4} = 1.85$

Key Vocabulary

decimal (p. 579)
decimal point (p. 579)
hundredth (p. 580)
tenth (p. 580)

Vocabulary Check

Complete each sentence with the correct vocabulary word.

1. In 0.56, the ____?____ is between the 0 and 5.

2. A(n) ____?____ is a number that uses place value, numbers, and a decimal point to show part of a whole.

3. The underlined digit in 1.<u>3</u>6 is in the ____?____ place.

4. Since the number 0.36 has a 6 in the ____?____ place, the fraction is written as $\frac{36}{100}$.

5. The underlined digit in 0.4<u>2</u> is in the ____?____ place.

6. The ____?____ is always directly to the right of the ones place.

Lesson-by-Lesson Review

14-1 Tenths and Hundredths (pp. 579–581)

4-2.10

Example 1
Write eight tenths as two different decimals.

Write tenths.　　Write hundredths.

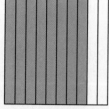　　

eight tenths　　eighty hundredths
0.8　　0.80

The decimals 0.8 and 0.80 are equivalent decimals.

7. Write a fraction and a decimal the shaded part.

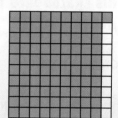

Write as a fraction and as a decimal.

8. three tenths

9. twenty-two hundredths

Write each fraction as a decimal.

10. $\frac{1}{10}$　　**11.** $\frac{60}{100}$

14-2 Relate Mixed Numbers and Decimals (pp. 582–585)

4-2.10,
4-2.11

Example 2
Write $7\frac{52}{100}$ as a decimal.

Hundreds	Tens	Ones	Tenths	Hundredths
		7	5	2

Mixed Number $7\frac{52}{100}$
Read seven and fifty-two hundredths
Write 7.52

Write each as a mixed number and decimal.

12. forty-six and seven tenths

13. fifty-one and three hundredths

Write each mixed number as a decimal.

14. $30\frac{3}{100}$　　**15.** $7\frac{8}{10}$

16. Measurement A Burmese python is eight and twenty-three hundredths of a meter long. Write its length as a mixed number.

tegy: Make a Model (pp. 586–587)

17. There are 12 coins in a piggy bank that equal $2. What could be the coins in the piggy bank?

18. Raul paid $12.50 for a shirt and socks. The socks cost $1.75. How much was the shirt?

19. One-fourth of 36 houses receive 1 newspaper each day. The rest of the houses receive 2 newspapers each day. How many newspapers are delivered each day to the 36 houses?

20. Chandra wants to arrange 18 square tables into one larger rectangular-shaped table with the least perimeter possible. How many tables will be in each row?

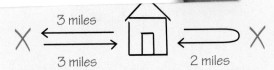

jogging route   skateboard route

3 mi + 3 mi + 2 mi = 8 mi

So, Leo traveled 8 miles.

Check Work backward to check.
8 − 2 − 3 − 3 = 0 ✓

So, the answer is correct.

14-4 **Locate Fractions and Decimals on a Number Line** (pp. 588–589)

4-2.10,
4-2.11

Example 4
Locate $4\frac{1}{2}$ on the number line.

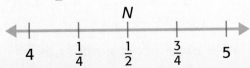

First find 4. Then, find the $\frac{1}{2}$ mark between 4 and 5.

Points on a number line can be represented by a letter.

So, $N = 4\frac{1}{2}$.

Tell which letter represents each mixed number on the number line. Write as a decimal.

21. $5\frac{9}{10}$

22. $16\frac{1}{2}$

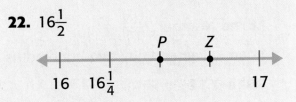

14-5 Compare and Order Decimals (pp. 590–592)

4-2.7

Example 5
Compare 7.26 and 7.62.

Hundreds	Tens	Ones	Tenths	Hundredths
		7	2	6
		7	6	2

Since the ones column has the same digits, compare the tenths place.

6 > 2. So, 7.62 > 7.26.

Compare. Use >, <, or =.

23. 6.50 ● 6.5   **24.** 2.06 ● 2.05

25. 0.58 ● 0.59   **26.** 0.78 ● 0.87

Order from greatest to least.

27. 54.06, 54.6, 54.04, 54.4

28. 80.17, 80.2, 80.3, 80.36

29. 4.3, 4.25, 4.4, 4.56

30. A runner ran a 100-meter dash in 10.65 seconds. Another runner ran the same distance in 10.49 seconds. Whose time is faster?

14-6 Problem-Solving Investigation: Choose a Strategy (pp. 594–595)

4-1.1

Example 6
Algebra What is the rule for the pattern 0, 3, 6, 9, 12, ■? What number comes next?

Each number is 3 more than the number before it

0, 3, 6, 9, 12, ■
  +3 +3 +3 +3

So, the rule is +3.

Use the rule, +3, to find the next number in the pattern. So, the next number in the pattern is 12 + 3 or 15.

Use any strategy to solve.

31. Steph is making a necklace with 15 beads. One third of the beads are red. The rest are black. How many are black?

32. Jonathan has a $20 bill. He buys a puzzle for $12.69. What will be his change?

33. Andrea pays the train fare of $2.75. What coins can Andrea use to pay for the fare using quarters, dimes, and nickels?

34. A scientist collected samples of bark from 258 trees. She took 4 samples from each tree. How many samples did she take in all?

14-7 **Fraction and Decimal Equivalents** (pp. 596–599)

4-2.10

Write a fraction and decimal to describe the shaded area.

Example 7

Thirty-two squares are shaded. So, that is $\frac{32}{100}$ or 0.32.

Example 8

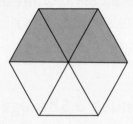

Three triangles are shaded. So, that is $\frac{3}{6}$ or 0.5.

Write a fraction and decimal to describe the shaded part of each model.

35.

36.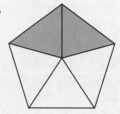

37. Della gave her brother part of a sandwich and said, "Here is your $\frac{1}{2}$ of the sandwich." Her brother said, "Actually, you ate $\frac{2}{4}$ of it." Who is correct? Explain.

14-8 **Decimals, Fractions, and Mixed Numbers** (pp. 602–604)

4-2.7,
4-2.9

Example 9
Order 6.34, $6\frac{1}{4}$, 6.5, and $6\frac{21}{100}$ from greatest to least.

Write the fractions as decimals. Then, compare.

$6\frac{1}{4} = 6.25$ $\qquad$ $6\frac{21}{100} = 6.21$

The order is 6.5, 6.34, $6\frac{1}{4}$, $6\frac{21}{100}$.

Use a number line to order from greatest to least.

38. $9\frac{1}{2}$; 9.9; $9\frac{36}{100}$; 9.75

39. 54.71; $54\frac{67}{100}$; $5\frac{5}{10}$; 56.75

40. Some of the fastest Olympic 100-meter times in seconds are 9.85, $\frac{992}{100}$, 9.87, and $\frac{984}{100}$. Order these times from greatest to least.

For Exercises 1 and 2, tell whether each statement is *true* or *false*.

1. To compare fractions and decimals, you can write the fractions as decimals and then compare.

2. Some decimals can be represented as more than one equivalent fraction.

Compare. Use >, <, or =.

3. 1.75 ⬤ $1\frac{3}{4}$

4. $3\frac{2}{100}$ ⬤ 3.2

5. Write a fraction and a decimal for the shaded part.

6. **MULTIPLE CHOICE** Which of the number sentences is false?

   A $\frac{1}{4} = 0.25$ **C** $1.2 = 1\frac{1}{4}$

   B $0.75 = \frac{6}{8}$ **D** $0.2 = 0.20$

7. A teacher is arranging 24 desks in a classroom in even rows. How many desks should be placed in each row so that the teacher has the smallest perimeter to walk around?

Write as a fraction and as a decimal.

8. nine tenths

9. twenty hundredths

Write each mixed number as a decimal.

10. $4\frac{7}{10}$ 11. $18\frac{65}{100}$

Write a fraction and a decimal to describe the shaded part of the model.

12. 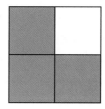   13.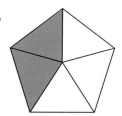

Use a number line to order from greatest to least.

14. 7.8; 7.78; 8.78; 8.7

15. $\frac{3}{4}$; 2.25; $2\frac{3}{4}$; 1.75

16. 9.3; $9\frac{1}{4}$; $9\frac{3}{4}$; 9.5

17. **MULTIPLE CHOICE** Look at the number line. Which order of numbers correctly shows the location of the points?

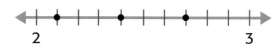

   F 2.1, 2.2, $2\frac{7}{10}$ **H** 2.01, 2.04, $2\frac{7}{100}$

   G 2.1, $2\frac{4}{10}$, 2.7   **J** $2\frac{1}{10}$, 2.1, $2\frac{4}{10}$

18. **WRITING IN ►MATH** Claire was given the following problem: $\frac{7}{10} = 0.$▪. Explain how you would find the correct answer.

PART 1   Multiple Choice

Read each question. Then fill in the correct answer on the answer sheet provided by your teacher or on a sheet of paper.

1. On the number line below, what number does point *K* represent?

   A 7.3   **C** 7.4

   B 7.35   **D** 7.45

2. Which symbol makes the number sentence true?

   1.45 ● 1.42

   F <   **H** =

   G >   **J** +

3. The clock below shows what time school ends. Volleyball practice begins 1 hour 15 minutes after school ends. At what time does volleyball practice begin?

   A 3:30   **C** 4:00

   B 3:45   **D** 4:15

4. Which of the following has the greatest value?

   F 11.5   **H** 1.15

   G 5.11   **J** 0.51

5. The function table shows some input and output values.

Input (x)	Output (y)
1	1
2	4
3	7
4	10
5	■

   What is the missing value?

   A 8   **C** 11

   B 10   **D** 13

6. Cindy grew $\frac{4}{5}$ of an inch in a year. Which decimal is equivalent to $\frac{4}{5}$?

   F 0.7   **H** 0.8

   G 0.75   **J** 0.85

7. What solid figure has two circular faces?

   A cone   **C** prism

   B cylinder   **D** sphere

8. Which decimal does the model show?

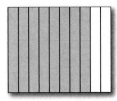

  F 8   **H** 0.8

  G 0.88   **J** 0.08

9. Kim has saved $59 to buy a bicycle helmet. She does not have enough money yet to buy the helmet. Let h represent the amount she still needs to buy the helmet. Which expression shows how much the helmet costs?

  A $59 + h$ **C** $h - 59$

  B $59 - h$ **D** $h + (59 + h)$

10. On the number line below, what number does point M represent?

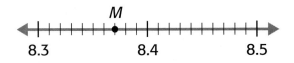

  F 8.4   **H** 8.37

  G 8.38   **J** 8.3

Preparing for PASS

For test-taking strategies and practice, see pages R42–R55.

PART 2   **Short Response**

Record your answers on the answer sheet provided by your teacher or on a sheet of paper.

11. Write 0.35 as a fraction.

12. Order the decimals in the table from greatest to least.

Track Practice	
Runner	**Miles**
Darin	1.24
Kirk	1.5
Damon	1.31
Mauricio	1.45

PART 3   **Extended Response**

Record your answers on the answer sheet provided by your teacher or on a sheet of paper.

13. Use the number line below to answer each of the following questions.

  a. Which letter represents 2.7? Explain.

  b. Which letter is closest to 2.3? Explain.

NEED EXTRA HELP?														
If You Missed Question...	1	2	3	4	5	6	7	8	9	10	11	12	13a	13b
Go to Lesson...	14-4	14-5	12-10	14-5	5-8	14-7	9-1	14-1	5-1	14-4	14-7	14-5	14-4	14-4
SC Academic Standards	4-2.11	4-2.7	4-5.6	4-2.7	4-3.3	4-2.10	4-4.4	4-2.11	4-3.4	4-2.11	4-2.10	4-2.7	4-2.11	4-2.11

CHAPTER 15

Add and Subtract Decimals

 **BIG Idea** How do I subtract decimals?

You can use models to subtract decimals.

Example The Monarch butterfly is the state insect of Illinois. One Monarch butterfly has a wingspan of 0.41 feet, and another has a wingspan of 0.28 feet. The model shows that the wingspan of the first butterfly is 0.41 − 0.28 or 0.13 feet longer than the other.

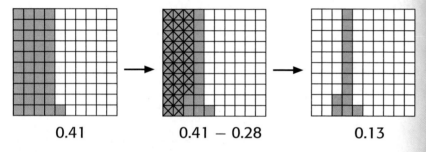

| 0.41 | 0.41 − 0.28 | 0.13 |

What will I learn in this chapter?

- Round decimals.
- Estimate decimal sums and differences.
- Add and subtract simple decimals.
- Solve problems by working backward.

Key Vocabulary

decimal

decimal point

estimate

sum

difference

 **SC Math Online** > **Student Study Tools**
at macmillanmh.com

FOLDABLES®
Study Organizer

Make this Foldable to help you organize information about decimals. Begin with one sheet of $8\frac{1}{2}" \times 11"$ paper.

① **Fold** the paper lengthwise about 3 inches from the bottom.

② **Fold** the paper in thirds.

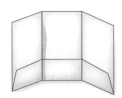

③ **Open** and staple the edges to form 3 pockets.

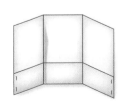

④ **Label** as shown. Place two index cards in each pocket.

Chapter 15 Add and Subtract Decimals   **615**

You have two ways to check prerequisite skills for this chapter.

Option 2

SC Math Online ⟩ Take the Chapter Readiness Quiz at <u>macmillanmh.com.</u>

Option 1

Complete the Quick Check below.

QUICK Check

Round each number to the indicated place value. (Lesson 1-6)

1. 852; hundreds   **2.** 2,614; tens   **3.** 26,703; ten thousands

4. Alexis has $1,363 in her bank account. To the nearest thousand, how much money does she have in her account?

Write a decimal for the shaded part of each figure. (Lesson 14-1)

5. 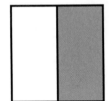   **6.** 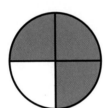   **7.**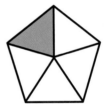

8. Tim ate part of the sandwich as shown. Write a decimal to represent the amount of the sandwich Tim ate.

Graph each decimal on a number line. (Lesson 14-4)

9. 0.15   **10.** 0.38   **11.** 1.75

12. What decimal does the letter *D* represent?

```
              D
   ←──┼────┼────┼────┼────┼──→
     3.0        3.5        4.0
```

Round Decimals

MAIN IDEA

I will round decimals.

SC Academic Standards

4-2.11 Represent improper fractions, mixed numbers, and **decimals.**

SC Math Online

macmillanmh.com
- Extra Examples
- Personal Tutor
- Self-Check Quiz

GET READY to Learn

A bridge in Japan is about 1.22 miles long. What is 1.22 rounded to the nearest whole number?

You can use a number line or rounding rules to round a two-place decimal like 1.22.

Real-World EXAMPLE Round Decimals

1 **BRIDGES** A bridge in Japan is about 1.22 miles long. Round 1.22 to the nearest whole number.

One Way: Use a Number Line

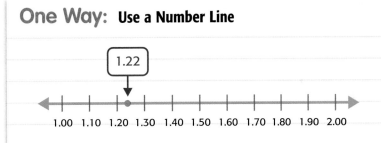

1.22 is between 1 and 2. It is closer to 1.
So, round 1.22 to 1.

Another Way: Use Rounding Rules

Use the same process that you use with rounding whole numbers.

| Underline the digit to be rounded. In this case, the digit is in the ones place. | 1.22 | Then look at the digit to the right. Since 2 is less than 5, the digit 1 remains the same. |

To the nearest whole number, 1.22 rounds to 1.

EXAMPLE   Round Decimals

2 **Round 38.52 to the nearest whole number.**

Use the rounding rules.

> Underline the digit to be rounded. In this case, the digit is in the ones place.

33.5̲2

> Then look at the digit to the right. Since that digit is 5, add one to the underlined digit

To the nearest whole number, 38.52 rounds to 39.

Real-World EXAMPLE   Round Decimals

3 **SPORTS** During one golf season, Tiger Woods had an average score of 68.41. Round this score to the nearest tenth.

Use the rounding rules.

> Underline the digit to be rounded. In this case, the digit is in the tenths place.

68.4̲1

> Then look at the digit to the right. Since 1 is less than 5, the underlined digit remains the same.

To the nearest tenth, 68.41 rounds to 68.4.

CHECK What You Know

Round to the nearest whole number. See Examples 1 and 2 (pp. 617–618)

1. 3.24   **2.** 9.87   **3.** 36.61   **4.** 83.14

Round to the nearest tenth. See Example 3 (p. 618)

5. 4.13   **6.** 8.45   **7.** 25.94   **8.** 67.28

9. Measurement Use the table to round the length of each bird to the nearest tenth of a foot.

10. **Talk About It** How is rounding decimals similar to rounding whole numbers? How is it different?

World's Smallest Birds	
Bird	**Length (feet)**
Pygmy parrot	0.29
Bee hummingbird	0.20
Gouldian finch	0.33
New Zealand wren	0.29

Source: *Scholastic Book of World Records*

Round to the nearest whole number. See Examples 1 and 2 (pp. 617–618)

11. 1.54   **12.** 6.38   **13.** 31.72   **14.** 49.63

15. 54.37   **16.** 59.72   **17.** 64.26   **18.** 81.48

Round to the nearest tenth. See Example 3 (p. 618)

19. 2.58   **20.** 7.31   **21.** 37.54   **22.** 42.07

23. 55.70   **24.** 63.05   **25.** 79.49   **26.** 97.33

For Exercises 27 and 28, round to the nearest whole number.

27. One of the world's largest insects is a stick insect. It is 1.83 feet long. About how long is this insect?

28. Caley wants to buy a shirt for $22.53. About how much money will she need to buy the shirt?

29. One of the most valuable cars in the world is worth $2.29 million dollars. How much is this car worth to the nearest tenth?

30. Measurement Rebeca rounded the weights of various sports balls to the nearest whole number. Are her estimates reasonable? Explain.

31. Measurement A city in Peru receives only 0.09 inches of rainfall each year. Is it reasonable to say that the city receives about 1 inch of rain each year? Explain.

Ball	Actual Weight (oz)	Estimate (oz)
Soccer	14.5	15
Tennis	2.1	2
Lacrosse	5.18	5

Real-World PROBLEM SOLVING

School Mr. Johnson is working on first quarter report cards. Use the table to the right to answer the questions.

32. For Angelo to earn an A, he must achieve a 93 or above. Mr. Johnson rounds his students' grades to the nearest whole number. Will Angelo get an A? Explain.

33. To the nearest whole number, who earned a higher score, Nara or Jodie?

34. To the nearest whole number, which two students earned the same grade?

Mr. Johnson's Class

Student	Grade
Angelo	92.52
Nara	88.27
Jena	85.46
Doug	76.81
Jocelyn	84.53
Jodie	88.59

H.O.T. Problems

OPEN ENDED Give a reasonable rounded estimate for each decimal.

35. 23.81 pounds

36. 30.85 feet

37. 16.37 miles per gallon

CHALLENGE Round to the nearest tenth.

38. $1\frac{1}{4}$

39. $2\frac{3}{4}$

40. $4\frac{53}{100}$

41. **WRITING IN ►MATH** Explain how to find the greatest decimal in tenths that rounds to 75. What is the decimal?

PASS Practice   4-2.7, 4-2.11

42. Order the numbers shown from greatest to least. (Lesson 14-8)

   A 2.46, $2\frac{1}{2}$, 2.64, $2\frac{1}{3}$

   B 2.64, $2\frac{1}{2}$, $2\frac{1}{3}$, 2.46

   C 2.64, $2\frac{1}{2}$, 2.46, $2\frac{1}{3}$

   D $2\frac{1}{3}$, 2.46, $2\frac{1}{2}$, 2.64

43. The length of a vehicle is 205.83 inches. Find the total length to the nearest whole number. (Lesson 15-1)

   F 200 inches

   G 205 inches

   H 206 inches

   J 210 inches

Spiral Review

Use a number line to compare. Use >, <, or =. (Lesson 14-8)

44. 1.75 ● $1\frac{3}{4}$

45. $7\frac{6}{100}$ ● 7.6

46. 46.2 ● $46\frac{1}{4}$

Write a fraction and decimal to describe the shaded part of each model. (Lesson 14-7)

47.
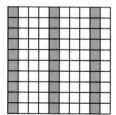

48.
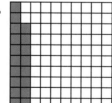

49.
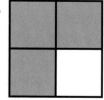

50. Alano, Sidney, and Tasha play instruments. Each student plays either the flute, the violin, or the cello. Sidney does not play the violin or the cello. Alano does not play the cello. What instruments do Alano, Sidney, and Tasha play? (Lesson 12-5)

Match Up
Round Decimals

You will need: 10 index cards

0.13	0.1	38.54	38.5
0.15	0.2	38.56	38.6
2.14	2.1	2.46	2.5
8.73	8.7	8.77	8.8
12.31	12.3	12.35	12.4

Get Ready!

Players: 2 players

Get Set!

Cut each index card in half. Then label each card with one decimal as shown.

Go!

- Shuffle the cards. Then spread the cards out facedown.

- Player 1 turns over two cards.

- If one decimal equals the other decimal after being rounded to the tenths place, Player 1 keeps the cards. Player 1 continues by choosing two more cards.

- If one decimal does not equal the other decimal after being rounded to the tenths place, the cards are turned over and Player 2 takes a turn.

- Continue playing until all matches are made. The player with the most cards wins.

GET READY to Learn

Martina is going white water rafting with her family. On the first day, they will travel 6.5 miles before lunch and 8.7 miles after lunch. *About* how far will they travel on the first day?

Rafting Trip

Before Lunch
6.5 miles

After Lunch
8.7 miles

MAIN IDEA

I will estimate decimal sums and differences.

SC Academic Standards

4-2.12 Generate strategies to add and subtract decimals through hundredths.

SC Math Online

macmillanmh.com

• Extra Examples
• Personal Tutor
• Self-Check Quiz

To estimate the sum of decimals, you can round each decimal to the nearest whole number and then add.

Estimate Decimal Sums   Key Concept

Words   To estimate the sum of two or more decimals, round each decimal to the nearest whole number. Then add.

Example $7.8 $\longrightarrow$ $8
$+ $4.20 $\longrightarrow$ $+ $4
                                    $12

Real-World EXAMPLE   Estimate Sums

1 TRAVEL About how far will Martina and her family travel on the first day?

You need to estimate 6.5 + 8.7. Round each addend to the nearest whole number. Then add.

6.50 $\longrightarrow$ 7
+ 8.7 $\longrightarrow$ + 9

Round 6.5 to 7.
Round 8.7 to 9.

So, Martina and her family will travel about 16 miles.

Remember

When rounding to the nearest whole number, think about the whole number that comes before and after the number to be rounded.

Estimate Decimal Differences
Key Concept

Words To estimate the difference of two decimals, round each decimal to the nearest whole number. Then subtract.

Example

$$\$28.75 \longrightarrow \$29$$
$$-\,\$13.49 \longrightarrow \dfrac{-\,\$13}{\$16}$$

Real-World EXAMPLE   Estimate Differences

2 Mallory wants to buy a cell phone that costs $37.99. She has $45.25. About how much money will she have left to buy ring tones after she buys the phone?

Estimate $45.25 − $37.99

Round each decimal to the nearest whole number. Then subtract.

$$\$45.25 \longrightarrow \$45$$
$$-\,\$37.99 \longrightarrow -\,\$38$$

> Round $45.25 to $45.
> Round $37.99 to $38.

$$\begin{array}{r} 3\ 15 \\ \$\cancel{45} \\ -\ \$38 \\ \hline \$\ \ 7 \end{array}$$

So, Mallory will have about $7 left to buy ring tones.

CHECK What You Know

Estimate. Round to the nearest whole number. See Examples 1 and 2 (pp. 622–623)

1. 1.5
   + 2.3

2. 5.4
   − 3.61

3. 24.9
   + 9.8

4. 62.8 − 9.5

5. $8.75 + $3.25

6. 46.37 − 7.3

7. Reed is running in a charity run that is 3.12 miles long. Reed has run 1.2 miles so far. About how many miles does he have left to run?

8. **Talk About It** Explain how you could estimate to find the sum of 2.1 and 3.3.

Lesson 15-2 Estimate Decimal Sums and Differences   623

Practice and Problem Solving

Estimate. Round to the nearest whole number.

See Examples 1 and 2 (pp. 622–623)

9. 2.5
  + 4.8

10. 9.8
  + 8.2

11. 8.5
  + 11.7

12. 19.6
  + 2.4

13. $17.50
  + $6.25

14. 28.49
  + 12.83

15. 9.7
  − 7.2

16. 5.2
  − 4.6

17. 34.5 − 5.4

18. 29.7 − 8.9

19. $49.54 − $25.15

20. 78.29 − 39.85

Algebra Estimate by rounding to the nearest whole number.
Then compare. Use >, <, or =.

21. 18.34 + 3.67 ● 12.29 + 7.95

22. 14.58 − 6.91 ● 21.62 − 12.19

23. The hawk moth is the fastest flying insect. It can fly up to 33.3 miles per hour. A hornet can fly up to 13.3 miles per hour. About how much faster can the moth fly than the hornet?

24. Amit is buying some action figures for $12.29. He is also buying a pack of trading cards for $1.25. If he pays with a 20 dollar bill, about how much change will he get back?

25. Oscar is 4.3 feet tall. The giant ragwood plant is 8.9 feet tall. Is 8 − 4 a reasonable estimate of the difference in Oscar's and the plant's height to the nearest whole number? Explain.

26. Kyle ran one mile in 7.58 minutes. He ran a second mile in 8.23 minutes. Is 7.6 + 8.2 a reasonable estimate of the combined times to the nearest tenth? Explain.

Real-World PROBLEM SOLVING

Science The table shows the speeds in which planets travel during their orbits, or trips around the Sun.

27. To the nearest whole number, what is the difference between the fastest and slowest orbital speeds of the planets listed?

28. About how much faster does Mercury travel than Earth?

29. Earth's orbital speed is faster than two other planets on the table. About how much faster does Earth travel than each of these planets?

Orbital Speeds of Planets	
Planet	**Speed (miles per second)**
Mercury	29.75
Venus	21.76
Earth	18.51
Mars	14.51
Jupiter	8.12

Source: *Scholastic Book of World Records*

H.O.T. Problems

30. OPEN ENDED Write an addition and a subtraction problem that involves decimals and results in an estimated answer of $12.

31. CHALLENGE Estimate 32.4 + 21.5 + 17.95 to the nearest whole number.

32. **WRITING IN ►MATH** Explain how you would estimate the difference of 9 and 5.52.

PASS Practice 4-2.11, 4-2.12

33. The deepest plant root is 393.7 feet deep. What is the total depth of the root rounded to the nearest whole number? (Lesson 15-1)

  A 300 feet

  B 390 feet

  C 394 feet

  D 400 feet

34. On Friday, Noah drove 166.5 miles. On Saturday, he drove 68.4 miles. On Sunday, he drove 72.75 miles. Approximately how many miles did Noah drive in three days? (Lesson 15-2)

  F 200 miles

  G 210 miles

  H 300 miles

  J 310 miles

Spiral Review

Round to the nearest whole number. (Lesson 15-1)

35. 28.5

36. 43.4

37. 84.2

Use a number line to compare. Use >, <, or =. (Lesson 14-8)

38. $3 \bullet 2\frac{7}{10}$

39. $7.03 \bullet 7\frac{3}{100}$

40. $\frac{25}{5} \bullet 5$

41. Identify the pattern in the shapes at the right. Continue the pattern by drawing the next four shapes. (Lesson 9-3)

42. Algebra The table shows a pattern. Identify the rule. Then find the missing numbers. (Lesson 5-8)

Rule: ■				
Input	2	3	4	5	■
Output	5	7	9	■	13

Problem-Solving Strategy

MAIN IDEA I will solve problems by working backward.

 SCAS 4-1.1 Analyze information to solve increasingly more sophisticated problems.

Rey has lacrosse practice in the evenings. He gets home from school and eats a snack for 15 minutes. Then he spends 1 hour doing his homework. It takes him 15 minutes to get to practice. Practice is at 5 P.M. What time does Rey get home from school?

Understand	**What facts do you know?**
	• Rey eats for 15 minutes.
	• He works on homework for 1 hour.
	• It takes 15 minutes to get to practice at 5 P.M.
	What do you need to find?
	• What time Rey gets home from school.
Plan	Work backward to solve the problem.
Solve	Start with the end result. Then work backward one step at a time.

5 P.M. − 15 minutes = 4:45 P.M.
practice · · · · time to get
starts · · · · · to practice

4:45 P.M. − 1 hour = 3:45 P.M.
· · · · · · homework

3:45 P.M. − 15 minutes = 3:30 P.M.
· · · · · · · · time spent
· · · · · · · · eating

So, Rey gets home from school at 3:30 P.M.

Check	Look back. You can use addition to check.
	15 minutes + 1 hour + 15 minutes = 1 hour and 30 minutes. He gets home at 3:30 P.M. One hour and 30 minutes later is 5 P.M. The answer is correct. ✔

Refer to the problem on the previous page.

1. Explain why 15 minutes was subtracted from 5 P.M. in the first step of solving the problem.

2. Suppose practice started at 4:30 P.M. What time would Rey get home from school?

3. Suppose it takes Rey 45 minutes to complete his homework. What time would he get home from school?

4. Look back to Exercise 3. Check your answer. How do you know it is correct? Explain.

► PRACTICE the Strategy

SCAS • PASS
Extra Practice, p. R40

Solve. Use the work backward strategy.

5. Debbie bought a movie ticket. She then let her friend borrow $3. She now has $7. How much money did she have originally?

6. Adrian volunteers at an animal shelter. It takes him 20 minutes to walk each dog shown. It takes him 15 minutes to give each dog a bath. He finished walking and bathing the dogs at 6 P.M. What time did he start?

7. A number is multiplied by 3. Next, 8 is subtracted from the product. Then, the difference is divided by 4. The result is 7. What is the number?

8. Shantel jogs a mile in 8 minutes. She warms up for 10 minutes. She stretches for 5 minutes after she jogs. She jogs 2 miles, including warming up and stretching. She finishes at 8 A.M. What time does she start?

9. Nadina has two times as many pennies as dimes. The number of quarters she has is shown below. She has 4 more dimes than quarters. How much money does she have?

10. A number is divided by 3. Next, 25 is added to the quotient. Then, the sum is multiplied by 4. The result is 116. What is the number?

11. **WRITING IN ►MATH** Explain how you used the work backward strategy in Exercise 10.

You can use grid paper to explore adding decimals.

ACTIVITY

Use models to add decimals. Find 1.5 + 0.29.

Step 1 **Model 1.5.**

To show 1.5, shade one whole 10-by-10 grid and $\frac{50}{100}$ of a second grid.

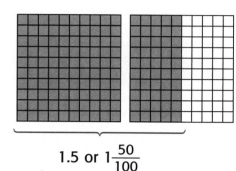

1.5 or $1\frac{50}{100}$

Step 2 **Model 0.29.**

To show 0.29, shade $\frac{29}{100}$ of the second grid using a different color.

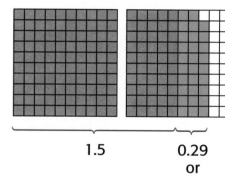

1.5   0.29
           or
           $\frac{29}{100}$

Step 3 **Add the decimals.**

Count the total number of shaded squares. Write as a decimal.

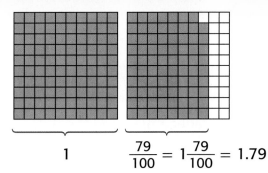

$$1 \qquad \frac{79}{100} = 1\frac{79}{100} = 1.79$$

Think About It

1. Why did you draw two 10-by-10 grids to show 1.5?

2. Why did you shade 50 squares of the second grid?

3. Why did you shade 29 squares of the second grid?

4. How did you find the sum of the decimals?

 CHECK What You Know

Add. Use the models.

5. 1.15 + 0.57

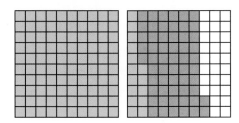

6. 0.25 + 0.46

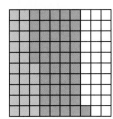

Add. Use models if needed.

7. $\begin{array}{r} 0.45 \\ + 0.30 \\ \hline \end{array}$	**8.** $\begin{array}{r} 0.16 \\ + 0.58 \\ \hline \end{array}$	**9.** $\begin{array}{r} 1.12 \\ + 1.50 \\ \hline \end{array}$
10. $\begin{array}{r} 0.19 \\ + 1.62 \\ \hline \end{array}$	**11.** $\begin{array}{r} 1.09 \\ + 1.58 \\ \hline \end{array}$	**12.** $\begin{array}{r} 1.42 \\ + 0.26 \\ \hline \end{array}$

13. 0.44 + 1.39

14. 1.28 + 2.10

15. 2.05 + 1.9

16. **WRITING IN ►MATH** Write the steps to use to find 2.34 + 1.76.

Explore 15-4 Addition of Decim

Add Decimals

MAIN IDEA

I will add decimals.

SC Academic Standards

4-2.12 Generate strategies to add and subtract **decimals through hundredths.**

SC Math Online

macmillanmh.com

• Extra Examples
• Personal Tutor
• Self-Check Quiz

GET READY to Learn

Darlene practiced the flute 1.5 hours on Saturday. On Sunday, she practiced 2.3 hours. How long did she practice during the two days?

In the previous Explore Activity, you used models to add decimals. You can also use paper and pencil to add decimals.

Real-World EXAMPLE   Add Decimals

① **MEASUREMENT** How many hours did Darlene practice the flute during the two days?

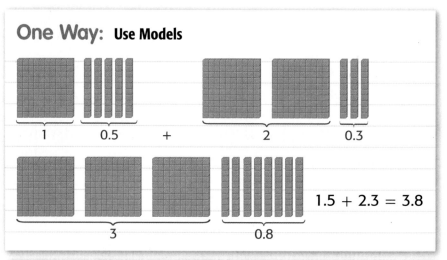

One Way: Use Models

1   0.5   +   2   0.3

3   0.8 $1.5 + 2.3 = 3.8$

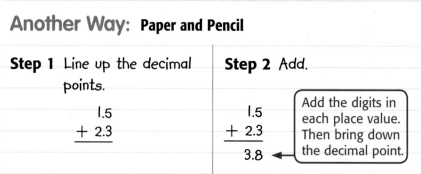

Another Way: Paper and Pencil

Step 1 Line up the decimal points.

$$\begin{array}{r} 1.5 \\ + 2.3 \\ \hline \end{array}$$

Step 2 Add.

$$\begin{array}{r} 1.5 \\ + 2.3 \\ \hline 3.8 \end{array}$$

Add the digits in each place value. Then bring down the decimal point.

So, Darlene practiced a total of 3.8 hours.

Real-World EXAMPLE Add Decimals

2 **FISH** Australia has 17.22 percent of the world's coral reefs. Fiji has 3.52 percent of the world's coral reefs. What percentage of the world's coral reefs do these countries have in all?

You need to find 17.22 + 3.52. **Estimate** 18 + 4 = 22

Step 1 Line up the decimal points.

$$\begin{array}{r} 17.22 \\ +\ 3.52 \\ \hline \end{array}$$

Step 2 Add.

$$\begin{array}{r} \overset{1}{1}7.22 \\ +\ 3.52 \\ \hline 20.74 \end{array}$$ Add the digits in each place value. Regroup if necessary.

So, these two countries have 20.74 percent of the world's coral reefs.

Check for Reasonableness

The sum of 20.74 is close to the estimate of 22. So, the answer is reasonable. ✔

Remember

Line up the decimal points before you add to make sure you are adding the same place values together.

 CHECK What You Know

Add. Use estimation to check for reasonableness. See Examples 1 and 2 (pp. 630–631)

1.
$$\begin{array}{r} 1.4 \\ +\ 0.7 \\ \hline \end{array}$$

2.
$$\begin{array}{r} 4.72 \\ +\ 3.9 \\ \hline \end{array}$$

3.
$$\begin{array}{r} 9.8 \\ +\ 7.33 \\ \hline \end{array}$$

4. 4.82 + 6.27

5. $25.85 + $8.49

6. 54.90 + 38.41

For Exercises 7 and 8, use the poster shown.

7. Andre has his birthday dinner at Medieval Era, a dinner theatre with knights jousting. What is the total cost for Andre and his father?

8. Suppose Andre's mother is also going to his birthday dinner. What is the total cost?

9. **Talk About It** Why is it important to line up the decimal points before you add?

Medieval Era

Adults $48.95   Children $33.95

Practice and Problem Solving

Add. Use estimation to check for reasonableness. See Examples 1 and 2 (pp. 630–631)

10. 0.7
  + 0.2

11. 0.4
  + 0.6

12. 1.1
  + 0.39

13. 5.1
  + 7.56

14. 8.76
  + 6.95

15. 7.09
  + 4.68

16. $9.82
  + $5.33

17. $12.33
  + $5.79

18. 47.28 + 36.05

19. $51.20 + $29.75

20. 3.21 + 14.7 + 9.35

21. Two bones in a leg are the femur and tibia. The average adult male femur is 19.88 inches long. The tibia is 16.94 inches long. How long is the average adult male's leg?

22. Maureen used 28.5 minutes of her cell phone plan on Saturday and 35.75 minutes on Sunday. How many minutes did Maureen use on these two days?

South Carolina Data File

Riverbanks Zoo and Garden in Columbia, South Carolina, is home to more than 2,000 animals and more than 4,200 species of plants.

23. Jamie is 11 years old. Suppose Jamie and his mom and dad want to camp overnight in the zoo. How much would it cost?

24. Heath, Rodney, and Mia go to the zoo on a field trip with their fourth grade class. If they bring $25, will they have enough money to enter the zoo? Explain.

Riverbanks Zoo and Garden
Columbia, South Carolina
Admission Rates
Adults $9.75
Children (3-12 years) .. $7.25
Children (under 3)..... FREE
Family on Safari Overnight Camp
Adults $16.75
Children (3-12 years) $14.25
Children (under 3)..... FREE

Source: Riverbanks Zoo and Garden

H.O.T. Problems

25. WHICH ONE DOESN'T BELONG? Three of the decimals shown below have a sum equal to 14.04. Identify the number that does not belong with the other three.

| 1.15 | 2.57 | 5.03 | 6.44 |

26. WRITING IN ►MATH Explain how to find the sum of 136.28 and 264.57.

Round to the nearest whole number.
(Lesson 15-1)

1. 4.55

2. 25.24

3. 8.58

4. 36.34

5. Measurement A bald eagle's nest is 2.4 meters wide. How wide is this to the nearest whole number?
(Lesson 15-1)

6. MULTIPLE CHOICE The height of a monster truck is 15.4 feet. What is the height of the truck rounded to the nearest whole number?
(Lesson 15-1)

A 14

C 15.4

B 15

D 16

Estimate. Round to the nearest whole number. (Lesson 15-2)

7.   2.4
     + 3.8

8.   9.4
     − 5.82

Algebra Estimate by rounding to the nearest whole number. Then compare. Use >, <, or =. (Lesson 15-2)

9. 13.73 + 8.04 ● 9.8 + 12.52

10. 46.91 − 19.8 ● 53.4 − 20.26

11. Tamika Catchings, a professional basketball player, scores an average of 19.2 points per game. About how many points would Tamika score in two games? (Lesson 15-2)

12. A number is divided by 4. Next, 8 is added to the quotient. Then, the sum is multiplied by 2. The result is 28. What is the number? (Lesson 15-3)

13. Measurement Bruno is going on vacation and needs to leave for the airport at 1 P.M. What time does Bruno need to wake up? (Lesson 15-3)

Task	Time to Complete (hours)
Clean house	3.25
Eat lunch	0.75
Pack suitcase	1.5

Add. Use estimation to check for reasonableness. (Lesson 15-4)

14. 14.5 + 7.8

15. 37.08 + 19.56

16. MULTIPLE CHOICE Brad buys a movie ticket for $4.75, a pretzel for $1.50, and a soda for $2.25. How much money did Brad spend? (Lesson 15-4)

F $8.50

H $9

G $8.75

J $9.25

Algebra Describe the pattern. Then identify the missing numbers. (Lesson 15-4)

17. 0.8, 1.6, ■, 3.2, ■, ■

18. 1.23, 3.25, ■, ■, 9.31, ■

19. **WRITING IN ►MATH** Tell whether 40 is a reasonable estimate for the sum of 28.4 + 14.68. Explain. (Lesson 15-2)

15-5 Problem-Solving Investigation

MAIN IDEA I will choose the best strategy to solve a problem.

SCAS **4-1.1 Analyze information to solve increasingly more sophisticated problems.**

P.S.I. TEAM +

JENNIFER: Two friends and I all have different kinds of pets. We have a lizard, a cat, a gerbil, and a snake. I do not have a cat. Rondell's pet is not a gerbil or a snake. Lorena's two pets are not lizards. My pet does not begin with the letters s or g.

YOUR MISSION: Find which person owns each pet.

Understand	You know the clues for each person's pet. You need to find which person owns each pet.	
Plan	Make a table to show what you know. Then use logical reasoning to find which person owns each pet.	
Solve	Make a table. Write *yes* or *no* for each fact that you are given. Once you write yes in the table, you can write no in the rest of the boxes in that row and column.	

	Cat	Gerbil	Lizard	Snake
Jennifer	No	No	Yes	No
Lorena	No	Yes	No	Yes
Rondell	Yes	No	No	No

	So, Jennifer owns a lizard. Lorena owns a gerbil and a snake. Rondell owns a cat.
Check	Look back. The solution matches the facts given in the problem. So, the answer is correct. ✔

Use any strategy shown below to solve. Tell what strategy you used.

PROBLEM-SOLVING STRATEGIES
• Work a simpler problem.
• Use logical reasoning.
• Draw a picture.
• Make a model.
• Work backward.

1. Reina is going bowling. Which route would be the shortest? Explain.

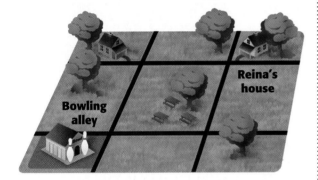

2. Students voted for a new mascot. Six out of ten students voted for a tiger. There are 300 students. How many students voted for a tiger?

3. A number is divided by 3. Then the quotient is subtracted from 20. The result is 8. What is the number?

4. Haley's comet can be seen from Earth about every 76 years. The next time it can be seen will be in 2062. When could the comet last be seen?

5. Dean bought three comic books for $6. At the same price, how much would 10 comic books cost?

6. Laurie spent 30 minutes on math homework. She spent half as much time doing her science homework. She spent 5 minutes longer on her reading homework than her science homework. How much time did Laurie spend on her homework?

7. The toy car below cost $2.50. At the same price, how many toy cars can Domingo buy with $10?

8. **Algebra** A type of bacteria doubles in number every 12 hours. After 2 days, there are 48 bacteria. How many bacteria were there at the beginning of the first day?

9. The product of two numbers is 24. Their difference is 5. What are these two numbers?

10. Audrey biked the trail below. Find the value of y.

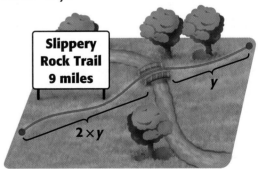

Slippery Rock Trail 9 miles

$2 \times y$

11. **WRITING IN ►MATH** The two busiest subway systems in the world have 3.1 and 2.84 billion passengers each year. The answer is 5.94 billion. What is the question?

Explore

Subtraction of Decimals

You can use grid paper to explore subtracting decimals.

ACTIVITY

Use models to find 2.75 − 1.15.

Step 1   Model 2.75.

To show 2.75, shade two whole grids and $\frac{75}{100}$ of a third grid.

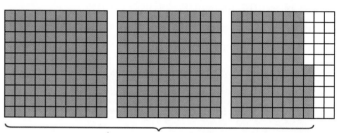

$$2.75 \quad \text{or} \quad 2\frac{75}{100}$$

Step 2   Subtract 1.15.

To subtract 1.15, cross out 1 whole grid and 15 squares of the third grid.

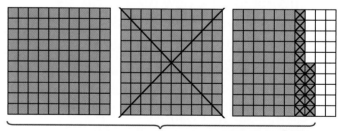

$$2.75 - 1.15 \quad \text{or} \quad 1\frac{15}{100}$$

Step 3 Find the difference.

Count the number of shaded squares left.

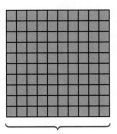 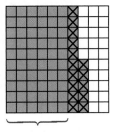 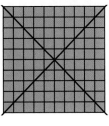

$$1 \qquad \frac{60}{100} = 1\frac{60}{100} = 1.6$$

Think About It

1. How did you model 2.75?

2. How did you model subtracting 1.15 from 2.75?

3. How did you find the difference?

✓CHECK What You Know

Subtract. Use the models.

4. 1.46 − 0.34

5. 2.8 − 1.23

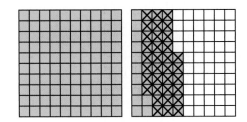 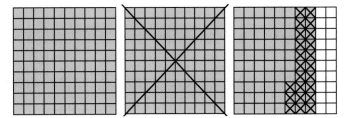

Subtract. Use models if needed.

6.   0.55
  − 0.29
	7. 0.99
	  − 0.46
		8. 1.4
		  − 1.11

9.   2.6
  − 1.09
	10. 2.81
	  − 1.29
		11. 3.77
		  − 1.08

12. 2.98 − 1.84

13. 3.45 − 2.73

14. 3.93 − 2.94

15. **WRITING IN ►MATH** Explain how to find 3.46 − 2.62.

MAIN IDEA

I will subtract decimals.

SC Academic Standards

4-2.12 Generate strategies to add and **subtract decimals through hundredths.**

SC Math Online

macmillanmh.com
• Extra Examples
• Personal Tutor
• Self-Check Quiz

GET READY to Learn

Albert Einstein was a very intelligent man who made many important scientific discoveries. His brain had a mass of 1.23 kilograms. This is less than the mass of an average adult male brain, which has a mass of about 1.4 kilograms. What is the difference in mass?

In the previous Explore Activity, you used models to subtract decimals.

Real-World EXAMPLE   Subtract Decimals

1 **MEASUREMENT What is the difference in mass between Albert Einstein's brain and the mass of an average adult male brain?**

Step 1 Draw a model of 1.4 on a hundredths grid.

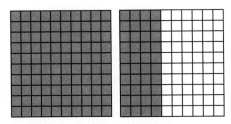

Step 2 Subtract 1.23.

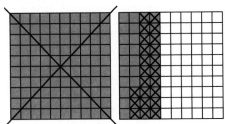

$$1.4 - 1.23 = 0.17$$

So, Einstein's brain had a mass of 0.17 kilogram less than the mass of an average adult male brain.

You can also use paper and pencil to solve.

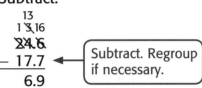 **Real-World EXAMPLE**   **Subtract Decimals**

2 **MEASUREMENT** **The average rock python is 24.6 feet long. The average king cobra is 17.7 feet long. How much longer is the rock python than the king cobra?**

Subtract 24.6 − 17.7 to find how much longer the rock python is than the king cobra.

Estimate 24.6 − 17.7 ⟶ 25 − 18 = 7

Step 1   Line up the decimal points.

$$\begin{array}{r} 24.6 \\ -\ 17.7 \\ \hline \end{array}$$

Step 2   Subtract.

$$\begin{array}{r} \overset{13}{}\ \\ 1\ \overset{13}{\cancel{3}}\ 16\ \\ \cancel{24.6}\ \\ -\ 17.7\ \\ \hline 6.9\ \end{array}$$

 Subtract. Regroup if necessary.

So, the average rock python is 6.9 feet longer than the average king cobra.

Check for Reasonableness
The answer, 6.9, is close to the estimate of 7. So, the answer is reasonable. ✔

Since 17.7 + 6.9 = 24.6, the answer is correct.

Rock Python

 CHECK What You Know

Subtract. Use estimation or addition to check. See Examples 1 and 2 (pp. 638–639)

1.
$$\begin{array}{r} 1.4 \\ -\ 1.0 \\ \hline \end{array}$$

2.
$$\begin{array}{r} 0.8 \\ -\ 0.49 \\ \hline \end{array}$$

3.
$$\begin{array}{r} \$1.67 \\ -\ \$0.58 \\ \hline \end{array}$$

4. 4.67 − 2.36

5. $8.72 − $2.95

6. 25.74 − 12.08

7. The height of the tallest woman in the world is 7.58 feet. The height of the tallest man in the world is 8.92 feet. How much taller is the tallest man than the tallest woman?

8. Explain how subtracting decimals is similar to subtracting whole numbers. How is it different?

Practice and Problem Solving

Subtract. Use estimation or addition to check. See Examples 1 and 2 (pp. 638–639)

9. 2.7
      − 1.4

10. 5.5
       − 3.8

11. 7.2
       − 0.9

12. 4.6
       − 1.45

13. 6.84
       − 3.56

14. $9.67
       − $7.05

15. 11.92
       − 8.87

16. $19.38
       − $14.55

17. 21.80
       − 15.91

18. $25.09 − $12.40

19. 34.94 − 28.17

20. 56.87 − 38.05

For Exercises 21 and 22, use the table.

21. How many more people play tennis in the most popular state than in the least popular state?

22. What is the total number of people in Florida, Texas, and New York who play tennis?

Most Popular States for Tennis	
State	**Number of Players (millions)**
California	3.2
Florida	1.4
Illinois	1.0
New York	1.7
Texas	1.4

Source: United States Tennis Association

23. Julina is buying pet supplies. She has $25.50. She buys cat food for $8.99, a collar for $4.79, and cat toys for $3.25. How much money will Julina have left?

24. The average American eats 57.4 kilograms of fresh fruit and 67.2 kilograms of fresh vegetables each year. What is the difference in the yearly amount of fruit and vegetables an American eats?

Real-World PROBLEM SOLVING

Science The table at the right shows the heights of different dinosaurs.

25. What is the difference in height between the two shortest dinosaurs?

26. How much taller is a Tyrannosaurus than a Araucanoraptor?

27. Which two dinosaurs have a height difference of 1.45 feet?

Dinosaur Heights	
Dinosaur	**Height (feet)**
Abrictosaurus	1.3
Araucanoraptor	2.75
Bagaceratops	1.5
Microvenator	2.5
Supersaurus	66.0
Triceratops	9.5
Tyrannosaurus	23.0

Source: Arts & Letters Corporation

H.O.T. Problems

28. FIND THE ERROR Morgan and Lloyd are finding $46.27 - 28.16$.
Who is correct? Explain.

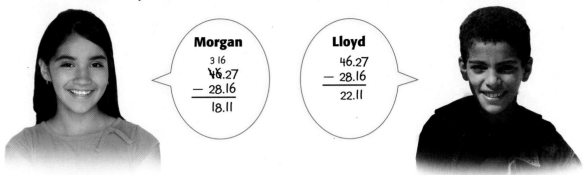

Morgan

$$
\begin{array}{r}
\overset{3\ 16}{\cancel{4}\cancel{6}.27} \\
-\ 28.16 \\
\hline
18.11
\end{array}
$$

Lloyd

$$
\begin{array}{r}
46.27 \\
-\ 28.16 \\
\hline
22.11
\end{array}
$$

29. OPEN ENDED A number is subtracted from 24.84. The difference is greater than 9 and less than 10. What is the number?

PASS Practice 4-2.12

30. At the school store, Benito bought a package of pens for $1.34 and a set of map pencils for $2.78. What was the total cost? (Lesson 15-4)

A $1.44

B $3.02

C $4.02

D $4.12

31. Sandy and her father have $100. They buy a fishing pole for $39.95 and cooking gear for $29.39. Which additional item could they buy? (Lesson 15-6)

$35.75 $64.99 $29.95 $75.50

F Backpack   H Lantern

G Camp stove   J Sleeping bag

Spiral Review

32. Mila volunteers at a food bank at 9 A.M. It takes 30 minutes to drive to the food bank, 20 minutes to eat breakfast, and 45 minutes to get ready in the morning. What is the latest time she can set her alarm to wake up? (Lesson 15-5)

Add. Use estimation to check for reasonableness. (Lesson 15-4)

33. $0.75 + 0.62$ **34.** $4.49 + 0.76$ **35.** $8.40 + 6.87$

Estimate. Round to the nearest whole number. (Lesson 15-2)

36. $2.5 + 4.3$ **37.** $8.4 - 5.7$ **38.** $22.9 + 5.4$

Problem Solving in History

Olympic Games

The Olympic games have been taking place since ancient times.

There are currently summer and winter games. Each season occurs every four years and includes different sports. There are over one hundred summer events including cycling, gymnastics, swimming and diving, and track and field, among others. A highlight of the summer games has always been the gymnastic events. These events mix strength, agility, style, and grace. Some of the events that take place in the gymnastic competition are floor exercise, horizontal bar, parallel bars, pommel horse, rings, and vault. Gymnasts are scored on a scale of one to ten, with ten being a perfect score and very difficult to earn.

Recent Olympic Games Men's Individual Scores

Gymnast	Floor	Horse	Rings	Vault	Parallel Bars	High Bar	Total Score
Paul Hamm (U.S.)	9.73	9.70	9.59	9.14	9.84	9.84	57.84
Kim Dae-Eun (South Korea)	9.65	9.54	9.71	9.41	9.78	9.73	57.82
Yang Tae-Young (South Korea)	9.51	9.65	9.73	9.70	9.71	9.48	57.78

Recent Olympic Games Women's Individual Scores

Gymnast	Vault	Uneven Bars	Beam	Floor	Total Score
Carly Patterson (U.S.)	9.38	9.58	9.73	9.71	38.34
Svetlana Khorkina (Russia)	9.46	9.73	9.46	9.56	38.21
Zhang Nan (China)	9.33	9.46	9.66	9.60	38.05

* All scores have been rounded to the nearest hundredth.　**Source:** International Olympic Committee

As of January 1, 1999, trampoline became a gymnastic event at the Olympic games.

Real-World Math

Use the information on page 642 to solve each problem.

1. A summer Olympic games will be taking place in London, England, in the year 2012. What years will the four previous Olympic games have been held?

2. What is the top female gymnast's total score rounded to the nearest whole number?

3. How much higher is Paul Hamm's score in the parallel bars than the vault when both scores are rounded to the nearest tenth?

4. What is the sum of Carly Patterson's two highest event scores when rounded to the nearest tenth?

5. Kim Dae-Eun's scores were higher than Paul Hamm's scores in two of the events. Identify the events. Find the difference in their scores for each event to the nearest tenth.

6. The gymnasts that earn the top three total scores win gold, silver, and bronze medals. Suppose the scores were rounded to the tenths place. Would this scoring change the medals that were given out to the male athletes? Explain.

7. Which place value would the female gymnast's scores have to be rounded to in order to have a three-way tie for gold? Explain.

FOLDABLES Study Organizer **GET READY** to Study

Be sure the following Key Vocabulary words and Key Concepts are written in your Foldable.

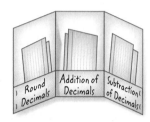

) Round
) Decimals   Addition of
Decimals   Subtraction(
of Decimals(

Key Concepts

Round Decimals (p. 617)

• Round 4.36 to the nearest whole number.

4.36

> Look at the digit to the right of the place you want to round to. Since it is less than 5, round down.

So, 4.36 rounds to 4.

Estimate Sums and Differences (p. 622)

• Round each addend to the nearest whole number. Then add.

8.6 + 7.2 ⟶ 9 + 7 = 16

Add and Subtract Decimals (pp. 630, 638)

Find 1.27 + 0.36.

```
  1.27
+ 0.36
  1.63
```

Find 0.78 − 0.45.

```
  1.78
− 0.45
  1.33
```

Key Vocabulary

decimal (pp. 579, 617)
decimal point (pp. 579, 617)
difference (pp. 71, 622)
estimate (pp. 58, 622)
sum (pp. 58, 622)

Vocabulary Check

Complete each sentence with the correct vocabulary word.

1. The answer to an addition problem is the ____?____.

2. A(n) ____?____ is a period separating the ones and the tenths in a number.

3. A(n) ____?____ indicates about how much.

4. The answer to a subtraction problem is the ____?____.

5. A(n) ____?____ is a number with one or more digits to the right of the decimal point.

6. A(n) ____?____ is a number that is close to an exact amount.

Lesson-by-Lesson Review

15-1 Round Decimals (pp. 617–620)

4-2.11

Example 1
Round 12.16 to the nearest tenth.

One Way: Use a Number Line

12.16

12   12.2   12.4   12.6   12.8   13

12.16 is closer to 12.2 than 12.1.

Another Way: Use Place Value

| Underline the digit to be rounded. | Then look at the digit to the right. Since 6 is closer to 10 than 0, round 1 to 2. |

12.1**6**

So, round 12.16 up to 12.2.

Round to the nearest whole number.

7. 4.12   **8.** 3.65

9. 12.40   **10.** 69.95

11. Measurement Marni hiked 3.65 miles on Saturday. About how many miles did she hike?

12. A baby panda weighs 4.36 ounces. About how many ounces does the baby panda weigh?

13. Travis spent $5.32 at lunch. About how much did he spend?

Round to the nearest tenth.

14. 7.45   **15.** 9.81

16. 32.78   **17.** 44.54

15-2 Estimate Decimal Sums and Differences (pp. 622–625)

4-2.12

Example 2
Estimate 8.63 + 6.15.

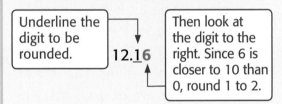

$$\begin{array}{r} 8.63 \rightarrow 9 \\ + 6.15 \rightarrow + 6 \\ \hline 15 \end{array}$$

Round 8.63 to 9.
Round 6.15 to 6.

So, 8.63 + 6.15 is about 15.

Example 3
Estimate 25.25 − 12.76.

$$\begin{array}{r} 25.25 \rightarrow 25 \\ - 12.76 \rightarrow - 13 \\ \hline 12 \end{array}$$

Round 25.25 to 25.
Round 12.76 to 13.

So, 25.25 − 12.76 is about 12.

Estimate. Round to the nearest whole number.

18. 4.88
       + 14.56

19. 35.15
       − 14.93

20. 9.51
       + 7.43

21. 99.65
       − 24.67

22. A basketball costs $17.95. It is on sale for $9.99. About how much less is the sale price than the original price?

15-3 **Problem-Solving Strategy: Work Backward** (pp. 626–627)

Example 4

4-1.1

Felipe's basketball team is having a car wash. It takes 10 minutes to wash a car. Felipe's team finished washing 12 cars at 5 P.M. What time did the car wash start?

Understand

What facts do you know?

- It takes 10 minutes to wash a car.
- Felipe's team finished washing 12 cars at 5 P.M.

What do you need to find?

- The time the car wash started.

Plan   Work backward.

Solve   Start with the end result. Then work backward.

$$12 \quad \times \quad 10 \quad = \quad 120$$

cars   minutes to   minutes to
         wash 1 car   wash 10 cars

5 P.M. − 120 minutes = 3 P.M.

[120 min = 2 hr]

The car wash started at 3 P.M.

Check   It took 120 minutes or 2 hours to wash the cars. Two hours before 5 P.M. is 3 P.M. So, the answer is correct.

23. A number is added to 3. The sum is multiplied by 5. The result is 45. What is the number?

24. **Measurement** Howard is doing his chores. He swept the floor for 20 minutes. He dusted for 10 minutes less than he swept. He cleaned his room for 45 minutes longer than he dusted. How long did it take Howard to clean his room?

25. Gabriela took 18 pictures of animals. She took 2 pictures of gorillas. She took twice as many pictures of penguins. She took 6 pictures of giraffes. The rest of the pictures are of sea lions. How many pictures did Gabriela take of sea lions?

26. Harrison, Colin, and Ruthie's favorite colors are red, blue, and green. Colin likes blue the best. Ruthie does not like green. What is Harrison's favorite color?

27. A number is divided by 7. Nine is added to the quotient. Then 5 is subtracted from the sum. The result is 9. What is the number?

15-4 **Add Decimals** (pp. 630–632)

4-2.12

Example 5
Find 2.7 + 12.38.

Step 1 Line up the decimal points.

$$\begin{array}{r} 2.70 \\ + 12.38 \end{array}$$

Place a zero in the hundreths place.

Step 2 Add.

$$\begin{array}{r} 1 \\ 2.70 \\ + 12.38 \\ \hline 15.08 \end{array}$$

Add the digits in each place value. Regroup if necessary.

So, 2.7 + 12.38 = 15.08.

Add. Use estimation to check for reasonableness.

28.
$$\begin{array}{r} 3.6 \\ + 0.8 \end{array}$$

29.
$$\begin{array}{r} 6.82 \\ + 4.7 \end{array}$$

30. 5.03 + 18.9   **31.** 34.82 + 8.31

32. Measurement Lance Armstrong's fastest average speed during a Tour de France bicycle race was 25.45 miles per hour. At this rate, how far would Lance travel in two hours?

15-5 **Problem-Solving Investigation: Choose a Strategy** (pp. 634–635)

4-1.1

Example 6
There are 27 plants in a garden. There are twice as many tomato as cucumber plants and three more pepper than cucumber plants. There are 9 pepper plants. How many of each kind of plant is in the garden?

Use logical reasoning to solve.

There are 9 pepper plants.

There are 3 more pepper than cucumber plants. So, the number of cucumber plants is 9 − 3 or 6.

There are twice as many tomato as cucumber plants. So, the number of tomato plants is 2 × 6 or 12.

Check

9 + 6 + 12 = 27
So, the answer is correct. ✓

Use any strategy to solve.

33. Monifa is putting up a tent for camping. The tent has four corners. Each corner needs three stakes. How many stakes does Monifa need?

34. Edwin is buying the books shown. How much will the books cost?

$3.75
$5.99

35. Use three of the following symbols +, −, ×, or ÷ to make the following math sentence true. Use each symbol only once.

3 ▪ 4 ▪ 6 ▪ 1 = 18

15-6 Subtract Decimals (pp. 638–641)

4-2.12

Example 7

A spider is one of the slowest moving animals. It travels at a speed of 1.2 miles per hour. A sloth is even slower. It travels at a speed of 0.07 miles per hour. How much faster is a spider than a sloth?

To find out how much faster a spider is than a sloth, subtract 0.07 from 1.20.

Step 1 Line up the decimal points.

```
  1.20
- 0.07
```

Step 2 Subtract. Regroup if needed.

```
  1 10
  1.2̶0̶    ◄── Subtract the digits in
- 0.07         each place. Regroup.
  ────
  1.13
```

The model shows 1.20 − 0.07 = 1.13.

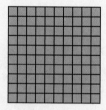 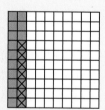

So, a spider is 1.13 miles per hour faster than a sloth.

Check

You can use addition to check.

```
  1.13
+ 0.07
  ────
  1.20
```

So, the answer is correct. ✓

Subtract. Use estimation or addition to check.

36.
```
  2.6
- 0.7
```

37.
```
  8.3
- 1.5
```

38.
```
  6.9
- 3.81
```

39.
```
  8.57
- 5.9
```

40. 26.08 − 16.4

41. 59.81 − 41.26

42. The longest space walk was 8.93 hours long. The second longest space walk was 8.48 hours long. How much longer was the longest space walk than the second longest space walk?

Measurement For Exercises 43 and 44, use the table. It shows the snakes that have the longest fangs.

Snakes' Fangs	
Snake	**Fang Length (cm)**
Australian Taipan	1.8
Black Mamba	2.5
Bushmaster	3.8
Diamondback Rattlesnake	2.5
Gaboon Viper	5.1

Source: *Scholastic Book of World Records*

43. What is the difference in length of the Gaboon Viper's and Black Mamba's fangs?

44. Which two snakes have the greatest difference in length of fangs? What is the difference?

Estimate. Round to the nearest whole number.

1. $26.7 - 9.09$ **2.** $\$31.56 + \$5.01$

3. Measurement Boston, Massachusetts, receives an average of 3.6 inches of rain in April. It receives an average of 3.3 inches of rain in May. About how much rainfall does Boston receive during these two months?

4. Eva has four coins. Two are the same and equal 50¢. One coin is a nickel. One coin is worth ten cents. What coins does Eva have?

Subtract. Use estimation or addition to check.

5.   6.9
      $- 2.48$

6.   74.64
       $- 12.8$

7. Marie is 4.25 feet tall. Marie's brother is 3.5 feet tall. How much taller is Marie than her brother?

8. MULTIPLE CHOICE What is 67.34 rounded to the nearest tenth?

 A 67   **C** 67.34

 B 67.3   **D** 68

Add. Use estimation to check for reasonableness.

9. $4.97 + 8.4$

10. $6.26 + 29.4$

Round to the nearest tenth.

11. 3.05   **12.** 84.72

13. Hermán rode 16.72 kilometers on his bike. After he rested, he rode another 11.35 kilometers. How many kilometers did he ride altogether?

14. MULTIPLE CHOICE Raymond and his father are planning a camping trip. The advertisement for a campsite is shown below.

If Raymond and his father have $45 to spend on a campsite, how many nights will they be able to stay?

 F 2   **H** 4

 G 3   **J** 5

Algebra Find the missing number.

15. $n + 1.2 = 3.6$

16. $2.8 + n = 4.5$

17. A number is subtracted from 15. The difference is multiplied by 4. Then the product is divided by 8. The result is 3. What is the number?

18. **WRITING IN ►MATH** Explain how to estimate $12.46 + 34.9$ by rounding each number to the nearest whole number.

PART 1 Multiple Choice

Read each question. Then fill in the correct answer on the answer sheet provided by your teacher or on a sheet of paper.

1. Terrez drove 42.5 miles in one hour. He drove 51.3 miles in the next hour. How many miles did he drive?

   A 93.8 miles   C 98.3 miles

   B 93.9 miles   D 938 miles

2. Carlita biked on Monday and on Wednesday. How many miles did she bike on the two days?

Distance Biked	
Day	**Distance (mi)**
Monday	3.5
Wednesday	3.75

   F 6.25 miles   H 7.25 miles

   G 6.75 miles   J 7.75 miles

3. Pamela is 52.6 inches tall. Roberto is 54.2 inches tall. How much taller is Roberto than Pamela?

   A 2.6 inches   C 1.6 inches

   B 2.4 inches   D 1.4 inches

4. Joy has $70. She buys these items.

   If she rounds each amount to the nearest whole number, about how much change should she receive?

   F $10   H $18

   G $15   J $20

5. What kind of triangle always has 3 acute angles and 3 sides the same length?

   A right   C isoceles

   B scalene   D equilateral

6. During one week, Thurston ran 4.2 miles. The following week he ran 5.75 miles. About how much farther did Thurston run the following week?

   F 1 mile   H 3 miles

   G 2 miles   J 10 miles

7. What is 35.18 rounded to the nearest tenth?

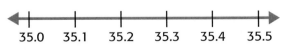

   A 35.1   C 35.3

   B 35.2   D 35.5

8. Arturo bought a kite for $19.95 and string for $4.19. Which is the closest estimate of the total amount spent?

F $20   **H** $24

G $22   **J** $25

9. Liseta earns $34.75 each week walking dogs. About how much will she earn in 3 weeks?

A $105   **C** $204

B $180   **D** $210

10. Which of the following is represented by the model?

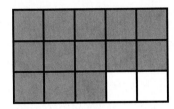

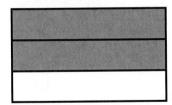

F $\frac{2}{13} > \frac{1}{3}$ **H** $\frac{1}{3} = \frac{2}{3}$

G $\frac{2}{3} > \frac{13}{15}$ **J** $\frac{13}{15} > \frac{2}{3}$

PART 2   Short Response

Record your answers on the answer sheet provided by your teacher or on a sheet of paper.

11. One bag of apples weighs 7.23 pounds, and another bag weighs 6.45 pounds. How much do the two bags of apples weigh together?

12. Which point on the number line is greater than 6.5 and less than 7.0?

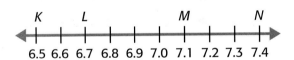

PART 3   Extended Response

Record your answers on the answer sheet provided by your teacher or on a sheet of paper.

13. Mr. Perry sold the items shown below in a yard sale.

Item	Original Price ($)	Selling Price ($)
CD	16.99	1.50
Stuffed animal	12.50	0.75
Table	74.89	12
Vase	22.49	3.50

If Mr. Perry sold all four items, how much money would he make? Explain.

NEED EXTRA HELP?													
If You Missed Question...	1	2	3	4	5	6	7	8	9	10	11	12	13
Go to Lesson...	15-4	15-4	15-6	15-2	9-5	15-2	15-1	15-2	15-2	13-5	15-4	14-5	15-4
SC Academic Standards	4-2.12	4-2.12	4-2.12	4-2.12	4-4.6	4-2.12	4-2.11	4-2.12	4-2.12	4-2.9	4-2.12	4-2.7	4-2.12

FOCUS ON
South Carolina
Beyond the Focal Points

GRADE 4

Contents

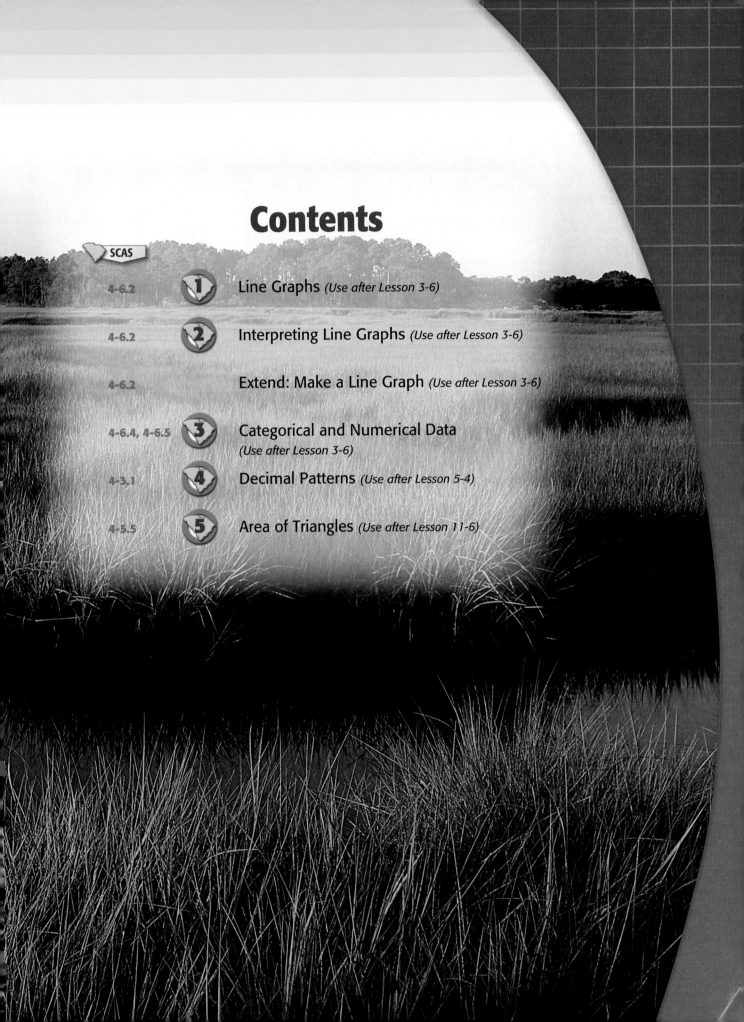

Line Graphs

GET READY to Learn

Lindsey and Jaden are measuring the growth of a flower. The graph shows the growth of the flower over four months. Find how tall the flower grew in four months.

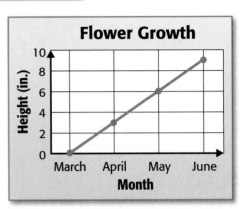

A **line graph** shows how data changes over time. You can use a line graph to make predictions about future events.

Real-World EXAMPLE Interpret a Line Graph

1 **FLOWERS Refer to the graph above. How tall did the flower grow in four months?**

Find the fourth month shown on the graph. The fourth month is June.

Move up to find where the point is located on the graph. Then compare the height of the point to the scale on the left.

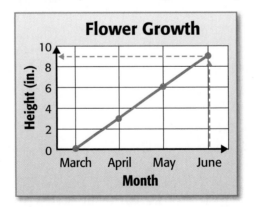

The point is located between 8 and 10 on the graph's scale. So, the plant grew 9 inches in four months.

Real-World EXAMPLE   Interpret a Line Graph

2 MEASUREMENT The graph shows the growth of a baby panda over four weeks. How much weight did the baby panda gain 0 between the first week and the fourth week?

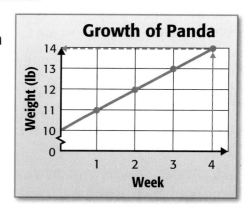

You need to subtract the panda's weight at week 1 from its weight at week 4.

During week one, the panda weighed 11 pounds. During week four, the panda weighed 14 pounds.

$14 - 11 = 3$

So, the baby panda gained 3 pounds between the first week and the fourth week.

Online Personal Tutor at macmillanmh.com

CHECK What You Know

For Exercises 1–6, use the line graph. See Examples 1 and 2

1. At what time is the least amount of snow on the ground?

2. How much snow is on the ground at 8:00 P.M.?

3. How many more inches of snow were on the ground at 9 P.M. than at 6 P.M.?

4. How many fewer inches of snow were on the ground at 7 P.M. than at 10 P.M.?

5. How much snow fell over the 4-hour period shown on the graph?

6. **Talk About It** Predict how much snow will be on the ground at midnight.

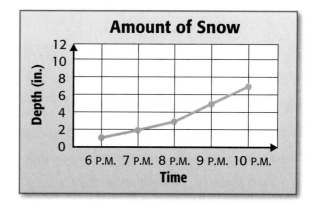

Math Online Extra Examples at macmillanmh.com

655

For Exercises 7–11, use the graph that shows the number of words read. See Examples 1 and 2

7. How many words were read in two minutes?

8. How many words were read in five minutes?

9. At this rate, how many words will be read in six minutes?

10. How many fewer words were read in two minutes than in four minutes?

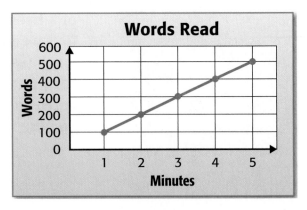

11. How many more words were read in five minutes than in one minute?

For Exercises 12–16, use the graph that shows the distance a car travels. See Examples 1 and 2

12. How many miles did the car travel in two hours?

13. How many miles did the car travel in three hours?

14. What distance did the car travel between two and four hours?

15. How long does it take the car to travel 200 miles?

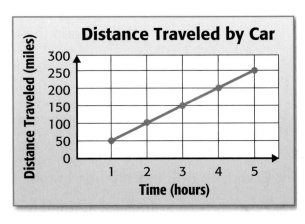

16. How many more miles did the car drive in five hours than in two hours?

H.O.T. Problems

17. **WRITING IN** ►**MATH** The graph shows the rate of a submarine's descent underwater. Write two sentences that describe the data.

18. **OPEN ENDED** Give an example of a set of data that is best represented in a line graph.

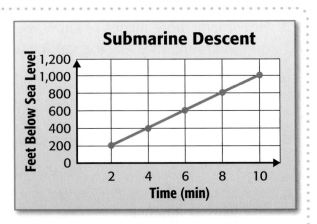

Math Online Self-Check Quiz at macmillanmh.com

Interpreting Line Graphs

GET READY to Learn

A **line graph** shows how data changes over time. You can use a line graph to show change over time as **increasing, decreasing,** or **varying** and to make predictions about future events.

MAIN IDEA

I will interpret data shown in a line graph.

◀ **SC Academic Standards** ▶

4-6.2 Interpret data in tables, **line graphs,** bar graphs, and double bar graphs **whose scale increments are greater than or equal to 1.**

4-3.6 Illustrate situations that show change over time as either increasing, decreasing, or varying.

New Vocabulary

line graph
increasing
decreasing
varying

◀ **SC Math Online** ▶

macmillanmh.com

EXAMPLES Interpret a Line Graph

1. **Refer to the graph at the right. How tall did the flower grow in four months?** The fourth month is June.

   Move up to find where the point is located on the graph. Then compare the height of the point to the scale on the left.

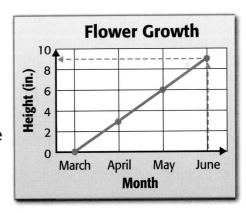

   The point is located between 8 and 10 on the graph's scale. So, the plant grew 9 inches in four months.

2. **The graph shows the growth of a baby panda over four weeks. The graph shows the growth of a baby panda over four week. Is the panda's weight increasing, decreasing, or varying over time? Explain.**

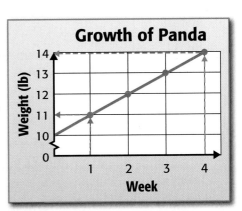

   The shape of the line graph tells you whether the panda's weight is increasing, decreasing, or varying over time.

   Since the line climbs up steadily from week to week, the panda's weight is increasing.

657

For Exercises 1–3, use the line graph.

1. At what time is the least amount of snow on the ground?

2. How much snow is on the ground at 8:00 P.M.?

3. **Talk About It** What hour(s) recorded the heaviest snowfall? How do you know?

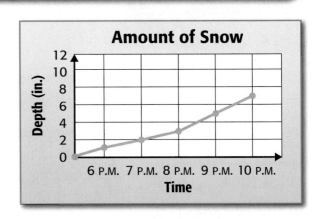

Amount of Snow

Practice and Problem Solving

For Exercises 4–7, use the line graph.

4. Is the school population increasing, decreasing, or varying over time?

5. How much did the population grow between 1995 and 2005?

6. During which time period did the population stay the same?

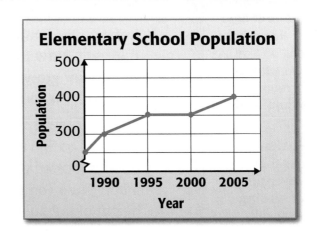

Elementary School Population

7. Predict the population in 2020. Explain your reasoning.

Represent each set of data in a line graph.

8.

Plant Growth	
Week	Height (in.)
1	1
2	2
3	3
4	5
5	8

9.

One Day's Temperatures	
Time	Temperature (°F)
12 P.M.	62°
1 P.M.	65°
2 P.M.	72°
3 P.M.	66°
4 P.M.	64°

10. Collect and organize data about a week's daily high temperatures in your city. Display the data on a line graph.

11. Analyze the graph you made in Exercise 11. Are the temperatures increasing, decreasing, or varying over time? Explain.

Extend

Make a Line Graph

In the following activity, you will collect and represent data in a line graph.

ACTIVITY

Concepts in MOtion

Animation
macmillanmh.com

MAIN IDEA

I will represent data in a line graph.

SC Academic Standards

4-6.2 Interpret data in tables, **line graphs,** bar graphs, and double bar graphs **whose scale increments are greater than or equal to 1.**

You Will Need
colored pencils
grid paper
newspaper

Step 1 Collect data.

Collect weather data from one day. Record the temperatures in a table like the one shown.

Time	Temperature (°F)
9 A.M.	
10 A.M.	
11 A.M.	
12 P.M.	
1 P.M.	

Step 2 Create a graph.

Draw two axes and label them. Then write a title at the top of the graph. Choose an appropriate scale for your graph.

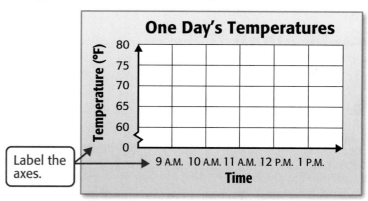

Label the axes.

Step 3   Graph the data.

Above 9 A.M., place a point at the correct temperature. For example, if the high was 60, then place a point at 60. Continue graphing the rest of the data. An example is shown.

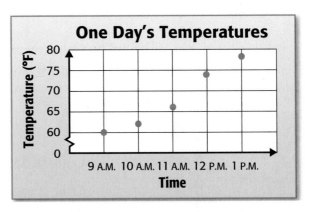

Step 4   Draw a line.

Connect the points with straight lines.

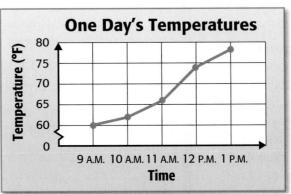

Think About It

1. Describe how a line graph shows how data changes over time.

2. Explain how you labeled the axes and chose a scale for the data.

CHECK What You Know

Represent each data set in a line graph.

3.

Plant Growth	
Week	Height (in.)
1	1
2	2
3	3
4	5
5	8

4.

One Day's Temperatures	
Time	Temperature (°F)
12 P.M.	62°
1 P.M.	65°
2 P.M.	72°
3 P.M.	66°
4 P.M.	64°

5. **WRITING IN ►MATH** Give an example of a set of data that is best displayed in a line graph.

Categorical and Numerical Data

3

SC Math Online
macmillanmh.com

MAIN IDEA

I will tell the difference between categorical and numerical data.

SC Academic Standards

4-6.4 Distinguish between categorical and numerical data.

4-6.5 Match categorical and numerical data to appropriate graphs.

New Vocabulary

categorical
numerical

GET READY to Learn

Data can be categorical or numerical.

Categorical Data	Numerical Data

Student Eye Color

blue	brown	green
blue	brown	green
blue	brown	green
brown	brown	green
brown	brown	green

Student Height (in.)

60	57	54	61
58	59	57	58
55	60	56	63
61	58	62	59

Categorical data uses labels to place data into groups or categories. **Numerical data** uses numbers to place data into groups.

CHECK What You Know

Tell whether each set of data is categorical or numerical.

1.

Running Time (min)				
36	32	40	39	43
35	43	37	31	34
42	40	37	38	42
31	38	43	34	36

2.

Student Pets			
bird	cat	dog	fish
bird	cat	dog	hamster
cat	dog	fish	hamster
cat	dog	fish	lizard

3. **Talk About It** Give an example of a question you could ask that would result in categorical data. Give an example of a question that would result in numerical data.

Tell whether each set of data is categorical or numerical.

4.

Favorite Color			
blue	green	pink	red
blue	green	pink	red
blue	green	purple	red
blue	pink	purple	yellow

5.

Student Age			
9	9	10	10
9	9	10	10
9	10	10	11
9	10	10	11

6.

Distance Biked (mi)			
4	6	2	7
2	3	5	3
5	4	6	5
3	7	5	6

7.

Instruments Students Play			
clarinet	drums	guitar	flute
clarinet	guitar	guitar	trumpet
drums	guitar	flute	trumpet
drums	guitar	flute	violin

The titles of data sets are given. Tell whether each set of data would be categorical or numerical. Explain your reasoning.

8. Students Favorite Fruits

9. Shoe Sizes

10. Weights of Puppies

11. Items in School Store

Tell whether each set of data is categorical or numerical. Then tell whether a bar graph, double bar graph, or line graph would best display each set of data. Explain.

12.

Tree Growth (in.)	
Week	Height (in.)
1	2
2	3
3	5
4	7

13.

Favorite Type of Book		
adventure	animal	mystery
adventure	animal	mystery
adventure	animal	sports
adventure	mystery	sports
adventure	mystery	sports
animal	mystery	sports

14.

Number of Books Read			
5	7	4	9
3	2	8	6
6	4	5	3
8	9	6	4
7	3	9	6

15.

Favorite Sports			
boys		girls	
baseball	football	basketball	soccer
baseball	football	basketball	soccer
baseball	football	basketball	soccer
basketball	soccer	soccer	tennis
basketball	soccer	soccer	tennis

Decimal Patterns

4

MAIN IDEA

I will analyze decimal patterns.

SC Academic Standards

4-3.1 Analyze numeric, nonnumeric, and repeating **patterns involving** all operations and **decimal patterns through hundredths.**

Review Vocabulary

pattern

SC Math Online

macmillanmh.com

> **GET READY to Learn**

In Lesson 5-4, you learned that a **pattern** is a sequence of numbers, figures, or symbols that follow a rule. You have extended patterns containing numbers and figures. Now you will extend patterns containing decimals.

EXAMPLES

Identify and describe each pattern. Then extend each pattern by finding the next three decimals in the pattern.

1 **3.2, 3.5, 3.8, 4.1, 4.4**

You can identify and describe the pattern by looking at what happens to get from one number to the next.

3.2, 3.5, 3.8, 4.1, 4.4

$+0.3 \quad +0.3 \quad +0.3 \quad +0.3$

The numbers in the pattern are increasing by 0.3. So, the rule is add 0.3.

$$\begin{array}{ccc} 4.4 & 4.7 & 5.0 \\ +0.3 & +0.3 & +0.3 \\ \hline 4.7 & 5.0 & 5.3 \end{array}$$

So, the next three decimals in the pattern are 4.7, 5.0, and 5.3.

2 **7.25, 7.0, 6.75, 6.5, 6.25**

You can identify and describe the pattern by looking at what happens to get from one number to the next.

7.25, 7.0, 6.75, 6.5, 6.25

$-0.25 \quad -0.25 \quad -0.25 \quad -0.25$

The numbers in the pattern are decreasing by 0.25. So, the rule is subtract 0.25.

$$\begin{array}{ccc} 6.25 & 6.00 & 5.75 \\ -0.25 & -0.25 & -0.25 \\ \hline 6.00 & 5.75 & 5.50 \end{array}$$

So, the next three decimals in the pattern are 6.00, 5.75, and 5.50.

Identify, describe, and extend each pattern by finding the next three decimals in the pattern.

1. 1.4, 1.6, 1.8, 2.0, 2.2

2. 3.9, 4.4, 4.9, 5.4, 5.9

3. 9.1, 8.7, 8.3, 7.9, 7.5

4. 14.7, 13.9, 13.1, 12.3, 11.5

5. **Talk About It** Look at the pattern. 9.2, 8.7, 8.2, 7.7, 7.2
What is the rule for this pattern? How did you find the rule?

Practice and Problem Solving

Identify, describe, and extend each pattern by finding the next three decimals in the pattern.

6. 17.03, 17.12, 17.21, 17.30, 17.39

7. 19.10, 19.25, 19.40, 19.55, 19.70

8. 22.46, 22.40, 22.34, 22.28, 22.22

9. 474.8, 475.4, 476, 476.6, 477.2

10. 3.54, 3.51, 3.48, 3.45, 3.42

11. 35.18, 34.83, 34.48, 34.13, 33.78

12. Write a decimal pattern that uses the rule of +0.8.

13. Brianna's past five hundred-yard dash times were 16.45, 16.24, 16.03, 15.82, and 15.61. If this pattern continues, what will Brianna's next three times be?

14. **WRITING IN ►MATH** Explain the differences between a whole number patterns and decimal patterns. How are they alike? How are they different.

Area of Triangles

GET READY to Learn

Notice that a parallelogram is made of two congruent triangles. So, the formula for the area of a triangle can be found by dividing the formula for the area of a parallelogram by two.

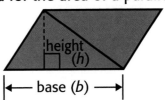

Area of a Triangle		Key Concept
Words	To find the area of a triangle, multiply the base and height of the triangle and then divide the product by 2.	**Model**
Symbols	$A = (b \times h) \div 2$	

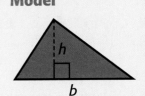

EXAMPLE Find the Area of a Triangle

1 **Find the area of the triangle.**

Use the area formula of a triangle.

$A = (b \times h) \div 2$ Area formula of a triangle.

$A = (8 \times 4) \div 2$ Replace b with 8 and h with 4.

$A = 32 \div 2$ Multiply.

$A = 16$ Divide. $32 \div 2 = 16$

The area of the triangle is 16 square centimeters.

CHECK What You Know

Find the area of each triangle.

1.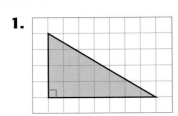

2.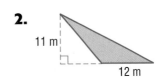

Find the area of each triangle.

3.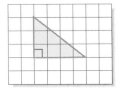

4.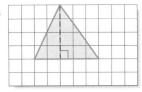

5.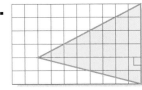

6.
3 ft
6 ft

7.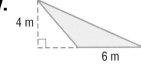
4 m
6 m

8.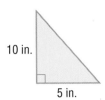
10 in.
5 in.

9.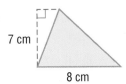
7 cm
8 cm

10.
10 ft
9 ft

11.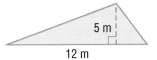
5 m
12 m

12. height: 6 in., base: 7 in.

13. height: 9 cm, base: 4 cm

14. height: 8 m, base: 10 m

15. height: 12 ft, base: 11 ft

16. ROOFING Ansley is going to help his father shingle the roof of their house. What is the area of the triangular portion of one end of the roof to be shingled?

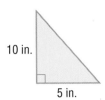
4 yd
7 yd

17. CRAFTS Emilia made the paper box shown at the right. What is the area of the top of the box?

9 cm
10 cm

18. FLOWER BEDS A flower bed in a parking lot is shaped like a triangle as shown. Find the area of the flower bed in square feet. If one bag of topsoil covers 10 square feet, how many bags are needed to cover this flower bed?

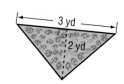
3 yd
2 yd

Problem-Solving Projects

Problem-Solving Projects

PROJECT 1

SCAS 4-1.5 Use correct, complete, and clearly written and oral mathematical language to pose questions, communicate ideas, and extend problem situations.

Make a Game

Have you ever made up a board game? In this project, you can invent a new board game or combine two board games that already exist.

Getting Started

Day 1 Choose the Subject
- Decide what your game will be about by choosing one of the chapters that was covered in math class this year.
- Determine which concepts in the chapter you want to focus on, such as multiplication facts, two-dimensional figures, or fractions.

Day 2 Brainstorm Ideas
- Work as a group to determine what facts, figures, or important vocabulary will be a part of your game.
- Discuss different ways this game can be played.
- Design several alternative ways to play the game.

- Discuss a point system.
- How many points can you earn and how can you earn them?
- Can you lose points? How?

Day 3 Rules and Regulations

- Choose one of the alternative games that were designed on Day 2.
- Write clear instructions for the game. Include any rules or regulations that may affect the scoring and outcome of the game. All players must have a fair chance of winning.
- Give some examples of how to play and score the game.

Day 4 Create and Practice

- Review the instructions for the game. List any items that you will need to make, such as pictures of shapes or flash cards.
- Make all items that are needed to play the game.
- Make a score card or board to keep track of the score.
- Practice your game to make sure that it works.

Day 5 Presentation Day

- Present the instructions along with the rules for the game to the class.
- Ask for volunteers to play your game.
- Play and enjoy.

Wrap Up

- Could you use this game for other math concepts? Describe what changes would need to be made.
- Do all players of your game have a fair chance of winning? Explain.
- How would the game have been different if you chose a different alternative game?

PROJECT 2

SCAS **4-1.5** Use correct, complete, and clearly written and oral mathematical language to pose questions, communicate ideas, and extend problem situations.

Plan a Family Celebration

Plan a celebration for your family. It can be a known holiday, special event, or you can create your own holiday.

Getting Started

Day 1 Decide What to Celebrate

- Decide on a special occasion for your family. Some examples are a family reunion, Independence Day, or "Juneteenth."
- Choose the day and time to have this celebration.
- Use a calendar to calculate the number of weeks, days, and hours that you have until the celebration.
- Create a timeline to help you organize how to prepare for the celebration.

Day 2 The Number Makes a Difference

- Think carefully about the number of people you want to invite.
- Plan a meal that will feed everyone.
- Using cookbooks and family recipes, choose foods for the celebration.
- Double the recipes if needed.
- Calculate the amounts of each ingredient you will need.
- Calculate a total for all food items.

Day 3 What's the Cost?

- Use the list of ingredients as a shopping list.
- Determine the cost of each item by using the Internet or advertisements from a grocery store.
- Add the prices together to find the total cost of the ingredients.
- Choose any other food items you might want to serve. Determine their cost and add it to your previous total.

Day 4 What Else Do I Need to Buy?

- Make a list of any nonfood items that may be needed.
- Research the cost for these items.
- Make a table to show the amount spent on food and nonfood items.
- Determine the total cost for food and nonfood items.

Day 5 Presentation Day

- Present your celebration to the class. Use your timeline to describe your plan.
- Share what you will serve, the total cost for each item, and the amount spent for each individual.
- Explain your reasoning for the total cost.

Wrap Up •

- Why did you choose this celebration?
- Would you like your family to use your plan for this celebration?
- Did the price of the food help you decide what you would have at your celebration?

PROJECT 3

SCAS 4-1.5 Use correct, complete, and clearly written and oral mathematical language to pose questions, communicate ideas, and extend problem situations.

Make your Home your Own

Have you ever wanted to design a community? When city planners construct a new development, they create a model of the development. Then that development becomes a community.

Getting Started

Day 1 Where Do You Live?

- Research your community. What interesting information can you find?
- Find the total area of the land used for your community.
- Find the area used for parks and recreation.
- Determine the area used for housing.

Day 2 Make It Better

- Think about what makes your community a nice place to live.
- Survey the class for ideas on how to improve communities.
- Create a bar graph to display the data you have collected.

Day 3 Various Viewpoints

- Discuss with other students whether their surveys showed similar data. If not, explain why.
- Research the cost of one idea from the survey.
- Identify three ways that you can raise money to improve your community.

Day 4 Map It Out

- Examine the scale of a map of your community. The scale is a chosen distance that represents an actual distance. For example, you may wish to use a scale of 1 inch = 1 mile.
- Recreate the map of your community using a different scale than what is shown on the map.
- Look at your classmates' maps. What do you notice about the scales and the sizes of the maps?

Day 5 Presentation Day

- Present your community research, survey, and map to the class.
- Is there anything you wanted to add to your community that no one else thought of?

Wrap Up ···

- How would changing the scale of your map affect the map?
- How can you work toward improving your community?
- Who can help you achieve your community improvement goals?

SCAS 4-1.5 Use correct, complete, and clearly written and oral mathematical language to pose questions, communicate ideas, and extend problem situations.

Plan a Trip

Plan a road trip in which you will determine the destination, cost, and route for the trip.

Getting Started

Day 1 Plan the Trip

- Plan a trip that includes at least three states and is about 500 miles from home.
- Use a map or atlas to determine all possible combinations of states you can visit.
- Choose the route for your trip. Add all the distances to determine the total miles to your final destination.
- Multiply by two to determine the round-trip mileage.
- Estimate all costs for the trip.
- Create a table to organize and display this data.

ROUTE
US
66

Day 2 Research Items Needed for Your Trip

- Estimate how long the trip will take if you travel 60 miles per hour.
- Determine how many stops for gas you will need to make if your car can travel 30 miles per gallon and holds 18 gallons of gas.
- Write an equation to determine how much you will spend on gas for the entire trip if gas costs $2.50 per gallon.
- Place the cost of the gas in the table from Day 1.

Day 3 What To Do When You Get There

- Research what you would like to do when you reach your final destination.
- Design a calendar for the week. Account for how each hour is spent.
- Draw a clock next to each event to show the time it will occur. Write the elapsed time for each event.
- Research prices on the places you will visit and the food you will eat. Add these figures to the table that was created on Day 1.

Day 4 What Is the Cost?

- Research prices for the hotel. Place this on the table from Day 1.
- Calculate the total cost of the trip using the table from Day 1.
- Prepare a poster to present to the class that shows the information about your trip.

Day 5 Presentation Day

- Present your trip to the class.
- Include a summary of where you would go, your calendar, the total cost, and the poster you created.

Wrap Up

- How many possible destinations did your group identify?
- Why did you choose your destination?
- Did the costs of places help you decide where you wanted to go?
- Estimate how much faster you will arrive at your destination if you travel 65 miles per hour. Explain.

Student Handbook

Built-In Workbooks

Reference

How to Use the Student Handbook

The Student Handbook is the additional skill and reference material found at the end of books. The Student Handbook can help answer these questions.

What If I Need More Practice?

You, or your teacher, may decide that working through some additional problems would be helpful. The **Extra Practice** section provides these problems for each lesson so you have ample opportunity to practice new skills.

What If I Need to Prepare for a Standardized Test?

The **Preparing for Standardized Tests** section provides worked-out examples and practice problems for multiple-choice, short-response, and extended response questions.

What if I Want to Learn Additional Concepts and Skills?

Use the Concepts and Skills Bank section to either refresh your memory about topics you have learned in other math classes or learn new math concepts and skills.

What If I Forget a Vocabulary Word?

The **English-Spanish Glossary** provides a list of important, or difficult, words used throughout the textbook. It provides a definition in English and Spanish as well as the page number(s) where the word can be found.

What If I Need to Find Something Quickly?

The **Index** alphabetically lists the subjects covered throughout the entire textbook and the pages on which each subject can be found.

What If I Forget Measurement Conversions, Multiplication Facts, or Formulas?

Inside the back cover of your math book is a list of measurement conversions and formulas that are used in the book. You will also find a multiplication table inside the back cover.

Extra Practice

Lesson 1-1
Pages 17–19

Write the value of the underlined digit.

1. 1,637   **2.** 37,904   **3.** 56,572   **4.** 209,631

Write each number in word form and expanded form.

5. 2,493   **6.** 6,319   **7.** 7,085   **8.** 9,160

9. 28,482   **10.** 71,045   **11.** 523,608   **12.** 347,281

Write each number in standard form and expanded form.

13. fifty-six thousand, seven hundred twenty

14. two hundred thirty-four thousand, eight hundred three

Lesson 1-2
Pages 22–25

Write each number in word form and expanded form.

1. 9,005   **2.** 19,860   **3.** 26,010   **4.** 360,508

5. 408,040   **6.** 26,053,107   **7.** 730,000,520   **8.** 800,530,700

Write each number in standard form and expanded form.

9. nine million, twenty-four thousand, ten

10. six hundred thirty-five million, eight hundred fifty-seven thousand, five

11. Write in word form and standard form.

$300,000 + 20,000 + 1,000 + 50 + 8$

Lesson 1-3
Pages 26–27

Solve. Use the four-step plan.

1. Mrs. Beal's students earned a class party. An extra large pizza cost $28. If she bought 3 pizzas, how much did she spend?

2. Carisa can draw 3 pictures in the morning and 3 pictures in the afternoon. If she draws for 5 days, how many pictures can she make?

3. Tom watched 45 movies this year. Each movie was two hours long. How many hours did he spend watching movies this year?

4. A basketball game has 4 quarters. If 5 players each score 2 points during each quarter, how many total points are scored?

Lesson 1-4

Pages 28–30

Compare. Use >, <, or =.

1. 9,719 ● 9,791

2. 3,780 ● 3,080

3. 34,925 ● 34,952

4. 89,629 ● 89,635

5. 47,283 ● 42,283

6. 72,036 ● 72,300

7. 325,614 ● 235,614

8. 758,438 ● 758,438

9. 7,863,403 ● 7,863,304

10. 9,604,138 ● 9,064,946

Copy and complete to make the number sentence true.

11. 4,■58 < 4,859

12. 34,199 = 3■,199

13. 214,166 > 2■4,166

14. 5,877,820 > 5,877,8■0

Lesson 1-5

Pages 32–34

Order the numbers from greatest to least.

1. 1,443; 1,434; 1,444; 1,344

2. 6,519; 6,600; 3,941; 4,872

3. 19,400; 9,400; 19,004; 10,440

4. 52,951; 49,384; 51,954; 52,865

5. 85,610; 85,185; 85,611; 85,625

6. 94,846; 49,846; 84,694; 46,948

7. 275,391; 2,086,344; 258,983

8. 361,259; 361,084; 61,999; 846,465

9. 568,208; 559,876; 59,986; 58,869

10. 768,635; 792,456; 741,056; 78,318

11. 3,849,257; 38,492,570; 38,492,057

12. 4,608,056; 4,608,942; 4,608,924

Lesson 1-6

Pages 36–39

Round each number to the given place-value position.

1. 451; hundred

2. 949; hundred

3. 4,965; thousand

4. 20,368; thousand

5. 36,801; hundred

6. 42,204; ten thousand

7. 70,988; thousand

8. 83,756; ten

9. 437,947; ten thousand

10. 455,877; ten

11. 849, 604; thousand

12. 934,567; hundred thousand

Lesson 1-7

Use the four-step plan to solve.

1. Lisa lives 7 miles from school. She bikes to school and back every day. How many miles does she bike in 1 school week?

2. A chicken runs 5 miles an hour. An ostrich runs 40 miles an hour. How many hours would it take a chicken to run the same distance it took an ostrich to run in two hours?

3. Aaron bought a shirt that cost $27 and a hat that cost $3. How much change will he receive if he pays with two $20 bills?

4. A bag of 15 oranges costs $20. Oranges that are sold individually cost $2. Is it cheaper to buy 15 oranges in a bag or 15 oranges sold individually? Explain.

Lesson 2-1

Copy and complete each number sentence. Identify the property or rule used.

1. $20 - \blacksquare = 0$

2. $14 + 37 = \blacksquare + 14$

3. $7 + (4 + 8) = (7 + 4) + \blacksquare$

4. $197 + 0 = \blacksquare$

5. $233 - \blacksquare = 233$

6. $72 + 9 = \blacksquare + 72$

7. $(14 + 3) + 8 = 14 + (3 + \blacksquare)$

8. $863 + 44 = \blacksquare + 863$

9. $21 + (\blacksquare + 9) = (21 + 17) + 9$

10. $541 - \blacksquare = 0$

Lesson 2-2

Estimate. Round to the indicated place value.

1. $43 + 29$; tens

2. $664 + 49$; tens

3. $1,329 + 755$; hundreds

4. $9,488 + 2,061$; thousands

5. $\$34,163 + \$29,982$; hundreds

6. $59 - 34$; tens

7. $859 - 42$; tens

8. $2,495 - 468$; hundreds

9. $\$6,295 - \$1,402$; thousands

10. $37,423 - 18,196$; ten thousands

Lesson 2-3

Pages 62–63

Tell whether an estimate or exact answer is needed. Then solve.

1. Nina bought a CD that cost $11. She gave the cashier a $20 bill. About how much change should she get back?

2. Carlos wants to buy a new football that costs $32. He earns $6 every week delivering newspapers. How many weeks will it take to save enough money for the ball?

3. The 29 students in Jin's science class are riding in vans on a field trip. Each van can hold 8 students. How many vans will be needed?

4. Mika spends about $1\frac{1}{2}$ hours practicing the piano each day, Monday through Friday. About how many hours does she practice each month?

Lesson 2-4

Pages 64–67

Find each sum. Check your work by estimating.

1. 456
    + 233

2. $3,879
    + $ 348

3. 5,678
    + 2,431

4. $38,406
    + $ 6,744

5. 60,483
    + 98,218

6. $32,819
    + $67,375

7. 357,816
    + 93,402

8. $572,938
    + $118,476

9. $983,107
    + $645,815

Lesson 2-5

Pages 72–74

Subtract. Use addition or estimation to check.

1. 721
    − 563

2. $807
    − $328

3. 926
    − 644

4. $1,766
    − $ 819

5. 9,663
    − 5,201

6. $6,741
    − $3,983

7. $24,509
    − $ 7,625

8. 55,788
    − 34,223

9. 71,864
    − 49,667

Lesson 2-6
Pages 76–77

Use any strategy to solve. Tell what strategy you used.

1. Mr. Lee spent about $23 on paintbrushes, $50 dollars on paint, and $15 on colored chalk. How much did he spend on art supplies?

2. Tia is hanging lights around her window. The window is a square with sides that are 28 inches. How many inches of lights will Tia need?

3. The cats in the animal shelter eat 18 pounds of food each day. How many pounds of food do the cats eat each week?

4. Casey has $6. He buys a sandwich for $2, a salad for $2, and milk for $1. How much money will he have left?

Lesson 2-7
Pages 80–83

Subtract. Use addition to check.

1. $400 − $298
2. 800 − 567
3. 1,000 − 703
4. 3,600 − 1,695
5. 5,000 − 2,367
6. $9,000 − $4,890
7. 7,000 − 5,804
8. 6,400 − 3,166
9. 9,600 − 1,879
10. $2,200 − $883
11. $4,700 − $2,864
12. 8,600 − 7,621
13. 7,000 − 4,386

Lesson 3-1
Pages 95–97

Organize each set of data in a tally chart and a frequency table.

1. George recorded the types of pets that his classmates have. His recordings are shown at the right.

Pets		
cat	cat	dog
cat	dog	lizard
dog	fish	bird
bird	dog	fish

2. Tina conducted a survey to find out the favorite sports of the children in the park. Her recordings are shown at the right.

Favorite Sports		
soccer	baseball	football
soccer	basketball	football
football	football	basketball
basketball	soccer	tennis

Lesson 3-2

Pages 98–101

Find the mode and median of the set of data. Identify any outliers.

1.

Students in Each Grade					
Grade	1	2	3	4	5
Number of Students	26	22	27	24	22

2.

Roller Coaster Riders at an Amusement Park							
Roller Coaster	1	2	3	4	5	6	7
Number of Riders	46	38	41	17	45	39	36

Lesson 3-3

Pages 102–103

Solve. Use the make a table strategy.

1. Akira mailed invitations to his birthday party. The postage to mail each invitation was 42¢. Akira paid 252¢ in all for postage. How many invitations did he send?

2. During the soccer season, for every 3 penalty kicks he took, Jamil scored on 2 of them. If he scored on 12 penalty kicks, how many penalty kicks did he take?

3. Nick earns $7 an hour walking dogs. He works the same number of hours each week. Nick earns $252 in 1 month. How many hours does he work each week if there are 4 weeks in a month?

4. Maria bought some six-packs of soda. She bought 48 cans of soda in all. How many six-packs of soda did she buy?

Lesson 3-4

Pages 104–107

Organize each set of data in a line plot.

1. Number of seeds that sprouted

Seeds That Sprouted	
Week	Seeds
Week 1	6
Week 2	9
Week 3	11
Week 4	10
Week 5	9
Week 6	6
Week 7	9

2. Miles hiked by campers

Miles Hiked per Day	
Day	Miles Hiked
Monday	5
Tuesday	7
Wednesday	6
Thursday	4
Friday	5
Saturday	4
Sunday	3

Lesson 3-5

Pages 108–110

For Exercises 1–4, use the graph shown.

1. Which animal has the longest life span?

2. Which animal has a life span of 70 years?

3. Which animal has a life span that is 45 years longer than a gorilla's life span?

4. How many years would three generations of humans last?

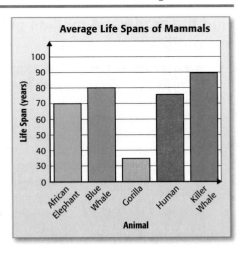

Lesson 3-6

Pages 112–114

For Exercises 1–4, use the graph shown.

1. Which fruit did the farm produce the most of?

2. Which fruit did the farm produce the least of?

3. How many more pounds of strawberries were produced than pounds of plums?

4. Which two fruits added together equal the amount of the fruit that the farm produced the most of?

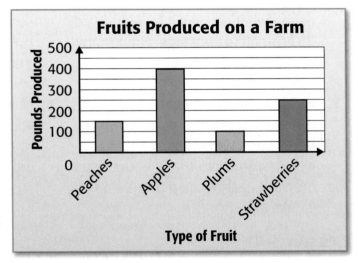

Lesson 3-7

Pages 118–119

Use any strategy to solve. Tell what strategy you used.

1. Luis has an aquarium with 47 fish. There are 12 orange fish, 13 blue fish, 9 white fish, and 8 yellow fish. The rest of the fish are red. How many are red?

2. There were 45 action, 60 comedy, 25 drama, and 50 mystery movies rented from a video store in one day. How many more comedies than dramas were rented?

Lesson 3-8

Pages 124–127

1. Draw a grid to find the number of possible outcomes if two counters are tossed once. Each counter is red on one side and yellow on the other.

2. Draw a grid to find the number of possible outcomes if a coin is tossed and a 0–5 number cube is rolled.

3. Draw a tree diagram to find the number of possible outcomes if a coin is tossed and a spinner with four equal sections labeled 1, 2, 3, and 4, is spun.

4. Draw a tree diagram to find the number of possible outcomes if a spinner with three equal sections labeled 1, 2, and 3, is spun twice.

Lesson 3-9

Pages 128–130

Describe the probability of each outcome. Write *certain, likely, equally likely, unlikely,* or *impossible.*

1. What is the probability of rolling a number?

2. What is the probability of rolling a number that is less than 5?

3. What is the probability of rolling an even number?

4. What is the probability of rolling a number that is greater than 6?

Lesson 4-1

Pages 147–149

Algebra Copy and complete each fact family.

1. $3 \times 8 = \blacksquare$ $8 \times \blacksquare = 24$
   $24 \div \blacksquare = 3$ $24 \div 3 = \blacksquare$

2. $9 \times \blacksquare = 72$ $8 \times \blacksquare = 72$
   $72 \div 9 = \blacksquare$ $72 \div 8 = \blacksquare$

Algebra Divide. Use a related multiplication fact.

3. $27 \div 3 = \blacksquare$

4. $54 \div 9 = \blacksquare$

5. $36 \div 6 = \blacksquare$

6. $88 \div 11 = \blacksquare$

7. $32 \div 8 = \blacksquare$

8. $50 \div 5 = \blacksquare$

Lesson 4-2

Pages 150–153

Identify the property or rule shown by each number sentence.

1. $7 \times 4 = 4 \times 7$

2. $0 \div 15 = 0$

3. $3 \times (4 \times 5) = (3 \times 4) \times 5$

4. $24 \div 1 = 24$

5. $36 \div 36 = 1$

6. $(5 \times 8) \times 6 = 5 \times (8 \times 6)$

Algebra Copy and complete each number sentence. Identify the property or rule used.

7. $6 \div \blacksquare = 1$

8. $16 \times \blacksquare = 0$

9. $14 \div \blacksquare = 1$

10. $\blacksquare \times 8 = 8 \times 5$

Lesson 4-3

Pages 154–157

Multiply or divide. Use arrays or area models if needed.

1. 3×8

2. 5×5

3. 4×7

4. 2×9

5. $\begin{array}{r} 9 \\ \times\ 4 \\ \hline \end{array}$

6. $\begin{array}{r} 2 \\ \times\ 7 \\ \hline \end{array}$

7. $\begin{array}{r} 3 \\ \times\ 6 \\ \hline \end{array}$

8. $\begin{array}{r} 12 \\ \times\ 3 \\ \hline \end{array}$

9. $27 \div 3$

10. $32 \div 4$

11. $30 \div 5$

12. $15 \div 3$

13. $45 \div 5$

14. $28 \div 4$

15. $24 \div 4$

16. $45 \div 3$

Lesson 4-4

Pages 158–159

Tell which operation you would use to solve each problem. Then solve.

1. Sanjay and 3 of his teammates together scored 52 points in a basketball game. They each scored the same number of points. How many points did each boy score?

2. Sherri jogged 9 miles last week, which is 3 times as many miles as her sister and half as much as her brother. How many miles did her sister and brother jog?

3. There are 6 rows of desks in a classroom. There are 7 desks in each row. How many desks are in the classroom?

4. Roger earns $3,600 a year delivering papers. How much does he earn in one month?

Lesson 4-5

Pages 160–162

Multiply or divide. Use arrays or area models if needed.

1. 9×6 **2.** 6×8 **3.** 7×7 **4.** 8×10

5. 5×8 **6.** 9×5 **7.** 6×10 **8.** 7×9

9. $42 \div 6$ **10.** $48 \div 6$ **11.** $90 \div 10$ **12.** $56 \div 7$

13. $35 \div 5$ **14.** $81 \div 9$ **15.** $36 \div 6$ **16.** $72 \div 8$

Lesson 4-6

Pages 166–169

Multiply or divide. Use arrays or area models if needed.

1. $\begin{array}{r} 3 \\ \times\ 11 \\ \hline \end{array}$ **2.** $\begin{array}{r} 4 \\ \times\ 12 \\ \hline \end{array}$ **3.** $\begin{array}{r} 11 \\ \times\ 6 \\ \hline \end{array}$

4. 8×12 **5.** 7×11 **6.** 4×12

7. $11\overline{)88}$ **8.** $11\overline{)110}$ **9.** $12\overline{)48}$

10. $120 \div 12$ **11.** $99 \div 11$ **12.** $96 \div 12$

Lesson 4-7

Pages 170–171

Use any strategy to solve. Tell what strategy you used.

1. Manuel earns $4 for every 3 dozen cookies he sells. How much will Manuel earn if he sells 9 dozen cookies? 12 dozen cookies?

2. Laura has 24 jazz CDs and 7 country CDs. She has 2 times as many pop CDs as country CDs. How many CDs does she have in all?

3. Kim wants to buy a snowboard that costs $160. She has $88 in the bank. If she earns $6 an hour babysitting, how many hours will Kim have to work to earn enough money to buy the snowboard?

4. An art gallery has paintings on display in 7 rooms. There are 12 paintings in each room. How many paintings are on display in the art gallery?

Lesson 4-8

Pages 172–174

Multiply.

1. $6 \times 3 \times 4$ **2.** $5 \times 7 \times 3$ **3.** $8 \times 2 \times 5$

4. $9 \times 3 \times 2$ **5.** $6 \times 4 \times 5$ **6.** $9 \times 1 \times 4$

7. $8 \times 4 \times 3$ **8.** $3 \times 3 \times 12$ **9.** $10 \times 3 \times 5$

10. $6 \times 11 \times 1$ **11.** $9 \times 4 \times 2$ **12.** $12 \times 2 \times 4$

Lesson 4-9

Pages 176–179

Find all of the factors of each number.

1. 36   **2.** 18   **3.** 16

4. 35   **5.** 11   **6.** 24

7. 48   **8.** 40   **9.** 23

Identify the first six multiples for each number.

10. 4   **11.** 7   **12.** 6

13. 12   **14.** 8   **15.** 9

16. 10   **17.** 11   **18.** 3

Lesson 5-1

Pages 193–195

Find the value of each expression if $x = 6$ and $c = 7$.

1. $c + 5$ **2.** $x - 3$ **3.** $c + 9$

4. $7 + x$ **5.** $c - 2$ **6.** $14 - x$

7. $(x - 2) + 9$ **8.** $16 - (c + 5)$ **9.** $5 + (6 + x)$

Write an expression for each situation.

10. five less than y **11.** the sum of b and seventeen

12. d minus twenty-four   **13.** fifty-one subtracted from f

Lesson 5-2

Solve each equation.

1. $4 + b = 12$ **2.** $7 + m = 18$ **3.** $p - 8 = 6$ **4.** $18 - 13 = y$

5. $9 - x = 2$ **6.** $q + 14 = 22$ **7.** $8 + d = 18$ **8.** $7 + 6 = f$

Write and solve an equation for each situation.

9. Twelve less than a number is sixteen. What is the number?

10. Eight subtracted from a number equals thirteen. What is the number?

11. The sum of nine and a number is twenty-eight. Find the number.

12. A number plus eleven equals twenty-five. What is the number?

Lesson 5-3

Identify any missing or extra information. Then solve if possible.

1. Monkeys at the zoo eat 9 bananas and 4 apples each day. How many pieces of fruit do the monkeys eat in one week?

2. Sandra has $21. She wants to buy cans of tennis balls for $4 each. There are 3 tennis balls in each can. How many cans can she buy?

3. Marco has soccer practice 3 days a week. He has 17 teammates. Practice lasts for 2 hours each day. How many hours does Marco practice soccer each week?

4. Kayla earns $5 per hour. She is saving to buy a new game that costs $36 dollars. How many weeks will Kayla have to work to earn enough money for the game?

Lesson 5-4

Identify, describe, and extend each pattern.

1. 3, 7, 11, 15, 19, ▉

2. 27, 22, 17, 12, 7, ▉

3. 2, 5, 3, 6, 4, ▉

4. 5, 1, 7, 3, 9, ▉

5. Sara jogs on a track five days a week. What is the rule for the pattern shown in the table?

6. Trevor practices the guitar every day. What is the rule for the pattern shown in the table?

Distance Jogged					
Day	1	2	3	4	5
Laps	8	16	24	32	40

Time Spent Practicing					
Day	1	2	3	4	5
Minutes	45	90	135	180	225

Lesson 5-5

Write an equation that describes each pattern. Then use the equation to find the next three numbers.

1.

Rule: ■						
Input (*b*)	4	6	10	14	20	24
Output (*x*)	13	15	19	■	■	■

2.

Rule: ■						
Input (*y*)	11	15	19	23	27	31
Output (*c*)	4	8	12	■	■	■

3.

Rule: ■						
Input (*f*)	$24	$32	$40	$48	$56	$64
Output (*q*)	$16	$24	$32	■	■	■

4.

Rule: ■						
Input (*m*)	$16	$19	$22	$25	$28	$31
Output (*p*)	$27	$30	$33	■	■	■

Lesson 5-6

Find the value of each expression if $v = 4$ and $x = 8$.

1. $x \div 4$

2. $6 \times v$

3. $x \div v$

4. $v \div v$

5. $x \times 7 =$

6. $5 \times v$

7. $(v \times 4) \div x$

8. $32 \div (x \div v)$

9. $(x \div 2) \times 9$

Write an expression for each situation.

10. a number divided by 5

11. The product of 3 and a number

12. a number divided by 10

13. 9 times a number

Lesson 5-7

Use any strategy to solve. Tell what strategy you used.

1. Ty wants to buy posters that cost $7 each. He has $50. How many posters can he buy?

2. Ian is eating pizza with 5 friends. They ordered 3 pizzas. If each pizza is cut into 6 slices, how many slices can each person have?

3. A vine in the park grows 2 inches every week. The vine is 13 inches tall now. How many inches tall will the vine be in 2 weeks? 4 weeks? 8 weeks?

4. Amy is putting photos in an album. Each page in the album can hold 4 photos. There are 32 pages in the album. How many photos can Amy put in the album?

Lesson 5-8

Pages 220–223

Write an equation that describes each pattern. Then use the equation to find the next three numbers.

1.

Input (a)	Output (q)
2	12
4	24
6	36
8	▦
10	▦
12	▦

2.

Input (g)	Output (v)
21	3
28	4
35	5
42	▦
49	▦
56	▦

Lesson 6-1

Pages 237–239

Multiply. Use basic facts and patterns.

1. 4×5
4×50
4×500
$4 \times 5,000$

2. 3×7
3×70
3×700
$3 \times 7,000$

3. 8×6
8×60
8×600
$8 \times 6,000$

4. 3×9
3×90
3×900
$3 \times 9,000$

5. 5×6
5×60
5×600
$5 \times 6,000$

6. 7×4
7×40
7×400
$7 \times 4,000$

Multiply. Use mental math.

7. 7×80

8. 60×6

9. 90×3

10. 500×7

11. 9×400

12. $8,000 \times 5$

Lesson 6-2

Pages 240–241

Decide whether each answer is reasonable. Explain your reasoning.

1. Ebony practices the guitar 30 minutes every day. Is it reasonable to say that she practices the guitar 3,000 minutes each month?

2. The soccer fields in a park are each 130 yards long. Is it reasonable to say that 4 soccer fields are a total of 1,560 feet long?

3. The chickens on a farm produce about 4,200 eggs per week. Is it reasonable to say that the chickens produce 600 eggs each day?

4. An album can hold 24 stamps on each page. There are 200 pages. Is it reasonable to say that the album can hold 48,000 stamps?

Lesson 6-3
Pages 242–244

Estimate each product. Then tell if the estimate is *greater than* or *less than* the actual product.

1. 584
$\times$ 3

2. 484
$\times$ 5

3. 723
$\times$ 8

4. 3 $\times$ 692

5. 6 $\times$ $472

6. 9 $\times$ $460

7. 7 $\times$ 1,986

8. 8 $\times$ $5,420

9. 5 $\times$ 6,752

10. 3 $\times$ $478

11. 6 $\times$ $9,810

12. 8 $\times$ 3,755

Lesson 6-4
Pages 246–248

Multiply. Check for reasonableness.

1. 18
$\times$ 6

2. 28
$\times$ 5

3. $17
$\times$ 9

4. 2 $\times$ 99

5. 6 $\times$ 25

6. 7 $\times$ $43

7. 5 $\times$ 73

8. 4 $\times$ $86

9. 9 $\times$ 39

10. 3 $\times$ $92

11. 8 $\times$ 78

12. 7 $\times$ $56

Lesson 6-5
Pages 250–251

Use any strategy to solve. Tell what strategy you used.

1. Jesse bikes 224 miles each month. He bikes the same number of miles each week. How many miles does Jesse bike each week? Assume that there are four weeks in each month.

2. Movie tickets are $7 for adults and $4 for children. What is the total cost if three adults and five children go to the theater?

3. Rita is making muffins. There are 36 muffins in each batch. How many muffins will be in 3 batches? How many muffins will be in 7 batches?

4. At the zoo, the big cats are in a row. The lions are last. The jaguars are to the left of the tigers. The cheetahs are to the left of the jaguars. In what order are the big cats?

Lesson 6-6

Pages 252–255

Multiply. Check for reasonableness.

1. 538
   × 3

2. 392
   × 6

3. $256
   × 8

4. 734
   × 7

5. $493
   × 6

6. $724
   × 4

7. $6 \times 5{,}630$

8. $6 \times \$8{,}562$

9. $5 \times 2{,}845$

10. $4 \times 3{,}488$

11. $8 \times 2{,}376$

12. $9 \times 5{,}670$

Lesson 6-7

Pages 258–261

Multiply. Check for reasonableness.

1. 408
   × 4

2. 507
   × 8

3. 906
   × 7

4. $2 \times 6{,}009$

5. $7 \times \$3{,}408$

6. $5 \times 9{,}206$

7. $3 \times \$8{,}702$

8. $6 \times 4{,}090$

9. $9 \times \$6{,}205$

10. $4 \times 7{,}084$

11. $8 \times 9{,}502$

12. $5 \times 5{,}047$

Lesson 7-1

Pages 273–275

Multiply.

1. 18
   ×30

2. 24
   ×50

3. 48
   ×90

4. 47
   ×60

5. 75
   ×40

6. 56
   ×90

7. 64
   ×30

8. $49
   ×60

9. 85
   ×70

10. $28
    ×30

11. 92
    ×70

12. 63
    ×90

Lesson 7-2

Estimate. Tell whether the estimate is *greater than* or *less than* the actual product.

1. 38 ×26
2. 63 ×44
3. 59 ×37
4. $98 ×57
5. 43 ×82
6. $67 ×38
7. 322 × 64
8. 668 × 27
9. 982 × 34
10. 441 × 33
11. 877 × 59
12. 799 × 87

Lesson 7-3

Solve. Use the act it out strategy.

1. There are 4 tennis players at the court. Each one played one set of tennis against every other player. How many sets of tennis were played?
2. Keisha has 450¢ in her piggy bank. She has the same number of dimes and quarters. She has half as many nickels as dimes. What coins does she have?
3. Linda is 12 years old. Her mother is 2 years less than 3 times her age. How old is Linda's mother?
4. Jaime has 17 coins in his pocket. The coins have a value of 120¢. What coins does he have?

Lesson 7-4

Multiply.

1. 17 ×25
2. 56 ×33
3. $84 ×42
4. 62 ×55
5. 74 ×93
6. $65 ×48
7. 36 ×56
8. 49 ×77
9. $44 ×83
10. 64 ×95
11. $58 ×17
12. 75 ×73

Lesson 7-5

Pages 288–291

Multiply.

1. 104
  ×18

2. 186
  ×32

3. 207
  ×49

4. 275
  ×64

5. 377
  ×53

6. 309
  ×81

7. 452
  ×37

8. 438
  ×27

9. 588
  ×39

10. 542
  ×64

11. 663
  ×46

12. 738
  ×56

Lesson 7-6

Pages 294–295

Use any strategy to solve. Tell what strategy you used.

1. Natalie is thinking of two numbers with a sum of 13 and a product of 36. What are the two numbers?

2. The fish at the pet store eat 28 jars of food every week. How many jars of food will the fish eat in 4 weeks? in 6 weeks? in 8 weeks?

3. Ramón saves $15 every week to buy a skateboard. The skateboard costs $105. How many weeks will it take him to save half as much as he needs to buy the skateboard?

4. Every fourth grader washed 4 cars at the car wash. The fourth graders washed 284 cars in all. How many fourth grade students are there?

Lesson 7-7

Pages 296–298

Multiply.

1. 1,877
  × 24

2. 2,345
  × 62

3. 3,906
  × 59

4. 5,792
  × 48

5. 6,504
  × 96

6. 7,708
  × 85

7. 8,544
  × 38

8. 12,304
  × 65

9. 17,455
  × 92

Lesson 8-1

Pages 313–315

Divide. Check each answer.

1. 36 ÷ 3

2. 60 ÷ 5

3. 54 ÷ 3

4. 70 ÷ 5

5. 98 ÷ 7

6. 91 ÷ 7

7. 79 ÷ 3

8. 66 ÷ 4

9. 95 ÷ 7

Lesson 8-2

Pages 316–319

Copy and complete each set of patterns.

1.
48 ÷ 6 = ▇
480 ÷ 6 = ▇
4,800 ÷ 6 = ▇

2.
63 ÷ 9 = ▇
630 ÷ 9 = ▇
6,300 ÷ 9 = ▇

3.
$40 ÷ 8 = ▇
$400 ÷ 8 = ▇
$4,000 ÷ 8 = ▇

4.
72 ÷ 9 = ▇
720 ÷ 9 = ▇
7,200 ÷ 6 = ▇

5.
$27 ÷ 3 = ▇
$270 ÷ 3 = ▇
$2,700 ÷ 3 = ▇

6.
35 ÷ 7 = ▇
350 ÷ 7 = ▇
3,500 ÷ 7 = ▇

Divide. Use patterns.

7. 420 ÷ 6

8. 300 ÷ 5

9. $280 ÷ 7

10. $210 ÷ 3

11. 5,600 ÷ 7

12. 7,200 ÷ 8

13. 8,100 ÷ 9

14. 1,600 ÷ 4

15. 3,000 ÷ 6

16. $2,700 ÷ 3

17. 4,500 ÷ 9

18. 5,400 ÷ 9

Lesson 8-3

Pages 320–321

Solve. Use the guess and check strategy.

1. Ren bought 5 CDs for $55. One of the CDs cost $5 more than the others. How much did each CD cost?

2. Carmen has 49 more mystery novels than adventure novels. She has 223 novels in all. How many mystery novels and adventure novels does Carmen have?

3. The chickens on a farm eat 3 times as much grain as the turkeys do per week. The chickens and turkeys eat a total of 52 pounds of grain every week. How much grain do the chickens and turkeys each eat every week?

4. A toy store has at least 10 wagons and at least 10 tricycles on sale. There are a total of 89 wheels. How many tricycles and how many wagons are on sale?

Lesson 8-4

Pages 322–324

Estimate. Check your estimate.

1. $24 \div 4$
2. $510 \div 7$
3. $433 \div 5$
4. $476 \div 8$
5. $\$537 \div 6$
6. $298 \div 4$
7. $337 \div 8$
8. $\$259 \div 5$
9. $1,244 \div 6$
10. $2,240 \div 3$
11. $\$6,580 \div 9$
12. $8,256 \div 9$

Lesson 8-5

Pages 326–329

Divide. Use estimation to check.

1. $7\overline{)47}$
2. $8\overline{)39}$
3. $9\overline{)71}$
4. $6\overline{)33}$
5. $5\overline{)44}$
6. $8\overline{)62}$
7. $9\overline{)25}$
8. $6\overline{)45}$
9. $554 \div 8$
10. $462 \div 9$
11. $368 \div 6$
12. $659 \div 8$

Lesson 8-6

Pages 330–331

Use any strategy to solve. Tell what strategy you used.

1. At the drugstore, pencils are on sale for 10 for $1. Pens are on sale for 4 for $2. How much do 20 pencils and 12 pens cost?

2. A plant produces about 45 new flowers every 2 weeks. After 8 weeks, how many flowers will the plant have produced?

3. There are 9 seals at a zoo. Altogether, the seals eat about 750 fish each day. About how many fish does each seal eat every day?

4. Mei hiked for 20 minutes every morning from her campsite to the lake. She hiked back to the campsite every afternoon. Mei hiked for a total of 8 hours to and from the lake. How many days was Mei at camp?

Lesson 8-7

Pages 332–334

Divide. Use estimation to check.

1. $3\overline{)693}$　　**2.** $2\overline{)764}$　　**3.** $7\overline{)875}$　　**4.** $4\overline{)936}$

5. $3\overline{)1,677}$　　**6.** $6\overline{)2,558}$　　**7.** $5\overline{)3,697}$　　**8.** $9\overline{)2,938}$

9. $1,539 \div 2$　　**10.** $7,564 \div 8$　　**11.** $4,255 \div 7$　　**12.** $2,687 \div 4$

Lesson 8-8

Pages 336–338

Divide. Use estimation to check.

1. $3\overline{)315}$　　**2.** $4\overline{)837}$　　**3.** $4\overline{)\$432}$　　**4.** $9\overline{)976}$

5. $3\overline{)625}$　　**6.** $4\overline{)438}$　　**7.** $2\overline{)414}$　　**8.** $7\overline{)756}$

9. $3\overline{)\$317}$　　**10.** $5\overline{)1,039}$　　**11.** $3\overline{)\$2,721}$　　**12.** $9\overline{)9,459}$

13. $1,615 \div 2$　　**14.** $4,363 \div 4$　　**15.** $\$611 \div 3$　　**16.** $1,236 \div 4$

Lesson 8-9

Pages 342–345

Divide. Use estimation to check.

1. $2\overline{)3,664}$　　**2.** $3\overline{)4,671}$　　**3.** $5\overline{)5,847}$　　**4.** $6\overline{)7,248}$

5. $4\overline{)6,184}$　　**6.** $8\overline{)9,872}$　　**7.** $7\overline{)9,256}$　　**8.** $6\overline{)57,888}$

9. $8\overline{)18,816}$　　**10.** $9\overline{)33,786}$　　**11.** $7\overline{)25,984}$　　**12.** $6\overline{)23,678}$

13. $9,634 \div 8$　　**14.** $59,510 \div 5$　　**15.** $67,651 \div 9$　　**16.** $95,785 \div 5$

Lesson 9-1

Pages 359–361

Tell the number of faces, edges, and vertices. Then identify each figure.

1.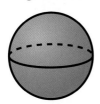

2.

3.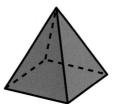

4.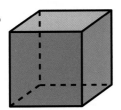

5.

6.

Lesson 9-2

Pages 362–365

Identify each polygon.

1.

2.

3.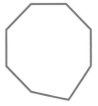

Tell whether each shape is a polygon.

4.

5.

6.

Lesson 9-3

Pages 366–367

Solve. Use the look for a pattern strategy.

1. A flowering plant produces 15 seeds on the first day of spring. On the second day, it produces 23 seeds. On the third day, it produces 31 seeds. Describe the pattern. How many seeds will the plant produce on the sixth day?

2. Copy and complete the table. What is the pattern?

Input	Output
3	21
5	35
7	▣
▣	56

Lesson 9-4

Pages 368–370

Write the measure of each angle in degrees and as a fraction.

1.   **2.** 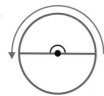 **3.**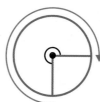

Classify each angle as *right, acute,* or *obtuse*.

4. 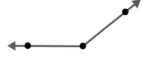 **5.**  **6.**

Lesson 9-5

Pages 372–375

Classify each triangle. Use *acute, right,* or *obtuse* and *isosceles, equilateral,* or *scalene*.

1. 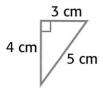 3 cm, 4 cm, 5 cm **2.** 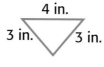 4 in., 3 in., 3 in. **3.** 5 ft, 2 ft, 6 ft

4. 5 ft, 5 ft, 5 ft **5.** 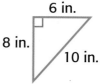 8 yd, 6 yd, 11 yd **6.** 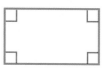 6 in., 8 in., 10 in.

Lesson 9-6

Pages 376–378

Classify each quadrilateral in as many ways as possible.

1.   **2.**  **3.**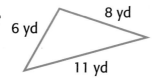

4.   **5.**  **6.**

Lesson 9-7

Pages 380–381

Use any strategy to solve. Tell what strategy you used.

1. What is the next number in the pattern 4, 14, 34, 64, 104?

2. For every 30 minutes that Julia swims, she rests for 15 minutes. In 3 hours of swimming, how many minutes will she rest?

Lesson 10-1

Pages 395–397

Tell what number each letter on the number line represents.

1.

1,347   1,349   1,351

2.
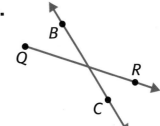
4,200   4,400   4,600

3.
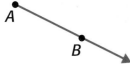
6,500   6,900   7,300

4.
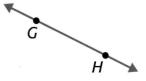
9,250   9,300   9,350

Tell what number point *X* represents on each number line.

5.
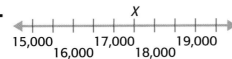
15,000   17,000   19,000
16,000   18,000

6.
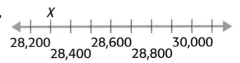
28,200   28,600   30,000
28,400   28,800

Lesson 10-2

Pages 400–403

Identify each figure.

1.
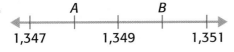
A
B

2.
S
R

3.

G
H

Describe each figure.

4.
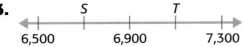
F
L
G
M

5.
B
Q
R
C

6.
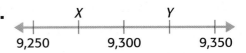
K
Q
P
L

Solve. Use the make an organized list strategy.

1. Jim has 1 blue jacket, 1 green jacket, and 1 brown jacket. He has 1 tan hat and 1 black hat. How many different combinations of a jacket and hat can he wear?

2. Lee, Diego, Tara, and Irena will ride the Ferris wheel. Two people can sit in each car. What pairs are possible for the four friends to ride the Ferris wheel?

Lesson 10-4

Identify the letter that is located at each ordered pair.

1. $(2, -4)$
2. $(-3, 4)$
3. $(7, 6)$
4. $(-4, -2)$
5. $(-2, 1)$
6. $(4, 0)$
7. $(-7, -6)$
8. $(7, -6)$
9. $(0, 0)$

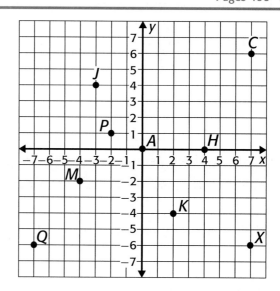

Lesson 10-5

Identify each transformation. Write *rotation*, *reflection*, or *translation*.

1.

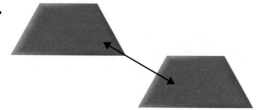

2.

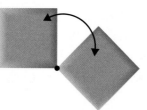

3.

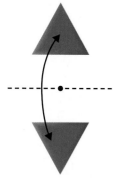

4.

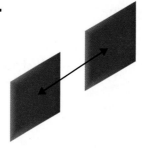

Lesson 10-6

Pages 416–417

Use any strategy to solve. Tell what strategy you used.

1. Sam is replacing the wheels on 6 bicycles. He is also replacing the wheels on 4 tricycles and 3 wagons. How many wheels is Sam replacing in all?

2. Suna wants to make 5 bracelets and 3 necklaces. She plans to use 3 shells for every bracelet and 4 shells for every necklace. How many shells does she need?

3. Evan has twice as many pairs of mittens as boots. He has 6 times as many pairs of socks as boots. He has 18 pairs of socks. How many pairs of boots and mittens does he have?

4. Mike makes $4 an hour babysitting. Omar makes $6 an hour gardening. How many hours will Mike have to work to make the same amount that Omar makes in 8 hours?

Lesson 10-7

Pages 418–420

Tell whether the figures appear to be congruent. Write *yes* or *no*. If they are, describe the movements that show the congruence.

1.

2.

3.

4.

5.

6.

Lesson 10-8

Pages 422–424

Tell whether each figure has line symmetry. Write *yes* or *no*. Then tell how many lines of symmetry the figure has.

1.

2.

3.

Tell whether each figure has rotational symmetry. Write *yes* or *no*.

4.

5.

6.

Lesson 11-1

Pages 441–443

Estimate. Then measure each to the nearest inch, $\frac{1}{2}$ inch, and $\frac{1}{4}$ inch.

1.

2.

Choose the best estimate for each length.

3.

4.

A 2 inches   **C** 22 feet   **F** 14 inches   **H** 14 feet

B 2 feet   **D** 2 yards   **G** 140 inches   **J** 14 yards

Lesson 11-2

Pages 444–445

Complete.

1. 24 in. = ▩ ft

2. 3 ft = ▩ in.

3. 15 ft = ▩ yd

4. ▩ ft = 48 in.

5. ▩ yd = 24 ft

6. ▩ in. = 5 ft

7. A sign at an amusement park says that a person must be 52 inches tall in order to ride a roller coaster. If Kwam is 4 feet 6 inches tall, is he tall enough to ride the roller coaster?

8. A python at a zoo is 6 yards 2 feet long. A cobra at the same zoo is 17 feet long. Which snake is longer? Explain.

Lesson 11-3

Pages 446–447

Solve. Use the solve a simpler problem strategy.

1. Mark painted a mural on each of the 4 walls of his room. It took him 6 hours and 25 minutes for each wall. How long did it take him to finish?

2. Anita bought a sandwich for $3, a salad for $2, a glass of juice for $1, and a cookie for $1. How much did she spend for lunch?

3. Tony's house is 8 blocks from school. If Tony walks to and from school every day, how many blocks does he walk during two school weeks?

4. The price of oranges at Super Mart is 6 for $2. The price of oranges at Food Palace is 9 for $3. Which is the better value? How much does each orange cost at each store?

Lesson 11-4

Pages 450–452

Measure each object to the nearest centimeter.

1.

2.

Choose the best estimate.

3.

4.

A 1 millimeter   **C** 1 meter   **F** 26 millimeters   **H** 26 meters

B 1 centimeter   **D** 1 kilometer   **G** 26 centimeters   **J** 26 kilometers

Lesson 11-5

Pages 456–459

Estimate the perimeter. Then find the exact perimeter.

1. 7 cm, 12 cm (rectangle)

2. 3 mm, 8 mm, 9 mm, 3 mm (L-shape)

3. 13 ft on each of eight sides (octagon)

Estimate. Then find the perimeter of each rectangle in units.

4.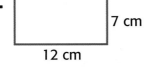

5.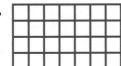

6.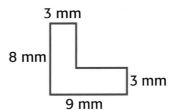

Lesson 11-6

Pages 460–462

Estimate the area. Then find the exact area of each square or rectangle.

1.

2. 3 m, 4 m (square)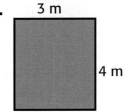

3. 3 in., 6 in. (rectangle)

Lesson 11-7

Pages 466–467

Use any strategy to solve. Tell what strategy you used.

1. The perimeter of a rectangular yard is 20 meters. What are the possible lengths of the sides?

2. Stella bought 5 pencils for 25¢. How much would she pay for 15 pencils?

3. Each bunch of flowers has 12 tulips and 23 daisies. There are 6 bunches of flowers. How many flowers are there in all?

4. There are 324 apples. There are 68 fewer apples than oranges and 127 more apples than limes. How many limes and oranges are there?

Lesson 11-8

Pages 468–471

Write the approximate temperature in degrees Fahrenheit and Celsius.

1.

2.

3. The thermometer reads 2° Celsius. Would Gabrielle go swimming or build a snowman?

4. An average person's body temperature is about 99° Fahrenheit. About how many degrees Celsius is this temperature?

Lesson 12-1

Pages 486–489

Choose the most reasonable estimate for each capacity.

1.

   A 15 fluid ounces
   B 15 pints
   C 15 quarts
   D 15 gallons

2.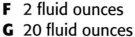

   F 2 fluid ounces
   G 20 fluid ounces
   H 2 quarts
   J 2 gallons

3.

   A 6 fluid ounces
   B 6 cups
   C 6 pints
   D 6 quarts

4.

   F 6 fluid ounces
   G 60 fluid ounces
   H 6 cups
   J 6 pints

5.

   A 1 fluid ounce
   B 1 cup
   C 1 quart
   D 1 gallon

6.

   F 1 fluid ounce
   G 1 cup
   H 1 pint
   J 1 quart

Lesson 12-2

Pages 490–491

Complete.

1. 6 c = ■ pt

2. 32 fl oz = ■ c

3. 8 qt = ■ pt

4. 2 gal = ■ qt

5. ■ fl oz = 5 c

6. 10 pt = ■ c

Compare. Use >, <, or =.

7. 3 qt 1 gal

8. 3 c ● 4 fl oz

9. 3 qt ● 5 pt

Lesson 12-3

Pages 492–495

Choose the more reasonable estimate for each capacity.

1.

11 mL   11 L

2.

710 mL   710 L

3.

1 mL   1 L

4.

235 mL   235 L

Lesson 12-4

Pages 498–500

Choose the most reasonable estimate for the weight of each object.

1.

A 8 ounces
B 80 pounds
C 8 pounds
D 8 tons

2.

F 70 ounces
G 7 pounds
H 700 pounds
J 7 tons

3.

A 8 ounces
B 8 pounds
C 80 pounds
D 8 tons

4.

F 1 ounce
G 10 ounces
H 1 pound
J 10 pounds

Extra Practice

Solve. Use logical reasoning.

1. Mr. Myers is thinking of a number between 20 and 30. The number is not even, not prime, and not divisible by 3. What is the number?

2. There are three buildings on a block. The bank is to the left of the school. The museum is not first. What is the order of the buildings?

3. A group of 3 adults and 7 students rode a ferry. The cost for the entire group was $36. If the cost of a student to ride was $3, what was the cost for an adult?

4. The Bears won 18 games. The Lions won one game for every three games the Bears won. The Sharks won 8 more games than the Lions. How many games did the Lions win?

Complete.

1. 2 lb = ▧ oz

2. 4,000 lb = ▧ T

3. 64 oz = ▧ lb

4. 2 T = ▧ lb

5. 1 lb and 2 oz = ▧ oz

6. 3 T and 400 lb = ▧

7. **Algebra** Copy and complete the table below.

Pounds	▧	5	▧	8	▧
Ounces	48	▧	96	▧	160

Choose the more reasonable estimate for the mass of each object.

1.

   4 g   4 kg

2.

   350 g   350 kg

3.

   250 g   250 kg

3.

   300 g   300 kg

Lesson 12-8

Pages 512–515

Find the volume of each figure.

1.

2.

Estimate the volume of each figure.

3.

4.

Lesson 12-9

Pages 518–519

Use any strategy to solve. Tell what strategy you used.

1. Leila bought a hat for $5, mittens for $7, and a scarf for $11. The cashier gave her $7 in change. How much did Leila give the cashier?

2. Radio station ABC plays songs that are 3 minutes long. How many songs can the station play in 50 minutes?

3. Emilio's sister is twice his age. In 6 years, his sister will be 3 times his age right now. How old are Emilio and his sister?

4. A model home has 8 windows on the first floor and 7 windows on the second floor. There are 180 windows all together. How many model homes are there?

Lesson 12-10

Pages 520–523

The following are times of tennis matches. Find the length of each match.

1. Start Time   End Time

2. Start Time   End Time

Find each elapsed time.

3. The clock shows when Lydia started ice skating. It is 12:45 when she stops.

4. The clock shows when Helki's hockey practice started. It is 6:30 when it stops.

Lesson 13-1

Pages 537–539

Write the fraction that names part of the whole.

1.

2.

3.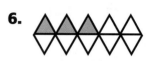

4.

5.

6.

Draw a picture and shade part of it to show the fraction.

7. $\frac{3}{7}$ 8. $\frac{6}{7}$ 9. $\frac{2}{10}$ 10. $\frac{4}{5}$ 11. $\frac{7}{8}$

Lesson 13-2

Pages 540–543

Write the fraction for the part of the set that is blue. Then write the fraction for the part that is *not* blue.

1.

2.

3.

4.

5.

6.

Lesson 13-3

Pages 544–545

Solve. Use the draw a picture strategy.

1. Four dogs are standing in a row. The Great Dane is ahead of the poodle. The terrier is not next to the poodle. The collie is to the right of the terrier and is not first. What is the order of the dogs?

2. There are 30 children at the park. $\frac{1}{2}$ are playing soccer. $\frac{1}{3}$ are playing football. The rest are on the swings. How many children are on the swings?

3. There are 16 CDs on a shelf. $\frac{1}{4}$ of the CDs are jazz. 5 are classical music, and 3 are blues. The rest are pop music. How many CDs are pop music?

4. There are 4 books on display. The cookbook is next to the history book but not next to the art book or the novel. The art book is third. What is the order of the books?

Lesson 13-4

Pages 548–551

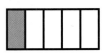

Write the fraction for the part that is shaded. Then find an equivalent fraction.

1.

2.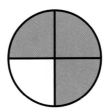

3.

Find an equivalent fraction for each fraction.

4. $\frac{3}{12}$ 5. $\frac{4}{10}$ 6. $\frac{1}{4}$ 7. $\frac{4}{6}$ 8. $\frac{3}{7}$

9. $\frac{6}{18}$ 10. $\frac{3}{8}$ 11. $\frac{6}{9}$ 12. $\frac{1}{2}$ 13. $\frac{4}{20}$

Lesson 13-5

Pages 554–557

Compare. Use >, <, or =.

1.
$\frac{4}{5}$ ● $\frac{3}{5}$

2.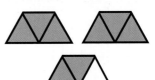
$\frac{6}{9}$ ● $\frac{2}{3}$

3.
$\frac{1}{3}$ ● $\frac{3}{6}$

4. $\frac{2}{5}$ ● $\frac{1}{6}$

5. $\frac{6}{9}$ ● $\frac{5}{10}$

6. $\frac{3}{8}$ ● $\frac{1}{2}$

7. $\frac{7}{8}$ ● $\frac{7}{12}$

8. $\frac{5}{5}$ ● $\frac{4}{5}$

9. $\frac{3}{9}$ ● $\frac{9}{12}$

Lesson 13-6

Pages 560–563

Write a mixed number and an improper fraction for each model.

1.

2.

Write each as an improper fraction or a mixed number. Use models if needed.

3. $3\frac{2}{3}$ 4. $3\frac{1}{4}$ 5. $3\frac{3}{10}$ 6. $\frac{21}{4}$

Lesson 13-7

Pages 564–565

Use any strategy to solve. Tell what strategy you used.

1. Juan has 9 coins that equal 85¢. None of them are pennies. What are the coins?

2. Ramona started reading at 4:20. She stopped reading at 5:15. For how many minutes did she read?

3. Ten students are in the library. Three students leave the library as 5 students go in. How many students are in the library now?

4. There are 20 fish in an aquarium. $\frac{1}{5}$ of the fish are blue. $\frac{1}{4}$ of the fish are red. The rest are yellow. How many yellow fish are there?

Lesson 14-1

Pages 579–581

Write a fraction and a decimal for each shaded part.

1.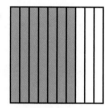

2.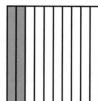

3.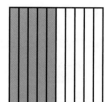

4.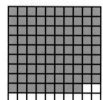

5.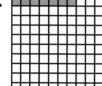

6.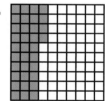

Lesson 14-2

Pages 582–585

Write each as a mixed number and decimal.

1.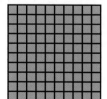

2.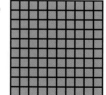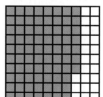

Write each mixed number as a decimal.

3. $4\frac{6}{10}$

4. $36\frac{33}{100}$

5. $83\frac{45}{100}$

6. $99\frac{8}{10}$

7. $15\frac{74}{100}$

8. $75\frac{3}{10}$

9. $62\frac{87}{100}$

10. $24\frac{5}{10}$

Lesson 14-3

Solve. Use the make a model strategy.

1. Marcus has 20 coins. One fourth are dimes. One fifth are nickels. The rest are quarters. How much are Marcus's coins worth?

2. There are 3 plants in a garden. The first plant is 3 times taller than the second and 2 times taller than the third. The plants are a total of 22 feet tall. How tall is each plant?

3. Simon is hanging wallpaper on 3 walls of his room. Each wall is 10 feet wide and 8 feet tall. Each roll of wallpaper covers 40 square feet. How many rolls of wallpaper does Simon need?

4. Emily walked halfway home from school. She walked back 3 blocks to find a book. Then she walked home. She walked 20 blocks in all. How many blocks is it from Emily's house to school?

Lesson 14-4

Pages 588–589

Tell which letter represents each mixed number on the number line. Write as a decimal.

1. $1\frac{1}{5}$

2. $1\frac{4}{5}$

3. Name the point N represents on the number line below.

4. Latisha is measuring her height. the top of her head reaches the fifth mark out of 7 marks between 1 feet and 5 feet. How many feet tall is Latisha?

5. A zookeeper measured the length of a newborn kangaroo. The kangaroo ends at the fourth mark out of nine marks between 0 and 1 inch. How many inches long is the kangaroo?

Lesson 14-5

Pages 590–592

Compare. Use >, <, or =.

1. 6.7 ● 0.67

2. 3.96 ● 3.09

3. 55.5 ● 55.50

4. 0.67 ● 0.76

5. 13.80 ● 13.8

6. 4.91 ● 4.9

Order from greatest to least.

7. 2.08, 2.98, 2.88

8. 53.03, 53.33, 53.13

9. 65.02, 6.86, 6.5

10. 0.78, 0.87, 0.08

Lesson 14-6

Pages 594–595

Use any strategy to solve. Tell what strategy you used.

1. A basement is rectangular in shape. One wall is 16 feet long. If the area is 304 square feet, what is the length of the other walls?

2. What is the next number in the pattern? What is the rule?

   8, 5, 12, 9, 16, 13, 20, 17

3. Bina began her chores at 3:30 P.M. She stopped at 4:20 to walk her dog. She started her chores again at 5:15 and stopped at 5:45. How long did Bina do her chores?

4. A pepperoni pizza is cut into 10 slices. A veggie pizza the same size is cut into 6 slices. Which is greater: 4 slices of pepperoni pizza or 3 slices of veggie pizza?

Lesson 14-7

Pages 596–599

Write a fraction and decimal to describe the shaded part of each model.

1.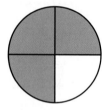

2.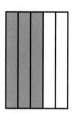

3.

4.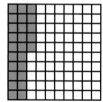

5.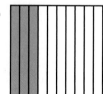

6.

Lesson 14-8

Pages 602–604

Use a number line or model to compare. Use >, <, or =.

1. $\frac{25}{5}$ ● 4

2. 12.34 ● 12.3

3. $6\frac{1}{2}$ ● 6.89

4. $8\frac{1}{10}$ ● 8.75

5. 72.07 ● 72.70

6. 52 ● 5.02

Use a number line to order from greatest to least.

7. $67\frac{2}{100}$, 67.0, 67.70

8. 50.80, $\frac{4}{10}$, $\frac{4}{5}$

9. $\frac{25}{100}$, $\frac{2}{3}$, 33.3

10. $\frac{70}{100}$, 0.75, $\frac{4}{10}$

Lesson 15-1

Pages 617–620

Round to the nearest whole number.

1. 19.8   **2.** 46.21   **3.** 73.81   **4.** 32.41

5. 55.79   **6.** 38.11   **7.** 82.7   **8.** 25.5

Round to the nearest tenth.

9. 16.72   **10.** 93.39   **11.** 47.11   **12.** 33.76

13. 29.28   **14.** 73.64   **15.** 51.82   **16.** 85.83

17. A CD costs the amount shown. What is this amount rounded to the nearest whole number?

18. The European mole is 12.7 centimeters long. What is this amount rounded to the nearest whole number?

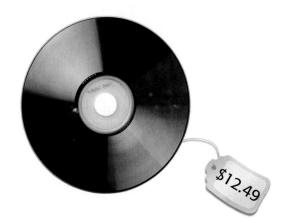

$12.49

Lesson 15-2

Pages 622–625

Estimate. Round to the nearest whole number.

1.   4.7
      + 2.1

2.   5.3
      + 4.2

3. $14.96
      + $23.17

4.   17.67
      + 23.78

5.   9.8
      −3.7

6. 13.3
      −7.2

7.   26.2
      −14.8

8. $25.85
      + $16.27

9.   34.95
      − 18.50

10. 27.8 − 14.7

11. $38.91 − $26.78

12. 59.5 − 23.12

13. $83.32 − $54.86

Solve. Use the work backward strategy.

1. Pedro has $3.75 left from lunch. He bought the items shown in the table below. How much money did he have before lunch?

Pedro's Lunch	
Item	**Cost**
taco	$1.60
salad	$2.45
milk	$0.95

2. Allison completed the chores shown in the table below. If she finished her chores at 8:30, what time did she start?

Allison's Chores	
Chore	**Time to Complete (minutes)**
Rake leaves	30
Pull Weeds	15
Mow Grass	45

3. What is the least number of coins worth 25¢ or less that could be used to make $3.49? What are the coins?

4. A number is divided by 4. Next, 7 is subtracted from the quotient. Then, the difference is multiplied by 3. The result is 15. What is the number?

Lesson 15-4

Add. Use estimation to check for reasonableness.

1. 0.5
    $+0.7$

2. 0.8
    $+ 0.7$

3. 2.3
    $+ 0.15$

4. 6.4
    $+ 9.34$

5. 7.65
    $+ 9.38$

6. $\$7.25$
    $+\$6.49$

7. 14.79
    $+ 5.55$

8. 11.46
    $+ 4.93$

9. $22.48 + 18.67$

10. $17.99 + 12.99$

11. $42.52 + 21.84$

12. $6.4 + 3.6 + 2.8$

13. $5.2 + 8.3 + 7.4$

14. $6.6 + 4.7 + 9.9$

Lesson 15-5

Pages 634–635

Use any strategy to solve. Tell what strategy you used.

1. There are two numbers whose product is 48 and difference is 8. What are the numbers?

2. A number is multiplied by 3. The product is subtracted from 50. The result is 11. What is the number?

3. A flower shop is selling roses at the price shown at the right. How much would 12 roses cost?

5 roses for $4

4. Dion surveyed 500 students to find out their favorite color. Blue was the favorite color of 7 out of 10 students. How many students' favorite color is blue?

Lesson 15-6

Pages 638–641

Subtract. Use estimation or addition to check.

1.
   4.8
   − 2.3

2.
   6.9
   − 3.3

3.
   8.3
   − 2.7

4.
   5.2
   − 2.8

5.
   3.78
   − 1.44

6.
   7.56
   − 4.43

7.
   $9.45
   − $2.06

8.
   8.55
   − 4.38

9.
   12.61
   − 8.75

10.
    $19.23
    − $12.86

11.
    $26.74
    − $16.95

12.
    48.03
    − 27.12

13. 54.50 − 46.72

14. 38.04 − 23.60

15. 41.93 − 15.98

16. $62.35 − $28.90

17. 76.40 − 39.24

18. 93.19 − 65.38

Preparing for Standardized Tests

Throughout the school year, you may be required to take several tests, and you may have many questions about them. Here are some answers to help you get ready.

How Should I Study?

The good news is that you've been studying all along—a little bit every day. Here are some of the ways your textbook has been preparing you.

- **Every Day** The lessons had multiple-choice practice questions.

- **Every Week** The Mid-Chapter Check and Chapter Test also had several multiple-choice practice questions.

- **Every Month** The Test Practice pages at the end of each chapter had even more questions, including short-response and extended-response questions.

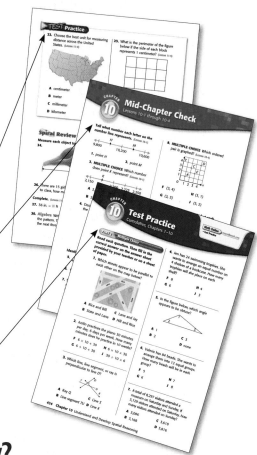

Are There Other Ways to Review?

Absolutely! The following pages contain even more practice for standardized tests.

Tips for SUCCESS

Before the Test

- Go to bed early the night before the test. You will think more clearly after a good night's rest.
- Become familiar with common measurement units and when they should be used.
- Think positively.

During the Test

- Read each problem carefully. Underline key words and think about different ways to solve the problem.
- Watch for key words like *not*. Also look for order words like *least, greatest, first,* and *last*.
- Answer questions you are sure about first. If you do not know the answer to a question, skip it and go back to that question later.
- Check your answer to make sure that it is reasonable.
- Make sure that the number of the question on the answer sheet matches the number of the question on which you are working in your test booklet.

Whatever you do…

- Don't try to do it all in your head. If no figure is provided, draw one.
- Don't rush. Try to work at a steady pace.
- Don't give up. Some problems may seem hard to you, but you may be able to figure out what to do if you read each question carefully or try another strategy.

Multiple-Choice Questions

Multiple-choice questions are the most common type of questions on standardized tests. You are asked to choose the best answer from four possible answers.

To record a multiple-choice answer, you may be asked to shade in a bubble that is a circle or an oval. Always make sure that your shading is dark enough and completely covers the bubble.

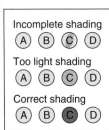

Incomplete shading
Ⓐ Ⓑ Ⓒ Ⓓ

Too light shading
Ⓐ Ⓑ Ⓒ Ⓓ

Correct shading
Ⓐ Ⓑ ● Ⓓ

Example

1. **The graph shows how many sit-ups a student did each day.**

If this pattern continues, how many total sit-ups will be done on Friday and Saturday?

A 88   **B** 48   **C** 40   **D** 8

Read the Problem Carefully You know how many sit-ups were done each day from Monday to Thursday. Find how many total sit-ups will be done on Friday and Saturday.

STRATEGY

Patterns Can you find a pattern to solve the problem?

Solve the Problem Look for a pattern. The student did 8 sit-ups on Monday, 16 on Tuesday, 24 on Wednesday, and 32 on Thursday. Each day, the student did 8 more sit-ups.

Extend the pattern to find how many sit-ups were done on Friday and Saturday. Then add the numbers to find the total.

$32 + 8 = 40$ sit-ups on Friday

$40 + 8 = 48$ sit-ups on Saturday

$$\begin{array}{r} 40 \\ +48 \\ \hline 88 \end{array} \text{ total sit-ups}$$

So, 88 sit-ups were done on Friday and Saturday.

The correct choice is A.

Example

2 The shaded part of the figure represents the fraction $\frac{4}{6}$. Which fraction represents the part that is not shaded?

F $\frac{1}{2}$ G $\frac{1}{3}$ H $\frac{1}{4}$ J $\frac{4}{5}$

Read the Problem Carefully You are asked to find which fraction represents the part of the figure that is not shaded.

> **STRATEGY**
>
> **Elimination** Can you eliminate any of the choices?

Solve the Problem The part that is not shaded is less than half of the figure. Since the answer is less than $\frac{1}{2}$, the choices $\frac{1}{2}$ and $\frac{4}{5}$ can be eliminated. The figure can be divided into 3 equal parts. One of the three, or $\frac{1}{3}$, of the figure is not shaded.

So, the correct choice is G.

Example

3 A family traveled 900 miles. They traveled half of the distance on the first day. How many total days did they travel if they traveled 150 miles each day for the rest of the trip?

A 3   B 4   C 5   D 6

Read the Problem Carefully You are asked to find the total number of travel days. You know how many miles were traveled each day and the total number of miles traveled.

> **STRATEGY**
>
> **Work Backward** Can you work backward from the total to find the number of days?

Solve the Problem First find the number of miles traveled the first day. Then add 150 miles each day until you reach 900 miles. Count the number of travel days.

Day 1 $900 \div 2 = 450$ miles
Day 2 $450 + 150 = 600$ miles   ⎫ The family traveled
Day 3 $600 + 150 = 750$ miles   ⎬ for 4 days.
Day 4 $750 + 150 = 900$ miles ←   ⎭

So, the family traveled for 4 days.

The correct choice is B.

Multiple-Choice Questions   **R45**

Multiple-Choice Practice

DIRECTIONS
Read each question. Choose the best answer.

1. Josh counted 29 desks in each of 3 classrooms in the 4th grade hall. If there are 8 classrooms in the 4th grade hall, about how many desks are there in all?

   A 250

   B 240

   C 200

   D 180

2. Which number sentence best represents the model below?

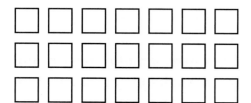

   F $7 + 7 = 14$

   G $3 \times 7 = 21$

   H $3 + 7 = 10$

   J $3 + 3 + 3 = 9$

3. What rule best describes the pattern of ordered pairs?

   (1, 10)   (2, 20)   (3, 30)
   (4, 40)   (5, 50)   (6, 60)

   A Add 10.

   B Add 9.

   C Multiply by 10.

   D Divide by 10.

4. When you multiply a number by 100, you move the decimal point of the number 2 places to the right.

$$630 \times 100 = 63,000$$

   What is 409×100?

   F 49,000

   G 40,900

   H 4,900

   J 4,090

5. Which of the following objects has a capacity of about 1 gallon?

   A    **C**

   B   **D**

6. Which of the following is the best estimate for the weight of a car?

   F 1,900 tons

   G 1,900 ounces

   H 1,900 grams

   J 1,900 kilograms

7. Look at the three-dimensional figures below. Which figure has exactly two faces?

A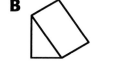

C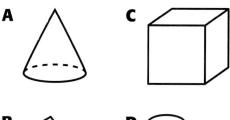

B

D

8. Which quadrilateral has 2 pairs of parallel opposite sides and 4 right angles?

F parallelogram

G pentagon

H square

J trapezoid

9. A piggy bank contains 1 quarter, 3 dimes, 2 nickels, and 2 pennies. If Lindsay picks a coin without looking, what is the probability she will pick a dime?

A 3 out of 5   **C** 5 out of 8

B 3 out of 8   **D** 5 out of 3

10. Refer to the bar graph below. It shows the number of absent students each day last week at Reggie's school.

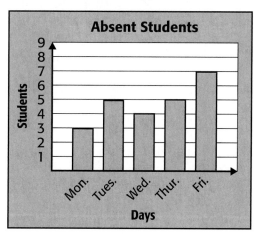

How many students were absent on Thursday and Friday combined last week?

F 5 students   **H** 11 students

G 7 students   **J** 12 students

11. Each player in a game spins the spinner below on his or her turn. What is the probability that Carla will spin an odd number on her next turn?

A 3 out of 5   **C** 2 out of 5

B 3 out of 2   **D** 2 out of 3

Short-Response Questions

Short-response questions ask you to find the answer to the problem as well as any method, explanation, and/or justification you used to arrive at the solution. You are asked to solve the problem, showing your work.

The following is a sample rubric, or scoring guide, for scoring short-response questions.

Credit	Scores	Criteria
Full	2	Full Credit: The answer is correct and a full explanation is provided that shows each step in arriving at the final answer.
Partial	1	Partial Credit: There are two different ways to receive partial credit. • The answer is correct, but the explanation provided is incomplete or incorrect. • The answer is incorrect, but the explanation and method of solving the problem is correct.
None	0	No credit: Either an answer is not provided or the answer does not make sense.

Example

STRATEGY

Find the Operation
Which operation can be used to perform repeated addition?

2 **Pencils are on sale at a store. Four pencils cost $1. How many pencils can be bought with $6?**

Full Credit Solution

First, I will decide which operation to use. Since each dollar can buy four pencils, I can use repeated addition or multiplication. I will use multiplication to find $6 × 4 pencils.

6 dollars
× 4 pencils
24 pencils

The steps, calculations, and reasoning are clearly stated.

So, $6 can be used to buy 24 pencils.

The correct answer is given.

Partial Credit Solution

In this sample solution, the answer is correct. However, there is no explanation for any of the calculations.

$6,4 pencils

24 pencils ← There is no explanation of how the problem was solved.

Partial Credit Solution

In this sample solution, the answer is incorrect. However, the calculations and reasoning are correct.

Each dollar can be used to buy 4 pencils, so I can use repeated addition or multiplication. I will use multiplication to find 6 × 4.

$$\begin{array}{r} 6 \text{ dollars} \\ \times \ \ 4 \text{ pencils} \\ \hline 12 \text{ pencils} \end{array}$$

← The student did not multiply correctly.

12 pencils can be bought with $6.00.

No Credit Solution

In this sample solution, the answer is incorrect, and there is no explanation for any calculations.

6 + 4 = 10 ← The student does not understand the problem and adds 6 and 4.

There are $10.

Short-Response Practice

DIRECTIONS
Solve each problem.

1. Mrs. Henderson brought 42 boxes of raisins to her daughter's class. She gave 33 of the boxes away to the students. How many boxes of raisins were left?

2. What fraction is represented by the shaded part of the figure below?

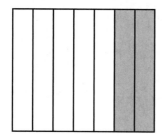

3. There are 14 buses at Millwood Elementary School. Each bus holds up to 56 students. How many students in all can be transported by the buses?

4. Juan walks at the park every morning for exercise. The table shows the total number of miles he has walked after different numbers of days.

Morning Walks	
Number of Days	Number of Miles
1	6
2	12
3	18
4	24

If Juan walks the same distance each day, how many miles will he have walked in a week?

5. Binta has 11 pages of stickers in a binder with 12 stickers on each page. She calculates that she has $11 \times 12 = 132$ stickers in all. Which number sentence can she use to check her calculation?

6. Molly's patio has the dimensions shown below.

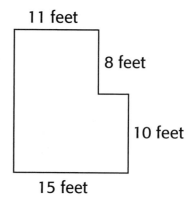

What is the area of the patio?

7. Before leaving for school, Taye checks the outside temperature. What temperature is shown on the thermometer?

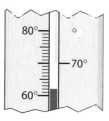

8. How many lines of symmetry does a square have?

9. What type of angles are formed by two perpendicular lines?

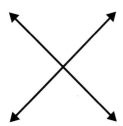

10. Draw a pair of figures that show reflection.

11. To play a board game, each player rolls a number cube and chooses a card at random from a deck. There are red and green cards in the deck.

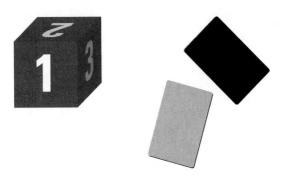

How many possible outcomes are there on each turn?

12. Refer to the rules for the game in Exercise 11. What is the probability that Eduardo will roll a 3 and select a red card on his next turn?

13. Look at the bar graph below. It shows the number of points scored by 4 players in a basketball game.

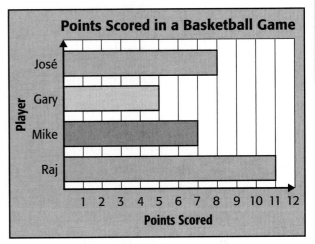

Points Scored in a Basketball Game

Which players scored a total of 12 points?

14. Refer to the bar graph in Exercise 13. How many points were scored in all?

15. Suppose Matt tosses a beanbag onto the game board below. What is the probability that the beanbag will land on a shaded space?

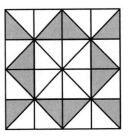

16. Kyle has 70 baseball cards. Write a number sentence that shows how many cards Kyle would have if he gave away half of his cards.

Extended-Response Questions

Most extended-response questions have multiple parts. You must answer all parts to receive full credit.

In extended-response questions, you must show all of your work in solving the problem. A rubric is used to determine if you receive full, partial, or no credit. The following is a sample rubric for scoring extended-response questions.

Credit	Score	Criteria
Full	4	Full Credit: The answer is correct and a full explanation is given that shows each step in finding the answer.
Partial	3, 2, 1	Partial Credit: Most of the solution is correct, but it may have some mistakes in the explanation or solution. The more correct the solution, the greater the score.
None	0	No credit: Either an answer is not provided or the answer does not make sense.

Make sure that when the problem says to *show your work,* you show every part of your solution. This includes figures, graphs, and any explanations for your calculations.

Example

 Find how much longer it took each student to read *Sounder* than *Charlotte's Web*. Make a bar graph to show the results.

Student	Charlotte's Web (hours to read)	Sounder (hours to read)
Lisa	9	27
Jason	15	45
Torres	6	18
Monique	12	36

Full Credit Solution

In this sample answer, the student explains what calculations need to be done and finds the correct solution.

First, I will list each student's name and write the expression that will show the difference. Then I will subtract.

Lisa:	Jason:	Torres:	Monique:
27 - 9 = 18	45 - 15 = 30	18 - 6 = 12	36 - 12 = 24

The steps, calculations, and reasoning are clearly stated.

The difference in hours spent reading the two books for each student is: Lisa: 18, Jason: 30, Torres: 12, and Monique: 24 hours.

> The correct answer is given.

Now I will use the data from the first part to make the bar graph.

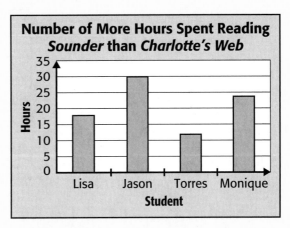

Number of More Hours Spent Reading Sounder than Charlotte's Web

Partial Credit Solution

This sample answer receives partial credit because the student explains how they got each answer, but did not create a bar graph.

First, I will list each student's name and write the expression that will show the difference. Then I will subtract.

Lisa	Jason	Torres	Monique
27	45	18	36
− 9	− 15	− 6	− 12
18	30	12	24

The number of more hours spent on *Sounder* than *Charlotte's Web* for each student is: Lisa: 18, Jason: 30, Torres: 12, and Monique: 24 hours.

No Credit Solution

A solution for this problem that will receive no credit may include incorrect answers and an inaccurate or incomplete bar graph.

Extended-Response Practice

DIRECTIONS
Solve each problem. Show all your work.

1. What is the smallest possible number you can make with the digits below? How did you decide how to arrange the digits?

$$5, 2, 8, 6, 4$$

2. Mark says the model below shows the fraction $2\frac{3}{4}$. Gina says that the model shows $\frac{11}{4}$. Who is correct? Explain.

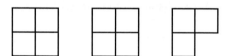

3. A pizza is cut into 8 equal slices. How many slices would you have to eat to have eaten $\frac{1}{4}$ of the pizza yourself? Draw a picture and write an equivalent fraction to show how to find the answer.

4. Look at the number sentences below.

$532 \times 10 = 5{,}320$

$75 \times 10 = 750$

$1{,}248 \times 10 = 12{,}480$

$49 \times 10 = 490$

How can these number sentences help you find the product of 35 and 10?

5. The table shows input and output numbers.

Input	Output
2	5
4	7
6	9
8	11
10	13

Describe what happened to each input number to result in the output number.

6. Describe two ways to find the perimeter of a soccer field with the dimensions shown below.

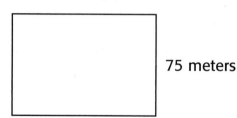

75 meters

110 meters

7. Suki returned home at the time shown on the clock, which is 2 hours 15 minutes after school ended. Explain how to find the time that school ended.

8. Artie estimates that the pitcher of lemonade has a capacity of 2 quarts. How can he find whether or not he is correct using a measuring cup that holds 1 cup?

9. Explain why the two figures below are congruent.

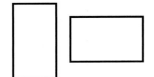

10. Use the figures below to write a definition for *isosceles triangles* and *right triangles.*

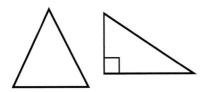

11. Suppose Kathi tosses a coin and records the result. Then she tosses a second coin and records the result. Let H represent a coin landing on heads, and let T represent a coin landing on tails. List all of the possible outcomes.

12. Four coins are placed in a bag. They add up to 41¢. What is the probability that a coin pulled from the bag has a value greater than 10¢? Show how you found the answer.

13. Two bags of grapes cost $5. Four bags of grapes cost $10. Suppose this pattern continues. Make a bar graph to show the cost of 6, 8, and 10 bags of grapes.

14. The double bar graph shows the number of points scored by two different players during the first 4 games of a basketball season.

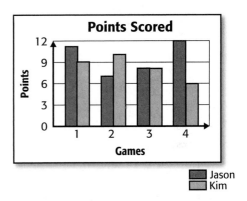

How can you find the overall difference in points scored by both players?

15. Compare and contrast a tally chart and a frequency table. How are they similar? How are they different?

16. There is ham, turkey, mayonnaise, mustard, and two types of bread in a refrigerator. How can a tree diagram be used to find the possible sandwich combinations?

Concepts and Skills Bank

 SCAS 4-1.3 Explain and justify answers to problems on the basis of mathematical properties, structures, and relationships.

Order of Operations

To find the value of an expression with more than one operation, you need to follow the **order of operations**.

Order of Operations   Key Concept

1. Do the operations in the parentheses first.

2. Multiply and divide in order from left to right.

3. Add and subtract in order from left to right.

EXAMPLE   Use the Order of Operations

1 **Find $3 + (2 \times 4) - 6$.**

$3 + (2 \times 4) - 6$ Write the expression.

$3 + \quad 8 \quad - 6$ Parentheses first. $(2 \times 4) = 8$

$3 + \quad 8 \quad - 6$ The is no multiplication or division,
                              so move to the next step.

$11 \quad - 6$ Add and subtract from left to right.
                  $3 + 8 = 11$ and $11 - 6 = 5$

5

So, $3 + (2 \times 4) - 6 = 5$.

Exercises

Find the value of each expression.

1. $(7 + 1) \times 3 - 5$ **2.** $(8 - 5) \div 3 + 2$

3. $13 + 4 - (7 \times 2)$ **4.** $5(2 + 3)$

5. $(5 + 4) \times 7 - 3$ **6.** $8 \times (14 - 8) + 7$

7. $6 \times (8 - 5) + 9$ **8.** $(8 + 6) \div (12 - 5)$

Write and find the value of an expression for the situation.

9. Measurement Todd walked 2 miles a day for 4 days and 3 miles on the fifth day. How many miles did he walk?

Divisibility Rules for 2, 5, and 10

A whole number is **divisible** by another number if the remainder is 0 when the first number is divided by the second. The divisibility rules for 2, 5, and 10 are stated below.

Divisibility Rules for 2, 5, and 10	Key Concepts
Words	**Examples**
A whole number is divisible by:	
• 2 if the ones digit is divisible by 2.	2, 4, 6, 8, 10, 12, …
• 5 if the ones digit is 0 or 5.	5, 10, 15, 20, 25, …
• 10 if the ones digit is 0.	10, 20, 30, 40, 50, …

A whole number is **even** if it is divisible by 2. A whole number is **odd** if it is not divisible by 2.

EXAMPLE Use Divisibility Rules

1 **Tell whether the number 340 is divisible by 2, 5, or 10. Then classify the number as even or odd.**

Use the divisibility rules to determine if 340 is divisible by 2, 5, or 10.

2: Yes, the ones digit, 0, is divisible by 2.

5: Yes, the ones digit is 0.

10: Yes, the ones digit is 0.

Since 340 is divisible by 2, it is an even number.

So, 340 is divisible by 2, 5, and 10, and it is an even number.

Exercises

Tell whether each number is divisible by 2, 5, or 10. They classify each number as even or odd.

1. 40	**2.** 65	**3.** 78	**4.** 91
5. 115	**6.** 136	**7.** 150	**8.** 194
9. 216	**10.** 280	**11.** 311	**12.** 345

13. Find a number that is divisible by both 2 and 5.

14. Find a number that is divisible by 2, 5, and 10.

SCAS **Reinforcement of 3-2.9** Analyze the effect that adding, subtracting, or **multiplying odd and/or even numbers has on the outcome.**

Even and Odd Numbers and Products

A whole number is **even** if it is divisible by 2. A whole number is **odd** if it is not divisible by 2.

Even Numbers	Odd Numbers
0, 2, 4, 6, 8, 10, 12, 14, 16, 18, 20, ...	1, 3, 5, 7, 9, 11, 13, 15, 17, 19, ...

The factors in a multiplication problem can help you determine if the product will be even or odd.

Odd and Even Products   Key Concepts

Words	Examples
even number × even number = even number	$2 \times 4 = 8$ or $6 \times 8 = 48$
even number × odd number = even number	$2 \times 3 = 6$ or $4 \times 5 = 20$
odd number × odd number = odd number	$3 \times 5 = 15$ or $7 \times 9 = 63$

EXAMPLE   Tell Whether a Product will be Even or Odd

1 **Tell whether the product of 14 and 23 will be even or odd.**

Classify each factor as even or odd. Then use the information in the Key Concept box to determine if the product will be even or odd.

The product of an even and odd number will be even. So, the product of 14 and 23 will be even.

Exercises

Tell whether each product will be even or odd.

1. 13×21 **2.** 34×56 **3.** 41×118 **4.** 73×129

5. 134×155 **6.** 143×167 **7.** 184×192 **8.** 212×257

SCAS 4-2.10 Identify the common fraction/decimal equivalents $\frac{1}{2} = .5, \frac{1}{4} = .25, \frac{3}{4} = .75,$ $\frac{1}{3} \approx .33, \frac{2}{3} \approx .67,$ multiples of $\frac{1}{10}$, and multiples of $\frac{1}{100}$.

Relate Fractions, Decimals, and Percents

Fractions, decimals, and percents are related. A **percent** compares a number to 100.

100%

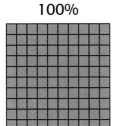

67%

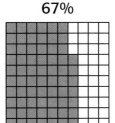

25%

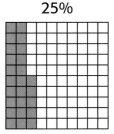

100 out of 100

$\frac{100}{100} = 1 = 1.0$

67 out of 100

$\frac{67}{100} = 0.67$

25 out of 100

$\frac{25}{100} = \frac{1}{4} = 0.25$

EXAMPLE   Write a Fraction, Decimal, and Percent

① **Write the amount shown by the model as a fraction, decimal, and percent.**

55 out of 100 squares in the model are shaded.

So, the amount shown by the model as a fraction, decimal, and percent is $\frac{55}{100}$, 0.55, and 55%.

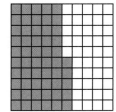

Exercises

Write the amount shown by each model as a fraction, decimal, and percent.

1.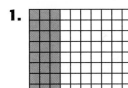

2.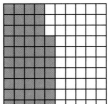

3.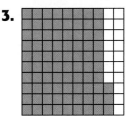

4. Carisa plays soccer. She makes 0.75 of the goals she shoots. What is the percentage of shots she makes?

5. Miguel read 35 of the 50 pages in his book. What percent of the book has Miguel read?

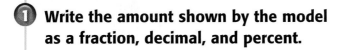

SCAS Reinforcement of 3-2.3 Apply an algorithm to add and subtract whole numbers fluently.

Skip Counting Forward and Backward

You can skip count forward and backward to find missing numbers in a function table.

EXAMPLES   Skip Counting on Function Tables

Use skip counting to find the missing number.

1

$y = 20x$	
Input (x)	**Output (y)**
1	20
2	40
3	60
4	▪

$+20$
$+20$
$+20$

2

$y = 1,000x$	
Input (x)	**Output (y)**
8	8,000
7	7,000
6	6,000
5	▪

$-1,000$
$-1,000$
$-1,000$

This function table shows $y = 20x$. You can skip count forward by 20 to find the missing number.

$60 + 20 = 80$

So, the missing number is 80.

The function table shows $y = 1,000x$. You can skip count backward by 1,000 to find the missing number.

$6,000 - 1,000 = 5,000$

So, the missing number is 5,000.

Exercises

Use skip counting to find the missing number.

1.

$y = 100x$	
Input (x)	**Output (y)**
5	500
6	600
7	700
8	▪

2.

$y = 50x$	
Input (x)	**Output (y)**
7	350
6	300
5	250
4	▪

3.

$y = 25x$	
Input (x)	**Output (y)**
10	250
9	225
8	200
7	▪

4.

$y = 10,000x$				
Input (x)	2	3	4	5
Output (y)	20,000	30,000	40,000	▪

Negative Numbers

The numbers +1 and +3 are **positive numbers**. They can be written with or without a + sign. The numbers −1 and −3 are **negative numbers**. A negative number has a − sign.

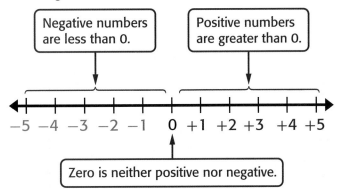

Negative numbers are less than 0.

Positive numbers are greater than 0.

Zero is neither positive nor negative.

EXAMPLES Write Positive and Negative Numbers

Write the number that represents each situation.

1 **WEATHER** **4 degrees below zero**

The temperature is below zero. The number is −4.

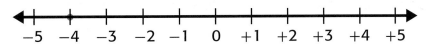

2 **FOOTBALL** **a gain of 3 yards**

The word *gain* means an increase. The number is +3 or 3.

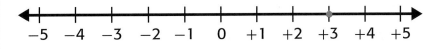

Exercises

Write the number that represents each situation.

1. move back 3 spaces

2. move 12 steps forward

3. score 10 points

4. owe $7

5. 8 degrees below 0

6. distance increases by 5 miles

7. earn $15

8. cut 10 seconds off a running time

Tell what number each letter on the number line represents.

9.

10.
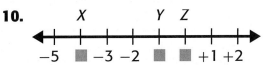

SCAS 4-4.7 Represent with ordered pairs of whole numbers the location of points in the first quadrant of a coordinate grid.

Graphing Functions

Functions can be placed in a table and then graphed. First, make a table for the function. Then graph the function using the ordered pairs found.

EXAMPLE **Graph a Function**

1 **Graph ten points on the graph of the function $y = 2x + 1$.**

Complete a table to find the ordered pairs. Then graph the ordered pairs. Connect the points with a straight line.

Input (x)	Output (y)	(x, y)
0	1	(0, 1)
1	3	(1, 3)
2	5	(2, 5)
3	7	(3, 7)
4	9	(4, 9)
5	11	(5, 11)
6	13	(6, 13)
7	15	(7, 15)
8	17	(8, 17)
9	19	(9, 19)

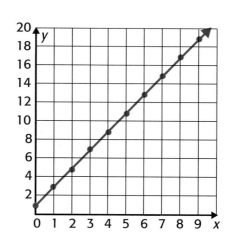

Exercises

Graph ten points on the graph of the function.

1. $y = 1x$

2. $y = 6x$

3. $y = x + 6$

4. $y = 2x - 1$

5. $y = 4x + 2$

6. $y = 5x - 3$

7. Laine gives $3 of her weekly allowance to a charity. The rule can be written as $y = 3x$. The function table shows the amount of money Laine has given to a charity after 1, 2, 3, and 4 weeks. Create a graph to show the amount of money given to charity after 10 weeks.

Input (x)	Output (y)	(x, y)
Weeks	Amount to Charity	
1	$3	(1, 3)
2	$6	(2, 6)
3	$9	(3, 9)
4	$12	(4, 12)

Units of Time

Time is a unit of measure. It measures the interval between two or more events. Like other units of measure, units of time can be converted.

- To convert from larger units to smaller units, multiply.
- To convert from smaller units to larger units, divide.

Units of Time
60 seconds (s) = 1 minute (min)
60 minutes = 1 hour (h)
24 hours = 1 day
7 days = 1 week
12 months = 1 year
52 weeks = 1 year
365 days = 1 year

EXAMPLES Convert Units of Time

MEASUREMENT Complete each conversion.

1 **5 hours = ■ minutes**

$$\begin{array}{r} 60 \\ \times 5 \\ \hline 300 \end{array}$$ Since 1 hour = 60 minutes, multiply by 60.

So, 5 hours = 300 minutes.

2 **42 days = ■ weeks**

$$7\overline{)42}^{\;6}$$ Since 7 days = 1 week, divide by 7.

So, 42 days = 6 weeks.

Exercises

MEASUREMENT Complete each conversion.

1. 52 weeks = ■ days

2. 7 days = ■ hours

3. 24 hours = ■ seconds

4. 3 years = ■ days

5. 120 months = ■ years

6. 15 minutes = ■ seconds

7. 49 days = ■ weeks

8. 4 weeks = ■ days

9. 1,470 days = ■ weeks

10. 216 months = ■ years

11. A calendar typically shows one year. Some calendars can show many years. If a calendar shows 5 years, how many months does it show?

12. James was looking at his calendar and noticed it was a 2-year calendar. How many weeks is that? how many days?

Concepts and Skills

Parts of a Circle

A **circle** is a two-dimensional figure in which all points are the same distance from a point called the **center**. The parts of a circle are shown below.

Parts of a Circle	Key Concepts
Words	A line segment that connects the center of a circle to a point on the circle is a **radius** of the circle.
Words	A line segment that connects two points on a circle and goes through the center of a circle is a **diameter** of a circle.

EXAMPLES Parts of a Circle

Identify the part of the circle.

①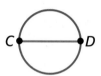

The line segment connects two points on the circle and goes through the center. This is a diameter.

②

The line segment connects the center of the circle to one point on the circle. This is a radius.

Exercises

Identify the part of the circle.

1.

2.

3.

Identify the part of the circle.

4. $\overline{LM}$

5. $\overline{ON}$

6. $\overline{NM}$

7. $\overline{ML}$

8. M

9. $\overline{PQ}$

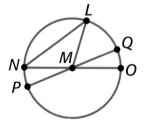

4-1.2 **Construct arguments that lead to conclusions about general mathematical** properties and **relationships.**

Similarity

In Lesson 10-7, you learned that congruent figures have the same size and shape. Figures that have the same shape but different sizes are **similar figures**.

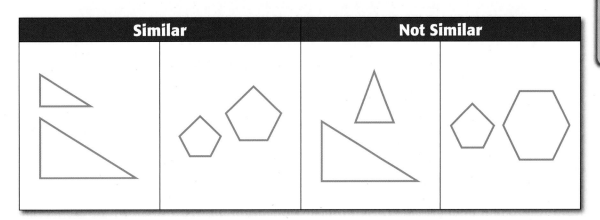

Similar	Not Similar

EXAMPLE **Identify Similar Figures**

Tell whether each pair of figures is similar. Explain.

The figures have the same shape but different sizes. So, they are similar figures.

The figures do not have the same shape or size. So, they are not similar figures.

Exercises

Tell whether each pair of figures is similar.

1.

2.

3.

4.

5.

6.

Perimeter of Irregular Figures

An **irregular figure** is made up of two or more figures. You can find the perimeter, or distance around an irregular figure.

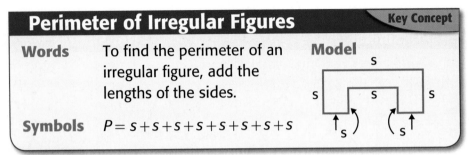

Perimeter of Irregular Figures	Key Concept
Words To find the perimeter of an irregular figure, add the lengths of the sides.	**Model**
Symbols $P = s+s+s+s+s+s+s+s$	

EXAMPLE **Estimate and Find Perimeter**

① **Estimate then find the perimeter of the figure.**

To estimate the perimeter you first need to round each side measure to the nearest ten.

$P = 19 + 8 + 6 + 7 + 13 + 15$

$P = 20 + 10 + 10 + 10 + 10 + 20$

$P = 80$

So the figure is about 80 centimeters.

Next, add the exact measures.

$P = 19 + 8 + 6 + 7 + 13 + 15 = 68$

So, the perimeter of this figure is 68 centimeters.

Check for Reasonableness
The answer, 68, is close to the estimate, 80. ✔

Exercises

Estimate then find the perimeter of each figure.

1.

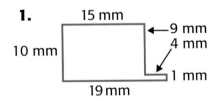

2.

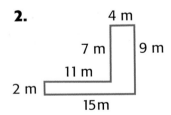

3.

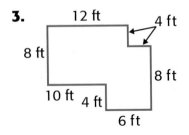

4.

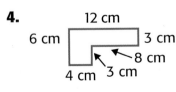

Concepts and Skills

Area of Irregular Figures

To find the area of an irregular figure, break the figure into smaller parts.

EXAMPLE   **Find the Area of a Figure**

1 **Find the area of the figure.**

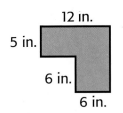

Step 1 Break the figure into smaller parts.
Look for rectangles and squares.

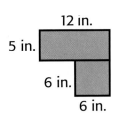

Rectangle

Square

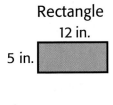

Step 2 Find the area of each part.

Rectangle
$A = \text{length} \times \text{width}$
$A = \ell \times w$
$A = 12 \text{ in.} \times 5 \text{ in.}$
$A = 60 \text{ square inches}$

Square
$A = \text{side} \times \text{side}$
$A = s \times s$
$A = 6 \text{ in.} \times 6 \text{ in.}$
$A = 36 \text{ square inches}$

Step 3 Add the areas.

The area of the figure is $60 + 36$ or 96 square inches.

Exercises

Find the area of each figure.

1.

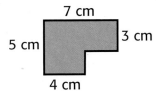

7 cm
5 cm
3 cm
4 cm

2.

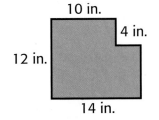

10 in.
4 in.
12 in.
14 in.

3.

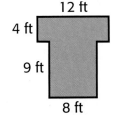

12 ft
4 ft
9 ft
8 ft

4.

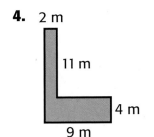

2 m
11 m
4 m
9 m

5.

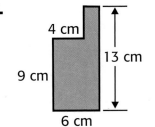

4 cm
13 cm
9 cm
6 cm

6.

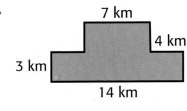

7 km
4 km
3 km
14 km

Concepts and Skills

SCAS **4-5.5 Generate strategies to determine** the **area** of rectangles and triangles.

Areas of Parallelograms

The areas of a parallelogram and a rectangle are related.

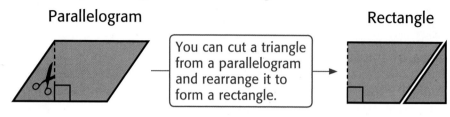

Parallelogram

You can cut a triangle from a parallelogram and rearrange it to form a rectangle.

Rectangle

To find the area of a parallelogram, multiply the base and the height.

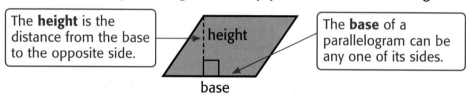

The **height** is the distance from the base to the opposite side.

height

The **base** of a parallelogram can be any one of its sides.

base

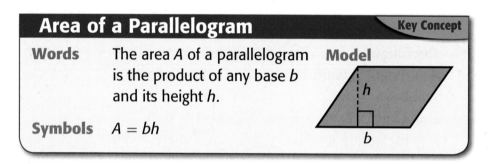

Area of a Parallelogram   Key Concept

Words   The area *A* of a parallelogram is the product of any base *b* and its height *h*.

Model

h

b

Symbols $A = bh$

EXAMPLE   Find the Area of a Parallelogram

1 **Find the area of the parallelogram.**

Use the area formula of a parallelogram.

$A = bh$ Area formula of a parallelogram.

$A = 6 \times 4$ Replace b with 6 and h with 4.

$A = 24$ Multiply.

The area of the parallelogram is 24 square centimeters.

4 cm

6 cm

Exercises

Find the area of each parallelogram.

1.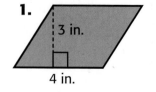
3 in.
4 in.

2.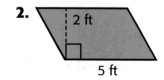
2 ft
5 ft

3.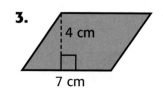
4 cm
7 cm

Areas of Triangles

Notice that a parallelogram is made of two congruent triangles. So, the formula for the area of a triangle can be found by dividing the formula for the area of a parallelogram by two.

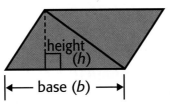

height (h)

base (b)

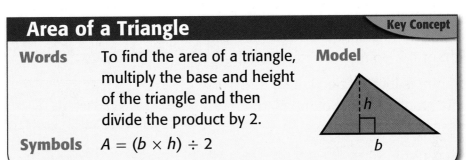

Area of a Triangle	**Key Concept**
Words To find the area of a triangle, multiply the base and height of the triangle and then divide the product by 2.	**Model**
Symbols $A = (b \times h) \div 2$	h b

EXAMPLE   **Find the Area of a Triangle**

1 **Find the area of the triangle.**

Use the area formula of a triangle.

4 cm

8 cm

$A = (b \times h) \div 2$ Area formula of a triangle.

$A = (8 \times 4) \div 2$ Replace b with 8 and h with 4.

$A = 32 \div 2$ Multiply.

$A = 16$ Divide. $32 \div 2 = 16$

The area of the triangle is 16 square centimeters.

Exercises

Find the area of each triangle.

1.
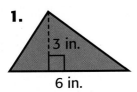
3 in.

6 in.

2.

10 m

5 m

3.
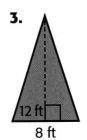
12 ft

8 ft

4-6.2 **Interpret data in** tables, **line graphs,** bar graphs, and double bar graphs **whose scale increments are greater than or equal to 1.**   4-3.6 **Illustrate situations that show change over time as either increasing, decreasing, or varying.**

Line Graphs

A **line graph** shows how data changes over time. You can use a line graph to make predictions about future events.

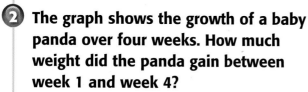

Interpret a Line Graph

1. **Refer to the graph at the right. How tall did the flower grow in three months?**
The third month is June.

   Move up to find where the point is located on the graph. Then compare the height of the point to the scale on the left.

   The point is located between 8 and 10 on the graph's scale. So, the plant grew 9 inches in three months.

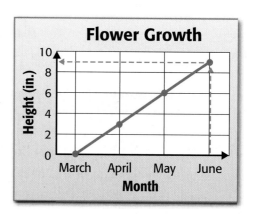

2. **The graph shows the growth of a baby panda over four weeks. How much weight did the panda gain between week 1 and week 4?**
Subtract the panda's weight at week 1 from its weight at week 4.

   Week 1: 11 pounds
   Week 4: 14 pounds

   $14 - 11 = 3$

   So, the baby panda gained 3 pounds between week 1 and week 4.

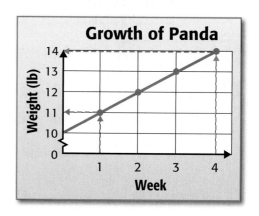

Exercises

For Exercises 1–3, use the line graph.

1. At what time is the least amount of snow on the ground?

2. How much snow is on the ground at 8:00 P.M.?

3. How much snow fell over the 5-hour period shown on the graph?

For Exercises 4–8, use the line graph.

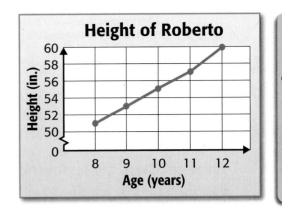

Height of Roberto

4. What was Roberto's height when he was 9 years old?

5. How many inches did Roberto grow between the ages of 10 and 12?

6. How many inches did Roberto grow from age 8 to age 12?

7. At this rate, predict how tall Roberto will be when he is 14 years old.

8. Can the data shown in the line graph be displayed in a bar graph? Explain.

For Exercises 9–13, use the line graph.

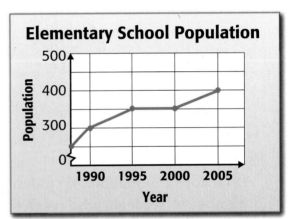

Elementary School Population

9. Is the school population increasing, decreasing, or varying over time?

10. What was the population in 1995?

11. How much did the population grow between 1995 and 2005?

12. During which time period did the population stay the same?

13. Predict the population in 2020. Explain your reasoning.

Represent each set of data in a line graph.

14.

Plant Growth	
Week	Height (in.)
1	1
2	2
3	3
4	5
5	8

15.

One Day's Temperatures	
Time	Temperature (°F)
12 P.M.	62°
1 P.M.	65°
2 P.M.	72°
3 P.M.	66°
4 P.M.	64°

16. Collect and organize data about a week's daily high temperatures in your city. Display the data on a line graph.

17. Analyze the graph you made in Exercise 16. Would a bar graph be a more effective way to display the data? Explain.

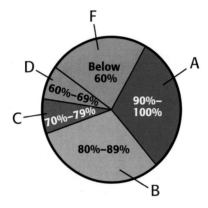

SCAS **4-6.4** Distinguish between categorical and numerical data. **4-6.5** Match categorical and numerical data to appropriate graphs.

Concepts and Skills

More Ways to Display Data

There are many ways to display sets of data. Three of them are shown.

EXAMPLES Different Displays of Data

Three teachers are reviewing the same test scores. The test scores are: 95, 68, 87, 100, 23, 56, 85, 93, 85, 70, 98, 45, and 85. Each teacher displayed the data in a different way.

① Teacher 1 displayed the data in a circle graph where it was organized by letter grade. A circle graph shows data as parts of a circle.

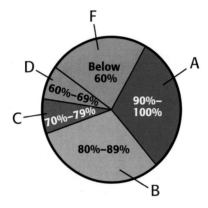

How does the number of students who received an A compare to the number of students who received a B?

The number of students who received an A or B on the test is the same because the sections marked as A and B on the circle graph are the same size.

② Teacher 2 displayed the data using a Venn diagram showing which students scored 70s or above and 70s or below. A Venn diagram is made of circles and shows the relationships between sets of data.

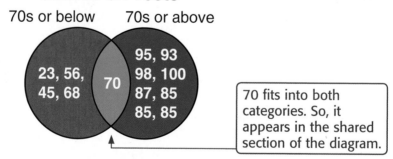

Scores on Tests

70s or below   70s or above

70 fits into both categories. So, it appears in the shared section of the diagram.

What score did most students receive: 70s or above or 70s or below?

There are 9 scores in 70s or above. There are 5 scores in the 70s or below.

So, most students' test scores were 70s or above.

3 Teacher 3 displayed the data using a stem-and-leaf plot. A stem-and-leaf plot is a display of data with digits to the left of ones digits as stems and ones digits as leaves.

What are the mode and the median of these test scores?

The median is the middle number in a set of data. In this set of data the middle number is 85.

The mode is the number that is repeated most. In this set of data it is 85.

So, both the median and mode are 85.

Stems	Leaves
2	3
4	5
5	6
6	8
7	0
8	5 5 5 7
9	3 5 8
10	0

Exercises

For Exercises 1–4, use the circle graph.

1. What fraction of students owns 2 dogs?

2. What fraction of students owns one dog?

3. How many dogs do most students own?

4. What is the greatest number of dogs a student owns?

Number of Dogs per Household

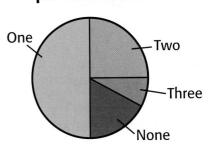

For Exercises 5–7, use the Venn diagram.

5. What may have been the survey question for this Venn diagram?

6. What is the favorite type of sport, indoor or outdoor?

7. What does the number 7 mean?

Favorite Sports

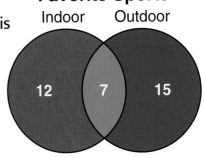

For Exercises 8–10, use the stem-and-leaf plot.

8. What is the greatest number in this set of numbers?

9. What is the median for this set of number?

10. What is the mode for this set of numbers?

Stems	Leaves
1	0 5 6
2	2 4 5 6
6	6 8
7	5 8 9
8	2 3 3 5
9	5

Minimum, Maximum, and Range

The **range** of a set of data describes how much the data varies. It is the difference between the greatest (**maximum**) and least (**minimum**) values of the set.

Range	Key Concept
Words	The difference between the greatest and least values of a data set. range = maximum − minimum

EXAMPLE   Find Range

1 **Find the range of the data set {39, 86, 21, 57, 14, 62}.**

Identify the maximum and minimum of the data set. Then find the range of the data set.

Step 1 Identify the maximum and minimum.

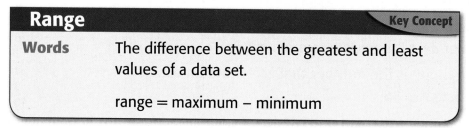

{39, 86, 21, 57, 14, 62}

maximum   minimum

Step 2 Subtract the minimum from the maximum to find the range.

86 − 14 = 72

So, the range of the data set is 72.

Exercises

Identify the maximum, minimum, and range of each data set.

1. Birthdays in May: {4, 22, 18, 2, 29, 15}

2. Ages: {18, 59, 83, 42, 27, 70}

3. Students per grade: {44, 61, 38, 59, 65, 42}

4. Bowling scores: {145, 98, 110, 128, 152, 105}

5. Cailin's test scores were 89, 92, 85, 76, 82, and 98. Find the maximum, minimum, and range of the data set.

6. The daily high temperatures during one week were 45, 53, 58, 62, 64, 55, and 57. Find the maximum, minimum, and range of the data set.

SCAS **Preparation for 5-6.3** Apply procedures to calculate the measures of central tendency (mean, median, and mode).

Mean

You have already learned how to find the median, mode, range, maximum, and minimum of a data set. You will now learn how to find the **mean** or average of a set of data.

Mean		Key Concept
Words	The **mean** of a set of data is the sum of the data divided by the number of pieces of data. $$\text{mean} = \frac{\text{sum of the data}}{\text{number of data items}}$$	
Example	Data set: 4, 2, 1, 5, 3 $$\text{mean: } \frac{4+2+1+5+3}{5} = \frac{15}{5} \text{ or } 3$$	

EXAMPLE   Find the Mean

1 **SPORTS** Henry is playing miniature golf. His scores on the first 6 holes are: 5, 2, 6, 3, 7, and 1. What is Henry's mean score?

Use the definition to find Henry's mean score.

$$\text{mean} = \frac{\text{sum of the data}}{\text{number of data items}}$$

$$= \frac{5+2+6+3+7+1}{6}$$

$$= \frac{24}{6}$$

$$= 4$$

So, Henry's mean score is 4.

Exercises

Find the mean for each set of data.

1. Weekly allowances: $3, $5, $4, $0, $2, $4

2. Number of siblings: 2, 1, 3, 0, 1, 3, 4

3. Number of songs on a CD: 9, 10, 14, 12, 15, 13, 11

4. Test scores: 87, 90, 84, 93, 86

SCAS **Preparation for 5-6.5** Represent the probability of a single-stage event in words and fractions.

Probability and Fractions

You have already used words to describe probability. You can also use a fraction to describe the probability of a desirable result, called a **favorable outcome**.

> ## Probability as a Fraction
> **Key Concept**
>
> $$\text{Probability} = \frac{\text{number of favorable outcomes}}{\text{total possible outcomes}}$$

EXAMPLE **Find Probability**

1. **Use words and a fraction to describe the probability of spinning a star.**

One out of six of the shapes is a star.

$$\text{Probability} = \frac{\text{number of favorable outcomes}}{\text{total possible outcomes}}$$

$$= \frac{\text{number of stars}}{\text{total number of shapes}}$$

$$= \frac{1}{6}$$

So, the probability of spinning a star is 1 out of 6, or $\frac{1}{6}$.

Exercises

The spinner is spun. Use words and a fraction to describe the probability of each outcome.

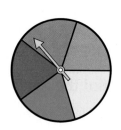

1. yellow
2. green or blue
3. white
4. *not* green
5. red
6. a color *not* in the United States' flag

7. Kylie has 6 pencils, 3 pens, 8 markers, and 2 highlighters in her back pack. If she chooses 1 item without looking, what is the probability that she will choose a pen?

Photo Credits

Unless otherwise credited, all currency courtesy of the US Mint.

v Thomas Barwick/Getty Images; **vi** Doug Martin; **vii** (br)Courtesy Dinah Zike, (others)Doug Martin; **xvi xvii** Isidor Stankov/iStockphoto; **xviii xix** Creatas/SuperStock; **xx xxi** Kevin Schafer/zefa/CORBIS; **xxii xxiii** Daniel A. Bedell/Animals Animals/Earth Scenes; **xviv xxv** Brand X/SuperStock; **xxvi xxvii** CORBIS; **xxviii xxix** Keren Su; **xxx xxxi** David Muench/CORBIS; **xxxiii** The McGraw-Hill Companies; **xxiv** Tim Fuller; **1** JOYCE & FRANK BUREK/Animals Animals/Earth Scenes; **2** David Muench/CORBIS; **3** David Muench/CORBIS; **4** Creatas Images/PictureQuest; **5** (t)Larry Allen/SuperStock, (b)Creatas/PunchStock; **6** William Struhs; **7** William Struhs; **8** Dynamic Graphics Group/PunchStock; **9** (t)Brand X Pictures/PunchStock, (b)Creatas/SuperStock; **10** Courtesy of the Columbia Museum of Art; **11** (l to r, t to b)Colin Young-Wolff/PhotoEdit, Spencer Grant, Dennis MacDonald, David Frazier/CORBIS; **12** Courtesy of South Carolina Stingrays; **13** Tom Grill/CORBIS; **14–15** Isidor Stankov/iStockphoto; **19** Elizabeth DeLaney/Index Stock Imagery; **20** Ed-Imaging; **23** Claver Carroll/JupiterImages; **24** (t)Brand X/SuperStock, (b)Pixtal/SuperStock; **26** Paul Seheult/Eye Ubiquitous/CORBIS; **28** Robert E Daemmrich; **32** (l)Ingram Publishing/Alamy Images, (r)G.K. Vikki Hart/Getty Images; **35** Ed-Imaging; **36** (t)Lon C. Diehl/PhotoEdit, (b)Matthias Kulka/CORBIS; **39** (l)Ed-Imaging, (r)Ryan McVay/Getty Images; **40** Ed-Imaging; **42–43** (bkgd)Stuart Westmorland/Getty Images, (inset)J. Berndes/A.B./Zefa/CORBIS; **52–53** The McGraw-Hill Companies; **54** (l)CORBIS, (r)C Squared Studios/Getty Images; **57** Ed-Imaging; **58** (t)Image Source/JupiterImages, (b)Index Stock Imagery; **60** Ralf-Finn Hestoft/CORBIS; **62** Gary Rhijnsburger/Masterfile; **65** (t)Brand X Pictures/Alamy Images, (b)2006 Photos To Go; **66** Ryan McVay/Getty Images; **70** Ed-Imaging; **73** CORBIS; **74** Raymond Forbes/age fotostock; **75 76** Ed-Imaging; **77** Getty Images; **78–79** (bkgd)Jeff Rotman/Getty Images, (inset)Paul Springett/Alamy Images; **81** C Squared Studios/Getty Images; **82** (tl)CORBIS, (others)Ed-Imaging; **83** CORBIS; **93** Kwame Zikomo/SuperStock; **96** G.K. Vikki Hart/Getty Images; **98** Creatas/SuperStock; **101** Ed-Imaging; **102** Oliver Benn/Royal Philharmonic Orchestra; **103** (l)2006 Photos To Go, (r)PhotoLink/Getty Images; **104** Darren Bennett/Animals Animals/Earth Scenes; **115 116 117 118** Ed-imaging; **119** (br)Ryan McVay/Getty Images, (others)The McGraw-Hill Companies; **120–121** (bkgd)Tony Craddock/Getty Images, (inset)Stockdisc/Getty Images; **124** David Young-Wolff/PhotoEdit; **126** Jeff Venier/Getty Images; **134** CORBIS; **139** (br)JupiterImages, (others)Stockdisc/PunchStock; **142–143** Denis Scot/CORBIS; **147** The McGraw-Hill Companies; **149** William Leaman/Alamy; **151** C Squared Studios/Getty Images; **152** BananaStock/Alamy Images; **154** Lon C. Diehl/PhotoEdit; **160** Getty Images; **162** Brian Hagiwara/PictureArts/CORBIS; **164** (l to r)Bettmann/CORBIS, John Van Hasselt/CORBIS Sygma, Webster & Stevens Collection/Museum of History and Industry, Seattle/CORBIS; **164–165** (bkgd)Tracy Hebden/Alamy Images, (l)SuperStock, (r)Rachel Epstein/PhotoEdit; **166** Tetra Images/Alamy Images; **167** D. Hurst/Alamy Images; **168** Kevin Schafer/zefa/CORBIS; **170** David Young-Wolff; **172 174 175** Ed-Imaging; **176** Dennis Macdonald/PhotoEdit; **177** Mark Richards/PhotoEdit; **178** StockTrek/Getty Images; **179** Ed-Imaging; **181** Getty Images; **190–191** Digital Vision/PunchStock; **193** Don Smetzer/PhotoEdit; **198** Stockdisc/JupiterImages; **200** (l)Ed-Imaging, (r)William Howard/Getty Images; **202** Ed-Imaging; **211** G.K. Vikki Hart/Getty Images; **212–213** (bkgd)Roine Magnusson/Getty Images, (inset)Joe McDonald/CORBIS; **214** Jim Cummins/CORBIS; **215** Getty Images; **216** Brand X Pictures/PunchStock; **217 218** Ed-Imaging; **220** Michael Newman/PhotoEdit; **226** Getty Images; **229** (l)C Squared Studios/Getty Images, (r)The McGraw-Hill Companies; **234–235** Denis Scott/CORBIS; **237** Jurgen Freund/JACANA/HOA-QUI/ImageState; **238** George Hall/CORBIS; **239** CORBIS; **240** C Squared Studios/Getty Images, G.K. Vikki Hart/Getty Images; **242** Ren Long/AP Images;

245 246 247 Ed-Imaging; **248** Joe Atlas/Brand X Pictures/PictureQuest; **249 250** Ed-Imaging; **252** Richard Hutchings/Digital Light Source/PhotoEdit; **254** age fotostock/SuperStock; **255** Ed-Imaging; **256–257** (bkgd)David Tipling/Lonely Planet Images, (inset)Daniel A. Bedell/Animals Animals/Earth Scenes; **258** Robin Lynne/Getty Images; **259** age fotostock/SuperStock; **261** (l)Jack Hollingsworth/Getty Images, (r)Ed-Imaging; **270–271** David Young-Wolff/PhotoEdit; **273** Cooperphoto/CORBIS; **275** Robert Lubeck/Animals Animals/Earth Scenes; **276** G.K. & Vikki Hart/Getty Images; **278** Colin Keates/Getty Images, (b)Ingram Publishing/age fotostock; **280** CORBIS; **284** Getty Images; **285** (l)Ryan McVay/Getty Images, (r)Michael Houghton/StudiOhio; **286** C Squared Studios/Getty Images; **288** Getty Images; **290** (bl)(br)Ed-Imaging, (t)Getty Images; **292–293** JupiterImages/Thinkstock; **294** BananaStock/JupiterImages; **296** Mark Newman/Photo Researchers; **297** Christian Petersen/Getty Images; **299** Ed-Imaging; **308–309** Dennis MacDonald; **311** Ed-Imaging; **313** Craig Lovell/CORBIS; **315** (l to r, t to b)G.K. & Vikki Hart/Getty Images, Patti Murray/Animals Animals/Earth Scenes, Brand X/Jupiter Images, Ed-Imaging; **321** Ryan McVay/Getty Images; **323** Stockbyte/Getty Images; **324** Kevin Fleming/CORBIS; **326** CORBIS; **327** Tony Freeman/PhotoEdit; **328** ThinkStock; **329 330** Ed-Imaging; **334** Brand X/SuperStock; **336** CORBIS; **339** Ed-Imaging; **340** Mauritius/SuperStock; **342** SuperStock, Inc./SuperStock; **343** Sergio Pitamitz/Robert Harding World Imagery/CORBIS; **348** (l)G.K. Vikki Hart/Getty Images, (r)Getty Images; **352** C Squared Studios/Getty Images; **356–357** Masterfile; **359** (t)G.K. Hart/Vikki Hart/Getty Images, (b)Thomas Northcut/Getty Images; **360** The McGraw-Hill Companies; **361** (l)C Squared Studios/Getty Images, (tl)Brand X Pictures/Getty Images, (tr)Stockdisc/PunchStock; **362** (t)Getty Images, (c)CORBIS, (b)Comstock Images/Alamy Images; **362B** S. Wanke/PhotoLink/Getty Images; **363** (l)Davies and Starr, (r)Getty Images; **364** (l)C Squared Studios/Getty Images, (r)Ed-Imaging, (t)Ryan McVay/Getty Images, (b)Bridgeman-Giraudon/Art Resource, NY; **365** Ed-Imaging; **370** The McGraw-Hill Companies; **371** Photos.com; **372** David Young-Wolff/PhotoEdit; **373** Lawrence Manning/CORBIS; **376** Werner H. Mueller/CORBIS; **377** (l to r, t to b)Alan King/Alamy Images, Stockbyte, Image Source/Alamy Images, Creatas/SuperStock, Purestock/JupiterImages, Peter Miller/eStock Photo; **378** (l to r, t to b)Jorg Greuel/Getty Images, Burke/Triolo/Brand X Pictures/JupiterImages, courtesy George Hart, www.georgehart.com/CORBIS, Thomas Northcut/Getty Images, DK Limited/CORBIS, Purestock/Alamy Images; **379 380** Ed-Imaging; **382–383** (bkgd)Visions of America, LLC/Alamy Images, **383** (l)Mary Ann Sullivan/Bluffton University, (r)Visions of America, LCC/Alamy Images; **385** JupiterImages; **392–393** Lawrence Manning/CORBIS; **396** Stockbyte/SuperStock; **399** (l)The McGraw-Hill Companies, (c)David Young-Wolff, (r)Tony Arruza/CORBIS; **400** CORBIS; **402** Brand X/ImageState; **404** Rob Gage/Getty Images; **407** through **417** Getty Images; **419** Photos.com; **420** (l to r, t to b)Ralph A. Clevenger/CORBIS, Ryan McVay/Getty Images, Ryan McVay/Getty Images, Ed-Imaging; **423** Comstock/Alamy Images; **424** Gallo Images/Getty Images; **425** Ed-Imaging; **426–427** (bkgd)The McGraw-Hill Companies, SuperStock, (2, 3)The McGraw-Hill Companies, The McGraw-Hill Companies, CREATAS, John Pitcher/age fotostock; **430** Getty Images; **436–437** Gary Gerovac/Masterfile; **438** (l)Design Pics Inc./Alamy Images, (r)Creatas Images/JupiterImages; **439** PhotoLink/Getty Images; **440** 2006 Photos to Go; **441** (l to r, t to b)Chris Newbert/Minden Pictures, C Squared Studios/Getty Images, The McGraw-Hill Companies, JupiterImages; **442** (l to r, t to b)G.K. Hart/Vikki Hart/Getty Images, Siede Preis/Getty Images, C Squared Studios/Getty Images, The McGraw-Hill Companies, C Squared Studios/Getty Images; **443** (l to r, t to b)Stockdisc/PunchStock, G.K. Vikki Hart/Getty Images, Siede Preis/Getty Images, 2006 Photos to Go; **444** STACY GOLD/National Geographic Society Images;

Photo Credits

446 C Squared Studios/Getty Images; 447 Getty Images; 449 Photos.com/JupiterImages; 450 (l to r, t to b)D. Hurst/Alamy Images, JupiterImages, Terri Chicko, Michael Grimm, D. Hurst/Alamy Images; 451 (l to r, t to b)Jeffrey Coolidge/CORBIS, Hans Christoph Kappel/npl/Minden Pictures, W.A.N.T. PHOTOGRAPHY/Animals Animals/Earth Scenes, Comstock Images, The McGraw-Hill Companies; 452 (l to r, t to b)The McGraw-Hill Companies, David Young-Wolff/PhotoEdit, Getty Images, Lon C. Diehl/PhotoEdit, CORBIS; 453 (tl, b)Getty Images, (tr)Photosindia.com/SuperStock, (c)JupiterImages; 454–455 (bkgd)CORBIS, (inset)James Hackett/eStock Photo; 455 CORBIS; 458 Michael Freeman/CORBIS; 459 (l)Getty Images, (r)The McGraw-Hill Companies; 463 466 Ed-Imaging; 467 (t)Getty Images, (b)age fotostock/SuperStock; 471 Ed-Imaging; 473 (tl)Getty Images, (tr)Stockbyte/PictureQuest, (b)C Squared Studios/Getty Images; 475 (tl)Getty Images, (tr)Creatas/PunchStock, (b)CORBIS; 479 (t)C Squared Studios/Getty Images, (b)USDA Natural Resources Conservation Service; 483–484 (bkgd)Keren Su/Getty Images; 485 Ed-Imaging; 486 (l to r, t to b)Lawrence Manning/CORBIS, (2–5)Ed-Imaging, G.K. Hart/Vikki Hart/The Image Bank/Getty Images; 487 (l to r, t to b)Burke/Triolo Productions/JupiterImages, Didier Robcis/CORBIS, 2006 Photos to Go, Photos.com/JupiterImages, Mark Steinmetz, David Young-Wolff/PhotoEdit, Colin Young-Wolff/PhotoEdit; 488 (l to r, t to b)Jeff Greenberg/PhotoEdit, JupiterImages, Burke/Triolo/JupiterImages, The McGraw-Hill Companies, Burke/Triolo Productions/Brand X/CORBIS, Spencer Grant/PhotoEdit, Getty Images; 489 The McGraw-Hill Companies; 490 Ed-Imaging; 492 (t)Amon/PhotoCuisine/CORBIS, (bl)Michael Newman/PhotoEdit, (br)Ed-Imaging; 493 (t)Comstock/JupiterImages, (c)Getty Images, (bl)Dynamic Graphics Value/SuperStock, (bc)Lawrence Manning CORBIS, (br)Elizabeth Whiting & Associates/CORBIS; 494 (l to r, t to b)Joson/zefa/CORBIS, David Young-Wolff/PhotoEdit, Lawrence Manning CORBIS, The McGraw-Hill Companies, Andy Crawford, DK Limited/CORBIS; 495 (l)Getty Images, (r)Andrea Rugg/Beateworks/CORBIS; 496 (t)Lew Robertson/JupiterImages, (c, b)Ed-Imaging; 498 (l to r, t to b)Rachel Epstein/PhotoEdit, Getty Images, Getty Images, Paul Gapper/worldphotos.org/Alamy Images, Caren Alpert/JupiterImages, Rachel Epstein/PhotoEdit; 499 (l to r, t to b)Getty Images, C Squared Studios/Getty Images, Thinkstock/Alamy Images, PunchStock, CORBIS/JupiterImages; 500 (l to r, t to b)Getty Images, CORBIS, Getty Images, David Stares/Alamy Images, G.K. Vikki Hart/Getty Images, Jeffrey Coolidge/CORBIS, Courtesy of the South Carolina Department of Parks, Recreation & Tourism; 501 (l to r, t to b)Michael Matisse/Getty Images, Photodisc/Getty Images, Envision/CORBIS, Russell Illig/Getty Images, G.K. & Vikki Hart/Getty Images; 502 Photodisc/Getty Images; 503 G.K. & Vikki Hart/Getty Images; 504 Envision/CORBIS; 506 Design Pics/FotoSearch; 507 (l to r, t to b)C Squared Studios/Getty Images, G.K. & Vikki Hart/Getty Images, 2006 Photos to Go; 508 Ed-Imaging; 509 (l to r, t to b)Big Cheese Photo/JupiterImages, Ron Chapple/JupiterImages, Photodisc/Getty Images, CORBIS; 510 (l to r, t to b)Monotype, LLC, Dave Mager/Index Stock Imagery, C Squared Studios/Getty Images, ThinkStock LLC, Image Farm Inc./Alamy Images, Charlie Roy/JupiterImages, C Squared Studios/Getty Images; 511 Ed-Imaging; 512 The McGraw-Hill Companies; 515 (l)Stockdisc/PunchStock, (r)Photos.com/JupiterImages; 516–517 (bkgd)Renee Morris/Alamy Images, (c)Iconotec/Alamy Images, (l)Mark Cassino/SuperStock, (r)Jupiter Images; 518 Ed-Imaging; 519 2006 Photos To Go; 520 2006 Photos To Go; 523 (l to r, t to b)Ed-Imaging, Ed-Imaging G.K. Vikki Hart/Getty Images, G.K. Vikki Hart/Getty Images; 525 (l)Masterfile, (tr)Hirdes/f1online/Alamy Images, (cr)Mick Broughton/Alamy Images, (br)JupiterImages; 526 (l to r, t to b)Colin Young-Wolff/PhotoEdit, Judith Collins/Alamy Images, Jan Tadeusz/Alamy Images, Purestock/Getty Images, Jeffrey Coolidge/Getty Images, Joe Schmelzer/Beateworks/CORBIS; 527 Rick Gayle Studio/CORBIS; 528 (l to r, t to b)

Ed-Imaging, G.K. Vikki Hart/Getty Images, The McGraw-Hill Companies, Ann Cutting/JupiterImages, Siede Preis/Getty Images; 529 (l)Siede Preis/Getty Images, (r)Getty Images; 531 (l to r, t to b) (2)The McGraw-Hill Companies, Brand X Pictures/Alamy Images, Jose Fuste Raga/CORBIS, Brand X Pictures/Punchstock, Mitch Diamond/Index Stock Imagery, Darren Bennett/Animals Animals/Earth Scenes; 534–535 (bkgd)Siede Preis/Getty Images, (inset)C Squared Studios/Getty Images; 540 The McGraw-Hill Companies; 541 (l)Don Farrall/Getty Images, (others)Stockdisc/PunchStock; 542 Rob Scholten/Foto Natura; 543 (l)Ed-Imaging, (r)Getty Images; 544 Stockdisc/PunchStock; 545 (l)Koopman/CORBIS, (c)Ton Kinsbergen/Beateworks/CORBIS, (r)C Squared Studios/Getty Images; 551 (t)Getty Images, (b)Ed-imaging; 552 Ed-Imaging; 557 Getty Images; 558–559 (bkgd)The McGraw-Hill Companies, (inset)Ed Taylor/Getty Images; 563 (l)Punchstock, (r)Getty Images; 564 Ed-Imaging; 568 The McGraw-Hill Companies; 570 Getty Images; 574–575 CORBIS; 579 MedioImages/SuperStock; 582 David Muench/CORBIS; 583 Martin Harvey/CORBIS; 584 Courtesy of the South Carolina Department of Parks, Recreation & Tourism; 585 (l)Ed-Imaging, (r)Getty Images; 586 through 594 Ed-imaging; 595 Michael Houghton/StudiOhio; 596 Greg Probst/CORBIS; 600–601 (bkgd)Digital Vision/Getty Images, (inset)Getty Images; 602 Stockdisc Classic/Alamy Images; 604 (l)Ed-Imaging, (r)Brad Wilson/Getty Images; 605 Ed-Imaging; 614–615 Steve Satushek; 617 Time & Life Pictures/Getty Images; 618 Sam Greenwood/NewSport/CORBIS; 621 Ed-Imaging; 623 Michael Houghton/StudiOhio; 624 Mauritius/SuperStock; 626 CORBIS; 627 G.K. Vikki Hart/Getty Images; 628 Ed-Imaging; 630 BigStockPhoto.com; 631 Deborah Meeks/SuperStock; 632 Comstock Images/PictureQuest; 634 Getty Images; 635 The McGraw-Hill Companies; 636 Ed-Imaging; 638 Bettmann/CORBIS; 639 John Cancalosi/Peter Arnold, Inc.; 641 (l)Image Source/Getty Images, (r)CORBIS; 642–643 (bkgd)Donald Miralle/Getty Images, (l)Empics/SportsChrome, (r)Rob Tringali/SportsChrome; LA0 Mark Steinmetz; LA1 Tim Fuller; LA2 Walter Geiersperger/CORBIS; LA3 PictureNet/CORBIS; LA5 (t)The McGraw-Hill Companies, (bl)Ed-Imaging, (br)CORBIS; LA6 Jeffrey L. Rotman/CORBIS; LA7 The McGraw-Hill Companies; LA9 (t)The McGraw-Hill Companies, (b)Ed-imaging; LA10 Tom Grill/CORBIS; LA11 The McGraw-Hill Companies; LA14 Stockbyte; LA18 Chev Wilkinson; P0 (t)Getty Images, (c)Punchstock, (b)Bob Daemmrich/PhotoEdit; P1 (t)Tim Fuller, (b)2006 Photos To Go; P2 BananaStock/Alamy Images; P4 (t)Food Image Source/O'Gara/Bissell/StockFood, (b)2006 Photos To Go; P5 Photos.com; P6 Sindre Ellingsen/Alamy Images; P7 Brand X Pictures/Alamy Images; P8 (t)Laurie Rubin/Getty Images, (b)Getty Images; R0 Ed-Imaging; R9 McGraw-Hill Companies Inc; R24 (l)gds/zefa/CORBIS, (c)Nancy R. Cohen/Getty Images, (r)Burke/Triolo Productions/Getty Images; R28 (tl)The McGraw-Hill Companies, (tr)Getty Images, (bl)D. Hurst/Alamy, (br)C Squared Studios/Getty Images; R29 (tr)C Squared Studios/Getty Images, (bl)C Squared Studios/Getty Images, (br)Photos.com/JupiterImages; R30 (l to r, t to b)The McGraw-Hill Companies, Ingram Publishing/SuperStock, The McGraw-Hill Companies, CORBIS, 2006 Photos To Go.com; R31 (l to r, t to b) JupiterImages, JupiterImages, Photos.com/JupiterImages, Stockdisc/PunchStock, Getty Images, Photos.com/Jupiter Images, 2006 Photos To Go; R32 (l to r, t to b)Getty Images, G.K. & Vikki Hart/Getty Images, JupiterImages; R39 through R41 Getty Images; R43 Ed-Imaging; R64 (l)The McGraw-Hill Companies, (r)Masterfile.

McGraw-Hill would like to acknowledge the artists and agencies who contributed to illustrating this program: **Cover** Mick McGinty represented by Mendola Artists; Argosy Publishing; Gary Ciccarelli, Keith Batcheller, Jean-Pascal Donnot represented by AA Reps. Inc; Dick Gage, Mark Collins, Richard Carbajal represented by Deborah Wolfe Ltd.

Glossary/Glosario

Cómo usar el glosario en español:
1. Busca el término en inglés que desees encontrar.
2. El término en español, junto con la definición, se encuentran en la columna de la derecha.

English

Español

A

acute angle (p. 369) An *angle* with a measure greater than 0° and less than 90°.

ángulo agudo Un *ángulo* que mide más de 0° y menos de 90°.

acute triangle (p. 372) A *triangle* with all three *angles* less than 90°.

triángulo acutángulo Un *triángulo* cuyos tres *ángulos* miden menos de 90°.

addend (p. 64) Any numbers being added together.

sumando Cualquier número que se suma a otro.

add (adding, addition) (p. 52) An operation on two or more *addends* that results in a *sum*.

$$9 + 3 = 12$$

suma (sumar, adición) Operación en dos o más *sumandos* que resulta en una *suma*.

$$9 + 3 = 12$$

algebra (p. 193) A branch of mathematics that uses symbols, usually letters, to explore relationships between quantities.

álgebra Rama de las matemáticas que usa símbolos, generalmente letras, para explorar relaciones entre cantidades.

angle (p. 368) A figure that is formed by two *rays* with the same *endpoint*.

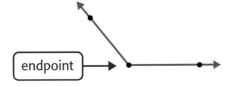

ángulo Figura formada por dos *rayos* con el mismo *extremo*.

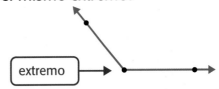

area (p. 460)   The number of *square units* needed to cover the inside of a region or plane figure without any overlap.

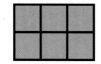

area = 6 square units

área   El número de *unidades cuadradas* necesarias para cubrir el interior de una región o figura plana sin traslapes.

área = 6 unidades cuadradas

Associative Property of Addition (p. 55)   The property states that the grouping of the *addends* does not change the *sum*.

$$(4 + 5) + 2 = 4 + (5 + 2)$$

propiedad asociativa de la suma Propiedad que establece que la agrupación de los *sumandos* no altera la *suma*.

$$(4 + 5) + 2 = 4 + (5 + 2)$$

Associative Property of Multiplication (p. 150)   The property that states that the grouping of the *factors* does not change the *product*.

$$3 \times (6 \times 2) = (3 \times 6) \times 2$$

propiedad asociativa de la multiplicación   Propiedad que establece que la agrupación de los *factores* no altera el *producto*.

$$3 \times (6 \times 2) = (3 \times 6) \times 2$$

B

bar graph (p. 108)   A graph that compares *data* by using bars of different lengths or heights to show the values.

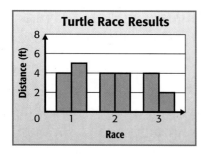

gráfica de barras   Gráfica que compara los *datos* usando barras de distintas longitudes o alturas para mostrar los valores.

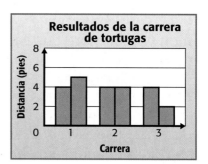

bilateral symmetry (p. 422)   The property of a figure that allows it to be folded so the two halves match exactly.

simetría bilateral   Propiedad de una figura que le permite ser doblada de manera que las mitades se correspondan exactamente.

Glossary/Glosario

C

capacity (p. 485)   The amount of liquid a container can hold.

circle (p. R64)   A closed figure in which all points are the same distance from a fixed point, called the center.

Commutative Property of Addition (p. 55)   The property that states that the order in which two numbers are added does not change the *sum*.

$$12 + 15 = 15 + 12$$

Commutative Property of Multiplication (p. 150)   The property that states that the order in which two numbers are multiplied does not change the *product*.

$$7 \times 2 = 2 \times 7$$

compatible numbers (p. 322)   Numbers in a problem or related numbers that are easy to work with mentally.

720 and 90 are compatible numbers for division because $72 \div 9 = 8$.

cone (p. 359)   A 3-dimensional figure with a curved surface, a circular base, and one *vertex*.

congruent figures (p. 418)   Two figures having the same size and the same shape.

capacidad   Cantidad que puede contener un envase, medida en unidades de volumen.

círculo   Figura cerrada en la cual todos los puntos equidistan de un punto fijo llamado centro.

propiedad conmutativa de la suma   Propiedad que establece que el orden en el cual se suman dos o más números no altera la *suma*.

$$12 + 15 = 15 + 12$$

propiedad conmutativa de la multiplicación   Propiedad que establece que el orden en el cual se multiplican dos o más números no altera el *producto*.

$$7 \times 2 = 2 \times 7$$

números compatibles   Números en un problema o números relacionados con los cuales es fácil trabajar mentalmente.

720 y 90 son números compatibles en la división porque $72 \div 9 = 8$.

cono   Figura tridimensional con una superficie curva, una base circular y un *vértice*.

figuras congruentes   Dos figuras con la misma forma y el mismo tamaño.

coordinate (p. 406) One of two numbers in an *ordered pair*.

In (1, 5), the 1 is the number on the *x*-axis. The 5 is on the *y*-axis.

coordenada Uno de los dos números de un *par ordenado*.

(1, 5) El 1 es el número en el eje *x* y el 5 está en el eje *y*.

coordinate plane (p. 406) A graph that displays a set of points and gives the position of a point on a line.

gráfica de coordenadas o cuadriculado Gráfica que representa un conjunto de puntos y da, en términos numéricos, la posición de un punto sobre una recta.

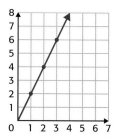

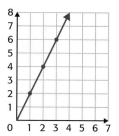

cube (p. 359) A 3-dimensional figure with six *congruent* square *faces*.

cubo Figura tridimensional con seis *caras* cuadradas *congruentes*.

cylinder (p. 359) A 3-dimensional *figure* having two *parallel congruent* circular *bases* and a curved surface connecting the two *bases*.

cilindro Figura tridimensional que tiene dos bases circulares *paralelas* y *congruentes* y una superficie curva que las une.

D

data (p. 95) Numbers or symbols, sometimes collected from a *survey* or experiment, to show information. Datum is singular; data is plural.

datos Números o símbolos que muestran información, algunas veces reunidos de una *encuesta* o un experimento.

decimal (p. 579) A number that uses *place value*, numbers, and a *decimal point* to show part of a whole.

decimal Número con uno o más dígitos a la derecha del punto *decimal*, tales como 8.37 ó 0.05.

decimal equivalents (p. 596) Decimals that represent the same number.

0.3 and 0.30

decimales equivalentes Decimales que representan el mismo número.

0.3 y 0.30

decimal point (p. 579) A period separating the ones and the *tenths* in a decimal number.

0.8 OR $3.77

punto decimal Punto que separa las unidades de las *décimas* en un número decimal.

0.8 ó $3.77

degrees (°) (p. 468) The units of measurement used to describe temperature.

grado (°) Unidad de temperatura.

denominator (p. 537) The bottom number in a *fraction*.

In $\frac{5}{6}$, 6 is the denominator.

denominador El número inferior en una *fracción*.

$\frac{5}{6}$ 6 es el denominador.

digit (p. 17) A symbol used to write numbers. The ten digits are 0, 1, 2, 3, 4, 5, 6, 7, 8, and 9.

dígito Símbolo que se usa para escribir números. Los diez dígitos son 0, 1, 2, 3, 4, 5, 6, 7, 8 y 9.

Distributive Property of Multiplication (p. 166) To multiply a *sum* by a number, multiply each *addend* by the number and add the *products*.

$$4 \times (1 + 3) = (4 \times 1) + (4 \times 3)$$

propiedad distributiva de la multiplicación Para multiplicar una *suma* por un número, puedes multiplica cada *sumando* por el número y suma los *productos*.

$$4 \times (1 + 3) = (4 \times 1) + (4 \times 3)$$

division (divide) (p. 142) An operation on two numbers in which the first number is split into the same number of equal groups as the second number.

división (dividir) Operación en dos números en que el primer número se separa en tantos grupos iguales como indica el segundo número.

dividend (p. 311) A number that is being divided.

$3\overline{)19}$ 19 is the dividend

dividendo El número que se divide.

$3\overline{)19}$ 19 es el dividendo

divisor (p. 311) The number by which the *dividend* is being divided.

$3\overline{)19}$ 3 is the divisor

divisor El número entre el cual se divide el *dividendo*.

$3\overline{)19}$ 3 es el divisor

double bar graph (p. 113)   A *bar graph* that compares two related groups of *data*.

gráfica de barras dobles   *Gráfica de barras* que compara dos grupos de *datos* relacionados.

edge (p. 359)   The *line segment* where two *faces* of a *solid figure* meet.

arista   El *segmento de recta* donde concurren dos *caras* de una *figura sólida*.

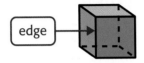

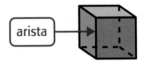

elapsed time (p. 520)   The amount of time that has passed from beginning to end.

tiempo transcurrido   Cantidad de tiempo que ha pasado entre el principio y el fin.

endpoint (p. 400)   The point at either end of a *line segment* or the point at the beginning of a ray.

extremo   El punto en cualquiera de los dos lados en que termina un *segmento de recta* o el punto al principio de un rayo.

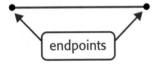

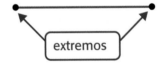

equally likely (p. 128)   Having the same chance of occurring.
In a coin toss, you are equally likely to flip a head or a tail.

equiprobable   Que tiene la misma posibilidad de ocurrir.
Al lanzar una moneda, es equiprobable que caiga cara o cruz.

equation (p. 198)   A sentence that contains an equals sign (=), showing that two *expressions* are equal.

ecuación   Oración matemátia que contiene el signo de igualdad, =, el que indica que las dos *expresiones* son iguales.

equilateral triangle (p. 373) A *triangle* with three *congruent* sides.

triángulo equilátero *Triángulo* con tres lados *congruentes*.

equivalent fractions (p. 548) *Fractions* that represent the same number.

$$\frac{3}{4} = \frac{6}{8}$$

fracciones equivalentes *Fracciones* que representan el mismo número.

$$\frac{3}{4} = \frac{6}{8}$$

estimate (p. 58) A number close to an exact value. An estimate indicates *about* how much.

47 + 22 is about 50 + 20 or 70.

estimación Número cercano a un valor exacto. Una estimación indica *aproximadamente* cuánto.

47 + 22 es aproximadamente 50 + 20; ó 70.

expanded form/expanded notation (p. 18) The representation of a number as a sum that shows the value of each digit.

536 is written as 500 + 30 + 6.

forma desarrollada/notación desarrollada Representación de un número como una suma que muestra el valor de cada dígito.

536 se escribe como 500 + 30 + 6.

expression (p. 193) A combination of numbers, variables, and at least one operation.

expresión Combinación de números, variables y por lo menos una operación.

F

face (p. 359) The flat part of a 3-dimensional figure.

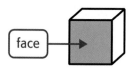

cara Parte llana de una figura tridimensional.

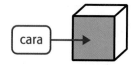

fact family (p. 147) A group of related facts using the same numbers.

5 + 3 = 8	5 × 3 = 15
3 + 5 = 8	3 × 5 = 15
8 − 3 = 5	15 ÷ 3 = 5
8 − 5 = 3	15 ÷ 5 = 3

familia de operaciones Grupo de operaciones relacionadas que usan los mismos números.

5 + 3 = 8	5 × 3 = 15
3 + 5 = 8	3 × 5 = 15
8 − 3 = 5	15 ÷ 3 = 5
8 − 5 = 3	15 ÷ 5 = 3

factor (p. 176) A number that divides a whole number evenly. Also a number that is multiplied by another number.

factor Número que divide exactamente a otro número entero. También es un número multiplicado por otro número.

fraction (p. 537)   A number that represents part of a whole or part of a set.

$$\frac{1}{2}, \frac{1}{3}, \frac{1}{4}, \frac{3}{4}$$

fracción   Número que representa parte de un todo o parte de un conjunto.

$$\frac{1}{2}, \frac{1}{3}, \frac{1}{4}, \frac{3}{4}$$

frequency table (p. 95)   A table for organizing a set of *data* that shows the number of times each result has occurred.

tabla de frecuencias   Tabla para organizar un conjunto de *datos* que muestra el número de veces que ha ocurrido cada resultado.

function (p. 208)   A relationship in which one number depends on another number.

función   Relación en que una cantidad depende de otra cantidad.

function table (p. 208)   A table of ordered pairs that is based on a rule.

tabla de funciones   Tabla de pares ordenados que se basa en una regla.

hexagon (p. 362)   A *polygon* with six sides and six *angles*.

hexágono   *Polígono* con seis lados y seis *ángulos*.

hundredth (p. 580)   A place value position. One of one hundred equal parts.
In the number 0.05, 5 is in the hundredths place.

centésima   Un valor de posición. Una parte de cien partes iguales.
En el número 4.57, 7 está en el lugar de las centésimas.

Identity Property of Addition (p. 55)
For any number, zero plus that number is the number.

$$3 + 0 = 3 \text{ or } 0 + 3 = 3$$

propiedad de identidad de la adición
Para todo numero, cero más el numero es el número.

$$3 + 0 = 3 \text{ ó } 0 + 3 = 3$$

Identity Property of Multiplication
(p. 150)   If you multiply a number by 1, the product is the same as the given number.

$$8 \times 1 = 8 = 1 \times 8$$

propiedad de identidad de la multiplicación   Si multiplicas un número por 1, el producto es igual al número dado.

$$8 \times 1 = 8 = 1 \times 8$$

Glossary/Glosario

impossible (p. 128)   An event that cannot happen. It has a probability of zero.

It is impossible to choose yellow.

imposible   Un evento que no puede suceder, cuya probabilidad es cero.

improper fraction (p. 560)   A fraction with a *numerator* that is greater than or equal to the *denominator*.

$$\frac{17}{3} \text{ or } \frac{5}{5}$$

fracción impropia   Fracción con un *numerador* mayor que o igual al *denominador*.

$$\frac{17}{3} \text{ ó } \frac{5}{5}$$

intersecting lines (p. 401)   *Lines* that meet or cross at a point.

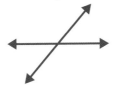

rectas secantes   *Rectas* que se intersecan o cruzan entre sí.

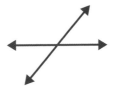

irregular figure (p. R66)   A shape that is made up of two or more shapes.

figura compleja   Figura compuesta por dos o más formas.

is greater than > (p. 28)   An inequality relationship showing that the number on the left of the symbol is greater than the number on the right.

$5 > 3$ 5 is greater than 3

es mayor que >   Relación de desigualdad que muestra que el número a la izquierda del símbolo es mayor que el número a la derecha.

$5 > 3$ 5 es mayor que 3

is less than < (p. 28)   The number on the left side of the symbol is smaller than the number on the right side.

$4 < 7$ 4 is less than 7

es menor que <   El número a la izquierda del símbolo es más pequeño que el número a la derecha.

$4 < 7$ 4 es menor que 7

isosceles triangle (p. 373)   A *triangle* with at least 2 sides of the same length.

triángulo isósceles   Un *triángulo* que tiene por lo menos 2 lados del mismo largo.

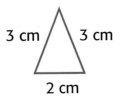

L

length (p. 441)   The measurement of a line between two points.

longitud   Medida de la distancia entre dos puntos.

likely (p. 128)   An event that will probably happen.
   It is likely you will choose a red tile.

posible   Un evento que probablemente sucederá
   Es posible que elijas una baldosa rojo.

line (p. 400)   A straight set of points that extend in opposite directions without ending.

recta   Conjunto de puntos dispuestos rectamente que se extienden en direcciones opuestas y sin fin.

line graph (p. R70)   A graph that uses points connected by *line segments* to represent data.

gráfica lineal   Gráfica que usa puntos unidos por *segmentos de recta* para representar datos.

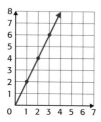

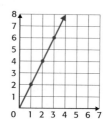

line of symmetry (p. 422)   A *line* on which a figure can be folded so that its two halves match exactly.

eje de simetría   *Recta* sobre la cual se puede doblar una figura de manera que sus mitades se correspondan exactamente.

line plot (p. 104)   A graph that uses columns of Xs above a *number line* to show frequency of data.

esquema lineal   Gráfica que usa columnas de X sobre una *recta numérica* para representar frecuencias de datos.

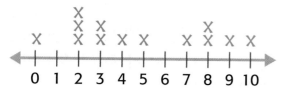

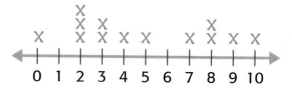

Glossary/Glosario

line segment (p. 400)   A part of a *line* between two *endpoints*. The length of the line segment can be measured.

line symmetry (p. 422)   A figure has *line symmetry* if it can be folded so that the two parts of the figure match, or are *congruent.*

segmento de recta   Parte de una *recta* entre dos *extremos*. La longitud de un segmento de recta se puede medir.

simetría lineal   Una figura tiene *simetria lineal* si puede doblarse de modo que las dos partes de la figura correspondan o sean *congruentes*.

median (p. 98)   The middle number in a group of numbers arranged in numerical order.

The median of 3, 5, 6, 7, and 8 is 6.

mediana   El número central de un grupo de números ordenados numéricamente.

La mediana de 3, 5, 6, 7 y 8 es 6.

minuend (p. 71)   The first number in a subtraction sentence from which a second number is to be subtracted.

$$8 \quad - \quad 3 \quad = \quad 5$$

minuend   subtrahend   difference

minuendo   El primer número en un enunciado de sustracción del cual se restará un segundo número

$$8 \quad - \quad 3 \quad = \quad 5$$

minuendo   sustraendo   diferencia

mixed number (p. 560)   A number that has a *whole number* part and a *fraction* part.

$$6\frac{3}{4}$$

número mixto   Número compuesto por un *número entero* y una parte *fraccionaria*.

$$6\frac{3}{4}$$

mode (p. 98)   The number(s) that occurs most often in a set of numbers.

7, 4, 7, 10, 7, and 2
The mode is 7.

moda   Número o números que ocurre(n) con mayor frecuencia en un conjunto de números.

7, 4, 7, 10, 7 y 2
La moda es 7.

multiple (p. 177)   A multiple of a number is the *product* of that number and any whole number.
15 is a multiple of 5 because $3 \times 5 = 15$.

múltiplo   Un múltiplo de un número es el *producto* de ese número y cualquier otro número entero.
15 es múltiplo de 5 porque $3 \times 5 = 15$.

multiply (multiplication) (p. 142)   An operation on two numbers to find their *product*. It can be thought of as repeated *addition*.

multiplicar (multiplicación)   Operación en dos números para calcular su *producto*. También se puede interpretar como una *adición* repetida.

Glossary/Glosario

net (p. 360) A flat pattern that can be folded to make a 3-dimensional figure.

red Patrón llano que se puede doblar para formar una figura tridimensional.

number line (p. 395) A line with numbers on it in order at regular intervals.

recta numérica Recta con números ordenadosa intervalos regulares.

numerator (p. 537) The number above the bar in a *fraction*; the part of the fraction that tells how many of the equal parts are being used.

numerador El número que está encima de la barra de *fracción*; la parte de la fracción que te indica cuántas partes iguales están siendo usadas.

obtuse angle (p. 369) An *angle* that measures greater than 90° but less than 180°.

ángulo obtuso *Ángulo* que mide más de 90° pero menos de 180°.

obtuse triangle (p. 372) A *triangle* with one *obtuse angle*.

triángulo obtusángulo *Triángulo* con un *ángulo obtuso*.

octagon (p. 362) A *polygon* with 8 sides.

octágono *Polígono* de 8 lados.

operation (p. 52) A mathematical process such as addition, subtraction, multiplication, or division.

operación Proceso matemático como la suma (+), la resta (−), la multiplicación (×) o la división (÷).

order of operations (p. R56)   Rules that tell what order to follow use in evaluating an expression:
(1) Do the operations in parentheses first.

(2) Multiply and divide in order from left to right.
(3) Add and subtract in order from left to right.

orden de las operaciones   Reglas que te indican qué orden seguir cuando evalúas una expresión:
(1) Evalúa primero las operaciones dentro de los paréntesis ( ).
(2) Multiplica o divide en orden de izquierda a derecha.
(3) Suma o resta en orden de izquierda a derecha.

ordered pair (p. 406)   A pair of numbers that are the *coordinates* of a point in a coordinate plane.

par ordenado   Par de números que son las *coordenadas* de un punto en un plano de coordenadas.

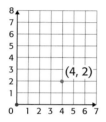

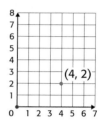

origin (p. 406)   The point (0, 0) on a *coordinate plane* where the vertical axis meets the horizontal axis.

origen   El punto (0, 0) en una *gráfica de* coordenadas donde el eje vertical interseca el eje horizontal, (0, 0).

outcome (p. 124)   A possible result of an experiment.

resultado   Resultado posible de un experimento.

outlier (p. 99)   A number in a set of data that is much larger or much smaller than most of the other numbers in the set.

valor atípico   Número en un conjunto de datos que es mucho mayor o mucho menor que la mayoría de los otros números del conjunto.

parallel lines (p. 401)   Lines that are the same distance apart. Parallel lines do not meet.

rectas paralelas   Rectas separadas por la misma distancia. Las rectas paralelas no se intersecan.

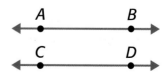

Glossary/Glosario

parallelogram (p. 376) A quadrilateral with four sides in which each pair of opposite sides are parallel and equal in length.

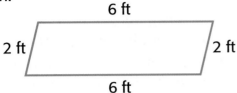

paralelogramo Cuadrilátero de cuatro lados en el cual cada par de lados opuestos son paralelos y de la misma longitud.

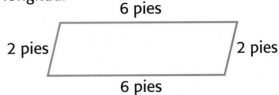

pentagon (p. 362) A *polygon* with five sides.

pentágono *Polígono* de cinco lados.

percent (p. R59) A ratio that compares a number to 100.

porcentaje Razón que compara un número con 100.

perimeter (p. 456) The distance around a shape or region.

perímetro Distancia alrededor de una figura o región.

period (p. 17) The name given to each group of three digits on a place-value chart.

período Nombre dado a cada grupo de tres dígitos en una tabla de valores de posición.

perpendicular lines (p. 401) *Lines* that meet or cross each other to form *right angles*.

rectas perpendiculares *Rectas* que se intersecan o cruzan formando *ángulos rectos*.

place value (p. 14) The value given to a *digit* by its position in a number.

valor de posición El valor dado a un *dígito* según su posición en un número.

polygon (p. 362) A closed *plane figure* formed using *line segments* that meet only at their *endpoints*.

polígono *Figura plana* cerrada formada por *segmentos de recta* que sólo se unen en sus *extremos*.

probability (p. 128)   A number between 0 and 1 that measures the likelihood of an event happening.

probabilidad   Número entre 0 y 1 que mide la posibilidad de que ocurra un evento.

product (p. 145)   The answer or result of a multiplication problem. It also refers to expressing a number as the product of its factors.

producto   Repuesta o resultado de un problema de multiplicación. También se refiere a la expresión de un número como el producto de sus factores.

pyramid (p. 359)   A 3-dimensional figure with a polygon as a base and triangular shaped faces that share a common vertex.

pirámide   Figura sólida con un polígono como base y caras triangulares que comparten un vértice común.

Q

quadrilateral (p. 362)   A shape that has 4 sides and 4 *angles*.
   square, rectangle, and parallelogram

cuadrilátero   Figura que tiene 4 lados y 4 *ángulos*.
   cuadrado, rectángulo y paralelogramo

quotient (p. 311)   The result of a *division* problem.

cociente   Respuesta o resultado de un problema de *división*.

R

range (p. R74)   The *difference* between the greatest and the least numbers in a set of data.

rango   La *diferencia* entre el mayor y el menor de los números en un conjunto de datos.

ray (p. 400)   A part of a *line* that has one *endpoint* and extends in one direction without ending.

rayo   Parte de una *recta* que tiene un *extremo* y que se extiende en una dirección sin fin.

rectangle (p. 376)   A *quadrilateral* with four *right angles*; opposite sides are equal and *parallel*.

rectángulo   *Cuadrilátero* con cuatro *ángulo rectos*; los lados opuestos son iguales y *paralelos*.

rectangular prism (p. 359)   A 3-dimensional figure with six faces that are rectangles.

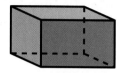

prisma rectangular   Figura tridimensional de seis caras rectangulares.

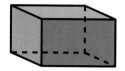

reflection (p. 412)   A type of transformation that flips a figure.

reflexion   Tipo de transformación en que seleda vuelta a una figura.

remainder (p. 312)   The number that is left after one whole number is divided by another.

residuo   Número que queda después de dividir un número entero entre otro número entero.

rhombus (p. 376)   A *parallelogram* with four *congruent* sides.

rombo   *Paralelogramo* con cuatro lados *congruentes*.

right angle (p. 369)   An *angle* with a measure of 90°.

ángulo recto   *Ángulo* que mide 90°.

right triangle (p. 372)   A *triangle* with one *right angle*.

triángulo rectángulo   *Triángulo* con un *ángulo recto*.

rotation (p. 412)   A type of transformation in which a figure is turned about a central point.

rotación   Tipo de transformación en que se hace girar una figura alrededor de un punto central.

rotational symmetry (p. 423)   A figure has rotational symmetry if, after a rotation of the figure about a point, the figure lies in its original position.

simetría de rotación   Una figura posee simetría de rotación si después de rotarla sobre un punto la figura yace en su posición original.

round (p. 37)   To change the value of a number to one that is easier to work with. To find the nearest value of a number based on a given *place value*.

redondear   Cambiar el valor de un número a uno con el cual es más fácil trabajar. Calcular el valor más cercano a un número basado en un *valor de posición* dado.

S

scalene triangle (p. 373)   A *triangle* with no *congruent* sides.

triángulo escaleno   *Triángulo* sin lados *congruentes*.

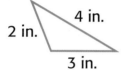

2 in. 4 in. 3 in.

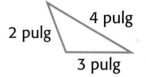

2 pulg 4 pulg 3 pulg

similar figures (p. R65)   Figures that have the same shape but different sizes.

figuras semejantes   Figuras que tienen la misma forma, pero diferente tamaño.

sphere (p. 359)   A solid or 3-dimensional figure that is set of all points that are the same distance from a given point, called the center.

esfera   *Figura tridimensional* formada por el conjunto de todos los puntos equidistantes de un punto dado llamado *centro*.

square (p. 376)   A rectangle with four *congruent sides*.

cuadrado   Rectángulo de cuatro *lados congruentes*.

square unit (p. 460)   A unit for measuring area.

unidad cuadrada   Unidad para medir el área.

Glossary/Glosario

standard form/standard notation
(p. 18)   The usual way of writing a number that shows only its *digits*, no words.

537   89   1642

forma estándar/notación estandard
Manera habitual de escribir un número que sólo muestra sus dígitos, sin palabras.

537   89   1642

subtract (subtraction) (p. 52)   An operation on two numbers that tells the *difference*, when some or all are taken away. Subtraction is also used to compare two numbers.

$14 - 8 = 6$

restar (resta)   Operación en dos números que indica la *diferencia*, cuando algunos o todos son eliminados. La sustracción también se usa para comparar dos números.

$14 - 8 = 6$

subtrahend (p. 71)   A number that is subtracted from another number.

$14 - 5 = 9$
↑
subtrahend

sustraendo   Un número que se sustrae de otro número.

$14 - 5 = 9$
↑
sustraendo

sum (p. 58)   The answer to an addition problem.

suma   Respuesta o resultado de un problema de suma.

surface area (p. LA22)   The area of the surface of a three-dimensional figure.

área de superficie   Área de la superficie de una *figura tridimensional*.

survey (p. 95)   A method of collecting data.

encuesta   Método para reunir datos.

tally chart (p. 95)   A way to keep track of *data* using tally marks to record the number of responses or occurrences.

What is Your Favorite Color?	
Color	**Tally**
Blue	⊬⊬ |||
Green	||||

tabla de conteo   Manera de llevar la cuenta de los datos usando marcas de conteo para anotar el número de respuestas o sucesos.

¿Cuál es tu color favorito?	
Color	**Conteo**
Azul	⊬⊬ |||
Verde	||||

tally mark(s) (p. 95)   A mark made to keep track and display *data* recorded from a survey.

marcas(s) de conteo   Marca que se hace para llevar un registro y representar datos reunidos de una encuesta.

Glossary/Glosario

tenth (p. 580)   One of ten equal parts or $\frac{1}{10}$.

décima   Una de diez partes iguales ó $\frac{1}{10}$.

three-dimensional figure (p. 359) A solid figure has three dimensions: length, width, and height.

figura sólida   Una figura sólida tiene tres dimensiones: largo, ancho y alto.

transformation (p. 412)   A movement of a figure.

transformación   Movimiento de una figura.

translation (p. 412)   A type of transformation in which a figure is slid horizontally, vertically, or both.

traslación   Tipo de transformación en que una figura se desliza en sentido vertical, en sentido horizontal o en ambos sentidos.

trapezoid (p. 376)   A *quadrilateral* with exactly one pair of *parallel* sides.

trapecio   *Cuadrilátero* con exactamente un par de lados *paralelos*.

tree diagram (p. 125)   A diagram of all the possible *outcomes* of an event or series of events or experiments.

diagrama de árbol   Diagrama de todos los *resultados* posibles de un evento o series de eventos o experimentos.

triangle (p. 362)   A *polygon* with three sides and three angles.

triángulo   *Polígono* con tres lados y tres ángulos.

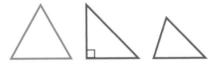

triangular prism (p. 359)   A prism whose bases are triangular with *parallelograms* for sides.

prisma triangular   Prisma cuyas bases son triangulares con *paralelogramos* como lados.

triangular pyramid (p. 359)   A pyramid whose base is a *triangle*.

pirámide triangular   Pirámide cuya base es un *triángulo*.

two-dimensional figure (p. 362)   A figure that lies entirely within one plane.

figura plana   Figura que yace completamente en un plano.

U

unlikely (p. 128)   An event that is improbable or it will probably *not* happen.

It is unlikely you will choose a yellow tile.

improbable   Evento que es improbable o que es probable que *no* suceda.

Es improbable que elijas una baldosa amarilla.

V

variable (p. 193)   A letter or symbol used to represent an unknown quantity.

variable   Letra o símbolo que se usa para representar una cantidad desconocida.

Venn diagram (p. R72)   A diagram that uses circles to display elements of different sets. Overlapping circles show common elements.

diagrama de Venn   Diagrama que usa círculos para mostrar elementos de diferentes conjuntos. Círculos sobrepuestos indican elementos comunes.

Factors of 42   Factors of 56

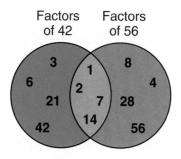

Factores de 42   Factores de 56

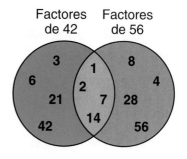

Glossary/Glosario

vertex (p. 359)   The point where two rays meet in an *angle*.

volume (p. 512)   The number of cubic units needed to fill a three-dimensional figure.

weight (p. 498)   A measurement that tells how heavy an object is.

x-axis (p. 406)   The horizontal axis (↔) in a coordinate graph.

x-coordinate (p. 406)   The first number in an *ordered pair* that indicates how far to the left or the right of the *y*-axis a point is. In (2, 3), 2 is the *x*-coordinate.

y-axis (p. 406)   The vertical axis (↕) in a coordinate graph.

y-coordinate (p. 406)   The second number in an *ordered pair* that indicates how far above or below the *x*-axis a point is. In (2, 3), 3 is the *y*-coordinate.

Zero Property of Multiplication (p. 150)   The property that states any number multiplied by zero is zero.

$$0 \times 5 = 0 \qquad 5 \times 0 = 0$$

vértice   Punto donde concurren dos o más rayos.

volumen   Número de unidades cúbicas necesarias para llenar una figura tridimensional o sólida.

peso   Medida que indica la pesadez un cuerpo.

eje x   El eje horizontal (↔) en una gráfica de coordenadas.

coordenada x   El primer número en un *par ordenado* que indica la distancia a la izquierda o a laderecha del eje *y* a la cual se encuentra un punto. En (2, 3), 3 es la coordenada *x*.

eje y   El eje vertical (↕) en una gráfica de coordenadas.

coordenada y   El segundo número en un *par ordenado* que indica la distancia hacia arriba o hacia abajo del eje *x* a la cual se encuentra un punto. En (2, 3), 3 es la coordenada *y*.

propiedad del producto nulo de la multiplicación   Propiedad que establece que cualquier número multiplicado por cero es igual a cero.

$$0 \times 5 = 0 \qquad 5 \times 0 = 0$$

Glossary/Glosario

Index

Index

Index

M

Mass, 508–511, 524, 528
  Estimating, 508–511, 528
  Grams (g), 508–511, 524, 528
  Kilograms (kg), 509–511, 524, 528

Math Activities
  Addition of Decimals, 628–629
  Equivalent Fractions, 546–547
  Fractions and Decimals, 577–578
  How Big is One Million?, 20–21
  Meaning of Multiplication and Division, 145–146
  Model Division, 311–312
  Multiply Two-Digit Numbers, 282–283
  Parallel and Intersecting Lines, 398–399
  Possible Outcomes, 122–123
  Subtract Whole Numbers, 70–71
  Subtraction of Decimals, 636–637

Math Tool Chest, 68, 131, 335, 421

Measurement, 8–9, 24, 57, 97, 100, 106, 110, 119, 137, 173, 203, 216, 249, 266, 295, 319, 321, 331, 381, 417, 420, 433, 436–517, 520–526, 528–531, 545, 568, 580–581, 583–585, 587, 589, 595, 597, 602–603, 607, 619, 633, 645
  Adding, 41, 60, 83, 87
  Of angles, 368–370, 387
  Area, 293, 460–467, 472, 476
  Balance scales, 496–497, 508

Capacity, 485–495, 524–526
Celsius (°C), 468–471, 478
Centimeters (cm), 448–452, 455, 472, 475
Clocks, 521–522, 530
Comparing, 554, 556, 591–592
Cups (c), 485–491, 524–525
Customary units, 241, 298, 304, 341, 342, 353, 439–445, 468–473, 478, 482, 485–491, 496–500, 504–507, 524–526, 528
Days, 252, 277
Degrees (°), 368–370, 387
Dividing, 318, 322, 324, 325, 333, 334, 349, 353
Estimating, 439–443, 448–449, 451–452, 473, 475, 486–489, 492–500, 508–515, 525–526, 528–529
Fahrenheit (°F), 468–471, 478
Feet (ft), 5, 241, 298, 304, 342, 352, 441–445, 472–473
Fluid ounces (fl oz), 486–491, 524–525
Gallons (gal), 485–491, 524–525
Grams (g), 508–511, 524, 528
Hours, 521–523, 530
Inches (in.), 5, 439–443, 445, 472–473
Kilograms (kg), 509–511, 524, 528
Kilometers (km), 450–452, 472
Length, 5, 241, 298, 304, 342, 353, 439–445, 448–455, 472–473, 475
Liters (L), 492–494, 524, 526
Mass, 508–511, 524, 528
Meters (m), 450–452, 455, 472
Metric units, 448–452, 468–472, 475, 478, 492–495, 508–511, 524, 526, 528
Miles (mi), 298, 304
Milliliters (mL), 492–494, 524, 526
Millimeters (mm), 450–452, 455, 472

Minutes, 521–522, 530
Multiplying, 238, 254, 260, 264, 274, 284, 286, 287, 290, 298, 303, 565
Ordering, 33
Ounces (oz), 8–9, 341, 482, 496–500, 504–507, 524, 526, 528
Perimeter, 436, 456–459, 464–465, 472, 475
Pints (pt), 485–491, 524–525
Pounds (lb), 8–9, 341, 482, 496–500, 504–507, 524, 526, 528
Quarts (qt), 485–491, 524–525
Rounding, 16, 36, 37
Rulers, 439–443, 448–452
Stopwatch, 520
Subtracting, 59, 72, 77, 82, 83, 87, 88, 201
Temperature, 468–471, 478
Thermometers, 468–470, 478
Time, 252, 274, 277, 520–524, 530
Tons (T), 498–500, 504–507, 524, 526, 528
Volume, 512–515, 524, 529
Weeks, 274
Weight, 8–9, 341, 482, 496–500, 504–507, 509, 524, 526, 528
Yards (yd), 241, 242, 352, 441–445, 472–473
Years, 252, 274, 277

Measurement Activities
  Estimate and Measure Capacity, 485
  Estimate and Measure Length, 439–440
  Estimate and Measure Weight, 496–497
  Metric Measurement of Length, 448–449
  Perimeter and Area, 464–465

Medians, 98–101, 105–107, 133

Mental math, 56–57
  Multiplying by 10, 100, 1,000, 237–239, 262–263, 273
  Solving equations, 198

Meters (m), 450–452, 455, 472

Metric units
Of capacity, 492–494, 524, 526
Celsius (°C), 468–471, 478
Centimeters (cm), 448–452, 455, 472, 475
Cubic centimeters, 512
Grams (g), 508–511, 524, 528
Kilograms (kg), 509–511, 524, 528
Kilometers (km), 450–452, 472
Of length, 448–455, 472, 475
Liters (L), 492–494, 524, 526
Of mass, 508–511, 524, 528
Meters (m), 450–452, 455, 472
Milliliters (mL), 492–494, 524, 526
Millimeters (mm), 450–452, 455 472
Of temperature, 468–471, 478

Miles, 298, 304

Milliliters (mL), 492–494, 524, 526

Millimeters (mm), 450–452, 455, 472

Missing information, 203, 226

Mixed numbers, 560–563, 566, 570
Decimals and, 582–585, 602–604, 607, 610
Modeling, 560–563, 566, 570, 582–584, 588–589, 602–603

Models
For addition, 630
Of decimals, 574, 577–585, 588–591, 596–598, 602–604, 606–608, 610, 614, 628–630, 636–638, 648
For division, 142, 146–149, 155–156, 161, 181, 311–312, 314
Of equations, 196–198
Of equivalent fractions, 546–549, 566, 569
Of expressions, 193, 214, 229
Of fractions, 534, 537–544, 546–551, 554–557,

560–564, 566–569, 577–585, 588–589, 596–598, 602–604, 606, 608, 610
Of improper fractions, 560–563, 570
Of mixed numbers, 560–563, 566, 570, 582–584, 588–589, 602–603
For multiplication, 145–149, 154–156, 158, 160–162, 166–168, 176, 181–182, 184, 246–247, 252–253, 258, 262, 264, 266, 270, 276–277, 282–285, 288, 300
For subtraction, 70–71, 614, 636–638, 648
Of whole numbers, 20–21

Modes, 98–101, 105–107, 133

Money, 579

Multiple-Choice Questions, *See Preparing for Standardized Tests*

Multiples, 177–178, 180, 186
Of one hundred, 237–239, 262–263
Of one thousand, 237–239, 262–263
Of ten, 237–239, 262–263, 273–275

Multiplication, 142–187, 234–305
Associative Property of, 150–153, 172, 180, 182, 273–274
To check division, 161, 167, 317, 322–324, 347, 350
Checking using addition, 240
Checking using division, 183
Commutative Property of, 150, 152, 180, 182, 273–274
To convert units, 444, 490, 504–505, 525, 528
Distributive property of, 166, 247, 282–283
Estimating products, 242–245, 247, 252–253, 258–259, 262, 264, 276–279, 285, 288–289, 296–297, 300–301, 303
Expressions, 214–216, 229
Factors, 145, 161

Facts, 154–157, 160–162, 182, 184
To find equivalent fractions, 548, 569, 597
Identity Property of, 150, 152, 180, 182
Modeling, 145–149, 154–156, 158, 160–162, 166–168, 176, 181–182, 184, 246–247, 252–253, 258, 262, 264, 266, 270, 276–277, 282–285, 288, 300
By one-digit numbers, 234–267
By one hundred, 237–239, 262–263
By one thousand, 237–239, 262–263
Partial products, 247, 252, 258, 270, 283–284, 297
Products, 145, 150, 177–178, 180
Properties of, 150–153, 166, 172, 180, 182, 247, 273–274, 282–283
Regrouping, 253, 259, 289, 296–297, 303–304
Relationship with division, 147–149, 155, 160–161, 167, 180–181, 183
Tables, 177
By ten, 237–239, 262–263, 273
By two-digit numbers, 270, 273–305
Of whole numbers, 5, 142–187, 234–305
Zero Property of, 150, 152, 180
Across zeros, 258–262, 266

Multiplication tables, 177

Nets, 360–361, 385

Number lines, 395–397, 406, 428–429
For comparing numbers, 28, 32, 47, 554–556, 569, 590–591
For decimals, 588–591, 596, 598, 602–604, 606, 608, 616–617, 645
For equivalent fractions, 547, 569

Index

Index